Lecture Notes
in Business Information Processing

32

T0237875

Series Editors

Wil van der Aalst
Eindhoven Technical University, The Netherlands
John Mylopoulos
University of Trento, Italy
Norman M. Sadeh
Carnegie Mellon University, Pittsburgh, PA, USA
Michael J. Shaw
University of Illinois, Urbana-Champaign, IL, USA
Clemens Szyperski
Microsoft Research, Redmond, WA, USA

Frank Bomarius   Markku Oivo
Päivi Jaring   Pekka Abrahamsson (Eds.)

Product-Focused Software Process Improvement

10th International Conference, PROFES 2009
Oulu, Finland, June 15-17, 2009
Proceedings

 Springer

Volume Editors

Frank Bomarius
Fraunhofer IESE
Fraunhofer-Platz 1, 67663 Kaiserslautern, Germany
E-mail: frank.bomarius@iese.fraunhofer.de

Markku Oivo
University of Oulu
Department of Information Processing Science
P.O.Box 3000, 90014 Oulu, Finland
E-mail: markku.oivo@oulu.fi

Päivi Jaring
VTT Technical Research Centre of Finland
Tietotie 3, 02150 Espoo, Finland
E-mail: paivi.jaring@vtt.fi

Pekka Abrahamsson
University of Helsinki
Department of Computer Science
P.O.Box 68, 00014 Helsinki, Finland
E-mail: Pekka.Abrahamsson@cs.helsinki.fi

Library of Congress Control Number: Applied for

ACM Computing Classification (1998): D.2, K.6

ISSN   1865-1348
ISBN-10   3-642-02151-4 Springer Berlin Heidelberg New York
ISBN-13   978-3-642-02151-0 Springer Berlin Heidelberg New York

This work is subject to copyright. All rights are reserved, whether the whole or part of the material is
concerned, specifically the rights of translation, reprinting, re-use of illustrations, recitation, broadcasting,
reproduction on microfilms or in any other way, and storage in data banks. Duplication of this publication
or parts thereof is permitted only under the provisions of the German Copyright Law of September 9, 1965,
in its current version, and permission for use must always be obtained from Springer. Violations are liable
to prosecution under the German Copyright Law.

springer.com

© Springer-Verlag Berlin Heidelberg 2009
Printed in Germany

Typesetting: Camera-ready by author, data conversion by Scientific Publishing Services, Chennai, India
Printed on acid-free paper   SPIN: 12693689   06/3180   5 4 3 2 1 0

Preface

On behalf of the PROFES Organizing Committee we are proud to present the proceedings of the 10th International Conference on Product Focused Software Process Improvement (PROFES 2009), held in Oulu, Finland. Since the first conference in 1999, the conference has established its place in the software engineering community as a respected conference that brings together participants from academia and industry.

The roots of PROFES are in professional software process improvement motivated by product and service quality needs. The conference addresses both the solutions found in practice as well as relevant research results from academia. To ensure that PROFES retains its high quality and focus on the most relevant research issues, the conference has actively maintained close collaboration with industry and subsequently widened its scope to the research areas of collaborative and agile software development. A special focus for 2009 was placed on software business to bridge research and practice in the economics of software engineering. This enabled us to cover software development in a more comprehensive manner and tackle one of the most important current challenges identified by the software industry and software research community – namely, the shift of focus from "products" to "services." The current global economic downturn emphasizes the need for new methods and solutions for fast and business-oriented development of products and services in a globally distributed environment.

PROFES conferences have continuously attracted attendees from industry, research, and academia. This confirms that the conference has provided topics that are up-to-date, important, and interesting. PROFES 2009 offered a unique forum for industry and academic professionals to discuss their needs and ideas especially from the perspective of software as a business.

The conference included two top keynote speakers: (1) David G. Messerschmitt, who is the Roger A. Strauch Professor Emeritus of Electrical Engineering and Computer Sciences (EECS) at the University of California at Berkeley, and also a Visiting Professor in the Department of Computer Science and Engineering at the Helsinki University of Technology (HUT) and (2) Steven Fraser, Director of Engineering from Cisco Research in San Jose, California, where he is responsible for Cisco Research Center operations.

PROFES also hosted the workshop on "Learning Software Organizations" (LSO2009), the workshop on "Smarter Investment by Aligning SPI Initiatives, Capabilities and Stakeholder Values" and several pre-conference tutorials.

We wish to thank the VTT Technical Research Center of Finland, the University of Oulu, and Fraunhofer IESE, for supporting the conference. We are also grateful to the authors for the high-quality papers, the Program Committee for their hard work in reviewing the papers, the Organizing Committee for making the event possible, and all the numerous supporters who helped in organizing this conference.

April 2009

Frank Bomarius
Markku Oivo
Päivi Jaring
Pekka Abrahamsson

Organization

Profes 2009 was organized by the VTT Technical Research Centre of Finland, University of Oulu, Fraunhofer IESE, Kaiserslautern, and University of Helsinki.

Organizing Committee

General Chair	Pekka Abrahamsson (University of Helsinki, Finland)
Program Chairs	Frank Bomarius (Fraunhofer IESE, Germany)
	Markku Oivo (University of Oulu, Finland)
Organizing Chairs	Päivi Jaring (VTT Technical Research Centre of Finland)
	Kaarina Karppinen (VTT Technical Research Centre of Finland)
Special Theme Chairs	Nilay Oza (VTT Technical Research Centre of Finland)
	Timo Koivumäki (VTT Technical Research Centre of Finland)

Program Committee

Zeiad Abdelnai Garyounis	University IT College, Libya
Silvia Abrahão	Universidad Politécnica de Valencia, Spain
Muhammad Ali Barbar	University of Limerick, Ireland
Bente Anda	Simula Research Laboratory, Norway
Teresa Baldassarre	University of Bari, Italy
Andreas Birk	SWPM - Software.Process.Management, Germany
Danilo Caivano	University of Bari, Italy
Gerardo Canfora	University of Sannio, Italy
Jeff Carver	Alabama University, USA
Marcus Ciolkowski	Fraunhofer Institute for Experimental Software Engineering, Germany
Reidar Conradi	Norwegian University of Science and Technology, Norway
Beniamino Di Martino	Second University of Naples, Italy
Torgeir Dingsøyr	SINTEF, Norway
Tore Dybå	SINTEF, Norway
Davide Falessi	University of Rome "Tor Vergata", Italy
Raimund Feldmann	Fraunhofer Center Maryland, USA
Jens Heidrich	Fraunhofer Institute for Experimental Software Engineering, Germany
Martin Höst	Lund University, Sweden
Frank Houdek	Daimler AG, Germany
Hajimu Iida	NAIST, Japan
Katsuro Inoue	Osaka University, Japan

Michel Jaring	Fluxica, Finland
Andreas Jedlitschka	Fraunhofer Institute for Experimental Software Engineering, Germany
Erik Johansson	Ericsson Mobile Platforms, Sweden
Natalia Juristo	Universidad Politécnica de Madrid, Spain
Janne Järvinen	F-Secure, Finland
Pasi Kuvaja	University of Oulu, Finland
Kari Känsälä	Nokia, Finland
Marek Leszak	Alcatel-Lucent, Germany
Lech Madeyski	Wroclaw University of Technology, Poland
Makoto Matsuhita	Osaka University, Japan
Kenichi Matsumoto	Nara Institute of Science and Technology, Japan
Alok Mishra	Atilim University, Turkey
Nils Brede Moe	SINTEF ICT, Norway
Maurizio Morisio	Politecnico di Torino, Italy
Mark Müller	Robert Bosch GmbH, Germany
Jürgen Münch	Fraunhofer IESE, Germany
Annukka Mäntyniemi	Nokia, Finland
Haruka Nakao	Japan Manned Space Systems Corporation, Japan
Risto Nevalainen	FiSMA ry, Finland
Mahmood Niazi	Keele University, UK
Paolo Panaroni	INTECS, Italy
Dietmar Pfahl	Simula Research Laboratory and University of Oslo, Norway
Minna Pikkarainen	VTT, Finland
Teade Punter	Embedded Systems Institute (ESI), The Netherlands
Austen Rainer	University of Hertfordshire, UK
Karl Reed	La Trobe University, Australia
Daniel Rodriguez	University of Alcalá, Spain
Outi Salo	Nokia, Finland
Kurt Schneider	Leibniz Universität Hannover, Germany
Carolyn Seaman	UMBC and Fraunhofer Center Maryland, USA
Darja Šmite	University of Latvia, Latvia
Michael Stupperich	Daimler AG, Germany
Guilherme Travassos	COPPE/UFRJ, Brazil
Markku Tukiainen	University of Joensuu, Finland
Mark van den Brand	Eindhoven University of Technology, The Netherlands
Rini van Solingen	Delft University of Technology, The Netherlands
Sira Vegas	Universidad de Politecnica de Madrid, Spain
Matias Vierimaa	VTT, Finland
Hironori Washizaki	National Institute of Informatics, Japan
Claes Wohlin	Blekinge Institute of Technology, Sweden
Bernhard Wong	University of Technology, Sydney, Australia

Sponsoring Institutions

City of Oulu, VTT, IESE and University of Oulu

Table of Contents

Agile Software Development

Process Models and SPI

Processes

Software as a Business

Industrial Case Studies

Workshops

Tutorials

The Consumer Juggernaut: Web-Based and Mobile Applications as Innovation Pioneer

David G. Messerschmitt

Department of Electrical Engineering and Computer Sciences
University of California at Berkeley, USA
messer@eecs.berkeley.edu

Abstract. As happened previously in electronics, software targeted at consumers is increasingly the focus of investment and innovation. Some of the areas where it is leading is animated interfaces, treating users as a community, audio and video information, software as a service, agile software development, and the integration of business models with software design. As a risk-taking and experimental market, and as a source of ideas, consumer software can benefit other areas of applications software. The influence of consumer software can be magnified by research into the internal organizations and processes of the innovative firms at its foundation.

Keywords: Software applications, world-wide web, user interfaces, development, business processes.

1 Introduction

Consumer software applications target individual members of our society, and provide them with productivity enhancements, fun and entertainment, and ways to interact and collaborate with family, friends, and colleagues. Other distinctive categories of software applications include those that serve organizations (businesses, education, government, military, etc.) and commerce. Consumer software applications can be (and frequently are) exploited in organizational contexts as well. With the advent of the Internet and the Web, as well as new computing platforms such as the smart phone, the space of consumer software applications has in recent years seen an explosion in innovation. Consumer software applications are highly innovative and experimental, and other categories of software can explicitly exploit or benefit from their pioneering spirit.

2 The Opportunity

Although the vendor industries in information technology (IT) have increasingly adopted an open innovation model [1], business and enterprise applications remain largely inwardly focused in their innovation. Many large enterprises expend considerable resources for customized solutions designed to meet their special needs or provide

F. Bomarius et al. (Eds.): PROFES 2009, LNBIP 32, pp. 1–7, 2009.
© Springer-Verlag Berlin Heidelberg 2009

competitive advantage, while the number of vendors providing standardized customizable solutions is small. The innovation model within a large company's information systems (IS) organizations falls in Pasteur's quadrant [2], relying on internal experience and expertise to identify specific opportunities for improving efficiency and effectiveness through information technology. Later as more generic needs spread throughout the relevant industry and the competitive advantage of customized solutions is undercut, it is typical to reduce cost and risk by adopting off-the shelf solutions (such as replacing a home-grown accounting system by a commercial enterprise resource planning solution).

In the meantime, consumer software applications have become very dynamic, moving beyond personal productivity and automation of existing functions into pioneering new territory. One characteristic of new technology development is uncertainty [3], which is a anathema to the manager of a large organization but more acceptable to entrepreneurs and early adopters among consumers. These applications are sometimes directly useful in enterprises, but more commonly there are opportunities for capturing innovation and value within enterprises inspired by these consumer technologies.

It is not unexpected that consumer markets would become a technology leader and application driver in software. The extraordinarily large market opportunity, the high competitive energy brought to bear, and the relatively large investments that are possible eventually overwhelm the greater focus of products aimed at specific organizational needs. This has happened previously in other areas of IT. For example, military technology has historically created important spin-offs to civilian and commercial use, the Internet being a premier example. Increasingly military applications have become dependent on commercial technology [4], while specific military needs are increasingly specialized and hence less likely to influence commercial markets. Another example is the supercomputers used for the highest end and most specialized needs imaginable, which today are most commonly built from large numbers of commodity commercial processors [5], those processors at the high end in turn largely justified by gaming and Web server applications. The supercomputer market could never justify investments approaching those already targeted at the commercial market.

In application software for enterprises, for similar reasons it has always been true that outside of specialized areas (such as enterprise resource planning, knowledge management, and applications customized to individual company processes) companies rely on standard commercial solutions at both the application and infrastructure levels. Both specialized solutions and commercial solutions should benefit from an infusion of new ideas.

In what follows we discuss some opportunities for other areas of the application software industry that arise from recent innovations in consumer applications.

3 The Cutting Edge of Consumer Software

It is useful to illustrate some areas where consumer software pioneered new innovations by focusing on three major examples.

Gaming has spawned innovations in graphics processors, software graphics, and programming tools. Embodied in gaming, in spite of its lighthearted motivations, is a richness of interaction and user experience that has profound implications for other application areas. Many areas of activity could benefit from such techniques and associated technology, suitably adapted and extended. This includes activities in the "real world" with a game-like character [6] and knowledge exploration and training and education [7]. SecondLife illustrates a game-like environment with a monetary and market element, and could be a precursor to more blatantly commercial market-places. Many other activities can benefit from interface elements like sensors and rich animation.

Social networking applications such as Facebook have moved beyond the view of a software application focused on the individual users. They treat their membership as a collection of communities, in a model called community networked services [8]. Earlier organizational applications focused on coordination of business processes such as customer service have pioneered the service of groups of users, but social networking is defining new ways to support (and more importantly expand) the informal and social needs of its users. As with gaming, many of the activities supported in social networking can be viewed as lighthearted or even trivial, but the general modalities captured therein may be applicable to a variety of serious purposes.

Audio, video, speech recognition are increasingly integrated into applications and help systems. A Google speech-recognition based search function has become popular on the mobile platform, and the ability for all users to post videos for all to see has stimulated a variety of new uses. The text to speech synthesis of the Kindle e-book reader bridges the gap between audiobooks and textual interfaces. Increasingly traditional journalism, product reviews and help systems rely on video in place of traditional textual interfaces.

The foregoing examples illustrate new functionality that has proven useful to consumers. Innovation has occurred in non-functional areas as well. Although it is not yet well documented, it appears that many of the new Web-based applications have a close connection to their end users in guiding the ongoing evolution of the service, as another concrete example of Pasteur's quadrant innovation [2] driven by end users, as has been common in many industries [10], [8]. As a driver for their business models, new services have found ways for users to collectively co-create value through their joint activities, and identified ways for the monetization of that value by the service provider [8]. New applications and services are much more likely to be distributed by software as a service (SaaS) [11] than the traditional software download and installation by the user. Mobile platforms, however, have illustrated the value of mixing the download and SaaS models. In a related but different vein, the opportunities from cloud computing [12] have been concretely illustrated by applications that allow consumers to store or backup data and perform processing on remote servers.

4 Capturing Innovations in Functionality

Inevitably many of these consumer applications are used within organizations and businesses, whether officially sanctioned and promulgated by an IS organization or informally introduced by the staff. Like the backdoor entry of the personal computer in an earlier era, this allows users to experiment and invent new uses while potentially creating a number of problems such as security holes or data loss. Consumer applications are not designed with specific organizational needs in mind, and in many cases neither do they directly meet compelling organizational needs. How, for example, would many of the video games be compelling? The consumer market is not only large, but less risk adverse and more appropriate for experimentation. It can serve as a source of ideas and inspiration, and a place where features can mature and be qualified. By their very nature, consumer applications have broad interest, and as such many of their most useful features are arguably more likely to be incorporated into vendor software than developed internally to organizations. The ideas incorporated therein are particularly applicable to customer-facing systems, and less likely to be incorporated into internal business processes. However, they should be valuable in the extemporaneous and informal processes of an organization, and inter-organizational interactions and collaborations [13] as well.

The three areas of innovation listed previously can illustrate this. New modalities of informal communication identified in social networking applications can improve the effectiveness of geography-spanning virtual teams [14], but an even bigger opportunity is to expand the informal lines of communication in an organization [15] that were previously associated with self-limiting physical proximity. Ways in which value can be co-created within a community [8] are clearly applicable to an organizational context. The use of media like audio and video can be dramatically expanded beyond voicemail and formal training videos to enhance communication and reduce some of the drudgery often associated with paperwork and documentation. It is a reasonable hypothesis that these sorts of informal connections among users are more effective than formal initiatives like knowledge management systems in capturing and conveying the tacit knowledge that is a crucially important resource for any effective organization [16]. Such informal networks may also help rejuvenate apprenticeship as a supplement to formal training programs.

Clearly there are many unknowns here. Studying the modalities for enhancing communication and collaboration in the consumer marketplace and their outcomes and effectiveness can contribute to understanding of how to achieve similar benefits in more formally structured organizations, and possibility how to restructure these organizations for greater effectiveness as well.

5 Capturing Other Benefits

While consumer applications can provide inspiration on new functionality, there can be other valuable spin-offs as well. A few examples will now be outlined.

One of the major challenges for applications software lies in the maturity of the industry. The earliest and easiest approach, the "low-hanging fruit" if you will, is the automation of existing functions and processes. For example, in the consumer area the earliest applications were word processing and email, functions that simply automated previously manual processes. Gaming and the Web began to introduce functionality not seen previously, and their success is evident. The greatest gains as measured by efficacy (accomplishing what is intended), effectiveness (accomplishing it well), and efficiency (accomplishing it with minimum resources) arise when new uses are found for technology, new uses that take advantage of its special capabilities. There is considerable historical evidence backing up this observation [17]. This process seems more evident in consumer software applications, at least recently. As greater understanding is developed into the mindsets and processes behind this, consumer software applications can serve as a model for speeding this process in other domains.

There are increasing demands on the information systems organization to become more business relevant, and the CIO to assume more of a role of a general business manager [18] that participates in decision making at the executive level. The nature of the business challenges facing a CIO are undoubtedly far different those faced by a consumer application vendor. However, firms in the most innovative parts of the consumer software marketplace require a tight coupling and dependence between business decisions and software design [19]. It seems generally true that a small group of managers, such as founders and early employees, serve as both technology visionaries and business managers. Studying the decision and consensus processes in such organizations and how they relate to commercial success can bring insights useful in larger software firms and end-user firms in a variety of industries in making their software design decisions more business-relevant.

The idea of value co-creation within the user community of a consumer application [8] remarkably parallels the type of value that arises in informal interactions and collaborations within an organization. For example, in both cases the individuals are expected to spontaneously form networks, and generally there is no need or desire to *directly* monetize any value that results. Rather, the benefits are indirect, manifested by for example more usage and user loyalty in the consumer case and greater exploitation of tacit knowledge and increased employee loyalty in the organizational case. Studying the forms and origins of value in either case, as well as how those relate to the design and features of the software, can bring valuable insights to the other.

The epitome of open innovation in software is open source [20], which has evolved from individual programmers to a collaborative method of software development among organizations. Both, but especially the individual contributions, are an example of end-user innovation [21]. While there has been considerable adoption of open-source solutions in enterprises, this has been mostly at the level of infrastructure (like operating systems or web servers) rather than applications. It remains largely unexplored whether open source would be a valuable modality for enterprises to share resources and expertise in application development [22]. Open source methodology and its predecessors have a long history in consumer application areas, and as such illustrate the potential.

Software development organizations have been adopting processes that are increasingly agile, embracing changing requirements and involving the end user more integrally in the design process [23], [24]. By all appearances many Web-based consumer applications have evolved at an unusually high rate, and tracked and benefited from user input and ideas to an unusual degree. It would be interesting to study their internal processes, which give the external appearance of agility. The extent to which processes are actually agile, and appreciating the mechanisms by which they are made agile, will require more empirical research. Clearly there is an opportunity to understand and capture and repurpose the techniques that have evolved. As well, consumer applications offer a good laboratory for experimenting with new ideas in development methodology.

While software distribution using software as a service (SaaS) [25] appears in the vendor enterprise market, particularly in applications that target small to midsize businesses, consumer applications have carried this trend to a greater extreme, and their experience should be a valuable asset. In addition, IS organizations exploit SaaS-like approaches for serving internal users, and can be both a source of ideas and inspiration and a beneficiary of better practices in managing SaaS. For example, SaaS despite its many advantages suffers potential security vulnerabilities and data security issues [26] that must be overcome.

6 Conclusions

The consumer applications market offers a ripe opportunity for empirical research and as a laboratory for experimentation and qualification of new ideas in business models, user support, end-user innovation, and software development. This is particularly true of the large number of emerging Web-based applications and emerging models for software application distribution on mobile platforms. Since these areas are still emerging and maturing, they are strongly influenced by innovative new ideas. This can be a fruitful area for academic research within the management and software engineering disciplines for some years to come.

References

1. Chesbrough, H.W., Vanhaverbeke, W., West, J.: Open innovation: Researching a new paradigm. Oxford University Press, USA (2006)
2. Stokes, D.E.: Pasteur's quadrant: Basic science and technological innovation. Brookings Institution Press (1997)
3. Teece, D.J.: Firm Organization, Industrial Structure, and Technological Innovation. Journal of Economic Behavior and Organization 31, 193–224 (1996)
4. Alic, J.A., Branscomb, L.M., Brooks, H.: Beyond spinoff: Military and commercial technologies in a changing world. Harvard Business School Press, Boston (1992)
5. Graham, S.L., Snir, M., Patterson, C.A. (eds.): Getting up to speed: The future of supercomputing. National Academies Press, Washington (2005)
6. Magerkurth, C., Cheok, A.D., Mandryk, R.L., et al.: Pervasive Games: Bringing Computer Entertainment Back to the Real World. Computers in Entertainment 3, 4 (2005)
7. Thomas, P., Macredie, R.: Games and the Design of Human-Computer Interfaces. Educational and Training Technology International 31, 134–142 (1994)
8. Messerschmitt, D.G., Peltonen, J., Laine, M.O.J., et al.: Community Networked Services: Learning from Web 2.0 (2008), SSRN: http://ssrn.com/abstract=1320947
9. von Hippel, E.: Democratizing innovation. MIT Press, Cambridge (2005)
10. von Hippel, E.: The sources of innovation. Oxford University Press, New York (1988)
11. Turner, M., Budgen, D., Brereton, P.: Turning Software into a Service. IEEE Computer 36, 38–44 (2003)
12. Hayes, B.: Cloud Computing. Communications of the ACM 51 (2008)
13. Österle, H., Fleisch, E., Alt, R.: Business networking: Shaping collaboration between enterprises. Springer, Heidelberg (2001)
14. Maznevski, M.L., Chudoba, K.M.: Bridging Space Over Time: Global Virtual Team Dynamics and Effectiveness. Organization Science, 473–492 (2000)
15. Kraut, R.E., Fish, R.S., Root, R.W., et al.: Informal communication in organizations: Form, function, and technology. In: Baecker (ed.) Readings in Groupware and Computer-Supported Cooperative Work, pp. 145–199. Morgan Kaufman, San Francisco (1990)
16. Eraut, M.: Non-formal learning, implicit learning and tacit knowledge in professional work. In: Anonymous: The Necessity of Informal Learning. Policy Press (2000)

17. David, P.A.: The Dynamo and the Computer: An Historical Perspective on the Modern Productivity Paradox. American Economic Review, 355–361 (1990)
18. Ross, J. W., Feeny, D. F.: The Evolving Role of the CIO. Sloan School of Management Working paper 4089 (1999),
    `http://web.mit.edu/cisr/working%20papers/cisrwp308.pdf`
19. Peltonen, J., Messerschmitt, D., Laine, M.: Web Business and Development Opportunities: Learning from Community Networked Services. In: Conference on Web Information Systems and Technologies (2009)
20. West, J., Gallagher, S.: Patterns of open innovation in open source software. Oxford University Press, Oxford (2006)
21. Hippel, E.: Innovation by User Communities: Learning from Open-Source Software. MIT Sloan Management Review 42, 82 (2001)
22. Dreiling, A., Klaus, H., Rosemann, M., et al.: Open Source Enterprise Systems: Towards a Viable Alternative. In: Hawaii International Conference on Systems Science, p. 227b (2005)
23. Beck, K., Beedle, M., van Bennekum, A. et al.: Manifesto for Agile Software Development, `http://agilemanifesto.org/`
24. Rajlich, V.: Changing the Paradigm of Software Engineering. Communications of the ACM 49, 67–70 (2006)
25. Olsen, E.R.: Transitioning to Software as a Service: Realigning Software Engineering Practices with the New Business Model. In: IEEE International Conference on Service Operations and Logistics and Informatics, pp. 266–271 (2006)
26. Clark, D.L.: Enterprise security: The manager's defense guide. Addison-Wesley Professional, Reading (2002)

Software "Best" Practices: Agile Deconstructed

Steven Fraser

Cisco Research Center, USA
sdfraser@acm.org

Abstract. Software "best" practices depend entirely on context – in terms of the problem domain, the system constructed, the software designers, and the "customers" ultimately deriving value from the system. Agile practices no longer have the luxury of "choosing" small non-mission critical projects with co-located teams. Project stakeholders are selecting and adapting practices based on a combination of interest, need and staffing. For example, growing product portfolios through a merger or the acquisition of a company exposes legacy systems to new staff, new software integration challenges, and new ideas. Innovation in communications (tools and processes) to span the growth and contraction of both information and organizations, while managing the adoption of changing software practices, is imperative for success. Traditional web-based tools such as web pages, document libraries, and forums are not sufficient. A blend of tweeting, blogs, wikis, instant messaging, web-based conferencing, and telepresence creates a new dimension of communication "best" practices.

1 Introduction

Over the past 15 years the author organized a series of panel discussions ([1],[2] , [3], [4], [5], [6], [7], [8], [9], [10], [11]) focused on the "soft" aspects of software development. A recurring theme has been the observation that communication patterns are often overlooked and that the software community continues to be challenged by failing to leverage the work of the past. As Craig Larman surveyed in [12], iterative and incremental processes pre-date the "Agile Software" movement by more than 30 years – or double that – depending on what is considered relevant. Fred Brooks commented in 2007 [13] that "I know of no other field where people do less study of other people's work." However, we've discovered that it is very difficult to achieve consensus on approach, e.g. methodology – let alone vocabulary – when dealing with software practices. Some authors [14] might even argue that there are no software "best" practices.

"Agile Software Development" and "Extreme Programming" (XP) group together individual practices in a manner similar to what Maxwell did for electromagnetics. Consider the "agile" case as equivalent to the "homogeneous" case in electromagnetics where the boundary conditions can greatly simplify the problem. In our experience, Agile software development generally remains in the comfort zone of small, co-located teams, building non-critical systems in the context of new "green field" development. Here there is an excellent collective understanding of customer requirements – or at least an opportunity to validate the understanding with a customer or customer proxy.

F. Bomarius et al. (Eds.): PROFES 2009, LNBIP 32, pp. 8–13, 2009.
© Springer-Verlag Berlin Heidelberg 2009

2 The Practice of Software Engineering

The practice of "Software Engineering" was coined in the late 1960s – at the NATO Workshop in Garmisch. Many of the challenges identified at the workshop remain to this day – from page 122 of the [15] report highlighting the positions of David and Fraser:

> »*The causes of this 'software gap' are many, but a basic one lies in the unfortunate telescoping of research, development and production of an operational version within a single project effort. This practice leads to slipped schedules, extensive rewriting, much lost effort, large numbers of bugs, and an inflexible and unwieldy product. It is unlikely that such a product can ever be brought to a satisfactory state of reliability or that it can be maintained and modified. Though this mixing of research, development, and production is a root cause of the 'software gap', there are many other contributory factors, from the lack of management talents to the employment of unqualified programmers and sheer incompetence in software design.*«

The impact of the 'software gap' has increased as software has crept into almost every aspect of our daily lives. Software engineering has been increasingly recognized as a "wicked problem" as characterized by Rittel and Webber [16]:

- System requirements are often not understood until the emergence of a prototype;
- Stakeholders have wildly divergent understanding of requirements;
- Requirements, constraints, and resources change during development; and
- Requirements are never "perfectly" solved for all stakeholders over all time.

Software itself consists of many components beyond the essential ingredients of executable code. Configurations, build scripts, executables, documentation, assembly processes, operating systems, libraries, requirements, use cases, and test cases are just some of the flavors of software. Software "stakeholders" are many – including programmers (the usual suspects), integrators, analysts, managers, customers, users, coaches, architects, testers, regulators, lawyers, channel sales, journalists, politicians, etc. However, the majority of this cast remains essentially invisible to the end users of software systems and only an inadvertent misstep might place an individual software engineer into the light of public scrutiny.

3 "Best" Practices

Shull and Turner [6] describe a *"best" practice as a: "repeatable activity, defined in such a way that someone other than the definer can implement it with demonstrable repeatability,"* and *"effectiveness is dependent on the context within which the practice is applied"*. While there are some, who suggest that "best practices" don't exist [14] – there are others (Steve McConnell), who facilitate discussion through a forum on the topic of "software best practices" [17].

Steve McConnell [18] summarized a number of rarely used – but key software development practices. He further suggested criteria to validate "new" practices as they mature, based on the work of Raghavan and Chand [19]: *"Will the practice work in the field? Are the claimed successes a result of the "practice" or the people? Are there side effects, risks, misapplications, adoption, overheads – that hinder adoption of the practice?"*

Much has been written [20], [12], [21], [22], [23] indicating that the sources of the practices encapsulated by "agile software development" are not really "new" – suggesting that they have been grouped and hyped for the 21st century. One unfortunate labeling was Barry Boehm and Richard Tuner's book title [20] "Balancing Agility and Discipline: A Guide for the Perplexed" which left readers with the unfortunate impression (in this author's opinion) that agile software development practices were not disciplined. In fact, much discipline and tooling support is required by agile practices which are generally far more prescriptive than traditional *ad hoc* development practices.

Agile software development practices first became prevalent in the late 1990s. The first book devoted to XP [24] was quickly followed by the first conference to specifically focus on XP and Agile software development practices which was held in Cagliari Italy, June 21-23, 2000 (*First International Conference on Extreme Programming and Flexible Processes in Software Engineering - XP 2000*). At that time – it was clear that a certain degree of enthusiast zeal ("agilista exuberance") had emerged – something was new! Kent Beck was later to relate at OOPSLA [25] *"In my mind as we began XP as a physics experiment, where you remove all the variables possible so what you're left with is repeatable. Some of the usual variables we eliminated: Geographic separation; Multiple customers; Expensive deployment; Stupid programmers; Growth-averse database technology; Computer-oriented programming language; GUI-intense system; Impersonal (>15 person) team; Wildly changing requirements (replacing a legacy system); [and] Disinterested business sponsors."*

• Architecture	• Peopleware and sustainable pace
• Coding standards	• Project planning
• Collaborative programming	• Refactoring
• Collective ownership	• Requirements engineering
• Continuous integration & tools	• Retrospectives
• Evolutionary & iterative design	• Risk management
• Data Hiding & abstraction	• Simple design
• Documentation	• Software economics & estimation
• Incremental releases	• Software metrics
• Metaphor	• Software reuse
• On-site customer	• Test-driven design
• Organizational learning	• Testing
• Patterns	• Use Cases & user stories

Fig. 1. Software "best" practices [from a distillation of this paper's references]

Reviewing the literature ([24], [26] [21], [27], [20], [12], [22], [23]) we've observed that "Agile" consists of a combination of the practices listed in Fig. 1. All of these practices date back at least to the 90s and most to the 60s, 70s, or 80s – and some as far back as the 50s. In the beginning, agile practitioners picked the projects to which they would apply "agile practices." Debates were quite frequent at conferences on whether – for example, XP required all 12 practices to be adopted and applied – or if a subset could be applied. This debate abated somewhat with the appearance of [21] which added to the practices of [24]. It also became evident that some developers misapplied practices. For example, some developers claimed to be doing XP – by not doing documentation! Several books have been published that question the tenants of XP – and while [28] is recommended, [29] is not.

4 Learning – An Iterative Process

The goal of a "best" practice is to deliver value at the appropriate level of quality – quickly and cost effectively. Unlike some of the "harder" engineering disciplines such as those governed by physics or chemistry, software is much more dependent on the human condition. Adoption and adaptation take time, as Pfleeger and Menezes [30] suggest. Ultimately, we must remember that "learning" – within an industry context – should be a journey of "applied value" for the stakeholders – rather than simply a "destination" in itself (2007), i.e. learning for the sake of learning. Manns and Rising [31] suggest a variety of patterns related to the introduction of change that should be applied to the introduction of software practices. Complementing Manns and Rising's work [31] is Cialdini's [32] patterns of influence.

Two different cost perspectives on process outcomes emerged in the 20th century [33] – Frederick Taylor (1856-1915) and his "Scientific Management" was motivated to optimize the *cost-of-acquisition* – this contrasts with the approach of William Deming (1900-1993) whose "continuous improvement" approach optimized the *cost-of-ownership*. The process of "continuous improvement" is one of both continuous learning and communication. There has been a move away from strictly hierarchical [34] teams with command-and-control organizational structures and co-located work groups. Tapscott and Williams [35] identify ways of thinking differently – for example: being open; peering; sharing; acting globally; building critical mass; supplying an infrastructure for collaboration; abiding by community norms; and letting the process evolve.

We believe that the emergence of collaboration tools including wikis, blogs, forums, instant messaging, tweeting, web-based meeting collaboration, and telepresence fosters the increased adoption of practices - particularly across non-collocated company teams. For "large" organizations where team size is the order of hundreds or thousands of engineering staff – "co-location" can become virtual. For example, in organizations such as Nortel, Qualcomm, Google, and Cisco – it is not unusual for virtual meeting attendees to outnumber in-room attendees – or for post-session viewers of "Video-on-Demand" recordings to out-number the real-time attendees.

5 Observations

The application of software "best" practices depends on individuals and context. Differences in culture, tooling, and legacy can create unforeseen challenges in adoption between organizations. For example, hierarchical [34] teams may not easily blend with teams where collaboration is the norm. While early in the 21st century, "Agile" practices were limited to small projects (teams/code-bases) – now there are an increasing number of organizations where "agile" practices have become main stream.

For example, Kati Vilkki [36] reported at XP2008 in her conference keynote that a product organization with approximately 500 staff at Nokia Siemens Networks now applies agile practices.

Some organizations discover "agile" through mergers and acquisitions. Integration challenges for both staff and software become evident when there are mismatches in communication. Traditional web-based tools alone – such as web pages, document libraries, and forums – are not sufficient for a successful transition. A blend of tweeting, blogs, wikis, instant messaging, web-based conferencing, and telepresence sustained by a mix of consulting and coaching have been reported as useful [11]. "Agile" demands that development team progress and communications become more visible to all – leading to a reduction in risk for all stakeholders.

We chose the title "Software Best Practices: Agile Deconstructed" to suggest: that the practices that constitute agile – predate agile; that "best" depends on context and people; and to observe that inter/intra team communication is an intrinsic ingredient of software production (agile or not). Going forward – there is much opportunity for university curriculum development and research on how software practices can be effectively applied in-the-large and in the growing context of legacy systems.

References

1. Fraser, S., Beck, K., Booch, G., Coleman, D., Coplien, J., Helm, R., Rubin, K.S.: How Do Teams Shape Objects? - How Do Object Shape Teams? In: OOPSLA, pp. 468–473 (1994)
2. Fraser, S., Booch, G., Buschmann, F., Coplien, J., Jacobson, I., Kerth, N.L., Rosson, M.B.: Patterns: Cult to Culture? In: OOPSLA, pp. 231–234 (1995)
3. Fraser, S., Cockburn, A., Brajkovich, L., Coplien, J., Constantine, L.L., West, D.: OO Anthropology: Crossing the Chasm (Panel Session). In: OOPSLA, pp. 286–291 (1996)
4. Fraser, S., Beck, K., Booch, G., Coplien, J., Johnson, R.E., Opdyke, B.: Beyond the Hype: Do Patterns and Frameworks Reduce Discovery Costs? In: OOPSLA, pp. 342–344 (1997)
5. Fraser, S., Astels, D., Beck, K., Boehm, B.W., McGregor, J.D., Newkirk, J., Poole, C.: Discipline and Practices of TDD (Test Driven Development). In: OOPSLA Companion, pp. 268–270 (2003)
6. Fraser, S., Beck, K., Booch, G., Constantine, L.L., Henderson-Sellers, B., McConnell, S., Wirfs-Brock, R., Yourdon, E.: Echoes? Structured Design and Modern Software Practices. In: OOPSLA Companion, pp. 383–386 (2005)
7. Fraser, S., Boehm, B.W., Brooks Jr., F.P., DeMarco, T., Lister, T., Rising, L., Yourdon, E.: Retrospectives on Peopleware. In: ICSE Companion, pp. 21–24 (2007)
8. Fraser, S., Brooks Jr., F.P., Fowler, M., Lopez, R., Namioka, A., Northrop, L.M., Parnas, D.L., Thomas, D.A.: No silver bullet reloaded: retrospective on essence and accidents of software engineering. In: OOPSLA Companion, pp. 1026–1030 (2007)
9. Fraser, S., Abrahamsson, P., Biddle, R., Eckstein, J., Kruchten, P., Mancl, D., Wild, W.: Culture and Agile: Challenges and Synergies. In: Abrahamsson, P., et al. (eds.) XP 2008. LNBIP, vol. 9, pp. 251–255. Springer, Heidelberg (2008)
10. Fraser, S., Lopez, R., Kathail, P., Schmidt, D.C., Shaw, M., Sullivan, K., Thomas, D.A.: Collaboration and Communication: Growing and Sustaining Ultra Large Scale (ULS) Systems. In: OOPSLA Companion, pp. 797–800 (2008)
11. Fraser, S., Lundh, E., Davies, R., Eckstein, J., Larsen, D., Vilkki, K.: Perspectives on Agile Coaching. In: Proceedings of XP 2009 - Agile Processes in Software Engineering and Extreme Programming (2009) (to appear)

12. Larman, C., Basili, V.R.: Iterative and Incremental Development: A Brief History. IEEE Computer 36(6), 47–56 (2003)
13. Fraser, S., Mancl, D.: No Silver Bullet: Software Engineering Reloaded. IEEE Software 25(1), 91–94 (2008)
14. Freeman, S.: There's No Such Thing as Best Practice. In: Proceeding of the 9th Int. Conf. on Agile Processes in Software Engineering and Extreme Programming, p. 250 (2008)
15. Naur, P., Randell, B. (eds.): Software Engineering: Report of a conference sponsored by the NATO Science Committee, Garmisch, Germany, Brussels, Scientific Affairs Division, NATO (October 1968)
16. Rittel, H.W.J., Webber, M.M.: Dilemmas in a General Theory of Planning in Policy Sciences, vol. 4. Elsevier Scientific Publishing Company, Amsterdam (1973)
17. McConnell, S.: McConnell's Construx Forum (2008),
    http://forums.construx.com
18. McConnell, S.: Closing the Gap. IEEE Software 19(1), 3–5 (2002)
19. Raghavan, S.A., Chand, D.R.: Diffusing Software-Engineering Methods. IEEE Software 6(4), 81–90 (1989)
20. Boehm, B., Turner, R.: Balancing Agility and Discipline: A Guide for the Perplexed. Addison-Wesley Professional, Reading (2003)
21. Beck, K., Andres, C.: Extreme Programming Explained: Embrace Change, 2nd edn. XP Series. Addison-Wesley Professional, Reading (2004)
22. Boehm, B.W.: A view of 20th and 21st Century Software Engineering. In: ICSE Proceedings, pp. 12–29 (2006)
23. Boehm, B.: Making a Difference in the Software Century. IEEE Computer 41(3), 78–84 (2008)
24. Beck, K.: Extreme Programming Explained: Embrace Change. Addison Wesley Longman, Amsterdam (2000)
25. Fraser, S., Reinitz, R., Beck, K., Jeffries, R., Lundh, E., Mee, R., Police, G., Pool, C.: To Be Extreme, or Not to Be Extreme. In: OOSPLA (2002),
    http://www.oopsla.org/2002/fp/files/pan-5.html
26. West, D.: Metaphor, Architecture, and XP. In: West, D. (ed.) Proceedings of the Third Interna-tional Conference on Extreme Programming and Agile Processes in Software Engineering, Alghero, Sardinia, Italy, May 26-29, pp. 101–104. University of Cagliari, Cagliari (2002)
27. Nord, R.L., Tomayko, J.E., Wojcik, R.: Integrating Software-Architecture-Centric Methods into Extreme Programming (XP). CMU/SEI-2004-TN-036 (2004)
28. McBreen, P.: Questioning Extreme Programming. Pearson Education, London (2003)
29. Stephens, M., Rosenberg, D.: Extreme Programming Refactored: The Case Against XP. Apress (2003)
30. Pfleeger, S.L., Menezes, W.: Marketing Technology to Software Practitioners. IEEE Software 17(1) (2000)
31. Manns, M.L., Rising, L.: Fearless Change: Patterns for Introducing New Ideas. Addison-Wesley, Reading (2004)
32. Cialdini, R.: Influence: Science and Practice, 5th edn. Allyn & Bacon (2008)
33. US General Accounting Office, Management Scoping Study. ACGOps-91-1 (1990)
34. Constantine, L.L.: Work Organization: Paradigms for Project Management and Organization. CACM 36(10), 34–43 (1993)
35. Tapscott, D., Williams, A.W.: How Mass Collaboration Changes Everything. Penguin Books (2007)
36. Vilkki, K.: XP2008 Keynote: Juggling with the Paradoxes of Agile Transformation (2008),
    http://www.lero.ie/xp2008/keynotesspeakers.html

Key Questions in Building Defect Prediction Models in Practice

Rudolf Ramler, Klaus Wolfmaier, Erwin Stauder, Felix Kossak,
and Thomas Natschläger

Software Competence Center Hagenberg
Softwarepark 21, A-4232 Hagenberg, Austria
{rudolf.ramler,klaus.wolfmaier,erwin.stauder,felix.kossak,
thomas.natschlaeger}@scch.at

Abstract. The information about which modules of a future version of a software system are defect-prone is a valuable planning aid for quality managers and testers. Defect prediction promises to indicate these defect-prone modules. However, constructing effective defect prediction models in an industrial setting involves a number of key questions. In this paper we discuss ten key questions identified in context of establishing defect prediction in a large software development project. Seven consecutive versions of the software system have been used to construct and validate defect prediction models for system test planning. Furthermore, the paper presents initial empirical results from the studied project and, by this means, contributes answers to the identified questions.

Keywords: defect prediction, software test management, machine learning.

1 Introduction

Quality is considered a key issue in any software development project. However, many projects face a tradeoff between cost and quality, as the time and effort for applying software quality assurance measures is usually limited due to economic constraints. In practice, quality managers and testers are in a daily struggle with critical bugs and shrinking budgets. Hence, they are eagerly looking for ways to make quality assurance and testing more effective and efficient. Defect prediction promises to indicate defect-prone modules in an upcoming version of a software system and, thus, allows focusing the effort on those modules. "The net result should be systems that are of higher quality, containing fewer faults, and projects that stay more closely on schedule than would otherwise be possible." [1].

This work is based on our experiences and initial empirical results from establishing defect prediction at an international company in the field of mass-market consumer products. In the studied project, defect prediction has been initiated to produce information for planning system testing and for allocating testing resources.

A large number of empirical studies on various aspects of defect prediction are available and several of these incorporate data from industrial projects (e.g., [1], [2], [3], [4]). Yet, few studies actually provide insights on how defect prediction can be

F. Bomarius et al. (Eds.): PROFES 2009, LNBIP 32, pp. 14–27, 2009.
© Springer-Verlag Berlin Heidelberg 2009

applied in an industrial setting, where defect prediction itself is subject to the afore-mentioned tradeoff between cost and quality. Among these are the study from Li et al. [5], who report experiences from initiating field defect prediction and product test prioritization at ABB, and from Weyuker [6], illustrating the research path towards making defect prediction usable for practitioners.

The objective of this paper is to identify and discuss the key questions that have to be addressed when constructing defect prediction models in practice. In addition, the paper presents our findings and insights from initiating defect prediction in a large industrial project, and by this means the paper contributes some answers to the identi-fied questions. The background of the project is described in Section 2 and the defect prediction approach in Section 3. The identified key questions are discussed in Sec-tion 4. Initial results from predicting defect-prone modules are presented in Section 5. Section 6 summarizes the paper and outlines future work.

2 Project Background

Defect-prediction has been applied in context of a large software development project conducted at an international company. The project concerns the development of an embedded software system for multi-media devices. It is an integrated part of mass-market consumer products such as mobile phones, handhelds and portable consoles.

In this domain, profit margins per product are often small and competition is fierce. Economic success can only be achieved by selling high numbers of products with a short time to market. Thus, software problems can have a devastating effect on the profitability of a product when they cause shipping delays or increased costs due to fixing defects found in the field. Once a product has been shipped, it is usually not possible to update the integrated software without announcing an expensive product callback. All critical defects have to be found and fixed before the product is released. Therefore, standards for software quality are very high. At the same time, however, any investment in quality assurance shrinks the already small profit margins and de-lays the market release. Hence, the budget and time available for quality assurance is constantly under pressure and occasionally testing has to be cut short to fit the release in a narrow window of opportunity.

The software system consists of more than 700 KLOC C++ code in about 180 soft-ware components. It has evolved to this size over several years of ongoing develop-ment. In this study we investigate seven consecutive versions of the software system, capturing the system's evolution over about one year.

Software development proceeds in fixed-length iterations that end with the release of a version. For a single version approximately 100 to 200 defects are reported and about the same number of defects are resolved. The majority of the defects are re-ported by the central testing department, which tests every released version and re-ports back defects while development continues with the next version (Figure 1).

Over the years a number of repositories and databases have been introduced that contain different aspects of the project's history. Figure 2 provides an overview of the development activities and the repositories and databases involved. For constructing defect prediction models, data from following repositories and databases has been made available [7]: (1) the issue management system containing reports on over 7,000

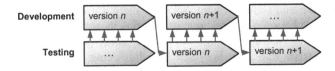

Fig. 1. Synchronization of development and testing

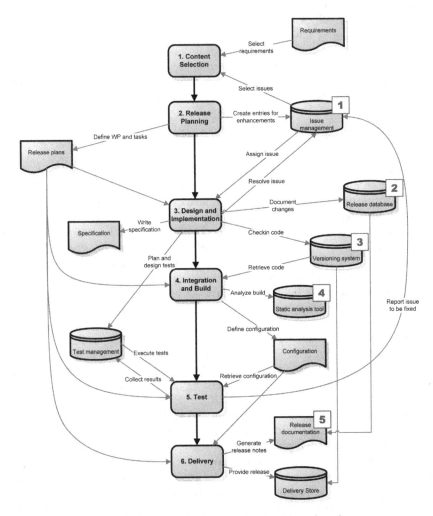

Fig. 2. Activities and data stores involved in an iteration

defects and enhancements, (2) the release database documenting all planned, released, and maintained versions of the software system, (3) the versioning system used for storing development artifacts and for tracking the changes to the source code, (4) a static analysis tool providing more than 200 metrics related to code, design and architecture, and (5) the release documentation for all released versions.

In this setting, defect prediction has been proposed as an aid for planning the system tests (activity 5 in Figure 2) after the build and integration phase. In particular, defect prediction has been expected to provide (a) an early estimation of the number of defect-prone modules to approximate the overall effort required for testing, and (b) a classification of the modules as defective or non-defective to allocate testing resources as not all modules can be tested by all testers and in all test environments. Furthermore, the classification is also intended for a first, simple prioritization of the modules for testing. Modules indicated as defect-prone will be tested first and with higher intensity.

3 Defect Prediction Approach

Defect prediction in the studied project followed the framework proposed by Wahyudin et al. [8]. This framework organizes the tasks for conducting defect prediction in three phases. First the goals and the prediction approach are defined. The intention of the first phase is to align practitioners' expectations with what can realistically be achieved by defect prediction within the specific project and organizational context. In the second phase the prediction model is constructed by collecting the necessary data, training the model using a learning algorithm, and validating the model's performance. Finally, in the third phase, the prediction model is applied on upcoming versions and the reliability of the prediction results is analyzed to trigger a calibration or reconstruction of the model. While the framework gives some guidance about how defect prediction should be organized in general, this paper presents details on how a prediction model should be constructed.

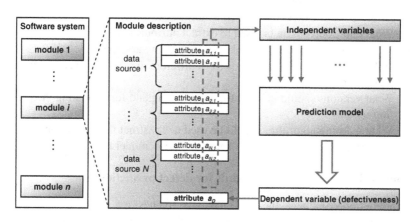

Fig. 3. Inputs and output of a defect prediction model

A *prediction model* incorporates various *attributes* of a software system and its *modules* as *independent variables*, which act as predictors for the *dependent variables* that characterize the defect-proneness of a software system's modules (see Figure 3).

Predictions – to be of practical use – have to be about the future, i.e., they have to provide information about defect-proneness before this information becomes available via other sources like inspection or testing. Thus, prediction models are usually constructed from historical data (using different *data sources*) such as code metrics and reported defects from previous versions or related projects. A broad range of different learning algorithms are available for constructing prediction models, each with specific benefits and limitations. How well a prediction model performs depends on the initially defined prediction objectives and the respective ways it is assessed.

Hence, many questions arise when defect prediction is introduced in a real-world software project. In the studied project, an initial cycle throughout the framework has been used to prototype the construction of the prediction model for gaining a better understanding of the requirements and expectations, for assessing the available data used to construct the model, and to evaluate the prediction performance that can be achieved in the context of the project. The questions that were identified when constructing the initial model as well as the related answers are described and discussed in the following section.

4 Discussion of Key Questions and Decisions

This section discusses the key questions that emerged throughout building and applying the first defect prediction model. It, furthermore, explains the decisions made in the studied project and refers to related research results. Following questions have been identified. Each will be addressed in a separate subsection.

Q1. What is the proper size of a module for defect prediction?
Q2. How can defective modules be identified?
Q3. How should defects be associated to versions?
Q4. How should the defectiveness of a module be defined?
Q5. What data sources can be used to extract attributes?
Q6. What attributes should be used as independent variables?
Q7. Will a combination of attributes from different data sources achieve better prediction results?
Q8. What versions should be used for constructing and for validating the prediction model?
Q9. What learning algorithm should be used to construct the prediction model?
Q10. How should the performance of the prediction model be measured?

Q1: What is the proper size of a module for defect prediction?

Defect prediction calculates the expected defectiveness of modules of a software system. Many studies on defect prediction talk about "modules" as the entities carrying the predicted attributes. However, the term module is vaguely defined in general and the different interpretations of what constitutes a module range from program functions or methods in an object-oriented system to classes (e.g. [4], [9]) and source files (e.g., [1]). Other studies look at even coarser grained entities such as components and sets of related files (e.g. [3], [10]) or smaller entities like distinct changes made to a system (e.g., [11]).

In the studied project, the entities stored in the analyzed repositories and databases were of different levels of granularity. For example, changes were logged at the level of source code lines in the versioning system and at the level of affected files in the release database, while metrics for code and design analysis were calculated for methods, classes and components. The level of granularity shared between the different repositories and databases and, thus, suitable to link the data retrieved from these different sources were files.

However, quality managers and testers understood and discussed the software system in terms of its components. Components were, for example, used to plan QA measures and to allocate testing resources. In the studied system, components were defined as a set of related files implementing a specified functionality. Hence, we decided to use components as modules in defect prediction.

By aggregating the attributes of files to components it turned out that components were a good abstraction from technical details, such as the split of classes into C++ header files and implementation files. Furthermore, the aggregation to components is in line with the findings of Koru et al. [12], who advise practitioners to "collect measurement and defect data at a macro level, shifting the static measures and defect data to a higher abstraction level" [12].

Q2: How can defective modules be identified?

Defect prediction aims to predict the values of dependent variables, which characterize the defectiveness of the software system's modules. Which module contains a defect is determined by debugging and is documented when the defect is resolved. In many cases, several modules have to be changed in order to resolve a defect. It is a common practice in scientific studies to count all modules as defective which are affected by a fix (see, e.g. [13]).

In practice, a broad range of influencing factors has an impact on the number of reported defects. First of all, what counts as defect is more often than not a subjective decision. Although distinct definitions exist in theory as well as in process guidelines of companies, we found several borderline cases and conflicting classification principles in the studied project. For example, the same modification to a component may be classified as defect in the issue database while it is classified as enhancement in the release database, and vice versa. Depending on the objective of the classification used in a particular repository, different ways for counting are applied. Hence, in the studied project, we decided to rely on the defect counts retrieved from the issue database, for which it had been confirmed that reports about defects most likely reflect actual faults in the system.

Q3: How should defects be associated to versions?

The defectiveness of a module changes over time as existing defects are fixed and new ones are introduced. Thus, defect numbers have to be related to the software system's versions. In general, a defect is associated to the version on which it has been reported. However, the assumption that defects are only present in the reported version is flawed, first, because a defect reported for a particular version may have been introduced but missed in an earlier version and, second, because a defect may not be fixed immediately in the next version. So the defect is actually present in all versions from its introduction to the version before it has been fixed. Failing to correctly identify all versions containing the defect, results in a paradox situation. The prediction model would be expected to classify a module as defective in one version and as non-defective in the next version, although the module and all associated attributes have not changed.

In the studied project, not all released versions were integrated in hardware devices. When integration finally took place, several defects that were introduced but missed in previous versions were revealed. Due to the short release cycles and constrained budgets, fixes were also scheduled for later versions and remained open in the next version. A careful analysis of the overall product development strategy revealed that in some cases the number of actually open defects of a version was more than 60 percent higher than the number of defects reported for this version [14]. In order to gain reliable measures for constructing defect prediction models, the number of open defects per version had to be calculated by tracing defects to their introduction and fix versions as an additional step in data preparation.

Q4: How should the defectiveness of a module be defined?

For predicting defect-prone modules, the actual defects have to be linked to software modules. Scientific studies commonly assume that the defectiveness of a module is determined by the number of defects, which have been resolved in this module (see, e.g., [13]). This single variable is used to expresses the defectiveness in different ways. The number of defects per module can be used to build regression models (e.g., [13]), to classify the modules (e.g., in defective or non-defective [12]), or to calculate a module's defect density (e.g., [1]).

In the studied project, a prediction model based on a binary classification of the modules (defective or non-defective) has been used as first step. This model has been found adequate for meeting the initially defined objective of defect prediction. It divides all modules in two sets, one of potentially defective modules and one of potentially non-defective modules, which are used as input for test planning. The number of predicted defects per module has not been considered for the beginning. Nevertheless, the binary classification approach can be extended to a two-step prediction model as proposed by Kutlubay et al. [15] later on, which combines a binary classification with a regression analysis.

Q5: What data sources can be used to extract attributes?

Various attributes of a software module such as static code metrics (e.g., [13], [16]) or process metrics and change metrics (e.g., [2], [16]) have been used as independent variables in prediction models. The available studies demonstrate the applicability and value of these properties for defect prediction.

In the studied project, the practical choice of attributes serving as independent variables for the initial prediction model has mainly been driven by the availability of historical data. A number of different software repositories and corporate databases have been identified as potential data sources. However, mining these repositories and databases revealed that the effort for collecting data appropriate for defect prediction is very high [7]. The different repositories and databases were designed for a specific purpose other than defect prediction. Hence, the data quality in terms of accuracy, completeness, consistency, and timeliness has often been found inappropriate and the integration of heterogeneous data sources was hampered by only partly matching data sets and substantial semantic gaps. The release database, the versioning system, and a static analysis tool were found suitable for extracting attributes for prediction.

Even when a repository has been identified as an appropriate data source, in practice it remains a strategic decision to include the data from this repository for prediction. The selected repositories have to be maintained as part of the project's development infrastructure also in future and workflows and tools have to be aligned with data quality requirements from defect prediction. So, for example, the company in the studied project opted for the static analysis tool as main data source, which fitted into the company's infrastructure plans, although the initial prediction results did not allow to clearly favor static analysis over other sources.

Q6: What attributes should be used as independent variables?

The attributes used as independent variables in the initial prediction model have been extracted from the selected data sources. After the indispensable step of preparing and integrating the data sources in the studied project, a large number of attributes could be retrieved or calculated from each source. For example, the static analysis tool provided about 200 code-, design-, and architecture-related metrics ready to use. Many more metrics were calculated from the other repositories. From the versioning system, for example, several metrics related the number of changes to different time ranges like last week, last month, last six months, last year, and last release.

Depending on the capabilities of the learning algorithm used to construct the prediction model, it may be necessary to preselect metrics with a significant influence on the depending variables. For example, the performance of linear regression models will suffer from irrelevant attributes whereas classification trees are more robust as they select the most significant attributes as initial nodes (see [17]).

In the studied project, all metrics extracted from the different data sources were incorporated in constructing prediction models. A cross-correlation analysis confirmed that the available metrics contributed unique information. A pre-selection of the attributes has not been considered necessary since the applied learning algorithms were able to select the most relevant attributes automatically.

Q7: Will a combination of attributes from different data sources achieve better prediction results?

In general it is assumed that a combination of different attributes will produce best prediction results. Furthermore, some researchers argue that defect prediction can benefit from a combination of multiple partial defect indicators [9]. Turhan et al. [18], for example, enhance static code metrics with architectural information with the aim to construct more accurate prediction models.

However, preparing and mining data sources for attributes is an expensive activity. Thus, although it would be desirable to build prediction models with attributes from a multitude of different repositories and databases, in practice, the number of involved data sources needs to be minimized to keep the costs for prediction reasonably low.

In the studied project, first predictions based on attributes extracted from the versioning system and static analysis produced best overall results. A union of all available attributes derived from the different analyzed data sources did not significantly improve prediction results. This finding is in conformance with results from other studies (e.g., [16]) and encourages continuing with static analysis as data source.

Q8. What versions should be used for constructing and for validating the prediction model?

Predictions have to provide information about a future state of the modules, before this information is acquired by testing, inspection or other means. Therefore, prediction models are constructed from historical data, usually from previous versions [1] or related projects [3], for which the attributes used as dependent and independent variables are available. The constructed models are then validated with the actual data from the upcoming version. In contrast, scientific studies often use a hold-out strategy to validate the constructed model, as Lessmann et al. [19] affirm: "Binary classifiers are routinely assessed by counting the number of correctly predicted modules over hold-out data." This approach has been repeatedly criticized [5] and prediction results not validated with actual future data tend to raise concerns of practitioners.

In the studied project, seven consecutive versions with a consistent set of metrics were available. For six of these seven versions prediction models were constructed. Thereby, for predicting the defective modules of a version n, the data from the previous version n-1 has been used. From the viewpoint of the constructed model, the subsequent version was used for validation.

Using future versions for validation holds a potential threat to validity. A low number of changed modules between the version used for construction and the version used for validation means that large parts of the system remained untouched and their attributes stayed the same. Learning algorithms with the ability to capture the current state would thus achieve good prediction performance by just repeating what is already known.

In the studied project, the change rates as well as the defect rates were generally high. In addition, a repeated validation of defect prediction only for changed or new modules produced equal results in terms of prediction performance.

Q9: What learning algorithm should be used to construct the prediction model?

Various types of learning algorithms have been applied for defect prediction, including statistical methods, classification trees, neural networks, and analogy-based approaches (e.g., [1], [10], [13], [20]). Some studies assume that "sophisticated models are preferable to simple linear regression and correlation models because the relationship between defects (response variable) and static measures (predictor variables) might not be a monotonous linear relationship." [21] However, findings concerning the superiority of one method over another do not seem to be conclusive. For example, Lessmann et al. [19] report that "the importance of the classification model may have been overestimated in the previous research ... Given that basic models, and especially linear ones ... give similar results to more sophisticated classifiers, it is evident that most data sets are fairly well linearly separable. In other words, simple classifiers suffice to model the relationship between static code attributes and software defect." [19] Consequently, these authors came to the conclusion that "the assessment and selection of a classification model should not be based on predictive accuracy alone but should be comprised of several additional criteria like computational efficiency, ease of use, and especially comprehensibility." [19] Furthermore, in some other studies the choice of learning algorithms seems to be influenced by the availability of tools for data mining, e.g., the open source framework WEKA [17].

In the studied project, an investigation of algorithms from the open source tool WEKA and the commercial tool MLF showed the usefulness of decision tree learners such as MLF's FS-ID3 [22] as preferable. The criteria for selecting a learning algorithm have been, first, prediction performance in combination with ease of use and, second, the comprehensibility of the constructed model. When looking at the predictive performance it has to be mentioned that most algorithms require some amount of tuning the algorithm's hyper-parameters in order to produce satisfying results. So ease of use, i.e., the ease of tuning, had a significant impact on the prediction performance and both criteria were considered together. In addition, quality managers and testers preferred algorithms that provided insight into the relationship between metrics and defects. Managers were able to interpret the classification trees produced by FS-ID3, which considerably increased the trust in prediction results.

Q10: How should the performance of the prediction model be measured?

Typically the performance of a binary prediction model is summarized by the so called confusion matrix, which consists of the following four counts: number of defective modules predicted as defective (true positives, tp), number of non-defective modules predicted as defective (false positives, fp), number of non-defective modules predicted as non-defective (true negatives, tn) and number of defective modules predicted as non-defective (false negatives, fn). Basically one is looking for a prediction model which has high numbers of tp and tn along with low numbers of fp and fn. Many different performance measures like $precision = tp/(tp+fp)$, $recall = tp/(tp+fn)$ or $accuracy = (tp+tn) / (tp + fp + tn + fn)$ are computed from these basic numbers and are used in the literature (see e.g., [9], [12]).

A cost function based on the defect prediction objective should be defined, which assumes the lowest value for the optimal prediction model (see e.g., [20]). Nevertheless, most studies do not include a dedicated cost function as the particular objective for doing defect prediction can only be defined in a real-world setting, most of the available data mining tools report the confusion matrix and the performance measures based on it, and last but not least many learning algorithms are based on optimizing a specific performance measure derived from the confusion matrix.

In the studied project, the goal was to use defect prediction as planning aid for test managers. In this application it has been interesting how much an optimized testing strategy based on defect prediction gains in comparison to a random testing strategy. We will exemplify this idea further in the next section.

5 Overview of Defect Prediction Results

This section gives an overview of our first results that have been achieved by predicting defect-prone components in the studied project. We report results for six analyzed versions of the considered software system, which together span about one year of ongoing software development. Table 1 gives an overview of the analyzed versions.

Table 1. Overview of version analyzed in the studied project

Version	0	1	2	3	4	5	6	Avg.
Number of components	137	147	141	154	171	165	181	157
Number of new or changed comp.	n.a.	141	134	142	135	156	138	141
Number of defective components	77	85	89	91	99	106	84	90
Percentage defective components	56%	58%	63%	59%	58%	64%	46%	58%
Total KLOC	539	605	565	647	682	711	723	639

The number of components per software version varies over time with an average of 157 components per version. In each iteration, the majority of these components – 90 percent on average – are affected by development activities as the number of new or changed components shows. It can also be seen that the number of defective components is rather high and varies around 58 percent. It has been described under questions Q2 and Q3 how the defects are associated to components and versions.

For each version we constructed prediction models from the data of the previous version. The models were then tested on the current version. Table 2 summarizes the performance assessments for these prediction models. Four different models were constructed, reflecting the different data sources available for extracting defect indicators. Thus, results are shown for the models constructed from data from the release management database, the versioning system, the static code analysis repository, and the combination of these three sources. The results of the prediction were compared with the actual data and the performance measures accuracy, precision and recall (defined in the previous section under question Q10) were reported. Bold accuracy indicates the best results for a version. The performance levels confirm the conclusion of Menzies et al. [9] that defect prediction models are useful for classifying defect-prone and defect-free modules and, hence, for guiding the assignment of testing resources.

Following hypothetical example demonstrates the efficiency improvement and, thus, the usefulness of defect prediction for the studied project. The best prediction result has been achieved for version 4. Focusing testing – as a rule of thumb – on the 93 modules classified as defect-prone (*tp+fp*) would already reveal defects from 77 truly defective modules (78 percent of all truly defective modules). A random testing strategy, in contrast, would reveal defects from only 54 truly defective modules from 93 tested modules. Hence, in case testing has to be stopped early and some modules have to be left untested, the effect from testing can be increased up to 43 percent if test planning is based on the results from defect prediction. Even in the worst case (version 1) the gain can be up to 29 percent over a random testing strategy.

Table 2. Summary of defect prediction results obtained in the studied project

Version	1	2	3	4	5	6
Release management						
Accuracy	*0.67*	*0.60*	*0.64*	*0.64*	*0.64*	*0.71*
Precision	0.81	0.90	0.77	0.79	0.75	0.78
Recall	0.55	0.42	0.55	0.53	0.63	0.54
Versioning system						
Accuracy	*0.61*	*0.74*	*0.71*	*0.75*	***0.68***	***0.75***
Precision	0.81	0.84	0.84	0.83	0.92	0.77
Recall	0.41	0.72	0.63	0.73	0.53	0.64
Static code analysis						
Accuracy	*0.66*	***0.76***	***0.73***	*0.54*	*0.67*	*0.73*
Precision	0.73	0.81	0.70	0.92	0.86	0.74
Recall	0.65	0.77	0.93	0.22	0.57	0.67
Combination of above						
Accuracy	*0.67*	*0.68*	*0.71*	***0.78***	***0.68***	*0.73*
Precision	0.75	0.92	0.75	0.83	0.92	0.69
Recall	0.64	0.54	0.77	0.78	0.53	0.77

6 Summary and Further Work

In this paper we presented our preliminary findings from constructing defect prediction models for a large industrial software system with the objective to support planning and management of system testing. The prediction models have been constructed for six subsequent versions of the system from data of their predecessor versions. In total, these six versions reflect the history of about one year of ongoing software development in the studied project. We identified ten questions that corresponded to key decisions in constructing the prediction models. These questions concern aspects such as the granularity level at which predictions should be made, the measure for a module's defectiveness, the sources of prediction data, and the choice of learning algorithms and validation measures.

A number of studies exist that can be appreciated as examples for the various possible choices one has in answering each of the questions. Some studies even address a particular question and conclude with a helpful advice. However, the appropriate answer to each of the questions can only be given in the context of a particular prediction objective and a specific project background. For each question we therefore discussed what influenced the decisions in the real-world project we studied. In addition, we gave some references to the existing body of literature and contrasted common approaches with contradictory observations from the studied project.

The questions led to the following setting for defect prediction. Components have been used as prediction modules (Q1), which were classified as defective or non-defective (Q4) based on the information retrieved from the issue repository (Q2). The defects actually open in a version have been determined by tracing the reported defects to all affected versions (Q3). The metrics computed from the release database, the versioning system and a static analysis tool (Q5) constituted the prediction attributes (Q6), whereby the union of all metrics from the different data sources did not show a substantial improvement over the metrics from the single best source (Q7). The prediction models for a particular version n have been created from the data of their predecessor version $n-1$ (Q8) using different learning algorithms. The FL-ID3 decision tree learner from MLF exhibited interpretable results in combination with best overall prediction performance (Q9), which has been measured in terms of accuracy, precision and recall (Q10).

Taking the best results for each version, the highest accuracy (0.78) has been achieved for version 4 and the lowest (0.67) for version 1. In both cases a testing strategy based on the prediction results is clearly superior to a random approach. Hence, the initial results from the studied project underline the applicability and usefulness of defect prediction for practice, especially as prediction performance may be further improved by fine-tuning the applied learning algorithm.

The key questions provide valuable guidance for constructing defect prediction models in a real-world setting and highlight areas for further research. For example, we currently study the contribution of the different data sources to the overall prediction performance in order to allow better choices on mining repositories and databases for prediction attributes. Furthermore, we investigate industrial projects to define relevant factors for cost functions that enable economically justifiable assessments of prediction results.

References

1. Ostrand, T.J., Weyuker, E.J., Bell, R.M.: Predicting the Location and Number of Faults in Large Software Systems. IEEE Trans. on Software Engineering 31(4), 340–355 (2005)
2. Nagappan, N., Ball, T.: Use of Relative Code Churn Measures to Predict System Defect Density. In: 27th Int. Conf. on Software Engineering, St. Louis, MO, USA. ACM, New York (2005)
3. Nagappan, N., Ball, T., Zeller, A.: Mining Metrics to Predict Component Failures. In: 28th Int. Conf. on Software Engineering, Shanghai, China. ACM, New York (2006)
4. Subramanyam, R., Krishnan, M.: Empirical Analysis of CK Metrics for Object-Oriented Design Complexity: Implications for Software Defects. IEEE Trans. on Software Engineering 29(4), 297–310 (2003)
5. Li, P.L., Herbsleb, J., Shaw, M., Robinson, B.: Experiences and Results from Initiating Field Defect Prediction and Product Test Prioritization Efforts at ABB Inc. In: 28th Int. Conf. on Software Engineering, Shanghai, China. ACM, New York (2006)
6. Weyuker, E.J.: Software Engineering Research: From Cradle to Grave. In: 6th European Software Engineering Conference and ACM SIGSOFT Symposium on the Foundations of Software Engineering, Dubrovnik, Croatia. ACM, New York (2007)
7. Ramler, R., Wolfmaier, K.: Issues and Effort in Integrating Data from Heterogeneous Software Repositories and Corporate Databases. In: 2nd Int. Symposium on Empirical Software Engineering and Measurement, Kaiserslautern, Germany. ACM, New York (2008)
8. Wahyudin, D., Ramler, R., Biffl, S.: A Framework for Defect Prediction in Specific Software Project Contexts. In: 3rd IFIP TC2 Central and East European Conference on Software Engineering Techniques, Brno, Slovakia. Springer, Heidelberg (2008)
9. Menzies, T., Greenwald, J., Frank, A.: Data Mining Static Code Attributes to Learn Defect Predictors. IEEE Trans. on Software Engineering 33, 2–13 (2007)

10. Khoshgoftaar, T.M., Seliya, N.: Analogy-Based Practical Classification Rules for Software Quality Estimation. Empirical Software Engineering 8(4), 325–350 (2003)
11. Kim, S., Whitehead Jr., E.J.: Classifying Software Changes: Clean or Buggy? IEEE Trans. on Software Engineering 34(2), 181–196 (2008)
12. Koru, A.G., Hongfang, L.: Building Defect Prediction Models in Practice. IEEE Software 22, 23–29 (2005)
13. Denaro, G., Pezze, M.: An empirical evaluation of fault-proneness models. In: 24th Int. Conf. on Software Engineering, Orlando, Florida. ACM, New York (2002)
14. Ramler, R.: The Impact of Product Development on the Lifecycle of Defects. In: Workshop on Defects in Large Software Systems, Seattle, WA, USA. ACM, New York (2008)
15. Kutlubay, O., Turhan, B., Bener, A.B.: A Two-Step Model for Defect Density Estimation. In: 33rd Euromicro Conf. on Software Eng. and Advanced Applications, Lübeck, Germany. IEEE, Los Alamitos (2007)
16. Moser, R., Pedrycz, W., Succi, G.: A Comparative Analysis of the Efficiency of Change Metrics and Static Code Attributes for Defect Prediction. In: 30th Int. Conf. on Software Engineering. ACM, New York (2008)
17. Witten, I.H., Frank, E.: Data Mining: Practical Machine Learning Tools and Techniques, 2nd edn. Morgan Kaufmann, San Francisco (2005)
18. Turhan, B., Kocak, G., Bener, A.: Software Defect Prediction Using Call Graph Based Ranking (CGBR) Framework. In: 34th Euromicro Conf. on Software Engineering and Advanced Applications. IEEE, Los Alamitos (2008)
19. Lessmann, S., Baesens, B., Mues, C., Pietsch, S.: Benchmarking Classification Models for Software Defect Prediction: A Proposed Framework and Novel Findings. IEEE Trans. on Software Engineering 34(11), 485–496 (2008)
20. Menzies, T., Di Stefano, J., Ammar, K., McGill, K., Callis, P., Chapman, R., Davis, J.: When Can We Test Less? In: 9th Int. Symposium on Software Metrics, Sydney, Australia. IEEE, Los Alamitos (2003)
21. Koru, A.G., Tian, J.: An Empirical Comparison and Characterization of High Defect and High Complexity Modules. J. Systems and Software 67(3), 153–163 (2003)
22. Natschläger, T., Kossak, F., Drobics, M.: Extracting Knowledge and Computable Models from Data - Needs, Expectations, and Experience. In: 13th Int. Conf. on Fuzzy Systems, Budapest, Hungary. IEEE, Los Alamitos (2004)

Investigating the Impact
of Software Requirements Specification Quality
on Project Success

Eric Knauss, Christian El Boustani, and Thomas Flohr

FG Software Engineering, Leibniz Universität Hannover
Welfengarten 1, D-30167 Hannover, Germany
{knauss,el.boustani,flohr}@se.uni-hannover.de

Abstract. Different Software Requirements Specifications (SRS) are
hard to compare due to the uniqueness of the projects they were created in. Without such comparison, it is difficult to objectively determine
if a project's SRS is good enough to serve as a foundation for project
success. We define a quality model for SRS and derive required metrics
using the Goal-Question-Metric approach. These metrics were applied
in roughly 40 student's software projects. Based on this we find a quality threshold for project success. This paper contributes in three areas:
Firstly, we present our quality model. It was derived from literature, and
contributes to the discussion of how to objectively measure requirements
quality. Secondly, we share our evaluation approach and our experiences
measuring SRS quality. Others could profit, when planning to measure
requirements quality. Finally, we present our findings and compare them
to related studies in literature.

Keywords: Quality of Requirements, Metrics for Requirements.

1   Introduction

One of the main difficulties faced by Quality Management during the requirements analysis in software projects is to decide, whether a software requirements
specification (SRS) is *good enough*. This is due to two major problems:

1. It is hard to measure *how good* a SRS is, i.e. determine the quality of a SRS
   in a quantifiable way.
2. If the quality of a SRS is determined, it still remains an open question,
   whether the value is *good enough* or not. The quality of the SRS has to be
   compared to other projects.

Basically, our hypothesis is that the quality of a SRS strongly influences the
probability of its project success. In this paper we show that the quality can
be measured mainly based on formal and objective metrics. This is important,
because it allows to assess the chances of a project based on SRS quality internally. If quality is below a certain quality threshold, the project is more likely

F. Bomarius et al. (Eds.): PROFES 2009, LNBIP 32, pp. 28–42, 2009.
© Springer-Verlag Berlin Heidelberg 2009

to fail. In order to determine this threshold we investigated roughly 40 projects based on the Goal-Question-Metric method. Based on our results we found two specific thresholds:

A lower threshold: Projects that have a SRS's quality below this value are highly endangered.
A higher threshold: Projects that have a SRS's quality above this value are likely to succeed.

These results have been discussed in [1]. In this contribution, we focus on the methodology and comparison of our results. We start with an overview of literature dealing with quality of requirement in Sect. 2. Based on this literature we decided what aspects to measure. We give examples of some promising and more sophisticated metrics in literature and discuss why they are not appropriate to our work.

The Goal-Question-Metric method basically demands for a top-down approach. Therefore, we start by stating our measurement-goal and our hypotheses. We also define, when a hypothesis is supported and when it is falsified. This is done in Sect. 3.

In Sect. 4 we explain how the measurement was done. We summarize our findings and discuss them. Finally, we compare them to the results of other empirical studies.

Next, we need to show how trustworthy our results are: We think that our empirical results are valuable to others and want to make them comparable (and hence transferable). Therefore, we discuss the validity of our results in Sect. 5.

We summarize our results in Sect. 6. We also give hints on how to enhance the reliability of similar studies.

2   Requirements Quality in Literature

Quality aspects and metrics for requirements have been widely discussed in literature. The difficulties are well known and were often discussed (e.g. see [2]). Obviously, it is very difficult to obtain objective data. For example, it is hard to determine, whether a requirement specification is complete or not. Without the original stakeholders it is impossible to decide if it contains all the requirements.

There are many textbooks [3,4,5,6] that describe how to write high-quality requirements specifications. The quality gateway in [5] is a well known example: Only *good* requirements can pass it. A *good* requirement fulfills several quality criteria. For example, only requirements are allowed to pass the quality gateway that state how to decide whether they are met. However, this process does not help to compare the requirements specifications of different projects.

Rupp [6] gives a more analytical approach to requirement's quality. Well-known quality aspects, like completeness, are revisited. But where the Robertsons [5] defined completeness based on requirements templates, [6] shows how to find incomplete requirements based on natural language. Both approaches help to enhance the quality of SRS, but do not help to quantifiable compare it. Nevertheless, the quality aspects in these textbooks are the foundation of our work.

Davis [3] gives some suggestions on how to quantify the quality of a requirements document: Findings are weighted according to their severity. Accordingly, the overall quality of a document is the amount of findings multiplied by their weight. We integrated this suggestion as well as the proposed weights into our approach. In order to compare two SRS, we had to normalize the result by the amount of their requirements.

Besides the rather basic quality-metrics for requirements discussed above, many more sophisticated ones were suggested in science. For example, the clearness of terms is discussed in the CLEAR-method [7]. Another example is the discussion of the ambiguity of *and* respectively *or* in natural language [8]. Based on our measurement goals we had to discard these promising metrics, because they either constructively influenced the RE-process or were simply too difficult to measure.

3 Study Goals

The GQM (Goal-Question-Metric) method suggests a top-down way of goal-oriented measurement. The basic steps are defining measurement goals, describing the goals in a more detailed way using a table (the Abstraction Sheet), to formulate questions, and to derive metrics from the Abstraction Sheet that help to answer the questions in a quantifiable way (see [9]).

By filling out the Abstraction Sheets we formulated hypotheses about how good the quality goals are reached at the moment. Those hypotheses are expected measurements results. After the elicitation of data we are able to verify the hypotheses and determine if they were correct or not. We only give a sketch of our GQM-tree, examples of metrics, and our main hypotheses here.

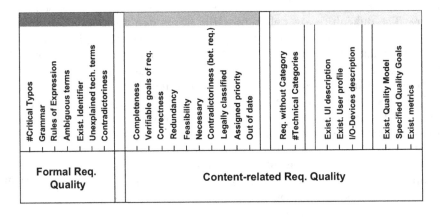

Fig. 1. Measurement goals and metrics for Requirements Quality

Figure 1 gives an overview of goals and metrics in our study. We planned to systematically measure the quality of Software Requirements Specifications (SRS). We have two subgoals: the formal requirements quality and the content related requirements quality. The main goal is to assess the quality of a SRS and to draw a connection to project success. The term *formal requirements quality* refers to verbalization rules as in [6] (e.g. completely specified process words, avoidance of incomplete comparisons, etc.). In contrast, *content related requirements quality* refers to goals that need interpretation to some extend. For example to judge, whether the SRS contains a quality model or not, the assessor has to search for quality aspects and decide, if they were sufficiently detailed. Content related requirements quality is subdivided into general, technical, UI, and quality aspects.

3.1 Project Settings

The objects of this study are software projects conducted in university teaching. These software projects (SWP) are part of the curriculum of our bachelor in computer science. All participants had basic courses in programming languages, data structures and algorithms, as well as in software engineering and project management. Participants with additional knowledge in one or more advanced courses like databases, artificial intelligence, or requirements engineering were evenly distributed among the project teams.

Each project team consists of five members. The students had to elect a project manager among themselves for their course. The projects last one term (four months) and students spent approximately 16 hours a week for their project.

We try to let our students experience a realistic software project. Therefore, each project has a customer with real interest in the final software product. This is important to determine project success. In addition, we limit the time our students may spend to interview the customer. Time for technical questions or advice is also limited.

Our students have to follow a strict waterfall development process. They start with an analysis phase, go on to design phase, and finally implement the software in the last phase, before the customer accepts (or sometimes even rejects) the software in a final test.

We measure the quality of SRS at the end of the analysis phase. At this point the requirements are frozen and the design phase builds upon them. Our motivation for this work is to identify projects that are in trouble. We run up to 9 projects in parallel. All projects reach the end of the requirements analysis at the same time. A typical SRS has more than 30 pages and contains more than 50 functional requirements. If we want to help, we need to find the project that needs our sparse resources the most.

3.2 Hypotheses

In order to judge a project's success we interviewed each customer and asked him to rate the success based on the following scale:

⊞ The project's results (i.e. software) are used in the intended way.

⊞ The project's results could be used in the intended way, but there are better solutions available to reach the customer's goals.

⊟ Projects in this category failed to reach some of the customer's goals. The customer believes that these goals are reachable within a month of rework.

■ This category consists of projects that failed to deliver working software. These projects failed the acceptance tests and the customer does not believe that it would pay off to continue the project.

Note that our definition of project success differs from [10]: Our projects cannot overrun time and budget, because they are stopped at the end of term. If they cannot deliver, they have failed (category ■). Only projects in category ⊞ are considered successful.

Concerning the relationship between SRS quality and project success we have the following hypotheses:

Hypothesis 1. Projects with a high quality-score are more likely to succeed (category ⊞).
Influencing factors: Relationship between formal quality aspects and quality of the SRS's content as reported in [11]. A high quality SRS might also be a sign of well-organized teams, more likely to succeed in delivering valuable software.
Hypothesis holds if we find an upper threshold with more than 75% of the projects scoring above, fall in category ⊞ or ⊞.

Hypothesis 2. Projects with very low quality-score are much more likely to fail (category ■).
Influencing factors: A low-quality SRS is bad enough. But teams that produce a bad SRS might have additional problems. For example, team members may work against each other or may have a bad time-managing. These difficulties may multiply as the project proceeds.
Hypothesis holds if a lower quality-threshold can be found, with more than 75% of projects scoring below, fail (⊟ or ■).

4   Conduction and Findings

This section describes, how our study was conducted. It gives an example of a metric and shows our results. We also discuss the implications for our metrics and compare our results to others.

4.1   Strategy of Measurement

Concerning the elicitation of the quantitative data we defined basic constraints. Because we wanted to compare 40 SRS and because of our limited resources we had to limit the time for the elicitation. We planned to spend less than 240 minutes per SRS.

We were interested in the relationship between formal quality aspects and project success. Therefore, we decided not to take the customers point of view into account (i.e. we did not measure whether the requirements were complete from the customer's point of view).

To enhance the speed of measurement we introduced a software tool to support the assessment of a SRS. The whole text of a SRS was copied and pasted into the tool. The tool separated each sentence and asked the assessor to decide whether it was a functional, technical, UI, or quality requirement. After that it presented each requirement and asked the assessor to look for each metric. Figure 2 shows the general process of assessing a SRS.

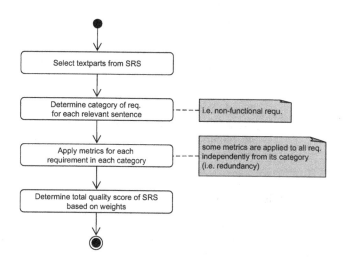

Fig. 2. Activities of analyzing a SRS

For some metrics the tool included heuristic support. For example a full-text search presented candidates for contradictory requirements. According to [12] a metric should fulfil the following requirements:

Simplicity: Effort of interpretation should be adequate. Therefore, we give the results in percentage or in numbers.

Validity: Reasonably correlation between metric and measured property. Metrics were created using the GQM-Method, the heuristic tool-support only indicates possible flaws.

Stability: Stability of the metric against manipulation of lower subordinated consideration. We consider this to be fulfilled because of using percentage and numbers.

Timeliness: Elicitation must be early enough to be able to adjust the process. This is met, because the measurement of the SRS takes place in the first stage of the project.

Analyzability: One should be able to put data of measurements in relation. Our results are given in percentage or comparable numbers.

Repeatability: Objective measurement-criteria must exist. Subjective exertion of influence must not be possible. This is only partly fulfilled because of the subjective factors in some metrics (see section 5).

Table 1 gives an example of a metric.

Table 1. Example of a metric based on 1

Metric	Formular
Verifiable goals of reqs.	$\frac{\sum verifiable\ aspects\ of\ req.}{\sum allaspects\ of\ req.}$
Simplicity:	Yes, because of percentage scale
Stability:	Yes, because of percentage scale
Timeliness:	Yes, because of measurement of the SRS in the first stage of the project
Analysable:	Yes, because percentage number can be easily compared
Repeatability:	Partly, because the decision whether or not an aspect of an requirement is verifiable, may differ from person to person

4.2   Results and Discussion

Figure 3 show an excerpt from the data we obtained. This data covers the 16 projects conducted in the last two years. The colors of the bars reflect the part of the goal-tree in figure 1:

Gray: Results of metrics that belong to the *formal requirements quality* measurement goal.

Light gray: Results of general metrics that hold for all requirements and belong to the general *content related requirements quality* measurement goal.

White: *Content related requirements quality* metrics that are specific for non-functional requirements.

In order to compare SRS of different projects, we want to determine a total score for a single SRS. To do so, we take a list from quality aspects for requirements, that is based on widespread standards [13] and pragmatic extensions [6]. For every aspect we add a weight, that indicates how important this quality aspect is estimated to be according to Davis proposals [3].

Let $m_i(srs)$ be metric i applied to all requirements of the SRS and w_i the weight of a quality-aspect from the Tab. 2, that is associated with the metric i as specified in our GQM-Model. The total score of a SRS with respect to quality of requirements is:

$$f(srs) = \sum_i w_i * m_i(srs) \tag{1}$$

Table 2. Weights of quality-aspects of requirements

Quality-aspect	Weight (w)
Correctness	10
Feasibility	10
Without contradiction	10
Up to date	9
Verifiable goal of req.	8
Comprehensibility	5
Quality of Necessary	3
Completeness	2
Unambiguousness	2
Assigned priority	1
Legally classified	1

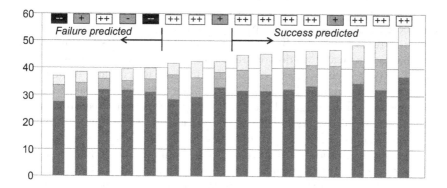

Fig. 3. Quality scores of SRS for 16 projects

Low values (below 40) indicate low SRS quality, with a high risk for errors. Values above 44 indicate high quality. Interestingly, these results generally supported each project advisor's gut feeling.

Based on our hypotheses in Sect. 3 we investigate our software projects' requirement specifications. We are interested in the dependency of a project's quality score and its success. The results support our hypotheses:

Hypothesis 1 holds: All projects that scored more than 44 Points were successful (category ++ or +). The results in Fig. 3 give even stronger support: 87% of the projects that score more than 44 on the quality-assessment fall into category ++.

Hypothesis 2 holds: All projects that failed (category - and --) scored below 40 points and we found only one project from category ++ below this threshold. Therefore, 80% of the projects below the lower threshold were not satisfactory.

Investigations of the remaining projects support this. In contradiction to the results in Fig. 3 they also show that projects that score somewhere between the upper and lower quality-threshold have a remaining risk of failure. Based on these results we do not suppose that the upper threshold could be set lower.

4.3   Comparison to Related Studies

Forsberg [14] investigated the relationship between time spent for RE and project success. Accordingly, it is advisable to spent about 20% of the time with requirements engineering. Our work cannot add to these results because our students could not decide how much time to spend for RE. All projects spent roughly 20% of their time for requirements analysis. Because of this timeboxing, we are able to draw a connection between SRS quality and project success.

In [15] So and Berry investigated how adjustments of the RE-process improved requirements engineering. This work compared two releases of a large software product. The encouraging result is that RE efforts pay-off. The evidence is based on the decreased number of bug reports and change requests. Again, we cannot directly add to these results, because our development process does not include change management and we do not track bugs after release. Therefore, our definition of project success differs too much. However we can add evidence that good requirements engineering increases customer satisfaction.

Olsson et al. [16] investigated the relationship of functional requirements and non-functional requirements (NFR) at Sony-Ericsson. Accordingly, about 40 % of the requirements specified were non-functional. This result is very interesting for our work: It shows a quantifiable (i.e. comparable) difference (despite project size) between our students' projects and high-quality industrial software projects. Table 3 shows the relationship derived from our data. The difference is much lower than expected. However, the non-functional requirements in our projects were poorly specified (e.g. there were no testable quality requirements).

Table 3. Relationship of functional requirements and non-functional requirements

Percentage of technical requirements	10%
Percentage of UI requirements	2,8%
Percentage of quality requirements	17,2%
Percentage of non-functional requirements	30%

Kamata and Tamai [17] investigate the relationship between the quality of a SRS and project success. In difference to our approach they rely upon data derived from normal quality assurance activities. Quality Agents rate each section of a SRS based on 100 criterions. Their approach of measuring requirements quality seems to rely on subjective criterions and the Quality Agent's experience. Based on the maturity of the organization, the evaluaton results can be considered repeatable.

The quality of a SRS is computed by mapping the ratings to requirement arti-facts (i.e. subsections proposed for SRS in [13]). This allows Kamata and Tamai to identify critical sections for project success. In addition, computing a SRS quality profile based on a accepted SRS structure enhances the comparability of their approach. In order to compare our results to the results of Kamata and Tamai, we performed several steps:

1. *Describe fundamental differences of the approaches.* In contrast to [17], we focused on mostly formal metrics. We tried to make our metrics as objec-tive as possible instead of relying on experienced assessors. In addition, we measured the quality as a whole. The main result is the same: Both our work reports that a correlation between SRS quality and project success exists. Table 4 shows how the different definitions of project success can be compared.

2. *Map our results to the proposed structure.* In order to compare the results we normalized the results of each metric to values between 0 and 1. Some of our content-related metrics can be mapped to the proposed structure. The others measure quality of the specification as a whole. So we filtered each finding of such a metric by the section of our specification where it was found. Then, we mapped the sections of our specification to the proposed structure. Finally, we can give a rating between 0 and 5 for each section of the proposed structure for our projects.

Based on this mapping, we can compare the profiles of our successful and failed projects to the corresponding profiles reported in [17]. Our goal was to investigate if we could identify critical sections in our projects, too. As shown in Fig. 4 we did not achieve good results. One reason for this is that our metrics do not measure quality in each section in a fair way:

Table 4. Comparing Definitions of Project success

	In Costs	Over Costs
Over Time	- / +	--
In Time	++	+ / -

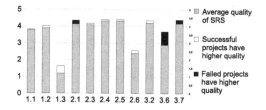

Fig. 4. Quality of our SRS per section mapped to IEEE template [13]

We have many metrics that apply to sections 1.3 and 3.2 but only our general metrics for formal requirements quality apply to section 3.7. Based on our obser-vations we would support Kamata and Tamai in that not all sections are equally important for project success. However, our GQM-study cannot contribute to these results, because it was focussed on other measurement goals.

5   Evaluation of Validity

This section presents the threats to validity we identified during our work (according to Wohlin et al. [18]) in order to let others decide if our work is relevant for them.

5.1   Construction Validity

Construction Validity describes issues that are caused by the construction of the empirical evaluation.

The construction of our study is influenced by the design of the practical programming course we investigated. Apart from our study, students should learn to accomplish a whole software project. Therefore, we were not allowed to exchange the SRS between the groups investigated. This leads to the issue that our model might measure the performance of the students groups instead of the project success. Good students achieve good results (i.e. good SRS, good design, and finally good projects). The investigation of this issue remains future work.

5.2   Conclusion Validity

Conclusion validity mainly concerns the possibility to draw statistically significant conclusions from the empirical study.

The main problem we see here is the reliability of measures. Since some measures rely on human judgement to some degree a certain bias is probable. This problem was mitigated by conducting the measurements by the same person. To apply the measurements in a company (where measurements will be conducted by different persons) we suggest to develop measurement guidelines over time to reduce the influence of human judgement. We take a closer look on repeatability in section 5.5.

A minor threat concerns the statistical power. 16 specifications were intensely reviewed by one person. The considerable number of the remaining 24 specifications were reviewed by different persons. Our original measurement results seem to hold for these 24 specifications, too.

5.3   Internal Validity

Internal validity concerns the influences on independent variables beyond the knowledge of the reviewer.

Since all measurements were conducted by one single person measures could be applied in a different way over time, because the person got more familiar with the measurement process. The second problem concerns the fatigue. There is a considerable probability that the person got tired over time, affecting measurements in a untraceable way. This problem is considered to be low, because only one SRS was measured per day.

In addition, other factors during the later phases of the projects might have influenced the empirical results. This issue is moderated by the fact that all observed projects followed the same process. Furthermore, we carefully observed the groups and did a post-mortem analysis, but could not observe any such factors.

5.4 External Validity

External validity concerns the ability to draw conclusions beyond the scope of our empirical study e.g. transfer our results to industry.

A rather superficial threat to external validity is that all investigated projects were conducted in a university setting. Consequently, transferability of the results poses a problem. The fact that all our projects have a common background setting helps to achieve a better result concerning data quality (which strengthens conclusion validity). Industry strength projects could be assessed in the same way and compared to our findings, because the application of our metrics is not limited in any way. We opted for conclusion validity instead of external validity in order to gain more data points.

5.5 Discussion of Repeatability

A more severe threat concerns the repeatability: How do different assessors affect the result? We let four different persons assess the same project. The results of one person differed drastically from the others as shown in figure 5.

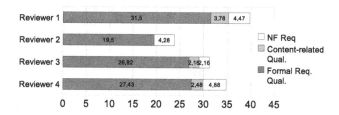

Fig. 5. Assessment of repeatability shows room for improvement

We analyzed each variably classified requirement. The main reasons for the derivation were:

1. False positives, e.g. requirement was classified as passive voice but was formulated in active voice.
2. Scope of interpretation, e.g. finding process words.
3. Generally subjective measures, e.g. understandability, redundancy, and technical terms

The effect of false positives and scope of interpretation can be reduced by more extensive training, keyword-lists, and heuristic tools. Furthermore, these errors are systematic: if one person assesses a project twice, the result will be more or less the same. Therefore, we expect that the ranking of the projects will be more or less the same, despite different quality-scores. Bad projects will be rated worse than good projects.

Another problem is the complexity and long duration of the assessment. An assessment of a typical SRS took between 120 and 180 minutes. In addition, some of the measurements are rather complex, like finding inconsistencies between different requirements.

Based on these threats to validity there are also some issues concerning the mapping between SRS quality and project success. Because of the different scores the reference project got depended on the reviewer, there is no absolute threshold for the quality-score. However, with all reviewers creating a consistent ranking of the projects, we can give a relative quality thresholds.

Table 5 shows types of measurement faults we identified. The first column gives the type and the second column a typical example. The third column shows how we would address this problems in future work.

Table 5. Overview of Measurement Faults

Type	Example	Mitigation Strategy
1 False Positives	*found* passive voice *but was* active voice	• training • keyword-lists
2 Scope of Interpretation	*identification of process words*	• heuristic tool support
3 Generally subjective measures	*understandability*	• quantify and limit the effects

6 Conclusion and Outlook

In this work we had two goals. On the one hand we wanted to measure the quality of software requirements specifications. On the other hand we wanted to depict project risk based on this quality.

In order to do this, we had to investigate a set of software projects. Based on the GQM-method we could support our hypotheses that the quality of a requirement specification influences the probability of project success. In our setting we were even able to give a threshold: projects that are worse than this value are very likely to fail.

With this assessment of the SRS' quality we have a powerful instrument for our software projects: Based on the results we can decide whether a project is allowed to go on or whether its SRS needs major rework. Based on our assessment we also observed that the overall quality of our projects' SRS increased since last year. Such observations are essential for software organizations that want to improve themselves, because the effects of process improvements become visible.

As a side-effect we found out that even simple verbalization policies (e.g. the requirement template [6] or the use case template [19]) strongly improved the requirement quality. Such policies simply let fewer room for errors.

However, our approach has some known limitations. Our assessment cannot replace the validation of requirements. There is still the need of customer collaboration, e.g. aspects regarding the content cannot be quantified using the SRS only. Nevertheless, our assessment helps finding hazardous points in the SRS, that can be addressed during validation. Therefore, it helps increasing the efficiency of Reviews. The main drawback of our work is the limited repeatability. In section 5 we argued that this does not limit the validity of our results. However, this causes our specific threshold to be worthless for others, leaving each organization with the need to find and calibrate their own threshold.

For this reason we plan to enhance the elicitation of our metrics. On the one hand we will improve the preparation courses of our quality agents. In addition we will provide them with more detailed instructions on how to interpret a given metric. On the other hand we want to introduce more heuristic tool support. With the reduced cognitive load of separating false positives from true ones, we hope to enhance repeatability as well as elicitation speed.

Finally, we were able to compare our teaching projects to industry projects. Despite being considerably smaller and at some points not as good as their real-world siblings, we saw that our projects are highly comparable. Because of this we expect others being able to build upon our results.

References

1. Knauss, E., El Boustani, C.: Assessing the Quality of Software Requirements Specifications. In: Proceedings of 16th International Requirements Engineering Conference, Barcelona, Spain, pp. 341–342 (2008)
2. Costello, R.J., Liu, D.B.: Metrics for requirements engineering. In: Selected papers of the sixth annual Oregon workshop on Software metrics, New York, USA, pp. 39–63 (1995)
3. Davis, A.M.: Just Enough Requirements Management: Where Software Development meets Marketing (2005)
4. Gause, D.C., Weinberg, G.M.: Exploring Requirements: Quality Before Design (1989)
5. Robertson, S., Robertson, J.: Mastering the Requirements Process (1999)
6. Rupp, C.: Requirements-Engineering und -Management: professionelle, iterative Anforderungsanalyse für die Praxis (2004)
7. Wasson, K.S.: A Case Study in Systematic Improvement of Language for Requirements. In: Proceedings of the 14th IEEE International Requirements Engineering Conference, Minneapolis, USA, pp. 6–15 (2006)
8. Chantree, F., Nuseibeh, B., de Roeck, A., Willis, A.: Identifying Nocuous Ambiguities in Natural Language Requirements. In: Proceedings of the 14th IEEE International Requirements Engineering Conference, Minneapolis, USA, pp. 56–65 (2006)
9. van Solingen, R., Berghout, E.: The Goal/Question/Metric Method: a practical guide for quality improvement of software development (1999)
10. The Standish Group: CHAOS Chronicles v3.0. Technical report (2003)
11. Wilson, W.M., Rosenberg, L.H., Hyatt, L.E.: Automated analysis of requirement specifications. In: ICSE 1997: Proceedings of the 19th international conference on Software engineering, New York, USA, pp. 161–171 (1997)

12. Liggesmeyer, P.: Software-Qualität. Testen, Analysieren und Verifizieren von Software (2002)
13. IEEE: IEEE Recommended Practice for Software Requirements Specifications. IEEE Std 830-1998 (1998)
14. Forsberg, K., Mooz, H.: System Engineering Overview. In: Thayer, R.H., Dorfman, M., Davis, A.M. (eds.) Software Requirements Engineering, Los Alamitos CA, pp. 44–72 (1997)
15. So, J., Berry, D.M.: Experiences of Requirements Engineering for Two Consecutive Versions of a Product at VLSC. In: RE 2006: Proceedings of the 14th IEEE International Requirements Engineering Conference (RE 2006), Washington, DC, USA, pp. 216–221 (2006)
16. Olsson, T., Svensson, R.B., Regnell, B.: Non-functional requirements metrics in practice - an empirical document analysis. In: Proceedings of Workshop on Measuring Requirements for Project and Product Success, in conjunction with the IWSM-Mensura Conference (2007)
17. Kamata, M.I., Tamai, T.: How Does Requirements Quality Relate to Project Success or Failure? In: Proceedings of 15th International Requirements Engineering Conference, Delhi, India, pp. 69–78 (2007)
18. Wohlin, C., Runeson, P., Höst, M., Ohlsson, M.C.: Experimentation In Software Engineering: An Introduction, 1st edn. (1999)
19. Cockburn, A.: Writing Effective Use Cases (2000)

Prediction of Software Quality Model Using Gene Expression Programming

Yogesh Singh, Arvinder Kaur, and Ruchika Malhotra

University School of Information Technology, GGS Indraprastha University,
Delhi 110403, India
Ys66@rediffmail.com, arvinderkaurtakkar@yahoo.com,
ruchikamalhotra@yahoo.com

Abstract. There has been number of measurement techniques proposed in the literature. These metrics can be used in assessing quality of software products, thereby controlling costs and schedules. The empirical validation of object-oriented (OO) metrics is essential to ensure their practical relevance in industrial settings. In this paper, we empirically validate OO metrics given by Chidamber and Kemerer for their ability to predict software quality in terms of fault proneness. In order to analyze these metrics we use gene expression programming (GEP). Here, we explore the ability of OO metrics using defect data for open source software. Further, we develop a software quality metric and suggest ways in which software professional may use this metric for process improvement. We conclude that GEP can be used in detecting fault prone classes. We also conclude that the proposed metric may be effectively used by software managers tin predicting faulty classes in earlier phases of software development.

Keywords: Metrics, Object-oriented, Software Quality, Empirical validation, Fault prediction, Gene expression programming.

1 Introduction

Faulty software classes cause software failures, increase development time, maintenance costs and decrease customer satisfaction. Effective prediction models can help software developers focus quality assurance activities on fault-prone classes and thus improve software quality by using testing resources more efficiently. Static metrics and fault data collected at class level can be used to construct fault prediction models in practice. There have been empirical studies evaluating the impact of these metrics on software quality and constructing models that utilize them in predicting quality attributes of the system, such as [1-21]. However, there is a need of data based studies to empirically validate these metrics for predicting faulty classes. In this work, we find the impact of OO metrics on fault proneness of a class using open source software Jedit [22]. We also develop a software quality metric, which can be used to predict faulty classes.

F. Bomarius et al. (Eds.): PROFES 2009, LNBIP 32, pp. 43–58, 2009.
© Springer-Verlag Berlin Heidelberg 2009

Genetic algorithms have been successfully applied to protein structure prediction [23], defect prediction [24], and memory bound computations [25]. GEP is a type of GA as it uses population of individuals, selected them according to fitness function, and introduces genetic variation using various operators [26]. In GEP mutations insure that the resultant expression is not mathematically incorrect. "Experiments have shown that GEP is 100 to 60,000 times faster than older genetic algorithms" [27]. Thus, we build a model to predict faulty classes using the GEP. In GEP an expression is computed in order to predict faulty/non faulty classes. We analyze and validate this expression in order to predict faulty/non-faulty classes. Finally, we propose this expression as a quality metric for predicted fault prone classes. The lower values of this metric will imply higher build and release quality.

The main contributions of this study are summarized as follows: First, we empirically validated OO metrics using GEP. This method is being successfully applied in various disciplines and there is a need to evaluate its performance in predicting software quality models. Second, we used open source software system. These systems are developed with different development methods than proprietary software. In previous studies mostly proprietary software were analyzed. Third, we develop a software quality metric that can be used by software quality practitioner in earlier phases of software development to predict faulty classes. The proposed metric may also be used as quality benchmark to assess and compare software products. The results showed that the proposed metric predict faulty classes with good accuracy. However, since our analysis is based on only one data set, this study should be replicated on different data sets to generalize our findings.

The paper is organized as follows: Section 2 provides an overview of GEP. Section 3 summarizes the metrics studied, describes sources from which data is collected and gives hypothesis to be tested in the study. Section 4 presents the research methodology followed in this paper. The results of the study are given in section 5. Section 6 presents the definition and validation of the developed metric. The application of the developed software quality metric is presented in section 7. Finally, conclusions of the research are presented in section 8.

2 An Overview of Gene Expression Programming

A genetic algorithm (GA) is a search procedure with a goal to find a solution in a multidimensional space. GA is generally many times faster than exhaustive search procedures. There is a problem in finding a way to efficiently mutate and cross-breed symbolic expressions so that the resultant expressions have a valid mathematical syntax.

Candida Ferreira provided a solution to this problem [26]. Ferreira developed a system for encoding expressions so that a wide variety of mutation and cross-breeding techniques perform faster while guaranteeing that the resultant expression will always be a valid mathematical syntax. This procedure is known as GEP. GEP was presented as a new technique for the creation of computer programs. GEP uses chromosomes composed of genes organized in a head and a tail. The chromosomes are subjected to modification by means of mutation, inversion, transposition, and recombination. The technique performs with high efficiency that greatly surpasses existing adaptive techniques.

2.1 Converting Expression Tree into k-Expression

GEP encodes the symbols in genes. This notation is called the karva language [26]. Expressions encoded using karva language are called k-expressions.

For example, the expression a+b*c can be encoded in the expression tree shown in Figure 1.

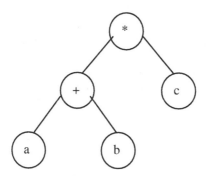

Fig. 1. Expression Tree for a+b*c

To convert the expression tree using karva language, start at the left-most symbol in top line, scan symbols from top to bottom, and left to right. The resultant k-expression is *+cab.

The process of converting an expression tree into a k-expression and vice versa can be done quickly by a computer.

2.2 Genes

The fixed number of symbols encoded in karva language constitutes a gene. A GEP gene has a head and a tail. The head can contain functions, constants, and variables whereas a tail can only contain variables and constants. The number of symbols in the head of a gene is passed as an argument in the analysis. The number of symbols in the tail is determined by the following equation

$$\text{tail} = \text{head (Max-1)} + 1 \tag{1}$$

where tail is the number of symbols in the tail
 head is the number of symbols in the head
 Max is the maximum number of operands required by any function
 The tail provides a store of terminal symbols consisting of variables and constants that can be used as arguments for functions in the head. For example, head can be +,*,/ and tail can be abde. The expression is shown in Figure 2.

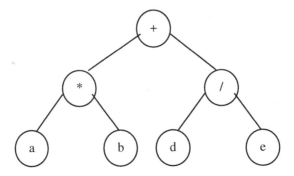

Fig. 2. Expression for Head +,*, / and Tail abde

During mutation, symbols in the head can be replaced by terminal symbols or functions whereas terminals (variables and constants) can replace symbols in the tail (see Figure 3).

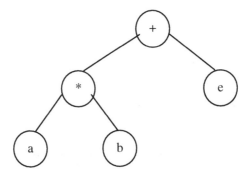

Fig. 3. Resultant Expression after Mutation

GEP ensures that the following rules are followed inorder to generate valid expression during mutation:

1. Symbols in the head are replaced with functions, constants, and variables.
2. Symbols in the tail are only replaced with variables and constants
3. The tail is of sufficient length (see equation (1))

2.3 Chromosomes

A chromosome consist of one or more than one genes of equal length. If there are more then on chromosomes in the gene, then a linking function is used to join the genes in the final function.

Consider the following example:

Gene 1: +ab
Gene 2: *cd

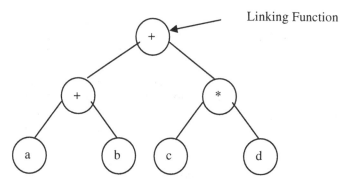

Fig. 4. Example of a 2-Gene Chromosome

The following steps are used in the training of a model using GEP:

1. Create an initial population of chromosomes.
2. Attempt to create chromosomes that model the data well.
3. Try to find a simpler function.

2.4 GEP Process

In order for a population to improve from generations to generations to predict the target variable (fault proneness in our study), mutation, inversion, transportation, and recombination are performed.

Mutation
Mutation can occur anywhere in the chromosomes but the structural organization of the chromosomes should not be changed. Mutation replaces symbols in heads of genes by function or variables and constants and symbols in tails are replaced only by variables and constants. Thus, the structural organization of chromosomes remains intact and the correct programs are produced by the mutation in the form of new individuals.

Inversion
Inversion reverses the order of symbol in a gene section.

Transposition
Transposition selects a group of symbols and moves them to a different position in the same gene.

Recombination
Two chromosomes are selected randomly and generic portion is exchanged between them inorder to produce two new chromosomes. There are three types of recombinations: one-point, two-point, and gene recombination.

3 Research Background

In this section, we present the summary of metrics studied in this paper (Section 3.1) and empirical data collection (Section 3.2).

3.1 Dependent and Independent Variables

The binary dependent variable in our study is fault proneness. The goal of our study is to empirically explore the relationship between OO metrics and fault proneness at the class level. Fault proneness is defined as the probability of fault detection in a class. We use GEP to predict probability of fault proneness. Our dependent variable will be predicted based on the faults found during software development. The software metrics [28-36] can be used in predicting these quality attributes. In this study, we empirically validated metrics given Chidamber and Kemerer [32] (see Table 1). These metrics are explained with practical applications in [28].

Table 1. Metrics Studied (Chidamber and Kemerer [32] suite)

Metric	Definition
Coupling between Objects (CBO)	CBO for a class is count of the number of other classes to which it is coupled and vice versa.
Lack of Cohesion (LCOM)	It measures the dissimilarity of methods in a class by looking at the instance variable or attributes used by methods. Consider a class C_1 with n methods $M_1, M_2...., M_n$. Let (I_j) = set of all instance variables used by method M_j. There are n such sets $\{I_1\},.......\{I_n\}$. Let $P = \{(I_i, I_j) \mid I_i \cap I_j = 0\}$ and $Q = \{((I_i, I_j) \mid I_i \cap I_j \neq 0\}$. If all n sets $\{(I_1\},.........(I_n)\}$ are 0 then P=0 $$LCOM = \mid P \mid - \mid Q \mid, \text{ if } \mid P \mid > \mid Q \mid$$ $$= 0 \text{ otherwise}$$
Number of Children (NOC)	The NOC is the number of immediate subclasses of a class in a hierarchy.
Depth of Inheritance (DIT)	The depth of a class within the inheritance hierarchy is the maximum number of steps from the class node to the root of the tree and is measured by the number of ancestor classes.
Weighted Methods per Class (WMC)	The WMC is a count of sum of complexities of all methods in a class. Consider a class K1, with methods M1,........ Mn that are defined in the class. Let C1,..........Cn be the complexity of the methods. $$WMC = \sum_{i=1}^{n} Ci$$ If all method complexities are considered to be unity, then WMC = n, the number of methods in the class.
Response for a Class (RFC)	The response set of a class (RFC) is defined as set of methods that can be potentially executed in response to a message received by an object of that class. It is given by RFC=|RS|, where RS, the response set of the class, is given by $$RS = M_i \cup_{all\ j} \{R_{ij}\}$$
Number of Public Methods (NPM)	It is the count of number of public methods in a class.
Lines Of Code (LOC)	It is the count of lines in the text of the source code excluding comment lines

To incorporate the correlation of independent variables, a correlation based feature selection technique (CFS) is applied to select to select the best predictors out of independent variables in the datasets [37]. The best combinations of independent variable were searched through all possible combinations of variables. CFS evaluates the best of a subset of variables (OO metrics in our case) by considering the individual predictive ability of each feature along with the degree of redundancy between them.

3.2 Empirical Data Collection

We used JEdit open source software in this study [38]. JEdit is a programmer's text editor developed using Java language. JEdit combines the functionality of Window, Unix, and MacOS text editors. It was released as free software and the source code is available on www.sourceforge.net/projects/jedit. The LOC of JEdit is 169,107. The number of developers involved in this project was 144. The project was started in 1999.

The metric data was computed using metric tool, Understand for Java [39]. The metrics proposed by Chidamber and Kemerer [32] were computed using this tool. The number of bugs was computed using SVC repositories. The release point for the project was identified in 2002. The log data from that point to 2007 was collected. The header files in C++ were excluded in data collection. The word bug or fixed was counted. Details on bug collection process can be found in [40].

4   Research Methodology

In this section, the steps taken to analyze coupling, cohesion, inheritance and size metrics for classes taken for analysis are described. The procedure used to analyze the data collected for each measure is described in following stages (i) data statistics and outlier analysis (ii) correlation among metrics (iii) performance measures.

4.1 Descriptive Statistics and Outlier Analysis

The role of statistics is to function as a tool in analyzing research data and drawing conclusions from it. The research data must be suitably reduced so that the same can be read easily and can be used for further analysis. Descriptive statistics concern development of certain indices or measures to summarize data. The important statistics measures used for comparing different case studies include mean, median, and standard deviation. Data points, which are located in an empty part of the sample space, are called outliers. Outlier analysis is done to find data points that are over influential and removing them is essential. Univariate and multivariate outliers are found in our study. To identify multivariate outliers, we calculate for each data point the Mahalanobis Jackknife distance. Mahalanobis Jackknife is a measure of the distance in multidimensional space of each observation from the mean center of the observations [1, 41].

The influence of univariate and multivariate outliers was tested. If by removing an univariate outlier the significance (see Section 3.4) of metric changes i.e., the effect of that metric on fault proneness changes then the outlier is to be removed. Similarly, if the significance of one or more independent variables in the model depends on the presence or absence of the outlier, then that outlier is to be removed. Details on outlier analysis can be found in [42].

4.2 Correlation among Metrics

Correlation analysis studies the variation of two or more variables for determining the amount of correlation between them. In order to analyze the relationship among design metrics we use Spearman's Rho coefficient of correlation. We preferred to use a non-parametric technique (Spearman's Rho) for measuring relationship among OO metrics as we usually observe the skewed distribution of the design measures.

4.3 Evaluating the Performance of the Models

The performance of binary prediction models is typically evaluated using confusion matrix (see Table 2). In this study, we used the commonly used evaluation measures. These measures include Sensitivity, Precision, Specificity, and ROC analysis.

Table 2. Confusion matrix

Observed	Predicted	
	1.00 (Fault-Prone)	0.00 (Not Fault-Prone)
1.00 (Fault-Prone)	True Fault Prone (TFP)	False Not Fault Prone (FNFP)
0.00 (Not Fault-Prone)	False Fault Prone (FFP)	True Not Fault Prone (TNFP)

Precision
It is defined as the ratio of number of classes correctly predicted to the total number of classes.

$$\text{Precision} = \frac{TFP + TNFP}{TFP + FNFP + FFP + TNFP} \tag{2}$$

Sensitivity
It is defined as the ratio of the number of classes correctly predicted as fault prone to the total number of classes that are actually fault prone.

$$\text{Sensitivity} = \frac{TFP}{TFP + FNFP} \tag{3}$$

Sensitivity
It is defined as the ratio of the number of classes correctly predicted as not fault prone to the total number of classes that are actually not fault prone.

$$\text{Specificity} = \frac{TNFP}{FFP + FNFP} \tag{4}$$

Completeness
It is defined as the number of faults in classes classified fault-prone, divided by the total number of faults in the system.

Receiver Operating Characteristic (ROC) Analysis
ROC curve, which is defined as a plot of sensitivity on the y-coordinate versus its 1-specificity on the x coordinate, is an effective method of evaluating the quality or performance of predicted models [11]. While constructing ROC curves, one selects many cutoff points between 0 and 1 in our case, and calculates sensitivity and specificity at each cut off point. The optimal choice of cutoff point (that maximizes both sensitivity and specificity) can be selected from the ROC curve [11, 43]. Hence, by using ROC curve one can easily determine optimal cutoff point for an predicted model.

Area Under the ROC Curve (AUC) is a combined measure of sensitivity and specificity. In order to compute the accuracy of the predicted models, we use the area under ROC curve.

Cross Validation

In order to predict accuracy of model it should be applied on different data sets. We therefore performed holdout validation of models [44]. The data set is randomly divided into testing and validations data sets.

5 Analysis Results

This section presents the analysis results, following the procedure described in Section 4. Descriptive statistics (Section 5.1), GEP results (Section 5.2).

5.1 Descriptive Statistics

Table 3 show "min", "max", "mean", "std dev", "75% quartile" and "25% quartile" for all metrics considered in this study.

Table 3. Descriptive Statistics for OO metrics

Metric	Min.	Max.	Mean	Std. Dev.	Percentile (25%)	Percentile (75%)
WMC	0	407	11.72	31.201	3	10
DIT	0	7	2.496	1.976	1	3
NOC	0	35	0.715	3.100	0	0
CBO	0	105	12.64	14.13	4	17
RFC	0	843	174.97	269.5	20.75	84.25
LCOM	0	100	46.23	33.51	0	75
NPM	0	193	7.78	17.12	1	8
LOC	3	6191	206.21	529.66	32.75	171.75

The following observations are made from Table 3:

- The size of a class measured in terms of lines of source code ranges from 3-6191.
- The values of DIT and NOC are less, which shows that inheritance is not much used in all the systems; similar results have also been shown by other studies [7, 9, 10].
- The LCOM measure, which counts the number of classes with no attribute usage in common, has high values (upto 100).

We calculated the correlation among metrics as shown in Table 4 which is an important static quantity. Zhou and Leung (2006), Gyimothy, Forenc, and Siket [13] and Basili et al. [4] calculated the correlation among metrics. WMC metric is correlated with all the metrics except DIT, NOC and RFC. There is a correlation between DIT and RFC metrics, between RFC and CBO metrics, LCOM and CBO and between LCOM and NPM metrics. LOC metric is correlated with all the metrics except DIT and NOC metrics. Therefore, it shows that these metrics are not totally independent and represents redundant information.

Table 4. Correlations among Metrics

Metric	WMC	DIT	NOC	CBO	RFC	LCOM	NPM	LOC
WMC	1							
DIT	-0.17	1						
NOC	-0.005	-0.363	1					
CBO	**0.53**	0.314	-0.297	1				
RFC	0.245	**0.813**	-0.336	**0.619**	1			
LCOM	**0.632**	0.073	-0.105	**0.531**	0.340	1		
NPM	**0.822**	-0.086	-0.032	0.447	0.281	**0.570**	1	
LOC	**0.698**	0.154	-0.227	**0.841**	**0.500**	**0.620**	**0.572**	1

5.2   Gene Expression Programming (GEP) Results

In this section, we present the results of combined effect of OO metrics on fault
proneness (same as multivariate analysis). The subset of attributes was selected using
CFS method described in Section 3.1. NPM, CBO, RFC, DIT, and LOC were selected
from the set of eight metrics.

In Table 5, we summarize the parameters to and determined by GEP. 576 generations were used to train the model to predict faulty classes and an additional generation
to simplify the expression. We used 4 genes per chromosome and addition function to
link the genes.

Table 5. GEP Parameters

Population size	50
Gene per chromosome	4
Gene head length	8
Generations required to train the model	576
Generations required for simplification	1
Linking Function	Addition
Fitness function	Number of correct predictions with penalty

The fitness function measures the number of correct predictions and penalties the
situation where there is no correct predictions for some target categories of dependent
variable.

$$Fitness = \frac{TFP + TNFP}{TFP + FNFP + FFP + TNFP}$$

If there are some correctly classified fault prone and not fault prone classes the
fitness is the proportion of correctly predicted classes, but if there is no correct prediction foe either faulty or non faulty classes then the fitness is 0.

The model was applied to 274 classes and Table 6 presents the results of correctness of the fault proneness model predicted. As shown in Table 6, out of 134 classes,

Table 6. Accuracy of Model Predicted using Training Data

Observed	Predicted	
	0.00	1.00
0.00	111	29
1.00	35	99

actually fault prone, 99 classes were predicted to be fault prone. The sensitivity of the model is 73.8 percent. Similarly, 111 out of 140 classes were predicted not to be fault prone. Thus, specificity of the model is 79.28 percent. Table 7 shows the sensitivity, specificity, precision and AUC of model predicted using GEP method.

Table 7. Result of Model Training

GENE EXPRESSION PROGRAMMING	
Cutoff	0.5
Sensitivity	73.5
Specificity	79.28
Precision	76.64
AUC	0.77

6 Software Quality Metric Definition and Validation

Based on the results obtained from model prediction using GEP, we propose the generated expression as a software quality metric that can be used to predict faulty classes. The metric is defined as follows:

Metric: Fault Factor (FF)

Definition: Consider a class C_1, then the fault factor of the class is defined as follows:

$$FF = 2 * NPM * NPM + CBO + (2 * (LOC + DIT)) + 2 * LOC + (2 * NPM) +$$
$$(((NPM + DIT) * NPM - LOC)) + \sqrt{RFC}) \tag{5}$$
$$\text{if } 2 * NPM * NPM + CBO + (2 * (LOC + DIT)) + 2 * LOC + (2 * NPM) +$$
$$(((NPM + DIT) * NPM - LOC)) + \sqrt{RFC}) < 0, \text{ then}$$

FF = 0
Where

NPM = Number of public methods in a class
CBO = Count of import and export coupling in a class
LOC = Lines of code in a class
DIT = Number of ancestors of a class
RFC = Number of external and internal methods in a class

When we validated the above predicted model using FF metric on 74 classes, 25 out of 38 were correctly classified as non faulty and 27 out of 36.classes were predicted to be faulty (see Table 8). Thus, the sensitivity is 75% and specificity is 65.78%. The AUC of the model is 0.704. Table 9 shows the sensitivity, specificity, precision, and AUC of model predicted using the developed metric..

Table 8. Accuracy of Model Predicted Using Validation Data

Observed	Predicted	
	0.00	1.00
0.00	25	13
1.00	9	27

Table 9. Result of Model Validation

GENE EXPRESSION PROGRAMMING	
Cutoff	0.5
Sensitivity	75
Specificity	65
Precision	69.3
AUC	0.704

7 Application of the FF Metric

Software developers can use the FF metric developed in the previous section in earlier phases of software development to measure the quality of the systems. From the design phase, one can make software measurements and then predict which classes will need extra attention during the remainder of development. The classes with higher values of FF metric will be predicted to be non faulty and the classes with less value of FF metric will be predicted as faulty. This can help management focus resources on those classes that cause most of the problems. Also, if required, developers can reconsider design and thus take corrective actions. In order to draw strong conclusions, however, more studies should evaluate the effectiveness of the proposed metric.

These design measurements can be used as quality benchmarks to assess and compare products, after one calculated the value of FF metric. More such studies can provide quality benchmarks across organizations, whereas within an organization, quality benchmarks can be set comparing metric values with the existing operational good quality software. If deviation is found in the metric values further investigation to know the cause of deviation could be done. Thus, corrective actions could be taken before final delivery or future releases of the software. This is particularly important when systems are maintained over a long period and new versions are released regularly. Based on our observation the classes with value of FF between 2 and 392 should be classified as non faulty and the classes with values less than 2 should be classified as faulty.

Planning and resource allocating for inspection and testing is difficult. The FF metric developed in the previous section could be of great help for planning and executing testing activities. The bar chart shown in Figure 5, shows that 15.6% of classes (12 out of 134 faulty classes) misclassified as non faulty have only 1-3 number of faults. Thus, the classes with high number of faults were mostly correctly classified to be fault prone. Thus, for example, if one has the resources available to inspect 26 percent of the code. From the values calculated by the FF metric one can tell that classes with the lowest predicted metric values and total LOC upto 26% should only be tested. If these classes are selected for testing one can expect maximum faults to be covered.

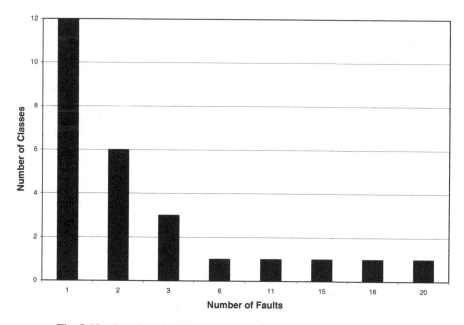

Fig. 5. Number of Faults Misclassified with Respect to Number of Classes

8 Conclusion

This paper empirically evaluates the performance of GEP algorithm in predicting fault-prone classes. We developed a software quality metric using the expression generated from GEP. The faulty classes were predicted using OO metrics proposed by Chidamber and Kemerer. The developed metric was validated using open source software. The results indicate that that the performance of GEP is at least competitive. This study confirms that construction of model using GEP is feasible, adaptable to OO systems, and useful in predicting fault prone classes.

The precision of developed metric FF is 69.3 percent, its accuracy in predicting faulty classes is 75 percent, and specificity is 65 percent. While research continues, practitioners and researchers may apply the proposed metric for predicting faulty classes. The FF metric can help in improving software quality in the context of software testing by reducing risks of faulty classes go undetected. As discussed, one important application of the proposed metric FF is to build quality benchmarks to assess fault proneness of OO systems that are newly developed or under maintenance, for example, in the case of software acquisition and outsourcing. Thus, one can conclude that FF metric appears to be well suited to develop practical quality benchmarks.

The future work may include conducting similar type of studies with different data sets to give generalized results across different organizations. We plan to replicate our study to predict model based on genetic algorithms. We will also focus on cost benefit analysis of models that will help to determine whether a given fault proneness model would be economically viable.

References

1. Aggarwal, K.K., Singh, Y., Kaur, A., Malhotra, R.: Empirical Analysis for Investigating the Effect of Object-Oriented Metrics on Fault Proneness: A Replicated Case Study. Software Process Improvement and Practice 14(1), 39–62 (2008)
2. Aggarwal, K.K., Singh, Y., Kaur, A., Malhotra, R.: Investigating the Effect of Coupling Metrics on Fault Proneness in Object-Oriented Systems. Software Quality Professional 8(4), 4–16 (2006)
3. Barnett, V., Price, T.: Outliers in Statistical Data. John Wiley & Sons, Chichester (1995)
4. Basili, V., Briand, L., Melo, W.: A Validation of Object-Oriented Design Metrics as Quality Indicators. IEEE Transactions on Software Engineering 22(10), 751–761 (1996)
5. Bieman, J., Kang, B.: Cohesion and reuse in an object-oriented system. In: Proceedings of the ACM Symposium on Software Reusability, pp. 259–262 (1995)
6. Binkley, A., Schach, S.: Validation of the coupling dependency metric as a risk predictor. In: Proceedings of the International Conference on Software Engineering, pp. 452–455 (1998)
7. Briand, L., Daly, W., Wust, J.: Exploring the relationships between design measures and software quality. Journal of Systems and Software 5, 245–273 (2000)
8. Briand, L., Wüst, J., Lounis, H.: Replicated Case Studies for Investigating Quality Factors in Object-Oriented Designs. Empirical Software Engineering: An International Journal 6(1), 11–58 (2001)
9. Cartwright, M., Shepperd, M.: An Empirical Investigation of an Object-Oriented Software System. IEEE Transactions of Software Engineering 26(8), 786–796 (1999)
10. Chidamber, S., Darcy, D., Kemerer, C.: Managerial use of Metrics for Object-Oriented Software: An Exploratory Analysis. IEEE Transactions on Software Engineering 24(8), 629–639 (1998)
11. El Emam, K., Benlarbi, S., Goel, N., Rai, S.: A Validation of Object-Oriented Metrics, Technical Report ERB-1063, NRC (1999)
12. El Emam, K., Benlarbi, S., Goel, N., Rai, S.: The Confounding Effect of Class Size on the Validity of Object-Oriented Metrics. IEEE Transactions on Software Engineering 27(7), 630–650 (2001)

13. Gyimothy, T., Ferenc, R., Siket, I.: Empirical validation of object-oriented metrics on open source software for fault prediction. IEEE Trans. Software Engineering 31(10), 897–910 (2005)
14. Harrison, R., Counsell, S.J., Nithi, R.V.: An Evaluation of MOOD set of Object-Oriented Software Metrics. IEEE Trans. Software Engineering SE-24(6), 491–496 (1998)
15. Lee, Y., Liang, B., Wu, S., Wang, F.: Measuring the Coupling and Cohesion of an Object-Oriented program based on Information flow (1995)
16. Li, W., Henry, S.: Object-Oriented Metrics that Predict Maintainability. Journal of Systems and Software 23(2), 111–122 (1993)
17. Olague, H., Etzkorn, L., Gholston, S., Quattlebaum, S.: Empirical Validation of Three Software Metrics Suites to Predict Fault-Proneness of Object-Oriented Classes Developed Using Highly Iterative or Agile Software Development Processes. IEEE Transactions on software Engineering 33(8), 402–419 (2007)
18. Pai, G.: Empirical analysis of Software Fault Content and Fault Proneness Using Bayesian Methods. IEEE Transactions on software Engineering 33(10), 675–686 (2007)
19. Tang, M.H., Kao, M.H., Chen, M.H.: An Empirical Study on Object-Oriented Metrics. In: Proceedings of Metrics, pp. 242–249 (1999)
20. Tegarden, D., Sheetz, S., Monarchi, D.: A software complexity model of object-oriented systems. Decision Support Systems 13(3-4), 241–262 (1995)
21. Zhou, Y., Leung, H.: Empirical analysis of Object-Oriented Design Metrics for predicting high severity faults. IEEE Transactions on Software Engineering 32(10), 771–784 (2006)
22. promise, http://promisedata.org/repository/
23. Moreira, B.C., Fitzjohn, P.W., Offman, M., Smith, G.R., Bates, P.A.: Novel Use of a Genetic Algorithm for Protein Structure Prediction: Searching Template and Sequence Alignment Space. PROTEINS: Structure, Function, and Genetics 53, 424–429 (2003)
24. Sheta, A.F.: Estimation of the COCOMO Model Parameters Using Genetic Algorithms for NASA Software Projects. Journal of Computer Science 2(2), 118–123 (2006)
25. Tikir, M., Carrington, L., Strohmaier, E., Snavely, A.: A Genetic Algorithms Approach to Modeling the Performance of Memory-bound Computations. In: SC 2007, Reno, Nevada, USA, November 10-16 (2007)
26. Ferreira, C.: Gene Expression Programming: A New Adaptive Algorithm for Solving Problems. Complex Systems 13, 87–129 (2001)
27. Sherrod, P.: DTreg Predictive Modeling Software (2003)
28. Aggarwal, K.K., Singh, Y., Kaur, A., Malhotra, R.: Empirical study of object-oriented metrics. Journal of Object Technology 5(8), 149–173 (2006)
29. Aggarwal, K.K., Singh, Y., Kaur, A., Malhotra, R.: Software Reuse Metrics for Object-Oriented Systems. In: Third ACIS Int'l Conference on Software Engineering Research, Management and Applications (SERA 2005), pp. 48–55. IEEE Computer Society, Los Alamitos (2005)
30. Briand, L., Daly, W., Wust, J.: Unified Framework for Cohesion Measurement in Object-Oriented Systems. Empirical Software Engineering 3, 65–117 (1998)
31. Briand, L., Daly, W., Wust, J.: A Unified Framework for Coupling Measurement in Object-Oriented Systems. IEEE Transactions on software Engineering 25, 91–121 (1999)
32. Chidamber, S., Kemerer, C.: A metrics Suite for Object-Oriented Design. IEEE Trans. Software Engineering SE-20(6), 476–493 (1994)
33. Henderson-sellers, B.: Object-Oriented Metrics, Measures of Complexity. Prentice-Hall, Englewood Cliffs (1996)
34. Hitz, M., Montazeri, B.: Measuring Coupling and Cohesion in Object-Oriented Systems. In: Proc. Int. Symposium on Applied Corporate Computing, Monterrey, Mexico (1995)

35. Lake, A., Cook, C.: Use of factor analysis to develop OOP software complexity metrics. In: Proceedings of the 6th Annual Oregon Workshop on Software Metrics, Silver Falls, Oregon (1994)
36. Lorenz, M., Kidd, J.: Object-Oriented Software Metrics. Prentice-Hall, Englewood Cliffs (1994)
37. Hall, M.: Correlation-based feature selection for discrete and numeric class machine learning. In: Proceedings of the 17th International Conference on Machine Learning, pp. 359–366 (2000)
38. jedit, http://sourceforge.net/projects/jedit/
39. scitools, http://www.scitools.com/index.php
40. Watanabe, S., Kaiya, H., Kaijiri, K.: Adapting a Fault Prediction Model to Allow Inter Language Reuse. In: PROMISE 2008, Leipzig, Germany, May 12–13 (2008)
41. Hair, J., Anderson, R., Tatham, W.: Black Multivariate Data Analysis. Pearson Education, London (2000)
42. Belsley, D., Kuh, E., Welsch, R.: Regression Diagnostics: Identifying Influential Data and Sources of Collinearity. John Wiley & Sons, Chichester (1980)
43. Hanley, J., McNeil, B.: The meaning and use of the area under a Receiver Operating Characteristic ROC curve. Radiology 143, 29–36 (1982)
44. Stone, M.: Cross-validatory choice and assessment of statistical predictions. J. Royal Stat. Soc. 36, 111–147 (1974)

Method for Software Cost Estimating Using Scope Champions

Yegor Bugayenko

TechnoPark Corp.
568 9th Street South 202
Naples, Florida 34102
egor@technoparkcorp.com

Abstract. There are many methods of software cost estimating (COCOMO, function points analysis, three-point estimate, use case points, class points, XP user stories, SLOC prediction and others), with their advantages and drawbacks. One common problem with all methods is the necessity to estimate the whole requirements specification, item by item. At the end, either this process is expensive or the numbers are inaccurate. This paper presents a method of software cost estimating using a limited number of functional requirements, called Scope Champions. Estimators produce more detailed and grounded numbers that are used in a final estimation formula. The method reduces the costs of estimating and increases accuracy.

Keywords: software cost estimating, size estimating, cost optimization, requirements analysis.

1   Introduction and Problem Statement

Any project needs estimates (cost, time and resource) as key artifacts, which are based on scope definition [1].

There are many well-established and proven methods of software size and cost estimating, which are based on software specifications and organizational assets, e.g. historical data. In a general case, any method includes *a)* requirements analysis, *b)* numbers deriving and *c)* final calculation.

These three steps could be repeated several times iteratively, e.g. like in Wideband Delphi [2]. Each step may be completed manually or with a special tool and/or algorithm, e.g. function point analysis [3], COCOMO [4], PERT [1], XP user stories [5,6], SLOC prediction [7], by analogies [8], with use case points [9], class points [10], neural networks, and others.

No matter what tools and algorithms are used, the whole process has two significant disadvantages, which very often make it difficult to achieve optimal results or even to finish the estimating in time.

First, even a mid-size software project may contain hundreds of functional and non-functional requirements [11]. The time required by estimators for proper

F. Bomarius et al. (Eds.): PROFES 2009, LNBIP 32, pp. 59–70, 2009.
© Springer-Verlag Berlin Heidelberg 2009

understanding and analysis of requirements almost always is much bigger than the budgeted time for the whole estimating process. The obvious outcome of this situation is a limited understanding of requirements by estimators, which leads to inaccuracy in the estimators' judgement [12, pp. 33–54].

Second, estimators tend to approximate the numbers. With a big amount of small estimates, this leads to a certain deviation in the final calculation (either to the higher or to the lower boundary of the approximation). The deviation grows much faster than the amount of the estimates does.

A good solution to the outlined problems could be a method that will decrease the amount of efforts required for deriving numbers, at the same time improving the accuracy of the estimate.

2   The Method of Scope Champions

The purpose of this method is to improve the accuracy of existing software estimating methods by decreasing the amount of efforts required for the estimating process and focusing on selected elements of the scope.

In properly managed software projects, product scope is defined by software requirements specification (SRS) [11], that includes functional and non-functional requirements to the product. A numbered list of requirements defines the boundary of the product scope, while non-functional requirements supplement them with quality attributes [13,6].

The method consists of three steps: a) select Scope Champions, b) estimate Scope Champions, and c) calculate the product scope estimate.

Scope Champion is a selected functional requirement, the biggest and the most complex element of scope, according to the estimators' expert judgement. Scope Champions are picked up from a complete set of requirements on the same level of abstraction.

When Scope Champions are selected, isolated estimates for them are made by estimators. Using the estimates and the formula, proposed as part of this method, the final product scope estimate is calculated. The formula is:

$$Y \approx 0.56 \times \frac{n}{m} \times \sum_{i=1}^{m} Y_i \tag{1}$$

Where $\{Y_1, Y_2, \ldots, Y_m\}$ are estimates of Scope Champions, m is a total amount of Scope Champions, and n is the total amount of functional requirements in SRS. Y is a final product scope estimate.

Accuracy of the final estimate is improved because a) the estimators judgement is based on more detailed analysis, and b) the final estimate is much easier to validate and review.

The method can be used with other scope-defining artifacts, i.e. use case models [6], software architecture [14], design model [15], test plan [16], and others. The results obtained should be applied together, which will give higher accuracy for the total.

3   Formal Proof of the Method

There is a simple mathematical explanation of the proposed method, which is based on probability theory and Central Limit Theorem [17, pp. 317–323].

The product scope estimate X is a summary of all individual estimates X_i of functional requirements (n):

$$X = \sum_i^n X_i \tag{2}$$

It is assumed that the list of requirements consists of a *complete* set of elements on the same *level of abstraction*. The set of requirements is *complete* if it covers the whole product scope and it is impossible to add any more requirements to it without changing the level of abstraction.

Thus, it is assumed that all requirements estimates satisfy the following criteria:

$$min < X_i < max$$
$$min < X_i < min \times R \tag{3}$$
$$R > 1$$

Where R is a ratio-constant, that indicates that there is certain difference between maximum estimate and minimum estimate of requirements from the list.

We also assume that all estimates X_i are unbiased estimates of the mean μ, where μ equals to:

$$\mu = \frac{max + min}{2} \tag{4}$$

Figure 1 shows the graph of probability distribution. The horizontal axis is an expected X, summary of all X_i. The vertical axis is a probability of given X.

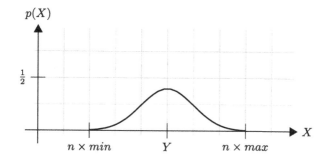

Fig. 1. Function $p(X)$ (vertical axis) is a probability of the event when the summary of all individual estimates X_i is equal to X (horizontal axis). The distribution of $p(X)$ is normal.

According to central limit theorem, the sum of all X_i is an approximately normally distributed value, i.e. following a "normal" distribution [18, pp. 152-154].

Since the estimates are unbiased, the sum of them is distributed normally, each estimate X_i is in the interval $[min \ldots max]$, and max depends on min as defined in (3), we assume that the mean Y could be calculated like:

$$Y = \mu \times n =$$
$$= \frac{max + max/R}{2} \times n =$$
$$= max \times \frac{1 + R}{2R} \times n =$$
$$= max \times Z \times n$$

(5)

Manually selecting a small number of functional requirements (which are the most complex, according to expert judgement), we estimate them: $\{Y_1, Y_2, \ldots, Y_m\}$.

Since we estimated the most complex requirements from the whole set, we may assume that the average of them is "very close" to max. Using this assumption, the product scope estimate equals to:

$$max = \frac{1}{m} \times \sum_{i=1}^{m} Y_i$$
$$Y = Z \times \frac{n}{m} \times \sum_{i=1}^{m} Y_i$$

(6)

Figure 2 illustrates the dependency between R from equation (3) and the constant for equation (6). It is visually clear that the constant (Z) will be somewhere in interval $(1/2; 1]$ and will never reach $1/2$.

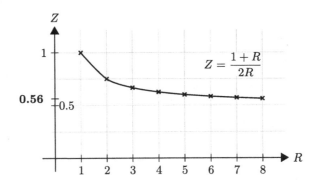

Fig. 2. There is a dependency between R (horizontal axis) and Z (vertical axis), where R is a difference multiplier between the biggest and the smallest estimates, and Z is the multiplier used in final formula (6)

It is assumed that R will be not only bigger than 1, but also bigger than 5. In other words, the most complex requirement will be at least 5 times more complex than the smallest one. In most cases this is true and the value of 0.56 will be the best for any given software project.

$$Y \approx 0.56 \times \frac{n}{m} \times \sum_{i=1}^{m} Y_i \qquad (7)$$

The constant 0.56 was found experimentally and could be changed, according to the analysis of the requirements structure. Other positive numbers in interval $(1/2; 1]$ can be used, keeping it close to the lowest boundary $(1/2)$.

4   Practical Example of the Method Application

The software we estimated was a scalable web platform for web-traffic tracking, billing and management, designed in SOA architecture, developed on J2EE platform. There were 280 functional requirements in SRS.

Figure 3 illustrates a workflow of the method, starting from specified requirements and finishing with the estimated product cost.

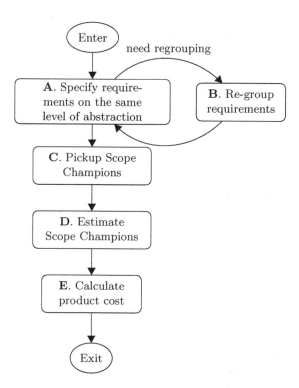

Fig. 3. Method flow chart, that illustrates key steps that should be performed in order to obtain the project scope estimate with Scope Champions

	Description
	. . .
R4.1	Register new account for Advertiser
R4.1.1	Remind password with security check
R4.2	Get suggestions for best keywords
R4.3	Review history of XML API requests
R4.5	Configure IP filtering for XML API
R4.6	Register new campaign
R4.6.1	On-fly campaign parameters correction
R4.7	Create new ad and upload creatives
R4.7.1	Ad cloning from another campaign
R4.7.2	Add new creatives to the existing ad
R4.7.3	Delete existing creatives from the ad
R4.8	Request a status of manual approval process
R4.8.1	Re-initiate manual approval of the ad
R4.9	Clone campaign (copy existing one)
R4.10	Start campaign
R4.10.1	Schedule the moment of campaign start
	. . .

Fig. 4. Sample list of functional requirements in the Software Requirements Specification (SRS) document, actually a part of a much longer list

First, in step **A**, requirements are defined by system analyst and listed in a SRS document [19,11]. We do not show the whole document here, just a number of requirements, see figure 4.

We specified functional requirements in textual form with title and details. In figure 4 there are just titles, which more or less effectively explain the sense of each requirement.

All calculations and estimates were in staff-hours, related only to programming efforts in the project. Requirements engineering, architecture, testing, deployment, configuration management and other disciplines were not estimated. We calculated the numbers using the estimate of programming effort.

In step **B** requirements should be refined and re-grouped in order to achieve one level of abstraction allocation of all of them. The re-grouping should be performed manually with expert judgement and may involve either decomposition or aggregation of existing requirements. We assumed that requirements were already on the same level of abstraction and didn't do any re-grouping.

This assumption was made by our system analyst's expert judgement. As explained before, functional requirements must be on one level of abstraction before they could be used in the method. We do not know any formal method of such "requirements normalization" [20,21] and use informal expert judgement [24].

If requirements are engineered and modeled with some formal logic-based approach [21], normalization could be done according to some more or less strict rules. Also, with formal requirements model, it's possible to change the constant from equation (6) to a more meaningful and specific number.

In step **C** Scope Champions were picked up from the full list of requirements. Scope Champions are the most complex and "expensive" requirements, according to current expert judgement. Small amount of Scope Champions should be selected, disregarding the size of the project and total amount of functional requirements. We selected five Scope Champions: R4.7, R19, R47.5, R180, and R289.

In step **D** we estimated Scope Champions with a three-point estimating method [1]

We started with a preliminary UML [22,23] class diagram (figure 5) that helps to undertstand key risks and assumptions in the solution domain. A software architect, designer and programmer participated in the analysis. Class diagram was used as the most valuable view of the technical domain in the given project. Beside class diagram other approaches could be used by estimators, like dynamic views (state-machine, activity or interaction diagrams).

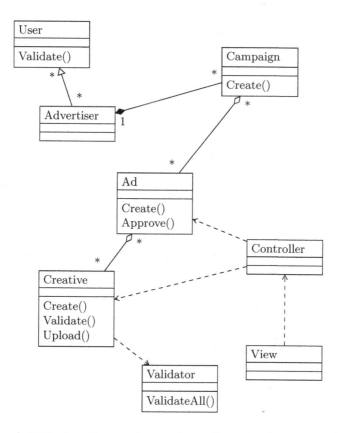

Fig. 5. Sample UML class diagram for one Scope Champion (requirement), created by the estimator in order to understand the technical scope and provide more accurate numbers for this individual requirement

Eight classes were identified as the best candidates for R4.7 requirement implementation participants. Some classes will be used only for the implementation of this particular requirement, but the majority of them will be used in other requirements.

Then, we estimated the R4.7 requirement using the class diagram (figure 6) and took into account all discovered risks and assumptions.

Class Method	BC	WC	ML	SLOC
Advertiser	1	6	2	50
Campaign	-	4	1	30
::Create()	1	3	2	40
Ad	-	6	3	40
::Create()	1	7	2	60
::Approve()	2	5	2	90
Creative	1	6	2	60
::Upload()	2	4	2	20
::Validate()	1	3	1	20
::Create()	1	3	2	25
Validator	3	9	6	120
Controller	1	3	1	15
View	2	8	3	50
Total	16	67	29	620
PERT Average	**33.2**			

Fig. 6. A detailed estimation result of one Scope Champion, made by one estimator. The estimation was made using PERT method (three-point estimate) and is based on the UML diagram. In other words, the estimate is based on more thourough scope understanding.

This estimation of R4.7 took two hours of work for three people (six staff-hours total). Five requirements estimates costed us totally 34 staff-hours. For all five functional requirements we received the numbers listed in figure 6.

Requirement	Estimate	Time spent, staff-hours
R4.7	33.2	6
R19	29.0	5
R47.5	28.5	9
R180	34.0	5
R289	24.8	9
Total	149.5	34

Fig. 7. Estimates received from estimators for 5 Scope Champions and the total time spent for each requirement estimation, in staff-hours

Using the formula from equation (6) we calculated the product cost estimate, which equals to 4700 staff-hours:

$$Y = 0.56 \times \frac{280}{5} \times (33.2 + 29 + 28.5 + 34 + 24.8) \approx$$
$$\approx 4700 \tag{8}$$

The bottom line is that we had a SRS document with 280 functional requirements, we spent 34 staff-hours and created an estimate which was accurate and self-explained. We performed technical analysis of the problem, found key technical risks and assumptions and produced a number of preliminary class diagrams. We did all this for just 34 staff-hours, while the project size was close to five thousand staff-hours (just programming).

5   Lessons Learned

The lessons learned in the estimating of the size of this project are:

"Transparency" The documents produced by this estimating method were more than clear to all project participants. We easily presented them to the project sponsor, executive management and programmers. No additional explanation was required. Such transparency is a very rare outcome of traditional estimating methods (if 34 staff-hours are spent for estimating).

"Speed of delivery" We spent 3 working days for project estimating, which is three times less than we could spend if we estimate all 280 requirements, even with less attention to details.

"Customer satisfaction" The project sponsor was satisfied with the level of details and transparency of the estimate we prepared.

"Team motivation" By working with Scope Champions, the project team was self-motivated. Mostly due to the limited and boxed scope of work (just 5 requirements). Before that, with traditional methods, we experienced difficulties in team motivation, when it was necessary to work with 280 requirements.

6   Threats to Validity

There are a number of potential "what-if"-s, that may hamper the use of the method in industrial projects. The most critical of them are:

"*What if the assumption that all requirements are described at the same level of abstraction is invalid?*" Here we recall a fundamental assumption of iterative software development — when system analyst baselines the requirements this means that we are getting the best and the most thorough understanding of the scope at this particular moment.

The estimate we get at this moment is the best estimate we can get according to our current understanding of the scope. When architects and designers go into technical analysis of the requirements and discover that some of them are too small or too big (are not on the same level of abstraction) we get back to the system analysis, refine requirements and re-estimate them again.

With any other well-known method we will do the same, but with scope champions we spend less effort for such re-estimating session.

"*What if the selected scope champions are not the most complex requirements (in implementation)?*" During estimation session estimators may be unsure what requirements are the best candidates for Scope Champions. Such uncertainty is an indicator of SRS defects, which shall be fixed by system analyst either before estimate session or on the next iteration. The bigger the uncertainty the higher Z constant in equation 6. Maximum value in interval $(1/2; 1]$ means that estimators are absolutely not sure in their selection of Scope Champions.

"*What if the effort associated with the regrouping (normalization) of requirements is too big?*" Requirements normalization, i.e. making all of them located at the same level of abstraction, is an important task for project planning and tracking. Functional requirements as atomic scope components (valuable for project customer) are the only objective earned value in the project. If they are not normalized, project planning and tracking will be compromised.

7   Conclusion

This method has been successfully implemented and tested in TechnoPark Corp., since March 2007. The results obtained so far are accurate and precise, while estimators are more focused and attentive while using this method. They were not, when they worked with the three-point estimate approach, applied to all functional requirements in SRS.

There is a still a space for research. First of all, the mechanism of requirements normalization should be developed. So far, no formal approach to this task is known [21,20].

Second, the constant that is used in the method (0.56) should get some calculation method. Obviously, it should depend on some requirements metrics.

Third, the method may be applied not only to SRS and functional requirements, but to other scope-definition documents, like test plan [16], software architecture document [14], software design description [15], etc. Moreover, when the method is applied to a number of documents, final result will be more grounded and accurate.

References

1. Project Management Institute, Project Management Body of Knowledge (PMBOK) Guide v.3, 3rd edn. PMI Press (2004)
2. Boehm, B.: Software Engineering Economics. Prentice-Hall, Englewood Cliffs (1981)
3. International Organization for Standardization, ISO 20926, Software Engineering — IFPUG 4.1 Unadjusted functional size measurement method — Counting practices manual (2003)
4. Boehm, B.: Software Cost Estimation with Cocomo II. Addison-Wesley, Reading (2000)

5. Beck, K., Fowler, M.: Planning Extreme Programming. Addison-Wesley, Reading (2000)
6. Cockburn, A.: Agile Software Development. Addison-Wesley, Reading (2001)
7. Albrecht, A.J., Gaffney, J.E.: Software Function, Source Lines of Code, and Development Effort Prediction: A Software Science Validation. IEEE Transactions on Software Engineering 9(6), 639–648 (1983)
8. Shepperd, M., Schofield, C.: Estimating software project effort using analogies. IEEE Transactions on Software Engineering 23(11), 736–743 (1997)
9. Mohagheghi, P., Anda, B., Conradi, R.: Effort estimation of use cases for incremental large-scale software development. In: ICSE 2005: Proceedings of the 27th international conference on Software engineering, St. Louis, MO, USA, pp. 303–311. ACM, New York (2005)
10. Kanmani, S., Kathiravan, J., Kumar, S.S., Shanmugam, M.: Class point based effort estimation of OO systems using fuzzy subtractive clustering and artificial neural networks. In: ISEC 2008: Proceedings of the 1st conference on India software engineering conference, Hyderabad, India, pp. 141–142. ACM, New York (2008)
11. Software Engineering Standards Committee of the IEEE Computer Society, The Institute of Electrical and Electronics Engineers, Inc., IEEE Recommended Practice for Software Requirements Specifications, IEEE Std 830-1998 (Revision of IEEE Std 830-1993), NY, USA (1998)
12. McConnell, S.: Software Estimation, Demistifying the Black Art. Microsoft Press, Redmond (2006)
13. Wiegers, K.: Software Requirements, Thorny Issues and Practical Advise, 2nd edn. Microsoft Press, Redmond (2003)
14. Software Engineering Standards Committee of the IEEE Computer Society, The Institute of Electrical and Electronics Engineers, Inc., Recommended Practice for Architectural Description of Software-Intensive Systems, IEEE Std 1471-2000, NY, USA (2000)
15. Software Engineering Standards Committee of the IEEE Computer Society, The Institute of Electrical and Electronics Engineers, Inc., Recommended Practice for Software Design Descriptions, IEEE Std 1016-1998, NY, USA (1998)
16. Software Engineering Standards Committee of the IEEE Computer Society, The Institute of Electrical and Electronics Engineers, Inc., IEEE Standard for Software Test Documentation, IEEE Std 829-1998, NY, USA (1998)
17. Klenke, A.: Probability Theory, Comprehensive Course. Springer, London (2006)
18. Renyi, A.: Probability Theory. Dover Publications Inc., New York (2007)
19. IBM, Rational, Rational Unified Process in Rational Method Composer (2007)
20. Nuseibeh, B., Easterbrook, S.: Requirements engineering: a roadmap. In: ICSE 2000: Proceedings of the Conference on The Future of Software Engineering, Limerick, Ireland, pp. 35–46. ACM, New York (2000)
21. Cheng, B.H.C., Atlee, J.M.: Research Directions in Requirements Engineering. In: FOSE 2007: 2007 Future of Software Engineering, pp. 285–303. IEEE Computer Society, Los Alamitos (2007)
22. Podgorelec, V., Heričko, M.: Estimating software complexity from UML models. SIGSOFT Software Engineering Notes 32(2), 1–5 (2007)
23. Object Management Group: Unified Modeling Language (UML), Superstructure, Version 2.0 (2005)
24. Crow, J., Vito, B.D.: Formalizing space shuttle software requirements: four case studies. ACM Transactions Software Engineering Methodologies 7(3), 296–332 (1998)

25. Gervasi, V., Zowghi, D.: Reasoning about inconsistencies in natural language requirements. ACM Transactions Software Engineering Methodologies 14(3), 277–330 (2005)
26. Jain, H., Vitharana, P., Zahedi, F.M.: An assessment model for requirements identification in component-based software development. SIGMIS Database 34(4), 48–63 (2003)
27. Jeffords, R.D., Heitmeyer, C.L.: A strategy for efficiently verifying requirements. SIGSOFT Software Engineering Notes 5(28), 28–37 (2003)
28. Kit, L.K., Man, C.K., Baniassad, E.: Isolating and relating concerns in requirements using latent semantic analysis. SIGPLAN Notes 10(41), 383–396 (2006)
29. Loconsole, A.: Empirical Studies on Requirement Management Measures. In: ICSE 2004: Proceedings of the 26th International Conference on Software Engineering, pp. 42–44. IEEE Computer Society, Washington (2004)
30. Maiden, N., Manning, S., Robertson, S., Greenwood, J.: Integrating creativity workshops into structured requirements processes. In: DIS 2004: Proceedings of the 5th conference on Designing interactive systems, pp. 113–122. ACM Press, New York (2004)
31. Maiden, N., Gizikis, A., Robertson, S.: Provoking Creativity: Imagine What Your Requirements Could Be Like. IEEE Software 21(5), 68–75 (2004)
32. Trendowicz, A., Heidrich, J., Münch, J., Ishigai, Y., Yokoyama, K., Kikuchi, N.: Development of a hybrid cost estimation model in an iterative manner. In: ICSE 2006: Proceedings of the 28th international conference on Software engineering, Shanghai, China, pp. 331–340. ACM, New York (2006)
33. Lee, S.W., Rine, D.C.: Missing requirements and relationship discovery through proxy viewpoints model. In: SAC 2004: Proceedings of the 2004 ACM symposium on Applied computing, pp. 1513–1518. ACM, New York (2004)

A Measurement Framework for Team Level Assessment of Innovation Capability in Early Requirements Engineering

Björn Regnell[1,2], Martin Höst[1], Fredrik Nilsson[3], and Henrik Bengtsson[2]

[1] Dept. of Computer Science, Lund University, Sweden
http://www.cs.lth.se
[2] Sony Ericsson, Lund, Sweden
http://www.sonyericsson.com
[3] Dept. of Design Sciences, Lund University, Sweden
http://www.design.lth.se
{bjorn.regnell,martin.host}@cs.lth.se,
fredrik.nilsson@plog.lth.se

Abstract. When developing software-intensive products for a market-place it is important for a development organisation to create innovative features for coming releases in order to achieve advantage over competitors. This paper focuses on assessment of innovation capability at team level in relation to the requirements engineering that is taking place before the actual product development projects are decided, when new business models, technology opportunities and intellectual property rights are created and investigated through e.g. prototyping and concept development. The result is a measurement framework focusing on four areas: innovation elicitation, selection, impact and ways-of-working. For each area, candidate measurements were derived from interviews to be used as inspiration in the development of a tailored measurement program. The framework is based on interviews with participants of a software team with specific innovation responsibilities and validated through cross-case analysis and feedback from practitioners.

Keywords: requirements engineering, measurement, metrics, innovation.

1 Introduction

How do we know that we are innovative? This question was asked by a manager for a software team with explicit responsibility to create and analyze innovative product features before actual product development projects are started. In early market-driven requirements engineering [1, 2], it may be a long lead-time to feedback counted from initial concept invention to response from market success (or failure). Still, managers of teams that work with the conceptualisation of novel product ideas need to steer the innovative work in the right direction before market feedback is given.

The above question of determining innovation capability in pre-development activities was the starting-point for a research effort resulting in the framework for

F. Bomarius et al. (Eds.): PROFES 2009, LNBIP 32, pp. 71–86, 2009.
© Springer-Verlag Berlin Heidelberg 2009

measuring innovation capability in teams (MINT), presented in this paper. Our interpretation of innovation here includes not only a creative, radical idea but also that the idea is implemented in products and/or services and results in recognized, novel and significant value for its users. In line with this interpretation we use the term (product) innovation capability to imply the capacity of an organisational entity to create novel product feature concepts that are successfully incorporated in product development and (eventually) creating significant value for product stakeholders.

The question of how to know the innovative capability of a team leads to the follow-up question: What are the aspects of innovation capability that can be measured? Innovation capability is a multi-faceted phenomenon including individuals' skills, team work, organisational aspects as well as specific properties of the domain in which the innovation is carried out. Several issues are "soft" and related to human judgement and it can be assumed that an assessment of innovation capability needs inclusion of subjective evaluation with not only quantitative data, but also qualitative data based on the views of individuals. Subsequently, we thus use the term measurement in a broad sense, also including qualitative data using nominal and ordinal scales in addition to quantitative data on absolute and ratio scales.

We have conducted an investigation into aspects of innovation capability through a qualitative analysis of semi-structured interviews with 5 members of a team with specific responsibilities of software innovation for future products. The coding of the interview transcriptions was input to a brainstorming session where innovation capability measurement candidates were defined and then grouped and structured into a three level framework. The research approach is further elaborated in Section 2.

The main contribution of this paper is described in Section 3 and is comprised of the empirically based three-level framework denoted MINT. The MINT framework is aimed for organisations considering assessment of innovation capability on team level, and the measurement areas, factors and candidates are supposed to be used as inspiration material when developing a situated measurements program. The validation of the framework is based on feedback from practitioners and a detailed cross-case analysis with another case study of a team also with the responsibility to be innovative, but in a different context [3].

The innovative aspects of requirements engineering have been recognized in e.g. [4, 5, 6], however not specifically addressing innovation capability measurement. The literature on general engineering management in relation to innovation is extensive, however limited with respect to team level studies, see further Section 4 on related work. Section 5 concludes the paper.

2 Research Approach

The general focus of the presented research is to develop support for continuous improvement of innovation capability through measurement in the innovation process at team level. In market-driven software development [2], requirements engineering is also needed at a strategic level before development projects are started [1]. These early requirements are closely related to an organisation's innovation capability, as pre-development activities can pave the way for investments in radical development rather than incremental refinement based on existing customers' voices.

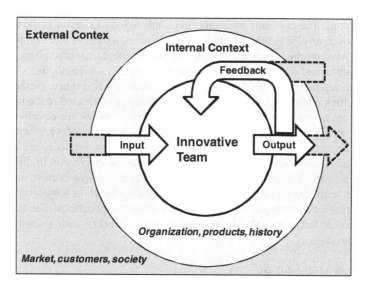

Fig. 1. Conceptual model of research focus

Based on literature studies [7, 8, 9, 10], knowledge of the case company, and our pre-understanding of innovative teams and contexts, a conceptual model was depicted that guided our research design, see fig. 1. The *innovative team* represents an organisational unit that has a specific focus to develop radically new products or features for future markets that can enable the company to meet future competition rather than current competition. The use of teams is something several authors accentuate [8, 9, 10] and effective team work is put forward as a central activity for innovation. Other parts of the company may have teams that work with normal product development targeting incremental improvement of existing products, while the innovative team drives special projects with higher risks and often longer time horizons. The innovative team operates in an *internal context* representing the rest of the company. The internal context also encompasses soft aspects such as company values, culture and history of the organisation. The internal context is by Davida et al [9] called the internal marketplace on which organisational antibodies that may hamper innovation within the organisation may exist as well as proponents for novelty. The innovative team is provided with *input* in the form of goals and assignments, and also the input resources provided such as competent engineers and accompanying budget to enable accomplishment of the goals. The *output* can range from novel features of products to new ways of doing business i.e. novel business models. Finally, the team acts in relation to an *external context* including markets, competitors, other industries and society, from which behaviours and trends can be observed.

2.1 Case Company

The case company was chosen based on its participation in a long-term research collaboration effort in software engineering, where the company has expressed interest in innovation management issues. The case company is Sony Ericsson Mobile

Communications. The company mission is to establish Sony Ericsson as the most attractive and innovative global brand in the mobile handset industry. The company undertakes world-wide product research, design and development, manufacturing, marketing, sales, distribution and customer services. The company has several thousand employees working with research and development in e.g. Sweden, UK, France, Netherlands, India, Japan, China and the US. The presented case study is conducted at the site in Lund, Sweden, where a major part of the company's software assets are developed using a product line engineering approach integrating sub-contracted software with in-house software in an evolving application platform on which new products are configured. The organization has several units and teams that focus on innovation in different technical areas and with different time frames. Based on management interest we chose one specific team with special responsibility of coordinating the most long-term innovation efforts with particular strategic value in mobile software applications. The team composition is dynamic but it includes more than 10 core members with a strong record in software innovation.

2.2 Research Methodology

The case study is conducted in an exploratory, qualitative, action research mode [11], where identified innovation metrics are grounded in interviews with five software engineering practitioners. The research was conducted in the following steps:

1. Definition of interview instrument.
2. Conduct interviews.
3. Transcribe and divide into sentences, phrases or sections.
4. Identify a first version of metrics based on phrases.
5. Sort identified metrics into high level groups.
6. For each group, go through and join, reformulate etc to find more metrics.
7. Validate the results by (a) feedback from the innovative team, and (b) cross-case analysis in a different organization.

Step 1. The interview instrument was defined based on the research questions and the researchers' prior knowledge of the organization and the area in general. These questions were validated with the use of four external innovation researchers. This resulted in a set of 36 interview questions, grouped into sub-topics such as characterization of organization, innovation climate in the team, incentives for innovation, mission for group, resources to the group, deliverables from the team, etc. Together with the interview questions an interview guide with guidelines on how long time to spend on each question, and a recommended order of questions, was developed. A summary of the topic and sub-topics of the interview instrument is given in Table 1.

Step 2. Five persons were interviewed, and each interview lasted for about one and a half hour. All interviews were recorded in audio format, and notes were taken. The interviews were semi-structured [12, 11] where the interview guide acted as a checklist in order to see to that all relevant topics were covered. The interviews were conducted by two researchers interviewing one interviewee. According to [12], advantages of being two researchers are that a second researcher can focus on what is said and relate this to the interview guide while the other researcher can improvise based on what is said, and that it is possible for the researcher to discuss what was said afterwards and verify their interpretations. The selection of people to interview was made based on discussions with the team manager.

Table 1. Overview of the interview instrument

Interview topics	Sub-topics
Internal Context	Management, colleagues, departments, organisation
External Context	Market, customers, external stakeholders
Innovation Process (at team level)	Characterization, Current situation, Innovation Climate, Incentives, Future, Challenges
Input	Assignment, Resources
Output	Deliverables, Results, Effects
Feedback	Goals achieved, External/internal feedback, Measurement, Assessment

Step 3. All interviews were transcribed into text. The transcripts were then processed by dividing them into sentences to make it possible to treat every sentence individually. The sentences order was kept making it easy to see the sentences before and after each sentence. The transcripts from the interviews ranged from about 5,000 words to about 12,000 words. The transcripts are not presented in detail due to confidentiality reasons.

Step 4. Almost 300 potential innovation metrics were identified through brainstorming sessions where innovation-related metrics were formulated based on the assumed meaning or inferred implications of the transcribed sentences. The brainstorming involved the creativity of the researchers in order to transform the statements of the informants into measurement. This resulted in a first list of potential metrics, which in **Step 5** were grouped by the researchers. To some extent the groups were based on the researchers' prior knowledge about the area, but care was taken to be open-minded, and not to be too limited by prior knowledge. New groups emerged at two different levels of abstraction. The highest level concerns main interfaces of the innovative teams, and the more detailed level consists of sub-areas of the higher level groups (eventually leading to the areas and factors in Fig. 2).

Step 6. The identified metrics of every sub-group were studied and refined. Some metrics were very similar and could therefore be reformulated and combined into a new metric, while others were kept apart as they were different. Based on this a final set of examples of metrics were suggested for every sub-group.

Step 7. The results were improved through a cross-case comparison to a similar interview study conducted in another organization. If the results in the two studies are similar this may serve as an initial validation. The other organization, which the results are compared to, works with innovations in the healthcare sector. This team focus mainly on product and service innovations but also on innovations related to management processes. The result was also presented to the interviewed organization. The final results were then adjusted based on the cross-case comparison.

2.3 Validity Discussion

The threats to validity for a case study can be classified into construct validity, internal validity, external validity, and reliability [13]. *Construct validity* concerns to what extent the constructs that are studied really represent what the researcher have in mind. In this study there is a potential threat that different people may interpret the term "innovation" differently. However, much attention was given to discuss the meaning of this during the interviews. For constructs related to the organization its products, the risk is lower as the researchers have a long-term collaboration experience with the organization. The intention was also to control this threat by having two interviewers at all interviews. *Internal validity* is concerned with threats to conclusions about cause and effect relationships, which is not a major objective of this study. *External validity* is concerned with generalization of the results from the chosen population and the tasks that have been studied. This threat is partly addressed by the validation step where the results are compared to another type of organization. The people to interview were chosen with the objective to cover as many different views and roles as possible within a given time frame. We believe that a good sample of people from the team was made. *Reliability* is concerned with to what extent the data and the analysis are dependent on the specific researchers. Hypothetically, if another researcher later on conducted the same study, the result should be the same. In this study all findings have been derived by at least two researchers, and then reviewed by the other researchers, which means that this threat has been made smaller. The threat is also addressed by having a defined interview guide, and by being two interviewers at every interview. To summarize, we believe that the validity threats of our results are in control, although the identified metrics should not be seen as a final list general to all organizations.

3 Results

The results of this study includes various findings from the interviews (Section 3.1) and the three-level MINT framework (Section 3.2) that is proposed as inspiration and guidance in the development of tailored measurements programs for innovation capability assessment and improvement. The MINT framework was developed in three steps: (1) a first version was conceived based on interview data from the Sony Ericsson case, (2) a new version with minor changes was developed based on validation within the Sony Ericsson case, (3) a revised version including a limited restructuring based on a validation with a parallel case from the healthcare domain. Section 3.3 and 3.4 describe initial efforts on internal and external validation respectively.

3.1 Discussion of Some General Findings from Interviews

We have selected four findings that stand out as salient issues in interviews:

1. the importance of spending effort on promoting the results of the innovative team in the rest of the organization in order to enable innovation realization,
2. the application of a useful development process focused on prototyping and concept development with little overhead and small increments,

3. the increased focus on quality requirements when prototype development is transformed to traditional product development, and
4. the expressed high demands on technical skills needed in order to be accepted as a member of the innovative team.

The first finding addresses the expressed importance for the innovative team to pave the way for their innovations within the organization. It is by no means certain that the investigated innovations are included in developed products. There is a limited number of new features in new products and many ideas have been rejected by prioritizing other features. In this case the team sees it as its responsibility to spend significant effort to promote the ideas that they really believe in.

The development within the team is focused on software prototypes as executable concept demonstrators. In some cases, also hardware prototypes are developed. The development of prototypes is seen as a requirement for successful promotion of the investigated innovations within the organization, as executable prototypes are more convincing in demonstrating the potential value of a new concept compared to a non-working paper product. An evaluation based only on e.g. market opinions and interviews is considered insufficient. This is expressed as *"It is the main reason for us to develop prototypes"* by one of the team members.

The prototype software is not developed in the same way as normal product-grade software. The requirements concerning code quality are not the same, and the development process is different compared to when product-quality software is developed.

When a prototype has been developed, and a decision has been taken to introduce a concept in products, the lead time is, as for all new features, of high priority. This means that there is an interest to transfer as much knowledge and as much software as possible, from the prototype projects to traditional product project. That is, there is a clear shift in the organization with respect to the interest in a feature. From being a long-term innovation which is investigated at a conceptual level, it is transformed to a prioritized product feature with a relatively shorter time frame. This is expressed as *"If we have found an innovation to be promising we want to include it as soon as possible"* by one of the team members. The interviewees also express the challenge of shifting from prototype code to product-grade quality code and the risk that the members of the innovative team work too much on normal product development rather than on radical innovation.

It was found that the typical requirements on the people in this type of team include technical knowledge in combination with social skills, as well as being "innovative". However, the technical skills, including knowledge of the product structure and skill in software development is viewed as critical. It is also important to have general knowledge of the whole product. One developer stated: *"Other developers at [the company] work in one module, while we work in the whole [product]. We have tried to include people from different groups of the company in our team."*

3.2 The MINT Framework

The main result of the interview study is the MINT framework that is intended to be used as an inspiration and guidance when developing a situated measurements program for assessing and improving innovation capability. The MINT framework is comprised of three levels: measurement areas, measurement factors and measurement inspiration, subsequently described in Fig. 2 and Tables 2-5.

Innovation Elicitation. This area consists of measurement inspiration related to activities that are devoted to identification of ideas for innovation projects. The area is divided into factor depending of if ideas are actively generated or collected from existing resources, as well as if the originate from internal or external stakeholders. The ideas elicited are the basis for project proposals for the innovative team. Feedback to on the proposals is important for stakeholders so that they can see that their proposals are considered.

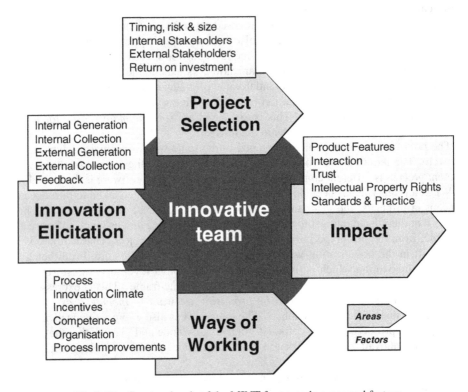

Fig 2. The first two levels of the MINT framework: areas and factors

Project Selection. The project proposals that are considered best are chosen and innovation projects are started for proof-of-concept and prototype development. Different criteria can be used in project assessment, including e.g. risk, effort needed and time horizon for when the market is estimated to be ready for the innovation. By choosing a mix of projects with different characteristics with respect to such criteria, a balanced project portfolio can be created that may give beneficial variation and increased chances of success in innovation work.

Impact. In order to realize a great idea and make it an innovation, it needs to be handed over to and taken care of by the normal product development organization, where product-grade quality can be achieved through a systematic implementation and quality assurance. The innovative team acts as ambassador for its project results and communicates their benefits in order to explain why further development efforts should be allocated. The overall goal is to have a beneficial impact on and a renewal of the whole organization and its business.

Ways-of-working. This factor concerns the ways-of-working of the innovative team, including the process of innovation projects as well as organizational abilities related to competence, the innovation climate in relation to the team's group dynamics, and continuous process improvement.

Measurement Inspiration. The third level of the MINT framework is comprised of selected examples of measurements intended as inspiration to definition of tailored assessment of innovation capability. Tables 2-5 below include the empirically grounded inspiration.

Table 2. Measurement inspiration related to the area of Innovation Elicitation

Innovation Elicitation	
Factors	*Measurement inspiration*
Internal collection	Number of incoming proposals from different sources
	Number of analyzed patents in patent portfolio
	Number of and time between activities of collaboration with patent team.
External collection	Number of and time between collection activities focused on specific external stakeholders (different types of users, customers, competitors, owners, public authorities, etc.)
	Number of visited events (conferences, convents, courses, etc.)
	Number of investigation of other companies (potential threats, technology providers, takeover, etc.)
	Number of patents or prototypes further developed based on existing patent portfolio
Internal generation	Number of and time between activities of presenting the work of the innovative team.
	Longitudinal change of proposal (e.g. to see peaks after presentation activities)
	Number of and time between activities of systematic idea generation (e.g. different types of brainstorming and elicitation workshops)
External generation	Number of observation studies of users.
	Number of projects based on ideas from external stakeholders
	Number of workshops with customers on future needs
Feedback	Number of submitted proposals from persons with rejected proposals (it is important that people continue to give proposals even if not all ideas becomes projects)
	Elapsed time from proposal to feedback
	Effort spent to give feedback

3.3 Validation within the Case

It remains in future work to validate the MINT framework in other case organisations. However, several actions were taken in order to validate the findings within the studied case. First, the interview transcripts were sent to interviewees who all (after some minor corrections) found the transcripts a valid representation of their views of the

Table 3. Measurement inspiration related to the area of Project Selection

Project Selection	
Factors	*Measurement inspiration*
Timing	Estimated lead time to market launch of project results
	Ratio of short-term and long-term projects
	Estimated lead time to hand-over of projects results to internal stakeholders
Risk	Subjective assessment of project risk (feasibility, technical challenge, etc
	Number of parallel tracks or options investigated (in case of technology uncertainties)
	Number of terminated/unsuccessful projects (a certain degree of risk-taking is good)
Size	Estimated project effort
	Distribution of project size (effort) in portfolio
Internal stakeholders	Distribution of projects over different types of internal stakeholders
	Number of projects that challenge current business models or paradigms
	Number of projects that focus on incremental enhancement of existing product features
External stakeholders	Number of projects based on radical future scenarios
	Number of projects with end-user relevance
	Number of projects with future customer or new market relevance
Return on Investment	Estimated Return on Investment
	Potential loss (alternative cost) of not selecting a projects (worst case scenario).
	Number of and time between of decision input from steering committee on which projects to prioritize

topic. Second, an initial version of the MINT framework was then presented at a 2h seminar with 16 team members present including all but one of the interviewees, where discussions on how to apply the framework were initiated. The seminar participants had different views on which factors that are most important to start with when implementing a measurement program, but the general opinion recognized the value of having concrete example metrics for each factor as inspiration when formulating metrics. No factors were found missing; instead it was stressed that the framework was extensive and that it was necessary to focus the implementation of a measurement program to only a few highly relevant metrics. Third, a future project was planned where a set of factors from the MINT framework were chosen as input to the definition key performance indicators for the innovative team. Thus the MINT framework was by the team and its management found useful as starting-point for innovation capability assessment.

3.4 Comparison with Parallel Case

The same research focus of Fig. 1 and interview instrument of Table 1 were used in a parallel study [3] of an innovative team in a public sector organization that delivers health services within the regional government. The innovation focus of the external parallel case is mainly product and service-oriented innovation in the health care and medical technology domains, and only indirectly related to software, thus giving a variation in term of both organisation and domain. The intention of this validation is to address external validity of the results (c.f. Section 2.3). The analysis and coding of interview transcriptions was done in the same way in both cases through brainstorming sessions that generated a high number of potential metrics of innovation capabilities.

Table 4. Measurement inspiration related to the Impact area

Impact	
Factors	*Measurement inspiration*
Product features	Number of released product features that have been impacted by the team's work
	Number of projects plans that have been impacted by the team's work
	Number of change requests that originate from the team's work
	Number of end users of released product features that from the team's work
	Number of results from the team accepted by product planning (or other stakeholders)
	Subjective assessment of the extent to which the team's results have had positive (compared to neutral or negative) impact on released products
Interaction	Number of persons in the team's contact network
	Number of stakeholders that are covered by contact network
	Share of project effort spent on internal marketing
	Number of visitors at events where the teams work is presented (e.g. demo shows)
	Number of company employees outside the team that know about the team's work
	Number of collaboration activities with internal and external stakeholders
	Effort spent on hand-over and integration of results into products
	Number of internal promotion meetings with relevant stakeholders
Trust	Number of invitations of team members to presentations, meetings, courses etc.
	Subjective assessment of the quality of the team's results by the receiving stakeholders
	Number of accesses in the document management system of the team's project reports
	Results of questionnaires on results quality by participants at presentation events
	Subjective assessment by internal stakeholders on the team's credibility in various strategic technology areas
Intellectual property rights	Number of patent proposals, number of patents applications, number of filed patents, (per year, per person) etc.
	Effort spent of patent proposals
	The team's share of the company patent incentive program
	The team's share of company patents (proposed and filed)
Standards and practice	Number of standardisation organisations and practice-shaping networks that the team is participation in (actively contributing or passively monitoring)
	Number of occasions where the team's work has impacted standards and practice
	Share of standardisation bodies that are impacted vs standardisation bodies that would be relevant to impact
	Subjective assessment of ability to impact standardisation and practice vs competitors
	Effort spent on driving standards and shaping practice

A cross-case comparison was then performed between the cases which resulted in minor changes to the framework and the set-up of measures. The comparison of generated measurement candidates revealed that a majority were similar or related. The changes to the framework involved inclusion of process measures and measures of standards and practice. Also, more metrics found in the cross-case analysis related to common team aspects such as the competence factor resulted in a restructuring of the areas of the framework and the introduction of the ways-of-working area in Fig. 2, which gave a more coherent grouping of related factors. In summary, the comparison of the framework on the three levels supported our belief that the MINT framework has some degree of general validity also outside the initial case study in which the first version of the framework was conceived.

Table 5. Measurement inspiration related to the area of Ways-of-Working

Ways-of-Working	
Factors	*Measurement inspiration*
Process	Subjective assessment of the efficiency of the team's ways of working
	Share of total effort spent on creative work compared to e.g. administration
	Subjective assessment of the effectiveness of innovation assessment methodology
	Number of projects that shifts from innovation to normal development
	Estimated remaining investment needed to implement the innovation in real products
	Share of prototype construction (e.g. lines of code) that can be reused directly in normal product development
Climate	Number of consecutive non-booked time slots in each team member's calendar
	Share of time that is devoted to each tem member's own proposals
	Time between deadlines for each project member
	Subjective assessment of the teams climate with respect to open, constructive debates
	Subjective assessment negative climate factors (personal conflicts, fear of failing, overloading, etc.)
Incentives	Monetary rewards for achieved personal and group goals
	Monetary rewards for patent proposals
	Number of personal and group recognitions of achievements
Competence	Distribution of team member's background, experience, age, gender etc.
	Number of competence area that are mastered within the team
	Subjective assessment of how well strategic competence areas are covered
	Number of job rotations per year
	Number of projects that each team member has managed or participated in
Organization	Project resources (effort , budget, etc.)
	Number of projects per year, number of involved persons per project
	Lead time per project
	Share of budget on outsourced projects
Process improvement	Number of process improvement proposals from team members
	Number or process improvement proposals that are based on stakeholder feedback on the team's results
	Number of implemented process improvement proposals
	Subjective assessment of number of process improvement proposals that have had impact on the team's ways-of-working
	Subjective assessment of the benefit of each process change
	Number of process changes that are considered significant improvements

4 Related Work

The innovative aspects of requirements engineering have been recognized already in 1995 by Potts [6]. More recent work on innovation in requirements engineering includes investigation of creativity in requirements elicitation workshops by Maiden and Robertson [4, 5]. In the literature on general engineering management, several studies on innovation measurements can be found that relates to the presented framework. However, while there has been much focus on innovation and innovation capabilities on organizational level, as well as on the individual level, less focus has been placed on the team level. The same accounts for measurement and assessment methods of innovation and innovation capabilities. Furthermore, a majority of innovation metrics focus on product or process performance and are of a post-hoc character i.e. when products or processes reach the market. Reported performance innovation metrics in industry are percent of revenue from new products (NPs), percent of growths in NPs, overall profits generated by NPs [14]. Other reported metrics include number of patents and number of ideas generated in various suggestion facilities.

Measuring the climate for group innovation is addressed by Anderson and West [8]. This is the only reference, to the authors´ knowledge, that emphasizes measurement of innovation at team level. They present a multidimensional measure of facet-specific climate for innovation in group called Team Climate Inventory and pinpoint that "most previous measures of [innovative] climate have evaluated organizations as a whole…" [8, p.254]. They conclude that by focusing on specific aspect of climate and specific group level outcomes the predictive accuracy is high.

Other sources provide different aspects and dimensions to innovation measurement and assessment. One of the most comprehensive sources is the literature review by Adams et al [7] on innovation management measurements. Based on their review a framework of seven areas for measurement of innovation is provided. They point to the need for both practitioners and academics to measure innovation and stress the absence of frameworks for innovation management measurements as well as "the relatively small number of empirical studies on measurement in practice" [7, p.389]. Griffin and Page [15] argue that a company can assess failure or success of development projects by using appropriate sets of measures with alignment to project and innovation strategies. The framework presented by Griffin and Page is relevant when products are placed on the market i.e. post hoc measures (e.g. customer acceptance, market share goals, competitive advantage) and provides insights for innovation on the organizational (corporate) level. The same measurement focus can be found in Huang et al. [16] i.e. on corporate level and on post-hoc measures. Based on their study on the measurement of new product success in Australian small and medium sized enterprises, it is concluded that firms should use multiple criteria when measuring new product success. The most contributing factors to customer success were found to be customer satisfaction and customer acceptance, i.e. post-hoc measures.

Davila et al. [9] present another view, based on a business model for innovation with appropriate measures based on four phases; input, process, output, and outcome. For each of these phases they present a plethora of measures. They also define three roles of measurement systems: (1) *plan*, involving a design and monitoring strategy; (2) *monitor*, including tracking of execution efforts and performance evaluation; and (3) *learn*, in order to identify new opportunities. The framework they provide shows some similarity with the MINT framework on the second level of measurement areas.

Chiesa et al. [17] present a framework for technical innovation audit. Their framework consists of four core processes: 1) the identification of new product concepts – concept generation; 2) taking the innovation from concept to launch – product development; 3) the development of innovation in production – process innovation; and 4) the development and management of technology per se. In addition they define three enabling processes: 1) recourses – the deployment of human and financial resources; 2) system and tools – the effective use of appropriate systems and tools; and 3) leadership – providing the top management leadership and direction. However, the focus in both Davial et al. and Chiesa et al. is mostly on an organizational (corporate) level, hence team-level innovation measurement on climate, processes and performance is not addressed explicitly.

Other literature on measurement of innovation extends the main stream focus on product and technology by addressing other innovation areas such as service innovation, aesthetic innovation and the measurement thereof. For example, Alcaide-Marzal, and Tortajada-Esparza [18] approach innovation and its assessment in industries that are not focused on technological innovation but instead on aesthetic innovation. In their review of innovation surveys they investigate the occurrence of the following aspects; goals of innovation, inputs to innovation, outputs of innovation, innovation diffusion, and aesthetic design. Hipp and Grupp [19] focus on service innovations and state that "Scientific research in measurement methods and indicator creation describing service innovations and their effects on the economic, technological, and social environment has only just started" [19, p.531].

5 Conclusion

Innovation management is an important part of the business of software developing companies in competitive industries, which makes it a central part of market-driven requirements engineering. This work is often carried out by innovative teams that develop prototypes in order to investigate the feasibility of new ideas. A major problem in this kind of work is that the time until feedback from the market is too long to serve alone as a basis for assessment of on-going work.

The problem of assessing the capability of this type of management has been investigated, and a framework for measurement has been formulated based on interviews. The defined dimensions of the framework concern how innovation ideas are identified, how investigation projects are defined and managed, how innovative teams carry out their work, and what impact innovations have on the rest of the organization and on the business. For each of these dimensions a number of sub-areas have been defined, and for every sub-area a set of metrics have been defined.

The identified framework is related to other defined frameworks, e.g. [9], but specifically derived for innovative teams in software-intensive industries. The framework includes a rich set of examples of metrics, and a sub-set of these can be selected or modified when a metrics program is tailored for a specific organization. The intention is not that all defined metrics should be used in every situation, but rather that they act as inspiration. Further work includes case-studies where the framework is used for this purpose, i.e., where metrics programs are planned and executed based on it.

Acknowledgements. The Product Innovation Engineering program (www.piep.se), a Swedish research and development program for increased innovation capability in organizations, has contributed to this work together with the VINNOVA industrial excellence centre in Embedded Application Software Engineering (EASE). Special thanks to the anonymous interviewees for their dedicated participation in this study. Thanks also to the following researchers for valuable input on the study design and analysis: Dr Sofia Ritzén, Prof. Tobias Larsson, and Dr Erik Sundin.

References

1. Ebert, C.: Requirements BEFORE the Requirements: Understanding the Upstream Impacts. In: Proceedings of the 2005 13th IEEE International Conference on Requirements Engineering (RE 2005), Paris, France, pp. 117–124 (2005)
2. Karlsson, L., Dahlstedt, Å.G., Nattoch Dag, J., Regnell, B., Persson, A.: Challenges in Market-Driven Requirements Engineering - an Industrial Interview Study. In: Proc. 8th Int. Workshop on Requirements Engineering: Foundation for Software Quality (REFSQ 2002), Essen Germany, pp. 37–49 (2002)
3. Nilsson, F., Regnell, B., Höst, M., Lindström, B.: Improving innovation capabilities in public healthcare – the application of an innovation measurement framework. In: The European Health Management Association Conference, Austria (2009) (in press)
4. Maiden, N., Robertson, S.: Integrating creativity into requirements processes: experiences with an air traffic management system. In: Proceedings of the 2005 13th IEEE International Conference on Requirements Engineering (RE 2005), Paris, France, pp. 105–114 (2005)
5. Maiden, N., Gizikis, A., Robertson, S.: Provoking Creativity: Imagine What Your Requirements Could Be Like. IEEE Software 21(5), 68–75 (2004)
6. Potts, C.: Invented requirements and imagined customers: requirements engineering for off-the-shelf software. In: Proceedings of the Second IEEE International Symposium on Requirements Engineering (RE 1995), NewYork, UK, pp. 128–130 (1995)
7. Adams, R., Bessant, J., Phelps, R.: Innovation management measurement: A review. International Journal of Management Reviews 8, 21–47 (2006)
8. Anderson, N.R., West, M.A.: Measuring Climate for Work Group Innovation: Development and Validation of the Team Climate Inventory. Journal of Organizational Behavior 19, 235–258 (1998)
9. Davila, T., Epstein, M.J., Shelton, R.: Making innovation work: How to manage it, measure it, and profit from it. Wharton School Publishing (2006)
10. Tidd, J., Bessant, J.: Managing innovation - Integrating Technological, Market and Organizational Change, 4th edn. John Wiley & Sons, Ltd., Chichester (2009)
11. Robson, C.: Real World Research, 2nd edn. Blackwell, Malden (2002)
12. Hove, S.E., Anda, B.: Experiences from Conducting Semi-Structured Interviews in Empirical Software Engineering Research. In: 11th IEEE International Symposium on Software Metrics (2005)
13. Yin, R.K.: Case Study Research Design and Methods, 3rd edn. Sage Publications, Thousand Oaks (2003)
14. Cooper, R., Edgett, S., Kleinschmidt, E.: Benchmarking best NPD practices. Research Technology Management 47, 31–43 (2004)

15. Griffin, A., Page, A.L.: PDMA Success measurement project: Recommended measures for product development success and failure. Journal of product innovation management 13, 478–496 (1996)
16. Huang, X., Soutar, G.N., Brown, A.: Measuring new product success: an empirical investigation of Australian SMEs. Industrial marketing management 33, 117–123 (2004)
17. Chiesa, V., Coughlan, P., Voss, C.A.: Development of a technical innovation audit. Journal of product innovation management 13, 105–136 (1996)
18. Alcaide-Marzal, J., Tortajada-Esparza, E.: Innovation assessment in traditional industries, A proposal of aesthetic innovation indicators. Scientometrics 72, 33–57 (2007)
19. Hipp, C., Grupp, H.: Innovation in the service sector: The demand for service-specific innovation measurement concepts and typologies. Research Policy 34, 517–535 (2005)

Why a CMMI Level 5 Company Fails to Meet the Deadlines?

Darja Smite and Cigdem Gencel

Blekinge Institute of Technology, Ronneby, Sweden
{Darja.Smite,Cigdem.Gencel}@bth.se

Abstract. Reliable effort and cost estimation remains to be a challenging issue even for mature software organizations. Although, these organizations collect historical data to base their future estimates, changes in circumstances (such as application type, development platform, etc.) prevent their successful utilization. As a result, companies often suffer from underestimated and unrealistic schedules. Managing software projects that involve a large number of globally distributed stakeholders makes estimation and planning even more challenging. Related studies show that even knowledgeable project managers often underestimate hidden costs and sources of delay associated with distributed development. Therefore, management activities such as estimation of development effort, planning and control require special attention. In this paper we discuss experiences gained from a highly distributed software project, which aimed at development of a product based on a new platform and architectural solution. The project was conducted in a CMMI Level 5 company and still failed to meet initial plan constraints. We thus provide an overview of management decisions in the light of their consequences, and discuss potential areas of improvement.

Keywords: Software Project Management, Effort Estimation, Distributed Software Development, Global Software Engineering.

1 Introduction

Considerable effort has been put forth by the software engineering community to define and improve the software engineering process as well as its proper management. Project management and software engineering frameworks such as [1], [2] accumulated considerable amount of knowledge to facilitate project managers. As appreciated by other engineering disciplines, the benefits of process improvement on projects success have also started to be realized by the software engineering organizations.

Moreover, unique tools and techniques were developed to address challenges related to management of software development projects [3], [4], [5]. Many investments have been especially directed to support project upfront planning activities, in particular to find reliable duration, effort and cost estimation models for project outcome prediction. Unfortunately, although different models are reported to be successfully used by different groups and for particular domains, they do not have unanimous acceptance by the software community as being not performing well enough.

F. Bomarius et al. (Eds.): PROFES 2009, LNBIP 32, pp. 87–95, 2009.
© Springer-Verlag Berlin Heidelberg 2009

Therefore, the mature and wise companies have started to collect historical data and use it for future project predictions. However, when a team is introduced to new tasks, technologies, engineering methods or settings, historical data can be of little use. Moreover, diverse and changing nature of application types, which a company develops, limits the usage of the collected historical data for reliable estimation.

Most of software nowadays is developed by global software teams. Effort estimation is recognized as one of the top problems in globally distributed software projects and two thirds of these projects were reported to suffer from faulty effort estimates [6]. Distributed work is relatively new and is recognized as considerably more complex than even the most difficult collocated projects [7]. Thus many problems associated with geographic, temporal and cultural distance take inexperienced project managers by surprise. As a consequence, a large number of project failures plague the global software industry [8].

In this paper we discuss a software engineering project that failed to meet the deadlines due to underestimated scope and unforeseen consequences of corrective actions. The studied project team experienced new tasks, new technologies, new engineering methods and new settings of a global highly distributed software project.

The paper is organized as follows. Section 2 provides case organization and project description. In section 3, we illustrate measurements gathered during the project, analyze project management challenges and actions taken by the software organization, and discuss reasons of failure. Finally, section 4 concludes the study.

2   Case Study

2.1   Methodology

This study is a single-case study [9] and the object of our investigation is a recently finished software development project that experienced huge problems with underestimated effort and duration. The study is based on multiple data sources: interviews and project documentation and is exploratory in nature. This means that the researchers did not have a preconceived theory in mind, but rather focused on understanding the reasons behind project events and their influence on the project performance, and let conclusions evolve through data analysis.

During this study, we used multiple data sources in our analysis. We have had continues discussions with the team leader who was responsible for software development that were held in person, through electronic means (Skype) and through email communication. We have also had access to various sources of project information, such as project plans, measures, and post-mortem analysis data. At the end, our conclusions were reviewed and approved by the project team leader and project manager from the case organization.

In our case study, we have addressed the threats to construct validity by involving two researchers in the data analysis. Internal validity was addressed by approving our observations with the project managers from the studied company. A possible threat to internal validity is the limited number of team members involved in the investigation. However, we believe that reliable project documentation was the key source of information for our research questions. We thus generally believe that there is no speculation or subjective judgment in our conclusions.

This study serves as an industrial experience report and lessons learned.

2.2 Case Organization Description

The context for this study is one of the top 100 IT services companies in the U.S. that evolved through acquisition and is spread across several locations including software development centers in Eastern and Northern Europe (for confidentiality reasons we do not disclose the true name of the company). The studied company offers outsourcing services for customers around the world and is marketed as a leader in distributed agile development. While it extended its operation in global markets, quality certification has been given a high priority and the processes have been both CMMI Level 5 and ISO-9001 certified for stability, efficiency and maturity. At the present time the company has around 1500 employees and offers such services as global software development, application and architecture reviews, component-based development, enterprise application integration and migration, as well as maintenance.

2.3 Case Project Description

During this study we have investigated a project that was particularly interesting due to a unique combination of new approaches applied. This was a distributed agile project that delivered web-based software application for a call centre built on a new technology platform and architectural solutions. For more detail see Table 1.

Table 1. Project description

Project Characteristic	Description
Application type	Web-based software application for a call centre
Application size	60,000 SLOC PHP & JavaScript; 1,000 SLOC Java; 57, 000 SLOC Java code including copied third part code (SLOC includes comments and empty lines)
Technology platform	Java, PHP, CSS, JavaScript
Development tools	Eclipse IDE
Development methodology	Incremental development with application of Scrum

The studied project at times was highly distributed across six offshore development locations all subsidiaries of the studied company and involved a distributed customer (Fig. 1). The project team consisted of a Project Management Team, a Business Analyst Team, a Quality Assurance Team and Development Teams that involved experts from several locations.

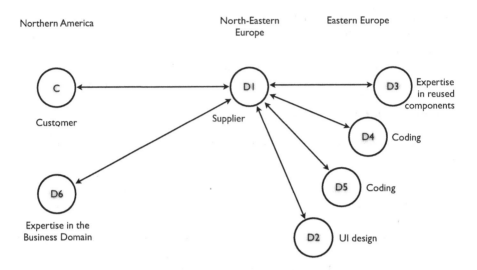

Northern America

North-Eastern Europe

Eastern Europe

Fig. 1. Sites involved in the project

2.4 Project Management

As the studied company is CMMI Level 5 and ISO 9001:2000 certified, the studied project initially followed a set of best practices. Project manager and a software development team leader were involved in management activities. When the team lacked experience with the development platform, architecture and programming language experts from remote locations were involved at time to fill the gaps in the necessary expertise. As a part of the strategy of delivering quick and qualitative solution, the software product was to be built on reusable components that were developed by the offshore locations of the company.

Since the company was branding itself as the leader in distributed agile development, the project initially chose to follow Scrum practices for project management. Project tasks and activities were scheduled in a project plan that was regularly updated. In illustration, by the end of the project after 10 month of development, the

Table 2. Collected Measures for the Project

Collected Measures	Values
Number of defects /number of features	10
Number of defects found by the Customer	87
Number of defects found by the Quality Assurance	299
Number of defects found by the Development team	279
Number of Test Plans	9
Number of Test Cases	479

plan was updated 35 times. Project management was supported by a variety of tools that collect measures, e.g. status reports on task progress. The measures collected during the project to ensure quality are given in Table 2.

The studied project failed to meet the initial deadlines and effort estimates, which served as a motivation for our investigation. There were significant deviations in effort and duration figures (see Table 3).

Table 3. Project Estimate Deviations

Measures	Estimate	Actual	Deviation
Total estimated effort (person/months)	37,5	66,5	177%
Calendar duration estimate (days)	50	222	404%

The reasons why the studied company failed this project are elaborated in the following section.

3   Findings and Discussion

3.1   Effort Underestimation

Although XYZ has some historical data, which includes past productivity figures, these could not be used to make a good estimate for this case because of the following reasons:

- Development of a new application type with no prior experience;
- Application of a new development platform and architectural solution;
- Underestimated complexity of the product;
- Unforeseen limitations of the reusable components;
- Lack of experience with the chosen engineering methods.

First, the application to be developed was a new kind of application for the development organization. They did not have any previous experience in developing such applications.

Second, the development organization planned to use a new development platform, for which the developers had no experience. The team also used a new software architectural solution. This decision was based on the necessity to gain first customer reference for the company's future marketing activities.

Third, the product to be developed appeared to be more complex than expected. Poorly described set of initial requirements (20 features - each described by a couple of sentences) resulted in the lack of understanding of the customer needs. Considerable amount of time was spent in discussions between the quality assurance team and the development team about interpretations of requirements. Business analysis, initially planned 15 working days, achieved actual duration of 165 working days. Similarly, several initially unplanned development activities resulted in a huge delay for the product delivery. E.g. an unplanned module to be implemented was planned to require 19 working days, but actually took 96 working days; two other unplanned activities resulted in 167 and 191 working days respectively. In addition, the chosen software components at the end did not match the expectations.

Fourth, a number of components that were developed in other geographically distributed locations of XYZ were assumed to be ready for reuse. Accordingly, no effort was planned for any tailoring activities. However, these assumptions appeared to be faulty and the team spent more than 5 person-months modifying them to fit the needs of the customer.

Finally, the project team had no previous experience with the chosen software engineering method. In particular, Scrum practices were relatively new for the development team and the project management. Despite the potential benefits of the methodology, deviations from the agile principles prevented early reaction to the project challenges. The project was formally organized around 6 sprints with a demo meeting at the end of each increment. The main emphasis in each sprint was put on the new functionality; however the results were not delivered to the customer. Therefore, limited feedback was received. Thus, when the product was finally delivered, it led to significant changes due to unmet needs of the customer. This is reflected in the new versions of the project plan through new development activities.

The project team leader described the project by stating that it contained "buzzword-oriented architecture, assumption-oriented design and excuse-oriented execution". As a result, the required effort and duration of the project increased dramatically. Poorly planned activities further caused user acceptance testing to continue much longer than estimated. It was planned to be 45 working days, whereas it actually took 121 working days.

The management continued to be overly optimistic in planning and the project kept failing to meet the new estimated deadlines. A set of corrective actions did not bring expected results and additional rework was necessary, which resulted in almost exponential growth of necessary time for completion of the project (see Fig. 2).

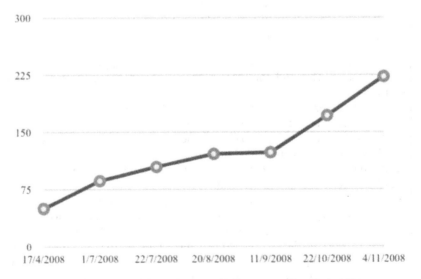

Fig. 2. Evolution of the Estimates with Respect to Plan Update Dates

3.2 Unforeseen Effects of the Corrective Actions

To overcome the underestimated problems such as failure to meet the deadlines and the lack of on-site resources and expertise, the project management team made a decision to involve three other remote locations of XYZ, which actually caused the project inevitably to become a failure.

Initial plan included the tasks to be distributed across three locations of the company. Different activities by type were to be conducted by the most experienced team members. This means that one site had to work on integration of components; another on business analysis and the main site performed the rest of the work. Though development activities were not initially planned to be distributed, project problems forced the project manager to distribute coding tasks across four locations in total. Similar to the mistakes made by other companies discussed in related studies [10], the case project underestimated the communication, coordination, trust and commitment challenges as well. Thus, poorly controlled dependencies resulted in late deliveries and parts of remotely developed pieces of software had to be re-built. As a consequence, once initiated for good reasons, collaboration with these remote locations was not further prolonged.

Although empirical studies show that an agile delivery strategy is recognized to have a positive influence on the scope, timelines and cost of the project [11] and at the same time is found to be useful for reducing communication, coordination, and control problems that have been associated with global software development [12], the project management failed to use these benefits due to deviations from the chosen methodology. In particular, the project started as an agile project and intended to follow Scrum practices, however failed to strictly maintain the practices throughout the project. Close collaboration with the remote locations was challenged by temporal and geographic distance. The project maintained product and sprint backlogs with requirements and user stories. However, the team leader (Scrum master) individually coordinated tasks for each developer. Lack of experience with Scrum and the pressure of deadlines prevented establishment of a cohesive agile team and application of self-management. In addition, coordination by mutual adjustment across locations was challenged by a lack of previous experience of working together, lack of trust and commitment, and "us versus them" attitude. Finally, daily Scrum meetings across multiple locations were challenged by the limitations of computer-mediated communication and were thus often withdrawn.

Configuration management is another challenging task in globally distributed projects [13]. Due to unplanned involvement of remote team members into development activities, the project infrastructure was not prepared to facilitate distributed software development. Thus, the team experienced significant difficulties in relation to configuration management and required additional effort for integration of the pieces developed by remote locations. Accordingly, the configuration management activity initially planned 5 working days appeared in the newer version of the plan to take 76 working-days and at the end took 154 working-days.

4   Conclusions

In this paper, we discussed a case project conducted in a CMMI Level 5 company that failed to meet initial plan constraints. We elaborated the possible causes for a high-maturity level organization to fail a project and observed that no company is immune to fail addressing unforeseen problems.

The basic reason for the project to become a candidate for a failure was initially underestimated effort and unrealistic schedules. This was unavoidable since the company cannot utilize the historical data they collected in the past years. Moreover, unfortunately, there exists no effort estimation model, which is accepted to successfully address all possible circumstances in software engineering projects, And especially, in distributed work. Therefore, we emphasize a need to collect project related data in benchmarking datasets that can be utilized by the organizations worldwide. Otherwise, only with the local efforts put by the organizations, it seems that these failure stories continue to be told. During the last 10 years, such effort has been put on forming publicly available benchmarking datasets such as the one by the International Software Benchmarking Standards Group (ISBSG) [14] to enable organizations share and use the others' experiences gained. However, without the commitment of the software organizations to provide data to these datasets, improvement in effort estimation area will stay minimal.

Global software development puts new challenges on project managers since geographic separation leads to more difficult effort estimations, project planning and control [15]. Effort required for communication, coordination and integration of the developed pieces of software in the studied case project was underestimated due to over optimistic expectations. These can be explained by lacking experience of working together across locations involved in the project.

Our study also shows that task distribution to remote locations under the pressure of deadlines drove the project to even deeper problems. In the studied case, project management decided to share the pain and stress with remote colleagues. Nonetheless, lack of cohesiveness and commitment from remote colleagues caused failure. However, it is worth mentioning that due to initially underestimated scope, schedule and project staffing, managers are often left with little choice of corrective actions. Therefore, the choice to distribute some of the effort to remote locations seemed natural. And this trend for distributed software development seems to increase as well. Therefore, global software development requires urgent tools and methods that help to overcome the difficulties and enable efficient distributed work.

Unfortunately, the case study does not allow evaluating the suitability and advantages of agile approaches for globally distributed environment, since agile principles and practices at the end were not complied. However, we can conclude, that a lack of previous experience and familiarity with the chosen methodology along with the changing members of the team prevented the project to experience potential benefits. Software community requires more empirical evidence of specific methodologies, such as agile approaches, applied in organizations practicing distributed development.

Acknowledgement

We would like to sincerely thank the team leader from the studied case project, who provided all the data and spent his precious time in discussions that helped us to make this study. This research is conducted within BESQ Research Centre at Blekinge Institute of Technology.

References

[1] A Guide to the Project Management Body of Knowledge (PMBOK® Guide), 3rd edn. Project Management Institute (2004)

[2] A Guide to the Software Engineering Body of Knowledge (SWEBOK). IEEE Computer Society (2004)

[3] Jones, T.C.: Estimating Software Costs. McGraw-Hill, New York (1998)

[4] Boehm, B.W.: Software Engineering Economics. Prentice-Hall, Englewood Cliffs (1981)

[5] Thayer, H.R.: Software Engineering Project Management, 2nd edn. IEEE CS Press, Los Alamitos (2001)

[6] Smite, D.: Project Outcome Predictions: Risk Barometer Based on Historical Data. In: Proc. of the ICGSE conference, Germany, August 2007, pp. 103–112. IEEE Computer Society, Los Alamitos (2007)

[7] Karolak, D.W.: Global Software Development: Managing Virtual Teams and Environments. IEEE Computer Society, Los Alamitos (1998)

[8] Prikladnicki, R., Audy, J.L.N., Evaristo, R.: A Reference Model for Global Software Development: Findings from a Case Study. In: Proc. of IEEE Int. Conf. on Global Software Engineering (ICGSE 2006), Florianópolis, Brazil, pp. 18–25. IEEE Computer Society Press, Los Alamitos (2006)

[9] Yin, R.K.: Case Study Research: design and methods, 2nd edn., vol. 5. Sage Publications, Newbury Park (1994)

[10] Ramesh, B., Cao, L., Mohan, K., Xu, P.: Can Distributed Software Development Be Agile? Communications of ACM 49(10), 41–46 (2006)

[11] Chow, T., Cao, D.-B.: A Survey Study of Critical Success Factors in Agile Software Projects. The Journal of Systems and Software 81, 961–971 (2008)

[12] Holmström, H., Fitzgerald, B., Ågerfalk, P.J., Conchúir, E.Ó.: Agile Practices Reduce Distance in Global Software Development. Information System Management 23(3), 7–18 (2006)

[13] Battin, R.D., Crocker, R., Kreidler, J., Subramanian, K.: Leveraging resources in global software development. IEEE Software 18(2), 70–77 (2001)

[14] ISBSG Dataset 10 (2007), http://www.isbsg.org

[15] Taxén, L.: An integration centric approach for the coordination of distributed software development projects. Information and Software Technology 48, 767–780 (2006)

Towards Multi-Method Research Approach in Empirical Software Engineering

Vladimir Mandić, Jouni Markkula, and Markku Oivo

University of Oulu, Department of Information Processing Science, Rakentajantie 3,
90014 University of Oulu, Finland
vladimir.mandic@tol.oulu.fi, Jouni.Markkula@oulu.fi, Markku.Oivo@oulu.fi

Abstract. This paper presents results of a literature analysis on Empirical Research Approaches in Software Engineering (SE). The analysis explores reasons why traditional methods, such as statistical hypothesis testing and experiment replication are weakly utilized in the field of SE. It appears that basic assumptions and preconditions of the traditional methods are contradicting the actual situation in the SE. Furthermore, we have identified main issues that should be considered by the researcher when selecting the research approach. In virtue of reasons for weak utilization of traditional methods we propose stronger use of Multi-Method approach with Pragmatism as the philosophical standpoint.

Keywords: Empirical Methods, Experimentation in Software Engineering, ESE, Multi-Method Research, Reporting Experiments.

1 Introduction

Researchers in the field of software engineering (SE) are facing dilemma: which empirical research approach should be taken? As Shaw [1] has pointed out that there is no shared understanding of preferred research approaches inside SE community, and therefore there is no clear response to the question. This encourages us to revisit the issue.

Researchers are usually confronted by following questions: Can the traditional scientific approach[1] of experimentation be effectively utilized for SE setting? What is an alternative? What should be taken in account while considering alternative approaches? Questions stated here resemble first decisions that a researcher has to make.

The objective of our research was to explore the current literature in order to seek sufficient sources regarding problems of utilizing quantitative methods like experimentation, statistical hypothesis testing, and experiment replications. Based on our literature study and analysis, we are able to suggest some alternative approaches. The results of the our analysis are packed in a simple decision making process. This process can help the researchers in their decisions regard the selection of research approaches and appropriate methods.

---

[1] Examples of traditional research concepts are statistical hypothesis testing and experiment replications.

F. Bomarius et al. (Eds.): PROFES 2009, LNBIP 32, pp. 96–110, 2009.
© Springer-Verlag Berlin Heidelberg 2009

This paper is result of the literature analysis. Literature review process was not systematic in terms as Kitchenham [2] suggests. The process started by reviewing two book classics on experimentation in SE [3,4]. After that, the review was complemented and deepened with additional references on specific issues, such as statistical hypothesis testing, experiment replications, and experiment reporting. Also the method of following bibliographical trails [5] was used. The following resources were used for the analysis: Google Scholar, IEEE Xplore, SpringerLink, Wiley InterScience, ACM, and reference databases available in University of Oulu Library. From the large number of potential references we selected 46 most relevant references for further analyzis. The structure of analyzed references is given in Table 1.

Table 1. Reference structure

Ref. Type	Journal	Book	Ed. Book	Conference
Percentage of total	54%	15%	20%	11%

The references were categorized using the following criteria:

1. **Meta-studies:** meta-studies on the topic of empirical and experimental methods in software engineering. Number of references: 7.
2. **Reporting experiments:** papers that report some empirical studies. Number of references: 7.
3. **Empirical methods:** papers that define methods and techniques for empirical research or comment on utilization of the methods in SE. Number of references: 26.
4. **Other:** References which were not categorized by first three criteria. Number of references: 6.

By reviewing the literature we found that researchers in the field of software engineering still seems to base their findings more on experiences and personal feelings then on empirical evidences (section 2). One of the most powerful scientific methods, experimentation, was introduced to SE research as one possible solution to the problem (section 3). However, due to the strong dependence of the objects under investigation upon context and the field immaturity, adaptation of the experimentation is lacking sufficient level of statistical significance (as shown in section 4). A concept of corroboration and/or refutation of findings through replications of the experiments is important for justifying results and knowledge creation process. Reported studies on experimentation in SE settings revealed us that external replications are not easily applicable (section 5). Besides reporting quantitative result, a structured qualitative analysis is needed to overcome contextual dependences and to explain design of experiment at such level of details to enable external replications (section 6). Multi-method approach advocates use of other methods in combination with purpose of achieving more creditable results (section 7). At the end we discuss how the approach can produce a near-close effect as the concept of experiment replications (section 8).

2   Motivation for the Use of Empirical Methods in Software Engineering

In the field of software engineering so called "advocacy research", has often been used in last decades [6,7,8,9]. Shortly we can illustrate this approach with a following scenario [6, p. 87]:

Authors describe a new concept in considerable detail; recommend the concept to be transferred to practice. Time passes, and other researchers derive similar conclusions. Eventually the consensus among researchers is that the concept has clear benefits. Yet practitioners often seem unenthused. Researchers, satisfied that their communal analysis is correct, become frustrated. Heated discussion and finger-pointing ensues.

Given scenario is lacking empirical proofs that the proposed new concept is beneficial. Such empirical proofs can dramatically change the scenario. All communal analysis will shift from a personal, subjective, judgment regarding substance to objective reasoning based on the empirical evidence.

One of the roles of the experimentation is to enable researchers in the field of software engineering to derive conclusions based on empirically made observations.

The main concern of the researchers is with what degree of certainty it is possible to claim that a hypothesis is true or false [7, p. 457].

Basili [10] describes analogies with other fields of research. Separation on two groups of people and existence of strong feedback loop among them is the common element in all those analogical models. The basic idea is to have a clear separation on two groups: researchers and practitioners. In this tentative model we can identify three loops:

Loop 1. Describes activity of the researcher. A researcher relies on the global body of knowledge, and entire process which is encapsulated by the loop 1, has a basis in academic research and academic writing. The researcher's role is to understand the nature of processes and products, and relationships between them [10, p. 443].

Loop 2. Describes activity of the practitioner. Practitioners use tools, methods and techniques in daily work. The feedback of using tools, methods and techniques always exists; the question is how well is it formulated and/or documented.

Loop 3. Is the feedback loop, which was the main reason to consider this kind of model. According to Basili *et al.* [7,10] this kind of a loop has a significant influence on knowledge creation process.

Unfortunately, the implementation of the proposed model is not straightforward, even worse it is questioned if it is feasible at all. Some problems that affect communication paths between researchers and practitioners are [11]:

(1) Data sharing, this includes problems of work sharing and intellectual property rights.

(2) Data Interpretation problem is illustrated with following questions made by Basili [11]: *When we find agreement how much can we generalize, how do*

we incorporate the context variables in the interpretation, how do we assign the degree of confidence in the interpretation? When we find disagreement do we expand the model, identify two different contexts, or reject the model?

Vegas *et al.* [12] propose some possible mechanisms for dealing with those issues like licensing, software support tools, and etc. General conclusion is that each field has its own particular problems and issues and we have to tailor such rules for the SE field [12, p. 116].

We will formulate another question regarding feasibility of the proposed approach in software engineering field. *Has the global body of knowledge reached "critical mass", and became capable of supporting the separation on the researchers and the practitioners?*

Physics and medicine certainly fall in well-developed disciplines [13, p. 1145]. Well-developed disciplines have well defined a relationship structure within body of knowledge.

Such established structures provide a comfortable environment for researchers, and enables them to create new concepts, theories, with high degree of confidence. *Researchers in the field of software engineering are facing: human subjects with large ability variations, ill-defined processes, products with poorly defined characteristics, a limited number of facts, nothing that can be regarded as a universal constant,...* [14, p. 188].

Can the lack of the structure in the software engineering body of knowledge be compensated with strong, direct, feedback loop from the practice to the researcher? Our response to the question: yes, it has to be.

3   Basic Terminology of the Software Engineering Experimentation

First we will define the basic terminology adopted from Wohlin *et al.* [4], alternative terminology is commented and referenced.

In Figure 1 the basic elements of an experiment are illustrated. Figure is adopted from [4, p. 34], with an addition of *context*. It is very important to be aware of an existing context and its influence on experiment. Partially the

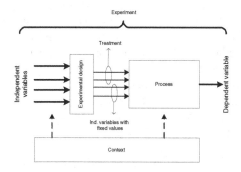

Fig. 1. Illustration of the experimental process

influence of the context will be taken in account through experimental design. It is not possible to model, take in account, all numerous variables existing in the context. The objective of experimental design is to reduce the context interference to the level of noise. Context plays important role in reporting and sharing results of the experiments, therefore it is advisable to document it as detail as possible [15,16]. Endres *et al.* [17] formulated *Conjecture*: *Empirical results are transferable only if abstracted and packaged with context*. Kitchenham *et al.* [18] proposed an entire set of guidelines for dealing with context during experiment.

The variables that are in the focus of a study are called *dependent* or response variables, all other variables are called *independent*.

Independent variables can have constant value during experiment and then they are *fixed variables*.

Independent variables that change value (in controlled manner) during experiment are called *factors*. One particular value of the factor is called *treatment*. Alternative terminology for treatment is *alternative or level* [3, p. 60].

Subjects of the experiment are usually people that have to apply a treatment. *Object* is any artifact of the process on which a treatment is applied. Objects can be referred as *experimental units* [3, p. 57]. An experiment consists of a set of *tests or trials*, where each test is a combination of treatment, subject and object.

Cook *et al.* [19] define **quasi-experiments** as experiments that have treatments, outcome measures, and experimental units, but do not use random assignment to create comparison from which treatment-cause change is inferred.

Experimental Design. Figure 1 illustrates the role of the experimental design in an experiment. The goal of experimental design is to isolate variation of the interest. Juristo *et al.* [3, p. 84] give an overview of the experimental designs based on parameters like: number of factor, number of alternatives per factor, and existence of the blocking variables. The basic experimental designs are: one-factor design, block design, factorial design, nested design, fractional design, and factorial block design.

Randomization in Experimental Designs. Randomized design means that the factor alternatives are assigned to experimental units in absolutely random order. Concerning SE, both the factor alternatives and the subjects have to be randomized, as the subjects (people) have a critical impact on the value of dependent variable [3]. The request for randomizing both subjects and factor alternatives might sound odd, unless the idea of randomizing subjects is a proposal how to deal with a fact that in SE field subject characteristics vary a lot even within same class (Example: productivity of the programmers with same number of years of experience). Still remains a question how well the randomization of the subjects can effectively solve the problem. When the idea of randomization was introduced into experiments, the goal was to ensure that errors were independent. With new applications of the significance testing, a representative sample has been added. Miller [14] observed that very often a mistake is made by using randomization to "discard" representativeness.

More often feasibility of the random sampling in the field of software engineering is questioned. Miller *et al.* [20] define the sampling problem as: *Regardless of the characteristic under investigation, the software engineering field has no defined sampling frame (i.e. description of the entire population) for its practitioners, and hence we cannot know if the sample is truly representative of the underlying population.* However there are no universal sampling frameworks in other fields as well, practice is that research setting determines sampling strategy. But we can notice that other fields have some elementary, basic, knowledge about population which is used for defining sampling strategy. That kind of basic knowledge is lacking in the field of SE.

4   Quantitative Aspect of the Experimentation

Quantitative methods are maybe the only approach that can provide researchers with concrete information about certainty of their conclusions. Other approaches are also considered to be suitable for the field of software engineering at this moment, like explorative studies and qualitative confirmatory analysis [9].

Experimental analysis is dependent on the characteristics of data that are collected or measured during experiment. Depending on the nature of data several measurement scales can be used: nominal, ordinal, interval, or ration. Information about measurement scale is important because it determines which statistical methods can be and cannot be used for analyzing results. Generally methods are divided in two groups: parametric and non-parametric methods [3,4]. Most common methods are given in Table 2.

Table 2. Overview of parametric/non-parametric tests for different designs

Design	Parametric	Non-parametric
One factor, one treatment		Chi-2
		Binomial test
One factor, two treatments,	t-test	Mann-Whitney
completely randomized design	F-test	Chi-2
One factor, two treatments,	Paired t-test	Wilcoxon
paired comparison		Sign test
One factor,	ANOVA	Kruskal-Wallis
more than two treatments		Chi-2
More than one factor	ANOVA	

Statistical hypothesis testing. The Neyman-Pearson type of significance testing is the form of testing a null hypothesis, where the null hypothesis is formulated with the purpose if it is rejected to allow the researcher considering an alternative hypothesis and conclude that an effect exists [20, p. 286]. Basic steps of statistical hypothesis testing are [14, p. 183]:

1. The construction of a null hypothesis;
2. The collection of data;
3. A statistical test against the null hypothesis is undertaken;
4. The generated P−value[2] is considered against the null hypothesis; and one or more interpretations are made.

The probability of committing Type I error is statistical significance, denoted by Greek letter α.

Test significance value, α is set in advanced, after having all data form experiment the P−value is calculated and compared to α [14].

Statistical power analysis. As a part of statistical significance testing is statistical power analysis. Power analyses involve three components [20]:

- **The significance criterion** (α).
- **The sample size** (n): the larger the number of samples, the smaller the error, the greater accuracy.
- **The effect size** (γ): the degree to which the phenomenon under study is present in the population (sample).

Methods how to calculate or estimate sample size are given in [3,20].The only critical step in this process is estimate of the effect size. Coehn has established a convention that *small effect* is not observable with bare eyes, *medium effect* is observable with researcher's eyes and *large effect* is high over an average.

In the study [21, p. 749] a systematic literature analysis has been performed in order to conclude how Coehn's convention maps to the field of software engineering. The findings of the study showed that in SE effect size is for 50% smaller for small effect size and about 25% to 20% for medium and large effects. This decrease in effect size calls for larger sample size, which is very often difficult to achieve in SE experiments.

5   Software Experiment Replication

The first experiment is usually referenced as an original, later experiments which have the same null hypothesis as original are called replications. Replicated experiments can be categorized in two groups [22]:

Exact replications or partial replications of the original, they have the same alternative hypothesis as the original, usually in the form H_1^{rep}: The results of the replication will be in same direction as the first (original) experiment [23].

Replications with goal to improve on the original. This type of replicated experiment will have different, improved formulation of the alternative hypothesis.

---

[2] The P−value can be viewed as the probability that results obtained due to chance, therefore small values are taken to indicate that results where not just a chance.

First type of the replicated experiments is common for *internal replications,* when the same researcher performance replicated experiment, while second type would be expected in *external replication.*

Replication of the experiments is important for at least two reasons: (1) it is the best way to validate experiment (experimental results and experimental design) [22, p. 237] and (2) as the instrument of Popperian inference. General statements (hypotheses) cannot be proved, but they can be disproved. This is the basic idea of Popper's conjuncture [24].

The statistical hypothesis testing is an instrument of Popperian inference; or more correctly that statistical hypothesis testing was designed as an instrument of the hypothetic-deductive scientific method and that this method and Popperian inference are effectively equivalent approaches [14].

Following this philosophy, we can note that replication of the experiments (test) is crucial for making a theory to become well-proved and trusted. How to get that level of replications in software engineering?

Several studies have shown that experimentation is not utilized well enough in software engineering at the level of the original experiment (first experiment) [6,25,26], and the field is far away from performing replications. Brooks *et al.* [27] noted that in cases when people are dominant factor, controlled experiments are less effective. Miller [22] defined dimensions of the replication framework for software engineering field. Those dimensions can be seen as major categories of causes for the weak utilization of the replications in SE. We present those causes in the cause-effect diagram Figure 2.

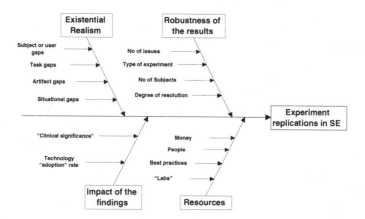

Fig. 2. Major categories of the problems regarding experiment replications in the field of software engineering

Existential realism. Software engineering experiment differs from the real world. Numerous differing points are characterized as: *subject gaps, task gaps, artifact gaps,* and *situational gaps* [22]. Factors affecting different types of gaps are varying from socio-psychological up to mixed influence of socio-technological factors.

Experimental results are robust when they produce relatively stable results across a range of minor variations in experimental setting. High robustness can be a motivation factor for replicating experiments. If experiment results are robust, replicated experiments even if they reject original hypothesis they can be used by researchers to generate new conclusions.

Impact of the findings is dealing with question: Will the finding convince practitioners in real world setting to change, adapt or adopt new practices? This issue is correlated with technology transfer and adaption rate of the technology.

Resources. Beside material resources an attention is raised on non-existing experimental practices for software engineering. Basili [10] pointed out that 'laboratories' exist only where practitioners build software systems. This fact complicates entire experimental process and increases cost.

Analyzing results of the replicated experiments. Once, having results of the replicated experiments, the method for analyzing the results should be selected. Based on practices in the social sciences, two groups of analyzing methods are identified [22]: (1) Meta-analytical procedures and (2) informal approach.

Meta-analysis provides a simple quantitative framework for comparing and combining results of the experiments. Most common techniques used in software engineering are: comparative and additive meta-analysis. Both methods are usually done to compare results of two experiments.

6   Reporting Experiments

Communication between communities of the researchers and practitioners is very important, especially when reporting results of the experiments in such way to enable, encourage, others to replicate or conduct similar experiments. Therefore a mutually accepted standard or form, of the reporting results is welcome. According to Miller [22] only three serious initiatives were proposed. First one is Basili's approach for classifying experiments. Originally this scheme was developed for a meta-study on experimentation in software engineering and later was used as basis for experimental paradigm [28,16]. Main elements of the scheme are: definition, planning, operation, and interpretation. Beside the original idea for developing the scheme, it is possible to use it as a guideline for reporting experiments.

Second scheme developed by Lott *et al.* [29] has many similarities with first one, including the use of GQM to derive the subsequent scheme. The main elements of this scheme are: (1) goals, hypothesis and theories, (2) Experimental planning, (3) Experimental procedures, and (4) results. Third scheme, actually entire package for experimentation, is developed by Kamsties and Lott. Unfortunately it is least likely that entire package can be implemented in software engineering.

Beside those three schemes, recently Jedlitschka *et al.* [30] proposed a new scheme based on comparative study of existing schemes, mainly in software engineering area. The scheme suggests following elements: structured abstract, introduction, related work, experiment planning, execution, analysis, interpretation, discussion and conclusions, future work, acknowledgements, references, and appendices.

7 Multi-Method Research Approach

The multi-method or mixed-method approach originates from the social sciences [31,32]. The basic idea of the approach is to investigate a phenomenon using a combination of empirical research methods, with intention that the combination of the methods complements each others. The combination may include quantitative and qualitative methods to collect, analyze, and interpret both types of data [33]. This approach offers potential for more stable and generalizable results in empirical software engineering research.

Discussions on utilizing multi-method approach for information systems research started in late 80's and early 90's [34,35], continued in 2000's [33,36,37]. Despite the agreement of the researchers in information systems that there are benefits of utilizing multi-method approach, there is no such agreement among researchers in the field of software engineering. Reported SE related studies using multi-method are still very rare. One example is use of multi-method approach to study collaboration of global virtual teams [38]. Wood et al. [23] used multi-method to investigate object-oriented technology with particular focus on how the inheritance levels affect maintainability of software.

The use of multi-method approach is shaded with philosophical discussions if such methodological pluralism is acceptable [39,37,36]. Particular methods are paired with paradigms or philosophical standpoints [37, p. 243], which raises the question whether mixing of the methods would mean mixing of the paradigms. The question evolved in debate over *incompatibility* vs. *compatibility* thesis.

Howe [39] points out that: *The incompatibility thesis, like the drunkard's search*[3], *permits the "lights" to determine what is to be looked for and where.* Howe took bottom-up approach in proving his *compatibility thesis* [39]. He discussed what quantitative and qualitative means at levels of *data, design and analysis*, and *interpretation of results*. The conclusion was that mixing of the methods is acceptable if it provides additional evidences, and it does not imply mixing of the paradigms. Conclusion made by Howe is known as *compatibility thesis*.

Mingers [37] arguments that phenomena studied by researchers in the field of information systems are extremely complex. Such complexity can be studied if it is decomposed on dimensions of *the multidimensional world*. Therefore it is less likely that one method can be successfully applied to all dimensions.

The multi-method approach is not limited to the combining qualitative and quantitative methods. Also the combination of different quantitative methods is

---

[3] Kaplan's story illustrating the "principle of the drunkard's search." *There is a story of a drunkard searching under a street lamp for his house key, which he had dropped some distance away. Asked why he didn't look where he had dropped it, he replied, "It's lighter here!"* (Kaplan, 1964).

possible. When designing a multi-method research, the following strategies can be used [23,32]:

Evolutionary or sequential is followed when there is little research conducted on a particular phenomenon, or where research hypothesis require increased focus.

Complementary or concurrent or triangulation aims to enhance the validity of research findings. Different research methods are used independently to study phenomenon. An example how to structure a study which uses triangulation as method is given in [40].

Transformative strategy, procedures which use theoretical lens or perspective in qualitative research. Examples of the perspectives are: Feminist perspective, Critical theory, and Racialized discourse [32].

Guidelines for categorizing mixed methods can be found in *mixed method research framework* [33]. The classification matrix (Table 3) is based on *purpose* dimension: triangulation, complementary, development, initiation, and expansion. And *approach* dimension how the method is applied: sequential, parallel and independent.

Table 3. Mixed method (Multi-method) research framework [33, p. 1]

| | | APPROACH | | |
		Sequential	Parallel	Independent
PURPOSE	Triangulation			
	Complementarity			
	Development			
	Initiation			
	Expansion			

The following methods are usually combined: *observational studies, pre-experiment studies, quasi-experiments, controlled experiments, surveys*. More comprehensive list of the methods can be found in *taxonomy of information systems research approaches* [35, p. 96]. The taxonomy classifies methods by the object of a study: (1) society, organization/group, (2) individual, (3) technology, and (4) methodology. In studying technology or methodology objects, both groups of approaches (qualitative and quantitative) can be utilized. In studying socio-psychological phenomena qualitative approaches are suggested.

The main challenge of the multi-method design/planning is how to select a good combination of methods. For that purpose Wood *et al.* [23] proposed a set of criteria:

- **Internal validity:** The extent to which causal conclusions can be made from the study.
- **External validity:** The extent to which results may be generalized to the population under study and other settings.

Reaching a high validity is a balancing game because some validity types are opposing each other [7, p. 457]: *...make it less likely that the validity types can all be satisfied at the same time: e.g., making a study more realistic to achieve a high external validity is in tension with the ability to manipulate the context to get a high internal validity.*

- **Ease of replication:** The ease with which the study can be repeated under the same conditions.
- **Potential for theory generation:** The potential to generate new causal theories.
- **Potential for theory confirmation:** The potential to test a theory providing robust conclusions.
- **Cost per subject:** The relative cost of the study.

Based on this characterization, Daly *et al.* [41] provide the following advice:

A Maximize internal validity, external validity, and ease of replication by selecting a combination of the methods that jointly satisfy these criteria. For example a controlled experiment (high internal validity) and a survey (high external validity), both being relatively easy to replicate, provide good coverage of the criteria [41].
B Since the cost of a multi-method approach is usually significant, combine methods to minimize overall cost.
C Determine the need for theory generation and theory confirmation, considering whether the perspective of the approach is complimentary or evolutionary. For example, if it is evolutionary, observational studies may be use for theory generation combined with controlled experiments for theory confirmation.

In the context of the multi-method approach, observational studies may be used to characterize, baseline, and/or identify relationships. They are also very often seen in combination with other methods.

8   Conclusions

In order to avoid the habit of *advocacy research*, it is necessary to justify conclusions with empirical evidences. Empirical evidences have also a psychological effect as a very strong element of persuading other researches and practitioners to trust the validity and usefulness of the results. Without this persuasion, especially practitioners will not strive to use the result of the research. This phenomenon is known as *clinical significance* and it is a major factor for not having wide replications of software experiments within researcher's community. Also, the everyday use of methods and tools in practice can be considered as a form of replication, unfortunately reported in a very free form of experience reports or lessons learned.

The complexity of the phenomena under study in the field of SE sets a very sophisticated conditions and constraints on performing software experiments and replications. Existential realism argues that a gap between experimental setting and real world situations is too large. Because of the lack of sufficient body of knowledge which would allow researchers to bridge the gap. In such kind of situations qualitative research approaches are much more applicable then quantitative.

Robustness of results could be achieved with high statistical significance in experimentation. Unfortunately, it is common to have low statistical significance in SE experiments which is followed with less robust results. Use of different methods with purpose of triangulation can significantly increase robustness of the results, especially if the methods are applied independently.

The impact of the findings can be improved only if trust and confidence in new theories and research findings is increased. That can be achieved by using multi-method approach. This approach is compatible with Pragmatism as the philosophical standpoint. It is an effective tool for confirming results with sufficient flexibility to cope with specifics of the software engineering research.

Our proposal is based on analysis of available literature and previous experiences in the field of software engineering. The proposal is not a silver bullet, but it is good starting point. The main advantage of the multi-method approach is the possibility to balance method's rigor for a given research setting. Probably the biggest disadvantage is that it requires the researcher to be proficient in several empirical methods instead of just one method.

This preliminary literature analysis will be a base for the future work. We plan to expend literature review in more systematic way. Our further contributions on this topic will be focused on exploring relationships between different philosophical standpoints and empirical methods, and their applicability in software engineering settings.

Acknowledgements. This article is based on the work carried out in the VASPO project (Value-based Software Process Improvement and Organizational Change Management) financed by the Finnish Funding Agency for Technology and Innovation (Tekes).

References

1. Shaw, M.: What makes good research in software engineering? International Journal of Software Tools for Technology Transfer 4(1), 1–7 (2002)
2. Kitchenham, B.: Guidelines for performing systematic literature reviews in software engineering. Technical report, TR-EBSE-2007-01, UK (2007)
3. Juristo, N., Moreno, A.: Basics of Software Engineering Experimentation. Kluwer Academic Publishers, Dordrecht (2003)
4. Wohlin, C., Runeson, P., Horst, M., Ohlsson, M., Regnell, B., Wesslen, A.: Experimentation in Software Engineering: An Introduction. Kluwer Academic Publishers, Dordrecht (2000)
5. Turabian, K.: A Manual for Writers of Research Papers, Theses, and Dissertations. The University of Chicago Press, Chicago (2007)
6. Fenton, N., Pfleeger, S., Glass, R.: Science and substance: A challenge to software engineers. IEEE Software 4(11), 86–95 (1994)

7. Basili, V., Shull, F., Lanubile, F.: Building knowledge through families of experiments. IEEE Transactions on Software Engineering 25(4), 456–473 (1999)
8. Oivo, M.: New opportunities for empirical research. In: Basili, V.R., Rombach, H.D., Schneider, K., Kitchenham, B., Pfahl, D., Selby, R.W. (eds.) Empirical Software Engineering Issues. LNCS, vol. 4336, p. 22. Springer, Heidelberg (2007)
9. Oivo, M., Kuvaja, P., Pulli, P., Similä, J.: Software engineering research strategy: Combining experimental and explorative research (eer). In: Bomarius, F., Iida, H. (eds.) PROFES 2004. LNCS, vol. 3009, pp. 302–317. Springer, Heidelberg (2004)
10. Basili, V.: The role of experimentation in software engineering: Past, current, and future. In: 18th International Conference on Software Engineering, pp. 442–449. IEEE, Berlin (1996)
11. Basili, V.: Measurement and model building, introduction. In: Basili, V.R., Rombach, H.D., Schneider, K., Kitchenham, B., Pfahl, D., Selby, R.W. (eds.) Empirical Software Engineering Issues. LNCS, vol. 4336, pp. 68–69. Springer, Heidelberg (2007)
12. Vegas, S., Basili, V.: Measurement and model building, discussion and summary. In: Basili, V.R., Rombach, H.D., Schneider, K., Kitchenham, B., Pfahl, D., Selby, R.W. (eds.) Empirical Software Engineering Issues. LNCS, vol. 4336, pp. 115–120. Springer, Heidelberg (2007)
13. Curtis, B.: Measurement and experimentation in software engineering. In: Proceedings of IEEE, pp. 1144–1157. IEEE, Los Alamitos (1980)
14. Miller, J.: Statistical significance testing – a panacea for software technology experiments? Journal of Systems and Software 2(73), 183–192 (2004)
15. Zelkowitz, M., Wallance, D.: Experimental validation in software engineering. Information and Software Technology 11(39), 735–743 (1997)
16. Basili, V., Selby, R., Hutchens, D.: Experimentation in software engineering. IEEE Transactions on Software Engineering 12(7), 733–743 (1986)
17. Endres, A., Rombach, D.: A Handbook of Software and Systems Engineering: Empirical Observations, Laws and Theories. Pearson Education, Harlow (2003)
18. Kitchenham, B., Pfleeger, S., Pickard, L., Jones, P., Hoaglin, D., El Emam, K., et al.: Preliminary guidelines for empirical research in software engineering. IEEE Transactions on Software Engineering 8(28), 721–734 (2002)
19. Cook, T., Campbell, D.: Quasi-Experimentation: Design and Analysis Issues for Field Settings. Houghton Mifflin Company, USA (1979)
20. Miller, J., Daly, J., Wood, M., Roper, M., Brooks, A.: Statistical power and its subcomponents - missing and misunderstood concepts in empirical software engineering research. Information and Software Technology 4(39), 285–295 (1997)
21. Dybå, T., Kampenes, V., Sjøberg, D.: A systematic review of statistical power in software engineering experiments. Information and Software Technology 8(48), 745–755 (2006)
22. Miller, J.: Replicating software engineering experiments: a poisoned chalice or the holy grail. Information and Software Technology 4(47), 233–244 (2005)
23. Wood, M., Daly, J., Miller, J., Roper, M.: Multi-method research: An empirical investigation of object-oriented technology. Journal of Systems and Software 1(48), 13–26 (1999)
24. Popper, K.: The Logic of Scientific Discovery. Routledge Classics, New York (1959)
25. Ramesh, V., Glass, R., Vessey, I.: Research in computer science: an empirical study. Journal of systems and Software 2(70), 165–176 (2004)

26. Sjøberg, D., Hannay, J., Hansen, O., By Kampenes, V., Karahasanovic, A., Liborg, N.K., et al.: A survey of controlled experiments in software engineering. IEEE Transactions on Software Engineering 31(9), 733–753 (2005)

27. Brooks, A., Roper, M., Wood, M., Daly, J., Miller, J.: Replication's role in software engineering. In: Shull, F., et al. (eds.) Guide to Advanced Empirical Software Engineering, pp. 365–379. Springer, London (2008)

28. Basili, V., Selby, R.: Paradigms for experimentation and empirical studies in software engineering. Reliability Engineering and System Safety 1(32), 171–191 (1991)

29. Lott, C., Rombach, D.: Repeatable software engineering experiments for comparing defect-detection techniques. Empirical Software Engineering 1(3), 241–277 (1996)

30. Jedlitschka, A., Ciolkowski, M.: Reporting experiments in software engineering. In: Shull, F., et al. (eds.) Guide to Advanced Empirical Software Engineering, pp. 201–228. Springer, London (2007)

31. Easterbrook, S., Singer, J., Storey, M.A., Damian, D.: Selecting empirical methods for software engineering research. In: Shull, F., et al. (eds.) Guide to Advanced Empirical Software Engineering, pp. 285–311. Springer, London (2008)

32. Creswell, J.: Research Design: Qualitative, Quantitative, and Mixed Method Approaches. Sage Publications, Inc., London (2008)

33. Petter, S., Gallivan, M.: Toward a framework for classifying and guiding mixed method research in information systems. In: The 37th Hawaii International Conference on System Sciences, Big Island, HI, USA, pp. 1–10 (2004)

34. Nunamaker, J., Chen, M., Purdin, T.: Systems development in information systems research. Journal of Management Information Systems 7(3), 89–106 (1991)

35. Galliers, R.: Research issues in information systems. Journal of Information Technology 2(8), 92–98 (1993)

36. Sawyer, S.: Studying organizational computing infrastructures: Multi-method approaches. In: Baskerville, R., et al. (eds.) Organizational and Social Perspectives on Information Technology, IFIP TC8 WG8.2 International Working Conference on the Social and Organizational Perspective on Research and Practice in Information Technology, pp. 213–232. Kluwer, Aalborg (2000)

37. Mingers, J.: Combining is research methods: Towards a pluralist methodology. Information Systems Research 12(3), 240–259 (2001)

38. Steinfield, C., Huysman, M., David, K., Yang Jang, C., Poot, J., Huis in 't Veld, M., et al.: New methods for studying global virtual teams: Towards a multifaceted approach, Wailea Maui, Hawaii, USA. In: The 34th Hawaii International Conference on System Sciences 2001, pp. 1–10 (2001)

39. Howe, K.: Against the quantitative-qualitative incompatibility thesis. Educational Researcher 17(8), 10–16 (1998)

40. Bratthall, L., Jørgensen, M.: Can you trust a single data source exploratory software engineering case study? Empirical Software Engineering 7(1), 9–26 (2002)

41. Daly, J., El Emam, K., Miller, J.: An empirical research methodology for software process improvement. In: El Emam, K., et al. (eds.) Elements of Software Process Assessment and Improvement. Wiley-IEEE Computer Society Press, London (1998)

The Role of Empirical Evidence for Transferring a New Technology to Industry

Maria Teresa Baldassarre, Giovanni Bruno, Danilo Caivano,
and Giuseppe Visaggio

University of Bari – Dept. Informatics, Via Orabona 4, 70126 Bari, Italy
{baldassarre,bruno,caivano,visaggio}@di.uniba.it

Abstract. Technology transfer and innovation diffusion are key success factors for an enterprise. The shift to a new software technology involves, on one hand, inevitable changes to ingrained and familiar processes and, on the other, requires training, changes in practices and commitment on behalf of technical staff and management. Nevertheless, industry is often reluctant to innovation due to the changes it determines. The process of innovation diffusion is easier if the new technology is supported by empirical evidence. In this sense our conjecture is that Empirical Software Engineering (ESE) serves as means for validating and transferring a new technology within production processes. In this paper, the authors report their experience of a method, Multiview Framework, defined in the SERLAB research laboratory as support for designing and managing a goal oriented measurement program that has been validated through various empirical studies before being transferred to an Italian SME. Our discussion points out the important role of empirical evidence for obtaining management commitment and buy-in on behalf of technical staff, and for making technological transfer possible.

Keywords: Technology transfer, innovation diffusion, empirical evidence.

1 Introduction

Diffusion is the process by which an innovation is communicated through certain channels, over time, among the members of a social system. As so, an innovation is an idea, practice or object perceived as new by the unit adopting it, either it be an individual or an entire organization. Nowadays it is quite evident that we are surrounded by software in our every day life. Nevertheless, the transfer of new software engineering techniques from research to practice still strives to succeed. It's as if the two worlds of research and practice are still quite distant, as if "the researcher builds to study, the practitioner studies to build". Consequently, methods and techniques defined by researchers are often difficult to transfer into industry.

It is well known that technological innovation is a key factor for the competitiveness of an enterprise. It can be introduced in the production cycles as process or product innovation for improving effectiveness and efficiency of business goals and also for adapting products to market needs. Innovation is not always well seen and accepted in

F. Bomarius et al. (Eds.): PROFES 2009, LNBIP 32, pp. 111–125, 2009.
© Springer-Verlag Berlin Heidelberg 2009

that it introduces a change of techniques and methods that are ingrained in the production processes. Because of the changes required, technological innovation must take into consideration both organizational and technical factors. The first refer to the level of commitment of the organization wanting to introduce the innovation. The second concerns who is going to use the technology. Both technical and organizational factors "are important in setting the tone and culture in the organization and depend heavily on the interest and support of managers" [1]. So, the organization in its whole plays an important role in influencing innovation adoption and diffusion.

Given these premises the process of innovation diffusion can be made easier if the new technology, defined by researchers, is supported by empirical evidence. To this intent, in a previous work [2] authors have investigated the importance of Empirical Software Engineering (ESE) as means for validating and transferring a new technology within production processes. The importance of experimentation for introducing new techniques and methods has been faced in [3] where the author proposes an experimentally-based technology transfer lifecycle as mechanism for driving the introduction of software engineering technologies into industrial environments and as means for eliciting co-operation between laboratory and industry.

In this sense, this paper represents a further investigation on the role of empirical evidence for allowing technological transfer. The authors illustrate how the technology transfer lifecycle has been adapted and applied for transferring a method (Multiview Framework) developed in a laboratory context and validated through various types of empirical studies before being transferred to industry, and how it was then transferred to a local Italian SME.

The remaining part of the paper is organized as follows: the next section we comment on issues concerning innovation diffusion in literature; section 3 illustrates the experiment based technology transfer lifecycle, followed by details of our experience carrying out the lifecycle (section 4). The description starts from the definition of the method, proceeds with its validation through empirical studies and finally concludes with its transfer and diffusion to industry. At last, conclusions are drawn.

2   Related Literature

A strategic aspect for any organization is to continuously innovate its production processes in order to achieve improvements in business acquisition. Shifting to a new software technology involves inevitable changes to ingrained and familiar processes, and requires training, changes in practices and commitment on behalf of technical staff and management. In [4] the authors conclude that "it takes on the order of 15 to 20 years to mature a technology to the point that it can be popularized and disseminated to the technical community at large". Obviously, markets cannot wait so long, especially considering time-to-market pressures. So, many organizations end up falling for new promising technologies before their declared benefits are actually supported by empirical evidence [1, 5].

In [6] Rogers studied technology transfer in different types of organizations and identified various patterns in the way and time implied for adopting a new technology. He distinguishes among: Innovators who launch a new idea in the system by importing the innovation from outside of a system's boundaries; Early adopters who are a more integrated part of the organization's culture. They decrease uncertainty about a new innovation by adopting it and then socialize their subjective evaluation to peers; Early majority: although they interact with their peers, they seldom hold positions of opinion leadership. Their attitude is more of a "follow the leader". Late majority: innovations are approached with a skeptical an cautious air, and this category of innovators usually will not adopt until most others in their organization have done so. Their adoption is most likely the result of external pressures; Laggards, they will join the crowd when they are sure that the innovation will not fail.

Berniker [7] and Zelkowitz [8] have also carried out similar studies and have identified models for transferring technologies in the first case and risk levels in the second, that can be traced with Rogers' categories. Basically, from these three studies it arises that different adopters use different styles. So, for example, innovators are people-movers and will accept a high level of risk in trying the new technology. Early adopters use a communication model i.e. they let others go on first, and when they read about the success of the technology on behalf of others they will introduce it in their own organization. Early majority are even more cautious because the technology must not only have been successfully adopted by others, but it has to have been appropriately packaged (on-the-shelf model) so that adoption is easier and not effort prone. Late majority conform to a vendor model of technology transfer in that they use examples of other customers' experiences as a way for committing to the innovation and being sure of the low level of risk. Finally laggards adopt a technology only when they are forced to. Rules imposed by the organization or by external parties. So, as it can be seen, technology transfer is not only made up of a new idea but it also requires an appropriate audience with a specific adoption style. Usually, as the level of risk decreases because the body of knowledge and empirical evidences are more convincing, practitioners tend to be less reluctant in adopting the technology. In particular the two main elements in the technology transfer process can be identified as either promoters, those who accelerate technology adoption, or inhibitors, those who interfere with or prevent technology adoption.

In [9] the author carried out a survey on the effectiveness of technology transfer within Information Systems (IS) organizations. Results pointed out that the perceived effectiveness of technology transfer on behalf of managers differed according to its level of maturity. In other words, whether the technology was in its infancy, was being tried for the first time or was mature enough to become an integrated part of the organization's production processes. So, the maturity of a technology acted as a promoter.

Clearly, a technology must answer business or technical issues, or specific requirements experienced by an organization. In this sense basic research is called to perceive such needs and provide solutions through new models and technologies to transfer and apply in industry. Nevertheless, these two communities are often found to be quite distant one from another. In [10] authors point out how researchers and practitioners have different ideas on the criteria to use for evaluating the success of a technology. In particular, the study surveyed 90 researchers and practitioners on their perceptions of the most appropriate empirical methods for validating a new technology. Results were discordant: practitioners attributed higher value to methods relevant to their specific context, i.e. case studies, field studies, retrospective analysis, replicated and controlled experiments on industrial cases; researchers expressed preferences in validation methods to be used in isolation in laboratory, i.e. theoretical proof, static analysis, and simulation. So, the body of evidence provided by researchers and practitioners seem to follow two parallel paths.

Furthermore, in [2] the authors overview ten years of experience in carrying out empirical studies that range from surveys, case studies, and formal experiments to assess which are more suitable for transferring a new technology from academia to an industrial context.

Therefore, if we are to achieve successful technology transfer, it is important to find ways for basic research results to be reported, understood, and convincing for practitioners. This paper faces these issues and moves towards closing the gap between research and practice, academia and industry, basic research and applied research, so that results achieved and collected evidence can serve as promoters for obtaining management support, overcoming cultural inertia and assuring successful technology transfer. In the next sections we express what is intended as technology transfer process and in which terms it has been applied by our research group for enacting innovation diffusion.

3 Technology Transfer Process

Resistance to innovation is not a novelty. Often new technologies are not accepted by project staff because they are considered not appropriate to market needs and the project managers are not convinced of benefits produced. Also, the risk of innovation often slackens both project staff and management to buy-into the new idea [3]. Our hypothesis is that introduction of a new technology can be facilitated if it is supported by evidence on its efficacy and effectiveness.

As so, ESE can support providing such evidence, introducing and then diffusing the innovation within the industrial environment. It is expected that introduction of a new technology in some way improves processes, products and resources. In this sense evidence should help determine if the new technology actually determines such improvement by investigating the cause-effect relations between variables of interest. According to Rogers [6] innovations supported by evidence that assess the previous aspects will be adopted more rapidly than other ones.

Evidence alone is not enough for transferring a technology. Rather, once effectiveness of a technology has been proven, specific models must support its transfer and diffusion in industry. Such a process creates new knowledge as the innovation is acquired and more evidence as it is adopted. In other words, knowledge and evidence are both involved and play an important role in the technology transfer process.

3.1 Knowledge Creation and Flow

The diffusion of any innovation goes through all or at least part of the phases of what is known as Knowledge Lifecycle [11] because it must first be acquired by single individuals and then gradually transferred to the rest of the technical staff, up to the entire organization. The original definition of this lifecycle has been considered and interpreted in relation to introduction and transfer of a new technology, let it be a process or product, within an industrial environment. We have defined it Knowledge Lifecycle during Innovation (KLI). Figure 1 synthesizes our representation of the model.

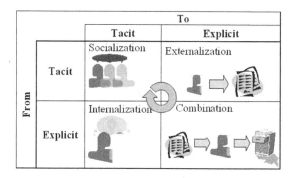

Fig. 1. Knowledge Lifecycle during Innovation (KLI)

At first the innovator internalizes the knowledge related to the new technology he is willing to introduce (tacit knowledge and individual learning occurs); tacit knowledge is then socialized between the innovator and other project team members, and among them, during training sessions or team work (informal communication and group learning occur); during externalization acquired knowledge is formalized and made independent from the innovator. Tacit knowledge is made explicit to all stakeholders of the organization (explicit knowledge and formal learning occur); once new knowledge is acquired and formalized, each individual can combine it to previous one. So, abstract knowledge models are extracted from explicit ones. An innovation is completely acquired when it is integrated and combined with previous knowledge.

Summarizing, innovation diffusion transforms tacit knowledge, i.e. operational skills that few stakeholders possess, including practical judgment capabilities, into explicit knowledge, i.e. formalized knowledge through models, guidelines, processes and so on. Moreover, transfer occurs through learning at both an individual and group level, i.e. modification in stakeholders' behavior according to experience and acquisition of new knowledge after adopting the new technology.

3.2 Importance of Evidence

Once basic research has defined a new technology, models that address key aspects of technology diffusion are needed, i.e. "the process by which an innovation is communicated through certain channels over time among members of a social system" [6]. So, evidence alone is not enough for adopting a new technology, rather it must be formalized, packaged and made transferable through specific models. Till now knowledge on technology transfer models in software engineering is anecdotal.

The authors have referred to the experimentally based technology transfer process commented in [3], and have tailored it to their experience. A graphical representation is given in Figure 2. It can be seen as a state diagram where each node is a possible state one can be in, and the arcs define how to pass from one state to another.

More precisely with refer to the figure, given a "current practice", researchers identify the weaknesses of original techniques through observational studies, literature review and experiences reported. These weaknesses motivate "creation of a new technology or a new methodology". The proposed method needs experimental validation

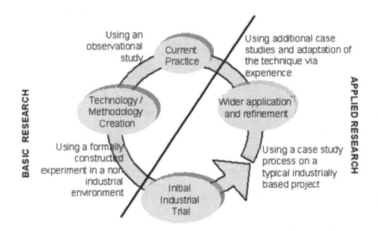

Fig. 2. Experimentally based technology transfer lifecycle

to assess the improvement perceived. This is done at first through formal controlled experiments and their replications in a laboratory context. It is a first step towards collecting evidence on the benefits of the new technology and for motivating industry in adopting the technique (Initial Industrial Trial). Following, the technology is transferred to industry through a case study on a typical industrially based project. Transfer also involves training technical staff on the use of the techniques. Further, live trials of the technique lead to adaptations and refinements of the proposed technique in order to tailor it to the specific context through experience (Wider application and Refinement).

The nature of software engineering suggests it be a laboratory science, in which the researcher's role is to understand processes, products and the relation among them. On the other hand, the practitioner's role is to design improved systems by using available knowledge. Consequently, our technology transfer process combines the characteristics of researchers and practitioners in the context of software engineering, and achieves a symbiosis between research and practice so that practitioners are able to benefit from research results.

With respect to the KLI, first of all the researcher, who by definition is an innovator and promoter of innovation, comes up with a "new idea" following to observational studies. The idea at this point is still internalized as tacit knowledge. Next, the idea is socialized to others before being formalized in a technology or methodology. At this point the tacit knowledge becomes explicit knowledge and externalization occurs. In other words the tacit idea is formally represented so that others can understand, adopt it and perceive the strengths (and in some cases weaknesses) of the technology. As so, the technology is ready to be transferred to practice i.e. others can use it and as they use it learning occurs, individuals acquire the new technology and combine the derived knowledge with their own knowledge and experiences.

It is in this sense knowledge lifecycle and technology transfer process, research and practice are combined in a synergic blend, two worlds that become one.

4 Empirical Studies for Transferring Multiview Framework

Given the general considerations on the technology transfer process and on the knowledge lifecycle that an innovation goes through, we now report our experience on how the process in Figure 2 has been carried out for creating a new technology, providing empirical evidence, and finally transferring it in an Italian SME by applying the technology to an industrial project.

In the next paragraphs, we will illustrate the technology transfer process with refer to Multiview Framework, defined in the SERLAB research laboratory as support for designing and managing a goal oriented measurement programs.

4.1 From Current Practice to Technology/Methodology Creation

The technology transfer process has been applied in the context of goal oriented measurement (Goal Question Metrics approach) [12] for achieving Software Process Improvement, which represents one of the research areas of the authors.

Analysis of literature and experiences collected by the authors of the paper, have pointed out the importance of measurement for assessing SPI. Quality is defined as the set of desired characteristics that a software process or product must have in order to satisfy its requirements. How it is measured inevitably depends on the context and on the viewpoint from which measurement is being carried out. Software engineers use goal oriented quality models, such as Goal Question Metrics (GQM) [12] for measuring software quality because they adapt to business and project characteristics better than other methods and can be combined and integrated with process and organization maturity models such as CMM and ISO [13]. In spite of evidence of successful application of goal oriented measurement programs in industrial contexts such as Motorola [14], HP[15], AT&T [16], Schlumberger RPS [17], SEL [18] there are still many aspects that the conventional GQM methodology strives to overcome: in real projects the dimensions of the quality model are not decided solely by the quality manager, but also depend on project characteristics and business needs. Also, a large quality model makes interpretation more complex, introduces dependencies among goals, requires more effort to manage the entire measurement plan which may include measurements related to process, product, project management and cost/benefit aspects as well as quality. GQM, as reported in the literature [12], is not enough to manage all these issues.

These first observational studies have motivated the researchers of this paper to define a new methodology, Multiview Framework, able to face the previously described open issues. It is based on GQM and guides quality managers, through a set of well formalized steps, to define, tailor, and manage a large goal-oriented quality model.

4.2 From Technology/Methodology Creation to Initial Industrial Trial

4.2.1 Multiview Framework in Pills

The Multiview Framework (MF) addresses the weaknesses in the conventional GQM methodology such as dimensions, complexity and dependencies between goals of a measurement plan. For clearness, we describe some details of the approach. This is not a complete and exhaustive, however it is enough for understanding the basic characteristics of the methodology. More details are in [19]. Multiview Framework (MF) characterizes a software project being evaluated and provides a model for defining a goal oriented measurement program according to the project characterization. It is made up of 4-step.

Step 1. Project Definition: In this first step the project must be defined in terms of processes executed to obtain the final products requested; deliverables; project management activities to plan and control the project; activities for evaluating fitness of investment.

Step 2. Goal Setting: The goals of the measurement plan must be defined, keeping in mind the project definition. They are defined with the GQM-goal template.

Step 3. Cross-Validation: The measurement plan structure is validated by tracing the goals in a Goal-View table to assure that there is one goal for each object of study.

Step 4. Interpretation Complexity: Decision tables [20, 21] are used to depict goal interpretation. Every table column of the decision table indicates which actions should (or should not) be executed for a specific combination of condition entries. The complexity of the interpretation is equal to the total number of rules, or action entries that make up the decision table.

4.2.2 Evidence through a Retrospective Analysis
Following to the description of the proposed model, we applied the MF to a measurement plan that had been designed during the execution of an industrial project. The goals were defined according to the original GQM approach. The four steps of the MF were applied to the previous measurement plan [19]. This first validation was a retrospective analysis [22] and was based on analysis of how the structure of the measurement plan would have been if the MF method had been used to design it.

The original measurement plan was identified with "NS-GQM" (non structured). The measurement plan resulting from the application of the MF was referred to as "S-GQM" (structured).

After applying the model, we analyzed and compared data related to the NS-GQM and S-GQM. Overall results pointed out that the number of goals was greater in the S-GQM (11 vs 8 in NS-GQM), the average interpretation complexity was less (18.45 vs 44.87 in NS-GQM). This was due to the lower number of metrics for each goal (20.18 vs. 32.75 average in NS-GQM), achieved as a consequence to applying the technique to the NS-GQM. More details are in [23].

4.2.3 Evidence through a Controlled and a Replicated Experiment
Further empirical evidence was achieved through a formally constructed experiment in a non industrial context, i.e. a synthetic environment experiment [22] in an artificial setting such as a university class room with graduate students.

The controlled experiment aimed at assessing comprehensibility and efficiency of a quality model obtained by applying MF, compared to one using the conventional GQM paradigm. To this end, the two different quality models (NS-GQM and S-GQM) defined in the retrospective analysis were used. So, two research goals were investigated:

RG1: Analyze S-GQM obtained by applying MF
For the purpose of comparing it to NS-GQM
With respect to efficiency (effort)
From the point of view of a quality evaluator
In the context of a controlled experiment

RG2: Analyze S-GQM obtained by applying MF
For the purpose of comparing it to NS-GQM
With respect to comprehensibility (error proneness)
From the point of view of a quality evaluator
In the context of a controlled experiment

A two-treatment, two period (2X2) cross-over design [24] was used. More precisely, the experiment was organized in two experimental periods (RUN_1 and RUN_2), and subjects were randomly assigned to either one of two groups (Group_A and Group_B). Each group received the treatments according to two different sequences: S-GQM followed by NS-GQM for Group_A (Sequence1), and NS-GQM followed by S-GQM for Group_B (Sequence2). In this way each subject is measured twice, one for each treatment, i.e. each subject acts as his/her own control. This type of design was most appropriate given the sample size. A graphical representation of the experimental design is given in Figure 3.

Group/ Run	RUN 1	RUN 2
GROUP A	S-GQM/ MT1	NS-GQM/ MT2
GROUP B	NS-GQM/ MT1	S-GQM/ MT2

Fig. 3. Experimental Design

The experiment was designed to emulate software project monitoring during two periods in the project lifecycle. So, operationally, during each run, each subject was asked to: analyze the measures of a selected subset of metrics (MT1 or MT2) related to either of the treatments (S-GQM or NS-GQM), use decision tables, and interpret each goal. The controlled experiment with university graduate students as subjects was followed by a strict replication whose subjects (master degree students) were more representative of practitioners in that they collaborated with industrial partners for many project works. Both the controlled experiment and its replication were carried out following guidelines in [25].

The replication aimed at validating that the results of the first controlled experiment were repeatable. This replication was classified as "strict replication" [26] in that it did not vary any of the research hypotheses and it reuses instrumentation of the original experiment. It is important for increasing confidence in the validity of experimental results in that it confirms that results from the original experiment are repeatable and have been appropriately documented by the original experimenters

[27]. Being this a replication with the intent of validating previously obtained results, the research goal was defined as follows:

> **RG**: Replicate a previous experiment
> For the purpose of assessing the repeatability of the experiment
> With respect to comparing MF-quality models with GQM-based quality models
> From the point of view of experimental rigour
> In the context of an internal replication varying only the subjects

Data analysis for both studies was carried out after investigating the distribution of collected data. We analyzed the differences between effort and error proneness obtained from each group in using S-GQM and NS-GQM. For the hypotheses testing, an α-value was fixed at 5%. The dependent variables, aiming at assessing effort and error proneness of S-GQM compared to NS-GQM were tested to investigate if the differences in their values were statistically significant. For space reasons we cannot illustrate and comment all of the details and graphs on data analysis. However, more details can be found in [23, 28]. Here we give conclusive and overall results.

First of all, both studies led to positive and analogous results: The cross-over analysis carried out on the collected data identified significant differences in subject responses for effort and error rates throughout the entire observation period. It provided evidence that less effort and lower error rates occurred for interpretation using S-GQM plans compared to NS-GQM plans. These considerations are also supported by meta-analysis effect size estimations used to compare the two independent studies. Such results point out the validity of the treatment. In other words, the Multiview Framework leads to a better structured quality model with lower complexity, fewer dependencies and easier to manage during measurement activities.

Finally, we carried out meta-analysis as a means for comparing studies and combining results of the two experiments in order to determine if the two studies (controlled experiment and its replication) produce significantly different results. In particular effect size estimates were calculated [29]. For this aim, the Cohen's d model was used [30]. It is calculated as the difference between treatment means divided by the standard deviation and has been calculated for dependent variables in both studies. Results are summarized in Table 1.

Table 1. Effect sizes in each experiment

	Effect Size Estimates	
	Original Experiment	Replication
Effort	1.60	1.82
Errors	1.04	1.08

Cohen suggests that effect sizes be classified into three groups: Small (≈0.2), Medium (≈0.4) and Large (≈0,8). This classification was intended to assist power analysis. The results shown in Table 1 point out the consistency between the two experiments examined and confirm a large effect size. Given an alpha value of 0.05, the power of both experiments was better than 0.8. So, assuming that a similar experiment is used, the experimental subjects can be considered as sufficient in any future replications to detect the expected effect and achieve an adequate power.

4.3 From Initial Industrial Trial to Wider Application and Refinement

The third phase of the innovation process for transferring a technology sees active involvement on behalf on industry. It is from this moment that the "new idea", previously formalized in a methodology or technology and validated in a controlled context is gradually introduced in industrial production processes and communicated to the social system (in this case an Italian SME). This step is the link that joins research and practice and brings together basic research with applied research.

In our specific case, the MF technology was presented to an Italian SME and integrated during the execution of an industrial project. Moreover, the project was called PH_ERP (Process Hiding of ERP Systems), aiming at developing an experience factory as support for developing SAP applications. It required definition of a measurement program to adopt while monitoring project execution, for this reason we chose it as candidate project for introducing and transferring our technology.

The organization did not adopt any specific framework for defining their measurement plans. So, although they carried out measurement activities, from identification of metrics, to collection and interpretation of measurement values, it was not systematic. Moreover, collected data was analyzed and represented in charts, tables and in reports. All stakeholders participated to feedback sessions and commented the measurement results. The main weakness of these sessions was that there were no guidelines on decision making when measurement values were below expected baselines and goals were not fulfilled, i.e. knowledge was not rigorously represented. So, in spite of stakeholders' experience, each time feedback sessions were convoked different criteria were inevitably adopted in decision making, and previously acquired knowledge could not be reused for interpreting new measurement values. Moreover, lack of guidelines made the interpretation process not repeatable i.e. the same measurement data given to two different stakeholders would have most likely led to different conclusions.

Evidence collected on the MF technology served as promoter for management buy-in. In particular, the results obtained in the retrospective analysis helped management to acknowledge the improvements that could have been made if the technology had been used. Following, although the controlled experiment was carried out in a synthetic environment the results represented a first validation of comprehensibility and efficiency of the model. It was possible to generalize these results through the replication of the study. The fact that experimental subjects were in some way representative of practitioners, played an important role for overcoming resistance of management and technical staff, i.e. benefits were perceived on behalf of industry.

To summarize, empirical evidence has pointed out to management how MF addresses several improvements compared to their current measurement activities. Moreover:

-   MF provides a systematic and operative support for defining a measurement program and interpreting data;
-   use of decision tables for interpretation keeps track of learning that occurs during the feedback sessions. In this sense, content of each table can be updated each time an improvement is assessed and therefore a baseline is changed, or a metric is added to a goal. In this way they support experience packaging;
-   the interpretation process becomes repeatable and independent from the stakeholders involved in the discussion of results because tacit stakeholder knowledge is made explicit. So, if different people are present in different moments, the same measurement data will lead to the same conclusions;
-   decision-making concerning initiatives to carry out in order to improve quality characteristics measured in each goal is more straightforward.
-   MF explicates the cause-effect relation between improvement actions to carry out and metrics of a measurement goal that they impact on;

Once management perceived the possible improvements and accepted to introduce the MF in the PH_ERP project, the next step was to obtain commitment of technical staff. After all, they were the ones going to actually "use" the technology.

In many cases, technical staff are refrained by their cultural inertia and, are scarcely inclined and skeptic to give up current and familiar technologies for a new one they know nothing about and that must be learnt. Such a barrier can be overcome by pointing out how the innovation is able to improve working conditions, and how it allows achieving the production goals assigned to the development teams.

It is therefore important to motivate those that act as innovators or early adopters within the organization, so they can be followed by early majority, late majority and laggards. In our case, this was achieved through training.

Operatively, two workshops were organized in conjunction with researchers (authors of this paper) and 30 practitioners of the Italian SME. In the first workshop practitioners were introduced to the general concepts of the MF methodology: systematic approach for goal oriented measurement, decision tables as support to interpretation, and finally the four step approach. These theoretical concepts were illustrated through a sample case study, representative of the industrial context. Next, an assignment was given: practitioners were asked to apply the concepts to the project they had previously worked on.

Our choice, as researchers, of giving this assignment was twofold: first, give practitioners a "hands on" approach to the MF methodology in a context they were familiar to, i.e. the project they had worked on before PH_ERP; second, perceive strengths and point out difficulties concerning MF. Being the previous projects concluded, practitioners carried out a sort of retrospective analysis (although certainly less rigorous) in which they acknowledged the improvements that could have been made if the innovation had been available. This was possible because each of them had "lived" through the previous projects. Some general topics of the projects used are reported in Table 2.

Table 2. Project Topics

Nr	Project Topics
I	Italian Bank Help Desk process
II	Data communication between SAP and external systems
III	Process Improvement in a Software Factory
IV	Process for creating "Building Blocks" in SAP solutions
V	Script Management in a telephone company

In the second workshop, assignments were presented and discussed. Although projects differed among practitioners conclusions were analogous: the systematic and structured organization that the MF methodology attributed to measurement plan definition and interpretation led to more rigorous measurement activities. Participation and interest was quite high on behalf of practitioners, i.e. 80% of the participants handed in and presented their assignment.

Following to the survey, some important comments that 30 responding practitioners conformed to were collected. They are briefly shown in Table 3.

Table 3. Comments from Survey

%	Comments of conforming practitioner opinions
80%	MF provides a systematic and operative support to definition of a measurement program and to interpretation of data;
82%	Definition of decision tables requires much effort but they are useful for achieving a more objective and straightforward interpretation
71%	MF explicates the cause-effect relation between improvement actions to carry out and metrics of a measurement goal that they impact on;

At the moment the MF is being adopted in the PH_ERP project. As it is adopted we are confident that results and acquired experiences will be useful for tailoring and improving the approach to what are practitioners' needs and not researchers' thoughts. In this way it can eventually be extended to all the organizations' production processes and development teams without being restricted to only those involved in the project alone. The final phase (*wider application and refinement*) of the technology transfer process is still being assessed.

5   Conclusions

With this paper authors have suggested a technology transfer process that is an approach towards binding the gap between research and practice. It sees involvement of both parts who must work together for transforming a "new idea" into a "new technology/methodology" able to improve industrial production processes and, produce a body of evidence used for refining and adapting the technique, following to experience. Among various types of empirical studies, the ones that favor diffusion of technological innovations are the ones that actively involve developers and exploit their skills and abilities. As so, when the improvement is perceived by management and technical staff, the experimental results are good motivations for assimilating them within the organization as a technological innovation. In these terms empirical evidence can avoid to be left to itself and be appropriately integrated in the technology transfer process. We have illustrated how the process has been successfully applied by our research group for transferring the MF technology in an Italian SME.

Experimentation, applied properly, is therefore a powerful means for obtaining the body of evidence necessary for introducing new software engineering technologies into industrial environments. Only in this way can cooperation across laboratory and industry be enacted.

References

1. Aaen, I., Siltanen, A., Sorensen, C., Tahvanainen, V.-P.: A Tale of Two Countries: CASE Experiences and Expectations. In: IFIP Transactions, pp. 61–91 (1992)
2. Ardimento, P., Baldassarre, M.T., Caivano, D., Visaggio, G.: Innovation Diffusion through Empirical Studies. In: Proceedings of the 17th International conference on Software and Knowledge Engineering (SEKE 2005), Taipei, China (July 2005)
3. Linkman, S., Rombach, H.D.: Esperimentation as a vehicle for software technology transfer–A family of software reading techniques. Information and Software Technology 39, 777–780 (1997)
4. Redwine, S.T., Riddle, W.E.: Software Technology Maturation. In: Proceedings of 8th International Conference on Software Engineering (ICSE 1985), pp. 189–200. IEEE Computer Society Press, Los Alamitos (1985)
5. Aaen, I.: Problems in CASE Introduction: Experiences from User Organizations. Information and Software Technology 36, 643–654 (1994)
6. Rogers, E.M.: Diffusion of Innovations, 4th edn. Free Press, New York (1995)
7. Berniker, E.: Models of technology transfer: a dialectical case study. In: Proceedings of the IEEE Conference: the New International Language, pp. 499–502 (July 1999)
8. Zelkowitz, M.V.: Assessing software engineering technology transfer within NASA. NASA technical report NASA-RPT-003095, National Aeronautics and Space Administration, Washington, DC (January 1995)
9. Rai, A.: External information source and channel effectiveness and the diffusion of CASE innovations: an empirical study. European Journal of Inf. Syst. 4(2), 93–102 (1995)
10. Zelkowitz, M.V., Dolores, R., Binkley, D.: Understanding the culture clash in software engineering technology transfer. University of Maryland technical report, June 2 (1998)
11. Nonaka, I., Takeuchi, H.: The Knowledge Creating Company. Oxford University Press, Oxford (1995)
12. Basili, V.R., Caldiera, G., Rombach, H.D.: Goal Question Metric Paradigm. Encyclopedia of Software Engineering 1, 528–532 (1994)
13. Pulford, K., Kuntzmann-Combelles, A., Shirlaw, S.: A Quantitative Approach to Software Management. Addison-Wesley, Reading (1995)
14. Daskalantonakis, M.K.: A Practical View of Software Measurement and Implementation Experiences within Motorola. IEEE TSE 18(11), 998–1010 (1992)

15. Grady, R.B.: Practical Software Metrics for Project Management and Process Improvement. Hewlett-Packard Professional Books (1992)

16. Barnard, L., Price, A.: Managing Code Inspection Information. IEEE Software 11(2), 59–69 (1994)

17. Solingen, R.V., Latum, F.V., Oivo, M., Berghout, E.W.: Application of Software Measurement at Schlumberger RPS: towards enhancing GQM. In: Proceedings of the 6th European Software Control and Metrics Conference, The Netherlands, May 17-19 (1995)

18. Basili, V.R., Green, S.: Software Process Evolution at the SEL. IEEE Software 11(4), 58–66 (1994)

19. Ardimento, P., Baldassarre, M.T., Caivano, D., Visaggio, G.: Multiview Framework for Goal-Oriented Measurement Plan Design. In: Bomarius, F., Iida, H. (eds.) PROFES 2004. LNCS, vol. 3009, pp. 159–173. Springer, Heidelberg (2004)

20. Pooch, U.W.: Translation of Decision Tables. Computing Surv. 6(2), 125–151 (1974)

21. http://www.econ.kuleuven.ac.be/tew/academic/infosys/research/prologa /prologa.htm

22. Zelkowitz, M.V., Wallace, D.R.: Experimental Models for Validating Technology. IEEE Computer, 23–31 (May 1998)

23. Ardimento, P., Baldassarre, M.T., Caivano, D., Visaggio, G.: Assessing Multiview Framework (MF) comprehensibility and efficiency: a replicated experiment. In: Information & Software Technology, April 2006. Kluwer Academic Press, Dordrecht (2006)

24. Senn, S.: Cross-Over Trials in Clinical Research, 2nd edn. John Wiley & Sons Ltd., Chichester (2002)

25. Wohlin, C., Runeson, P., Host, M., Ohlsson, M.C., Regnell, B., Wesslèn, A.: Experimentation in Software Engineering. Kluwer Academic Publishers, Dordrecht (2002)

26. Basili, V., et al.: Building knowledge through families of experiments. IEEE TSE 25(4), 456–473 (1999)

27. Cook, T.D., Campbell, D.T.: Quasi-Experimentation Design and Analysis Issues for Field Settings. Houghton Mifflin Company (1979)

28. Baldassarre, M.T., Caivano, D., Visaggio, G.: Comprehensibility and Efficiency of Multiview Framework for Measurement Plan Design. In: Proceedings of the International Symposium on Empirical Software Engineering, Rome, Italy, October 2003, pp. 89–99 (2003)

29. Kramer, S., Rosenthal, R.: Effect sizes and significance levels in small sample research. In: Hoyle, R. (ed.) Statistical Strategies for Small Sample Research. Sage publications, Beverly Hills (1999)

30. Cohen, J.: Statistical power analysis for the behavioural sciences. Academic Press, London (1977)

Towards a Framework for Using Agile Approaches in Global Software Development

Emam Hossain[1,3], Muhammad Ali Babar[2], and June Verner[3]

[1] UNSW-NICTA, Australian Technology Park
Sydney, Australia
Emam.Hossain@nicta.com.au
[2] Lero,University of Limerick
Castletroy, Limerick, Ireland
malibaba@lero.ie
[3] School of Computer Science and Engineering,UNSW
Sydney, Australia
jverner@cse.unsw.edu.au

Abstract. As agile methods and Global Software Development (GSD) are become increasingly popular, GSD project managers have been exploring the viability of using agile approaches in their development environments. Despite the expected benefits of using an agile approach with a GSD project, the overall combining mechanisms of the two approaches are not clearly understood. To address this challenge, we propose a conceptual framework, based on the research literature. This framework is expected to aid a project manager in deciding what agile strategies are effective for a particular GSD project, taking into account project context. We use an industry-based case study to explore the components of our conceptual framework. Our case study is planned and conducted according to specific published case study guidelines. We identify the agile practices and agile supporting practices used by a GSD project manager in our case study and conclude with future research directions.

Keywords: Agile approaches, Global Software Development, Case study.

1 Introduction

Agile Software Development (ASD) and Global Software Development (GSD) are promoted as a means of reducing time to market, increasing productivity, improving quality and gaining cost effectiveness and efficiency [1]. ASD has gained significant popularity because of a promise to handle requirements volatility throughout the development life cycle, promotion of extensive collaboration between customers and developers, and support for early and frequent delivery of a product [2]. GSD is also considered to be a cost effective software development paradigm driven by a number of factors, such as time to market pressures, taking advantage of using distributed resource pools, use of multiple time zones, shared best practices, and closer proximity to customer [3].

F. Bomarius et al. (Eds.): PROFES 2009, LNBIP 32, pp. 126–140, 2009.
© Springer-Verlag Berlin Heidelberg 2009

GSD project managers have recently begun using agile practices in their development environments [4, 5]. However, despite the expected benefits of using agile approaches with GSD, the overall combining mechanisms of the two approaches are yet to be fully understood [6]. To address this problem, we propose a conceptual framework that describes the use of various strategies to use agile approaches in GSD projects, based on the research literature. We also conducted an industry-based case study to test our framework and to help us better understand the use of agile strategies in a GSD project in a real life setting. We used a framework-based data collection approach, adopted from [7], to record project context factors as we believe that GSD project agility depends substantially on project context. In our case study, we identified the agile strategies used by the project manager to aid in a discussion of our framework components.

In the next section we discuss the background to our research. Section 3 describes our research problem in detail, while section 4 presents the proposed framework. Section 5 discusses our research methodology and case study, and we conclude with section 6, which discusses our future research directions.

2 Research Background

The fundamental concepts of an agile approach in software development are described in the agile manifesto. This manifesto states that the agile community values individuals and interactions over process and tools, working software over comprehensive documentation, customer collaboration over contract negotiation, and responding to change over following a plan [8]. The heart of an agile approach is in using agile practices that emanate from agile methods, such as XP and Scrum. On the other hand, GSD is a contemporary form of software development where project stakeholders are dispersed in distributed locations where socio-cultural distances may be involved. Because of geographical, temporal and in some cases, socio-cultural differences, GSD may suffer from a number of difficulties related to communication, coordination, control [12]. Thus, it is apparently difficult to apply many of the key agile concepts in distributed developments as agile development promotes a close collaboration and communication environment. However, despite the apparent difficulties in applying agile approaches within distributed settings, a number of GSD projects are currently using agile practices in their development environments [5, 9].

3 Our Research

As noted earlier, the combination of agile approaches with GSD is not fully understood although such a combination is expected to be beneficial [6]. Because of geographically dispersed teams, it can be very difficult to apply some agile practices, for example pair programming, daily stand up meetings, the planning game, and onsite customer participation in distributed projects. Also project contextual factors (for example, project size, collaboration modes, number of distributed sites, and team size) may limit the use of agile practices. Hence using agile approaches in distributed settings is not straightforward; rather practitioners need to fully understand what agile strategies will be effective for their specific development environment.

To address this challenge, the broad objective of our research is to explore and understand effective strategies to help GSD project managers with agility. To this end we develop and describe the components of our framework. As noted earlier, to understand, explain and explore agile strategies, we conduct an industry-based case study in a real life setting. We use the case study findings to further understand the components of our framework. We also investigate if there are any elements not present in the framework that should be considered for inclusion in a revised framework. Finally our research concludes with future research directions.

4   Conceptual Framework

This section defines, explains and describes the various elements of our proposed framework.

4.1 Development Process

In order to support agile approaches in GSD, we have identified a number of components from a literature survey that are included in our framework. The framework includes components and factors that need to be taken into account when a project manager considers using agile approaches for a GSD project. Our framework includes an agility assessment process that covers both project contextual factors and an organization's previous agile experience. The framework also includes agility supporting strategies that are categorized into five groups: plan, policy, people, process and infrastructure. To develop our conceptual framework, we taken several carefully planned steps, as described below:

- To identify framework components we studied existing frameworks and methodologies that discuss agility issues in a number of development scenarios (e.g. [10-11, 33]); and conducted an extensive survey of the GSD literature where agile approaches were used, as well as analyzing the heuristics of experienced GSD researchers and practitioners (e.g. [14]).
- We identified and categorized factors that drive project managers towards choosing agile strategies for their GSD projects (e.g. [14-27]).
- We investigated research papers (e.g. [7, 29]) that describe how project contextual information is recorded. After reviewing these studies, we identified a number of key project contextual factors useful when assessing a possible degree of project agility. Agility assessment is important; it is usually difficult for a GSD project to be agile and a project manger needs to carefully balance agility with a defined development process [6]. An organization's past agile experience is also considered to be part of the agility assessment.
- We reviewed reports describing agile approaches in GSD projects (e.g. [9, 12, 15-28]) and identified a number of agility supporting strategies used by GSD project managers. We categorized these strategies as plan, policy, infrastructure, process and people elements.

- Finally, we consolidated the components into a framework to aid a GSD project manager in deciding what agile strategies could be used within a project.

Figure 1 presents GSD project managers with a framework to assist them in assessing the degree of agility possible for a project. This framework also provides a basis for the consideration of suitable agility supporting strategies in GSD projects.

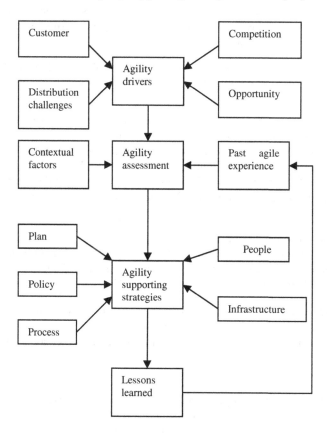

Fig. 1. Proposed conceptual framework for using agile approaches in GSD projects

4.2 Framework Usage

We do not claim that we have developed an exhaustive list of components that influence the agility of all GSD projects. Rather the proposed framework will help guide the identification of effective agile strategies for such projects. The framework is easily modifiable and extensible, as is necessary in research that is still in its inception stage. Our framework will also help to identify missing agile strategies in a GSD project when an agile approach is being considered. To provide an initial validation for our research, we conducted an industry-based case study of a project that uses some agile practices and some GSD supporting practices. From the case study, we identified effective, poorly executed and missing agile strategies in a GSD project that claimed agility. In future, a series of case studies will help to build up a body of knowledge that will guide GSD project managers in choosing effective agile strategies suitable for their particular development environment.

4.3 Framework Components

Framework components are classified as 1) agility drivers, 2) contextual factors, 3) past agile experience, 4) agility assessment, 5) agility supporting strategies and 6) lessons learned. We discuss each of these below.

Agility Drivers. Agility drivers are factors that influence GSD project managers to use agile approaches. We found that agility drivers can be broadly categorized into the following:

Competition. This category includes factors such as: increasing demand for project quality, a rapidly changing market, cost savings, maximizing project productivity, time, competitors, and the enhancement of technical capabilities, mergers and acquisitions, and scalability [4, 14-16]. Other factors such as, leveraging the distributed team's expertise, facilitating knowledge transfer, and supporting the international nature of a company, can also drive a GSD project manager toward using an agile approach [18].

Customer. The customer is one of the most important drivers in choosing an agile approach for a GSD project [15, 20]. For example, a customer may want to develop his product using XP [22]. Requirements volatility and rapid changes also drive GSD customers toward choosing an agile approach [17, 21].

Distribution challenges. GSD project managers also choose agile approaches to minimize various challenges related to communication, coordination and control [8, 12]. For example, to minimize delays in communication and to increase communication quality, a GSD project manager may use some agile practices (e.g. pair programming) [23].

Opportunity. Because an organization may wish to change its existing GSD development processes, it may perceive an opportunity to choose an agile approach as the most optimal method [15, 17, 21]. Previous project experience success also drives GSD project managers to use agile approaches [15, 16, 24]. A GSD project manager may also use some agile practices in a pilot project or in an experimental study in order to investigate the risks and benefits of agile methodologies [18, 25, 28]. Earlier development method failure (e.g. with the waterfall model), may drive GSD project managers towards agile approaches [27, 26]. A GSD project manager may use an agile approach to: increase a project's visibility, allow for early project estimation, or to help provide client business security [4, 19, 27]. Agile approaches are also used as an opportunity for distributed teams to standardize their processes and tools [19]. A shortage of onshore expertise and a match with an outsourced partner's development methodology, as well as a desire to capture domain knowledge and expertise, may also encourage a GSD project manager toward an agile approach [16].

Contextual Factors. Software projects can be influenced by as many as 250 different contextual factors; although most projects are affected by 10-20 major factors (for example project complexity, size, uncertainty, staff experience, contract nature etc.) [29]. Project stakeholder distribution provides an additional contextual factor in GSD projects and is related to geographical, temporal and socio-cultural distances [12]. Project contextual factors heavily influence the use of agile strategies and we consider the following project contextual factors should be considered as a minimum [7, 30].

Software classification. The software to be developed can be classified as [12, 30]. 1. System, 2. Commercial, 3. Information system, 4. Military, 5. End user/Private, 6. Other.

Project specific. Factors that include development quality, schedule, and risk etc should be considered. But initially we suggest: 1. Contract nature, 2. Project domain, 3. Requirements changes, 4. Staff months, 5. Budget, 6. Complexity, 7. Criticality.

Team characteristics. Specific distributed team information needs to be considered. 1. Team size, 2. Team experience, 3. Project manager's experience, 4. Team work culture.

Distance. The geographical, temporal and socio-cultural distances caused by project stakeholder distribution in a particular GSD project will also be recorded.

1. Geographical distance: This distance is considered as a directional measure of the effort required for one actor to visit another, at the latter's home site [6].
2. Temporal distance: This is a directional measure of the dislocation in time experienced by two actors wishing to interact [12].
3. Socio-cultural distance: Any differences in organizational culture, national culture and language, politics, individual motivation, and work ethics, etc [3].

Technology. Technology required for developing the project also needs to be considered, e.g. graphical packages, specific programming languages etc.

Past Agile Experience. A project experience repository can provide lessons learned and effectiveness ratings for agile approaches used in the past, as well as appropriate tools and agility supporting distributed practices. At the start of a project, a GSD project team with extensive prior project experience will have effective agility coping strategies [13]. Previous agile experience can also help to decide on the extent of agility, and need for 1) formal communication, 2) training, or 3) extensive documentation [20].

Agility Assessment. Agility assessment is an evaluation of a particular project's degree of agility based on several parameters. The project manager should make an assessment of a project's need for agility and the organization's capabilities before deciding to use an agile approach for the project [10]. Conboy and Fitzgerald [10] note that an appropriate agile approach should be selected based on the project's contextual factors. Boehm and Turner's [30] risk based model provides a good example of the assessment of a project's degree of agility; it determines required agility by analyzing a project's environmental risks, agile risk and plan-driven risk. We believe that a GSD project manager can estimate the extent of a project's possible agility by analyzing both project contextual factors and past agile project experiences.

Agility Supporting Strategies. Based on an initial assessment of the extent of agility, a GSD project manager needs to apply agility supporting strategies in an effective way. In any development environment, the core of an agile approach is based on a gradual evolution of effective processes, infrastructure, teams, plans, and policies [11]. For the effective use of agile strategies a GSD project manager should ensure appropriate plans are developed, effective teams formed, and provide the necessary infrastructure, ensure appropriate policies and follow defined processes.

Plan. A GSD project manager should develop plans that will initially describe how the project will be carried out. For example: a project manager can plan to distribute the project work based on the nature of the work (for example, highly volatile work should be co-located), form a team close to the business, provide agile training etc. [20].

People. The success of agility in a GSD project is very dependent on its people [16]. A number of research papers mention that in considering the use of agile approaches, a GSD project manager should decide if he can build distributed teams that include experienced agile developers [16-18].

Infrastructure. A GSD project manager should also ensure the necessary project infrastructure (hardware, software, licenses, tools etc.) to support the agile practices used in the globally distributed project is available [16, 20]. A GSD project manager should also carefully chose appropriate software tools relevant to communication, collaboration, project management, testing, and metrics/measurement etc.

Policy. A project manager should maintain policies to tackle any GSD project challenges that emerge. For example: a project team member training policy (technical, domain, process etc), a documentation maintenance policy or policies for using various agility supporting distributed practices (e.g. cultural liaisons) [15-19].

Process. Balancing agility within defined processes is one of the major challenges for GSD project managers [6]. A GSD project manager should ensure sufficient processes for the effective use of the agile approaches, and should also choose suitable agile practices for the development environment. Like many other researchers, we believe that not all agile practices are suitable for use in globally distributed projects. Thus, a GSD project manager should carefully choose appropriate agile practices suitable for their development environment. Although the agile manifesto suggests less emphasis on process and tools, we found that a GSD project manager must define processes for the use of agile practices in a GSD environment [6].

Lessons Learned. Both the degree of success achieved, and the challenges faced in a project, while using specific agile approaches, should be monitored and stored in a project experience repository [20]. Practices and tools which are proven to be effective for a particular project should be recorded and managed in the process repository.

5   Research Methodology and Case Study

In this section, we report on our industry-based exploratory case study. The case study is considered as a robust research method with a range of data collection approaches when a holistic in-depth investigation of a social phenomenon in its real life context is required [31]. The research question we investigate is: how can GSD project managers decide what agile strategies will be effective in a particular project environment? To make such a decision, a project manager needs an understanding of the everyday mechanics of team processes, project characteristics, distance and technology involved in existing GSD projects and the agile practices that are used effectively in such projects. In this research, we do not provide formal hypothesis testing or draw any general conclusions as GSD has many forms based on project contextual factors. We use a case study to gain greater understanding of how specific agile strategies were used within a particular GSD project context.

Our primary data collection method was the interview, supplemented by a review of relevant project documentation, onsite demonstrations of the software and informal conversations. We performed two face-to-face interviews (one with a project manager and one with an actively involved customer); each interview lasted about two hours. We provided a brief research plan to both participants before beginning the interview sessions. We asked our respondents about the facts of the matter as well as gaining their opinions about events that occurred. Project artifacts, such as documentation, were also used as an important data source. System specifications, the project plans, testing scripts and the completed software were made available to the researchers. Documentary information was also used to corroborate and augment evidence found from the interviews and discussion. A qualitative content analysis technique was used to extract the framework component data from the interviews. Qualitative data analysis was done by the lead author who coded both interviews, and developed separate codes for addressing each of the framework components. In doing the data analysis, our aim was to identify, describe and make sense of how the chosen strategies were used to make a GSD project agile. To improve the quality of our interpretation, we reported our initial findings back to both interviewees who provided us with valuable feedback that rectified omissions and misunderstandings.

5.1 Case Description

AusBest is an Australian based software development company that develops a range of software products. For some time the company has had developers in Australia and Malaysia. We call the project we investigated the "AGI project"; it is a service-based commercial software product developed by a team distributed in Australia and Malaysia. In a later section, we discuss our case in detail while describing elements of our framework. We discuss our various case study findings, in particular how our case GSD project's agile strategies differ from our proposed conceptual framework. This helps us to understand how a real life GSD project manager did or did not use agile strategies effectively.

Agility Drivers. AusBest's senior manager decided to go with an agile approach in order to minimize project cost. He felt that this would enable his company to release the product within the set time limits, to use their distributed resource pool effectively and help with cost reduction. Thus we can argue that as cost is a component of competition and that *"Competition"* was the key driver for the AGI project in its use of agile strategies.

Contextual Factors. Project contextual factors were as follows.

Software classification. The "AGI project" software is a graphical software engineering tool developed for *commercial* use for external customers.

Project specific factors. Key project specific factors are as follows.

1. Contract nature: The developer's contract specified that the project would be developed within a fixed price and schedule.
2. Project Domain: The project is a web based graphical service application.
3. Requirements change: There were a number of initial requirements changes but after that the requirements were stable and clear to the development team.
4. Staff months: In terms of effort the AGI project required approximately 20 person months and was developed over six months.
5. Budget: The project budget was slightly more than one hundred thousand Australian dollars.
6. Complexity: Although the project was small in size it was a complex graphical application; this increased the development complexity.
7. Criticality: The software was critical to setting up a new business venture.

Team characteristics. The characteristics of the project teams included:

1. Number of distributed teams: There were two development teams, distributed in Australia and Malaysia. The customer team was based in Australia.
2. Team size: The project manager was based in Sydney; the Sydney part of the team consisted of the project manager, two full time developers and one part time test engineer. The time involvement of Malaysian developers varied. They were mostly involved in back end development work, and had around 25 developers with one local development lead. The project work was assigned based on skills and availability as the Malaysian developers were involved in several other projects at the same time.
3. Overall team experience: Both Australian and Malaysian team members had previously worked on several distributed projects and had also participated in agile projects in the past. However, no team members had any prior experience of using agile practices in distributed projects.
4. Project manager experience: Although the project manager was experienced in project management he had no prior experience using agile approaches in a distributed project.
5. Team culture: The working culture of both sites tended toward informal. Later on the project manager tried to impose more explicit processes to provide better project visibility to the teams.

Distance. The project involved low geographical and temporal distance but had significant socio-cultural distances.

1. Geographical distance: The development team was distributed between Malaysia and Australia. Malaysia and Australia are relatively closely located and there are convenient air links and regular flights between the two countries.

2. Temporal distance: There was a two hours time difference (three hours in summer) between Sydney and Malaysia; hence we can argue that the project had a low temporal distance.
3. Socio-cultural: we used Hofstede's study [32] to measure the cultural differences between the Malaysian and Australian team. Hofstede's study use five cultural dimension (Power distance, Individualism, Masculinity, Uncertainty Avoidance, Long term orientation) to describe national cultural differences between two countries. From that study's indexes, we found there were significant differences in the cultural dimensions, power distance, individualism and moderate differences in masculinity, and uncertainty avoidance. Thus based on Hofstede's study [32], we can claim that there were significant socio-cultural distances between the Malaysian and Australian team members.

Technological. A variety of programming languages, methods and tools were used to develop the complex graphical software engineering tool. Initially, the development team members had a low level of expertise with the technologies used for the project. The Sydney team members received training in the use of the new programming languages and tools.

Past Agile Experience. The project manager claimed that AusBest had considerable previous agile project experience although applying agile practices in distributed projects was new for this company. The company's previous agile project success encouraged them to use some agile practices in this distributed project.

Agility Assessment. The project manager did not follow any particular model or method when assessing the possible degree of project agility during the initial stage of the development; this was due to the lack of agile experience of the project manager in distributed projects.

Agility Supporting Strategies. Although the project manager used a number of agile supporting strategies, we believe that the lack of defined project processes, plans and policies made project success difficult. The project manager had a number of difficulties because some processes were ignored.

Plan: Poor project planning was identified as a major challenge and this caused a number of difficulties. The project manager eventually developed a concrete plan for the project which was agreed with the customers. For example: minimizing task interdependence was an important focus in that plan.

People. The people were an important driver in this project's success. Although the project suffered from staff turnover the project manager utilized the company's large offshore resource pool effectively (a large part of the team was in off shore). The project manager moved as much work as he could to Malaysia which had a number of talented programmers and a team lead who was very committed to the project; the leader of the Malaysian team played a key role in making the project a success.

Infrastructure. The project manager ensured sufficient infrastructure was available to support the agile approaches used in the project. He also ensured that a number of tools were available to the teams including communication tools such as: telephone,

VOIP (Skype), email, teleconferencing, video conferencing, IM. The project manager used a wiki as a collaborative tool, and a tool called "Jira" as an issue tracker, bug tracker and project management tool. For testing purposes, automated testing tools (e.g. continuous integration tools) were also used.

Policies. The project manager maintained different policies for different agile strategies. For example, a training policy for the Sydney based front-end developers. There were also a number of policies for using agility supporting distributed practices, for example, policies for maintaining "just enough documentation" in order to minimize project misunderstanding and miscommunication. He frequently used the practice "visits" for both development teams, and spent every second month in Malaysia. The project manager also used other supporting practices such as multiple communication modes (e.g., sufficient communication and collaborative tools), and synchronized work hours to increase communication and reduce misunderstandings among distributed team members.

Process. Project management suffered due to a lack of defined processes; the project manager appeared to have no control over the project at some stages. Later, to take control, and to make project management visible to project stakeholders, the project manager set up some standard work processes and took greater ownership with more direct supervision. The project manager claimed that he used a number of agile practices including daily Scrum meetings, Scrum planning meetings, Scrum review meetings, Retrospectives, continuous code integration, and test driven development within their normal defined development process.

Lessons learned. Although the project manager did not maintain a formal project experience repository, he documented what practices were effective and any problems incurred while using the agile practices. He also documented effective agility supporting distributed practices and tools used in the project.

5.2 Discussion

The project was completed within time and budget and was considered a success by the customers and vendors. Both the customer and project manager were happy with the product developed. However, our framework-based analysis aids us in exploring a number of issues in relation to the use of agile strategies in this project. We found that this agile project contract was fixed price although this type of contract has not previously proven effective in an outsourcing environment [34]. The project manager also did not use some agile practices effectively and did not properly consider the possible extent of agility for the project during the initial stages of development. We believe that this was due to the project manager's inexperience in using agile methods in a distributed environment. Plans and policies were also lacking for the effective use of the agile strategies chosen. The customer maintained continuous pressure on the project manager to properly define project processes and to use the agile practices in a planned way. The customer actively participated in the project and had a very good relationship with both the project manager and AusBest's senior management. The project contract specified that payment was to be made incrementally, and when the customer was unsatisfied with the release, payments were not made. This meant that senior management investigated what was going on, and this was one reason for improvement in the processes and for a successful project outcome.

Although the agile manifesto opposes a focus on processes and tools, these are very important when using agile practices in distributed projects. Although poor project management and staff turnover are common risks for any software development project, our study reveals they are more challenging when using agile approaches in a distributed project. Experienced agile developers are also a key requirement for the successful use of agile approaches in distributed projects; our GSD project suffered substantially when experienced agile developers left the project.

Improper use of agile practices creates problems. The project manager did not use some agile practices effectively. The customer (who had extensive software development experience and actively participated in the project development) commented that some of the practices, including daily standup meetings, Scrum planning, and Test Driven Development (TDD) were not used properly. For example, one of the customers commented that the development team released code (working software) too frequently (almost every day!) with a large number of errors. This made it very difficult for the customer to perform acceptance testing. The customer complained that the testing took an unreasonable amount of time, and that the releases should be fewer, of higher quality, and with previously identified problems and bugs fixed before the next release. This led to a number of confrontational phone calls and visits to the vendor by the customer although later the project manager was more careful with the releases. This case study reinforces the importance of using teams of skilled developers for the effective use of agile approaches. Lack of developer language expertise can also impact on the effective use agile practices.

Thus, in our case study project the GSD project manager struggled with the framework components, "People", "Plan" and "Process". The project manager did not find any major difficulties due to socio-cultural and time zone differences. He successfully minimized project distribution challenges by ensuring a sufficient communication environment by providing suitable communication tools and supporting practices, for example, synchronized work hours, and frequent visits. The work culture of the Malaysian site also made it relatively easy for the project manager, as the Malaysians frequently started their work early to increase the number of overlapping hours with Sydney team. The GSD project manager helped to build trust by establishing a feeling of "teamness", and increased project visibility, and reduced misunderstandings and misinterpretations by using agile practices and appropriate supporting practices.

The project manager was also happy with the tools used in the project. The communication tools: telephone, VOIP (Skype), email, teleconferencing, video conferencing, and Instant Messaging (IM) were found effective. The wiki used by the project was also found effective for collaboration. The project manager effectively used an integrated testing tool and was happy with the tool "Jira" which was used as an issue tracker, bug tracker and also to support project management.

5.3 Case Study Limitations

The design of this case study is based upon the four criteria for judging the quality of research design recommended by Yin [31]. Construct validity, which is involved with establishing correct operational measures for the concepts being studied was not a limitation in our study. We developed a sufficient operational set of measures for collecting data. As our case study is exploratory in nature, not explanatory or causal, we need not consider internal validity. Our study is also not concerned with external validity as our study findings are not generalized to other GSD projects. Our single case study initiated an exploration of the use of various agile strategies in a GSD project. In this case study, we must consider reliability; data was collected based on a framework developed from the literature. However we cannot exclude bias on the part of our interviewees who reported what they thought happened. However, we did use multiple sources of evidence (documentation, discussion, interaction etc) to help us ensure sufficient reliability.

6   Conclusions and Future Research

There is an increasing interest in using agile approaches for GSD projects. GSD takes many forms, based on project contextual factors but process issues around using agile approaches in GSD are not clearly understood. GSD practitioners need further research to help them understand what agile strategies are likely to be effective for a particular type of project. We propose a conceptual framework based on existing GSD literature that describes the effective use of various agile strategies. Our goal is to introduce the different elements of our framework and to provide an initial test of its effectiveness with an industry-based case study. Various issues were identified, including the project manager's lack of experience, and failure to provide suitable processes, plans and policies. Such processes, plans and policies would help a GSD project manager to understand how to achieve effective agility in a development environment. Our case study reveals that the project manager did not assess project contextual factors for an appropriate degree of agility prior to starting this project.

A GSD project manager can reduce some project stakeholder distribution challenges by using appropriate agile practices; for example: we agree with the project manager's claim that distributed Scrum meetings, using video conferencing, reduces GSD project communication and coordination overhead. On the other hand, our case study has identified elements missing from our proposed conceptual framework as we did not initially include some important project contextual factors, such as staff turnover, contract type, customer-project management/management relationship, technology expertise, nature of the day to day work, and documentation practices.

In future, we will conduct a series of case studies to aid us in better understanding the use of agile strategies in GSD projects. This will include appropriate agile practices, agility supporting distributed practices and tools within a defined GSD project context. Thus, our research will contribute to answering a current GSD research question: What agile strategies are effective and when?

Acknowledgments. M. Ali Babar's research is partially supported by Science foundation Ireland under grant number 03/CE2/I303-1.

References

1. Ramesh, B., Cao, L., Mohan, K., Xu, P.: Can distributed software development be agile? Communications of the ACM 49, 41–46 (2006)
2. Abrahamsson, P., Salo, O., Ronkainen, J., Warsta, J.: Agile software development methods - Review and analysis. VTT Electronics (ed.). VTT Publications (2002)
3. Conchuir, E.O., Holmstrom, H., Agerfalk, P.J., Fitzgerald, B.: Exploring the Assumed Benefits of Global Software Development. In: Proceedings of the Conference on ICGSE 2006, pp. 159–168. IEEE Press, New York (2006)
4. Nisar, M.F., Hameed, T.: Agile methods handling offshore software development issues. In: Proceedings of the conference on INMIC 2004, pp. 417–422 (2004)
5. Taylor, P.S., Greer, D., Sage, P., Coleman, G., McDaid, K., Keenan, F.: Do agile GSD experience reports help the practitioner? In: Proceedings of the Conference on GSD 2006, pp. 87–93 (2006)
6. Agerfalk, P., Fitzgerald, B.: Flexible and Distributed software processes: Old Petunias in new bowls? Communications of the ACM 49, 41–46 (2006)
7. Williams, L., Kerbs, W., Layman, L., Anton, A.I., Abrahamsson, P.: Toward a Framework for Evaluating Extreme Programming. In: Proceeding of the Conference on EASE 2004, pp. 11–20 (2004)
8. Manifesto for Agile Software Development, http://www.agilemanifesto.org
9. Paasivaara, M., Durasiewicz, S., Lassenius, C.: Distributed Agile Development: Using Scrum in a Large Project. In: Proceedings of the Conference on ICGSE 2008, pp. 87–95 (2008)
10. Conboy, K., Fitzgerald, B.: Toward a Conceptual Framework for Agile Methods. In: Zannier, C., Erdogmus, H., Lindstrom, L. (eds.) XP/Agile Universe 2004. LNCS, vol. 3134, pp. 105–116. Springer, Heidelberg (2004)
11. Qumer, A., Hendersom-Sellers, B.: An evaluation of the degree of agility in six agile methods and its applicability for method engineering. Information and Software Technology 50, 280–295 (2008)
12. Holmstrom, H., Fitzgerald, B., Agerfalk, P.J., Conchuir, E.O.: Agile Practices Reduce Distance in Global Software Development. In: Information Systems Management, pp. 7–26 (summer 2006)
13. Lee, G., Delone, W., Espinosa, J.A.: Ambidextrous coping strategies in globally distributed software development projects. Communications of the ACM 49, 41–46 (2006)
14. Herbsleb, J.D.: Global Software Engineering: The Future of Socio- technical Coordination. In: Proceeding of the Conference on Future of Software Engineering, FOSE, pp. 188–298 (2007)
15. Sutherland, J., Viktorov, A., Blount, J., Puntikov, N.: Distributed Scrum: Agile Project management with Outsourced Development Teams. In: Proceedings of the Conference on HICSS'40 (2007)
16. Sutherland, J., Schoonheim, G., Rustenburg, E., Rijk, M.: Fully distributed Scrum: The secret sauce for Hyperproductive Outsourced Development Teams. In: Proceedings of the Conference on Agile 2008, pp. 339–343 (2008)
17. Berczuk, S.: Back to Basics: The Role of agile Principles in Success with a Distributed Scrum Team. In: Proceedings of the Conference on Agile 2007, pp. 382–388 (2007)
18. Hogan, B.: Lessons Learned from an eXtremely Distributed project. In: Proceedings of the conference on Agile 2006, pp. 321–326 (2006)
19. Yap, M.: Follow the Sun: Distributed Extreme Programming Development. In: Proceedings of the Conference on ADC 2005, pp. 218–224 (2005)

20. Sureshchandra, K., Shrinivasavadhani, J.: Adopting Agile in Distributed Development. In: Proceedings of the Conference on ICGSE 2008, pp. 217–221 (2008)
21. Farmer, M.: DecisionSpace Infrastructure: Agile Development in a Large, distributed team. In: Proceedings of the Conference on Agile Development Conference (ADC 2004), pp. 95–99 (2004)
22. Sison, R., Yang, T.: Use of Agile Methods and Practices in the Philippines. In: Proceedings of the Conference on 14th APSEC 2007, pp. 462–469 (2007)
23. Xiaohu, Y., Bin, X., Zhijun, H., Maddineni, S.R.: Extreme Programming in Global Software Development. In: Proceedings of the Conference on CCECE - CCGEI 2004, pp. 1845–1848 (2004)
24. Smits, H.: Implementing Scrum in a Distributed Software Development Organization. In: Proceedings of the Conference on Agile 2007, pp. 371–375 (2007)
25. Urdangarin, R., Fernades, P., Avirtzer, A., Paulish, D.: Experiences with Agile Practices in the global studio project. In: Proceedings of the Conference on ICGSE 2008, pp. 77–86 (2008)
26. Paasivaara, M., Lassenius, C.: Could Global Software Development Benefit from Agile Method? In: Proceedings of the Conference on ICGSE 2006, pp. 109–113 (2006)
27. Cottmeyer, M.: The Good and Bad of Agile Offshore Development. In: Proceedings of the Conference on Agile 2008, pp. 362–367 (2008)
28. Simon, M.: Internationally Agile. In: Inform IT 2002 (2002), http://www.informit.com/articles/article.aspx?p=25929
29. Jones, C.: Software Assessments Benchmarks and Best Practices. Addison Wesley, Boston (2000)
30. Boehm, B., Turner, R.: Balancing Agility and Discipline: A Guide for the Perplexed. Addison Wesley, Boston (2003)
31. Yin, R.K.: Case Study Research. Sage publications, Thousand Oaks (1994)
32. Geert Hofstede™ Cultural Dimensions, http://www.geert-hofstede.com/
33. Sharifi, H., Zhang, Z.: A methodology for achieving agility in manufacturing organizations: An introduction. Production Economics 62, 7–22 (1999)
34. Martin, A., Biddle, R., Noble, J.: When XP met outsourcing. In: Eckstein, J., Baumeister, H. (eds.) XP 2004. LNCS, vol. 3092, pp. 51–59. Springer, Heidelberg (2004)

Value Creation by Agile Projects: Methodology or Mystery?

Zornitza Racheva, Maya Daneva, and Klaas Sikkel

University of Twente, Drienerlolaan 5, Enschede 7500,
The Netherlands
{z.racheva,m.daneva,k.sikkel}@utwente.nl

Abstract. Business value is a key concept in agile software development approaches. This paper presents results of a systematic review of literature on how business value is created by agile projects. We found that with very few exceptions, most published studies take the concept of business value for granted and do not state what it means in general as well as in the specific study context. We could find no study which clearly indicates how exactly individual agile practices or groups of those create value and keep accumulating it over time. The key implication for research is that we have an incentive to pursue the study of value creation in agile project by deploying empirical research methods.

Keywords: business value, agile development, systematic review.

1 Introduction

In many organizations today, the IT departments undergo a cultural change through which the once-dominating cost-centric view of IT is being replaced by a value-centric view. For companies, to be able to support this transition in culture, they need to provide senior management with an explicit means to show the link between the IT solutions being adopted and the benefits resulting from them. This is particularly necessary in the context of agile software development, as new agile methodologies are being adopted and need to prove their merits. A key characteristic of any agile approach is its explicit focus on business value [1]. Essentially, in agile software project, the development process is a value creation process. Indeed, the agile community established a common understanding [2] that (i) the main purpose of an agile project is to deliver maximum business value for the client and that (ii) agile approaches deliver business value fast and early in the project.

In this paper, we take a closer look into the ways in which agile software practices create value in agile projects. We have set out to answer three research questions (RQ): RQ1: *What concepts of business value are used in agile context?* RQ2: *In which way do agile projects create business value?* RQ3: *In which way do specific or individual practices influence the creation of business value?* We consider RQ3 to represent a more concrete look into the process of creation of value and, thus, can be considered as a refinement of RQ2. In the course of our research action, however, it turned out that we could not answer RQ3. In spite of our efforts, based on the results

F. Bomarius et al. (Eds.): PROFES 2009, LNBIP 32, pp. 141–155, 2009.
© Springer-Verlag Berlin Heidelberg 2009

of the study we could not provide a complete answer to that question. The fact that we could not find enough evidence is in itself surprising, and is one of the results of the study. Nevertheless, as we have no enough evidence, in the course of the paper we will not discuss further this question.

To answer our research questions, we have performed a systematic review [3] of literature. In the next section, we provide background on agile software development and business value as its central theme, and on our motivation for caring out this research. Section 3 describes the details of our systematic review (SR) process and Section 4 presents the results. Section 5 assesses our answers to the research questions and discusses implications for researchers. Section 6 analyses the possible validity threats, in section 7 we compare our results to previous studies, and Section 8 concludes the paper.

2   Background and Motivation

2.1   Agile Software Development

This section is an introduction for readers who are less familiar with agile software project contexts and agile software development and management approaches.

Agile approaches to software project delivery and to software product development can be considered a paradigm, a project management philosophy, a culture, an attitude, and a state of mind. All these rest on the 'minimalist' principle of organizing work in the software development process, meaning a conscious choice in carrying out those tasks which directly create value for clients and leaving out anything that is deemed "waste" [4]. The latter refers to all work and work products not directly contributing to the development of the desired software, for example spending time on implementing features that are not specified by any user story or on producing an artifact not explicitly asked by the clients.The 'minimalist' principle is fundamental to the ability of the agile approaches to cope with project uncertainties. In that sense, this principle can be seen as a reaction to the 'plan-based' paradigm which assumes that problems are fully specifiable and that predictable solutions exist for every problem [4]. Agile approaches, such as Extreme Programming (XP), SCRUM or CRYSTAL, for example advocate requirements engineering (RE) through the software product development cycle in small and informal stages. That is, instead of engineering the requirements upfront, one lets requirements emerge during development. Agile software process practitioners deem this approach particularly valuable for software producers in a context that includes highly uncertain requirements, experimentation with new development technology, and clients willing to explore the ways in which an evolving product can help their business goals. If we compare agile RE and 'plan-based RE', one could notice two important differences [1]: (i) (re)prioritization happens at inter-iteration time, which means that the project team anticipates and plans as many reprioritization sessions as the number of project iterations, and (ii) (re)prioritization is based mostly on business value, that is, the highest priority features get implemented early so that most business value gets realized.

All agile software approaches share the same 'minimalist' principle, but, despite that, not all of them are directly comparable in terms of scope and content. For example, an important distinction exists between agile software development (ASD) and agile project management (APM) approaches. While the first class of approaches are defined as "evolutionary approaches which are collaborative and self-organizing in nature, producing high-quality systems that meets the changing needs of stakeholders in a cost effective and timely manner" [1], the APM approaches are defined as "the work of energizing, empowering and enabling project teams to rapidly and reliably deliver customer value by engaging customer and continuously learning and adapting to their changing needs and environments". We make the note, however, that in this paper we treat ASD and APM practices in the same way. That is, when we use the term 'agile practice' we mean a practice which can be part of either software development or project management. In the next sub-section, we narrow down the discussion to the concept of business value as business value is what motivates the adoption of agile practices in the first place.

2.2 Related Work

Systematic reviews of empirical studies of ASD and APM practice have been contributed by a few authors [1,4,5]. However, the research questions asked in these studies are different from ours. The first review [5] dates from 2002 and answers the question "What makes a development method an agile one?" This SR synthesizes existing literature to characterize the state-of-the-art practice and compare agile methods by pinpointing out their similarities and differences. Furthermore, a comparative analysis of nine agile methods was published in a report in 2002 [1]. We make the note that these two publications [1,5] found scarce empirical support to exist for the nine reviewed methods.

The second SR [4] dates from 2008 and its objective is to answer the questions of "What's currently known about the benefits and limitations of ASD?" and "What is the strength of the evidence in support of these findings?" These authors also investigated what the implication of ASD studies are for the software practitioners and software engineering researchers. This SR identified four categories of ASD publications: (i) those pertaining to ADS adoption, (ii) to human and social factors, (iii) to customer and developers perceptions and (iv) comparative studies of ASD processes and alternative ones. With respect to each category, the SR [4] indicated a number of reported benefits and limitations of agile development. A key finding of this SR was that "the strength of evidence is very low, which makes it difficult to offer a specific advice to industry and that the research community "needs to increase both the number and the quality of studies on ASD".

Clearly, the research questions of our SR were not the objectives of the previously published reviews. In this sense, the present study complements the existing research by other SR authors. In Section 8, we will compare our findings with those previously published and we will see points of convergence and divergence between us and other SR authors.

2.3 The Concept of Business Value

The term BV is being used in management and financial economics as an informal term that includes all forms of value that determine the health and well-being of the firm in the long-run In the context of agile development the term Business Value appears in the majority of publications at agile software development conferences (for example, the annual AGILE conference series, e.g. www.agile2008.org). Typically, it is used in phrases like 'companies should focus on delivering business value', or 'agile methods help deliver business value'.

That this term is central to the agile community is not surprising, as one could see from Section 2.1. What we found surprising, however, is that while studying the agile software development literature for more than a year, we consistently made two contradicting observations with respect to the concept of business value. On one side, practitioners are occupied with how to measure the creation of business value through the software development process by translating anything valuable into dollar value. On the other side, intuition suggests that in agile projects it makes sense to interpret business value as a multi-dimensional concept, just as it is in studies on business value of IT in general.

These observations motivated us to look deeper and in a more structured way at agile literature and get to know what is the understanding of business value that is particular to the agile context and in which particular ways agile practices contribute to the value creation process. Our goal is to uncover such knowledge, to identify the different viewpoints presented in current agile software engineering literature and to derive conceptual categories which are significant in developing a deeper understanding of the phenomenon of creating business value in agile software projects. In this paper, we talk about the term BV in general and as understood in the agile community. As seen from the definition used in the economic sciences, it is not a well defined concept. Still, if our purpose is to uncover how an ASM or an APM method increases (or influences) it, we need an operationalizable definition of this concept. In this sense our study can be considered as a firs step in this direction.

3 The Research Method

As per SR guidelines [3], we used the RQs for determining the content and structure of the SR, for designing strategies for locating and selecting primary studies, for critically evaluating the studies, and for analyzing their results. We implemented the following SR process:

We used the following search strings: (1) business value AND iterative development, (2) business value AND agile projects, (3) business value AND scrum, (4) business value AND XP. These search strings are the result of a learning process, that is, we experimented with a variety of combinations of these words in order to test synonyms used in literature and to cover the variety of agile software development and agile project management concepts. We want to underline that we performed searches with alternative strings: feature driven development AND business value; crystal clear AND business value; agile development AND benefits; lean development AND business value. They didn't return any papers. We considered it important to proceed like this because no standardized, consistent terminology exists with respect to the topic of our study.

We used the Boolean "OR" operator to concatenate the four search terms: 1 OR 2 OR 3 OR 4. Our search strategy included six electronic databases, namely (i) ACM Digital Library, (ii) IEEE Xplore, (iii) ISI Web of Science, (iv) Kluwer Online ScienceDirect – Elsevier, (v) SpringerLink, (vi) Wiley InterScience, and (vii) Scopus, ensuring our search was applied to journals, magazines, conference/workshop proceedings published since 2000. As the topic of business value in agile software development is closely related to the practice, we decided our search strategy to include the Agile Journal (www.agilejournal.com) which is the most popular practitioner-centric online publication venue of the agile community. The Agile Journal publishes monthly issues with articles on various subjects concerning ASD and APM. We make the note that there is an overlap between Scopus and the other databases we used in terms of citation data [6], e.g. the sources of IEEE and Springer are included in Scopus. As indicated in SR methodologists [7], the role of deploying a multiple-database-searching strategy is twofold: (1) to ensure a coverage including additional sources (unique coverage) and (2) to take advantage of differences in indexing across databases to increase the chances of retrieving relevant items that are in both databases (incremental retrieval).

We performed the searches between Nov 1 and Nov 28, 2008, applying the search query individually to each electronic database. We make the note that not all databases, which we used, allow for queries composed of complex Boolean expressions. For those ones, which did not process complex queries, we run separate searches and, then, we used the union of the results obtained. We adopted this practice because the second author used it in her earlier SR study [8] and found it to work well. We applied the search query to the titles, abstracts, conclusions, and keywords of the articles in the identified databases and conference proceedings. We excluded editorials, prefaces, summaries of articles and tutorials, workshops, panels and poster sessions. We also did not include PhD theses and technical reports. The published sources we reviewed were written in English only and included both qualitative and quantitative research, from scientists and practitioners.

We were surprised to retrieve only a small number of papers from the scientific electronic libraries. For example, there was 1 paper from Springer, 17 from Wiley, 19 from IEEE and 67 from Scopus. In the Agile Journal, the only search string we used was "business value", as we assumed that the publications would be relevant to the agile software development topic. The result was 50 articles.

After identifying the potential sources, we have screened all titles, abstracts and conclusions to extract the ones we consider relevant to our research effort. We consider relevant those papers in which (i) there is an explicit description of what the authors understand under the term 'business value', and/or (ii) there is some indications of the ways in which business value is created, accumulated, measured and tracked throughout the agile project. We highlighted all phrases that contain author's understanding of the nature of business value. We used this information threefold: first, to catalogue existing definitions of business value in agile, second, to compare them and identify areas where the definitions overlap, complement each other or diverge, and third, to build conceptual categories which could serve researchers and practitioners to clearly see what the current literature refers to, when using the term business value. In the next sections, we first present our results and offer a discussion on them (in Section 4). We, then form answers to our research questions in Section 5. We chose this lay-out in presenting and analyzing our findings as we believe that this helps the readers under-stand clearer how we derived the answers to our research questions.

4 Results

Our overall observation from reviewing the papers is that most of them turned out to be irrelevant according to our inclusion criteria described above. A large number of materials in fact did contain the terms business value and agile, but we found that business value itself was not elaborated in either of the two senses mentioned above.

Our SR indicates that the authors of the papers we reviewed consider business value a self-evident concept. It seems that business value concepts reflect condensed meanings of general terms which the authors of the papers assume everyone shares.

We found no paper that provides a rigorous definition of business value in agile context. With exception of five papers [9,10,11,12,13] in the literature we reviewed, the understanding of business value was either implicit, or taken for granted.

In what follows, we first discuss the definitions we catalogued from our review, and then we compare them to distil some characteristic features of the understanding of business value in the agile literature. Last, we present the results of our application of a coding process on the reading materials we deemed relevant. These results are conceptual categories which we think help understand and reason about the business value concept in agile project context.

4.1 Definitions of Business Value

The definitions we discovered are presented below in Table 1.

Table 1. Definitions and sources

Authors	Definitions
Barnett [9]	"…business value, as measured in business revenue, stock price, market share, or other business metrics. Value is in the eyes of the customer…"
Patton [10]	"Business value is something that delivers profit to the organization paying for the software in the form of an increase in revenue, an avoidance of costs, or an improvement in service".
Pettit [11]	"Business value is a communication vehicle: we use business value to communicate value, priorities, motivation'"".
Rawsthorne [12]	"Business value is what management is willing to pay for; value can only be defined by the ultimate customer. And it's only meaningful when expressed in terms of a specific product (a good or a service, and often both at once), which meets the customer's needs at a specific price at a specific time".
Poole [14]	"Might not be possible to define the business value of IT independently of other activities. What is business value: *Business value = F(x) + F(y) + F(z) + ….* That is, a complex function where we must balance multiple things …while they are changing!"

An interesting observation is that all of them are from practitioners' articles. We explain this with the facts that (i) we could not find scientific publications, particularly dedicated to explaining the notion of value in agile context, and (ii) we believe that the authors assume that the concept of business value is self-evident because it is extensively studied in economic sciences. (For more information on the topic of business value of IT, we refer interested readers to the reference [15]).

For the sake of completeness, we also mention published works of other authors who discuss ways of realizing value [16,17, 18]. We note that these works, however, don't provide any definition of value, which is the reason to leave them out of this study.

In addition to the above definitions, we identified seven other publications [13,19,20,21,22,23,24] which discuss the topic of business value without using explicitly the term "business value" itself but terms synonymous to it. We list these six for the sake of completeness:

(i) three papers [19,20,24] use the concept *Earned Value* in agile settings. All three base this concept on the earned value measure used in economic sciences, in order to track progress or velocity of an agile project. According to [19,20,24], Earned Value is a project management technique to measure, at a specific date, the progress and performance of a project against the plan, and to estimate future performance.

(ii) one paper [23] uses the term *perceived business value*. According to the authors, this concept means the particular context of multiple projects and optimizing value in this case.

(iii) one paper [13] proposes the concept of *Earned business value* (EBV). It defines a measure, which can be used to track the value of the requirements being delivered. The measure helps calculating the relative value of the work done compared to the whole project. Agile earned business value is a ration calculated by using the formula:

$$EBV = the\text{-}percent\text{-}of\text{-}value\text{-}delivered\,/\,the\text{-}percent\text{-}of\text{-}cost\text{-}consumed.$$

(iv) two published sources [21, 22] use the term *Economic value* interchangeably with business value. The second source [22] defines the Economic Value trough the net present value (NPV) in the formula:

$$NPV = AssetValue\,/\,(\,1 + DiscountRate\,)\,DevTime - DevCost$$

We note that the term 'Asset Value' (meaning the dollar returns of a project) is neither defined, nor traced back to tangible project characteristics. Instead, it is taken as a given in the calculations.

4.2 Comparison of the Concepts

Our comparison of the definitions presented in the previous section was done by applying the following steps: we first identified the original authors' terms used in discussing business value and then, we compared them to see points of convergence and divergence and to characterize these. This process of constant comparison is borrowed from Grounded Theory research methodologists [25] who suggest it as a qualitative analysis technique for research settings like ours. In our comparison, we also checked for each definition the context of its intended use. This analysis revealed the following characterizing features of the business value concepts we found in existing literature:

1. Business value in practice tends to be qualitative: Our observations from the reviewed sources do indicate that there are quantitative definitions of business value. However, we found evidence suggesting that these definitions, when used in practice, are applied at project level. We found no study suggesting that a quantitative definition of business value is used when authors attempt to see how much value is contributed by the deployment of an individual agile practice or by a group of practices. We could also find no study which provides evidence that business value and its accumulation over time has been tracked quantitatively throughout the project iterations. Clearly, if one is to see how agile development creates business value, one needs "to tie value back to some tangible gain for the business" [10]. For example, to "something that delivers profit to the organization paying for the software in the form of an increase in revenue, an avoidance of costs, or an improvement in service" [10]. However, our review indicates that tying back business value to gain is problematic.

2. Business value tends to be subjective: Our observations from the literature sources indicate hat often, the term "value" is used subjectively. Patton [10] illustrates clearly this by his experiences witnessing agile project stakeholders expressing value in the following ways: "I value something if it makes me feel good", or "If I'm representing the business, then I might view something that makes me feel good as a "business value".

3. The sources of business value drive requirements prioritization: Our observation is that, more often than not, when agile projects refer to "customer", they mean a multistakeholder setting in a client organization. In such a setting, if requirements are prioritized and re-prioritized from the perspective of the "customer" at inter-iteration time, then the relative priority, which is given to each stakeholder group behind the label "customer" is the actual driver for the prioritization process. Patton [10] illustrates this point drawing on the matter that "different people consider different things valuable" and that "prioritizing work becomes a tug-of-war in those circumstances". (Patton [10] warns that "If we share a common idea of what's valuable, then we needn't pull in opposite directions."

4. Business value of the IT solution requires a degree of trust: There is a limit to the confidence we can place in business value numbers. This means that business value is not an absolute "dollar value" [11]

5. The business value an IT solution tends to be dependent on non-IT business processes. Our observations from the reviewed publications suggest that business value might well be related to other aspects and processes of the business. Poole [14] even warns that it might not be possible to define the business value of IT independently of other activities.

4.3   Perspectives to Consider When Thinking of Business Value

We identified that the understanding of business value is traced back to the perspectives of the two key groups of participants in the agile project and, in turn, their roles.

Throughout our SR, two main groups of papers emerged: (i) those dealing with creation of business value for the client organization and (ii) those discussing how a development organization can manage a portfolio of multiple and concurrent agile projects being done for one or more client organizations [13]. The two groups of papers clearly indicated that each perspective represented a unique understanding of what is of value and how to achieve maximum value.

From the client's perspective, the value is defined by the clients themselves. Indeed, most of the literature sources we studied relate to business value as understood from the client's perspective.

Furthermore, from the perspective of an agile software development organization, the management defines the relative business value of each project in the portfolio of projects, which the organization is engaged in, as a software supplier. The management team typically uses projects' business value in the process of performing trade-off analysis and balance between resource demands coming from different projects. We make the note that in addition to the above, in case of a development team in a client-supplier contractual relationship, the value for the team is to satisfy the client's needs, so that the client will eventually come back the next time, which has a direct impact on the revenue of the developer [26]. This is different in the case of an IT-department within a company, where the IT-team has (i) to make business management happy, (ii) to help increase overall profit of the organization, and (iii) to balance between new development and other IT operations and maintenance tasks.

We make the note that we have consciously excluded the role of the end user. This is because, in the literature sources we reviewed, we could not find any evidence suggesting a linkage between the end user and the decisions influencing business value in agile projects. We believe that this is so because authors silently assume that the "customer" will take into consideration what is valuable for the end users in the client organization. Still, we think that this question is worth to be explored in detail in a future work, as it is very relevant for the value perspective.

4.4 Conceptual Categories Helping Understand Business Value

Our process of making analytic sense of the reading materials by means of coding and constant comparison brought us to five conceptual categories which we deem significant in understanding business value and its creation in agile projects. A conceptual category explicates ideas, event, or processes in our observations, which we collected while running the SR. We call these categories 'significant' because we believe we can use them to make an interpretative rendering that illuminates the studied phenomenon, namely business value creation in agile projects. We think that other researchers can use these categories to define what is happening in the project and begin to grapple with what it means. The categories we discerned are these:

1. *Vision*. Multiple indications [9,19,21,27] from literature suggest the creation of business value should be driven by the vision of the organization.
2. *Business goals*. Approximately half of the papers suggest that business value must be established from business deliverables often requiring input from a range of stakeholders[27, 26].
3. *Product goals*. The majority of the agile practitioners relate business value to software product goals. For example, [20, 27] cite experiences in which product

goals were re-defined after the effect of the IT solution is known. Re-definition of business objectives after change in the project context is also possible [27]. The authors mean, for example, change in the business environment, lows, competition. Each of these events might trigger a change in the business goals and consequently – in the defined objectives for the software.

4. *Product features*. Practitioners indicate that it would be of benefit if there is a way to quantitatively assess the business value of each feature of the software product. As Poole says [14], only by assigning business value, in hard currency, to each IT deliverable and even every feature of a deliverable, can business truly manage the relationship with IT effectively. More than ¾ of the publications are concerned with the question how to measure the part of the whole business value (at project level) which is included (encapsulated) in each feature. For example, [13] assigns to the whole set of features the value of 100%, and each separate feature is treated as a fragment of the whole functionality and, in turn, is measured in its relation to the whole. However, we found no study that describes a project in which this was done.

5. *Agile practices*. There seems to be a common agreement in the literature that some practices help more the process of creating value than others [21,28]. Gurses [28] highlights the importance of knowing the value that the particular agile practices create. However, we found no study which suggests how exactly certain groups of practices add more value and even what "more value" means in agile context.

To check whether we have grasped what is significant, we attempted to use these categories on examples of real-life projects described by practitioners in the agile literature. For the purpose of illustration, in this section we refer to the experiences reported by Yahoo's Advanced Products team [27]. At Yahoo!, this team develops innovative product ideas before formally launching them into the Yahoo! Network. The reported experiences [27] in using ASD and APM approaches date from 2006 and are about Mixd (http://mixd.yahoo.com), a group mobile messaging and media sharing tool for people who want to organize and remember gettogethers. This t was, built and launched by Yáhoo's Advanced Products team in a nine month timeframe. In what follows we show how the conceptual categories, described earlier in this section, can be used to makes sense of the business value creation in Yahoo's case.

As per Yahoo's 2007 annual report[1], Yahoo's purpose is formulated as "powering its communities of users, advertisers, publishers, and developers to create indispensable experience, built on trust". The *vision* of the company is to have these communities provided with internet services that are essential and relevant. In line of their vision, Yahoo set the *business goal* of the Mixd project "to get to the target youth market as quickly as possible, while still providing a compelling user experience, and iterate on the product quickly". The *product goal* was "to help communities of 18-25 year olds connect both online and offline, share ideas and information, and socialize with each other using their personal cell phones". Yahoo refers to the product goal as to 'core goals'. At the start of the agile process, as per the Yahoo's Mixd experience report [27], this goal was reformulated in a specific client-centric way as follows: "*it's 5pm on a Friday night and I want to hang out with my friends. What do I do?*". This

---

[1] The report is publicly available in pdf-format at Yahoo's web site.

was to reflect the Yahoo Advanced Team's assumptions that framed their actions at the beginning of each agile process-iteration which followed. The experience report indicates the translation of this product goal into the following key groups of *product features:* to allow people (i) to create add-hoc groups, (ii) share mobile photos and video and (iii) see it all on a website later. These product features - which support the 'core goal' as well, are called 'core features'. The report does not provide details on whether business value was quantified or not, it gives a detailed account on how the team involved their clients into the agile development process in a way that helped discover the 'core features' and ultimately develop a product with "more business value" than it was thought possible at the formulation of the original product concept. At the very first iteration, the Advanced Product Team started with a concept of a product which was a web-based invitation application (for example, similar to Evite: http://www.evite.com). Throughout the agile process and with consistently high user involvement - by means of regular feedback at inter-iteration time, Mixd ended up as a mobile social networking product. It was through these feedback points that Yahoo's team managed to change their course of action in a timely fashion so that it tuned the functionality to their users' wants and delivered in each iteration "new chunks of functionality working without breaking what already worked". At inter-iteration time, the Yahoo team filtered most product decisions by using their *product goal* and prioritized *product features* by asking if the feature was absolutely necessary to help the user accomplish their goal of hanging out with friends. The team "brutally cut features" which did not address the product goal. For example, one of the features included in the initial Mixd solution proposal was a way for the Yahoo user to get updates via email, instead of mobile phone. Yahoo's Advanced Products team thought "this was a terrific add-on for people who didn't want to get updates or converse on their mobile phone" [27]. They also found "This feature required a significant amount of effort, but could be completed in time for our launch. We once again bought up the core problem statement and realized that the feature diluted the key focus of the product and that it added extra UI complexity where we didn't need it. We cut the feature and instead focused on strengthening the other features".

5 Summary of Results and Implications

This study has addressed the questions of *What concepts of business value are used in agile context? (RQ1)* and *In which way do agile projects create business value? (RQ2).*

For RQ1, our findings are that (i) the majority of papers in agile software engineering literature do not define the concept of business value, (ii) the business value concepts rest on a definition of Earned Value as used in economic sciences, and (iii) authors rest on the premise that business value is translatable into dollar value. However, we found that this 'translation' is problematic.

For RQ2, we could not find sufficient evidence that allows us to formulate an answer. The publications included in our review offer almost no evidence pertaining to the specific ways in which agile practices create and keep accumulating business value throughout the project.

However, the fact that RQ2 could not be answered by means of a systematic litera-ture review is, in our view an important finding. The idea of focusing on business value is pivotal in the agile paradigm, yet in which way this value is created seems to evade precise description. Why? At this stage we can only speculate at this. Our intui-tion says the fault isn't in the agile practices, but in the very concept of business value, which turns out to be rather more slippery and volatile than the most of the authors of studied papers seem to assume implicitly. If business value often cannot be given very accurately, it follows that it is hard to describe exactly how an agile project contributes to it.

If we do want to further investigate the value of agile practices, a different type of research is called for. The key distinguishing feature of the agile practice is re-prioritization, based on an assessment of business value that appears to be uncertain and changing over time. The idea that re-prioritization is driven by calculating a cost function can be discarded as overly simplistic; it seems evident that some non-trivial decision making is involved. The key question, then, is how this decision making takes place. In order to gain a deeper insight in this process, we intend to empirically investigate this in agile software projects.

6 Limitations

There are three main validity concerns pertinent to our SR: (i) our selection of publi-cations to be included, (ii) our analysis of definitions, and (iii) potential bias by the researchers.

The search step of our SR was executed separately by the first and the second au-thors. The first author searched the ACM, Springer and IEEE and the second – Wiley, Elsevier and ISI Web of Science. Each of these authors individually screened titles, abstracts and conclusions and discarded the hits returned in the respective databases. The authors worked in isolation from each other in two locations and met only after this step was completed.

We make the note here that our access to 'relevant' sources depended on the ap-propriateness of the search strings used. As we treated their composition as a learning process [8], the list of search strings was adapted four times and the search was re-run with the new terms. For some search strings, we applied synonyms like "business impact" and "value oriented". We also tentatively AND-combined the search strings pair-wise and queried the databases. The resulting list of papers had reduced the num-ber of items, which were less than 10% of the items resulting from using one search string alone. In half of the cases with pair-wise combined strings, the resulting paper list was empty or contained only one or two papers. This is a hint that our search strings are only slightly redundant.

Furthermore, approximately half of the selected papers were reviewed by both re-searchers. For these papers, we consistently observed a consensus. Whenever there was disagreement, the points of disagreements were discussed until both researchers arrived at a consensus.

We believe that the threat to validity due to researchers' bias is minimal, because no one of the authors (i) has published a study which is included in the SR or (ii) is in a close research-collaboration relationship with the authors of included studies.

7 Comparing Our Findings to Previously Published Related Work

When comparing our SR and the earlier published SRs [1,4,5], we consider that our findings converge with the earlier published SRs in two respects: First, similarly to the other authors, we found that the existing sources of definitions of business value are practitioners' reports. As Abrahamsson et al indicated in 2002 [5], back at the time of their SR, the existing evidence consisted primarily of practitioners' success stories. Second, the key implication of out study is a strong incentive for carrying out empirical research. This converges with the finding of Dyba et al [4], as stated above.

Last, we make the note that the SR by Dyba et al is concerned with the concept of 'benefits' of agile practices and that we thought that the concept of 'benefits' in [4] could be related to the concept of business value. However, when we checked what the authors mean, we found that the notion of benefits in [4] is different from what we mean when referring to 'business value creation'. As a matter of fact, we counted automatically the occurrences of the word combination 'business value' in [4] and we found only two of them.

8 Conclusions and Future Work

A systematic review on concepts of business value in agile software engineering literature yielded the following findings:

1. In the literature on agile software engineering there is no elaborated definition of business value.
2. Practitioners offer definitions which translate business value into dollar value. However, we found that this 'translation' is problematic.
3. The notion of business value is slippery and highly volatile.

We acknowledge that at this point, the question "In which way business value is created in agile projects" remains unanswered by our systematic review approach. We only uncovered scarce indications about specific instances of value being brought by means of specific agile practices [10,16,17]. However, because these instances stem from anecdotic experiences, we could not deem them good enough for forming any conclusion.

We are really surprised that we couldn't find a more profound answer. This raises the question whether there is an existing representative body of knowledge on the subject, which might have been uncovered by means of other research approaches. Or is it time that researchers and practitioners look more closely at the phenomenon of value creation? This gives us the incentive to do further empirical research on how people make decisions in agile projects based on people's concepts of value. For this purpose we will apply another empirical method, following the recommendation in [29]. At the time of writing this paper, we are planning case study research at three agile software companies in the Netherlands.

Acknowledgements

This research has been funded by the Netherlands Research Foundation (NWO) under the QUADREAD project and the CARES project. The authors would like to thank Roel J. Wieringa, Siv Hilde Houmb, Erlend Engum, Luigi Buglione, Thijs Munsterman and Eltjo Poort and all the members of the QUADREAD research team for sharing ideas on the topic of business value. We are also indebted to the anonymous reviewers for their comments which helped us to improve the quality of this paper.

References

1. Abrahamsson, P., Salo, O., Ronkainen, J., Warsta, J.: Agile Software Development Methods: Review and Analysis, VTT Technoical Report (2002)
2. Agile Manifesto, http://agilemanifesto.org/principles.html
3. Kitchenham, B.: Procedures for Undertaking Systematic Reviews, Joint Technical Report, Computer Science Department, Keele University (TR/SE-0401) and National ICT Australia Ltd. (0400011T.1) (2004)
4. Dyba, T., Dingsoyr, T.: Empirical Studies of Agile Software Development: a Systematic Review. Journal of Information and Software Technology 50, 833–859 (2008)
5. Abrahamsson, P., Warsta, J., Siponen, M.T., Ronkainen, J.: New Directions on Agile Methods: a Comparative Analysis. In: Proc. of ICSE. IEEE CS Press, Los Alamitos (2003)
6. Bosman, J., Mourik, I.v., Rasch, M., Sieverts, E., Verhoeff, H.: Scopus reviewed and compared: The coverage and functionality of the citation database Scopus, including comparisons with Web of Science and Google Scholar, p. 63. Utrecht University Library, Utrecht (2006)
7. McGowan, J., Sampson, M.: Systematic reviews need systematic searchers. Journal of Medical Library Association 93(1), 74–80 (2005)
8. Herrmann, A., Daneva, M.: Requirements Prioritization Based on Benefit and Cost Prediction: An Agenda for Future Research. In: Proc of the Int. Conference on Requirements Engineering (RE 2008), pp. 125–134. IEEE, Los Alamitos (2008)
9. Barnett, L.: Agile Projects Must Measure Business Value. Agile Journal (January 2007), http://www.agilejournal.com/content/view/211/76/
10. Patton, J.: Ambiguous Business Value Harms Software Products. IEEE Software 25(1) (January/February 2008)
11. Pettit, R.: Business Value Applied: Aligning The Day To Day With Business Imperative. Agile Journal (January 4, 2007), http://www.agilejournal.com/content/view/206/33/
12. Rawsthorne, D.: Managing the Work in an Agile Project, http://www.netobjectives.com/files/resources/downloads/ManagingTheWork.pdf
13. Rawsthorne, D.: Calculating Earned Business Value For An Agile Project. Agile Journal (June 2006), http://www.agilejournal.com/articles/articles/calculating-earned-business-value-for-an-agile-project.html
14. Poole, M.: Business and IT – A Marriage Made in Heaven? Agile Journal (October 6, 2007), http://www.agilejournal.com/content/view/627/76/
15. Kraemer, K.L., Gurbaxani, V., Dunkle, D., Vitalari, N.: Business Value of Information Technology (Eight Dimensions of Business Value)

16. Favaro, J.M.: Managing Requirements for Business Value. IEEE Software 19(2), 15–17
17. Qumer, A.: Defining an Integrated Agile Governance for Large Agile Software Development Environments. In: Concas, G., Damiani, E., Scotto, M., Succi, G. (eds.) XP 2007. LNCS, vol. 4536, pp. 157–160. Springer, Heidelberg (2007)
18. Setia, P., Sambamurthym, B., Closs, D.: Realizing Business Value of Agile IT Applications: Antedecents in the Supply Chain Networks. Information technology Management Journal 9, 5–19 (2008)
19. Alleman, G.B., Henderson, M., Seggelke, R.: Making Agile Development Work in a Government Contracting Environment Measuring Velocity with Earned Value. In: Proc. of the Agile Development Conference, pp. 114–119 (2003)
20. Cabri, A., Griffiths, M.: Earned Value and Agile Reporting. In: Proc. of AGILE Conf., p. 6 (2006)
21. Favaro, J.M.: That Elusive Business Value: Some Lessons from the Top. In: Baumeister, H., Marchesi, M., Holcombe, M. (eds.) XP 2005. LNCS, vol. 3556, p. 199. Springer, Heidelberg (2005)
22. Muller, M., Padberg, F. (eds.): On the Economic Evaluation of XP Projects ACM SIGSOFT Software Engineering Notes, SESSION: Software process and workflow, September 2003, vol. 28, pp. 168–177 (2003)
23. Pinheiro, C., Maurer, F., Sillito, J.: Adopting Iterative Development: The Perceived Business Value. In: Prod. of the 9th International Conference on XP, Agile Processes in Software Engineering and Extreme Programming. Lecture Notes in Business Information Processing (2008) ,
24. Sulaiman, T., Barton, B., Blackburn, T., Agile, E.V.M.: – Earned Value Management in Scrum Projects. In: Proc. of AGILE Conf., p. 10 (2006)
25. Charmaz, K.: Constructing Grounded Theory: a Practical Guide Through Qualitative Research. Sage, Thousand Oaks (2007)
26. Logue, K., McDaid, K.: Agile Release Planning: Dealing with Uncertainty in Development Time and Business Value, Engineering of Computer Based Systems. In: Proc of 15th Annual IEEE International Conference and Workshop, pp. 437–442 (2008)
27. Gatz, S.A., Benefield, G.: Less, Never More: Launching a Product with Critical Features and Nothing More. In: Proc. of AGILE Conf., pp. 324–327. IEEE CS, Los Alamitos (2007)
28. Gurses, L.: Increasing Business Value by Adopting Agile Methods. Agile Journal (May 8, 2007), http://www.agilejournal.com/content/view/410/
29. Easterbrook, S., Singer, J., Storey, M.-A., Damian, D.: Selecting Empirical Methods for Software Engineering Research. In: Guide to Advanced Empirical Software Engineering. Springer, Heidelberg (2008); ISBN 978-1-84800-043-8 (Print) 978-1-84800-044-5 (Online)

Decision Support for Iteration Scheduling in Agile Environments

Ákos Szőke

Department of Measurement and Information Systems,
Budapest University of Technology and Economics, Budapest, Hungary
aszoke@mit.bme.hu

Abstract. Today's software business development projects often lay claim to low-risk value to the customers in order to be financed. Emerging agile processes offer shorter investment periods, faster time-to-market and better customer satisfaction. To date, however, in agile environments there is no sound methodological schedule support contrary to the traditional plan-based approaches. To address this situation, we present an agile iteration scheduling method whose usefulness is evaluated with post-mortem simulation. It demonstrates that the method can significantly improve load balancing of resources (cca. 5×), produce higher quality and lower-risk feasible schedule, and provide more informed and established decisions by optimized schedule production. Finally, the paper analyzes benefits and issues from the use of this method.

Keywords: agile planning, iteration planning, scheduling.

1 Introduction

Agile software development represents a major approach to software engineering. Recent surveys showed that in the last 10 years agile methods adoption expanded to the ≈ 70%, which can be explained by the fact that agile teams are generally more successful than traditional ones [1,2]. The most popular agile methods are Extreme Programming (XP) (58%), Scrum(23%), and Feature Driven Development (FDD) (5%) [3]. Several studies pointed out that Extreme programming provides ≈ 60% increase in productivity, quality and improved stakeholder satisfaction, and ≈ 60% and ≈ 40% reduction in products pre-, and post-release defect rates respectively [4].

Despite variety of methods all of them share the common principles specified in the *Agile Manifesto* [5]. The *Declaration of Interdependence (DOI)* [6] defines a set of management principles for agile methods [6]. The main practices respect to agile project planning includes *i*) Continuous improvement *ii*) Iterative development *iii*) Staged program delivery *iv*) Scenario-driven development, and *v*) Business-driven project pipeline [5,6,7,8].

From the project management point of view, agile software development delivery process is made up of the following phases: 1) *conceptualization* to define vision, high-level ranked deliverables and project roadmap, 2) *release planning*

F. Bomarius et al. (Eds.): PROFES 2009, LNBIP 32, pp. 156–170, 2009.
© Springer-Verlag Berlin Heidelberg 2009

to estimate deliverables and assign them into releases, 3) *iteration planning* to break down selected deliverables into technical tasks, 4) *iteration* to discuss the daily progress concerning writing tests, codes and fixing defects, 5) *iteration review* to demonstrate product increments to stakeholders and conduct iteration retrospective for the next iteration, and finally 6) *release* to package and deploy software to customers [3,9] (see Fig. 1).

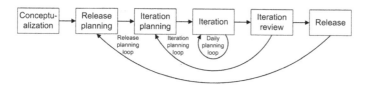

Fig. 1. Agile Software Development Delivery Process

Figure 1 points out that planning functions are generally described by a three-level management hierarchy in agile environments: *release* (coarse-grained), *iteration* (fine-grained), and *daily* plans. Each planning level is responsible for realizing the objectives of both the given and its superior level [3,9].

Problem Statement and Analysis. In 2008, an Agile Tools survey [10] showed that many developers-focused tools were come out (including JUnit testing, sub versioning, auto build, etc.) in the last decade, but most companies (> 52%) are still using old-fashioned project management tools like MS Project [11] or generic tools like spreadsheets. Surprisingly 18% of the respondents do not use any tool for project planning and tracking at all – although many commercial (such as Rally [12]) and open source (e.g. XPlanner [13]) agile project planning tools are available.

The lack of penetration of the modern agile planning tools can be explained by the weak embedded support of traditionally important project *scheduling functions* such as resource allocations and what-if analysis. Their implemented methods provide 'quick and dirty' scheduling solutions [12,13]: the team can distribute deliverables among releases and iterations in planning meetings – while all explicit and implicit objectives and constraints are taken into account informally. Typical constraints and objectives are **P1**) *precedences* (to express temporal precedences between realizations), **P2**) *balancing resource workloads* (to avoid resources overloading), and **P3**) *optimality* (to choose the best one from different plans). Informal approaches work well in smaller projects, however as the size and complexity increases scheduling becomes a very complex process and advocates tool support [14,15].

Related Work. Scheduling requirements for the upcoming version is complex decision-centric process [15]. Its complexity emanates from increasing market demand and extensive use of high technology while all explicit and implicit objectives and constraints must be taken into account. In order to deal with this decision problem some method have been proposed. Compared to the extensive research on requirements priorization [16], interdependencies [17,18], and estimation [19], only few researches investigated the release planning problem. In the early period, researchers focused on the method of assessing requirements value and estimating cost to prioritize requirements [20,16]. Later, several optimization methods were proposed to select requirements for the next release. In [17] release planning was formulated as Integer Linear Programming (ILP) problem, where requirement dependencies were treated as precedence constraints. The ILP technique is extended with stakeholders' opinions and some managerial steering mechanism that enabled what-if analysis in [14,21]. The IFM method provides insight into the impact of development decisions with an financially-informed approach to maximize Net Present Value [22]. In [23] a case study showed that integration of requirements and planning how significantly can accelerate UML-based release planning.

All previous methods relate to requirements priorization and selection and none of them bothers with the implementation aspect: how to realize the selected requirements.

Objectives. Our proposed method intends to provide a sound decision support to the **P1)**-**P3)** by constructing an *information model* to specify data semantics of agile planning, and an innovative heuristic *scheduling algorithm* for wide-ranging agile iteration scheduling problems. This method not only supports making delivery decisions even in complex situations but provides a 'quick and clean' solution for agile iteration scheduling.

Structure of the Paper. The rest of the paper arranged as follows: Sec. 2 presents the background information on agile planning; Sec. 3 details the information model and the scheduling algorithm; Sec. 4 introduces simulation experiment with our prototypic tools; Sec. 5 discusses our solution and findings; Sec. 6 offers a survey of related work; and finally Sec. 7 concludes the paper.

2   Background

In this section, first we introduce agile *release*, *iteration* and *daily* planning practices to provide the necessary background information for the proposed method.

2.1   Release Planning

Release planning is a fundamental part of any incremental software development process (ISDP). It deals with assigning requirements to releases of evolving software products. Two kinds of release planning are adhered to ISDP: *predictive* and *adaptive* planning [24]. Predictive planning produces a detailed plan covering the whole software life cycle. On the contrary, adaptive planning includes two plans: a coarse-grained long-time (release) and a fine-grained short-time (iteration) plan. In the present perpetually changing environment the overall goal of ISDP is to *maximize stakeholders' satisfaction in least time possible*, so adaptive planning is more suitable for ISDP [24,3,9].

In agile methods a deliverable system is decomposed into units of customer-valued functionalities, and they are defined as self-contained *features* [9]. A proper release plan should satisfy customer needs while provide maximal business value by selecting the right set of features (requirements and defect corrections) into the next release(es). Feature selection considers the demands of stakeholders – including users, managers, developers, or their representatives. As a consequence, it is often not obvious which choice is better, because several concurrent aspects must be taken into account. The simplest forms of release planning are done informally and one of the most well known is the Planning game [9,3]. Sophisticated methods include optimization-based priorization mechanism while considering different constraint (e.g. technological, resource, system) and optimality criterions (e.g. value, urgency) [14,15].

2.2   Iteration and Daily Planning

Once the maximal customer-valued features are selected for the next release the following step is to realize them. In agile approaches software is rolled out in *increments* over time with *iterative* development approach (c.f. Sec.1 *ii*, *iii*) to reduce overall risk of realization [9,3]. Therefore a release is made up several iterations (from 1 to 4 and with duration 1 or 2 weeks) which deliver intermediate features (i.e. technical tasks – c.f. Sec.1) to the customers, so they receive both a sense of value and an opportunity to provide early feedback.

Iteration schedule is operational level support for realization of technical tasks, it focuses on resource allocation to these tasks [9]. In traditional approaches scheduling is usually carried out by a project planner software package (e.g. MS Project [11]) that helps dealing with constraints (e.g. scarcity of resources and precedences between features) and objectives (e.g minimal execution time) – but it is constructed mainly manually and takes relatively long time (several hours). However it is too heavyweight for agile approaches since they promise rapid response to the given situation – even on a daily basis (c.f. Sec.1 *i*, *ii*, *v*). Instead, without adequate tool support in agile methodologies, iteration scheduling is based on *intuitive* human judgements whose inherent discrepancies are resolved during team's daily and iteration review meetings (see Fig. 1) [9,24].

3   Decision Support in Iteration Scheduling

In this section first, we construct an information model of agile planning by representing concepts, relations, constraints to specify data semantics for agile iteration scheduling (subset of agile planning). Then we point out that iteration planning problems can be characterized as a special kind of resource-constrained project scheduling problem (RCPSP). Finally, a prototypic tool, and the analysis of our proposed solution is presented.

Iteration scheduling process made up of the following major steps: 1) features are broken down into smaller parts i.e. *technical tasks* (each task is realized by one developer); 2) durations of tasks are estimated and precedences among them are identified (they affect the realization time and the sequencing of tasks); and finally 3) resources allocation to tasks are performed. Output of this process is an schedule: *what* task is realized by *who* and *when* (see Fig. 2).

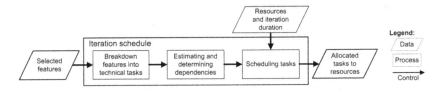

Fig. 2. Iteration Scheduling Process Overview

3.1   Conceptual Model of Agile Planning

In order to formulate the iteration scheduling model, first, we have to identify the main concepts of agile planning. These concepts are presented in the following list and visualized with UML notation in Fig. 3 [25,9,26].

- **Project:** is a planned endeavor, usually with specific *requirements* and rolled out in several deliverable stages i.e. *releases*.
- **Release:** produces (usually external) *selected* deliverable *features* for the customer, contains 1-4 iterations with start/end date and an iteration count.
- **Iteration:** is a development timebox that *delivers* intermediate deliverables with the realization of several technical tasks. It is characterized by available resource capacity – often expressed by iteration velocity.
- **Resource:** is human manpower who accomplish the demanded *feature* for the customer and they are *allocated* to *releases*.
- **Feature:** deliverables that the customer values. They can be classified two kind of set of elements: i) (new/change) *requirements* (functional and non-functional), and ii) *defect repairs* (fixed defects in former product variants).
- **Technical task:** fundamental working unit accomplished by one developer. In most cases requirements mandates several realization steps that requires cooperation of some developers. Proper coordination requires individually realizable working units thus each *requirement* and *defect repairs* should be broken down into several technical tasks. Technical tasks usually requires some working hour (*Wh*) realization effort that is estimated by developers.
- **Precedence:** realization precedences between *features*. Precedences emanate from the following sources (j', j denotes technical tasks) [18,17]:
  i) *functional implication* (j demands j' to function),
  ii) *cost-based dependency* (j' influences the implementation cost of j, so useful to realize j' earlier),
  iii) *time-related dependency* (expresses technological / organizational demands).

These concepts not only help to identify the objects and the subject of the optimization model but with the precise relationships it can also be used as database schema definition for an agile planning and scheduling application.

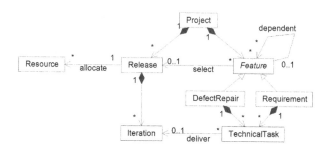

Fig. 3. Information Model of Agile Planning

3.2 Mapping Iteration Scheduling to RCPSP

In the following analogy between iteration planning and resource-constrained project scheduling optimization problem (RCPSP) is presented [27]. Generally, scheduling concerns the allocation of limited resources (manpower) to tasks over time in order to fulfill the predefined scheduling objective. In fact, many different objectives are possible – depending on the goals of the decision makers – but our aim is to 'maximize stakeholders' satisfaction in least time possible' (Sec. 2.1), thus the *makespan minimization* (i.e. finding the minimum execution time) is the most adequate. As agile methods recommend collaborative teamwork – without any development role (such as analyst, programmer, tester) – we only identify one kind of resource: the *developer*. The complexity of scheduling arises from the interaction between tasks by *implicit* and *explicit* dependencies. While the previous is given by scarcity of resources, the latter is emerged from different precedences (Sec. 3.1) between tasks that define the routing of the tasks [17].

To provide suitable scheduling method for wide-ranging iteration scheduling situations, we extended the ordinary RCPS problem with i) *pre-assignments* (i.e. assigning certain tasks to resources before scheduling) and ii) *timeboxed* iteration duration control. On the one hand, defect corrections and onward development of a formerly delivered functionalities legitimates *pre-assignments*, on the other hand, *timeboxed* iteration execution mandates an upper boundary control in time – which is not allowed to be exceeded otherwise schedule is treated infeasible.

3.3 Formulating RCPSP Model

Let $\mathcal{R}$ be the set of resources i and the following typical properties for scheduling be interpreted on technical tasks to schedule them (i.e. $j \in A$) [27]:

Effort: d_j – time estimation (in hours) is associated with each task. It is calculated by simple expert estimation (e.g. 2,4, or 8 working hour (Wh)).
Pre-assignment: a_j – in some cases resource pre-assignment is applied before scheduling. It is used by the scheduler algorithm during resource allocation.

Let the vector $S = (S_0, S_1, ..., S_{n+1})$ be start times for tasks' realizations – where $S_j \geqslant 0 : j \in A$ and $S_0 = 0$. The vector S is called a *schedule* of development.

In this definition the 0 and $n+1$ are auxiliary elements to represent iteration beginning and termination, respectively.

Temporal and Resource Constraints. Dependencies (temporal constraints – c.f. Sec. 3.1) can be defined by *precedence relations* (Eq. 1):

$$S_j - S_{j'} + d_{j'} \geqslant P_{j',j} \qquad : j',j \in A \tag{1}$$

Let the $R_i \in \mathbb{N}$ is a set of capacities of resources that have been assigned to the project. The effort estimation yields resource requirements $r_{j,i} \in \mathbb{Z}$ for each task j and each resource i. Now let S be some schedule and let t be some point in time. Then let $\mathcal{A}(S,t) \triangleq \{j \in A \,|\, S_j \leqslant t \leqslant S_j + d_j\}$ be the *active set of tasks* being in progress at time t. The corresponding requirement for resource $i \in \mathcal{R}$ at time t is given by $r_i(S,t) \triangleq \sum_{j \in \mathcal{A}(S,t)} r_{j,i}$. As a consequence, the resource constraints can be treated as follows (Eq. 2):

$$r_i(S,t) \leqslant R_i \qquad : i \in \mathcal{R} \tag{2}$$

Optimization Model. With the application of previous elements, RCPSP for iteration scheduling can be formulated as follows:

$$\text{Minimize } z = S_{n+1} \tag{3a}$$

subject to

$$S_j - S_{j'} + d_{j'} \geqslant P_{j',j} \qquad\qquad : j,j' \in A \tag{3b}$$
$$r_i(S,t) \leqslant R_i \qquad\qquad\qquad : i \in \mathcal{R} \tag{3c}$$
$$S_{n+1} \leqslant c \tag{3d}$$

where Eq. 3b, 3c are scheduling constraints (c.f. Eq. 1, 2), Eq. 3d is the timebox duration, and Eq. 3a is the makespan minimization objective.

3.4   Solving Iteration Scheduling

For the previous optimization model we developed an innovative scheduling algorithm. It is a constructive heuristic algorithm, which iteratively selects and assigns *technical tasks* to *resources*. In the program listing (Algorithm 1) lower-case/uppercase letters with indices denote vectors/matrices (e.g. $r_i, P_{j,j'}$). While bold-faced types show concise (without indices) forms (e.g. $\mathbf{P}$).

In the *require* section the preconditions are given. The vector $\mathbf{r}$ indicates the available resources (developers) in the iteration. Each d_j is the planned effort (duration) for technical task j – both development and defect correction. Every element of vector a_j contains a reference to a resource index ($a_j \in \{1..|\mathbf{r}|\}$) which indicates resource pre-assignment to task j. The $a_j = 0$ means that task j is not pre-assigned, thus the algorithm will find the best resource to its realization. Precedences between tasks (c.f. Eq. 3b) can be represented by a precedence matrix where $P_{j,j'} = 1$ means that task j precedes task j', otherwise $P_{j,j'} = 0$.

Algorithm 1. *List scheduling* algorithm with AF strategy
Require:

$r_i \in N, c \in N$ /* resources and iteration duration */
$a_j \in N : a_j \in \{1..|\mathbf{r}|\}, d_j \in N$ /* pre-assignments and duration of tasks */
$P_{j,j'} \in 0, 1 \wedge P_{j,j} = 0 \wedge P$ is DAG   /* precedences */

Ensure:

$S_{i,j} \in 0, 1 \wedge \forall j \exists! i \; S_{i,j} = 1$

```
 1: m ⇐ length(r), n ⇐ length(d)           /* number of resources and tasks */
 2: S ⇐ [0]_{m,n}                           /* assignment matrix initialization */
 3: rlist ⇐ ∅, slist ⇐ ∅       /* 'ready list' and 'scheduled list' initialization */
 4: for fj = 0 to n do
 5:    pot ⇐ findNotPrecedentedTasks (P)       /* find potentially tasks */
 6:    rlist ⇐ pot \ slist                     /* construct ready list */
 7:    if rlist == ∅ then
 8:       return ∅                             /* No schedulable task */
 9:    end if
10:    j ⇐ max {a_j} : j ∈ rlist           /* select a task using AF strategy */
11:    if a_j == 0 then
12:       i ⇐ selectMinLoadedResource (S)           /* without assignment */
13:    else
14:       i ⇐ a_j                                    /* with assignment */
15:    end if
16:    l ⇐ sum (S_{i,{1..n}})              /* calculate load of resource i */
17:    if (l + d_j) > c then
18:       return ∅                          /* Overloaded iteration */
19:    end if
20:    p ⇐ findNextPos (S, i)                     /* index for next task */
21:    S_{i,p} ⇐ j                 /* assign task j to resource i at position p */
22:    slist ⇐ slist ∪ {j}             /* add task j to 'scheduled list' */
23:    P_{{1,...,n},j} = 0         /* delete precedence related to scheduled task */
24: end for
25: return S
```

Both conditions $P_{j,j} = 0$ (no loop) and P is directed acyclic graph (DAG) ensures that temporal constraints are not trivially unsatisfiable. Iteration timebox is asserted by variable c. It it is used as an upperbound in resource allocation to prevent resources overloading. The result of the algorithm is a schedule matrix $\mathbf{S}$, where rows represent resources, and columns give an order of task execution. Thus $S_{i,p} = j$ means that task j is assigned to resource i at position p. The *ensure* section prescribes the postcondition on the return value ($\mathbf{S}$): every task j has to be assigned to exactly one resource i.

During scheduling steps, first the initial values are set (line $1 - 3$). The iteration value (n) is equal to the number of technical tasks (line 1). The algorithm uses a *ready list* (**rlist**) and a *scheduled list* (**slist**) to keep track of schedulable and scheduled tasks. *Potentially* schedulable tasks (**pot**) are unscheduled tasks from which the algorithm can choose in the current control step without violating any precedence constraint (line 5). Previously assigned tasks are subtracted from **pot** to form the ready list (line 6). As long as the ready list contains schedulable tasks, the algorithm chooses tasks from it – otherwise the schedule is infeasible (line 7) and as a consequence the algorithm aborts (line 8).

To select the next task to schedule from concurrently schedulable tasks (i.e. ready list) we constructed the custom 'Assigned First' *scheduling rule* (line 10) (c.f. Sec. 3.2). This rule chooses from the pre-assigned tasks ($a_j > 0$) before the unassigned ones ($a_j = 0$). As the selection sequence is discretionary we applied the *max* function to the choice. After selection the minimal loaded (min summa duration) resource is allocated to the selected task unless the task is pre-assigned to a given resource (line $11-15$) (c.f. Sec. 3.2). If the load of the resource i exceeds iteration timebox (c) then the schedule is treated infeasible (line $16 - 19$).

The following step is to find the index of next task position (p) (right after the previous task's index) at resource i (line 20) for task j for assignment (line 21). Finally, scheduled list (**slist**), is updated with scheduled task (lines 22), and no longer valid precedence relations are also deleted from **P** (lines 23). Iteration proceeds until all items are assigned to iterations (line $4 - 24$). After termination, **S** contains the task assignments to resources and the makespan is
$$z \Leftarrow \max_{i=1..m} \sum_{p=1}^{n} d_{S_{i,p}} - \text{c.f. Eq. 3a}.$$

Solution Analysis. This greedy strategy makes a series of local decisions, selecting at each point the best step without backtracking or lookahead. Thus local decisions miss the global optimal solution, but produce quick (time complexity is clearly $O(n + m)$) and usually sufficient results for practical applications.

Figure 4 illustrates the application of the algorithm on real application development data which was extracted from the backlog of IRIS at Multilogic [28]. The figure shows post-mortem scheduling result of an iteration – visualized by resource aspect Gantt diagram – where tasks' realizations plotted against time. The diagram points out that 94 tasks (with 2, 4, and 8 working hours (Wh)) are allocated to 6 resources, and the makespan is 78.

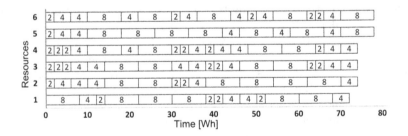

Fig. 4. Generated Iteration Schedule

3.5   Tool Support

Previously presented theoretical foundation is realized by our MS Sharepoint-based website at Multilogic and our scheduling toolbox on the Matlab platform [29,28,30]. Sharepoint is browser-based collaboration and a document-management platform, and its capability includes creating different lists (as database tables) – such as list of technical tasks and resources. The previously constructed agile planning information model (see Fig. 3) were implemented as Sharepoint lists. Thus, the portal was targeted as a collaborative workspace for developers, and a tool for the management to collect all planning information. With this web-based tool, developers can break-down requirements into technical tasks, indicate precedences, set effort estimation, status of tasks/defect corrections and they also can share these information to facilitate communication. Additionally, we have implemented the presented algorithm in Matlab to support iteration decisions based on data collected through the Sharepoint site.

4   Experiments

To evaluate our proposed scheduling method simulations were carried out. Applying the historical iteration planning data, as an input for the scheduling algorithm, made it possible to compare them [31]. The four past data sets extracted from the backlog of IRIS application that is developed by Multilogic Ltd [28].

In this section, first we set research questions, then present necessary background information, and finally we present and interpret our findings.

4.1   Research Questions

Our initial intend (see Sec. 1 **P1-3**) was to support decisions in agile iteration scheduling in the following aspects: 1) dealing with precedences, 2) tracking workloads, and 3) providing optimal (makespan minimized) delivery plan. To validate our proposed method the next questions were addressed: *How does optimization-based iteration scheduling compare with informal one in terms of* **Q1**) *resource workload over time,* **Q2**) *quality and* **Q3**) *feasibility of the plans.*

4.2   Context and Methodology

IRIS is a client risk management system (approx. 2 million SLOC) for credit institutions for analyzing the non-payment risk of clients. It has been continual evolution since its first release in the middle of 90s. The system was written in Visual Basic and C# the applied methodology was a custom agile process.

The planning process were made up of the following steps. First, during *release planning*, the requirements were selected (expressed in User stories [9]) from the backlog – considering stakeholders' demands. Then every User story was estimated by the team and distributed into iterations taking resources, precedences and iteration timebox into account. Second, during *iteration planning*, each User

Story was broken down into technical tasks and important defect corrections were also selected to the next product increment. Finally, resource allocation was determined intuitively by the team in intuitive way and the conflicts (precedences, resource overload) were managed during *daily meetings* (see Fig. 1).

4.3   Data Collection and Results

Four data sets (four iterations $(I_1^A, I_2^A, I_1^B, I_2^B)$ of two releases (R_A, R_B)) were selected to make a comparison between the algorithmic and the intuitive method. All iterations had same project members (6 developers /*Dev.*/), iteration length (80 working hours (2 weeks) /*IL*/), domain, customer, and development methodology, but they were characterized by different number of technical tasks (development /*DT*/ and defect correction /*CT*/ with 2, 4 and $8Wh$), User Stories /*US*/, precedences /*Prec.*/, and pre-assignments /*Ass.*/. Table 1 summarizes *state variables* that were used to capture facts that were likely affect the findings. These variables were collected from the SharePoint-based backlog.

Table 1. Iteration Planning Data

	Dev.	IL	US	DT	CT	TT = DT + CT	Prec.	Ass.
I_1^A	6	80 Wh	28	91(25,34,32)	3(2,1,0)	94(27,35,32)	11	19
I_2^A	6	80 Wh	35	89(16,46,27)	2(0,2,0)	91(16,48,27)	5	17
I_1^B	6	80 Wh	33	84(29,24,31)	5(2,1,2)	89(31,25,33)	15	22
I_2^B	6	80 Wh	34.5	79(13,31,35)	7(4,2,1)	86(17,33,36)	4	16

We constructed *Task effort* (TE_i) *response variables* to test **Q1**. This simple variable is computed by adding up estimated tasks' efforts that were assigned to resources i. Explanations of **Q2**, and **Q3** were produced with the utilization of the solution's inherent properties.

4.4   Analysis

To answer to the questions **Q1-3** simulations were performed on the previously described input data to compare the characteristics of the two approaches. The simulation output is summarized in Table 2.

On the left the four historical iteration schedules are presented $(I_1^A, I_2^A, I_1^B$ and $I_2^B)$. In the table D_is denote resources (developers); 2, 4, and 8 values are estimated effort (instead of indeces) of task realizations; and finally the previously introduced response variable (TE_i) can be seen. On the right column simulation results $(^*I_1^A, {}^*I_2^A, {}^*I_1^B$, and $^*I_2^B)$ are presented.

To compare the intuitive and the algorithmic cases quantitative (statistical) analysis were performed on the two response variables $(^*TE_i$ and $TE_i)$. The result is presented in Table 3 and summarized in boxplot (see Fig. 5).

From these, we conclude that optimized case i) did not exceed the time-box limit $(^*Max = 78Wh < 80Wh < Max = 102)$ which means lower level scheduling risk; ii) has less dispersion in total task allocation $(^*Std.dev = 3$ vs.

Table 2. Intuitive (left) and Optimized (right) Schedules

I_1^A	Schedule	TE_i	$*I_1^A$	Schedule	$*TE_i$
D_1	2 2 2 2 4 4 4 4 4 8 8 8 8 8 8 8 - -	84	D_1	8 4 2 8 8 8 8 2 2 4 4 2 8 8 4 - - - - -	72
D_2	2 2 4 4 4 4 4 4 8 8 8 8 8 8 8 - - -	84	D_2	2 4 4 4 8 8 2 2 4 8 8 8 8 4 - - - - -	74
D_3	2 2 2 2 2 2 2 4 4 4 4 8 8 - - - - -	46	D_3	2 2 2 4 4 8 8 4 4 2 2 4 8 8 8 2 2 4 4 -	74
D_4	2 2 2 2 2 4 4 4 4 4 4 4 8 8 8 - -	70	D_4	2 2 2 4 8 4 8 2 2 4 2 4 4 8 8 2 4 4 -	74
D_5	2 2 2 4 4 4 4 8 8 8 8 8 8 8 8 8 8 -	102	D_5	2 4 4 8 8 8 8 4 8 4 8 4 8 - - - - - -	78
D_6	2 2 2 2 2 2 2 4 4 4 4 4 4 4 4 8 8 -	64	D_6	2 4 4 8 4 8 2 4 8 4 2 4 8 2 2 4 8 - -	78
I_2^A		**450**	$*I_2^A$		**450**
D_1	2 2 2 2 2 2 4 4 4 4 4 8 8 8 8 - - -	64	D_1	2 4 4 4 8 8 8 2 8 4 4 8 8 - - - - - -	72
D_2	2 2 2 2 2 2 2 4 4 4 8 8 8 8 8 - - -	66	D_2	2 4 4 4 8 8 8 2 2 4 8 4 2 2 4 8 - - -	74
D_3	2 2 2 2 2 2 4 4 4 4 8 8 8 - - - - -	52	D_3	8 8 2 2 4 2 2 2 8 4 4 8 8 4 - - - - -	66
D_4	2 2 2 4 4 4 4 4 8 8 8 8 8 8 8 8 - -	90	D_4	4 8 8 8 8 2 4 4 2 8 8 8 - - - - - - -	72
D_5	2 2 2 4 4 4 4 8 8 8 8 8 8 8 8 8 - -	90	D_5	8 8 8 2 2 2 8 4 4 2 2 2 4 2 2 2 8 - -	70
D_6	2 2 2 2 2 2 4 4 4 8 8 8 8 8 - - - -	64	D_6	4 8 2 2 2 4 8 2 2 2 4 2 8 4 8 2 8 - -	72
I_1^B		**426**	$*I_1^B$		**426**
D_1	2 2 2 4 4 4 4 4 4 4 8 8 8 8 - - - -	66	D_1	2 4 4 4 8 4 8 4 2 4 8 4 8 4 4 - - - -	72
D_2	2 2 2 2 4 4 4 4 4 4 8 8 8 8 - - - -	64	D_2	4 2 2 4 4 8 2 4 4 4 2 4 8 4 8 4 8 - -	76
D_3	4 4 4 4 4 4 4 4 4 4 8 8 8 - - - - -	68	D_3	4 4 4 4 2 4 4 4 4 8 4 8 8 2 4 8 - - -	76
D_4	2 2 2 4 4 4 4 4 4 4 8 8 8 8 8 8 - -	82	D_4	4 4 8 8 8 4 8 8 8 2 2 4 8 - - - - - -	76
D_5	2 2 4 4 4 4 4 4 8 8 8 8 8 8 - - -	84	D_5	4 4 8 2 4 8 4 8 4 2 2 4 8 4 4 - - - -	70
D_6	2 2 2 2 4 4 4 4 4 4 4 4 4 4 4 8 8 8	76	D_6	2 4 4 4 8 2 8 4 2 4 8 4 8 4 4 - - - -	70
I_2^B		**440**	$*I_2^B$		**440**
D_1	4 4 4 4 4 4 4 4 4 4 4 - - - - - - -	44	D_1	4 4 4 8 2 4 8 8 8 4 8 2 4 4 - - - - -	72
D_2	2 2 2 2 2 4 4 8 8 8 8 8 8 8 8 - - - -	74	D_2	4 4 4 4 4 2 8 2 4 4 4 4 8 4 2 8 4 8 - -	78
D_3	2 2 2 4 4 8 8 8 8 8 8 8 8 - - - - -	78	D_3	8 8 8 8 8 4 8 8 8 8 - - - - - - - - -	76
D_4	4 4 4 4 4 4 4 4 8 8 8 8 8 8 8 - - -	88	D_4	4 4 4 8 2 8 2 8 4 8 8 8 - - - - - -	76
D_5	2 2 2 2 2 4 4 4 4 8 8 8 8 8 8 8 - -	82	D_5	2 2 4 4 4 4 2 8 2 8 4 2 2 2 4 8 2 4 8	82
D_6	2 2 2 2 4 4 4 4 4 4 8 8 8 8 8 8 8 8 -	88	D_6	2 4 8 8 8 4 8 8 4 8 2 4 8 - - - - - -	76
		454			**454**

Table 3. Comparison of Schedules

	Mean	Median	Min	Max	Std.dev.	c_v
I_{1-2}^{A-B}	75	73.7	44	102	14.6	0.1976
$*I_{1-2}^{A-B}$	74	73.7	66	78	3.0	0.0410

$Std.dev = 14.6$); iii) yields more balanced workload on resources – while the means are similar ($*Mean = 74 \approx Mean = 75$). As a consequence, in terms of coefficient variation (i.e. normalized measure of dispersion), the optimization-based scheduling provides $c_v/*c_v = \frac{Std.dev}{Mean} / \frac{*Std.dev}{*Mean} = \frac{0.1976}{0.0410} \approx 5$ times more balanced resource workload over time contrary to the intuitive method (c.f. **Q1**).

The algorithmic method easily resolves complex decision situation – as it handles precedences between tasks and avoids resource workloads – contrary to the intuitive case where these are managed intuitively during daily meeting. As a consequence these two capabilities of the algorithmic method ensure higher quality and lower-risk feasible plans in contrast to the intuitive case (c.f. **Q2-3**).

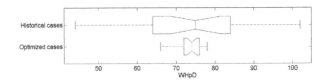

Fig. 5. Boxplots of Intuitive (above) and Optimized (below)

5   Discussion

First we constructed a general agile planning information model – including both releases and iterations – that helped us to identify the objects and the subject of our proposed optimization model. Its precise relationships can also be used as database schema definition for an agile planning and scheduling application such as our Sharepoint-based prototypic tool for collaborative data collection.

Then we formulated iteration scheduling model as a special case of RCPS problem to provide decision support in feature implementation sequencing. The formulated model considers temporal constraints (Sec. 3.1, 3.3), team's resources, and defines makespan minimization scheduling objective. As a matter of fact many different objectives are possible – depending on the goals of the decision makers – but in our scheduling case ('maximize stakeholders' satisfaction in least time possible') the makespan minimization is the most adequate. This interpretation of iteration schedule makes it possible to adapt extremely successful heuristic algorithms applied for solving RCPSP. To provide suitable scheduling method for wide-ranging iteration scheduling situations we extended the ordinary RCPS problem with i) pre-assignments (i.e. assigning certain tasks to resources before scheduling) and ii) timeboxed iteration duration control.

Generally, RCPS problems are combinatorial NP-hard problems and a variety approximation algorithms are proposed. The most popular heuristics in approximation algorithms are SPT or LTP (Shortest/Longest Processing Time first) [27]. However, we constructed and applied our AF *assigned task first* scheduling rule demanded by pre-assignments (defect corrections and onward development of a formerly delivered functionalities). Our proposed combinatorial algorithm is capable to provide acceptable results with good time complexity ($O(n + m)$) for practical applications.

This approach gives the business increased visibility, and it can also provide constantly up-to-date schedule decision support considering changes necessitated by shifting business priorities. Moreover, the decision maker can accommodate quick what-if scenarios and replanning on-the-fly. However, as our simulation carried out post mortem analysis, examination of the method is recommended in real development cases in order to investigate it in dynamical situations.

6 Conclusions

The growing pressure to reduce costs, time-to-market and to improve quality catalyzes transitions to more automated methods and tools in software engineering to support release-centered decisions [15]. In agile environments, which recommends small and iterative software releases, the decision is even more difficult due to the perpetual changes in requirements, constraints and objectives. To address this situation, we have presented a method including an information model to specify data semantics for agile planning, and an innovative heuristic scheduling algorithm for wide-ranging agile iteration scheduling problems. To evaluate our method four simulations were carried out that demonstrated how the method could 1) significantly improve load balancing of resources (cca. $5\times$), 2) produce higher quality and lower-risk feasible schedule, and 3) provide more informed and established decisions to agile teams.

We think that our proposed method is a plain combination of the present theories and methods, thus it lead us to generalize our findings beyond the result of the simulations.

Acknowledgements. The development is supported in part by the GVOP grant (GVOP-3.3.3-05/1.-2005-05-0046/3.0) and realized by the Multilogic Ltd [28].

References

1. Dybå, T., Dingsøyr, T.: Empirical studies of agile software development: A systematic review. Information & Software Technology 50, 833–859 (2008)
2. Ambler, S.W.: Survey says: Agile works in practice. Dr. Dobb's Journal (2006), http://www.ddj.com
3. Chow, T., Cao, D.B.: A survey study of critical success factors in agile software projects. Journal of System and Software 81, 961–971 (2008)
4. Layman, L., Williams, L., Cunningham, L.: Motivations and measurements in an agile case study. Journal of Systems Architecture 52, 654–667 (2006)
5. Manifesto for agile software development, http://www.agilemanifesto.org
6. Declaration of interdependence for agile software project management, http://pmdoi.org
7. Scott, W., Ambler, P.K.: Lean development governance. Technical report, IBM Rational Software (2007)
8. Qumer, A., Henderson-Sellers, B.: An evaluation of the degree of agility in six agile methods and its applicability for method engineering. Information & Software Technology 50, 280–295 (2008)
9. Cohn, M.: Agile Estimating and Planning. Prentice Hall PTR, Upper Saddle River (2005)
10. Dubakov, M., Stevens, P.: Agile Tools: The good, the bad, the ugly. Agile Journal (2008), http://www.agilejournal.com
11. Microsoft office project, sdk (2003), http://msdn2.microsoft.com
12. Rally homepage, http://www.rallydev.com
13. Xplanner homepage, http://xplanner.codehaus.org

14. Ruhe, G., Saliu, M.: The art and science of software release planning. IEEE Software 22, 47–53 (2005)
15. Aurum, A., Wohlin, C.: The fundamental nature of requirements engineering activities as a decision-making process. Information & Software Technology 45, 945–954 (2003)
16. Karlsson, L., Thelin, T., Regnell, B., Berander, P., Wohlin, C.: Pair-wise comparisons versus planning game partitioning–experiments on requirements prioritisation techniques. Empirical Software Engineering 12, 3–33 (2007)
17. Carlshamre, P., Sandahl, K., Lindvall, M., Regnell, B., Dag, J.: An industrial survey of requirements interdependencies in software product release planning. In: RE 2001: Proceedings of the Fifth IEEE International Symposium on Requirements Engineering, pp. 84–93. IEEE Press, Los Alamitos (2001)
18. Li, C., van den Akker, J.M., Brinkkemper, S., Diepen, G.: Integrated requirement selection and scheduling for the release planning of a software product. In: Sawyer, P., Paech, B., Heymans, P. (eds.) REFSQ 2007. LNCS, vol. 4542, pp. 93–108. Springer, Heidelberg (2007)
19. Boehm, B.W., Horowitz, E., Madachy, R., Reifer, D., Clark, B.K., Steece, B., Brown, W.A., Chulani, S., Abts, C.: Software Cost Estimation with Cocomo II. Prentice Hall PTR, Englewood Cliffs (2000)
20. Jung, H.W.: Optimizing value and cost in requirements analysis. IEEE Software 15, 74–78 (1998)
21. van den Akker, M., Brinkkemper, S., Diepen, G., Versendaal, J.: Software product release planning through optimization and what-if analysis. Information & Software Technology 50, 101–111 (2008)
22. Denne, M., Cleland-Huang, J.: The incremental funding method: Data-driven software development. IEEE Software 21, 39–47 (2004)
23. Szoke, A.: A proposed method for release planning from use case-based requirements. In: Euromicro SEAA 2008: Proceedings of the 34th Euromicro Conference, pp. 449–456. IEEE Press, Los Alamitos (2008)
24. Larman, C.: Agile and Iterative Development: A Manager's Guide. Pearson Education, London (2003)
25. Ambler, S.W., Jeffries, R.: Agile modeling: effective practices for extreme programming and the unified process. John Wiley & Sons Inc., New York (2002)
26. Unified modeling language version 2.0, http://www.uml.org
27. Schwindt, C.: Resource Allocation in Project Management. Springer, Heidelberg (2005)
28. Multilogic homepage, http://www.multilogic.hu
29. Microsoft sharepoint (2007), http://www.microsoft.com/sharepoint/
30. Mathworks homepage, http://www.mathworks.com/
31. Kellner, M., Madachy, R., Raffo, D.: Software process simulation modeling: Why? what? how? Journal of Systems and Software 46, 91–105 (1999)

Some Findings Concerning Requirements in *Agile* Methodologies

Pilar Rodríguez, Agustín Yagüe, Pedro P. Alarcón, and Juan Garbajosa

Technical University of Madrid (UPM)
SYST Research Group
E.U. Informatica. Ctra. Valencia Km. 7. E-28031 Madrid
prodriguez@syst.eui.upm.es, agustin.yague@upm.es,
{pedrop.alarcon,jgs}@eui.upm.es

Abstract. Agile methods have appeared as an attractive alternative to conventional methodologies. These methods try to reduce the time to market and, indirectly, the cost of the product through flexible development and deep customer involvement. The processes related to requirements have been extensively studied in literature, in most cases in the frame of conventional methods. However, conclusions of conventional methodologies could not be necessarily valid for Agile; in some issues, conventional and Agile processes are radically different. As recent surveys report, inadequate project requirements is one of the most conflictive issues in agile approaches and better understanding about this is needed. This paper describes some findings concerning requirements activities in a project developed under an agile methodology. The project intended to evolve an existing product and, therefore, some background information was available. The major difficulties encountered were related to non-functional needs and management of requirements dependencies.

1 Introduction

Software industry is facing the fact that time to market is progressively becoming shorter. Agile approaches appeared as an attractive alternative to adapt the development to the unavoidable market changes, characterized by a continuous dynamism and variability [1]. Agile methods are suitable when the customer needs are quickly emerging and changing [2,3]. Their popularity is growing as they are able to better meet customer needs, improved quality software, faster time to delivery and lower development cost [4]. Assessments of agile in relation with other process models can be found in literature [5,6,7].

The experience that is being obtained from scaling up agile process models to large industrial projects and organizations [8][1] is showing us a radical breach between agile and other more conventional or traditional approaches. Agile process models, differently from more conventional software engineering process models, are structured into values, principles and practices [9,10]. As reported in [8] one

---

[1] This article develops Katti Vilki's keynote presentation at *Agile* 2008 Conference.

F. Bomarius et al. (Eds.): PROFES 2009, LNBIP 32, pp. 171–184, 2009.
© Springer-Verlag Berlin Heidelberg 2009

of the reasons for this breach can be understood by the required application of agile values and principles to large projects and organizations; and not so much by the already well known practices such as continuous integration, integrated testing, or incremental delivery.

As it is nowadays accepted, the product quality is particularly dependent on how requirements engineering practices have been performed [11,12]. In [13,14] the differences between requirements specification in conventional and agile approaches are analyzed. Conventional methodologies are focused on *anticipation abilities* and can be termed as *plan based* [15,16] because these process models are defined in such a way that the later an error is discovered, the more expensive will be to correct it. They intend to identify a complete set of requirements in the requirement phase, what is always difficult to achieve. Once requirement phase is ended changes are always regarded as negative. Defining this complete set of requirements is essential for the soundness of the project, and if the problem domain is not well defined, this will affect negatively to the rest of the project [17,18,19]. As opposed to this, agile methods perceive each change like a chance to improve the system and increase the customer satisfaction. So, *responding to change over following a plan*[9] is one of the agile values. Agile teams do not try to avoid changes but try to understand what is behind them, seek to *embrace* them; the resulting set of requirements, after introducing a change, will be evaluated and rated searching for those requirements that will deliver the highest value to the customer. Therefore, change is considered as a normal and characteristic condition of software development.

One of the main aims of agile methods is to reduce the cost caused by these changes in requirements simplifying the requirements management and documentation tasks. Agile methods promote a fast and continuous communication between customers and development team. Face to face communication and frequent feedback are the most significant practices concerning to requirements engineering in these approaches [20]. The definition of tasks related to requirements is very often kept informal in agile approaches. Therefore, although there are evidences of the advantages that agile methodologies provide in small-scale projects, it is still difficult to scale to large projects applying among others the principle *responding to change over following a plan*.

Being Agile a relative young process model, there are few studies with relevant results about the elicitation and management of requirements. However, a recent survey [4] points out that inadequate project requirements and instability of requirements are among the important limitations of agile methods currently. Other papers, such as [20,13,21,22,23,24] report some problems in this area but do not analyze them in depth. Some of the open issues in agile methodologies concern elicitation of non-functional requirements and requirements documentation tasks.

In practice there are not studies that compare empirical results of agile and conventional projects referred to the same product. It is clear that it would be expensive to have two teams developing the same product. However in our case we had the opportunity to monitor the agile evolution of an existing product,

TOPENprimer, developed initially following a conventional approach. The existing requirements specification had been performed in compliance with IEEE[2] requirements specification standard 830-1998[25]. This was a good opportunity to get a better understanding of how Agile manages customer needs. That is how we were able to isolate specific requirements, understand the impact of missing requirements that were not identified at the supposedly appropriate moment of the agile development process. The study was performed considering the background on qualitative methods presented in [26].

The remainder of the paper is organized into four sections: Section 2 discusses related work about requirements engineering in agile approaches. Section 3 describes the case study in which the work is based and the process used in the development. Section 4, illustrates the identified issues with specific examples. Section 5 provides a reflection on the implications of the identified issues and possible correction mechanisms. Finally, Section 6 summarizes the findings and elaborate on future work.

2   Background and Related Work

Although some authors assert that agile methodologies are just old wine in new bottles [3], other studies show that product development in agile environments is very different to that in conventional environments [11,13,14,28]. Several experience reports, such as [29,30,31,32], describe success stories of using agile approaches. However, they do not usually provide enough context information or are merely a *lessons learned* report based on expert opinions do not focused on requirements. Others are designed to give recommendations and general rules for the agile methodologies use [3,33,34]. Requirements Engineering (RE) activities are considered critical to any software development process. It has been recognized that problems associated with the requirements area are among the major reason for software project failures [35,4]. The effort to explore and refine RE has grown up in the last years, as is pointed out by Nuseibeh in [11] and Cheng and Atlee in [12] in their studies about the current and the future in RE. However, there are still few studies about how real agile projects identify and manage the customer needs, and some authors suggest that the key issue is this [36]. Detractors argue that the quest for speed in software development may have the undesirable effect of weakening principles of purposefulness, appropriateness and truthfulness [37]. In contrast, current studies begin to identify and give solutions to existing problems. For example, in [21] to make an explicit requirements stage with customer is proposed or in [36] to add a conventional requirements stage. Araujo proposes to incorporate aspect orientation concepts in [38], in [39] it is proposed to deal with crosscutting requirements and in [40] to establish traceability. Other studies such as [22] are focused on giving high-level recommendations about identification and definition of customer needs in

---

[2] IEEE: Institute of Electrical and Electronics Engineers, Inc.

[3] Adapted from "Is Extreme Programming Just Old Wine in New Bottles: A Comparison of Two Cases" [27].

agile. In [41] the result of an experiment about the application of Requirements Interaction Management (RIM) process is showed. This study proposes changes in the agile requirement process, particularly in eXtreme Programming. Other publications, such as [20,13] identify some of the presented aspects in this paper but without going into them and point out the need to explicitly consider non-functional requirements management in Agile. However, none of these studies had the opportunity of compare the result of an agile and a conventional project referred to the same product as it is the case of this work. And finally, several studies such as [42,41,43,44] have been focused on interaction requirements and the conflicts related to this interaction. However, they are mostly focused on conventional methodologies.

3 Case Study: From TOPENprimer to TOPENbiogas

In this section we will provide a description of the case study in which the work is based. Subsection 3.1 describes the features of the product that has been evolved. The objective is to describe the project scope. In subsection 3.2, the used process is briefly described, focusing on the activities about customer needs management. Finally, in subsection 3.3 a list of some features existing in the initial product that were dropped in result product is presented; also a list of new features is included.

3.1 The Evolution Product Description

The case study was focused on the evolution of *TOPENprimer*. TOPENprimer was developed under a conventional methodology. It is based on the TOPEN (*Test Operation ENvironment*) architecture [45], that defines a domain specific environment for testing, monitoring and operating complex systems. TOPEN architecture is made up of four distributed components: *Topen Engine* is the kernel architecture. *Mission Information Base(MIB)* contains the database and the business rules. *Gateway* is the element that interacts with the *System Under Test (SUT)*. And, finally, *TOE* is the user graphical interface. TOPEN follows a software product line approach [45] and it is specially designed to be adaptable to different application domains with a limited cost. For this reason, the evolution to a new domain implied, in general, a well-identified number of changes. On the one hand, this limits the scope of the study but, on the other, makes the study manageable. However taking advantage of the agile approach no feature was taken for granted in advance. The project consisted in the required evolution of TOPENprimer to support a new application domain. The target application domain was a biogas power production plant that had to be tested and monitored. *TOPENbiogas* was the result product in this project. In parallel, a biogas power plant simulator was developed in order to validate TOPENbiogas before its deployment in the real plant. More details about the evolution project are available in [46]. Some features of the product scope are shown in table 1.

Table 1. Characteristics of initial product TOPENprimer

Contextual Factor	Characteristic Product	TOPENprimer
Structure	Architecture	Four distributed components
Size	System Code Lines	30667
	Number of classes	216
	Code Lines	MIB: 7779
	by Component	TopenEngine:8372
		Gateway: 907
		TOE: 13609
	Number of classes	MIB: 48
	by component	TopenEngine: 55
		Gateway: 10
		TOE: 103
Technical Factors	Programming Language	Java
	Communication	Sockets, RMI

3.2 The *Agile* Development Process Description

The work reported here has been carried out within *ITEA2 Flexi project* [47]. Scrum [48] was used as the management methodology as it widely extended and Flexi partners were familiar with it. The constant feedback loops constitute the core element of the methodology. The development process is divided into short iterations called sprints. Figure 1 shows the Scrum project cycle. The sprint starts with a *planning* and finishes with *review and retrospective* stages. Features to be implemented in the system are registered in an artifact called *Product Backlog* (PB). In our case each feature was defined of a simple and clear way in form of *User Story* [49], in business language and prioritized by business value. At the beginning of each sprint, the Product Owner decides which PB

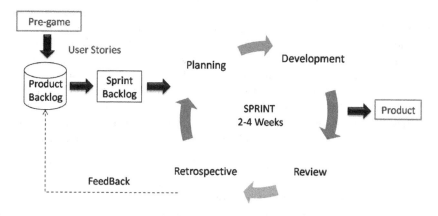

Fig. 1. *Agile* Development Model with SCRUM

items should be developed in that sprint. As can be seen in figure 1, there is not a specific task to pick up requirements. Pre-game is the most approximate stage because of its aims. In this stage, the scrum team, together with the customer, prepares a list of needs that the system should have in form of user stories.

3.3   Some New and Dropped Features

Some of the original TOPENprimer functionalities were modified. *Manager* facility was removed. *Managers* would have implemented operation views of the biogas plant; this feature is required to support cooperation of several stakeholders, e.g. an operator and an engineer. This could have been useful but it could be considered in a future upgraded version. A second issue was the Biogas plant visualization. Though the graphical user interface was important, it was agreed to postpone its implementation. A third issue was a Natural language facility. In TOPENprimer test/operation procedures are translated into natural language; the implementation of this feature was postponed. Finally, Operation Commands had some changes because some elements of the test/operation language (i.e. wait, for, repeat until, while, createNE or deleteNE) were not supported in the implemented version.

With respect to new features, a new kind of operation errors was considered because the complexity of the plant and its level of criticality were higher than that of slot machines. For instance, a gate cannot be close if it has not been opened before is a very critical restriction. Second, some internal identifiers were updated. This was transparent to the user, but implied a higher cost at MIB ·database level. Finally, command validation was done both at the real plant (simulator of real plant) and at TOPENbiogas. In TOPENprimer this validation was only done in the TOPEN environment.

4   Identified Issues in the Case Study

The Scrum methodology was tailored according to the specific project needs and the structure of the team. The project was developed in six sprints, fifteen days long each. The scrum team was made out of eight members (some of them with part-time). The customer provided the background documentation to define the User Stories and took part in the process, though a proxy customer was also used. This section describes some problems discovered during the study. Five fundamental issues were identified related to requirements working with Scrum methodology. In particular, the issues identified include requirements elicitation tasks, crosscutting requirements, derived requirements, granularity requirements and requirements documentation. These issues are not mutually exclusive.

4.1   Requirements Elicitation

Requirements elicitation activity intends to identify and understand customer needs. In agile approaches development tasks are not centered in a complete and well-defined set of requirements. User needs are incrementally elicited. In [14] this closed relation with the customer is reported as very successful. However, we have found that it often happens that the customer is focused on issues on what the system has to do, forgetting other aspects, that may be become critical, such as the use of resources, maintenance, portability, safety, security or design. Most of these could be classified as non-functional requirements[4]. This happens because the customer usually does not have a vision of technical aspects. The problem is not so much how to express these requirements but the impact that may have on the product if they are not introduced at the right development stage.

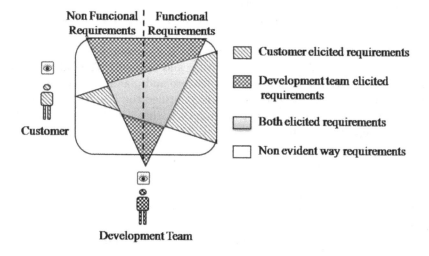

Fig. 2. System view from the team and customer

Actually it might be thought that most of the non-functional requirements should be known in the first stages of the development [13]. Although agile approaches contemplate an extensive use of refactoring techniques, the impact, e.g. to re-design a client-server architecture from a centralized could be dramatic. In our opinion, two main perspectives could be identified during the requirement elicitation: the customer view and the team view. Figure 2 shows it graphically. The customer perspective is functionality oriented leaving some product aspects out of its visibility, such as technical ones. At the other side, the development team perspective, depicted in the grid area, covers some requirements derived from the customer needs and some others of which the customer might not be aware of at all because of their nature. These include platform constraints, technical issues, and even development methodologies issues. As it can be shown in figure 2, there are some areas without any visibility. This is because at the beginning of the project all the requirements are not available.

---

[4] Within this paper, and referred to the experiment reported, non-functional includes what are called quality requirements for some authors "-ilities" and also design or other kind of requirements outside of functional.

4.2   Crosscutting Requirements

One of the features that had a strong impact on the project was the transversal nature of some requirements. This is the case of non-functional with respect to functional requirements, but non-functional requirements do not have the exclusivity of transversality. This is similar to the crosscutting concerns concept [38,50]. That is, non-functional requirements may be associated to many user stories. These crosscutting needs are difficult to break down into user stories such as in the case of safety. There is also no explicit way to express user stories interactions. A crosscut requirement is *spread* over several user stories, therefore, some tasks like planning, effort estimation or testing are affected. In the study case presented, this type of requirements has been managed under a new concept called System Story and that will be presented in the subsection 4.5. A specific example about this problem is shown in table 2. For example, if TOPENbiogas has to get access to the biogas plant locally and remotely; then all commands to be implemented have to consider this feature and planning, effort estimation and validation tasks are concerned. If it is identified too late it could have very serious implications on the product architecture what could delay unnecessarily get to an acceptable product.

Table 2. Example of Crosscutting Requirement

Formal Requirement Definition		
TOPEN environment can be accessed either locally or remotely		
System Story		
Id SS	**Who**	**What**	**Why**
SS6	Test Engineer	Access the environment locally or remotely	Operate and monitor Shredding Tank

4.3   Derived Requirements

Some required features could seem quite obvious and easy to obtain from the customer view. However, they could have an impact in the development tasks because some implicit related requirements are not still considered. In the study case, this type of hidden needs was classified as derived requirements (referring to those requirements that were derived from the analysis of other requirements). The communication protocols that use the TOPENbiogas commands are an example of this. These protocols are different if the environment works in local or remote access. In local, TOPENbiogas can check the components status *in situ* but not in remote. For this reason, the protocol has to be redefined to support other additional information when TOPENbiogas is working in remote access, as is shown in the table 2.

4.4   Granularity

Some user needs can be required at a lower level of detail. This happens not only in agile, of course, but in not conventional approaches the impact can be lower as long as a long and detailed requirement process takes place. The issue in agile is to minimize the impact in case a requirement has to be split into lower granularity level ones. This is the case, for example, of the variables that are used to monitor the *Shredding Tank*, one component of the biogas plant. In a first iteration, the Shredding Tank was considered as the component to monitor. However, as the project went on, lower granularity variables, that have to be monitored too, appeared. The features of these variables affected the operation commands format that originally was defined in a too simplistic way. The result was to have to re-implement all the components. A lot of work was, probably unnecessarily, lost.

4.5   Customer Needs Documentation in Form of Stories

Finally, we found an important problem when we tried to represent some customer needs as user stories, which were already known in the initial product TOPENprimer. Those TOPENprimer requirements classified as functional could be written in user stories without problems. The problem appeared when we tried to include some needs such as the required database management system or the response time of TOPENbiogas. We found difficulties because the inclusion of features classified by conventional methodologies as non-functional, in the widest sense of this term, is not clearly defined in agile methodologies. We tested different solutions along the development. One was that these needs were included into user stories themselves. We considered this alternative because user stories describe features required by user and, anyway, non-functional requirements are special user expectations. However, according to Kassab [51], non functional requirements management is different to functional. Besides, many non-functional requirements often concern multiple user stories. In our project a new concept called System Story was used. System Stories have been defined as *"an added element to Agile methodologies that is used to collect any feature that customer/stakeholders want the system have related to non-functional requirements that could not be allocated in user stories"*

5   Discussion

The results achieved in the previous section show that, in agile methodologies, customer requirements elicitation and management require further maturation [39]. Therefore effectiveness can improve in the future. This section presents a discussion and some analysis of the previous results.

5.1   User Stories Interaction

User stories represent product needs that are defined and implemented in reduced time slot. Agile teams manage a high number of user stories, that grows up during the development duration, e.g. the Product Backlog in Scrum or the analog element in other agile methods is a dynamic artifact. As consequence of

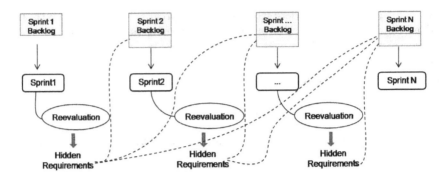

Fig. 3. Proposed life cicle for an *Agile* development

it, and from our own experience, the Product Backlog management is a complex task in agile methodologies like SCRUM. To consider that each user stories can be implemented independently of others is an error according to our experience. Several studies such as [42,41,43,44,17] have considered interaction of requirements and the conflicts related to this interaction. Most of the problems identified in section 4 are derived from these implicit requirement interactions what implies an overload to Product Backlog management.Although communication of team members is one of the principles of the Agile manifesto, some specific mechanisms to manage user stories dependencies should be advisable.

Table 3. Examples of User Story

		User Story	
Id US	**Who**	**What**	**Why**
US31	Test Engineer	To change the shredding speed of the Tank	To operate Shredding Tank
US40	Test Engineer	To receive alert of Tank over-temperature	To monitor Shredding Tank

5.2 A Way to Review Stages

It seems reevaluation after each sprint should include not only well identified needs, but also other requirements such as crosscutting or derived requirements. Obviously the risk is loosing agility. In the case study we use the revaluation and re-prioritization of requirements stage at the end of each sprint to evaluate user stories that involve functional requirements from the perspective of potential non-functional requirements that are usually identified in a less obvious way. Figure 3 shows the proposed process. An example in our case study was in the Gateway component. It didnot appear in user stories because it is transparent to the user but was discovered in a revaluation stage. This component had to be completely redesigned and implemented to be adapted to the new communication protocol of the biogas plant.

5.3   Managing Non-functional Needs

As it has been shown in the study case, non-functional requirements management is one of the tasks that causes more problems in agile methodologies and it have not been still found a right solution. There are two tendencies related to this problem. On the one hand, an important agile methodologies sector thinks that user stories are able to represent any system need, both functional and non functional, and they do not consider a possible needs classification in agile approaches. On the other hand, there is an increasingly number of studies that find many difficulties to deal all requirements in the same way. They think that all customer needs are not equal and, therefore, it is necessary to distinguish some requirements be-cause their importance or management is different. For example, Bostrom et al. in [52] make a differentiation with security requirements suggesting Abuser Stories and Security-related User Stories to consider these needs. In the case study presented, we have found numerous problems to deal all needs equal, mainly management problems, and we have chosen to make different between functional and non-functional needs appointing the concept to System Story (see section 4.5)

6   Conclusions and Future Work

This paper presents some finding for requirements processes. These findings might be currently limiting the success of agile approaches. Elicitation and management of customer needs, specially non-functional, is an issue that requires further research; to get a better understanding of the inner relation between functional and non functional may yield in improved Agile approaches. Requirements dependencies is another important issue underlying many identified problems in this work, such as the management of crosscutting or derived requirements. These identified issues may be also relevant in conventional processes but this paper is an attempt to stress that they may be more critical for Agile processes. Read in other way, Agile processes may get a higher benefit if the research community progresses within this direction. The work planned for the future is dealing with gaining a better empirical knowledge combined with formal approaches. Another issue is studying how improved team cooperation can help in situations in which the mentioned issues come up.

Acknowledgements

The work reported has been partially sponsored by the Spanish MEC and MICYT under OVAL/PM TIC2006-14840 and FLEXI FIT-340005-2007-37 (ITEA2 6022). Besides, we would like to express public gratitude to BiogasFuelCell for their help in the application domain and Answare-tech, a partner in FLEXI. We are also grateful to the rest of the team: A. Espinoza, G. Rueda, J. Pérez, J. Díaz, A. Gómez and R. Cavero.

References

1. Boehm, B.: A view of 20th and 21st century software engineering. In: ICSE 2006: Proceedings of the 28th international conference on Software engineering, pp. 12–29. ACM, New York (2006)
2. Lindvall, M., Basili, V.R., Boehm, B.W., Costa, P., Dangle, K., Shull, F., Tesoriero, R., Williams, L.A., Zelkowitz, M.V.: Empirical findings in agile methods. In: Wells, D., Williams, L. (eds.) XP 2002. LNCS, vol. 2418, pp. 197–207. Springer, Heidelberg (2002)
3. Nerur, S., Mahapatra, R., Mangalaraj, G.: Challenges of migrating to agile methodologies. Commun. ACM 48(5), 72–78 (2005)
4. Vijayasarathy, L.R., Turk, D.: Agile software development: A survey of early adopters. Journal of Information Technology Management 19(2) (2008)
5. Boehm, B.W., Turner, R.: Balancing agility and discipline: Evaluating and integrating agile and plan-driven methods. In: ICSE, pp. 718–719. IEEE Computer Society Press, Los Alamitos (2004)
6. Boehm, B.W., Turner, R.: Management challenges to implementing agile processes in traditional development organizations. IEEE Software 22(5), 30–39 (2005)
7. Larman, C., Basili, V.R.: Iterative and incremental development: A brief history. Computer 36(6), 47–56 (2003)
8. Vilki, K.: Juggling with the paradoxes of agile transformation. Flexi Newsletter 2(1), 3–5 (2008)
9. Beck, K., Beedle, M., van Bennekum, A., Cockburn, A., Cunningham, W., Fowler, M., Grenning, J., Highsmith, J., Hunt, A., Jeffries, R., Kern, J., Marick, B., Martin, R.C., Mellor, S., Schwaber, K., Sutherland, J., Thomas, D.: Manifesto for agile software development (2001)
10. Beck, K., Andres, C.: Extreme Programming Explained: Embrace Change, 2nd edn. Addison-Wesley Professional, Reading (2004)
11. Nuseibeh, B., Easterbrook, S.: Requirements engineering: a roadmap. In: ICSE 2000: Proceedings of the Conference on The Future of Software Engineering, pp. 35–46. ACM Press, New York (2000)
12. Cheng, B.H.C., Atlee, J.M.: Research directions in requirements engineering. In: FOSE 2007: 2007 Future of Software Engineering, Washington, DC, USA, pp. 285–303. IEEE Computer Society Press, Los Alamitos (2007)
13. Paetsch, F., Eberlein, A., Maurer, F.: Requirements engineering and agile software development. In: WETICE 2003: Proceedings of the Twelfth International Workshop on Enabling Technologies, Washington, DC, USA, p. 308. IEEE Computer Society, Los Alamitos (2003)
14. Sillitti, A., Ceschi, M., Russo, B., Succi, G.: Managing uncertainty in requirements: A survey in documentation-driven and agile companies. In: METRICS 2005: Proceedings of the 11th IEEE International Software Metrics Symposium, Washington, DC, USA, p. 17. IEEE Computer Society, Los Alamitos (2005)
15. Miler, R.: Managing Software or Growth without fear, control, and the manufacturing mindset. Addison-Wesley Professional, Reading (2003)
16. Boehm, B.W.: Software Engineering Economics. Prentice-Hall Advances in Computing Science & Technology Series. Prentice Hall PTR, Englewood Cliffs (1981)
17. Damian, D., Chisan, J.: An empirical study of the complex relationships between requirements engineering processes and other processes that lead to payoffs in productivity, quality, and risk management. IEEE Trans. Softw. Eng. 32(7), 433–453 (2006)

18. Damian, D., Chisan, J., Vaidyanathasamy, L., Pal, Y.: Requirements engineering and downstream software development: Findings from a case study. Empirical Softw. Engg. 10(3), 255–283 (2005)
19. Basili, V.R., McGarry, F.E., Pajerski, R., Zelkowitz, M.V.: Lessons learned from 25 years of process improvement: the rise and fall of the nasa software engineering laboratory. In: ICSE 2002: Proceedings of the 24th International Conference on Software Engineering, pp. 69–79. ACM, New York (2002)
20. Cao, L., Ramesh, B.: Agile requirements engineering practices: An empirical study. IEEE Software 25(1), 60–67 (2008)
21. Grünbacher, P., Hofer, C.: Complementing xp with requirements negotiation. In: Proceedings 3rd Int. Conf. Extreme Programming and Agile Processes in Software Engineering, pp. 105–108. Springer, Heidelberg (2002)
22. Eberlein, A., Leite, J.: Agile requirements definition: A view from requirements engineering. In: International Workshop on Time-Constrained Requirements Engineering, Essen, Germany (September 2002)
23. Dyba, T., Dingsoyr, T.: Empirical studies of agile software development: A systematic review. Information and Software Technology 50(9-10), 833–859 (2008)
24. Neill, C.J., Laplante, P.A.: Requirements engineering: The state of the practice. IEEE Softw. 20(6), 40–45 (2003)
25. IEEE: IEEE Std 830-1998: IEEE Recommended Practice for Software Requirements Specifications (1998)
26. Seaman, C.: Qualitative methods in empirical studies of software engineering. IEEE Transactions on Software Engineering 25(4), 557–572 (1999)
27. Merisalo-Rantanen, H., Tuunanen, T., Rossi, M.: Is extreme programming just old wine in new bottles: A comparison of two cases. J. Database Manag. 16(4), 41–61 (2005)
28. Ceschi, M., Sillitti, A., Succi, G., De Panfilis, S.: Project management in planbased and agile companies. IEEE Software 22(3), 21–27 (2005)
29. Sutherland, J.: Inventing and reinventing scrum in five companies (2001), http://www.agilealliance.org/system/article/file/888/file.pdf (accesed, May 2008)
30. Schwaber, K.: Agile Project Management With Scrum. Microsoft Press, Redmond (2004)
31. Mann, C., Maurer, F.: A case study on the impact of scrum on overtime and customer satisfaction. In: ADC 2005: Proceedings of the Agile Development Conference, Washington, DC, USA, pp. 70–79. IEEE Computer Society, Los Alamitos (2005)
32. Capiluppi, A., Fernandez-Ramil, J., Higman, J., Sharp, H.C., Smith, N.: An empirical study of the evolution of an agile-developed software system. In: ICSE 2007: Proceedings of the 29th international conference on Software Engineering, Washington, DC, USA, pp. 511–518. IEEE Computer Society, Los Alamitos (2007)
33. Baker, S.: Formalizing agility, part 2: how an agile organization embraced the cmmi. In: Agile Conference, p. 8 (July 2006)
34. Baker, S.W., Thomas, J.C.: Agile principles as a leadership value system: How agile memes survive and thrive in a corporate it culture. In: AGILE 2007: Proceedings of the AGILE 2007, Washington, DC, USA, pp. 415–420. IEEE Computer Society, Los Alamitos (2007)
35. Zowghi, D., Paryani, S.: Teaching requirements engineering through role playing: lessons learnt. In: Zowghi, D., Paryani, S. (eds.) Proceedings. 11th IEEE International Conference on Requirements Engineering, pp. 233–241 (September 2003)

36. Nawrocki, J.R., Michal Jasi, n., Walter, B., Wojciechowski, A.: Extreme programming modified: Embrace requirements engineering practices. In: RE 2002: Proceedings of the 10th Anniversary IEEE Joint International Conference on Requirements Engineering, Washington, DC, USA, pp. 303–310. IEEE Computer Society, Los Alamitos (2002)

37. Pinheiro, F.A.C.: Viewpoints: Requirements honesty. Requir. Eng. 8(3), 183–192 (2003)

38. Araujo, J., Ribeiro, J.: Towards an aspect-oriented agile requirements approach. In: Eighth International Workshop on Principles of Software Evolution, pp. 140–143 (September 2005)

39. Ribeiro, J.C., Araujo, J.: Asporas: A requirements agile approach based on scenarios and aspects. In: Second International Conference on Research Challenges in Information Science. RCIS 2008, pp. 313–324 (June 2008)

40. Lee, M.: Just-in-time requirements analysisthe engine that drives the planning game. In: Proc. 3rd Intl. Conf. Extreme Programming and Agile Processes in Software Eng. (XP 2002), pp. 138–141 (2002)

41. Woit, D.M.: Requirements interaction management in an extreme programming environment: a case study. In: ICSE 2005: Proceedings of the 27th international conference on Software engineering, pp. 489–494. ACM, New York (2005)

42. Robinson, W.N., Pawlowski, S.D., Volkov, V.: Requirements interaction management. ACM Comput. Surv. 35(2), 132–190 (2003)

43. Shehata, M., Eberlein, A., Fapojuwo, A.: Using semi-formal methods for detecting interactions among smart homes policies. Sci. Comput. Program. 67(2-3), 125–161 (2007)

44. Kim, M., Park, S., Sugumaran, V., Yang, H.: Managing requirements conflicts in software product lines: A goal and scenario based approach. Data Knowl. Eng. 61(3), 417–432 (2007)

45. Magro, B., Garbajosa, J., Perez, J.: A software product line definition for validation environments. In: 12th International Conference on Software Product Line, pp. 45–54 (September 2008)

46. Rodriguez, P., Yague, A., Alarcon, P., Garbajosa, J.: Metodologias agiles desde la perspectiva de la especificacion de requisitos funcionales y no funcionales. In: 13th Conference on Software Engineering and Databases, JISBD 2008 (2008)

47. The Flexi Research Project: Itea 2 flexi

48. Schwaber, K., Beedle, M.: Agile Software Development with Scrum. Prentice Hall PTR, Upper Saddle River (2001)

49. Cohn, M.: User Stories Applied: For Agile Software Development. The Addison-Wesley Signature Series. Addison-Wesley Professional, Reading (2004)

50. Murphy, G.C., Walker, R.J., Baniassad, E.L.A., Robillard, M.P., Lai, A., Kersten, M.A.: Does aspect-oriented programming work? Commun. ACM 44(10), 75–77 (2001)

51. Kassab, M., Daneva, M., Ormandjieva, O.: Scope management of non-functional requirements. In: 33rd EUROMICRO Conference on Software Engineering and Advanced Applications, pp. 409–417 (August 2007)

52. Boström, G., Wäyrynen, J., Bodén, M., Beznosov, K., Kruchten, P.: Extending xp practices to support security requirements engineering. In: SESS 2006: Proceedings of the 2006 international workshop on Software engineering for secure systems, pp. 11–18. ACM, New York (2006)

An Exploratory Investigation on Refactoring in Industrial Context

Yi Wang

Department of Information System
City University of Hong Kong, Kowloon, Hong Kong
ywang1@acm.org

Abstract. Refactoring, which is an efficient method to improve the quality of the existing code, has been widely used in practical software development and maintenance activities. The current refactoring researches are more focus on the technical aspect of refactoring but pay little attention to its use in real software development environment. However, software development and maintenance, in their nature, are human-centric activities. The lack of systematic empirical studies has resulted in the gap between current refactoring researches and industrial practices. To bridge this research gap, we conduct this exploratory study to learn more about the actual use of refactoring in the industrial context. Using a series of semi-controlled interviews as our major research method, we gathered first-hand information on how the refactoring is used by practitioners. We built a three-stage framework to describe the overall refactoring process. 19 basic factors are identified and categorized. We also identify the most important ones and the factors that may trigger potential conflicts between developers and the managers. Some related issues such as this study's implications are also discussed.

Keywords: Refactoring, Industrial context, Human factors.

1 Introduction

Refactoring, as a software engineering method used to incrementally improve the design of existing code, is being increasingly adopted in industrial software development. After its first presentation in last 80s [1], more and more software engineers already use refactoring in their daily developments [2]. Mainstream software development environments, such as Eclipse[1] and Visual Studio. net[2], now provide semi-automated refactoring modules, and thus further facilitate the adoption of refactoring in industrial software development environments. The value proposition of refactoring is its power to reconstruct existing software according to well-defined mechanics and principles, hence reversing the software decay process caused by traditional development methods [3]. Refactoring is now also a baseline approach of agile software development methodology [4]. All these developments suggest that refactoring becomes an important aspect of software design, whose impact is going to grow in future.

---

[1] http://www.eclipse.org
[2] http://msdn.microsoft.com/en-us/vstudio/products/default.aspx

F. Bomarius et al. (Eds.): PROFES 2009, LNBIP 32, pp. 185–198, 2009.
© Springer-Verlag Berlin Heidelberg 2009

However, much remains unknown about the factors that influence the refactoring practices in real software development context. We know little about what motive the programmers refactor the code, and what contribute to the success of the refactoring. Specifically, most research on refactoring has focused on technical aspects but has ignored human factors. Refactoring, as most other software development methods, is human-centric in nature. Besides, as software artifacts are created by and for human beings, human and organizational factors also play an important role in the success use of a specific development approaches; the human dimension is at least as important as the technical dimension [5]. Although several works (e.g. [6, 7, 8, 9] addressed this point, empirical studies on refactoring are still often organized in an ad hoc way and have not generated the needed empirical evidence. Therefore more and better formalized empirical research is necessary to improve our understanding of refactoring activities. Besides, identifying the factors influencing refactoring is a promising way to bring benefits to future software development practices. This can help practitioners to better deal with issues in refactoring and avoid potential failures.

In this paper, we present an empirical investigation to the refactoring usage in real world software development. Based on the existing literatures, we conducted semi-controlled interviews to the 10 software development practitioners to gather the information. In essence, our goal was to gain better and boarder understanding on the refactoring activities in industrial context. Therefore, our research questions can be specified as follows:

RQ1: What are the factors influence the refactoring in real software development?
RQ2: Can we build a framework for industrial refactoring activities with these factors?
RQ3: What are the theoretical and practical implications brought by the framework and the factors?

The remainder of this paper is organized as follows. Section 2 presents a preliminary conceptual framework that guides the whole process of this research. Section 3 briefly introduces the research methodology we adopted. Section 4 provides our interview results with the final framework, which is an improvement of the previous one. Some related issues are discussed in section 5. Section 6 concludes the whole paper and points out future research directions.

2 Preliminary Conceptual Framework

To frame our study, we make use of a three stages conceptual framework for the refactoring, based on reviews of prior literatures and several informal interviews to the software developers. The conceptual framework is shown as figure 1. The framework contains three sequence stages, which are: (1) Decision for Refactoring, (2) Refactoring Process, and (3) Refactoring Results. The three stages are sequential in time. Each of them contains several factors. Detailed illustrations to each stage and the factors will be described in the following three subsections.

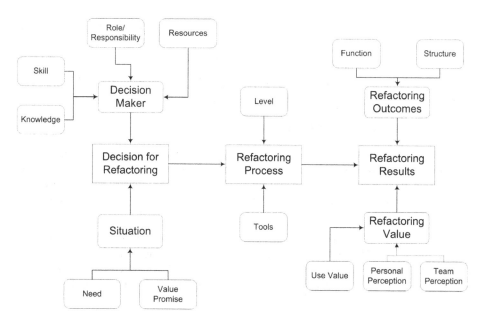

Fig. 1. The Preliminary Three Stages conceptual framework for the Refactoring in Real Software Development/Maintenance Activities

2.1 Stage 1: Decision for Refactoring

Before the refactoring activities, refactoring decisions must be made firstly. Every decision making process must to take some constrains into consideration. In another word, the decision makers have some concerns to push them make the decision of refactor their/others' programs. We divided these concerns into two categories, which are decision maker (subject who make the refactoring decision), and situation.

In the decision maker category, there are four items: (1) Skills, (2) Knowledge, (3) Role/responsibility, (4) Resources. It is obviously the first two have some connections. Detailed introduction is as follows.

- Skills: Personal skills are needed in the refactoring process, for example, carefulness, patience, communication skill. It obvious that successful refactoring ask for some specific personal skills [10, 11].
- Knowledge: "Knowledge" is also needed to ensure the success of refactoring. Generally, it includes programming language knowledge, testing and debugging, software engineering, etc [1].
- Role/Responsibility: The "Responsibility" of a specific vocational role influences the decision making of refactoring. From the view of programming ethnic [12,13], Good programmers often holds the opinion that they are responsible for their program's quality, so they tend to use refactoring to keep improving their existing code.
- Resources: "Resources" refers to the potential resources can be used in refactoring process. The resources can be divided into two categories, personal resources

and team resources. Personal resources often contain personal experiences, more powerful tools, etc. Team resources refer to the resources can be used by the team as a whole, for example, the support from the third party.

For the situation domain, two factors are emerged, which are "need" (refers to the need from stakeholders), and "value promise".

2.2 Stage 2: Refactoring Process

Due to the complexity and sophistication of the refactoring, the refactoring process is not an "isolate" process. No process is operated without constrains. There are some constraints that influence the Refactoring Process. These constraints are also the refactoring participants' major concerns in the refactoring process. Two types of constraints are identified as follows.

- Level: The refactoring can be divided into two categories: Low level and High level [1, 14]. The low level (primitive) refactoring is fine-gained (under the class or interface level), while the high level refactoring is operated on bigger granularity (major design changes) and can be treated as the composition of low level refactoring.
- Tools: Software engineers need to use some software tools to ease their tasks (e.g. finding code need refactoring, [15]) during the refactoring process. Besides some prototypes developed by researches, most frequently used IDEs, for example, Microsoft Visual Studio .net, and Eclipse, has contained some basic refactoring functions, but most of these IDEs only support primitive refactoring.

2.3 Stage 3: Refactoring Results

The refactoring results can be divided into two dimensions. The first one is "Refactoring Outcomes", which refers to the factors which are easy to define and measure. The other one is "Refactoring Values", which refers to the more abstract factors with value attributes of refactoring results.

The refactoring outcomes contain two factors:

- Function: Functions means the program's functions should be neither added nor reduced. The ideal refactoring keep the functions unchanged, this directly comes from the definition of refactoring. However, in many occasions, it is impractical to achieve this goal. To make all the original test cases pass is the common criteria in most refactoring practices [16].
- Structure: Structure refers to the way of how the source code organized; it is often an important indicator of the program quality. The refactoring is no doubt an efficient way of improving the program structure [3, 17, 18].

The refactoring values contain three factors:

- Use Value: Use value is generated through refactoring. Refactoring makes the programs are more easily to reuse, hence bring use value to the existing software systems [19, 20, 21]. Some bugs are also fixed during the refactoring process.
- Personal Perception: Personal perception refers to the perception based on the participant's personal experience in refactoring. Personal perception often

contains the personal experiences increasing, skill development, confidence, happiness, satisfaction and so on.
- Team Perception: the perception from the team level. For example, it can be other team members' reorganizations, rewards, and so on.

3 Empirical Methodology

We adopt the semi-structured interview as our main data collection approach. The data collection process is consisted of 10 interviews. The data collection procedure contains two steps, the first step is subjects' selection, and the second is interview. Both of them are briefly introduced respectively as follows.

3.1 Who Can Be the Interview Subjects?

Software developers and the junior level managers in creditable software development organizations are considered as target interviewees for this study. We selected 10 interviewees from 4 software companies (IBM: 4, Microsoft: 2, SAP 2, Wicrosoft (a joint venture of Microsoft and Shanghai local government): 2, 8 males and 2 females). The interviewees contain six software developers, four program/project managers. All interviewees are full-time employees. We do not enroll the senior level manager in our interviews, because senior level managers often do not participate in software development and maintenance activities directly. All these interviewees have at least 1 year software development/maintenance experience (Avarage: 4.65, Standard Deviation: 3.786). All of them have obtained bachelor degree, and six of them received post-graduate education. We try our best to ensure the diversity of the interviewees to make this study more representative and sound. The detailed background information of interviewees is shown in table 1.

The interviewees were all based in Shanghai and not selected randomly. Although we made this selection mainly for the convenience, this was still a wise decision. Shanghai has most high developed software industry in China. It is also a city with high diversity. We also paid enough attentions to make our interviews be more representative.

3.2 Interviews

The interview processes are semi-controlled. This means we have an interview plan to guide the interviews process. The interview plan contains a set of specific questions (for detailed information, please refer the appendix 1), which derive from the conceptual framework, which would be revised continuously according the up-to-date information gathered through the interviews. During the interview process, the interviewees were asked to describe what motivate them to make the refactoring decisions, what influence the refactoring process, and what the refactoring results are. Informants were also asked to describe their personal perceptions about the refactoring. Some other related questions are also asked. We also allow the interviewees to express themselves freely; they can talk anything they want. And we do not interrupt them. Each interview takes approximately 30 minutes. All interviews are taken detailed notes, and finally formed 76 pages of hand-writing notes with 182 entries. The same interviewer, using identical data collection protocols, conducted all the interviews for 10 interviewees.

Table 1. The backgrounds of the Interviewees

Interviewee	Org.	Job Role	Business Type	Edu. (highest)	Experience
No.1	Microsoft	SDE	Standard Dev.	BSc in CS	2
No.2	Wicrosoft	SDE	Tailored Dev. (I)	ME in CS	1.5
No.3	IBM	PM	Tailored Dev. (E)	BSc in CS	14
No.4	Microsoft	PM	Standard Dev.	MSc in CS	5
No.5	IBM	IT Spec.	Tailored Dev. (E)	ME in CS	3
No.6	IBM	SDE	Standard Dev.	BSc in Math.	6
No.7	Wicrosoft	PM	Tailored Dev. (E)	ME in CS	7
No.8	SAP	PM	Standard Dev.	BSc in CS	4
No.9	SAP	SDE	Standard Dev.	ME in CS	2
No.10	IBM	SDE	Standard Dev.	ME in SE	2

REMARKS. SDE: Software Development Engineer, IT Spec.: IT Specialist, PM: Project/Program Managers. (I): Internal, (E) External.

4   Final Framework and Results

According to the interviews we conducted, we revised the conceptual framework that presented in section 2 until it became stable (no new factors were identified). The revision was through an incremental way till the eighth interview. Finally, some new factors were added, and we made the categories of different factors more reasonable. We also defined the major relationships in the final framework to make it more complete and expressive. The revised framework is shown by figure 2. Detailed illustrations will follow the figure. We use two parts to illustrate this final framework. We first point out the differences between the preliminary framework and the final one, and then explain the major relationships in this framework.

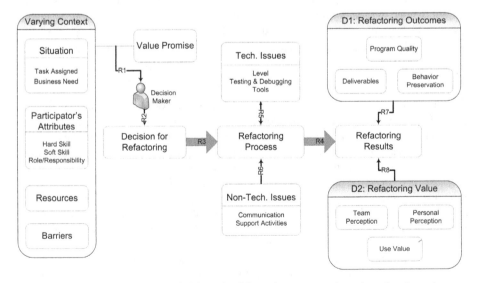

Fig. 2. The final framework which is revised from the conceptual one based on interviews

4.1 Changes to the Preliminary Framework

Compared with the preliminary conceptual framework, new factors are added in every stage. We also refine the categories of them. We introduce these changes according to the three stages respectively. At the end of this subsection, we use table 2 to summarize all changes between the preliminary framework and the final one.

(1) In "Decision for Refactoring"
In this stage, two factors are added; the first one is "Task Assigned", while the other is "Barriers". The "Task Assigned" describes such a situation that somebody is assigned to finish some refactoring tasks. The "Barriers" refers to the barriers that may be encountered by the developers during the refactoring process, for example, time limitation, lack of resources, etc. Meanwhile, three factors are substituted by new factors (please refer to the table 2). These substitutions are trying to ensure the items we adopt to describe these factors more precise and to avoid ambiguities.

Not only add the factors mentioned above, we also divide them into different categories. In the "Decision for Refactoring" stage, they fall into two categories, "Varying Context" and "Value Promise". As shown by its name, "Varying Context" contains the changeable factors that vary in different development environment, while the "Value Promise" of Refactoring is relatively identical for all refactoring practices. In the "Varying Context" category, there are two sub-categories: "Situation" and "Participant's Attributes" and two independent factors ("Barriers" and "Resources"). The "Situation" refers to the situations faced by the decision maker, while the "Participant's Attributes" refers to the personal attributes of the refactoring participants.

(2) In "Refactoring Process"
In this stage, three factors are added based on the interviews, they are: "Tasting and Debugging"[22], "Support Activities", and "Communication". We also divided them to two different categories, which are "Technical Issues" and "Non-Technical Issues". "Testing and Debugging" is really straightforward, so we do not make further explanation here. Besides, even test code itself also can be refactored [23]. It is used to describe the testing and debugging efforts aiming to ensure the correctness and reliability of software. The most important change is that we add the two "Non-Technical Issues" factors here. We also give the meaning of these two factors.

- Support Activities: "Support Activities" refers to the activities occurring in the refactoring process which try to ensure the refactoring process runs smoothly. Generally, these activities contain group meeting, workshops, and knowledge sharing.
- Communication: "Communication" refers to the communication activities occurring in the refactoring process. There are two kinds of communications. The first one is internal communication, which occurs between team members. The other one is external communication, which occurs between the refactoring team and other stakeholders (e.g. senior level managers, clients, etc.).

(3) In "Refactoring Results"
As we have done in the first two stages, we also make some changes here. We add one element named "Deliverables" in the "Refactoring Outcome" dimension. The item "Deliverables" refers to the software after some kinds of refactoring. It is the final deliverables to other stakeholders of refactoring activities.

Table 2. The changes between the preliminary framework and the final one

Changes on Basic factors			
Stage	**Original**	**Changed**	**Change Type**
Stage 1:	Need	Business Need	Substitute
Decision for	Skill	Soft Skill	Substitute
Refactoring	Knowledge	Hard Skill	Substitute
	N/A	Barriers	Add
	N/A	Task Assigned	Add
Stage 2:	N/A	Testing and Debugging	Add
Refactoring	N/A	Communication	Add
Process	N/A	Support Activities	Add
Stage 3:	Function	Behavior Preservation	Substitute
Refactoring	Structure	Program Quality	Substitute
Process	N/A	Deliverables	Add
Changes on Categories			
Stages	**Changes**		
Stage 1: Decision for Refactoring	"Varying Context" category is added. "Situation" downgrades to sub-category, and the "Participants Attributes" is added as sub-category. "Value Promise" becomes an independent element.		
Stage 2: Refactoring Process	Basic factors are divided into "Technical Issues" and "Non-Technical Issues".		
Stage 3: Refactoring Results	No major changes in this stage.		

We also use the "Program Quality" to substitute the "Structure". The "Program Quality" is more general than the "structure". In the refactoring process, not only source code structure improves but other aspects of program quality also do. For instance, refactoring eliminates some duplicated code, makes the software is easier to test and maintain [24]. The "Function" is also changed to "Behavior Preservation" [25, 26]. The latter one is more precise to describe the important feature (the program's external behaviors should not be changed in refactoring) of refactoring.

4.2 Relationships in the Final Framework

There are a set of relationships defined in the final framework, ordered from R1 to R8. The relationships set can be grouped into 5 subsets according their similarity:

$$\{R1\}, \{R2\}, \{R3, R4\}, \{R5, R6\}, \{R7, R8\}.$$

- R1: It means the "varying context" works together with "value promise" to influence the decision maker in stage 1.
- R2: It means the decision maker decides to start refactoring.
- R3 & R4: These two relationships belong to the sequential lockstep relationship. The previous one leads to the occurrence of the latter one.
- R5 & R6: These two relationships are used to describe both the "Technical Issues" and "Non-Technical Issues" affect the refactoring process.

- R7 & R8: These two show the relationships of two different dimensions with refactoring results respectively. These two are used show "Refactoring Outcomes" and "Refactoring Value" are two different aspects of "Refactoring Results".

4.3 The Importance of Each Factors

In figure 4, we provided the information on the importance of each factor. According to the criteria we specify in the illustration section of figure 4, five (26.3%) factors are the strong factors, six (31.6%) are neutral factors, and the left eight (42.1%) are weak factors. The strong factors contain "Hard Skill", "Level", "Communication", "Behaviour Preservation" and "Program Quality". These are the most important factors in the refactoring process. Both the developers and the managers should pay more attentions to these points in their future refactoring activities.

Stages	Elements	Int.1 SDE	Int.2 SDE	Int.3 A PM	Int.4 D M	Int.5 IT Spec.	Int.6 S SDE	Int.7 PG M	Int.8 P M	Int.9 SDE	Int.10 SDE	Weight	Remarks
Decision For Refactoring	Soft Skill		√			√	√			√	√	W	S in Dev.
	Hard Skill	√		√		√	√	√	√	√	√	S	
	Responsibility	√	√			√	√	√		√	√	N	S in Dev.
	Resources	√		√	√	√		√	√			W	
	Barriers	√				√	√			√		W	
	Business Need			√	√			√	√	√		W	S in Man.
	Assigned Task	√	√	√		√	√	√			√	N	S in Dev.
	Value Promise		√	√	√	√	√	√	√			N	S in Man.
Refactoring Process	Level	√	√		√	√	√	√		√	√	S	
	Tools	√	√		√	√	√			√	√	N	S in Dev.
	Testing	√	√			√	√		√	√	√	N	S in Dev.
	Support Activities			√	√			√	√			W	S in Man.
	Com Mech.	√	√	√	√	√		√	√	√		S	
Refactoring Results	Deliverables			√	√			√	√			W	S in Man.
	Behavior Presevation	√	√	√	√	√	√	√	√	√	√	S	
	Program Quality	√	√	√	√	√	√	√	√	√	√	S	
	Use Value			√	√		√	√	√	√		N	
	Team Perception		√	√	√		√	√				W	S in Man.
	Personal Perception	√	√			√	√			√	√	W	S in Dev.

S: Strong, N: Neutral W: Weak. These are used to describe the importance of the each element. If a factor is mentioned as important factors by no more than 6 interviewees, it is "Weak", if 7, it is "Neutral", and "Strong" for 8 and more.

Fig. 3. Interviewees' attitudes towards each factor. If they think a factor is important, we mark a " √ "on responsed cell.

Although the neutral and weak factors seem not as important as the five strong ones, they also provide some important implications. From the last column of figure 3, we can find that some factors are really important for some specific groups of practitioners (managers and developers). There are five factors which are strong in managers, while another five are strongly supported by the developers. The identifying of these factors helps the specific practitioners to better deal with related issue. For example, the managers maybe understand their subordinates better and identify their major tasks more clearly.

5 Disscussions

5.1 The Implications of the Factors' Importance

5.1.1 Factors with High Importance

As we mentioned before, it is no deny that the five strong factors are the most important ones. These high important factors can be divided into two categories. The first one is the factors that influence the overall success of the refactoring. It contains four factors, which are "Hard Skill", "Level", "Communication", and "Behavior Preservation". If they are ignored in the refactoring process, the refactoring activates will fail in all likelihood. For instance, if a refactoring participant does not have sufficient programming skill, how can he/she finish a refactoring task?

Another category is the key indicators of the refactoring result. It contains two factors, "Behavior Preservation" and "Program Quality". These two are the most important criteria to judge whether a refactoring success or not.

From above discussion, we can find that, the element "Behavior Preservation" belongs to both categories. This because of it is not only a factor that need to be considered during the every primitive refactoring step, but also a key indicator to evaluate the overall results of the refactoring process.

5.1.2 Factors with Potential Conflicts

Other factors need us pay more attentions are the neutral or weak factors that are strong for specific group of people. The last column of the figure 2 summarize these factors, these are 5 factors strong only for managers and another 5 for developers.

So, what are the implications showed by these factors? The answer for this question is really straight-forward. These factors show that there are many differences between managers and the developers. The differences span all three stages of the refactoring, we have pointed out them in section 4.2. In decision for refactoring stage, there are "Soft Skill" and "Role/Responsibility", which are strongly supported by the developers, while, "Business Need" and "Value Promise" are highly regarded by the managers. In the refactoring process, the developers tend to pay more attentions to the technical issues ("Tools" and "Testing and Debugging"). The managers, more concern on the "Support Activities". When comes to the refactoring results, the "Deliverables" and "Team Perception" are more preferred by the managers while "Personal Perception" is most developers' concern.

Base on above discussion, we can safely conclude that the differences between the developers and managers would trigger some misunderstanding between them, and lead to some potential conflicts directly or indirectly. For instance, if the managers do not show any interest to the technical issues such as testing and debugging, the developers may think their managers are in the wrong directions and do not have technical capability to lead them, hence, this misunderstanding may threat the success of the refactoring. Therefore, both managers and developers should pay some attention to these factors to avoid these conflicts in the refactoring practices.

5.1.3 Suggestions

After identifying these factors, we provided some suggestions to help the practitioners to better deal with these factors. Our suggestions for each category are summarized in following figure.

Factors With High Importance	Suggested Measures
• Hard Skill • Level • Communication • Behavior Reservation • Program Quality	Clearly define the hard skill needed and make comprehensive (self)evaluations to each participator. Be careful in conducting refactoring compositions. Build regular communication mechanism in the development team, encourage the communications occurring in any level. Check behavior reservation property in primitive level, at least ensure the pass of all original test cases. Clearly measure the program quantity to ensure the refactoring do not cause program quality decrease.
Factors With Potential Conflicts	**Suggested Measures***
DEVELOPER DOMAIN • Soft Skill • Role/Responsibility • Tools • Testing and Debugging • Personal Perception	Managers should spend some time to learn their developers' concerns rather than just force developers to finish some tasks. They should improve the communications with the developer. They also should pay more attention to some technical issues to better guide the project. They also need to provide chance for the developers to improve their personal skill.
MANAGER DOMAIN • Business Need • Value Promise • Support Activities • Deliverables • Team Perception	Developers should understand their managers business pressures. They should be openness, cooperative and constructive to the others, in order to avoid misunderstandings. They also need to find a balance between personal improvements and the success of the team/project.
* We only provided high level suggestions here rather than the one to one correspondent suggestion that we provided for the high important factors.	

Fig. 4. Suggestions for each identified factor

5.2   Are the Factors and Framework Fundamental?

It is difficult to ensure that our study has cover participants' all concerns on the refactoring. For the limitation of our research, we can not claim that the final framework describes all possible categories of issues on refactoring in the industrial context. With more data or experience with this topic, other related issues may be apparent. For now, we think it is more important to consider how well this framework supports the future practices and researches of refactoring. In particular, does it help to:

1. Provide clearer vision of refactoring to its participants,
2. Provide useful implications to future refactoring practices,
3. Help the practitioners to better deal with issues in the refactoring practice.

This study has great potential in this regard. It identifies the critical factors for the success of the refactoring practices, while providing some practical guidelines for future practices.

5.3   Are the Factors and Framework General?

We conducted 10 interviews to form this study; the interviewees come from 4 companies with two major types of software development roles. In these four companies, three (exclude Wicrosoft) are multinational ultra-large software development organizations. Although these interviewees work in these organizations' China branches, this is not a threat to the generality of this study. This because these organizations' China branches adopt the same development processes, methodologies, tools, and policies with other branches located in United States or India, etc. The employees are also educated and trained in the similar way with the foreign employees. Besides, they often engage in the global software development and collaborate with foreign colleagues. These all reduce the cultural influence to these individuals to the minimal level and ensure the generality of this study.

5.4 Summary

From the discussions in above and this section, we can easily find that, the three research questions specified in section 1.3 have been at least partly answered. We extracted the factors influence the real world refactoring activities, and build a stable framework for describing the panorama of refactoring with these factors. And what's more, we identified the importance for each factors and summarized some useful implications and suggestions for future refactoring practices based on the analysis to the collected data. However, we still need to continue the data analysis process to extract more useful facts and implications.

6 Concluding Remarks

This study focused on providing empirical investigation on the industrial refactoring practices. Our results demonstrate the existence of important factors for refactoring success. From a theoretical perspective, these findings add an important new dimension to empirical software engineering research in that they provide a panorama of the refactoring practice in the real software development and maintenance environment, and identify the key factors in different stages of the refactoring activity. From a practical perspective, this study suggests that, rather than trying to pursuit advanced refactoring techniques, software development teams should build a boarder view on the refactoring activities, and try to build fully understanding between people with different job role. This differs substantially from that found in most of the existing refactoring literatures, which focus almost entirely on design new refactoring tools and techniques. Besides, this study also brings some practical implications. For example, identifying the practitioners' concerns in the refactoring process and finding priority for these concerns could help the refactoring teams and individuals to deal with some potential problems they will encounter during the future refactoring activities.

Till now, this research is still in progress, we still need to provided deep analysis to the data we gathered and to learn more about the real refactoring usage and perception in the industrial context, for example, analyzing the interviewees opinions towards existing tools. We hope our future work could bring us more useful theoretical and practical implications. This study is need replicated in different contexts to increase the confidence towards the findings in this paper

References

1. Opdyke, W.F.: Refactoring: A Program Restructuring Aid in Designing Object-Oriented Application Frameworks. Ph.D. thesis, University of Illinois at Urbana-Champaign (1992)
2. Xing, Z., Stroulia, E.: Refactoring Practice: How it is and how it should be supported - An Eclipse Case Study. In: Proceedings of International Conference on Software Maintenance (ICSM 2006), pp. 458–468 (2006)
3. Fowler, M.: Refactoring: Improving the Design of Existing Programs. Addison-Wesley, Reading (1999)
4. Beck, K.: Extreme Programming Explained: Embrace Change. Addison Wesley, Reading (2000)
5. Constantine, L.: Peopleware Papers: The notes on the human side of software. Prentice Hall, Englewood Cliffs (2001)
6. Counsell, S., Swift, S.: Refactoring Steps, Java Refactorings and Empirical Evidence. In: Proceedings of 32nd Annual IEEE International Computer Software and Applications Conference (COMPSAC 2008), pp. 176–179. IEEE Computer Society, Los Alamitos (2008)
7. Murphy-Hill, E., Black, A.P.: Refactoring Tools: Fitness for Purpose. IEEE Software 25(5), 38–44 (2008)
8. Murphy-Hill, E., Black, A.P.: Breaking the Barriers to Successful Refactoring: Observations and Tools for Extract method. In: Proceedings of 30th International Conference on Software Engineering, Leipzig, Germany, May 2008. IEEE Computer Society, Los Alamitos (2008)
9. Murphy, G.C., Kersten, M., Findlater, L.: How Are Java Software Developers Using the Eclipse IDE? IEEE Software 23(4), 76–83 (2006)
10. Acuña, S.T., Juristo, N., Moreno, A.M.: Emphasizing Human Capabilities in software development. IEEE Software (9), 94–101 (2006)
11. Wake, W.C.: Refactoring Workbook. Addison-Wesley, Reading (2003)
12. Gill, T.: Visual Basic 6: Error Coding and Layering. Prentice-Hall, Englewood Cliffs (2000)
13. Gill, T.: Creating Blueprint-Quality Software Specifications. Prentice Hall, Englewood Cliffs (2001)
14. Roberts, D.: Practical Analysis for Refactoring. Ph.D. thesis, University of Illinois at Urbana-Champaign (1999)
15. Dudziak, T., Wloka, J.: Tool-supported Discovery and Refactoring of Structural Weaknesses in Code. M.S. thesis, Faculty of Computer Science, Technical University of Berlin (2002)
16. Mens, T., Tourwé, T.: A Survey of Software Refactoring. IEEE Transaction on Software Engineering 30(2), 126–139 (2004)
17. Demeyer, S., Ducasse, S., Nierstrasz, O.: Finding Refactorings via Change Metrics. In: Proceedings of International Conference on Object Oriented Programming, System, Language & Application (OOPSLA 2000). ACM SIGPLAN Notices, vol. 35(10), pp. 166–177 (2000)
18. Philipps, J., Rumpe, B.: Root of Refactoring. In: 10th OOPSLA Workshop on Behavioral Semantics (2001)
19. Cai, Y., Sullivan, K.J.: A Value-oriented Theory of Modularity in Design. In: Proceedings of the Seventh International Workshop on Economics-driven Software Engineering Research (EDSER 2005), pp. 1–4. ACM, New York (2005)
20. Favaro, J., Favaro, K., Favaro, P.: Value Based Software Reuse Investment. Annals of Software Engineering 5, 5–52 (1998)

21. Poulin, J.S., Caruso, J.M., Hancock, D.R.: The Business Case for Software Reuse. IBM System Journal 32(4), 567–586 (1993)
22. Dinh-Trong, T., Geppert, B., Li, J.J., Roessler, F.: Looking for More Confidence in Refactoring? How to Assess Adequacy of Your Refactoring Tests. In: Proceedings of the 8th International Conference on Quality Software. IEEE Computer Society, Los Alamitos (2008)
23. Meszaros, G.: xUnit Test Patterns: Refactoring Test Code. Addison-Wesley, Reading (2007)
24. Ducasse, S., Rieger, M., Demeyer, S.: A Language Independent Approach for Detecting Duplicated Code. In: Proceedings of 11th International Conference on Software Maintenance (ICSM 1999), pp. 109–118. IEEE Computer Society, Los Alamitos (1999)
25. Mens, T., Demeyer, S., Janssens, D.: Formalising behaviour preserving program transformations. In: Corradini, A., Ehrig, H., Kreowski, H.-J., Rozenberg, G. (eds.) ICGT 2002. LNCS, vol. 2505, pp. 286–301. Springer, Heidelberg (2002)
26. Mens, T.: A Formal Foundation for Object-Oriented Software Evolution. Ph.D. thesis, Department of Computer Science, Vrije Universiteit Brussel, Belgium (September 1999)

Appendix: The Interview Outline[3]

Section 1. Background Information

1. Basic Information (experience, education, etc.).
2. The use of refactoring method (frequency, degree of familiarity, etc.).

Section 2. Refactoring Related Information

3. What factors influence your decision making on refactoring? If possible, please specify the importance of them. (According to our conceptual model, the predefined factors are used as the hints for the interviewees).
4. During the refactoring process, what factors contribute to the refactoring results? Which is more important aspect (technical or non technical) in refactoring process? What are the reasons for your viewpoints? What about the importance of each factor?
5. How to evaluate the results of refactoring? Is the perceived success keep accordance with the improvements of the software artifacts?
6. What are your personal perceptions towards refactoring techniques?

Interviewee is free to provide any related information.

---

[3] This is only the short outline of the interviews, for the detailed interview questions, please contract the author via ywang1@acm.org. We also asked some specific questions according to the information provided each interviewee.

Absorbing Software Testing into the Scrum Method

Janne Tuomikoski[1] and Ilkka Tervonen[2]

[1] Ixonos Plc, Mobile Terminal & SW, Kiviharjunlenkki 1 B,
90220 Oulu, Finland
[2] University of Oulu, Department of Information Processing Science, P.O. Box 3000,
90014 Oulun Yliopisto, Finland
janne.tuomikoski@ixonos.com, ilkka.tervonen@oulu.fi

Abstract. In this paper we study, how to absorb software testing into the Scrum method. We conducted the research as an action research during the years 2007-2008 with three iterations. The result showed that testing can and even should be absorbed to the Scrum method. The testing team was merged into the Scrum teams. The teams can now deliver better working software in a shorter time, because testing keeps track of the progress of the development. Also the team spirit is higher, because the Scrum team members are committed to the same goal. The biggest change from test manager's point of view was the organized Product Owner Team. Test manager don't have testing team anymore, and in the future all the testing tasks have to be assigned through the Product Backlog.

Keywords: Scrum method, team structure, exploratory testing, test manager.

1 Introduction

The variety of agile methods, nowadays, includes a number of specific techniques (e.g. test-driven development) and practices (e.g. pair-programming) of software development. Among the first and perhaps best known agile methods are Scrum and XP. Scrum is aimed at providing an agile approach for managing software projects while increasing the probability of successful development of software, whereas XP focuses more on the project level activities of implementing software [1]. We use the term Scrum method, although it is originally defined as a framework [2]. This means that we provide some guidelines, how to merge testing tasks into development tasks – although as a framework it would give only general principles to manage software projects.

In this paper we focus on Scrum method and in particular, how to absorb software testing into the Scrum method. We conducted the research as an action research and during the research three iterations were done. Each iteration consisted of problem diagnosing, action planning, action taking, analyzing and specifying learning phases. The steps, presented in paper, started in the beginning of 2007 and ended by June 2008. It was mandatory to execute the transition in small steps, because the ongoing work couldn't be endangered. The transition started by changing development team

F. Bomarius et al. (Eds.): PROFES 2009, LNBIP 32, pp. 199–215, 2009.
© Springer-Verlag Berlin Heidelberg 2009

structures the Scrum teams alike. Piece by piece more Scrum methods like planning sessions and daily meetings were introduced inside the teams and transition continued.

The result showed that testing can and even should be absorbed to the Scrum method. Most important thing and power in the Scrum are self organizing teams, which deliver an increment of working software after each sprint. To achieve this situation, teams need expertise from different software development areas, in our case from testing and coding. Test engineers and developers together form a Scrum team, and each individual is able to commit totally on common goals of the team.

The biggest change from test manager point of view was the organized Product Owner Team. With the Product Owner Team we could support our Product Owner in building and maintaining the Product Backlog. The Product Owner Team could be also answer to our problem that how to handle and complete all the testing tasks in a way that does not mess up the work of test engineers and the Scrum teams. The test manager could generate the testing tasks and introduce those to the Product Owner Team to prioritize. Finally, those tasks would be placed at the Product Backlog as an equal task with other requirements.

This paper is structured as follows: in Section 2, the research settings are introduced; in Section 3, the steps for absorbing testing into the Scrum method are presented, and in Section 4, the conclusions are drawn.

2   Research Setting

The research was conducted in the company, which owns a long history in software development. The research method was action research and during the research period three iterations were done. The following sub-sections describe the research settings in more detail.

2.1   The Company and Software Under Study

Company where this research was done has over 20 years experience in software development. The software that Scrum teams are implementing has its roots back to over 10 years. The development process in the company followed mainly the waterfall process model, although some organizations in company had also experience from agile methods. Due to the schedule pressures and different kind of configurations and products the organization was forced to look at new ways of working in the beginning of 2006.

Organization consist of 17 design engineers (designers and programmers), seven test engineers, three architects, three UI designers, product manager, test manager, two project managers, error manager and one technology manager, who is leading the whole group, and is also responsible of financial issues. Developers and test engineers have in average 8 years experience from software development field. Development was based on object-oriented programming, and test driven development approach was used in some projects, but not regularly.

Application that is under development is part of the larger main software, which is mobile device operating system. This causes several interesting aspects to software development process.

* Integration to main software can be done only in bi-weekly cycles.
* Main software releases have strict rules, which cannot be violated, and thus only truly working software can be integrated into the main code line.
* Main software releases have own specified testing requirements which needs to be met, and thus it is not enough that testing is done only at the Scrum team's own application level.
* Application that is under development has complicated dependencies to different architecture levels, and thus testing and verification is not always possible to do only at application level. Even if application is working in development environment, testing and verification has to be done also in target main code line to verify that integration has been successful, and that all the different layers are working together on a way as required.
* From two to three different main releases are developed at the same time, so unfortunately teams cannot focus totally only on one release. This emphasizes especially in testing, where defect findings and corrections often needs to be verified in every different main release.
* Testing resources are limited, which causes that test engineers sometimes have to work over team and release boundaries to ensure that all testing work can be done.
* Organization is big, and targets can change rapidly, which causes pressure to software development.
* Offsite subcontracting is used, and sometimes subcontractors cannot test the delivery thorough, because of technical limitations or lack of other parts of software, which are accessible only for company's internal development.

All of those characteristics caused own challenges when absorbing testing to Scrum teams.

2.2 How the Research Was Conducted

Action research was selected as research method for this research. Susman and Evered [3] present a cyclical model for action research. The model consists of five phases that are diagnosing, action planning, action taking, evaluating and specifying learning. The first phase, called diagnosing, involves determination of the problems that require attention. The second phase is called action planning and it specifies the actions that may be taken to solve the problems. Theoretical framework is set by the researcher during the planning phase. Action taking is the third phase, during which the planned actions are implemented. During the fourth phase, evaluation, actions that were carried out are compared to intended objectives. The last phase, specifying learning, specifies lessons that were learnt during the action cycle. The last phase may also lead to the start of a new research cycle [3]. Because action research is a qualitative method, research diary and interview notes were collected and recorded during research.

Lot of different changes was done during research time, but in this paper we concentrate on the three major iterations. Fig. 1 depicts the schedule of these iterations in period 2007-2008 (Q1 – Q4 refer to quarter periods).

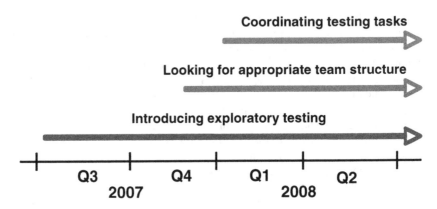

Fig. 1. Timeline for absorbing steps

In the first iteration we introduce exploratory testing as an improvement idea, which can be used to get immediate positive results of the Scrum methods usage for software testing area. This activity started in August 2007 and many sessions have been held after that. In the second iteration, which started in December 2007, we looked for appropriate team structure, which would support both constructing and testing activities. The third iteration started in January 2008 and it tells about testing task coordination in Scum method.

3   Absorbing Software Testing into the Scrum Method

We defined earlier that we use the term Scrum method, and thus provide some guidelines, how to merge testing tasks into development tasks. In the following subsections we briefly describe the Scrum method and introduce the three iterations, completed during the research period.

3.1   Core Characteristics of the Scrum Method

The Scrum method is typically defined by issues and roles such as Product Backlog, Product Owner, Sprint, Sprint Backlog, Scrum Master, Team, Daily Scrum, Sprint Demo, and with the process description, which ties these issues and roles together, as depicted in Fig. 2.

The three iterations, presented in this paper, focus on activities related to team organization in Sprint and Product ownership. Sprint planning is a core phase in the Scrum method, and it ties together different items, as Schwaber [4] defines *"Sprint planning meeting consist of two different parts. First part is spent with the Product*

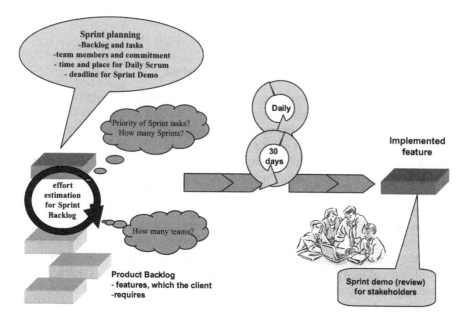

Fig. 2. The major issues and roles of the Scrum method

Owner, who is presenting the highest priority Backlog items to team. In this phase team can ask more information about items, like purpose, meaning and content of items. When the Team feels that they have enough information, they will select as much items to Sprint Backlog, as they believe they can build to a working piece of software during the one Sprint. After the selection is done, the Team commits for the Product Owner, that they will do the best they can to finish all the items they have selected. After commitment is given, the first part of Sprint planning meeting has ended".

3.2 Starting Point

The Scrum had been taken into use progressively in the organization. The process started in the beginning 2007, and the first pieces of Scrum were taken into use, when one development team that consists only of developers started to work in 30 days sprints. They held a kind of sprint planning meetings and estimated, how much work they could finish within next 30 days. This list of activities (Sprint Backlog) was split down in smaller tasks, which were further assigned to individual team members. Testing was not a part of team, and project manager acted as a Scrum Master and at the same time as a Product Owner. He was also the line manager for team members.

In the next phase all developers were split into two Scrum teams. The Product Backlog was created and all the development work was assigned through the Product Backlog. Teams continued planning their work in Sprints, but single tasks were not anymore assigned to individuals in planning sessions. Testing team was still separated from Scrum teams, but one to two test engineers were allocated so that they mainly worked for Scrum teams. Their priority was still in testing team's work. This team structure was messy, and we wanted to simplify and clarify it.

3.3 First Iteration: Introducing Exploratory Testing

Bach [5] defines exploratory testing as simultaneous learning, test design and test execution. Black [6] further characterizes it as a testing method, which is almost opposite to traditional test case based testing method. The effectiveness of exploratory testing is strongly based on individual test engineer's skills and ability to analyze system and it's behavior. Exploratory testing doesn't fit for everyone, and really requires experienced test engineers. As any other testing method, also exploratory testing has both advantages and disadvantages. Advantages are effectiveness, robustness, efficiency, safety and creativity. It's a known fact, that test cases or scripts tend to loose their power, when time goes, and those cases have been executed several times. But because exploratory testing is something that adopts in the situations, and tries to bring something new all the time, it is more likely to find more new defects with exploratory testing than with old and many times executed cases. As every process has its holes, exploratory testing gives a good change to extend coverage of predefined test cases. At the same time this coverage issue is one of exploratory testing's disadvantages. If only exploratory testing is executed it's really hard or even impossible to know what is testing coverage, because exploratory testing sessions are typically poorly documented.

Diagnosing: In both of Scrum teams, test engineers do manual functional testing of user interfaces. They have basic skills of code writing, and experience from software development, but the main thing was that they weren't doing the actual coding, module testing nor participating into code reviews. Same thing applies to developers, but vice versa. They all had a long history from coding, and of course they had done some basic testing during implementation work, but none of them was professional in software testing.

Action Planning: Couple of years ago the testing team participated in a course of exploratory testing. In the first trials exploratory testing didn't fulfil a promise given in the course, but after few exploratory testing sessions the team started to find out its power. Testing was quite fun, because we didn't need to go through again those same old test cases that has been executed hundreds of times and rarely revealed new defects. It was also uplifting to notice how own exploratory testing skills rabidly developed. At that same time we noticed that exploratory testing was easy way to familiarize oneself with new features and almost everyone could participate to exploratory testing sessions.

Jonathan Kohl's article [7] about exploratory testing in agile teams encouraged us: *"Recently exploratory testing has gained more exposure in the agile world. Some proponents have focused on using it as an end-of-iteration ritual in which the whole team and the customer are involved. This is a good idea, and I've used it much more that this on agile projects. I have done exploratory testing throughout development, from the first moment I have something to test, until we deliver software."*

We were very encouraged of this article and our own experiences from exploratory testing justified our decision to try exploratory testing together with whole team. Exploratory testing could be meaningful approach to testing for everyone, and each individual's knowledge could be used without too much time consuming planning and analyzing.

Action Taking: One of Scrum team's test engineers arranged the first exploratory testing session for the whole team. The session took place in the end phase of Sprint, when team had complete piece of working software in their hands. Testing was done already during the Sprint, and lot of defects was found and fixed, but still we were quite confident, that some defects could be found during exploratory testing session. Test engineer organized a meeting with coffee and cake, which relaxed the situation, and even the most sceptic engineers gladly joined the session.

In the beginning of the session, test engineer gave a short introduction on exploratory testing ideology. Yellow post-it notes were available for defect reporting, so after defect was found, everyone could quickly note down the steps to reproduce the defect. Quite often the defect reporting tools are more or less slow to use, and because continuous learning and observing are the key factors in exploratory testing. It is important that touch and the pace of testing is not lost because of slow defect reporting processes.

At the end of the session, after few hours of defect hunting and coffee drinking, session responsible test engineer collected defect reports, and team members had a final discussion of software's current state. After session, test engineer went through all the notes, separated real defects, and usability related problems, ignored the duplicate ones, created real defect reports, and recorder them to defect database.

Analyzing: Session went very well. Participants felt that session was a good alternation to normal daily routines. Session was also very open minded and free communication was allowed and even desirable. Thus session was good for team spirit, and improved communication between team members. One team member commented the organizing of exploratory testing session:

"The session was carried out different way than normal meetings. Coffee and cake was served and in the beginning of session, the session moderator announced that the team member who finds most defects will be given a small prize! Session was really useful and pleasant alternation to our normal daily routines".

The number of new revealed defects was unexpected in a good manner. Number of found defects was almost doubled compared to previous sessions, and this wasn't only because of new feature and code under test. Developers had really good understanding of the weak spots in code, and they could easily focus their testing on those spots. List of new defects wasn't the only thing what we expected from session, and it seemed that other results were also achieved. In exploratory testing session whole team noticed that the code they had wrote during sprint, really wasn't that perfect, and a lot of defects were still hiding somewhere. After session most participants agreed that they should concentrate more on testing and not to keep it only as a compulsory phase of the development process. One team member commented exploratory testing session's spirit:

"There was really good and open spirit, which lasted through the session. Discussion was open and information was shared freely. Even the members who usually don't speak a lot, started to praise the defects that they had found. Even the root cause for some certain defects was solved during the exploratory testing session, based on discussions between team members. That was something, which normally doesn't happen. Usually when team is correcting defects, each individual just takes one defect and starts investigating the root cause, and asks help only after he is stuck in investigations, and feels that cannot find the root cause."

It was also interesting to notice that number of found defects per exploratory testing sessions was about halved after each session. This was encouraging for team members, because they clearly recognied effectiveness of the sessions.

Specifying learning: Theories and articles of exploratory testing proved themselves. It is evident that exploratory testing is really powerful tool, and especially in agile development, where new features are developed really fast, and team can benefit from rapid feedback.

Session showed to everyone that each of team members can bring value for whole team. Developers and test engineers found different kind of defects, and each individual could use his or her own skills to uncover defects. Exploratory testing sessions also encouraged test engineers to use more adaptive ways in testing, rather than only strictly writing test cases and doing a lot of planning before testing.

3.4 Second Iteration: Looking for Appropriate Team Structure

Organizing design and coding in a Scrum way doesn't necessarily require much effort when team consist only of developers. But to establish true Scrum teams, that can handle all the software development activities from the design phase through the coding and testing to released software increment can be a challenge.

Diagnosing: Setup in organization was transforming towards true Scrum setup. There were two Scrum teams, which consist of developers only, and two former project managers were Scrum Masters for those teams. All the test engineers belong to testing team, but one or two test engineers were allocated to both Scrum teams. They participated in Scrum team's planning meetings, daily meetings, and tested things that Scrum teams developed. Test engineers were still sitting together with other test engineers.

Due to limited amount of resources, and test engineers that were allocated in Scrum teams, executed also other testing activities, which were not directly related to Scrum team's work. This double role of test engineers, and the fact that they were not a true members of Scrum teams caused a significant violation against Scrum's ideology. If Scrum teams should work together, they can benefit from enhanced communication, from rapid feedback loops, and teams can start self-organizing. If key team members cannot commit to goal, and give their 100% contribution to work, the benefits of teamwork will be lost.

In addition, our former project managers acted as Scrum Masters, and that was not the best solution. Project managers were also line managers for team members, and this caused that they had too much authority to team members, and teams weren't acting as freely as they should. We decided to to something for this issue.

Action Planning: There was a conflict between two objectives of test engineers, they had important information required in the Scrum team, but there was a lack of testing resources, which ment that if test engineers are merged into Scrum teams, there won't be enough testing resources to execute all the testing work that is not related to Scrum teams work. So, all the work to Scrum teams should come through same channel. Thus all the work can be planned and estimated in the Sprint planning, and team can take only that amount of work that they can finish during Sprint. We wanted to achieve a situation were we have fully committed true Scrum teams, which can do all the design, coding and testing work as a team. The desired team structure is shown in Fig. 3.

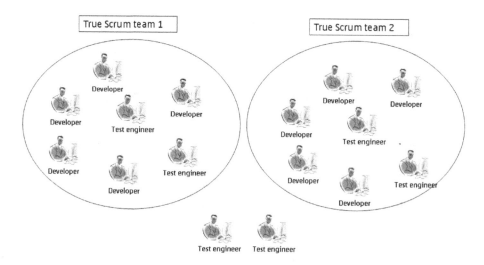

Fig. 3. Desired team structure

In this new structure a developer acts as Scrum Master in team 1 and test engineer in teams 2. Two test engineers are left outside the Scrum teams. In the beginning their function will be handling testing work that is not directly related to Scrum teams work.

Action Taking: Action started by analyzing all the testing team's work and trying to find out which of those responsibilities they could surrender. Analysis revealed that especially regression testing and bi-weekly executed basic acceptance testing consumed a lot of testing team's time.

Test engineers who were already participating to Scrum teams work, were taken away from testing team and they joined the Scrum teams as true and equal team members like all the developers already were. Scrum teams were sitting in an open-plan office and test engineers were located in together with teams. There was a screen between Scrum teams, but from the spot where test engineers were located, the screen was removed. Now test engineers are sitting together with the Scrum teams members, but they are still sitting close together so that communication, helping, and information sharing was not cut off. Office sitting layout is illustrated in Fig. 4.

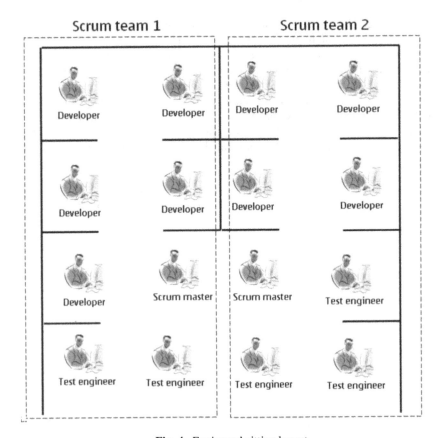

Fig. 4. Engineers' sitting layout

Because test engineers are equal team members, there was a clear need that also their work effort should be estimated in Sprint planning sessions. Earlier only developers work contribution was estimated and calculated in the Sprint planning sessions.

Analyzing: Now all the Scrum team members were located together in same sections, information exchange inside teams started to improve. When everyone was sitting so close to each other it was easier to ask also the smallest issues, which were normally left unasked, because no one bothered to walk across the office to ask. Team members also felt that they belong to same team and that everyone is working to achieve the same goal. Of course test engineers still had some old work to finish from previous setup, but progressively they could plan their work more closely together with team and concentrate on test developer's defect corrections and new features with fresh daily builds. Now testing was done alongside Scrum team development pace, not in a testing team's pace. After five sprints, developers were interviewed. One developer commented new structure:

"I think that this new team structure is working very well. Every morning we will get feedback and information of yesterday's defect fixes. If there exist some wishes or needs, they come out spontaneously during daily Scrum meeting, which is kept every

morning. Now communication between testers and developers is really natural and effective. Developers and testers are both committed to same goal, and other's work is supported very well. Everyone knows where we are at the moment, what each one have under work, and if someone is facing problems, we can try to find out solution together."

Two test engineers who didn't belong to neither of Scrum teams felt that they are a little bit on the sidelines. Of course they had their own responsibilities and works, but still they felt that they are missing information of all the new things that other guys are testing and coding. This is definitely a negative effect of this change, and in the future requires some corrective actions.

Now in Sprint planning test engineers workload was taken into account, which caused that their work overload was decreased. If it seemed in Sprint planning that test engineers cannot execute all the testing tasks that was related to development, they either drop off work from Sprint Backlog or planned Sprint's work so that some other team member participated in testing so that team managed to get everything done.

Specifying learning: Teams will get best results when they are working together as a whole. Team spirit, communication and information sharing are also the most important things in teamwork. When team members are located close to each other they can communicate easier and when even not work related issues can be easily shared, it tends to rise up team spirit.

Team's goals are still quite heavily biased towards implementation, and in the future this should be changed. Either there should be a new testing related goal, or the goals should be adjusted in a way that also takes into account testing.

3.5   Third Iteration: Coordinating Testing Tasks

Handling task and assigning them to teams is one of the important responsibilities that managers usually do in organizations. Well-run and organized project management gives good basement for engineers to do their work according to plans. But if project management fails, the whole project usually cannot be saved even with world's best engineers. This holds true also for team management in Scrum teams, although testing task coordination makes the situation more challenging.

Diagnosing: After previous iteration of implementing Scrum the world of test manager changed. Now when the test engineers are part of the Scrum team, test manager cannot anymore assign task directly for test engineers. Also he's role changed a little bit, because most of the testing was now related directly to Scrum team's work, and test engineers naturally had the best knowledge of each day's situation, and adjusted their work according to that. So test manager didn't anymore directly assign and control the execution of basic requirement testing.

After second iteration, there were changes to Scrum teams' structure. Former project managers acted as a Scrum Masters, which wasn't the best possible situation. They had to step away and new Scrum Masters had been nominated among the Team members. One former Scrum Master took a role as a line manager for every Scrum team member, so Scrum Masters didn't have anymore unnecessary authority towards team members. Now we had two project managers, one test manager, one error manager, one line manager and one product manager, whose roles and ways of working needed to be figured out.

Action Planning: The planning started with collecting ideas from different sources. After tens of read stories and articles we started to be quite confident, that we will definitely need one contact point for Scrum teams, which will be the Product Owner. Of course we already had the Product Owner, but his role and responsibilities needed some change, and thus we decided to rebuild the whole management setup.

To avoid conflicts it's required that there is only one Product Owner visible for team to whom they negotiate with. But in large scale projects this causes problems, because it's impossible to find out one individual who knows best every areas like testing, product management, customer side etc. And because the Scrum teams are also fixing defects, the Product Owner needs help from error management to prioritize everything to best possible order.

There are, however, few problems with a single Product Owner. The Product Owner should know technical issues so that he can understand and support the Scrum teams in a best possible way. But at the same time he should also have understanding of customer's needs, of testing issues and of defects.

We concluded to shared responsibilities in the ownership problem, and suggested as a solution the Product Owner Team. With the Product Owner Team we could support our Product Owner with building and maintaining the Product Backlog. The Product Owner Team could be also answer to our problem, how to handle and complete all the testing tasks in a way that it's not messing up the work of test engineers and Scrum teams. The test manager could generate testing tasks and introduce those to the Product Owner Team. The Product Owner Team could prioritize them and finally those tasks would be placed at the Product Backlog as equal tasks with other requirements.

Action Taking: Building of the Product Owner Team started with selection of the new Product Owner. Because we will have the whole team supporting new Product Owner, she/he doesn't need to be anymore product manager. To gain best possible value and support for the Scrum teams, and more time for the product manager, we decided that one of our project managers could be responsible for the Product Owner's role. The new Product Owner had strong background from coding, and he also knew lot of module testing and regression testing.

Next step was to decide members of the upcoming Product Owner Team. After analysing alternative compositions, we concluded to the structure, as depicted in Fig. 5. The Product Owner and the product manager were natural choices, and during planning phase we found that also the test manager's place would be in a team. We decided that it would be best if also the project manager and the error manager would join the team. In addition to these also skills of line manager and the head of technology area were appreciated and joined the team. This composition of skills would give the wide range of knowledge and opinions to the team. It would help a lot in requirement handling, preparation work and especially in prioritization. Another benefit would be that when they are working as a team, the information might spread with a natural way during normal daily work routines.

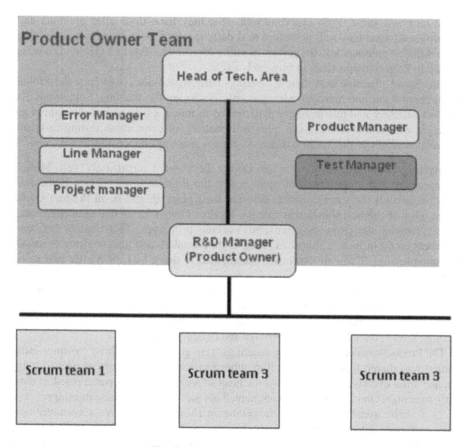

Fig. 5. New organization structure

The plan was that the test manager could assign and rise up testing tasks to the Product Backlog in a same way as all the requirements and other tasks were raised. Now we needed a meetings, were we could go through the new items on a Product Backlog, and a meeting where the items in the Product Backlog are prioritized, and where the new task candidates for the Scrum team's Sprints are chosen. We decided to start arranging weekly occurring meetings. First meeting was the Product Backlog meeting, where the Product Owner Team went through the new items. In this particular meeting the test manager introduced new testing items that he had generated. Also the architects and the user interface designers were participating to the meeting, whenever their support or information was needed. The second meeting was called as a backlog prioritization meeting. It was defined to be for arranging the backlog items to correct prioritized order and to choose the most suitable and important items for each Scrum team's Sprint Backlog. To this prioritization meeting participated regularly only the Product Owner, the product manager and the test manager. Some special guests were invited when needed.

The Product Owner Team also started to keep informal daily meetings. Informal because discussion wasn't so strictly limited as it is in Scrum's daily meetings, but the basic idea was same. First everyone told what they have done after previous daily meeting, and what they will do before next daily meeting. After round was over, there were still few minutes left for current burning topics. The Product Owner Team also started to keep retrospectives in bi-weekly cycle.

Into Sprint planning and review meetings participated always at least the Product Manager and the line manager who was only observing the meeting. Sometimes also product manager and test manager participated in meetings. In planning sessions test manager was available for given more information for team about testing tasks and test related issues in the Sprint backlog. In review meetings he's role was the same.

Analyzing: Organizing of the Product Owner Team went surprisingly well. Most of the members had a consensus of opinion that the Product Owner Team is the right solution, and all the team members felt that their place should be in Product Owner Team. One of the best things was that the Product Owner Team had quite free hands when planning the team structure and working processes. This caused that team members could influence almost as much as they wanted, and thus working processes become pleasing. Team structure was commented to diary 11.1.2008 after first workshop:

"New structure seems to be good, now I have support from different parties in management. Even same old testing team doesn't exist anymore, I still have good possibilities to influence to Scrum teams and especially to test engineers work through the Product Backlog and through the Product Owner."

The Product Owner Team's daily meetings were good idea. In those meetings information was shared flexibly, and each member had a basic knowledge of what is going on, and what everyone is doing. Also the head of technology area participated in these daily meetings. One team member commented his participation in daily meetings:

"It's really good that he is participating in these meetings. He's normally very busy and quite often very hard reach. This is good moment to hear news form his side; what is going on in upper organization, and if there is some new information that can be shared, we will get it sooner because we have daily meetings."

The Product Owner commented daily meetings:

"They are really good. It is good to know what everyone is doing and it's almost the only moment in a day when everyone is reachable at the same time. This daily status information helps me in my own work and helps to make decisions because I know daily what status in each area is."

Product Backlog meetings went well. After a couple of meetings, the Product Backlog started look as it should look from requirements point of view. But there still were few challenges with testing tasks. Earlier the testing tasks had been generated and executed in quite short and rapid cycles, because they were dependent on the development and releasing schedules. It seems that even with good test plans, a lot of testing work cannot be predicted well enough. A lot of testing tasks are generated during the normal work and also come from different departments of the organization. Because of this nature of testing, the Product Backlog will need constant updating from test manager side, and testing items might be added and removed from backlog quite rapidly, which might confuse someone who is following the Product Backlog constantly.

Prioritization of the testing tasks went extremely well. The Product Owner had strong background from software development and he fully understood the value of testing for software development. This caused that testing tasks easily got high priority in Product Backlog and time for testing was allocated in Sprint planning sessions with the support of Product Owner.

Assigning testing tasks through the Product Backlog seems to help test engineers' work. During interview one test engineer commented new testing task handling process:

"I feel that this new way of testing task assigning has gone well. Visibility for upcoming work in the future is now much better. Workload is now in better balance, because all the bigger tasks are split into smaller pieces, and upcoming workload is estimated. Now the work overload is almost always avoided. "

The Product Owner Team started to work relatively well. Few issues have risen up, and those could be investigated in the future. One of those issues is seating places. In our first trials the Product Owner Team members were sitting in separate rooms, which caused some communication problems. In the latest trials the Product Owner Team members are located in the same room (except line manager, who sits in the next room with door connection to tem's room). This improved communication between team members.

Specifying learning: The Product Owner Team seems to be good solution especially for large scale projects. It gives good change to use effectively each one's expertise and work is mainly handled in a controlled way with the Product Backlog. But to be effective Product Owner Team, team members have to remember few things. First, everyone needs to remember communicate and share information as much and as often as possible. Second, everyone needs to respect the Product Owner and remember that he in the end makes decisions and stands behind those decisions. We also recognized that Product Owner Team members should be located in the same room.

One issue has risen up, related to testing task handling. This iteration gave a good starting point for testing task handling, but the solution doesn't seem to be so simple. Sprint's tasks have to be very well defined, because without that teams cannot decide their goals, and makes commitment difficult. Also the follow up of tasks has to be done carefully that doesn't break the Scrum's rules. This test task handling process is one that needs further planning and developing, especially from test manager side.

4 Discussion and Conclusions

During this research only three iterations were done, but two of those were quite time consuming and changed daily routines of 40 people organization. Execution was quite easy to do, because organization was already in the middle of change, and everyone was open minded towards the Scrum. There was also strong support for Scrum from upper management, which of course reduced the unwanted resistance. The iteration where exploratory testing sessions started was the easiest one to execute, and its first results were immediate. It has also longer term effects, because share of information between team members tend to cause competence increase. But it takes time before these kinds of effects are visible, and they can be really challenging ones to measure.

The exploratory testing sessions and the new, modified team structure where test engineers are full team members strongly support each others. It's easier to execute exploratory testing sessions, when the team is working as a whole. First positive indications from team structure change came up already in the first retrospective after the change. Almost every team member indicated that test engineers' joining the Scrum team was the most positive issue.

The biggest change from test manager point of view was the formed Product Owner Team. Test manager didn't have testing team anymore, and in the future all the testing tasks needs to be assigned through the Product Backlog. This caused more work for Product Backlog maintenance, but at the same time it gave better visibility of overall workload. From Scrum team point of view this new way of testing task assignment is a positive thing, because now there is better visibility to the future work. But from the test manager point of view, this new process causes more work to do and decreased flexibility in task management. After all, the change was successful, because without the Product Owner Team the testing task handling would be in trouble, the test engineers couldn't be part of the Scrum teams.

After all, iterations worked very well together, supporting and completing each others. But, did we reach the situation where we wanted to be in the beginning of the research? We would say yes and no. After these iterations we had a controlled way to handle all the work that organization had – the Product Backlog. All the testing and development tasks were in the Product Backlog, where everyone could check the status of tasks. The items in Product Backlog change all the time, but still it gives a snapshot of the work status. The process where all work comes through the Product Backlog also helps to keep workload in balance. Major change in the Scrum teams was that they were rebuilt. The testing team was merged into the Scrum teams. The teams can now deliver better working software in a shorter time, because testing keeps track of the progress of development. Also the team spirit is higher, because the Scrum team members are committed to the same goal.

The limitations of our work are equal to Scrum method in general. If we stay at framework level, Scrum is not really going to tell exactly what to do. But, if we use it as a method, guidelines and reports how to adapt it in a specific situation are valuable for software practitioners. In this paper we aim to give valuable guidelines how to merge testing tasks into development tasks when using Scrum method in real life software development.

References

1. Salo, O., Abrahamsson, P.: Agile methods in European embedded softwaredevelopemnt organisations: a survey on the actual use and usefullness of Extreme programming and Scrum. IET Software 2(1), 58–64 (2008)
2. Kniberg, H.: and XP from the Trenches - How do we do Scrum (2006),
   http://www.infoq.com/minibooks/scrum-xp-from-the-trenches
3. Susman, G.I., Evered, R.D.: An Assessment of the Scientific Merits of Action Research. Administrative Science Quarterly 23, 582–603 (1978)

4. Schwaber, K.: Agile project management with Scrum. Microsoft Press, Redmond (2004)
5. Bach, J.: Exploratory Testing Explained (2003),
   http://www.satisfice.com/articles/et-article.pdf
6. Black, R.: Pragmatic Software Testing: Becoming an Effective and Efficient Test Professional. J. Wiley Publishing, Inc., Chichester (2007)
7. Kohl, J.: Exploratory Testing on Agile Teams (2005),
   http://www.kohl.ca/blog/archives/000152.html

Learning and Organizational Change in SPI Initiatives

Marikka Heikkilä

University of Jyväskylä, P.O. Box 35, FIN-40014 University of Jyväskylä, Finland
Marikka.Heikkila@jyu.fi

Abstract. Explaining how organizations chance has been a central and enduring quest of management scholars and many other disciplines. In order to be successful change requires not only a new process or technology but also the engagement and participation of the people involved. In this vein the change process results in new behavior and is routinized in practical daily business life of the company. Change management provides a framework for managing the human side of these changes. In this article we present a literature review on the change management in the context of Software Process Improvement. The traditional view of learning, as a "lessons learned" or post-mortem reporting activity is often apparent in SPI literature. However, learning can also be viewed as a continuous change process where specific learning cycle starts with creative conflict and ends up in formal norms and systems. Since this perspective has almost no visibility in SPI literature of past it could show a new direction to the future development of change management in SPI.

Keywords: Organizational change, learning, SPI.

1 Introduction

Many software firms see Software Process Improvement (SPI) as a strategic matter and are involved in organizational change initiatives to improve their software development practices. The fundamental goal of the SPI is improvement - for instance in software quality and reliability, employee and customer satisfaction, and profitability - by changing the organizational practices of firms [1]. Various maturity models can steer SPI initiatives since they offer different options for assessment and improvement, but successful SPI requires effective change management irrespective of the model adopted [2]. The challenge is that software developers must continue working productively while process changes are being implemented. Process improvement requires organizational and behavioral changes - changes in the way people communicate and collaborate as they do their work. Bringing about such changes requires management: a proven strategy, careful planning, flexibility and creativity in executing plans, and insight into issues surrounding organizational change. Thus organizational change management can be described as a process where structured approaches and tools are applied within organizations to enable its transition from a current state to a desired future state.

The literature on the change management field comes from psychology and organizational science. There are a multitude of approaches on change management and it

F. Bomarius et al. (Eds.): PROFES 2009, LNBIP 32, pp. 216–230, 2009.
© Springer-Verlag Berlin Heidelberg 2009

is rather difficult to point out a common denominator. But obviously there is a tight connection with the concept of learning organizations [3,1]. In the context of SPI, change is the result from an organizational learning process that centers on the topic of SPI initiatives. Only if organizations and individuals within organizations learn, they will able to master a positive change.

In this paper we combine literature on organizational learning and management to understand learning and change in organizational settings. We then apply these theories in analysis of SPI models, particularly CMM(I), SPICE and IDEAL. Thus we aim at better understanding of organizational learning in SPI context. Our contributions are consequently twofold. First, we review different theoretical perspectives on learning. Second, we utilize the literature to analyze SPI models to make suggestions how learning can be supported, encouraged and facilitated.

The paper is organized as follows. First, as theoretical background, literature on learning in organizations and change management is reviewed. Second, the recommendations and findings from the above mentioned literature are applied in the analysis of SPI models. The article ends with conclusions suggesting some amendments to current SPI models promoting, in a coordinated manner, the innovativeness and capabilities of the personnel.

2   Learning Organizations

Argyris and Schön [4] introduced a conceptualization of organizational learning. They identified three levels of 'learning loop' within an organization: single-loop learning is a simple behaviour adjustment in a mismatch or error situation, respecting the organization's current principles and rules. At a higher level, i.e. double-loop learning, the organization questions and modifies existing rules and procedures in response to mismatch or error. In other words, the organization tries to make sense of what is going on and what assumptions should be changed in order to achieve better results. The highest organizational learning loop is deutero-learning. This loop refers to the organizational problem solving capacity and capability to redesign policies, structures and techniques in the situation of constantly changing assumptions about the self and the environment. Deutero learning means understanding single-loop and double-loop learning in order to increment them. Thus the challenge for an organization – or network of organizations – is to provide its members with the necessary conditions for developing its capacity to assimilate knowledge and to solve problems [5] between the network partners [6,7].

Gattermann & Hoffmann [8] suggest that the success of deutero learning and the restructuring of values and rules can be assessed by the level of acceptance of change within organizations. Evidently, in order for that to take place, not only individuals but also organizations and networks must be provided with the conditions necessary for learning. Indeed, knowledge management literature suggests a variety of models and methods for knowledge creation and sharing through interaction (tacit knowledge) or through documents and information systems (explicit knowledge).

In line with the view of the firm as a 'sense-making system' [9,10] Nooteboom [11] explains the need for shared insights and models by pointing out that information is useless if it is not new, but it is also useless if it is so new that it cannot be understood. He argues that organizations should be able to reduce cognitive distance between its members, i.e. to achieve a sufficient alignment of mental models, to understand each other and achieve a common goal [11]. He also indicates the trade-off between need for cognitive distance for the sake of novelty and cognitive proximity and for the sake of efficient absorption. This is precisely the same challenge that Nonaka points out when he suggests that, one of the enabling elements for the process of organizational knowledge creation are requisite variety and redundancy of information. This need for variety and at the same time overlapping knowledge domains of individuals is concerned with balancing cognitive distance and cognitive proximity, as mentioned by Nooteboom [11].

2.1 Creativity and Chaos

Nonaka [12] proposes that new knowledge can be created by dialogue which brings up conflicting views. Open discourse and reference models seem to emerge in particular as important enablers for organizational learning and even more vital in the context of learning networks [12,13,14]. They are needed for members with differing backgrounds and history to achieve a shared desired vision for the future. That is, organizational learning occurs through shared insights, knowledge and mental models. Change is blocked unless all of the major decision makers learn together, come to share beliefs and goals and are committed to take the actions to change. Second, learning builds on past knowledge and experience, that is, on memory. Organizational memory depends on institutional mechanisms (e.g. policies, strategies and explicit models) used to retain knowledge.

Nonaka [12], referring to Brown and Duguid's [15] evolving communities of practice, points out the significance of links between individuals that span boundaries. He sees knowledge creation as a process that constantly makes extensive use of knowledge in the environment, especially that of customers and suppliers [12]. Thus, selecting people with the right mix of knowledge and capabilities for the creation process is critical [16]. Nonaka promotes the use of cross-departmental or even cross-organizational teams for organizational knowledge creation: "Teams play a central role in the knowledge-creating company because they provide a shared context where individuals can interact with each other and engage in the constant dialogue on which effective reflection depends. Team members create new points of view through dialogue and discussion. They pool their information and examine it from various angles. Eventually, they integrate their diverse individual perspectives into a new collective perspective. This dialogue can -- indeed, should -- involve considerable conflict and disagreement. It is precisely such conflict that pushes employees to question existing premises and make sense of their experience in a new way." [13].

Also Zimmerman [17] building on Stacey [18] points out that organizational learning often takes place in a complex setting. He proposed a matrix about learning and knowledge creation (in Fig. 1.). It has two dimensions: the degree of certainty and the level of agreement.

Many simple business processes are situated at a level in which it is certain what needs to be done and people involved agree on that. Here (area 1), traditional management approaches, e.g. management by objectives apply and work well. Organizations use techniques which gather data from the past and use that to predict the future. However, when members of the organization do not agree, or show resistance to the planned changes, the traditional methods fall short (area 2). Then politics become more important. Coalition building, negotiation, and compromise are used to create the organization's agenda and direction. Third case is where managers find themselves and their organizations in a situation characterized by a high agreement of stakeholders - what Senge calls "shared vision", but a substantial degree of uncertainty (area 3). In this region, the goal is to head towards an agreed upon future state even though the specific paths cannot be predetermined. A strong sense of shared mission or vision may substitute for a plan and comparisons are made not against plans but against the mission. This is the area when scenario design and participatory approaches for defining strategies are valuable.

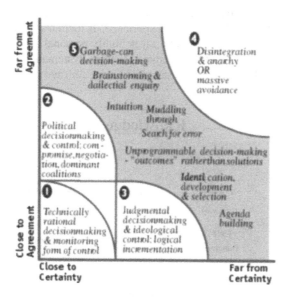

Fig. 1. Learning and knowledge creation

Situations where there are very high levels of uncertainty and the stakeholders are far beyond any agreement (area 4) often result in a breakdown or anarchy. The traditional methods of planning, visioning, and negotiation are insufficient in these contexts. Even though many political leaders are operating in exactly such an environment, in an organization managers would do everything to escape that situation which complexity scientists call "The Edge of Chaos". However, interestingly many contemporary management processes are situated in a field that fluctuates between the extremes that have been delineated above (area 5.). Here change is regarded as the norm. It is the zone of high creativity, innovation, and breaking with the past to create new modes of operating. In such environments, the main task of management is to facilitate the co-creation of the organization's future [17]. Methods proposed include several types of meetings and conferences advancing innovative co-operative thinking, and brainstorming (e.g. Open Space Technology, Appreciative Inquiry, World Café).

2.2 The Change Process

The lesson learned from the above discussion is that in order to be innovative and creative the companies should promote situations where members – or at least the major decision makers - of the organizations are able to express their differing views, share their information and eventually end up with a new collective perspective and solution. However, this should be done in a coordinated manner, so that the company does not end up in an anarchy and chaos. A change model [19] includes four steps: unfreezing, learning, internalization, and refreezing. The unfreezing is a cathartic process of increasing forces towards change and/or decreasing forces resisting change. After moving to a new equilibrium state through learning and internalization, the system is refrozen. In turn, Nonaka and Takeuchi [20] view on how the knowledge is diffused into the organization (in Fig. 2.) They note that there are two types of knowledge: tacit (subjective) knowledge and explicit (objective) knowledge. Tacit knowledge is the knowledge built on experience. It includes insights and intuitions, and is not easily visible and expressible. It is highly personal and is hard to formalize and share with others. Explicit knowledge is formal, systematic and easily communicated and shared in the form of hard data, formulae, codified procedures, or universal principles.

Knowledge Spiral

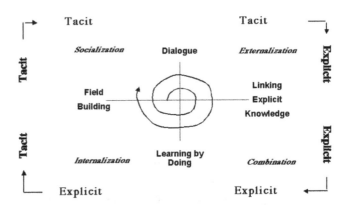

Fig. 2. Knowledge Spriral

Nonaka and Takeuchi represent the knowledge transfer process as a spiral, starting off with tacit knowledge that is externalized to someone else via dialogues. Then these explicit ideas are connected to the existing body of knowledge, combining them and internalizing them, making them tacit once again. The spiral points out that the process starts with dialogue, continuing with linking explicit knowledge, to learning by doing and finally to field building. Thus after the 'conflict and creativity' phase discussed above the company should engage in more rigid phase of learning by combining explicit information, followed by 'learning by doing' phase. Only when the new process knowledge is adopted into real work, and included into its tacit knowledge, the organizations has achieved sustainable process improvement. Thus in this learning process the approach starts with creative chaos, where mental models and brainstorming are applied to boost innovativeness in multi-departmental or multi-organizational teams, and finally curbs down to 'status quo' coordinated by shared work practices and formal rules (illustrated in Fig. 3.)

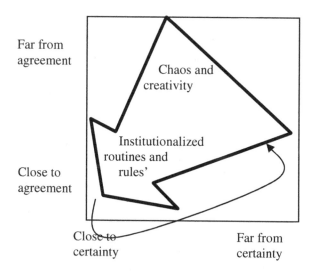

Fig. 3. The learning process

3   Organizations in Change

Whereas in the previous chapter we looked at organizational change from human learning perspective, here we would like to take another stance – organization.

Organizations have each own history and background, which affect the future decisions and actions. [21] defines organization's culture as "the accumulated learning that a given group has acquired during its history." This definition emphasizes learning aspect and also notes that culture applies only to that portion of the accumulated learning that is passed on to newcomers [21]. Huber [22] calls the learning related to institutionalized knowledge as congenital learning. (cultural transmission from other members). Other forms of learning identified by [22] were: experiential learning (via planned experimentation, self appraisal, and learning curves), vicarious learning (e.g., benchmarking other organizations' process, systems, and results), grafting (e.g., acquisitions and mergers, strategic alliances and partnering, and migration of top management), and Searching and Noticing (e.g. performance monitoring).

From organizational perspective, an organization consists of several variables, such as structure, people, technology and management [e.g. 23, 3]. These variables are highly independent, so that a change in one variable most often results in an intended or unintended change in other variables as well, which in turn cause new changes in the system. Dooley [19] points out that the magnitude of the change must be adjusted to the specific organization context (and to cognitive distance and proximity): the difference between the perceived organization state and the desired organizational state creates a "state gap" [19]. The gap motivates or demotivates an individual's readiness for change. If the gap is too big, change may be deemed impossible; if the gap is too small, change may be viewed as being unnecessary.

Level of Focus

Intervention seeks to modify		*Unit level*	*Individual or group level*
Informal behavior		Redefinition of - roles - responsibilities - relationships	Coaching/Counseling Training Process consultation Team building
Formal design		Compensation systems Information systems Organizational structure Measurement system	Replacement Recruitment Career pathing Succession planning Performance appraisal

Fig. 4. The order of changing activities in an organization (adopted from [24])

Beer et al.'s [24] described in their series of studies how to revitalize (i.e. to introduce permanent improvement) to an existing company's activities. The intentional change (in Fig. 4. called 'Intervention') should start from modifying informal behavior at the level of official social unit. This is to utilize the social coherence in order to achieve real change in the roles, responsibilities and relationships of the people (structure and processes). After that we should start coaching, training, etc. at the individual level and make sure that the momentum remains by creating vision of the roles of the people in the near and long term future (people). It is also important to award good performance (rewards). In the last stage – after the social organization is more-or-less stable- is the time to introduce the formal systems (structure and processes).

Specifically in the context of quality improvement Spector and Beer [25] propose the following steps.

1. Trigger change by combining external competitive pressure with clearly defined direction from the organization's leader.
2. Develop on the part of the top management team agreement on, and commitment to, the belief that quality improvement is the key strategic task of the organization.
3. Form ad hoc teams around processes to be improved.
4. Create an organization-wide change oversight team which promotes learning and systemic change and helps to overcome resistance.
5. Enable teams to analyze and take action through: the delegation of decision-making authority; the provision of necessary team skills; and the information necessary to understand, analyze, and re-engineer processes.
6. Align formal measurement and information systems with the cross-functional process approach.

Comparing this to the lessons learned from previous chapter, we can notice that here the clear guidance from the organization's leader is expected in the beginning to show the direction for the learning and improvement (step 1). This should direct the learning process towards agreement and certainty, not towards anarchy and breakdown. Then, during the 'conflict and creativity' phase the top management team is expected to come up with commitment (step 2), and also expert, ad hock teams are expected to come up with initiatives for process improvements (step 3). In these teams – in line with suggestions of e.g. [12,13,14] – members engage in a dialogue and create new points of view, pool their information and eventually integrate their diverse individual views into a new collective perspective. The idea of self-organization, instead of tight control, is operationalized in as "empowerment". Empowerment means not only giving teams the authority to make decisions, but also making information concerning all aspects of the context readily available [19] (steps 4 and 5). As there are multiple improvement teams working at the same time it is essential to establish also an organization-wide team to promote learning and systemic change and to help to overcome resistance. Thus the task of this head team is concerned with the highest organizational learning loop, deutero-learning [4], to facilitate organizational problem solving capacity and capabilities to redesign processes. Only as the final stage (step 6.) the company can establish formal information systems and measures.

To sum up, when organizations are to be changed, the literature seems to point out the importance of interactions between the organizational dimensions, multiple levels of teams and top management commitment. The process should advance starting from strategies to structures and processes (i.e. roles, responsibilities and relationships) to individual training and recruiting (people) and rewards, finally to formalize the planned structures and processes by systems, measures and controls. This process should start with top management teams showing commitment. Then special cross-functional teams after interaction and discussion end up with a solution for improvement. This multi-level and multi-team learning process is facilitated by an organization-wide team.

4 Software Process Management in Changing Learning Organizations

Continual process improvement is essential element of successful organizations. With process improvement the organizations can increase their efficiency and improve the quality of their products and services. For software companies, the software processes improvement (SPI) is crucial for surviving in a present day highly challenging business environment. Variety of quality and process improvement frameworks, normative models and standards (such as CMMI, ISO 9001, ISO 15504 (SPICE) and Bootstrap) are available for supporting process improvement. These norms contain maturity levels indicating good software practices and are primarily used to identify the weak areas in the existing software practice and to prioritize future improvements [26]. One of the goals in SPI is to have common procedures in the organization. If the organization wish to improve their maturity according to a normative model, then it is important that the new processes are institutionalized in the daily norms and tacit knowledge of the workers. This seems to be problematic, since for example in a survey [27] on CMM

Initiatives two thirds of the respondents agreed with the statement, "We understood what needed to be improved, but we needed more guidance about how to improve it." Indeed, one of the main concerns in SPI is how to create mechanisms to help the organization institutionalize continuous process improvement.

Currently the SPI literature focuses mainly on the aspects related to the norms for classifying software organizations, and metrics (i.e. how to assess whether an organization is compliant with the specific norm) [28]. Evolutionary approach to SPI is common: changes are implemented by a sequence (steps) of improvements over a period of time. For instance, the ultimate idea behind CMM is to create an organization at the highest maturity level that is able to continuously optimize its software processes and its software processes are institutionalized via policies, standards and organizational structures [29,30]. However, as [28] note, compliance to a norm does not automatically lead to success, but also other relevant aspects such as context and people should be considered [31]. Unfortunately, even though SPI is an organizational change mechanism the literature is lacking organizational change theory, and is thin in the area of organizational learning, and management of the SPI initiatives [28].

Next, using the organizational learning and change literature as a back drop, we assess the CMM(I), SPICE and IDEAL models first from management, and then from learning point of view.

4.1 Management

CMM(I) and ISO models can both be characterized as assessment-based models. Assessment-based techniques typically list a set of goals and sub-goals to achieve, provide a check-list to assess how much an organization achieves the goals, and may suggest tools to attain the goals. For example, ISO 15504-7 model (part of the forthcoming ISO 15504 standard) developed in a project called SPICE, approaches SPI with the following eight steps: Examine organisation's needs, Initiate process improvement, Prepare and conduct process assessment, Analyse results and derive action plan, Implement improvements, Confirm improvements, Sustain improvement gains, Monitor performance.

Like IDEAL, the ISO 15504-7 model deals with the management as a special issue, being something that is beyond the cycle itself. The management is seen as perhaps the most crucial issues of sustaining long-term improvement and ensuring that changes become permanent [32]. It includes organization, plan, measuring and reviewing tasks. SPI Literature is almost unique in recommending that improvement initiatives should be assigned to dedicated organizational units [28]. One of the most exact in this issue is perhaps IDEAL[sm 1], which defines several levels of groups concerned with SPI and is recommended to be used in parallel with CMM. In large organizations, in addition to practical operative working groups, there are four layers of management groups ensuring compliance to company's vision, coordinating and sharing of experiences (see Fig. 5.).

---

[1] The IDEAL[SM] model has been developed in Software Engineering Institute at Carnegie Mellon University (SEI).

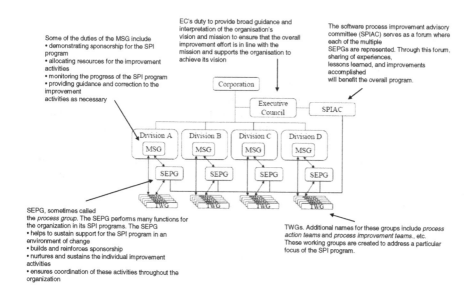

Some of the duties of the MSG include
• demonstrating sponsorship for the SPI program
• allocating resources for the improvement activities
• monitoring the progress of the SPI program
• providing guidance and correction to the improvement activities as necessary

EC's duty to provide broad guidance and interpretation of the organisation's vision and mission to ensure that the overall improvement effort is in line with the mission and supports the organisation to achieve its vision

The software process improvement advisory committee (SPIAC) serves as a forum where each of the multiple SEPGs are represented. Through this forum, sharing of experiences, lessons learned, and improvements accomplished will benefit the overall program.

SEPG, sometimes called the *process group*. The SEPG performs many functions for the organization in its SPI programs. The SEPG
• helps to sustain support for the SPI program in an environment of change
• builds and reinforces sponsorship
• nurtures and sustains the individual improvement activities
• ensures coordination of these activities throughout the organization

TWGs. Additional names for these groups include *process action teams* and *process improvement teams*, etc. These working groups are created to address a particular focus of the SPI program.

Fig. 5. Ideal: Typical SPI infrastructure in a large organization [33,32]

This arrangement assures that all levels of organization are involved in the SPI initiative: from senior management of executive council to people, working in or being customers to the process about to be changed, participating in TWG. As proposed in the organizational literature, wide scale participation is to guarantee that the entire organization is committed to follow the recommendations. "By involving practitioners in identifying and improving their own problems, the improvements will become situated in the proper context or practice, i.e. in their daily activities, making it far more likely that the practitioners will be committed to change their practice. By involving management, the SPI program will become linked to the organization's vision and appropriate resources to do improvements will be allocated and distributed." [2].

The members of SEPG (process group) should be experienced, have good interpersonal skills and be respected by peers [27,33,34]. This is because their role is to act as change agents and opinion leaders in the SPI initiative. Change agents initiate and support the improvement projects. They are teams (or individuals) external to the process that is to be improved. Opinion leaders, in turn, are competent individuals responsible for initiating, guiding and supporting the improvement at a local level. They also enjoy high respect in the social system that is to be changed [35].

The basic philosophy behind the IDEAL, as many other SPI models, is that the improvement or change is best done in project-like entities. The model itself is actually an attempt to establish good project management and engineering practices to process improvement program. Considering SPI initiatives as projects is one common way to approach planning of the initiative. In projects resources are allocated specifically to SPI initiatives, and their outcomes are specified as project deliverables. This improves visibility of the initiative [36], helps to ensure appropriate resources, and participation of experts from relevant parts of the organizations who can define working procedures that fit the organization and the new strategy [28].

The literature points out the need to obtain visible results backed up with data if possible, to keep the effort in focus, and to motivate and sustain interest in the SPI initiative [27]. Thus measurements that visualize the progress of the SPI effort are seen valuable. Applegate [3] suggests that to measure progress, it is necessary to benchmark initial performance and to conduct interval evaluations of process performance, stakeholder satisfaction and results. Process benchmarking can be done against leading firms in the industry or internally, or it can compare internally one development process with another highly successful development process. The company can also use baseline measurements, where the measurements are evaluated relative to a fixed norm, such as CMM [1]. The Goal Question [37], in turn, aims to deduce measurement from business goals of the organizations, instead of using the applied SPI model as a basis for measures.

Table 1. illustrates some aspects of organizational effectiveness that senior managers might want to measure [1,3].

Table 1. Organizational effectiveness measures [3]

Process performance	Stakeholder satisfaction	Results
• Time	• Customer/supplier satisfaction	• Market measures
• Quality	• Employee satisfaction	• Financial measures
• Cost		
• Innovation		

4.2 Learning

Even though especially CMM is aimed at improving software processes with an approach that is incremental and learning oriented, the instrumental and abstract role of the CMM organization is often forgotten. Instead the ideal model is taken as "self-evidently describing the evolution of the software organization 'as it is in itself' " [38,p. 20]. Thus, the software specialists are induced to push their organization along the prescribed learning curve and even in a learning oriented methodology - CMM - the abstract model and the related measurements come to dictate behavior, up to the point that many admit that CMM with its bias for 'technologies of reason' needs to be supplemented with proper concern for experimentation and true organizational learning.

As the previous section hints, the general view of SPI on learning is mostly operationalized as measures in addition to explicit role definitions. If used in most limited way, the metrics are used as a control mechanism. For instance, analysis by Ngwenyama & Axel Nielsen [39] reveals that even though the proponents advocate the idea that CMM would lead to a dynamic, flexible learning organization, the paradigm's core assumptions are based on rational rule-governed organization structures that are oriented toward stability, control, and productivity. The hierarchical structures of CMM work processes with their explicitly defined role responsibilities and strict management control are contradictory to building trust upon which a developmental culture thrives [39]. Indeed, one of the key challenges to SPI seems to be to simultaneously balance the objectives of control and learning: "Take as an example the implementation of TQM. TQM is steeped in a paradigm of control [19]. Concepts like reduction of variation, defined and standardized processes, management by fact, causal thinking, etc. all stem from the "Newtonian" paradigm of control and equilibrium, as manifested in the principles and practices of scientific management. Yet, TQM also has a learning component to it. Employee involvement, empowerment, and cross-functional coopera- tion are an important part of TQM. TQM thus has both mechanistic (control) and or- ganismic (adaptive learning) components. These learning components, in some ways, are in direct competition with the control components"[40].

Often, the measures are recommended to form a basis for the next improvement round. For instance, in IDEAL the last phase in process improvement cycle is Learning phase, where the overall adoption or improvement experience is reviewed to determine what was accomplished, whether the effort met the intended goals, and how the organization can implement change more effectively or efficiently in the future. Re- flecting this to learning models by Argyris and Schön [4] this view seems to support double-loop learning where the procedures are changed according to past experiences.

But, the company should facilitate organizational learning. When, for instance the experiences, lessons learned etc. were stored in a data base [41], forming part of ac- tively used organizational memory, the company is approaching more advanced 'deu- tero-level' learning. The improvement initiatives can also be supported by providing the groups with visualization tools, communication support, scheduling, reporting and controlling tools [41]. Experience factory is an example of a construct which separates practical problem solving and experience modeling. It aims to systematic reuse of previous knowledge by packaging experience related material relevant to a real user. This includes tailoring contents and format to a concrete anticipated usage situation. Experience is only valuable when set in context. It also point out that "we must base iteration, evolution, and learning on explicit information to form the seed for the next cycle." [42]. As a separate entity, an experience factory receives plans, status informa- tion, and experiences from all participating projects. Incoming data is organized in models, such as defect density models, Pareto charts of defect class baselines, algo- rithms, and so forth [42]. These models provide projects with immediate feedback.

In regard to assimilating tacit knowledge a few SPI articles and practical report sug- gests use of pilot projects, and mentoring [27]. Additionally, the multi level and cross- departmental SPI groups should advance a context where individuals with conflicting views can interact with each other and engage in dialogue. Otherwise, the means and tools to support learning in the route from 'creative chaos' towards rules and tacit knowledge is little discussed in the SPI literature. Maybe here the SPI literature could benefit from ideas presented in organizational learning on methods for advancing learning, such as in Fig. 1., and quality improvement steps proposed by [25].

5 Conclusions

This article provided a short presentation on literature on organizational learning and organizational change. A traditional way is to view learning as the "detection and cor- rection" of error [43], i.e. acting and learning due to conflict between what-is and what- was-supposed. Argyris and Schön [4] distinquish between three levels of learning, simple correction, changing procedures as a result of an error, and facilitating organiza- tional learning. The traditional of learning, as a "lessons learned" or post-mortem re- porting activity is often apparent in SPI literature [44]. The SPI paradigm seems to have adopted the views of Argyris and Schön [4] on learning where they aim at double-loop learning, i.e to to question and modify existing rules and procedures in response to mismatch or error. In this vein the organization plans to improve its processes gradually, that from learning point of view is generally regarded as being more favorable than radical changes. In the highest level of CMM(I) maturity, the goal is towards deutero-learning, where the double-loop learning is provided with proper organizational support and capabilities. Similar perspectives are proposed also in Experience factory.

However, there is also an alternative approach to learning suggested by literature. For instance Nonaka [12] proposes that new knowledge is created by dialogue which brings up conflicting views. This leads to a view where organizational learning is regarded as a continuous change process where specific learning cycle starts with creative conflict and ends up in formal norms and systems. This view can be recognized in the multi level organization structure of SPI groups. A few papers also advance use of mentoring and piloting in addition to formal training, but in general this 'learning via conflict' has almost no visibility in SPI literature.

Maybe, the SPI paradigm would benefit from taking a closer look on learning organization's models promoting creativity: the approach starts with creative phase, where mental models and brainstorming are applied to boost innovativeness in multi-departmental or multi-organizational teams, and finally curbs down to 'status quo' coordinated by shared work practices and formal rules.

We suggest that the software process improvement initiatives should pay more attention on how they facilitate learning and overcome the obstacles. Building on the organizational learning and change literature we propose the following steps to be considered more carefully in SPI models: First, the managers should communicate the objectives and methods for learning and provide also adequate resources and time for it. Second, innovation capability of people could be exploited more for instance by forming border-crossing teams and allowing more creative atmosphere in defining the objectives and means. Third, the management should commit and support personnel's learning and skill development. Fourth, learning and systemic change should be promoted with an organization level team. And, the final step in the change process is the adoption of formal metrics and systems.

References

1. Iversen, A., Ngwenyama, O.: Problems in measuring effectiveness in software process improvement: A longitudinal study of organizational change at Danske Data. International Journal of Information Management 26, 30–43 (2006)
2. Mathiassen, L., Ngwenyama, O., Aaen, I.: Managing Change in Software Process Improvement. IEEE Software 22(6), 84–91 (2005)
3. Applegate, L.: Managing in an information age: Transforming the organization for the 1990s. In: Baskerville, R., Smithson, S., Ngwenyama, O., DeGross, J.I. (eds.) Transforming organizations with information technology, pp. 15–94. Elsevier Science, Amsterdam (1994)
4. Argyris, C., Schön, D.: Organizational learning: A theory of action perspective. Addison Wesley, Reading (1978)

5. Cohen, W., Levinthal, D.: Absorptive Capacity: A New Perspective on Learning and Innovation. Administrative Science Quarterly 35, 128–152 (1990)
6. Doz, Y.L.: The evolution of cooperation in strategic alliances: initial conditions or learning processes? Strategic Management Journal 17, 55–83 (1996)
7. Gemünden, H.G., Ritter, T., Heyedebreck, P.: Network configuration and innovation success: An empirical analysis in German high-tech industries. International Journal of Research in Marketing (1996)
8. Gatterman, P.M., Hoffmann, S.C.: The relationship between learning orientation and innovation. In: 32nd EMAC Conference, Glasgow (2003)
9. Weick, K.E.: The social psychology of organizing, 2nd edn., p. 294. McGraw-Hill, Inc., New York (1979)
10. Weick, K.E.: Sensemaking in Organizations, 231 pages. Sage Publication Inc., Thousand Oaks (1995)
11. Nooteboom, B.: Learning by Interaction: Absorptive Capacity, Cognitive Distance and Governance. Journal of Management and Governance 4, 69–92 (2000)
12. Nonaka, I.: A Dynamic Theory of Organizational Knowledge Creation. Organization Science 5(1), 14–37 (1994)
13. Nonaka, I.: The knowledge-creating Company. Harvard Business Review 69(6), 96–104 (1991)
14. Senge, P.M.: The Fifth Discipline The Art & practise of the learning organization. Currency Doubleday, New York (1994)
15. Brown, J.S., Duguid, P.: Organizational learning and communities-of-practice: Toward a Unified View of working, learning and innovation. Organization Science 2(1) (February 1991)
16. Nonaka, I., Konno, N.: The Concept of BA: Building a foundation for knowledge creation. California management review 40(3) (Spring 1998)
17. Zimmerman, B.: Ralph Stacey's Agreement & Certainty Matrix (2001),
    http://www.plexusinstitute.org/edgeware/archive/think/
    main_aides3.html
18. Stacey, R.: Complexity and Creativity in Organizations. Berrett-Koehler Publishers (1996)
19. Dooley, K., Johnson, T.L.: TQM, Chaos and Complexity. Human Systems Management 14, 287–302 (1995)
20. Nonaka, I., Takeuchi, H.: The knowledge creating company. Oxford University Press, Oxford (1995)
21. Schein: Organizational culture, Sloan School of Management. MIT, Cambridge (1988)
22. Huber, G.: Organizational Learning: The Contributing Processes and the Literatures. Organization Science 2(1); Special Issue: Organizational Learning: Papers in Honor of (and by) James, G., pp. 88–115 (March 1991)
23. Galbraith, J.: Organizing to Deliver Solutions, Special Issue of Organizational Dynamics (May 2002)
24. Beer, M., Eisenstat, R.A., Spector, B.: The Critical Path to Corporate Renewal. Harvard Business School Press, Boston (1990)
25. Spector, B., Beer, M.: Beyond TQM Programmes. Journal of Organizational Change Management 7(2), 63–70 (1994)
26. Arent, J., Iversen, J., Andersen, C., Bang, S.: Project Assessments: Supporting Commitment, Participation, and Learning in Software Process Improvement. In: Proceedings of the 33rd Hawaii International Conference on System Sciences (2000)
27. Herbsleb, J., Zubrow, D., Goldenson, D., Hayes, W., Paulk, M.: Software quality and the Capability Maturity Model. Communications of the ACM 40(6) (1997)

28. Aaen, I., Arent, J., Mathiassen, L., Ngwenyama, O.: A Conceptual MAP of Software Process Improvement. Scandinavian J. Information Systems 13, 123–146 (2001)
29. Paulk, M.C., Curtis, B., Chrissis, M.B., Weber, C.V.: Capability maturity model, version 1.1. Software, VOL 10(4), 18–27 (1993)
30. Paulk, M.C.: How ISO 9001 compares with the CMM. Software 12(1), 74–83 (1995)
31. Dybå, T.: Enabling Software Process Improvement: An Investigation of the Importance of Organizational Issues. Empirical Software Engineering 7, 387–390 (2002)
32. Kinnula, A.: Software process engineering systems: models and industry cases, Oulun yliopisto (2001)
33. McFeeley, R.: IDEALSM - A User's Guide to Software Process Improvement. CMU/SEI-96- HB-001, Software Engineering Institute (February 1996)
34. Hardgrave, B., Armstrong, D.: Software process improvement: it's a journey, not a destination. Communications of the ACM 48(11) (2005)
35. Stelzer, D., Mellis, W.: Success factors of organizational change in software process improvement. Software Process: Improvement and Practice 4(4), 227–250 (2000)
36. Johansen, M.L.: Lessons Learned in a National SPI Effort. In: Proceedings of EuroSPI 1998, Gothenburg, Sweden, November 16-18, pp. 5–17 (1998)
37. Basili, V.R., Rombach, H.D.: The TAME project: towards improvement-oriented softwareenvironments. Transactions on Software Engineering 14(6), 758–773 (1988)
38. Ciborra, C.: The labyrinths of Information: Challenging the Wisdom of Systems. Oxford University Press, Oxford (2002)
39. Ngwenyama, O., Axel Nielsen, P.: Competing Values in Software Process Improvement: An Assumption Analysis of CMM From an Organizational Culture Perspective. IEEE Transactions on Engineering Management 50(1), 100–112 (2003)
40. Dooley, K.: A Complex Adaptive Systems Model of Organization Change. Nonlinear Dynamics, Psychology, and Life Sciences 1(1) (1999)
41. Sakamoto, K., Nakakoji, K., Takagi, Y., Niihara, N.: Toward computational support for software process improvement activities. In: Proceedings of the 20th international conference on Software engineering, Kyoto, Japan, April 19-25, pp. 22–31 (1998)
42. Schneider, K., Jan-Peter von Hunnius, J.-P., Basili, V.: Experience in Implementing a Learning Software Organization. IEEE Software (May/June 2002)
43. Senge, P.M.: Taking personal change seriously: The impact of Organizational Learning on management practice. Academy of Management Executive 17(2) (May 2003)
44. Levine, L.: Integrating Knowledge and processes in a Learning Organization. Information Systems Management 18(1) (Winter 2001)

The Role of Different Approaches in Inspection Process Improvement

Sami Kollanus

Department of Computer Science and Information Systems
P.O. Box 35 (Agora), FI-40014 University of Jyväskylä, Finland
sami.kollanus@jyu.fi

Abstract. There is a need to better understand improvement of software inspection practices. Typically process improvement is driven by different reference models like CMMI. In the previous work we found that such model based approach alone didn't provide sufficient support for inspection process improvement. This paper outlines an overall picture of inspection process improvement and four different approaches for it. These approaches are seen as complementary and the focus of the paper is on describing their role in the improvement process.

Keywords: software inspection, peer review, software process improvement.

1 Introduction

Software inspections were introduced more than 30 years ago [1] and several researchers have reported great savings or improved effectiveness gained from using inspections [2][3][4][5]. However, inspections are not so well applied in practice. Johnson [6] and Ciolkowski et al. [7] have both found that inspections and reviews are irregularly used in most of the software companies. In addition, our earlier work [8] proposes that there may be serious weaknesses in the current inspection practices even in the organizations, where inspections are well defined and regularly used.

It is reasonable to claim there is a need to better understand process improvement aspect on software inspections. However, there is very little such research made on the field. We conducted a comprehensive literature survey on inspection related research [9]. Only few of the surveyed 133 articles are related to inspection process improvement.

Software process improvement (SPI) has been strongly driven by reference models like CMM [10], CMMI [11] and ISO 15504 [12]. Various similar kinds of models have been suggested for specific process areas, for example testing [13], project management [14] and maintenance [15]. Our previous work [16][17] has focused on developing a maturity model for software inspection called ICMM (Inspection Capability Maturity Model). It has been developed based on the literature and experiences from eight case organizations. One of the key findings was that regardless of the positive experiences with ICMM, it didn't alone provide sufficient support for inspection

F. Bomarius et al. (Eds.): PROFES 2009, LNBIP 32, pp. 231–245, 2009.
© Springer-Verlag Berlin Heidelberg 2009

process assessment and improvement. This kind of model based process improvement has to be completed with some other aspects.

The goal of this paper is to sketch the overall picture of inspection process improvement and different approaches for it. Four different approaches and their role in inspection process improvement are presented. The work is based on both literature and the previous work with ICMM. The literature part is based on the previous literature survey [9] and completed with some relevant literature discussing SPI issues generally.

The second section will discuss the issues related to improvement process generally. Then sections 3-6 introduce four different approaches for inspection process improvement. The final conclusions are summarized in section 7.

2 Improvement Process

The previous inspection literature discusses very little about general organizational issues in process improvement. There are only few references, which more or less touch this viewpoint (ie. [18][19][20][21]). These few references don't include an overall picture of the improvement process in inspection context. It may be natural that they focus more on the substance, because the organizational viewpoint includes very few issues which are specific for inspections. And there is already a lot of research conducted on the general issues in software process improvement. Some key issues about the general SPI research are summarized in this section in order to create an overall picture of process improvement.

IDEAL model [22] is possibly the most known presentation about software process improvement as a process. The background of the model is based on the original *Capability Maturity Model* [10], which focused on the substance in various process areas, but doesn't provide practical support for process improvement. IDEAL model was developed to cover this need. It presents improvement process as 5 main phases, which divide into 14 activities (Figure 1). The circular form of the model emphasizes continuous nature of the improvement activities.

In the *Initiating phase*, the general objectives for the process improvement are defined. The current state of the organization is identified and analyzed in the *Diagnosing phase*. In the *Establishing phase*, long term strategies and concrete approaches for SPI are defined. In the *Acting phase*, solutions to the defined improvement areas are created, piloted, and deployed throughout the organization. The focus in the *Learning phase* is on learning from the experience and improving ability to adopt new technologies in the future.

A general model, like IDEAL, may be useful also for inspection process improvement. It may provide a good roadmap for the improvement activities on general level. In addition to this kind of process aspect, it is good to be aware of the typical success factors in process improvement. The following paragraphs include a short summary of the results from few different studies.

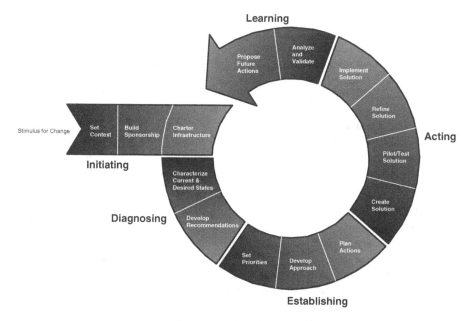

Fig. 1. IDEAL model [22]

Dybå [23] has summarized the key factors in SPI success to the following six items:

- **Business orientation:** SPI goals and actions are aligned with explicit and implicit
- business goals and strategies.
- **Involved leadership:** Leaders at all levels in the organization are genuinely committed to and actively participate in SPI.
- **Employee Participation:** Employees use their knowledge and experience to decide, act, and take responsibility for SPI.
- **Concern for Measurement:** The software organization collects and utilizes quality data to guide and assess the effects of SPI activities.
- **Exploitation of existing knowledge:** Exploitation involves improving existing capabilities by refining, standardizing, routinizing, and elaborating established ideas, paradigms, technologies, strategies, and knowledge.
- **Exploration of new knowledge:** exploration involves learning through discovery and experimenting with ideas, paradigms, technologies, strategies, and knowledge in hope of finding new alternatives

The items listed by Dybå are based on a comprehensive literature review. He uses them as hypotheses in his survey, which studied SPI success 120 organizations. He concluded that all six factors remarkably affected SPI success. They together explained more than 50 % of variation in SPI success.

Also several other studies have been focused on SPI success factors. Table 1 includes a summary of the results from five studies, which are based on varying research methods. There are clearly few common factors for the most of the results.

These are for example employee involvement, management commitment, measure-ment, resource allocation and well defined goals. Additionally, there are a number of various factors, which have been identified as remarkable at least in a single study. Also the most important factors have varied between the studies. Based on the varia-tion in the results, we can conclude that SPI success is a complex phenomenon that includes a lot of different factors. Therefore, there is no model that gives complete solutions for successful process improvement. The key issue is to know the organiza-tion and to find a fitting approach.

Most of the research studying SPI success is focused on factors which may have a positive effect on success. However, there are also some studies that have aimed to find barriers for successful SPI. For example, Goldeson and Herbsleb [24] studied both of the aspects in their survey. They found the following barriers for SPI success:

- excessive organizational politics
- "turf guarding"
- discouragement and cynicism from previous experience
- the feeling among the technical staff that process improvement gets in the way of their "real" work
- appraisals' recommendations too ambitious

Table 1. SPI success factors in five different studies

Success factor \ Study	Dybå [23]	Goldenson & Herbsleb [24]	Hall ym. [25]	Niazi ym. [26]	Stelzer & Mellis [27]
Employee involvement	x	x	x	x	x
Management commitment and support	-	-	x	x	x
SPI monitoring and measurement	x	x	x	-	-
Resource allocation	-	x	x	x	-
Well defined and realistic goals	-	x	x	-	x
Communication and co-operation	-	-	x	-	x
Change agents and key persons	-	-	x	-	x
Tailoring SPI approaches	-	-	x	-	x
Providing enhanced understanding	-	-	-	x	x
Leadership involvement	x				
Business orientation	x				
Exploitation of existing knowledge	x				
Exploration of existing knowledge	x				
Involved people are respected		x			
Well defined responsibilities		x			
Infrastructure for SPI			x		
Experienced staff				x	
Training				x	
Well defined SPI implementation methodology				x	
Managing the improvement project					x
Managing resistance to change					x
Stabilizing changed process					x

The issues discussed in this subsection are general and common to any kind of process improvement. They form a kind of framework in which also inspection process improvement take place. The rest of this paper focuses on issues that are specific in inspection context. The following subsections will describe different perspectives on inspection process improvement.

3 Reference Models for Inspection Process Improvement

Reference models here mean maturity or capability models that are developed to support inspection process improvement. These model types are based the approaches in the original CMM [10] and in ISO 15504 [12] which is often called SPICE. CMM is a *maturity model* which defines five stages for organizational maturity in software engineering context. The defined process areas prioritized so that the low level process areas are more critical to implement first. Based on this assumption, CMM is supposed to assess organizational maturity. This approach enables comparison between different organizations.

The aim of ISO 15504 [12] is not focused on organizational maturity, but capability of distinct process areas, which are assessed according to specific criteria. The goal for this approach is to enable more flexible process improvement compared to a maturity model like CMM. The comparison between ISO 15504 as a capability model and CMM as a maturity model is not valid anymore. Since the first version of current CMMI (updated CMM), the model has included also a capability model called continuous representation. And ISO (*International Organization for Standardization*) is in the process of developing its own stage model based on ISO 15504.

ICMM [16] is a maturity model for inspection process improvement that is based on our previous work. There are also few other related maturity models in the previous literature. CMMI [11] includes some requirements related to inspections, but they are described only on very general level. Some maturity models for software testing (i.e. [13][28]) include some ideas about inspections, but the descriptions are superficial. Earlier, Grady and Van Slack [4] have presented a maturity model for software inspections. However, their model focuses more on describing the history of the company wide implementation of inspections in HewletPackard.

The structure of ICMM (Figure 2) includes five stages which follow the ideas in CMMI. Inspection process areas are prioritized in the model based from the improvement point of view. It is a general assumption that for example the process areas defined on the second level should be implemented before the third level. According to our first experiences, ICMM worked well in identifying weaknesses in the current inspection practices [17]. However, the case organizations didn't have provide experience about the levels 4-5 or long term experience about using the model in inspection process improvement.

Tervonen et al. [29] have developed a capability model called i3GO that has later been improved by Harjumaa et al. [30]. The model divides inspection process into 12 distinct activities that are assessed through 29 indicators. The assessment result is a profile that describes how well each of the 12 activities is institutionalized in the organization.

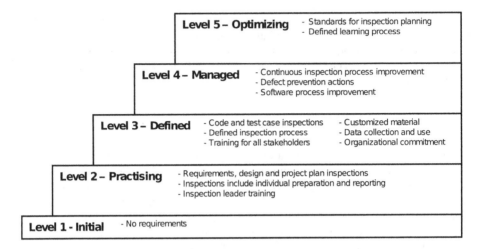

Fig. 2. ICMM model structure

Harjumaa et al. [30] report that i3GO has worked well in identifying weaknesses in the current inspection practices. There is little empirical experience about the model, which is common with ICMM. There are promising results about both of the models, but further research is needed in order to evaluate them. It is impossible to compare usefulness of the models due to very limited experiences. The basic structure is different in each model. ICMM as a stage model may provide more concrete support for designing improvement steps. On the other hand, i3GO provides more flexibility and more specific description about various inspection process areas. In any case, this kind of reference model provides an external framework, which may help in identifying weaknesses in the current practices.

4   Problem Based Approach

One of the key finding in our experiences with ICMM was that model based assessment alone did not provide enough support for inspection process improvement [17]. It may help in identifying the weaknesses that are directly related to the defined practices. However, there are various other practical problems which may occur in inspection practices. Our earlier work [31] introduces this kind of problems based on literature and a couple of case organizations. A good example is preparation for inspection meeting. Even an organization with well defined and regularly practiced inspections may have serious problems with preparation.

We suggest in our earlier work that model based inspection process improvement should be completed with a problem-based approach [31]. The article includes a suggestion of such process, which is includes the following five phases (these are in slightly improved form):

1. **Assess inspection practices:** The current state of inspection practices should be assessed based on some reference model like ICMM [16] or i3GO [30]. If this has not been done before, it can be undertaken at the same time with the problem

analysis. The assessment may reveal some problems which would be hard to detect otherwise.

2. **Collect experiences:** The second task is to collect experiences about possible problems with interviews or questionnaires. For example, the list presented in [31] can be used as a basis for this. The task is to find out what are the common problems in the organization.

3. **Identify actual problems:** The collected experiences probably do not directly reveal all the significant issues, but they may include some hints about other possible problems. This identification of the real problems should, therefore, include a more careful analysis by an expert with sufficient knowledge about inspections. The focus in this task is to analyze the degree of effect that the identified problems have on inspection effectiveness in the organization. All the suggested problems are listed and the importance of each identified problem is estimated in scale from 1 to 5 (1 is most important).

4. **Estimate required effort:** The task in this phase is to estimate the effort required to correct the problems. This is estimated in scale from 1 to 3. One in this scale means issues which are pretty easy to fix with small changes in inspection practices. Three means the problems which take a lot of time to be dealt with, for example changes in the whole organizational culture.

5. **Prioritize problems:** The final task is to prioritize the improvement actions to handle the identified problems. The estimated values from the tasks 3 and 4 are multiplied. The main rule is that the problems which get the lowest result values are the most beneficial to be handled first.

We found in the case organizations that the terms related to inspections may be ambiguous. Therefore interviews are possibly the best way to gather the data. Another finding was that the answers were not consistent. The interviewees were asked to estimate how common the suggested problems are in the organization (scale 1-5). Some of them described density of the problems while the others rather tried to describe how remarkable the problems are. In our case, the interviewees were asked to express the combination of these two dimensions with one score. Another option would be to request two distinct estimates.

Also some other than the suggested problems may come up during the process. An example in the case organizations was attitude towards inspections. Our question assumed that the authors may not be eager to give their documents under inspection. However, this was not experienced as a problem in any of the eight organizations, but the problems the inspectors' willingness to read others documents.

It good to realize that the problem based approach requires existing practices. It can be used to complete the weaknesses in model based approach when the basic practices are already deployed in the organization. The problem-based approach may be a continuous practice that is regularly used in monitoring an inspection process.

The faced problems may be related to the maturity level in an organization. Beecham et al. [32] made this kind of finding in their research that focused on software process improvement generally. They found that organizations on higher CMM level reported different problems from the others on lower CMM level. We got similar results related to inspection practices in the case organizations. Delay in inspection schedule is a good example of this. Some organizations do not face this problem, because they skip the whole inspection when the schedule gets tight. It may be a problem in an organization in which inspections are regular and institutionalized practice.

In the future, it could be possible to identify some common profiles which present typical problems in different situations. The profiles would possibly enable more effective identification of the problems. This kind of approach would be close to the idea of inspection patterns, which is introduced in the next section.

5 Inspection Patterns

There has been active discussion about *patterns* on the software engineering field during the recent years. Possibly the best known application are *design patterns* which describe communicating objects and classes that are customized to solve a general design in a particular context [33]. According to Gamma [33], a software pattern includes

- problem description including context in which it can be applied,
- solution to the problem,
- description of the expected benefits and costs.

This same idea has also been applied to software process patterns [34]. Harjumaa has applied the idea of process patterns specifically to software inspection improvement [19] [35]. He has defined a set of patterns that present typical situations with inspection practices in an organization. The key idea is to first identify the current state in the organization and the most important improvement needs. Then inspection patterns may help in defining a proper solution.

Harjumaa [19] defines the following 7 inspection patterns:

- **Greed:** Aims at finding more defects during inspections.
- **Early bird:** Aims at finding defects during earlier stages of development.
- **Substance:** Aims at finding more serious defects in inspections.
- **Comfort:** Aims at making the inspection process easier to run.
- **Promotion:** Aims at promoting the process so that it is carried out more often and in a larger number of projects.
- **Wisdom:** Aims at a more understandable, transparent and effective inspection process.
- **Precision:** Aims at making the process more rigorous, thus making it more effective.

Harjumaa [19] attach inspection patterns to model based assessment. First, existing practices are assessed and the most critical improvement needs are defined. Then it is possible to select the best fitting inspection pattern, which may help in defining concrete strategy for inspection process improvement. Inspection patterns are a kind of problem solving approach, but their focus is on very general level compared to the problem approach presented in the previous section.

Inspection patterns sound like a good idea for inspection process improvement. Reference models may help in identifying the current state of the practices, but they provide little support for designing concrete improvements. Well defined inspection patterns could answer this need, but there is still need for further research on this area.

Harjumaa gives only a superficial description of the patterns and would be hard to apply them in practice based on that information [19] [35].

6 Effectiveness Factors

The knowledge on different effectiveness factors in inspection process is not directly taken into account in the presented approaches. ICMM-model includes an assumption that the lower level practices are more important than the practices on the higher levels. Both problem based approach and inspection patterns includes some ideas about improving inspection effectiveness. However, none of these approaches doesn't provide improvement suggestions directly based on effectiveness factors. Therefore it may be beneficial to make a distinct evaluation of improvement suggestions from this point of view.

Effectiveness means here inspections' capability to find defects. The previous research includes several studies which discuss different effectiveness factors. The main results are summarized in the following points with the most important references:

- The most important factor is individual performance of the inspectors. [36][37][38]
- Most of the defects are found during individual preparation. [18][39][40]
- Inspection meetings don't have remarkable meaning in finding defects ([41][42][43]), but they may be important for some other purposes, i.e. training ([44][45]).
- An individual inspector has to use quite a lot of time in order to find major defects. For example, typical suggestions for code inspections are 60-200 LOC/hour. [3][18][46]
- Advanced reading techniques may help even experienced professional in finding defects effectively. [47][48][49][50][51]
- Proper training may improve inspection effectiveness. [52][53]

It is notable that the studies are usually controlled experiments focused on number of found defects and probably time used in inspection. Very few of them take economical aspect into account, which may remarkably affect the conclusions. For example, Porter et al. [54] and Biffl et al. [55] have both concluded that arranging two inspection rounds, instead of typical one, increased very little the number of found defects. The second round doesn't appear to be beneficial, if we look only the used time per found defect. However, Biffl et al. [55] also tried estimate the possible savings based on a sample data from industry and they found that the second round may pay for itself.

The main conclusion is that the inspectors' individual performance is the most important factor in inspection process. This phenomenon appears to be common to the whole software engineering field. Already Boehm made this finding related to the original COCOMO-model [56]. He studied different productivity factors in software engineering and concluded that development team had clearly the biggest impact on productivity. Some studies on software inspections ([36][38]) have found individual skills and experiment as important factors. In our case studies ([8][31]), the interviewees didn't regard insufficient skills as a problem, but the most significant problem in the inspection practices was motivation to read others' documents..

In improving inspection practices, it may be useful to evaluate improvement suggestions from the effectiveness point of view. Based on the conclusions presented above, it is most beneficial to focus on the issues related to skills and motivation of the inspectors. Different effectiveness factors should also be taken into account in defining inspection process. For example, it is crucial to understand that most of the defects are found in preparations phase.

The previous literature provides only a limited set of issues on inspection effectiveness. They may be useful in improving inspection practices, but the whole improvement can not be based on this knowledge. For example, there are several organizational factors that affect inspection success, but they are not directly related to the effectiveness point of view. In addition, effectiveness is generally very complex phenomenon and only a part of the potential effectiveness factors has been systematically studied. For example, some authors ([1][18]) suggest selecting independent inspectors outside of the development team in order to enable objective view on the documents. In our case organizations, the interviewees totally rejected this idea, because it often takes too much time from an outsider to inspect especially a technical document. Sometimes when applying a new technology, the author is the only one in the organization who is familiar with the technology.

7 Conclusions

This paper has tried to outline different aspects and approaches for inspection process improvement. Figure 3 summarizes the overall picture of inspection process improvement and the role of the presented approaches. The role of each approach is presented in relationship to the IDEAL model [22]. General understanding on software process improvement is a basis for inspection process improvement. This understanding includes organizational issues which are not specific for software inspections. The specific approaches for inspection process are mostly related to the diagnosing, establishing, and acting phases of the IDEAL model.

The diagnosing phase includes identification of the state of the current inspection practices. Reference models, like ICMM or i3GO, provide a framework which may help in assessing current practices and identifying weaknesses in them. One of the key finding in our case studies ([8][31]) was, that an organization with regular and well defined inspections may have serious problems with inspections in practice. Therefore the model based approach alone does not provide sufficient support for inspection process improvement. It should be completed with a problem based approach which is focused on identifying practical issues in inspection practices. The model based and problem based approaches together may be useful defining concrete improvement suggestions.

All the approaches presented in the paper are included in the establishing phase. Reference models provide help in identifying the practices, which need to be improved first. The problem analysis (section 4) may help in identifying practical problems in the current practices and in prioritizing improvement actions. After the initial assessment, the inspection patterns (section 5) may be useful in designing a proper improvement strategy. These different approaches are complementary and together

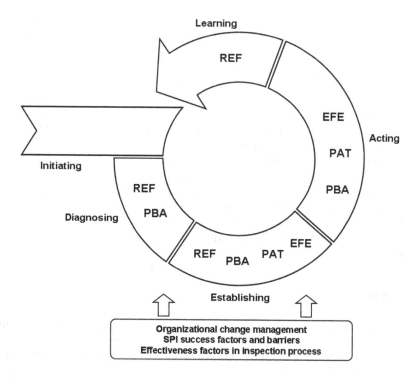

Fig. 3. Overall picture of inspection process improvement and the role of different approached in the improvement process (applied from IDEAL-model [22]). REF = Reference models, PBA = Problem-based approach, PAT = Inspection patterns, EFE = Effectiveness factors in inspection process.

they may be a useful toolset in defining the concrete action and strategy for inspection process improvement. However, they may not sufficiently take all the effectiveness issues into account. Therefore it is useful to make an additional analysis which is based on general effectiveness factors in inspection process (see section 6).

The acting phase includes the actual implementation of the process improvements. The problem analysis and the improvement patterns may help in this task. Well defined inspection patterns may provide a complete solution or at least help to find the right direction for improvement actions. Equally the problem analysis may lead to a solution. There may be a known possible solution to many of the practical issues in inspection practices (see [31]). Effectiveness factors in inspection process should also be taken into account, when the concrete implementation is defined.

Finally, reference models may be useful in the learning phase. They include practices which are related to process data collection and inspection process improvement generally.

Generally, organizational change management is possibly the most important issue in inspection process improvement, like in SPI overall. Several studies have tried to find out the most important success factors or the barriers in software process improvement. They have found a number of different factors which are not consistent between the studies. It can be concluded that due to the complexity of organizational change, there can't be a model or method which would guarantee success in it. Instead, the key issue in success is to know and understand the organization.

Throughout the whole improvement process, it is good to understand the general effectiveness factors in inspection process. The most important factor is always the individual performance of the inspectors in finding defects. So, an organization is probably successful with inspections if it is able get skilled enough employees to read others' documents with sufficient motivation. Even the best practices do not help without proper individual skills and motivation.

This paper has discussed four different approaches for inspection process improvement. The background for the study in the finding that the model based approach alone doesn't provide sufficient support for inspection process improvement. This finding may be relevant for the whole field of software process improvement which is strongly driven by different reference models. In the future work, it would be worth of studying, if the ideas presented in this paper can be generalized for the broader SPI field.

References

1. Fagan, M.: Design and code inspection to reduce errors in program development. IBM Systems Journal 15(3), 182–211 (1976)
2. Doolan, E.: Experience with Fagan's Inspection Method. Software - Practice and Experience 22(2), 173–182 (1992)
3. Fagan, M.: Advances in Software Inspections. IEEE Transactions on Software Engineering 12(7), 744–751 (1986)
4. Grady, R.B., Van Slack, T.: Key lessons in achieving widespread inspection use. IEEE Software 11(4), 46–57 (1994)
5. Russell, G.: Experience with inspection in ultra large-scale developments. IEEE Software 8(1), 25–31 (1991)
6. Johnson, P.M.: Reengineering Inspection. Communications of the ACM 41(2), 49–52 (1998)
7. Ciolkowski, M., Laitenberger, O., Biffl, S.: Software reviews, the state of the practice. IEEE Software 20(6), 46–51 (2003)
8. Kollanus, S., Koskinen, J.: Software inspections in practice: six case studies. In: Münch, J., Vierimaa, M. (eds.) PROFES 2006. LNCS, vol. 4034, pp. 377–382. Springer, Heidelberg (2006)
9. Kollanus, S., Koskinen, J.: Survey of software inspection research: 1991-2005. Computer Science and Information Systems Reports, Working Papers WP-40, Jyväskylä University Printing House, Jyväskylä, Finland, 39 p (2007)
10. Paulk, M., Curtis, B., Averill, E., Bamberger, J., Kasse, T., Konrad, M., Perdue, J., Weber, C., Withey, J.: Capability Maturity Model for Software. CMU/SEI-91-TR-24. Software Engineering Institute. Carnegie Mellon University, Pittsburgh (1991)
11. SEI. Capability Maturity Model Integration version 1.2. Software Engineering Institute (2006), http://www.sei.cmu.edu/cmmi/
12. ISO/IEC: ISO/IEC 15504 - Information Technology Process Assessment Parts 1-5 (2003-2006)

13. Burnstein, I., Homeyen, A., Suwanassart, T., Saxena, G., Grom, R.: A testing maturity model for software test process assessment and improvement. Software Quality Professional 1(4), 8–21 (1999)
14. Kerzner, H.: Strategic planning for project management using a project management maturity model. John Wiley & Sons, Chichester (2002)
15. April, A., Abran, A., Dumke, R.: SMcmm model to evaluate and improve the quality of the software maintenance process. In: 8th European Conference on Software Maintenance and Re-Engineering, Tampere, Finland, pp. 243–248 (2004)
16. Kollanus, S.: ICMM – Inspection Capability Maturity Model. In: IASTED International Conference on Software Engineering, pp. 372–377 (2005)
17. Kollanus, S.: Experiences from Using ICMM in Inspection Process Assessment. Software Quality Journal 17(2), 177–187 (2009)
18. Gilb, T., Graham, D.: Software Inspection. McGraw-Hill, New York (1993)
19. Harjumaa, L.: A pattern approach to software inspection process improvement. Software Process: Improvement and Practice 10(4), 455–465 (2005)
20. Jalote, P., Haragopal, M.: Overcoming the NAH syndrome for inspection deployment. In: 20th International Conference on Software Engineering, pp. 371–378. IEEE Computer Society, Washington (1998)
21. Wiegers, K.: Peer Reviews in Software: A Practical Guide. Addison-Wesley, Boston (2002)
22. SEI: IDEAL: A User's Guide for Software Process Improvement. CMU/SEI-96-HB-001. Software Engineering Institute, Carnegie Mellon University, Pittsburgh (1996)
23. Dybå, T.: An empirical investigation of the key factors for success in software process improvement. IEEE Transactions on Software Engineering 31(5), 410–424 (2005)
24. Goldenson, D., Herbsleb, J.: After the Appraisal: A Systematic Survey of Process Improvement, Its Benefits and Factors that Influence Success. SEI: CMU/SEI-95-TR-009. Software Engineering Institute (1995)
25. Hall, T., Rainer, A., Baddoo, N.: Implementing software process improvement: an empirical study. Software Process Improvement and Practice 7(1), 3–15 (2002)
26. Niazi, M., Wilson, D., Zowghi, D.: Critical success factors for software process improvement implementation: an empirical study. Software Process Improvement and Practice 11(2), 193–211 (2006)
27. Stelzer, D., Mellis, W.: Success factors of organizational change in software process improvement. Software Process - Improvement and Practice 4(4), 227–250 (1998)
28. Ericson, T., Subotec, A., Ursing, S.: TIM – A test improvement model. Software Testing, Verification and Reliability 7(4), 229–246 (1997)
29. Tervonen, I., Iisakka, J., Harjumaa, L.: Looking for inspection improvements through the base practices. In: Workshop on Inspection in Software Engineering, Paris (2001)
30. Harjumaa, L., Tervonen, I., Vuorio, P.: Using software inspection as a catalyst for SPI in a small company. In: Bomarius, F., Iida, H. (eds.) PROFES 2004. LNCS, vol. 3009, pp. 62–75. Springer, Heidelberg (2004)
31. Kollanus, S.: Issues in software inspection practices. In: Bomarius, F., Komi-Sirviö, S. (eds.) PROFES 2005. LNCS, vol. 3547, pp. 429–442. Springer, Heidelberg (2005)
32. Beecham, S., Hall, T., Rainer, A.: Software process improvement problems in twelve software companies: An Empirical Analysis. Empirical Software Engineering 8(1), 7–42 (2003)
33. Gamma, E., Helm, R., Johnson, R., Vlissides, J.: Design Patterns –Elements of Reusable Object-Oriented Software. Addison-Wesley, Reading (1995)

34. Coplien, J.: A Generative Development-Process Pattern Language, Pattern Languages of Program Design. Addison-Wesley, New York (1995)
35. Harjumaa, L.: Improving the Software Inspection Process with Patterns. Dissertation, University of Oulu, Finland (2005)
36. Knight, J.C., Myers, E.A.: An improved inspection technique. Communications of the ACM 36(11), 51–61 (1993)
37. Porter, A.A., Siy, H.P., Toman, C.A., Votta, L.G.: An experiment to assess the cost-benefits of code inspections in large scale software development. IEEE Transactions on Software Engineering 23(6), 329–346 (1997)
38. Sauer, C., Jeffery, D.R., Land, L., Yetton, P.: The effectiveness of software development technical reviews: a behaviorally motivated program of research. IEEE Transactions on Software Engineering 26(1), 1–14 (2000)
39. Christenson, D.A., Huang, S.T., Lamperez, A.J.: Statistical quality control applied to code inspections. IEEE Journal of Selected Areas of Communication 8(2), 196–200 (1990)
40. Laitenberger, O., Beil, T., Schwinn, T.: An industrial case study to examine a non-traditional inspection implementation for requirements specifications. Empirical Software Engineering 7(4), 345–374 (2002)
41. Porter, A.A., Johnson, P.M.: Assessing software review meetings: results of a comparative analysis of two experimental studies. IEEE Transactions on Software Engineering 23(3), 129–145 (1997)
42. Sabaliauskaite, G., Kusumoto, S., Inoue, K.: Assessing defect detection performance of interacting teams in object-oriented design inspection. Information and Software Technology 46(13), 875–886 (2004)
43. Votta, L.: Does every inspection need a meeting? ACM Software Engineering Notes 18(5), 107–114 (1993)
44. d'Astous, P., Robillard, P.N.: Characterizing implicit information during peer review meetings. In: 22nd International Conference on Software Engineering, pp. 460–466. ACM Press, New York (2000)
45. Johnson, P., Tjahjono, D.: Assessing software review meetings: A controlled experimental study using CSRS. In: 19th International Conference on Software Engineering, pp. 118–127. ACM Press, New York (1997)
46. Dunsmore, A., Roper, M., Wood, M.: The role of comprehension in software inspection. Journal of Systems and Software 52(2-3), 121–129 (2000)
47. Basili, V.R., Green, S., Laitenberger, O., Lanubile, F., Shull, F., Soerumgaard, S., Zelkowitz, M.: The empirical investigation of perspective-based reading. Empirical Software Engineering 1(2), 133–164 (1996)
48. Dunsmore, A., Roper, M., Wood, M.: The development and evaluation of three diverse techniques for object-oriented code inspection. IEEE Transactions on Software Engineering 29(8), 677–686 (2003)
49. Laitenberger, O., Atkinson, C., Schlich, M., El Emam, K.: An experimental comparison of reading techniques for defect detection in UML design documents. Journal of Systems and Software 53(2), 183–204 (2000)
50. Porter, A., Votta, L.G.: An experiment to assess different defect detection methods for software requirements inspections. In: 16th International Conference on Software Engineering, pp. 103–112. IEEE Computer Society Press, Los Alamitos (1994)
51. Thelin, T., Runeson, P., Regnell, B.: Usage-based reading — an experiment to guide reviewers with use cases. Information and Software Technology 43(15), 925–938 (2001)

52. Ebert, C., Parro, C.H., Suttels, R., Kolarczyk, H.: Improving validation activities in a global software development. In: 23rd International Conference on Software Engineering, pp. 545–554. IEEE Computer Society, Washington (2001)
53. Rifkin, S., Deimel, L.: Applying program comprehension techniques to improve software inspections. In: 19th Annual NASA Software Engineering Workshop, pp. 115–126 (1994)
54. Porter, A., Siy, H., Mockus, A., Votta, L.: Understanding the sources of variation in software inspections. ACM Transactions on Software Engineering and Methodology 7(1), 41–79 (1998)
55. Biffl, S., Freimut, B., Laitenberger, O.: Investigating the cost-effectiveness of reinspections in software development. In: 23rd International Conference on Software Engineering, pp. 155–164. IEEE Computer Society, Washington (2001)
56. Boehm, B.W.: Software Engineering Economics. Prentice-Hall, Englewood Cliffs (1981)

Scenario-Based Assessment of Process Pattern Languages

Antti Välimäki[1], Sari Vesiluoma[2], and Kai Koskimies[3]

[1] Metso Automation Inc, Finland
Antti.Valimaki@metso.com
[2] Teleca AB, Finland
Sari.Vesiluoma@teleca.com
[3] Tampere University of Technology, Finland
Kai.Koskimies@tut.fi

Abstract. Current standards and models for the quality of software development processes lead to a coarse-grained quality model which is heavy and difficult to focus for specific purposes. We propose a more light-weight method for
assessing processes that can be expressed as process pattern languages. The method is based on imitating an existing software architecture evaluation method,
ATAM, in the context of processes. The main advantages of the method are
more fine-grained assessment in terms of quality attributes possibility to tune
the assessment for a certain purpose, and a more light-weight assessment procedure. We illustrate the method in the case of two process pattern languages.

Keywords: Assessment, Process, ATAM, Global software development,
Knowledge, Agile project management, Organization patterns, Process patterns.

1 Introduction

Process models, such as OMT++ [1], Unified Process (UP) [2] or Scrum [3], describe
the phases, tasks, roles, artifacts etc. involved in a software development project. A
process model can be defined as a strict, step-by-step procedure, or more loosely as a
set of principles, practices and guidelines to be applied in a concrete software development process. Typically, the in-house process models of companies are relatively detailed and strict (like OMT++), while general process frameworks like UP and Scrum
are more of the latter kind. A loose process model can also be given as a process pattern language [4], that is, as an organized set of process patterns [5],[6],[7],[8],[9], project patterns [10], or organizational patterns [5],[11],[12],[13]. The advantage of the
pattern language approach is that the process model need not cover the entire process,
but it can concentrate on a certain viewpoint of the software development process. For
example, such partial process models have been given as pattern languages for managing knowledge sharing [14] and global software development [15],[16],[17] in software development.

Regardless of the way a process model is given, its main purpose is to improve the
quality of the software development work. Good quality can mean a flawless product,
timeliness, effectiveness, etc. Traditionally, process quality has been addressed by
general capability maturity models, such as SPICE (ISO 15504) [18] and Capability

F. Bomarius et al. (Eds.): PROFES 2009, LNBIP 32, pp. 246–260, 2009.
© Springer-Verlag Berlin Heidelberg 2009

Maturity Models Integrated (CMMI) [19], defining criteria for a process to be classified according to few maturity levels. Each maturity level specifies certain practices that are required for a process at that level. However, this approach has two major shortcomings. First, it gives only a rough measure for the general quality of a process, not answering questions like: what quality attributes are endangered if the process cannot reach a particular level? These kinds of questions arise if we wish to make a decision whether or not to adopt a process model that does not reach a particular level. Second, assessing the maturity level of a process becomes an unnecessarily heavy procedure in cases where only some particular aspect of quality is under scrutiny. For example, if a company is worried about the fault rate and wants to analyze its process with respect to fault management, it makes no sense to perform a general maturity level assessment. While general maturity models are suitable for holistic assessment of processes, we need more focused and lightweight assessment methods especially for viewpoint-specific processes and assessment motivations.

In many ways a process model can be compared to system architecture. The implementation of a process model is a concrete process instance, in the same way as the implementation of system architecture is the actual system. The system architecture determines the major quality attributes of the system, and the process model determines the major quality attributes of its instances realized in software development projects. The problem of determining the quality of a process model also resembles the problem of determining the quality of software architecture: in both cases, there are certain solutions supposedly contributing to some quality attributes, but the actual effect of these solutions to the quality is unclear. A further similarity is that in both cases, quality assessment is difficult on the basis of the general process or architecture model only, without considering the actual concrete realization of these models.

In the context of system architecture, a popular technique to assess the quality of software architecture is to apply scenario-based approaches, like ATAM (Architecture Tradeoff Analysis Method) [20]. In ATAM, the quality requirements are first derived from business goals and concretized using scenarios. That is, for each quality requirement (say, UI portability), a concrete situation testing the quality requirement is given, related to an imaginary implementation of the system (say, "the GUI of the system is made browser-based in a month"). Such scenarios are then analyzed against the solutions in the architecture, trying to identify those solutions which affect the realization of the scenario. If the scenario is considered realizable, the solutions contributing to this quality attribute are identified and marked as "safe". If the scenario is considered unrealizable, the solutions making the scenario difficult or impossible are identified as "risks". The general idea of ATAM is to create in this way links between the quality attributes and solutions in the architecture. To focus the assessment on the most important requirements, the scenarios are prioritized so that less essential scenarios can be ignored in the analysis.

We argue that a similar method can be applied for the quality assessment of software development processes as well. That is, the practices in a software process model (solutions) can be analyzed against concrete situations (scenarios) testing certain desired quality attributes in an imaginary instance of the process model. In that way, we can infer not only the overall quality level of a process model, but we also get a detailed explanation about which quality attributes are weak or strong in the process model, and why. We can also make observations on "safe" and "risky" practices in general: if a certain practice often appears as a "safe" solution, this practice is obviously beneficial, if another practice is many times labelled "risky", the value of the practice should be clearly questioned. The assessment process can be adjusted according to chosen goals or needs in a company, and carried out as lightly as possible.

A necessary prerequisite for this approach is that the individual practices of the process model are clearly identified, described and named. This is often not the case, of course. However, if a process is described as a pattern language, the solutions (patterns) are readily available. Here we do not discuss the question of "patternizing" a process model description, but assume that a process description is given as a pattern language, making the individual practices explicit. This can be compared to the assessment of software system architecture: the individual solutions of the architecture must be found and identified before an ATAM-like analysis can be performed.

The main contribution of this paper is a scenario-based assessment method of software development processes following the idea of ATAM, and its evaluation in the context of two process pattern languages, one intended for managing knowledge sharing in software development [14], and the other for global software development [15],[16],[17]. The assessment method is called Q-PAM (Quality-oriented Process Assessment Method).

We proceed as follows. First, we will briefly discuss the quality concept in the context of software processes in Section 2. The Q-PAM method itself is described in Section 3. In Section 4 we will discuss two case studies where we have applied the method for two pattern languages. We conclude with a discussion on the expected benefits and weaknesses of the method, and ideas for future work.

2   Quality in Software Engineering

In software engineering, the target is to produce results carrying an adequate level of software quality [21]. Software quality refers to e.g. the degree of a system or process to meet specific requirements and to the degree to meet customer needs and expectations [21]. The elements describing the quality of a piece of software have usually been referred to as quality attributes. Different software quality models have introduced selected sets of these quality attributes [22]. ISO 9126 standard [23] is one example of these software quality models.

ISO 9126 includes three perspectives to software product quality. They are internal quality, external quality and quality in use. Internal quality can be measured during development of the product, and external quality can be measured when the product is executed. Quality in use can be seen by the user while the product is applied in the intended fashion. The quality attributes, or, as the standard calls, quality characteristics, of external and internal quality are introduced in Fig 1. Quality in use includes the attributes effectiveness, productivity, safety, and satisfaction.

Also ISO 9000 [24] and CMMI have been referred to as quality models. However, their focus has been more on processes than on quality software results [22]. To summarize, at a very general level the quality in software engineering can be divided into the quality of the resulting software (product quality) and the quality of the processes (process quality) utilized to create the results.

Fig. 1. ISO 9126 quality attributes

To ensure adequate software quality, different kinds of software quality assurance activities are implemented and included into software engineering processes. Galin [21] lists different elements of software quality assurance, e.g. reviews, testing, procedures and work instructions, measuring, and quality management standards. These targets either to check reactively the quality (e.g. reviews, testing and measuring) or to ensure proactively that certain procedures are used to avoid possible quality problems in the resulting software (procedures and work instructions, and quality management standards).

Quality management standards or alike, e.g. ISO 9000, CMMI or ISO 15504, include all pre-selected sets of specific requirements for a software engineering organization to reach a certain maturity or capability. These standards are important as utilizations of international professional knowledge [21]. ISO 9000 is very general and targeted to assist all types of organizations to implement and operate effectively quality management systems. CMMI and ISO 15504 have their origins in software engineering work and are thus more software engineering specific quality models. All such process based quality models include implicit assumptions of what good quality in software processes means. Based on e.g. the quality management principles of ISO 9000 or the selection of process areas in CMMI some assumptions might be made about the underlying process quality attributes, but not much support has been given to really understand them.

In this work we will exploit ISO 9126 to derive quality attributes for processes, as part of the construction of quality profiles discussed in Section 3.2. However, this is only one possible technique of deriving process quality attributes, and the Q-PAM method does not take a standpoint of the technique. Indeed, a company could come up with the desired quality attributes as a result of an internal discussion on the goals of the assessment.

3   The Q-PAM Method

In the following we will first outline the Q-PAM method as a whole, and then explain the individual steps in more detail.

3.1 Method Overview

The first step in Q-PAM is to create a quality profile for the process (here, a process pattern language). The quality profile is a set of quality attributes considered essential in the assessment of the process. The quality profile thus depends not only on the quality requirements of the process, but also on the purpose of the assessment: the same process may be assessed with different profiles. Quality profiles are assumed to be obtained by extracting them from quality attribute lists available in standards. The construction of the quality profile is discussed in more detail in Section 3.2.

When the quality profile has been constructed, each quality attribute is associated with scenarios that serve as test cases for the quality attribute. A scenario is a concrete desired situation in an imaginary instance of the process where the existence or non-existence of the required quality attribute can be verified. The construction of the scenarios is discussed in Section 3.3. Scenarios can be prioritized for more focused processing, if needed.

The next step is the actual quality analysis. Each (possibly prioritized) scenario is analyzed against the process patterns: which patterns (if any) support the realization of the scenario, and which patterns counteract against the scenario (if any). A tag is attached to the scenario, characterizing the extent to which the pattern language is considered to pass the scenario test, on the basis of the analysis. The analysis step is discussed in more detail in Section 3.4.

3.2 Creating Quality Profile

A quality profile is a (possibly hierarchically structured) set of quality attributes. The term quality profile has been used here in a similar meaning as Bosch [25] has used it in the context of software architectures. In both cases, a profile is a means to capture a covering set of scenarios for a particular assessment purpose. A quality profile can be created on the basis of the requirements of a software development process (if such exist), a company's business goals, the purpose of the assessment, and/or a common quality framework. Here, we will use the quality attributes of ISO 9126 associated with external and internal quality as a basic source of the quality profile, interpreting and transforming the quality attributes for the context of processes. This is a straightforward technique that can be recommended in many cases, but we emphasize that other techniques could be used as well.

Let us consider a sample quality attribute in ISO 9126, efficient time behavior (that is, sub attribute of Time behavior under Efficiency). The standard defines this as "the capability of the software product to provide appropriate response and processing times and throughput rates when performing its function, under stated conditions". If we replace the words product and function with words process and task, respectively, this definition can be applied for processes as well, resulting in: the capability of the process to provide appropriate response and processing times and throughput rates when performing its tasks, under stated conditions. This kind of adaption is possible and reasonable to nearly all of the quality attributes in ISO 9126 regarding external and internal quality.

A quality profile obtained from a general quality model can be refined according to process specific characteristics or purpose of the assessment. For example, Efficiency could be refined as Project manager time usage, if the company is particularly interested in the efficient use of project manager resources. A more refined profile makes it easier to find scenarios related to the quality attribute.

3.3 Constructing Scenarios

The general idea of a scenario is to serve as a test case that can be run against the process patterns. For this purpose, a scenario should describe a concrete and measurable situation in an imaginary process instance (project). If the scenario represents a typical situation, a succeeding test suggests that the process pattern language normally supports the situation of the scenario. If the scenario represents a stress situation trying the limits of the process, a succeeding test gives an upper bound for the capacity of the process. A scenario can also test some specific part of the process that is of particular interest.

Each quality attribute in the quality profile should be associated with at least one scenario. For example, assume that we are assessing a process pattern language for requirements analysis, and the quality profile contains quality attribute Changeability (as a sub attribute of Maintainability). This quality attribute could be further refined as Organizational changeability. A scenario could be then given for this quality attribute as follows:

> Company X buys our company and wants to make our development process compatible with theirs. The requirements analysis part of our process is made compatible with X's process within half a year using nine man-months.

Note that this kind of a change scenario requires exact time specifications to be analyzable. All the implications or assumptions need not be visible in the scenario, but they must be reasonably inferable on the basis of the scenario. In the example, company X should refer to an actual company, with known process practices.

Scenarios are as valuable assets for processes as test cases are for systems, recording important information related to the process. Thus, all scenarios given for a quality profile should be documented and preserved. However, scenarios may have different weight in an assessment project, and there may be limited resources to carry out the assessment. To be able to concentrate on the essential ones among a large set of scenarios, the scenarios can be prioritized according to their importance.

3.4 Analysis

During the analysis phase, each of the (highly prioritized) scenarios is considered, and the involved process patterns are identified. The involved patterns are those patterns that potentially have affect on the scenario. Essentially, the analysis means that the effect of these patterns on the scenario is studied. For each pattern involved in the scenario, a positive conclusion is that the scenario situation is supported by the pattern, so that the application of the pattern helps to realize the scenario. A negative conclusion is that the pattern either does not provide support for handling a situation that it is supposed to support, or it hinders or complicates the situation described by the scenario. A rationale explaining either a positive or negative conclusion is associated with the scenario. In the case studies we have marked positive and negative conclusions with N (non-risk) or R (risk), respectively.

Sometimes it may be difficult to conclusively argue that a scenario is realizable using the process patterns, but there are patterns that provide some assistance in the scenario. Similarly, there may be patterns which do not prohibit a scenario, but may be to some extent counteracting against it. In these cases, it would be sensible to use a more fine-grained result than just a binary tag.

After each scenario has been analyzed and tagged, the assessment data is in principle available. However, if there are several quality attributes (with analyzed scenarios), it may be difficult to present this data in a condensed, complete form. For this purpose, the quality attributes can be grouped and each group can be characterized with a ratio of succeeded and failed scenarios. In this way, it is possible to find larger "problem areas" in the process. For example, if many scenarios related to different sub attributes of Efficiency fail, it seems reasonable to suggest that efficiency is a problem area in the process. Summary of the analysis of scenarios can be presented also by a table which is applied in the second case study.

4   Case Studies

We have applied the Q-PAM method to assess the quality of two pattern languages ([14], [15], [16], [17]). Both languages are motivated by practical needs and are made in industrial context. These languages have been created to support software development from two specific viewpoints, knowledge sharing and global software development. The assessment of the former has been made a little earlier than the assessment of latter. The implementation of the latter assessment has been somewhat influenced by our experiences of the first assessment, but the main ideas of Q-PAM as presented in this paper have been followed in both cases. The fact that these pattern languages have been developed by the authors does not essentially affect this study, since the actual assessment (and especially the creation of the scenarios) was carried out by an independent group. The role of the pattern language author in the assessment was similar to the role of the software architect in the ATAM method.

In both cases the assessment was implemented in a workshop consisting of two sessions. The first session included a brief introduction of the pattern language and of the Q-PAM evaluation method. The author of the pattern language proposed a quality profile that was refined together with the evaluators. The reminder of the first session was used for defining the scenarios. In both cases authors were not involved in creating scenarios. After the first session the author made a first draft for the analysis. It was examined in the second session scenario by scenario and corrected according to the findings in the workshop. In the following we discuss the case studies. We will briefly introduce the pattern languages, but for a more detailed account the reader is referred to literature [14], [15], [16], [17]. The assessment process is described, and the assessment technique is illustrated by presenting the analysis results of a representative scenario in both cases, explaining briefly the patterns involved in the analysis. We conclude both case studies with a summary of the results of the assessment and the experiences.

Here the focus is not in the actual implications of the assessments on these particular pattern languages, but rather we aim to illustrate the nature of the results and observations obtained in this kind of assessment based on the case studies.

4.1 Assessing a Pattern Language for Knowledge Sharing in Software Development

4.1.1 Target Pattern Language

The purpose of the Knowledge Sharing Pattern Language [14] is to enhance performance in software engineering work through improved knowledge sharing. This language includes 28 knowledge sharing patterns structured according to two dimensions: knowledge sharing interfaces and target knowledge types. The knowledge sharing interfaces include knowledge sharing in a project team, in an organization (between projects or projects and the base organization), and between the organization and other organizations. The target knowledge types include six types of knowledge areas: work status type of knowledge, knowledge regarding to requirements of a project, work results knowledge, work guidance, lessons learned type of knowledge, and competence.

These two dimensions are relevant because knowledge sharing takes place between different human stakeholders and different types of knowledge have different targets. The Knowledge Sharing Pattern Language is intended to be applied in a software development process regardless of the basic process model, being equally well suitable e.g. for traditional water-fall processes and agile processes.

4.1.2 Applying Q-PAM

Four faculty members from the Tampere University of Technology participated in the evaluation workshop along with the author. Three of the participants did not have any prior knowledge about the Knowledge Sharing Pattern Language. They were the main actors in this workshop. All participants had prior experience using the ATAM method in industrial context.

The author introduced a candidate quality profile in the first evaluation session. It was accepted after some discussion. Only a small subset of quality attributes from the ISO 9126 external and internal quality attributes was used. Reliability and maintainability related quality attributes (see Figure 1) were left out, because those are not critical in the case of the Knowledge Sharing Pattern Language. Similarly compliance (standards, conventions etc.) was left out of each quality attribute area. The rest of the unselected quality attributes were left out because of their low importance in this case.

The main part of the first workshop session was used for constructing the scenarios. The scenarios were decided by the three participants who did not have prior knowledge of the Knowledge Sharing Pattern Language. This way the independence of the scenarios with respect to the Knowledge Sharing Pattern Language was ensured. Eventually, 31 scenarios were defined. Those were not prioritized, because the evaluators anticipated that they will be able to analyze all during the second session. The prioritization, however, would have raised the value of the evaluation. In particular, relating the importance of a scenario (as suggested by the prioritization) with the information about the risk classification of the patterns involved in the scenario would have been valuable for evaluating the overall relevance of the results.

The results of the analysis of an exemplary scenario are presented in Table 1. For each scenario we have given a scenario id (e.g. S20), the type of the scenario in parenthesis (meta-level or process-level), and the scenario itself divided into the actual scenario and a response part. In this case study we found it useful to distinguish between meta-level and process-level scenarios. Here meta-level refers to a scenario that concerns the pattern language itself, while process-level refers to a scenario that concerns the application of some of its patterns. Separating these viewpoints clarified the discussions and helped in the formulation of the scenarios.

Table 1. Example analysis of a scenario

Scenario	S20 (process)	The chief architect of a project leaves the company.		
Response		A new, properly-educated person can effectively take his/her place in a month.		
Quality	Main Attribute	Resource Utilization (Efficiency)		
	Pattern	Analysis of Pattern Application	R	N
	Followed Progress	As a result of using this pattern the project is systematically following its progress compared to the project plan letting the new architect quickly find out the current situation in the project.		N
	Managed Versions	The pattern ensures identification and configuration management of the work results aswell as finding those. The new architect can find current right versions of project materials based on the rules for storing data.		N
	Discovered Lessons	Lessons learned have been registered in this project and can support the new architect to learn based on earlier experiences in this project.		N
	Work Guidance	Guidance existing for the project based on the standard processes of the company. The new architect has documentation about how the work is done in this project at general level. Also, if the architect has been in other projects in the same organization, the processes used are rather similar between projects.		N
	Shared Understanding	Targets for the project have been set, requirements defined and documented and deliverables and change management defined making it easy for the new architect to understand the purpose and aims of this project.		N
		The pattern language does not include very strong support for project memory in one project. This means, for example, that the patterns do not support definition of project folders, or what information should be stored and where.	R	
Result		**Some Support:** Several elements in the pattern language support storing of knowledge and sharing also in a discontinuity situation. There are, however, also some clear additional needs to have more support how to create a project specific "memory".		

The main quality attribute tells the quality attribute which is considered when defining the scenario. In the parentheses is the group this quality attribute belongs to in the ISO 9126 standard. The result part gives the overall conclusion regarding the support provided by the pattern language for this scenario: supporting, some support or no support. The associated explanation gives the reasoning for the conclusion based on the patterns. The columns R and N indicate whether or not the pattern includes a risk (R) or non-risk (N) for the realization of the scenario. An empty pattern name indicates a missing pattern, with an explanation of the (missing) required support for the scenario.

The patterns referred to in Table 1 are briefly introduced in Table 2. The solution part of the pattern is summarized with a short outline. For the actual pattern descriptions, the reader is referred to [26].

Table 2. Knowledge sharing patterns used in the example scenario

Name	Problem	Solution outline
Followed Progress	A project manager not knowing the project situation and progress status well enough.	Follow project progress on task basis and compare the realization to the project plan and schedule identifying, noticing the risks involved and changes required
Managed Versions	Difficulties in sharing the (intermediate) work results in the project team.	Establish configuration management, system integration practices and data management guidance in a project to manage project data and to have it available for relevant persons.
Discovered Lessons	In a project many experiences are gained but those are not systematically collected and understood.	Have a team exploring the relationship between action and outcome and producing lessons learned based on that.
Work Guidance	An organization with a need to establish or improve the guidance of work in the organization in order to allow for more efficient team work.	Define common targets and common ways of working and continuously improving them.
Shared Understanding	The aimed results of a project are not yet clear enough for all parties, especially between the customer and the supplier.	Instead of just starting to define requirements for a project, decompose the project target into different smaller parts. Negotiate these with the customer to have a shared understanding.

Of the resulting 31 scenarios, 14 scenarios were classified as being supported by the pattern language, 12 scenarios were classified as being partially supported (having supporting non-risk elements but also some risks), and 5 scenarios were classified as being not supported. At the process-level, 18 of the 23 scenarios get at least some support from the knowledge sharing patterns. Nine of those are fully supported by the knowledge sharing patterns and eight get some support. Five scenarios do not get any support from the Knowledge Sharing Pattern Language. At the meta-level, five scenarios of eight were classified as fully supported and three as partially supported. Based on this, the Knowledge Sharing Pattern Language as a whole seems to give reasonable support to the scenarios.

During the workshop, several improvement possibilities to the knowledge sharing patterns were found and the analysis resulted in better understanding of the limits of the Knowledge Sharing Pattern Language. For example, the analysis resulted in a finding that the Knowledge Sharing Pattern Language does not give very good support for achieving the right quality level of documentation, and that the pattern language would benefit of patterns giving better support for establishing a project memory, a systematic approach for storing of project related information.

An observation regarding the assessment process itself was that, in contrast to software architecture evaluation, typically a large portion of the solutions (patterns) is involved in a scenario, and these patterns are difficult to identify straight away. Thus, it was found useful to check the possible involvement of every pattern in the language when analyzing a scenario. Also the risk assessment was in some cases less unambiguous, giving rise to different views in the assessment team.

4.2 Assessing a Pattern Language for Global Software Development

4.2.1 Target Pattern Language

The purpose of the Global Software Development for Project Management (GSD) Pattern Language [15],[16],[17] is to enhance performance of project management work through improved global software project management practices. The GSD Pattern Language includes 18 process patterns. The current version of GSD Pattern Language includes process patterns supporting both traditional waterfall and agile project management.

4.2.2 Applying Q-PAM

Three faculty members from the Tampere University of Technology, three employees from Metso Automation and one employee from Teleca Inc. participated in the assessment workshop along with the author. Three of seven participants did not have any prior knowledge about the GSD Pattern Language and three of seven participants did not have prior experience using the ATAM method in an industrial context.

The author introduced a candidate quality profile in the first evaluation session based on ISO 9126. It was accepted with some changes after some discussion. At the highest level, the chosen quality profile consisted of *Functionality*, *Efficiency* and *Adaptability*. *Functionality* was refined as *Suitability*, *Accuracy* and *Security*. *Efficiency* was refined as *Time Behaviour* and *Resource Utilization*.

The analysis of one of the resulting scenarios is introduced in Table 3. The same notation is used as in Table 1. The patterns referred to in Table 3 are briefly introduced in Table 4. The solution part of the pattern is summarized with a short outline.

Table 3. Example analysis of a scenario

Scenario	S12	An offshore designer decides to decrease the contents of a feature by 50%. In this way, he/she can get the feature to suit one iteration but the problem is that he/she doesn't talk with the product manager. This problem should be visible in two weeks.		
Response		A problem need to be solved in GSD as fast as in centralized development.		
Quality	Main Attribute	Accuracy (Functionality), Time Behaviour (Efficiency)		
	Pattern	Analysis of Pattern Application	R	N
	Iteration Review	The pattern ensures that the change can be found at the latest in the next Iteration Review.		N
	Multi-Level Daily Meetings	As a result of using this pattern, a project manager might also notice the change during daily meetings		N
	Common Repositories and Tools	Common repositories and reports will improve visibility of a project between different sites and from repositories it is possible to find task lists and reports e.g about remaining work, in which it is possible to notice the change by this pattern.		N
	Communication Tools	Communication tools make it easier to clarify change when it has been found.		N
	Common Processes	With Common processes, there can be a risk if there isn't specific process guidelines to make a decision about making changes and/or all project members have not been trained well.	R	
Result		**Some Support:** The implementation of the scenario S12 is supported through four patterns in the language and one pattern can have a risk.		

Table 4. GSD Patterns used in the example scenario

Name	Problem	Solution outline
Iteration Review	It's difficult to know what the status of a project is.	Check the project status by a demo and present results to all relevant project members and stakeholders from different sites. Gather comments and change requests for further measures.
Multi-Level Daily Meetings	There are two or more sites which work together and there are problems to have a common meeting with a whole group every day.	Organize many daily meetings and organize another daily or weekly meeting between project managers from different sites to change information about the results of daily meetings. With foreigners, written logs can be one solution to ensure that communication messages are understood correctly in every site.
Common Repositories and Tools	Separate Excel files are difficult to manage and project data is difficult to find, manage and synchronize between many sites.	Provide a common Application Lifecycle (ALM) Management tools for all project artefacts (documents, source code, bugs, guidelines etc.) ALM provides almost real-time traceability, visualization and access to needed information etc. for all users in different sites. It can be implemented as a single tool set or it can be a group of different tools which has been integrated with each other
Communication Tools	Lack of communication and communication tools can vary between sites which make communication and co-operation difficult and tedious.	Have reliable and common communication methods and tools in every site. Use different tools at the same time as net meeting to show information, conference phones to have good sound and chat tool to discuss in written form if there are problems to understand e.g. English used in other sites.
Common Processes	Different processes and templates at different sites make communication inefficient.	Choose common upper level processes and allow local processes if they don't cause problems with upper level processes.

There were 57 different scenarios which have been prioritized by participants by voting, resulting in 10 prioritized scenarios to be analyzed. In this case we illustrate the results of the analysis with a scenario-pattern matrix (Table 5), where for each scenario the involved patterns are marked as N (non-risk) or R (risk). In addition, we have computed certain indicator values suggesting problematic scenarios or patterns. These indicators are intended only as hints, the actual conclusions can be made only after studying the seriousness of each risk separately. We have used the following indicators: IR (involvement ratio) = $(N+R)/S$ indicating the potential applicability scope of the pattern with respect to this set of scenarios, RR (risk ratio) = $R/(N+R)$ indicating the total degree of risk of the pattern with respect to the scenario set, and SI (support index) = $(N-R)/P$ indicating the level of support the pattern language provides for a scenario. Here N and R denote the number of N's and R's in a row/column, respectively, S denotes the number of scenarios and P the number of patterns. If IR is low, the pattern seems to be less relevant for the scenario set, if RR is close to 1, the pattern may cause more problems than benefits, if SI is negative the pattern language may counteract the

Table 5. Summary of the analysis of scenarios for GSD patterns

	S12	S3	S22	S16	S25	S31	S17	S19	S24	S28	IR	RR
GSD01												
GSD02		R									0,1	1,0
GSD03			R	N		N	R	N		N	0,6	0,3
GSD04			N								0,1	0,0
GSD05		R		R				R		R	0,4	1,0
GSD06	N	N		N	N	N	N				0,6	0,0
GSD07	N	N	N	R	N		N	N			0,7	0,1
GSD08		R		N	N		N				0,4	0,3
GSD09								N			0,1	0,0
GSD10												
GSD11												
GSD12	R			N		N		N			0,4	0,3
GSD13			N						N		0,2	0,0
GSD14	N	N	N		N	N		N	R		0,7	0,1
GSD15	N		N		N	N					0,4	0,0
GSD16								R			0,1	1,0
GSD17		N	N				R			N	0,4	0,3
GSD18		N	N			N		N	N	N	0,6	0,0
SI	0,2	0,1	0,3	0,1	0,3	0,3	0	0,3	0,1	0,1		

scenario. In this case we can conclude that although there are some suspicious patterns (GSD02, GSD05 and GSD16), as a whole the pattern language provides reasonable support for the scenarios.

During the workshop, several improvement possibilities to GSD patterns were found and the analysis resulted in better understanding of the limits of the GSD Pattern Language. For example, the analysis resulted in a finding that GSD patterns do not include all needed practices in critical fault management or knowledge transfer areas. GSD patterns also assume that the development environment is in a very good shape and that the communication network is working at a reasonable level. Some patterns originally intended for the beginning of a project were found useful also during a project.

5 Concluding Remarks

The Q-PAM method has been introduced and applied for assessing two pattern languages with selected quality profiles. In both assessments clear improvement ideas were gained as well as better understanding of the relationships of the languages to the required quality profiles. This kind of assessment can be seen as a tool for supporting the evolution of process pattern languages. A Q-PAM assessment, or a similar activity, should be carried out especially when there is doubt that current process practices are inappropriate in a changing environment, or when new practices are introduced in an organization. The assessment is a relatively cheap method to test the effect of the practices to the desired goals, and it can be easily tuned for particular purposes and for the amount of resources available.

Instead of Q-PAM, for example, the maturity models (e.g. CMMI or SPICE) could be used. Those are based on defined reference model and capability levels not explicitly addressing quality attributes and goals. However, they are quite massive and difficult to focus on e.g. to specific business driven quality attributes. Another alternative could be the method proposed by Martin et al. [10], starting from the goals and challenges of a company. The next step there is to create project patterns based on a company's processes. After that the new project patterns will be compared to earlier created ideal pattern library. The reference patterns guide the evaluation in the same way as the maturity models. Our scenario-based method is more straightforward to apply than [10] since it does not assume any reference models, but on the other hand the results of the assessment may be more sensitive to the abilities and experience of the assessment teams and to the selection of quality attributes.

The further development topics of the Q-PAM method include better ways to define the quality profile to be used in the evaluation. Here, the ISO 9126 based quality attributes have been used, but a more process oriented quality framework would be appropriate. Since the finding of scenarios is the key activity in these assessments, we should have more systematic support for producing efficiently a covering set of scenarios. A possible approach is to devise a set of generic scenario templates that can be customized for the process patterns is under study. We continue the work on Q-PAM along these lines.

Acknowledgment

This work is being supported by the Academy of Finland under grant 130685.

References

1. Jaaksi, A., Aalto, J.-M., Aalto, A., And Vättö, K.: Tried & True Object Development. In: Industry-Proven Approaches with UML. Cambridge University Press, Cambridge (1999)
2. Kruchten, P.: The Rational Unified Process: An Introduction, 3rd edn. Addison-Wesley, Reading (2003)
3. Schwaber, K., Beedle, M.: Agile Software Development with Scrum. Prentice Hall Series on Agile Software Development, Upper Saddle River (2002)
4. Alexander, C., Ishikawa, S., Silverstein, M., Jacobson, M., Fiksdahl-King, I., Angel, S.: A Pattern Language: Towns, Buildings, Construction. Oxford University Press, New York (1977)
5. Coplien, J.: A Generative Development-Process Pattern Language. In: Coplien, J., Schmidt, D. (eds.) Pattern Language of Program Design, pp. 183–237. Addison-Wesley, Reading (1995)
6. Ambler, S.: Process Patterns – Building Large-Scale Systems Using Object Technology. Cambridge University Press/SIGS Books (1998)
7. Hajimu, I.: Pattern-Oriented Approach to Software Process Evolution. In: Proceedings of IWPSE 1999 (1999)
8. Dittmann, T., Gruhn, V., Hagen, M.: Improved Support for the Description and Usage of Process Patterns. In: 1st Workshop on Process Patterns, OOPSLA 2002, Seattle (2002)

9. Bozheva, T., Gallo, M.E.: Framework of agile patterns. In: Richardson, I., Abrahamsson, P., Messnarz, R. (eds.) EuroSPI 2005. LNCS, vol. 3792, pp. 4–15. Springer, Heidelberg (2005)
10. Martin, D., Garcia, J., Amescua, A., Llorens, J.: Reusable Project Patterns to enhance Software Process Improvement. In: EuroSPI 2007 Industrial Proceedings, pp. 3.25--3.34 (2007)
11. Harrison, N., Coplien, J.: Organizational Patterns of Agile Software Development (August 2004) (manuscript),
    http://www.easycomp.org/cgi-bin/OrgPatterns?BookOutline
12. Coplien, J.O., Harrison, N.B.: Organizational Patterns of Agile Software Development. Pearson Prentice Hall, London (2005)
13. Biro, M., Messnarz, R., Ivanyos, J.: Managing Multi-Cultural and Multi-Social Projects in SPI. In: Proceeding of EuroSPI 2006, Joensuu, Finland (2006)
14. Vesiluoma, S.: Knowledge Sharing Pattern Language. In: Proceedings of Software Quality Management, SQM 2007, Tampere, Finland (2007)
15. Välimäki, A., Koskimies, K.: Mining best practices of project management as patterns in distributed software development. In: EuroSPI 2006 Industrial Proceedings, EuroSPI 2006, Finland, Joensuu, October 2006, pp.6.27–6.35 (2006)
16. Välimäki, A., Kääriäinen, J.: Product Managers' Requirement Management Practices As Patterns in Distributed Development. In: 8th International PROFES conference, Latvia, July 2-4 (2007)
17. Välimäki, A., Kääriäinen, J.: Patterns for Distributed Scrum – a Case Study. In: Mertins, K., Ruggaber, R., Popplewell, K., Xu, X. (eds.) International Conference on Interoperability of Enterprise, Software and Applications, Enterprise Interoperability III - New Challenges and Industrial Approaches, March 25– 28. Springer, Heidelberg (2008)
18. ISO/IEC TR 15504-2:1998(E), Information technology - Software process assessment – Reference Model (1998)
19. CMU/SEI-2006-TR-008, CMMI® for Development, Version 1.2, CMMI-DEV, V1.2
20. Clements, P., Kazman, R., Klein, M.: Evaluating Software Architectures: Methods and Case Studies. SEI Series in Software Engineering. Addison-Wesley, Reading (2002)
21. Galin, D.: Software Quality Assurance: From theory to implementation. Pearson Education Limited, Addison-Wesley (2004)
22. Miller, D.: Choice and Application of Software Quality Model. In: Daughtrey, T. (ed.) Fundamental Concepts for the Software Quality Engineer. American Society for Quality (2001)
23. International Organization for Standardization. Software engineering - Product quality - Part 1: Quality model. ISO/IEC 9126-1:2001 (2001)
24. International Organization for Standardization. Quality management systems – Fundamentals and vocabulary, ISO 9000:2000 (2000)
25. Bosch, J.: Design and use of software architectures. ACM Press, Addison-Wesley (2000)
26. Vesiluoma, S.: Understanding and Supporting Knowledge Sharing in Software Engineering. Ph.D thesis manuscript (2009)

Towards a Systematic Metric Based Approach to Evaluate SCAMPI Appraisals

Simona Pricope[1] and Horst Lichter[2]

[1] KUGLER MAAG CIE GmbH, Leibnizstr. 11,
70806 Kornwestheim, Germany
[2] RWTH Aachen University, Research Group Software Construction, Ahornstr. 55,
52074 Aachen, Germany
Simona.Pricope@kuglermaag.com, lichter@swc.rwth-aachen.de

Abstract. CMMI SCAMPI based appraisals are used worldwide to assess the process quality of organizations. In this paper we introduce a metric-based approach to assess and improve CMMI SCAMPI appraisals. To have a sound basis we at first present an appraisal meta model which defines all types of appraisal elements and their relationships. This meta model can be instantiated to get a concrete SCAMPI appraisal process, offering a precise roadmap for conducting appraisals. Based on the meta model two appraisal quality metrics are defined to systematically assess appraisal activities as well as phases and to support the improvement of appraisals. We describe the definition of these metrics in detail and give some metric interpretation guidelines.

1 Introduction

Nowadays the software market is expanding and the clients are requesting software products which are better, faster, and cheaper. That is why organizations are obligated to identify, structure and improve their processes systematically[1]. Different maturity models like CMMI, SPICE, Six Sigma or ISO 9000 are supporting software process improvement.

The maturity model CMMI (Capability Maturity Model Integration, [1]) is used all over the world and spans various classes of businesses. Between 2002 and 2007, SEI (Software Engineering Institute) registered worldwide 19% growth of CMMI use. Although giving guidelines for the development of software systems, CMMI does not assist directly the development of systems but the improvement of the processes that are applied for building these systems.

An additional support for software process improvement is the so-called appraisal. An appraisal is a procedure for verifying the implementation of CMMI and the current state of process improvement in the organization. By determining the current state of the processes an appraisal is a central part of each software process improvement project. SEI defines IDEAL [2], a SPICE[2] conformant process improvement

---

[1] "The quality of a software system depends on the quality of the process that is used for the development and maintenance of this software system" (W. Humphrey).
[2] Software Process Improvement and Capability Determination (ISO/IEC 15504).

F. Bomarius et al. (Eds.): PROFES 2009, LNBIP 32, pp. 261–274, 2009.
© Springer-Verlag Berlin Heidelberg 2009

model, consisting of the following five phases: Initiating, Diagnosing, Establishing, Acting, and Learning. According to this model an appraisal is conducted in the Diagnosing phase. The appraisal result is a diagnosis over the organization's maturity (quality of definition, description, planning, implementation and controlling of the software development processes). By means of an appraisal the strengths and weaknesses of an organization can be identified, recommendations can be developed and priorities set. Furthermore, the software processes are accordingly changed, applied in projects and analyzed. The lessons learned will be used further to improve the processes. The steps of the IDEAL phases have to be conducted iteratively. Thereby the processes of the organization will be improved continually and each improvement will be examined in a subsequent appraisal.

To harmonize appraisals SEI defines three appraisal classes (called A, B, and C) that are different concerning the amount of requirements an appraisal has to fulfill. These requirements are listed in detail in the ARC (Analyze Requirements for CMMI) document [3]. Since an appraisal is a complex procedure it is helpful or even necessary to follow a method or procedure for conducting it. The standard method for an appraisal is called SCAMPI (Standard CMMI Appraisal Method for Process Improvement, see [4], [5]). This method was developed by SEI and is applied by many CMMI users worldwide (e.g. see [6]). Unfortunately the official SCAMPI reference does not contain any activity-oriented graphical description of the appraisal process. Instead it is described in natural language which can cause misinterpretations. Other sources (e.g. [7]) are not detailed and precise enough. Furthermore the SCAMPI training courses offered by SEI provide only informal diagrams for a better understanding of the complex appraisal process (and this information is not publicly available). Hence it is near to impossible for an organization to conduct an appraisal without the support of appraisal experts and/or extra training. Because organizations want to adapt SCAMPI for their own use, a more formal and more detailed description of the appraisal method would help. We try to overcome this problem by explicitly modeling the appraisal method and by introducing appraisal metrics.

Another question that is of central importance is whether an organization is conducting an appraisal correctly (i.e. the intended way). This is crucial because the correctness and the validity of the appraisal result depend on the performed appraisal process. If the appraisal is conducted superficially then the results will be superficially too. A detailed inspection of the appraisal can identify weaknesses of the performed appraisal process. By discovering these weaknesses an organization can directly address the problems and solve them for future appraisals. In this way the organization aims not only to improve the software processes using CMMI but also to improve the appraisal process.

Therefore it is important to have a procedure to verify whether an organization has implemented the appraisal process correctly and to have an approach for evaluating the overall quality of the appraisal.

This paper is organized as follows. In Section 2 we introduce a meta model that allows to define SCAMPI appraisal processes and we exemplarily show how to instantiate the meta model. Based on the meta model we present in Section 3 two metrics to measure the quality of an appraisal. By means of these metrics the strength and weaknesses of an appraisal process can be discovered. First experience and conclusions conclude this paper in the last section. The research results described herein have been acquired in close cooperation with Generali Deutschland Informatik Services GmbH, Aachen.

2   Modeling the Appraisal Process

SCAMPI, the standard method for conducting an appraisal is used in organizations all over the world that aim for software process improvement with CMMI. One major problem in applying SCAMPI is its imprecise description which often causes misinterpretations. Furthermore SCAMPI does not completely specify this sequence of the activities that have to be performed. This can be a source for mistakes in conducting an appraisal leading to non-optimal appraisal results (e.g. incorrect appraisal results, appraisal failure, unmotivated teams). This is one of the reasons why organizations try to structure and adapt SCAMPI and especially class B appraisals for internal use. To support organizations we have developed a SCAMPI appraisal meta model. It can be easily instantiated to meet the requirements of organizations. It is explained in the following.

2.1   Appraisal Meta Model

In order to precisely define the elements of a SCAMPI appraisal process, we have developed a meta model, depicted by a UML class diagram (see Figure 1). This meta model is based on the SCAMPI appraisal description and on the appraisal method requirements defined in the ARC document. The elements of the meta model are explained in the following.

As the name already suggests *OrderedElements* are ordered concerning their execution sequence by means of the relationship *executed-before*. A *Phase* is a special ordered element and the top-level structural element of an appraisal; it has a defined start and end date.

An *Action* represents an abstraction of ordered elements that are performed by *Roles*. An action may *have to regard* associated *Conditions* and *produces* and/or *needs* one or more results.

For each condition a weight is defined. *Weights* represent the importance and influence of appraisal elements on the conformance and quality of an appraisal. There are three kinds of weight based on the source (and the importance) that introduces the respective element: The weight *ARC* is attributed to those elements specified in the ARC document, *SCA* to those elements defined in the SCAMPI reference document and *AON* (add-on) to those elements that are introduced in the appraisal process based on the experience of the organization or based on published experience reports and books. For this purpose we have conducted an intensive literature review. Many lessons learned contributing to the meta model are presented at the NDIA CMMI Technology[3] and at the annual SEPG conferences[4]. For some examples see [8], [9] and [10]. Further sources especially for AON-elements are [11] as well as [12].

---

[3] NDIA CMMI Conference Series, http://www.dtic.mil/ndia/
[4] SEPG Conference Series, http://www.sei.cmu.edu/sepg

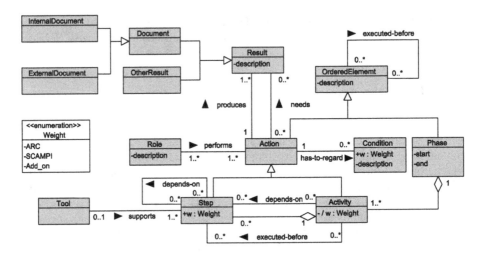

Fig. 1. SCAMPI appraisal meta model

Actions produce *Results* which are input for other actions or output of the whole appraisal. We distinguish two types of result: documents and other results. If a *Document* is accessible for everybody it is modeled as an *ExternalDocument*. In contrast, *InternalDocuments* can only be accessed by the appraisal team and typically contain confidential data. Results that cannot be represented as documents are called *Other-Result* (e.g. trained person, rooms, etc.).

A *Step*, as a special action, is performed by roles, may have to regard conditions and produces/needs results. Furthermore steps are ordered concerning their execution. As conditions, steps have a weight too. Steps may *depend* on each other which means, that if a result produced by a step must be updated all depending steps have to be executed once more.

An *Activity* is a special action consisting of steps. Activities are grouped into phases and must be finished at the end of the phase. This leads to a hierarchical aggregation structure of phases, activities, and steps. An activity may also have *executed-before* and *depends-on* relationships to steps. If an activity depends on a step then the activity must be executed again if the results of the step have to be updated. The weight of an activity is determined based on the weights of its steps and conditions.

Tools are means to support the execution of steps (e.g. software tools, spreadsheets or templates for documents).

2.2 Instantiating the Meta Model

Based on the meta model we have instantiated a SCAMPI class B appraisal reference process in the context of Generali Deutschland Informatik Services' process improvement project. It consists of the four standard phases: *Initiation, Preparation, Execution,* and *Termination,* ordered in this sequence (see Figure 2). Each phase contains activities, e.g. the phase Execution contains the activity *Generate Final Findings.*

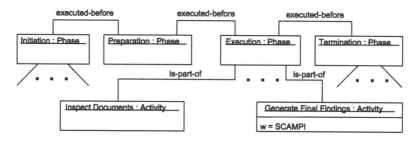

Fig. 2. Model for the appraisal reference process (excerpt)

In the following we explain exemplarily the object diagram modeling the activity *Generate Final Findings* (see Figure 3). The complete model of the SCAMPI class B reference process consisting of 32 activities can be found in [13].

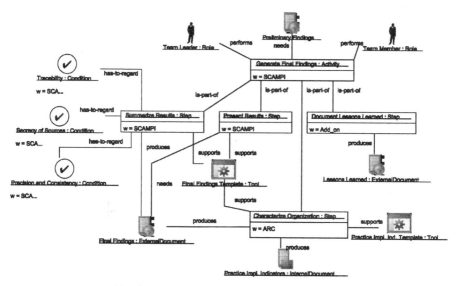

Fig. 3. Model of activity Generate Final Findings

The activity *Generate Final Findings* is performed by two roles (*Appraisal Leader* and *Appraisal Team*) and needs as input one external document (*Preliminary Findings*) produced in a preceding activity. It consists of four steps, three of them are defined in the SCAMPI document, one is defined in the ARC document and one is introduced by the organization (*Document Lessons Learned*). There are three conditions that have to be regarded by step *Summarize Results*, all defined in the SCAMPI reference document. The activity in general produces two external documents (*Final Findings* is jointly produced by steps *Summarize Results* and *Characterize Organization*; document *Lessons Learned* is produced by the respective step) and one internal document (*Practice Implementation Indicators*). There are two templates (tools) supporting the execution of the steps.

Together with detailed descriptions of the phases, activities, steps, results and conditions the resulting appraisal model explicitly documents the appraisal process, supports the appraisal conduction and guides the participants that are involved in the appraisal process.

3 Appraisal Quality Metrics

Until now a systematic evaluation means for CMMI appraisals is missing. There is an evaluation form handed over by SEI certified lead appraisers to evaluate the appraisal on a four-valued ordinary scale (very good, good, rather bad, bad). This kind of evaluation is very rough and not able to identify weaknesses and strengths of the appraisal process. Hence, an organization cannot achieve appraisal improvements by only using this kind of evaluation. In the following we describe a new metric-based evaluation approach.

3.1 Metric Design

The design of the appraisal quality metric is based on the hierarchical structure of the underlying meta model elements (see Figure 4): a phase consists of activities, an activity consists of steps and has associated conditions.

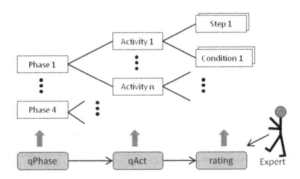

Fig. 4. Overview of the appraisal quality metric

Thus, steps and conditions are the atomic elements for the metric definition. The quality of steps and conditions must be rated subjectively. This can be done on a three-valued ordinal scale (poorly handled or absent, partially handled, adequately handled). Because this scale is very similar to the one used for evaluating CMMI practices and process areas (red, yellow, green) the personal involved in the appraisal should be familiar with this kind of rating. Another reason for choosing this scale is that subjective evaluations are by their nature error-prone and thus a more fine-grained scale would not improve the accuracy.

Since activities are the basic elements of the appraisal process, we have defined a metric to determine the quality of activities (called *qAct*) based on the ratings of their steps and conditions. Furthermore we introduced a metric for appraisal phases (called *qPhase*) which aggregates the results of the respective *qAct*-values.

3.2 Goals and Requirements

The overall goal of the proposed metrics is to evaluate appraisals (and their processes) that were conducted conformant to an instantiation of the meta model presented in the preceding section. Since the metrics *qAct* and *qPhase* deliver values for all activities and all phases the metric results shall allow analyzing the appraisal in greater detail and in a more precise way. In order to achieve this goal the metrics have to meet the following requirements:

R1: The subjective rating of the considered basic appraisal elements (steps and conditions) shall be considered appropriately. That means, the higher the amount of low subjective ratings, the faster the metric result has to decrease.

R2: The weight (i.e. the importance) of the elements (activities, steps and conditions) shall be considered appropriately. That means, the more important elements should have a higher influence on the decreasing of the metric result then the less important ones.

R3: The weight of the appraisal elements that were absent or poorly handled shall be identified. This points out the importance of the mistakes that has been done.

R4: Less important elements shall not compensate more important elements that were absent or poorly handled.

R5: The activities and phase results shall be comparable.

3.3 Quality Metric for Activities

As mentioned before steps and conditions are the atomic elements of activities. We define SC_a to be the set containing all steps and conditions of activity a. For each element $e \in SC_a$ the function *rate* returns its rating value:

$$rate(e) = \begin{cases} 0, & e\ was\ poorly\ handled\ or\ absent \\ 0.5, & e\ was\ partially\ handled \\ 1, & e\ was\ adequately\ handled \end{cases}$$

Depending on the value of the weight-attribute (ARC, SCA, AON (see section 2.1 Appraisal Meta Model) defined for steps and conditions, we call the elements in the following for sake of simplicity ARC-, SCA- and AON-elements respectively. Based on this classification we introduce for each activity a three sets, each containing its ARC-, SCA- and AON-elements, as follows:

$$SC_a^W = \{e|\ e \in SC_a \land e.w = W\} \quad \text{where W is a weight}$$

These sets are used to determine the corresponding sets R of all ratings of the respective elements:

$$R_a^W = \bigcup_{e \in SC_a^W} rate(e)$$

For determining the overall quality of an activity the metric has to regard all its steps and conditions. Hence, there are five different cases that the metric has to handle (see Table 1)[5]:

---

[5] It is easy to define the cases formally by using the SC_a^W sets.

Table 1. Cases to be handled by metric *qAct*

	Activity a has ...	and ...
	at least one ARC-element	
C1		at least one SCA- and AON-element
C2		at least either one SCA- or one AON-element
C3		neither SCA- nor AON-elements
C4	at least one SCA- and one AON-element but no ARC-element	
C5	only AON-elements	

In the following we explain the metric *qAct* for case C1. All other cases are defined accordingly; we will only present the resulting metric definitions at the end of this section.

To determine the quality of an activity, regard the ratings of its steps and conditions grouped according to their weight have to be regarded. This can be simply done by adding the so called calculated total ARC-, SCA- and AON-values (*Val*) for all elements of an activity a.

$$qAct(a) = Val_{ARC} + Val_{SCA} + Val_{AON}$$

To calculate the total ARC-, SCA- and AON-values a function is needed that does not violate the requirements introduced at the beginning of this section (especially R1 and R2). We investigated often applied functions like sum, product, minimum, median and arithmetic mean. Because the sum and product functions both violate R5 and the minimum and medium functions violate R1, we decided to choose the arithmetic mean function (m) although it has the drawback that its result decreases not fast enough if elements are not handled properly (and thus violating R1). To overcome this effect we raise the m-value by an appropriate exponent x. Since the m-value has to decrease faster if an ARC-element is absent or poorly handled than in case of a SCA- or AON-element (R2), we choose the exponent 4 for ARC-elements and 2 for SCA- and AON-elements respectively. We validated these exponents by a large number of experimental calculations to ensure that requirement R1 is always met. This leads to the following definition:

$$Val_W = m(R_a^W)^{x_W} \quad \text{where W is a weight and } x_{ARC} = 4, \; x_{SCA} = x_{AON} = 2$$

But only using different exponents is not sufficient for expressing the different importance and influence of ARC-, SCA- and AON-elements on the overall activity quality value. This illustrates the following example: If two ARC-elements and four AON-elements are rated each as 0.5 Val_{ARC} and Val_{AON} are equal but the ARC-elements are much more important than the AON-elements. For resolving this issue we introduce for each kind of weight an influence factor (*IF*) that is multiplied by the respective m-function value.

$$IF_{ARC} = 0.65, \quad IF_{SCA} = 0.21, \quad IF_{AON} = 0.14$$

Based on the experimental calculations we selected the influence factors in a way that ARC-elements represent 65% of the *qAct*-value (they are most important). The remainder (35%) is partitioned in 60% for SCA- and 40% for AON-elements. Hence, if an element is rated to 0 or 0.5 the average will drop. Applying these influence factors we yield the following metric definition:

$$qAct(a) = Val_{ARC} \cdot IF_{ARC} + Val_{SCA} \cdot IF_{SCA} + Val_{AON} \cdot IF_{AON}$$

$$= Val'_{ARC} + Val'_{SCA} + Val'_{AON}$$

According to requirement R4 the influence of SCA- and AON-elements ($Val'_{SCA} + Val'_{AON}$) should not be greater than the influence of one single ARC-element. There-fore a failure in at least one ARC-element (rated to 0 or 0.5) cannot be compensated by well done SCA- and AON-elements. To regard this requirement we restrict the influence of SCA- and AON-elements depending on the value of the ARC-elements. This can be achieved by multiplying the adjusted m-value of the ARC-elements by the influence of the SCA- and AON-elements:

$$qAct(a) = Val'_{ARC} + m(R_a^{ARC})^{y_{SCA}} \cdot Val'_{SCA} + m(R_a^{ARC})^{y_{AON}} \cdot Val'_{AON}$$

$$= Val'_{ARC} + Val''_{SCA} + Val''_{AON}$$

$$\text{where} \quad y_{SCA} = 3 \cdot 4, \quad y_{AON} = 3 \cdot 6$$

But again, the influence factors and the exponents of the m-functions are alone not sufficient to fulfill requirement R3 (the elements that were poorly handled or absent shall be identified). We illustrate this again by giving an example: Let activity a con-tain ten ARC-elements, x SCA-elements and y AON-elements. If one of the ARC-elements is rated to 0.5 and all SCA- and AON-elements to 1 the value of $qAct(a)$ is greater than 0.65. Hence, we need to define thresholds for the ARC- and SCA-elements in a way that if the $qAct$-value of an activity is less than the thresholds we will know that an ARC- respectively SCA-element was absent or poorly handled. Therefore we introduce the following threshold functions (tf):

$$qAct(a) = tf^{ARC} \cdot Val'_{ARC} + tf^{SCA} \cdot (Val''_{SCA} + Val''_{AON}) \quad \text{where}$$

$$tf^{ARC} = tf(SC_a^{ARC})$$

$$= \begin{cases} 1, & \forall e \in SC_a^{ARC} | rate(e) = 1 \\ \dfrac{E_{ARC}}{E_{ARC} + E_{SCA} + E_{AON}} = 0.65, & otherwise \end{cases}$$

$$tf^{SCA} = tf(SC_a^{SCA})$$

$$= \begin{cases} 1, & \forall e \in SC_a^{SCA} | rate(e) = 1 \\ \dfrac{E_{SCA}}{E_{SCA} + E_{AON}} = 0.6, & otherwise \end{cases}$$

Summing up the quality value of an activity a having ARC-, SCA- and AON-elements is calculated as follows:

$$qAct(a) = tf(SC_a^{ARC})$$
$$\cdot [m(R_a^{ARC})^4 \cdot IF_{ARC} + tf(SC_a^{SCA})$$
$$\cdot [m(R_a^{ARC})^{3 \cdot 4} \cdot m(R_a^{SCA})^2 \cdot IF_{SCA} + m(R_a^{ARC})^{3 \cdot 6}$$
$$\cdot m(R_a^{AON})^2 \cdot IF_{AON}]]$$

The remaining cases are defined analogously. In the following we only present the respective metric definitions.

Case 2: Activity a has ARC-elements and at least either one SCA- or at least one AON-element. In the following it is supposed that it has at least one AON-element.

$$qAct(a) = tf(SC_a^{ARC}) \cdot [m(R_a^{ARC})^4 \cdot IF_{ARC} + m(R_a^{ARC})^{3 \cdot 4} \cdot m(R_a^{AON})^2 \cdot IF_{AON}]$$

$$tf(SC_a^{ARC}) = \begin{cases} 1, & \forall e \in SC_a^{ARC} | \ rate(e) = 1 \\ \dfrac{E_{ARC}}{E_{ARC} + E_{AON}} = 0.7, & otherwise \end{cases}$$

where $IF_{ARC} = 0.7$, $IF_{AON} = 0.3$

Case 3: Activity a has ARC-elements and neither SCA- nor AON-elements

$$qAct(a) = m(R_a^{ARC})^2 \cdot IF_{ARC} \quad where \ IF_{ARC} = 1$$

Case 4: Activity a has at least one SCA- and AON-element but no ARC-elements:

$$qAct(a) = tf(SC_a^{SCA}) \cdot [m(R_a^{SCA})^2 \cdot IF_{SCA} + m(R_a^{AON})^2 \cdot IF_{AON}]$$

$$where \ IF_{SCA} = 0.6, \quad IF_{AON} = 0.4$$

The function $tf(SC_a^{SCA}))$ is the same as in Case 1.

Case 5: Activity a has only AON-elements:

$$qAct(a) = m(R_a^{AON})^2 \cdot IF_{AON} \quad where \ IF_{AON} = 1$$

When instantiating the meta model for a SCAMPI class B appraisal we did not discover any activity that has only SCA-elements. Of course, if other instantiations define activities containing only SCA-elements then the metric can be extended analogously.

3.4 Quality of Appraisal Phases

Based on the $qAct$-values for activities we now define the quality value of phases. For a phase p we define Act_p to be the set of all activities belonging to p.

Again we classify activities depending on their weights. The weight attribute of activities is derived and calculated according to the following function:

$$a.w = \begin{cases} ARC, & \exists e \in SC_a | \ e.w = ARC \\ SCA, & \exists e \in SC_a | \ e.w = SCA \wedge \nexists e_1 \in SC_a | e_1.w = ARC \\ AON, & otherwise \end{cases}$$

We call the activities in the following for sake of simplicity ARC-, SCA- and AON-activities respectively. As for steps and conditions we define three sets of activities depending on their weights:

$$Act_p^W = \{a | \ a \in Act_p \wedge a.w = W\} \quad where \ W \ is \ the \ weight$$

The sets containing all *qAct*-values of the activities with weight W for a phase p are defined as follows:

$$Q_p^W = \bigcup_{a \in Act_p^W} qAct(a)$$

Based on these sets we define the quality metric for appraisal phases as follows;

$$qPhase(p) = m(Q_p^{ARC}) \cdot IF_{ARC} + m(Q_p^{SCA}) \cdot IF_{SCA} + m(Q_p^{AON}) \cdot IF_{AON}$$

This metric is designed in analogy to the *qAct*-metric for the same reasons. We define as influence factors the values $IF_{ARC} = 0.65$, $IF_{SCA} = 0.21$ and $IF_{AON} = 0.14$ because the ARC- elements are more important than the SCA-elements, that are more important than the AON-elements. The m-function is again the arithmetic mean of the ARC-, SCA- and AON-activities results.

3.5 Metric Interpretation

Since the values of the metric are on a rational scale between 0 and 1 the values of both metrics, *qAct* and *qPhase,* are comparable. This permits to compare former appraisals with the current one and allows discovering whether an improvement has taken place or not. A metric value close to 1 means that the respective activity or phase was adequately handled, while a value close to 0 is an indicator that the activity or phase was absent or poorly handled. Based on the introduced thresholds we can define the following overall rating results of the metrics:

An important characteristic of the metric is its ability to identify the type of the element which was absent or poorly handled. This way the metric supports the organization to discover the strengths and weaknesses of the respective activity or phase. The influence factors *IF* and the threshold functions *tf* contribute together to define thresholds which can be used to analyze the obtained metric values. Table 3 shows the threshold based interpretation of the metric value for *qAct* (only Case 1) and *qPhase*.

Table 2. Metric interpretations

Value	Interpretation
0.00 – 0.64	poorly performed
0.65 – 0.85	satisfactory performed
0.86 – 1.00	Good

Table 3. Threshold based metric interpretation

Value	Interpretation
< 0.86	• all AON-elements were rated to 0 OR • at least one SCA-element was absent or poorly handled
< 0.65	• all AON- and SCA-elements are rated to 0 OR • at least one ARC-element was absent or poorly handled

4 Experience and Validation

The meta model, the derived SCAMPI class B appraisal reference model as well as the metrics were validated in cooperation with Generali Deutschland Informatik Services GmbH, Aachen.

Concerning the reference model we got some improvements hints regarding the granularity of some weak activity descriptions (for more details see Pricope, 2008). However, the appraisal members in general assess the reference model very helpful, "particularly the relationships, tasks, work results and responsibilities" (quotation of an appraisal team member) which were clearly identified.

To validate the metric we focused to check the important metric plausibility characteristics of metrics [14]. Plausibility means that the subjective ratings given by experts have to correspond closely to the metric results. To check the plausibility property we performed the following steps:

1. We developed a simple spreadsheet-tool for calculating *qAct* and *qPhase*.
2. All steps and conditions of the appraisal were rated and then the metric values were calculated.
3. We mapped the metric results to grades between 1 and 6 (German school grading scheme, see Table 4) because the original metric scale between 0 and 1 is to fine grained for a subjective assessment and could cause errors.
4. We asked appraisal-team members to assess all activities and phases of the appraisal by giving each a grade (1 to 6).
5. We compared the results of the metrics to the subjective assessment.

Table 4. Mapping of metric values to grading scheme

Metric	Grade	Interpretation
0.000 – 0.160	6	Fail
0.161 – 0.330	5	Poor
0.331 – 0.500	4	Sufficient
0.501 – 0.660	3	Satisfactory
0.661 – 0.830	2	Good
0.831 – 1.000	1	very good

The average deviation between the metric results and the subjective assessment was 0.448. This means that on average only every second metric result deviates by more than one point from the given grade (which is acceptable).

Because it is much easier to evaluate fine-grained elements (like steps and conditions) than whole activities or even phases, the metric is based on subjective evaluations of those elements. It can be applied like a checklist guiding the user through the evaluation process.

To summarize, we see the following benefits by applying a metric-based appraisal evaluation:

1. By analyzing the metric results the weaknesses of an appraisal process can be identified as well as its strengths. If the result of a phase or activity is low, we are able

to identify the weak elements (step or condition) by traversing the tree (see Fig 2) from the root to the leaves. This way we can decide if the appraisal results were negatively influenced and if they are still correct.

2. Experience and knowledge is quantified and can be reused for future appraisals.
3. The gained knowledge can support strategic decisions, e.g. whether the appraisal process must be further improved and more important we know what to improve, because we identified the weak appraisal elements.

5 Conclusions

In this paper we propose a systematic approach to improve SCAMPI appraisal processes based on a meta model and quality metrics for appraisals. The appraisal reference model, which is an instantiation of the meta model, supports and guides organizations to conduct appraisals by defining all the elements that should be present, conducted, produced and regarded.

The introduced appraisal quality metrics are able to evaluate the appraisal process (i.e. the activities and phases) and to identify opportunities for improvement. Furthermore, the application of the metrics leads to greater transparency of the appraisal process, since those activities and phases that have been poorly performed become visible. In contrast to a standard questionnaire the metrics take into consideration the weight and importance of the appraisal elements.

The appraisal quality metrics can not only be used for post-appraisal analyzes, but also for controlling the appraisal during the process. The results of the metrics can be analyzed after each appraisal phase to identify weaknesses of that phase early and to define appropriate counter measure for succeeding phases.

Until now we have made some first promising experience with the presented approach. But, it is obvious that the metrics have to be calibrated and adapted. For example the role element of the meta model, which is not considered by the metrics so far, should be integrated in the activity quality metric. We discovered that this element is also important and its absence may lead to deviations between the subjective evaluations of experts and the metric results.

To summarize we have developed a quality instrument that can be used to systematically assess and improve SCAMPI appraisals.

Acknowledgements

We would like to thank the Engineering Process Group of Generali Deutschland Informatik Services GmbH, Aachen for supporting this research.

References

1. SEI, CMMI: CMMI for Development, Version 1.2. CMU/SEI-2006-TR-008, ESC-TR-2006-008, Software Engineering Institute, Carnegie Mellon University, Pittsburgh, PA (2006)

2. McFeeley, R.: IDEAL: A User's Guide for Software Process Improvement. CMU/SEI-96-HB-001, ADA 305472, Software Engineering Institute, Carnegie Mellon University, Pittsburgh, PA, (1996)
3. SEI, CMMI: Appraisal Requirements for CMMI. Version 1.2 (ARC, V1.2) Technical Report, CMU/SEI-2006-TR-011, Software Engineering Institute, Carnegie Mellon University, Pittsburgh, PA (2006)
4. SEI, SCAMPI: Handbook for Conducting Standard CMMI Appraisal Method for Process Improvement (SCAMPI) B and C Appraisals. Version 1.1, CMU/SEI-2005-HB-005, Software Engineering Institute, Carnegie Mellon University, Pittsburgh, PA (2005)
5. SEI, SCAMPI: Standard CMMI Appraisal Method for Process Improvement (SCAMPI) A. Version 1.2: Method Definition Document, CMU/SEI-2006-HB-002, Software Engineering Institute, Carnegie Mellon University, Pittsburgh, PA (2006)
6. Ekdahl, F., Larsson, S.: Using Internal CMMI Appraisals to Institutionalize Software Development Performance Improvement. In: 32nd EUROMICRO Conference on Software Engineering and Advanced Applications (EUROMICRO 2006), pp. 216–223. IEEE Computer Society, Cavtat (2006)
7. Ahern, D., Armstrong, J., Clouse, A., Ferguso, J.R., Hayes, W., Nidiffer, K.: CMMI SCAMPI Distilled: Appraisals for Process Improvement. Addison-Wesley, Reading (2005)
8. Courtney-Clark, J.: Performing Consistent Appraisals in a Global Organization. In: 5th NDIA CMMI Technology Conference and User Group, Denver, Colorado, November 16-18 (2005),
   http://www.dtic.mil/ndia/2005cmmi/2005cmmi.html
9. Jansma, T.: CMMI Implementation for Software at JPL. In: 3rd NDIA CMMI Technology Conference and User Group, Denver, Colorado, November 18-20 (2003),
   http://www.dtic.mil/ndia/2003CMMI/2003CMMI.html
10. Oppenheimer, H.L.: The 3Rs and 4As of PIIDs. In: SEPG National Conference, Nashville, Tennessee, March 6-9 (2006),
    http://www.secc.org.eg/SEPG2006/Ingredients/PDF_files/195.pdf
11. Bush, M., Dunaway, D.: CMMI Assessments - Motivating Positive Change. Addison-Wesley Longman, Redwood City (2005)
12. Kasse, T.: Action Focused Assessment for Software Process Improvement. Artech House, Norwood (2001) ISBN-13: 978-1580532860
13. Pricope, S.: Development of an ARC-conformant CMMI Class B Appraisal Method. Master Thesis, RWTH Aachen University (2008) (in German)
14. Ludewig, J., Lichter, H.: Software Engineering – Grundlagen, Menschen, Prozesse, Techniken, 2nd edn. dpunkt.verlag, Heidelberg (2007) ISBN 3-89864-268-2

A New Way to Organize DFX in a Large Organization

Jarkko Hyysalo[1], Sanja Aaramaa[1], Jouni Similä[1], Samuli Saukkonen[1],
Pekka Belt[2], and Jari Lehto[3]

[1] University of Oulu, Department of Information Processing Science, M-Group,
P.O. Box 3000, FIN-90014 Oulu, Finland
{Jarkko.Hyysalo,Sanja.Aaramaa,Jouni.Simila,
Samuli.Saukkonen}@oulu.fi
[2] University of Oulu, Department of Industrial Engineering and Management,
P.O. Box 4610, FIN-90014 Oulu, Finland
Pekka.Belt@oulu.fi
[3] University of Oulu, Department of Information Processing Science,
P.O. Box 3000, FIN-90014 Oulu, Finland
Jari.A.Lehto@iki.fi

Abstract. Efficient requirements engineering and design is a demanding task. Design for excellence (DFX) offers a way to bring together different views and harmonizing practices. There are still impediments, for example, in having internal and external customers valued appropriately. The organizational implementation of DFX in itself is a debated question. We present a new way to organize the DFX concept in a large organization. The results are based on experiences of a large organization that operates in the area of ICT systems, and has had a successful implementation of the DFX concept for several years. Contrary to the traditional way of managing the DFX within R&D it is beneficial to organize it within also other parts of the operational subsystem, as this makes the concept and its improvement more visible and widespread in the organization. However, this requires seeing the concepts of problem domain and solution domain from a new angle.

Keywords: Design for excellence (DFX), DFX organizational implementation, requirements engineering, industrial management.

1 Introduction

Industrial companies, especially in the area of information and communications technology (ICT), are facing several challenges in modern days. Organizations' processes must be efficient and products have to yield high customer satisfaction. Customer needs and requirements can be changing, increasingly complex, very customer specific or hard to predict. However, fulfilling customer needs is of paramount importance. On the other hand standardized processes and products contribute greatly to efficiency and quality. A balance between standardization and customization must be found.

At the same time development times are getting shorter and schedules become tighter in order to bring products to the markets before competitors to gain a market

F. Bomarius et al. (Eds.): PROFES 2009, LNBIP 32, pp. 275–289, 2009.
© Springer-Verlag Berlin Heidelberg 2009

benefit. How to manage changing requirements and customer needs, while taking into account constraints of the design process and still bring a desirable, quality product to the markets? How to value and recognize internal and external customers appropriately? Solid requirements engineering processes and a tight connection between the organization's operations and product development process is needed.

Operations is often defined to include the processes of transforming inputs into final outputs. Together with production operations makes, assembles, and tests products, including components, systems and services. This includes organizations' logistics and distribution processes, and involves decision-making, coordination, and communication mechanisms to transform resources into products and services. [1]

It is a demanding task for requirements engineering and design to bring all the necessary views into the final product. Design For eXcellence (DFX) is one way to do this. DFX is traditionally managed within the R&D function of the organization. However, it can also be distributed to other parts of organization, as our industrial case will present. This offers some remarkable benefits compared to the traditional way.

Bralla [2] defines DFX as a knowledge-based approach that attempts to design products maximizing all desirable characteristics in product design and at the same time minimizing lifetime costs, including manufacturing costs. Desirable attributes can be for example quality, environmental friendliness, serviceability and manufacturability. In order to achieve these objectives the product design process itself has to be excellent. Therefore DFX's letter 'x' stands for two different aspects; 1) all desirable factors that a product should have, and 2) excellence and completeness of design.

Bralla sees DFX as a means of improving product design and development processes and eventually final products. Tools, methods and ways of forming design teams etc, which Bralla propose, all imply that DFX is a part of the company's R&D organization and thus managed also by designers. There is a limited number of published experiences on how companies implement DFX. However, there are dozens of open vacancy announcements in Web pages where companies seek for DFX managers or specialists.

There are attempts to improve the DFX concept, for example Sheu and Chen [3] build a model that adds backward design emphasizing downstream knowledge management and lessons learned for proactive cross functional product design management. They emphasize the meaning of other-than-design functions, and propose a management system adding other-than-design considerations to R&D and making them more recognized. This is in line with our model, however, Sheu and Chen still have the DFX concept managed within R&D. Our aim is to take this even further, and thus insert even stronger incentives to have all the stakeholders and disciplines considered as equally important.

The inherently cross-functional DFX process requires participation from various functions from the organization, including marketing, engineering, financing, manufacturing and supply chain. It brings together different views and harmonizes practices. Other benefits are also advances of requirements engineering and design in a coordinated way aiming for common goals.

The aim of this paper is to present a new effective way of organizing DFX in a large organization, thus our research question is: *How does a large system provider successfully organize DFX contrary to the traditional way?* As a subsequent research question we contemplate: *What benefits does the new way provide?* In order to answer the research questions we conducted a literature review on the subject how DFX can be organized and managed. However, the available literature is scarce on organizational implications. We also carried out a case study in an industrial company, which is a major systems provider, and has utilized the DFX concept for several years. The industrial case provides insights that highlight the value of DFX and also the role of the DFX management as a link between operations and the product development process.

The results of the paper provide value for both academics and professionals, who may utilize the results to learn how to manage and organize DFX in large organizations, and how DFX Management in Product Development (DMPD) process can be utilized to connect operations and the product development process. The case company operates in the ICT area, providing systems and services, however, the results can be used in several industrial areas in order to analyze and improve their requirements management and design processes.

2 Research Process

The goal for the study was to determine the DFX requirements flow and the visibility of the DFX concept in the case company. To form a sound understanding of DFX implementation, requirements and visibility, twenty interviews were executed in the case company. DFX managers were considered to have the widest knowledge about implementation of the DFX concept. Therefore 12 of the interviewees were DFX managers, including also the head of the DFX managers. In order to have also a practical point of view some old-timer hands-on-experienced were interviewed. This article is based on the analysis of the interviews, especially the interviews of the DFX managers.

The research process is described in the Figure 1. It follows loosely the process of building theory from case study research by Eisenhardt [4].

Fig. 1. The research process

In this study relevant research topics were identified and rough analyses were done on themes. Gathered material was compared to literature and other sources. Other important sources were company slides and presentations. In addition weekly meetings were held between researchers and company representatives, where open issues were discussed thoroughly. The meetings were also taped and transcriptions were made available to the researchers. The importance of these meetings must be stressed, as they were of paramount importance in order to gain full understanding of a large company's organizational issues. Then it was possible to continue with deeper analyses of original research themes and also start working on new interesting topics revealed in this research.

Interviews were executed in one month. Duration of each interview was approximately one hour. The first version of the questionnaire was updated after the first four interviews by changing a few words, adding some examples and two questions. The questionnaire was delivered to each interviewee in advance so they could be prepared. Each interview was managed by two or three interviewers. Most of the interviews were face to face. All interviews were recorded and tapes were sent for transcription, after that the researchers made short summaries from transcriptions. Within two weeks from interview a full transcription and summaries were emailed to interviewees and they were given one week to validate the information. Only a few interviewees made minor corrections or added something to the summaries.

In the second step, validated information was analyzed to formulate general descriptions of different DFX disciplines, lists of identified stakeholders, each discipline's greatest challenges, possible solutions, and requirements flow. These analyses were also reviewed by the interviewees. For cross-analyzing DFX disciplines the interviewees were grouped by different functions, for example manufacturing, processes, services and R&D. Finally, all the information was wrapped up to identify common challenges, especially in requirements flow and DFX visibility, and to find best practices and solutions within all DFX disciplines. At this phase common issues were compared to literature, and also an understanding of DFX implementation at the case company was built based on interviews and company material.

As the literature on organizational implementation of the DFX concept is not widely available, we used an alternative approach: a review of recruitment announcements published in the Internet. Recruitment announcements are part of the external dissemination, which is often handled better than internal dissemination. This way we were able to get enough data for our analysis. Web search was conducted using search words 'DFX manager jobs', (all words), which returned 12 300 hits. To narrow our search, the second search phrase was more exact, '"DFX manager" jobs' and search was restricted to pages that were published within a year. This returned 105 hits and all announcements were read. The third search was 'DFX manager jobs' within past year. Found announcements were sorted to three classes based on within which function the vacancy is managed: 1) similar to case company, 2) undefined (as it was not possible to tell from the announcement), and 3) differs from case company. Several announcements were left out, as they did not actually indicate that the DFX concept is implemented in the company. Most of the announcements only had qualification requirement of DFX knowledge for applicant, however, this was not enough for inclusion to our study. If responsibility included DFX, it was included. This narrowed our research considerably. Based on a study of these announcements, it is clearly evident that in most of companies DFX management is within R&D, as predicted.

3   Requirements Engineering Flow

Requirements engineering process includes requirements development (elicitation, analysis, specification and validation) and *requirements management* [5]. It is a systematic (engineering) approach to eliciting, organizing, and documenting the requirements of the system, and the process that establishes and maintains agreement between the customer and the project team on the changing requirements of the system. [6] Requirements engineering does not include design, implementation etc. activities of systems engineering, which are systematically included in DFX. Kotonya and Sommerville [7] define requirements management as the process of managing changes to the requirements. Many authors go in line with this definition [5], [8], [9]. They all characterize and define the tasks included in the management process, all stressing its nature of change. Leffingwell and Widrig [6] instead, define requirements management to include all the requirements engineering from elicitation to maintenance.

The concepts of *problem domain* and *solution domain* cf. [10], [11] are important in requirements engineering. Problem domain refers to a bounded part of the reality, which is the place where products make profits to the problem domain stakeholders. *Problem domain is the environment in which a problem is defined* – usually a problem that is to be "solved" by the product and the by-products related to it [12]. All the added-value used to pay the product is generated in the problem domain; no other domain can decide what is right or wrong. Other domains can only define restrictions for the problem domain. The problem domain includes and is composed of its stakeholders' concepts and relationships. A problem domain is simply looking at only the topics its stakeholders are interested in. The language and semantics of the domain originate also from its stakeholders only and may contain terminology conflicts, too.

Solution domain is an area, in which a solution of a problem is defined – the solution domain provides "solutions" to solve challenges of the problem domain. Solutions are usually manifested in the design and implementation of a system. The solution domain is usually understood by the developers of the system. [12] It is common that problem and solution domains both have their own concepts and entities with unique semantics.

Stakeholders are people who have a stake in a product. There are two main groups of stakeholders: customers and developers [8]. Examples of customer type of stakeholders are product users and product owners on the customer site. Hardware, software, mechanical engineers, manufacturing specialists, sourcing specialists, etc. can be named as examples in the developer category of stakeholders. Any person affected by the product or who has influence on product development, manufacturing, delivery etc. is a stakeholder.

By following the thoughts of Lauesen [9] the *requirements* can be categorized in *four levels*:

-    Goal-level requirements; there exist goal-level requirements both in problem domain and solution domain.
-    Problem Domain-level requirements.
-    Solution Domain-level requirements.
-    Design-level requirements.

The life-cycle of requirements discussed here starts from business goals and needs, and ends in features and constraints. The product specifications are the output of feature screening and prioritization.

The logical view of the requirements engineering workflow is depicted in high level in figure 2. The main logical structure is divided into three sets of tasks before the results are going to the feature screening decision-making. Pure decision-making activities are not presented in this figure as well as necessary feed-back loops, as they

Fig. 2. Overall structure of the requirements engineering workflow

are out of the scope of this study. The workflow is design from the view point of a single actor. There are no role based conditions along the workflow. However, along the logical flow separate tasks can be performed by separate actors as well as the workflow can be parallelized.

The high-level workflow is valid for problem level requirements engineering (customers' requirements) and for solution domain requirements engineering.

3.1 Requirements Engineering Flow in the DFX Context

In this study we will describe the requirements engineering work in more detail in the solution domain as the DFX is mainly a solution domain issue. This type of thinking requires a paradigm shift, as it is fundamentally different than traditional problem domain and solution domain thinking. The traditional view is that the problem domain is the business environment of the customer companies to which solutions are provided by the product development organization of the systems provider company.

In our case the problem domain is the product development organization of the systems provider company and the solution domain is the internal DFX management organization which provides guidelines and instructions to the product development organization. The original solution domain thus has become the problem domain. This also shows that the problem domain – solution domain thinking may and in fact should be applied recursively and iteratively when needed.

The DFX managers are one important category of stakeholders for a product program. Identification of DFX representatives as stakeholders should be done before starting a product program. Behind each DFX discipline, there is a *platform* of knowledge and technology to be adapted to the programs. These platforms are knowledge bases that include both product and the processes. Platform managers are responsible for defining and maintaining the platforms. Operations' platforms are Manufacturing platform, Sourcing platform, and Delivery platform (see figure 3). Manufacturing platform includes standard manufacturing processes and equipment to be used for example in manufacturing testing, board assembly, final assembly and product packaging. Sourcing platform consists of lists of recommended suppliers and recommended components, for example. Delivery platforms define, among others, standard distribution models. Service platforms develop and maintain standard services like remote operability. R&D platforms are developing and maintaining basic solutions and guidelines/instructions to be applied in product programs. The DFX capability management organization is responsible for defining and maintaining DFX requirements and targets based on agreed platform specifications. The requirements flow actually starts from the bottom of the figure, and requirements are defined at different levels: Company level, business unit level, business line level or program level. DFX capability management also develops competence of personnel implementing the DFX in programs in the DMPD process.

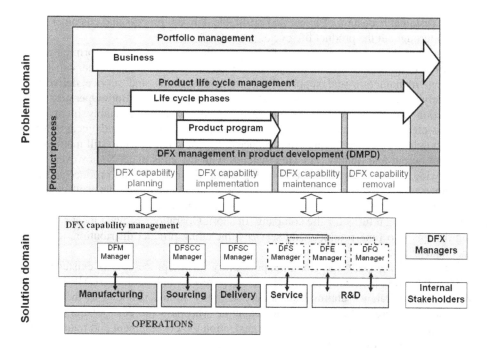

Fig. 3. Requirements engineering inside the DFX capability management, simplified model

During Product process the DFX requirements will be defined, prioritized and re-fined into product specifications during the early phases. During manufacturing the DFX requirements will be implemented with defined targets in products and services. During the maintenance and removal phases relevant DFX requirements especially those related to DFS (Design for Service) will also be dealt with. The role of DFX personnel (implementation managers) is to help the programs as well as to follow-up the implementation of DFX issues. During and in the end of a program lessons learned will be gathered and analyzed, too.

The left-hand part of the DMPD process is about the requirement negotiation and prioritization, and then after that starts the implementation of the requirements in the right-hand process. In the maintenance phase, you still keep implementing and fol-lowing the requirement process. Organizational implications of this will be discussed in the next chapter more thoroughly.

4 DFX Management in the Case Company

The DFX concept in general is a systematic and cross-functional design methodology – including design principles, requirements, metrics and target values. DFX optimizes usage of product, operations and service platforms and implements proactively the best practices in sourcing, manufacturing, demand/supply chain, services, environmental management, reliability and security in product process. The objective of DFX is to ensure sustainable design, efficient and profitable delivery process and customer satis-faction throughout the product life cycle.

In general the concept of operations includes the processes of transforming inputs into final outputs. It includes company's own, sub-contracted or partnership based sourcing, manufacture and supply. Product manufacturing and service delivery is often relying upon the efficient use of stable operating routines. Both Operations and production processes have to be managed effectively and predictably in order to achieve efficiency. Their aim is to reduce unwanted variability and uncertainty in product delivery and service and thus reduce defects and costs, while still maintaining constant output and quality. [1] This matches with the aims of DFX, however, DFX has a wider scope taking into account the whole life-cycle of the product and also customers' costs. On the other hand, Dodgson et al. [1] continue that well managed operations also deliver products and services at competitive price for the customer, whilst providing returns for the company. In short, Operations provide means of turn-ing designs into final products and services, including product distribution, and thus facilitate product and process delivery.

At the case company the global responsibility for the processes, its existence, de-velopment and implementation for DFX concept resides in Operations/DMPD organi-zation. In general, we claim that the responsibility should reside with the internal stakeholder where it most matters, for example who pays the costs of the develop-ment. In the case of a service oriented organization the development and management of DFX could be, for example, within service processes.

Large organizations are not born over night; they evolve from small basic func-tions. When companies evolve to be large global organizations, these basic functions affect the decision of which part of the organization takes the responsibility of DFX. For historical reasons in the case company the full responsibility of DFX was natu-rally located within Operations organization. In order to have on-going successful business all companies have to focus also on constant development of their processes and functions. In our case company the DFX principles have been executed success-fully over a decade, nevertheless there is still a need for improvement work, and con-tinuous discussions are held to find the optimal solution.

The aim of DFX is to optimize end-to-end cost from company and customer point of view, and to build core competence that leads to competitive advantage over the competitors. From the DFX point of view the following main organizational units are relevant:

- Organization of Product Lines (OPL). OPL is divided into business units, which are responsible for the development of products through product pro-grams and which have the ownership of products. In addition the R&D unit is divided into sub disciplines. Design for environment and quality are or-ganizationally located here.
- Financial unit, which provides the financial figures for cost accounting, but bears no other important direct relation to DFX.
- Operations, which is responsible for the delivery process, i.e. manufacturing and suppliers, and delivery of products to the customer sites. The delivery process includes also installation and related service activities. DMPD with its three DFX disciplines (supply management, manufacturing and demand/supply

chain) is located in Operations. Manufacturing is further split into sub disciplines out of which the major part are in DMPD.

- Services. After the delivery of the products to the customer site Services takes responsibility for them and starts the installation and maintenance activities. Design for Services DFX discipline with its four sub disciplines is located in Services.

In addition, there are other organizational units, however, they have no important direct relation to the organizational implementation of DFX.

4.1 DMPD within Operations

Although in our industrial case DFX is managed within Operations, the DFX requirements must be implemented into actual products as usually. Implementation responsibility still lies on product designers' shoulders. In order to have effective DFX process concurrent engineering is needed [2]. This means that DFX requirements are implemented within cross-functional design teams. According to Bralla cross-functional design teams' members represent manufacturing engineering and different DFX approaches such as service, quality and environment [2].

In our industrial case design teams are established basically in the same way as Bralla suggests, but the significant difference is the representatives', DFX managers' organizational 'home silo'. DFX managers are not a part of the R&D organization, instead they are part of the organization that pays the costs – DFX/DMPD. It does not make a difference to the individual who implements the DFX requirements which organization has the management responsibility of DFX, but to the company it does. This means that if product programs have responsibility of DFX they aim at their own local success and they may as well achieve it. Nevertheless success in a few product programs does not guarantee the success throughout the company. Placing responsibility of DFX management and development in Operations organization, as in our industrial case, leads more likely the company's success as a whole.

The cooperation between the DFX disciplines from different organizational units is organized through networking. Each DFX manager has the responsibility for his process. DFX networking manager has the total responsibility for these activities.

For each business portfolio a business unit DFX team is formed in the case company. The DFX managers are responsible for the content and principles of the disciplines, the business unit DFX teams implement the principles, the practical matters are solved within the teams. The teams function as the working channels to ensure the fulfillment of the requirements in the product development programs. The business unit DFX teams have an important role especially in the beginning phases of product life cycle.

4.2 DMPD Organization

The main task of the DMPD organization is to formulate all the operations requirements into words and figures and present them to the product programs. This is however not totally sufficient. It is also very important to be able to state the reasons for the requirements in a convincing way. Prioritizing the requirements and negotiating about them with the product development persons is the most time-consuming activity at least for the present. A general challenge is to make the product process more effective, and in general define requirements leading in work and cost reduction in some other phases of the product process.

The customer of DMPD is the product program prioritizing and deciding on the requirements to be implemented. In general, the decision making is based on the requirements documents including a business case description and cost/benefit analysis. The task of the DMPD organization is to make the program "buy" the requirements and their content, to make the persons in the program see what is meant by the requirements and their priorities. This seems to be a challenge for DFX requirements: it is quite straightforward to justify requirements having a concrete relation to some external customer needs compared to requirements arising from internal operations needs. To solve the dilemma more attention should be paid on analyzing and value based argumentation of DFX requirements, for example better cost/benefit analyses. After the programs produce the product the DMPD must have the required delivery capability, the required manufacturing capability and volume.

The DMPD process is a part of the Product Process. The main tasks of the DFX capability planning phase at the portfolio management level and product life cycle level are:

- Implementation of Operations' strategies and requirements, including evaluation of delivery capability requirements regarding purchasing, production, demand/supply chain, and service.
- Feasibility analysis from Operations point of view.
- Cost and risk analysis.
- Target setting with respect to Operations DFX metrics.
- Resource planning for Operations part

Based on the results of DFX capability planning the required delivery capability is created at the program level in the DFX capability implementation phase. This is then maintained in the DFX capability maintenance phase and eventually removed in the DFX capability removal phase. Major roles related to this in the case company in a glance are:

- Portfolio manager, who manages and controls all Operations activities regarding an entire product portfolio, including analysis, DFX capability implementation, maintenance and removal. He also leads all delivery, demand and supply chain, and is the purchasing and production capability manager of one portfolio. He is the Operations member in a business unit management team.
- DFX capability manager, who manages and controls all operations related activities regarding product capability planning, implementation, maintenance, and removal. It is important to notice, that DFX capability manager is a single Operations interface in programs – the link between a program and the DMPD.

A generic example of DMPD participation to business unit decision-making; when matters cannot be decided at the program level, the decision making is escalated step by step to higher levels of the organization, as usual.

5 Discussion

DFX has been utilized for several years in the industry. Traditionally it has been managed within R&D. The DFX concept provides common guidelines, instructions, and a harmonized way to aim for the common goal, instead of each group or department implementing its own plans. DFX aims to have all customers or stakeholders, internal and external, valued and recognized appropriately; production process and design taking into account the whole supply chain and visa versa.

The ICT business environment can be characterized by fierce price erosion that forces the companies to continuous process of improving their internal efficiency [13]. DFX can prove a functional means for addressing the strive for efficiency improvement and the needs of internal customers, as the case company experience proves. DFX provides the means to achieve functional integration, when used as a communication tool, and it is also a tangible way for managing requirements throughout the product development chain. The case company has utilized DFX extensively, especially Design for Manufacturing, for over a decade. The practices of the case company prove that DFX is not a philosophy, in contrast to literature, but rather works through principles and tools.

Several studies, see e.g., [14], [15], [16], [17] indicate that it is a common mistake to have product development based on a line of individual separate products, or to have different groups, function or companies in the supply chain basing their plans on individual specific needs. Even with the shared common goal, they may end up with contradicting plans. For example, if the products are developed based on the needs of separate product lines, it leads product design decision to be driven basically based on R&D requirements and direct cost optimization, and the outcome of this is inefficiency and poor customer service. Kaski [14] continues that often business process activities relate to product architecture and sales volumes as well. That is why he suggests total cost model instead of optimization of a single product. So, there is a need to align operations with the product creation process and all the other functions, especially if there are multiple development programs running simultaneously. How can this be implemented in a large organization if the traditional way is not efficient enough? This brings us to the research question 1.

A response to our research question 1, "*How does a large system provider successfully organize DFX contrary to the traditional way?*", and the main argument of our study is that DFX can be organized in a different way than it is usually done. Having DFX within Operations is certainly reasonable, and recommended. It can be organized as chapter 4 suggests, systematically through the concept of DMPD with emphasis on Operations, but also taking into account Services, R&D and Marketing operations. This is different from the traditional view cf. [2], [18] where DFX is mainly seen from the viewpoint of product development. Ensuring an adequate capability to deliver products is vital for business. Continuous streamlining of internal processes to maximize delivery capability is going on in the case company. They coordinate the activities of different DFX's through DFX management organization.

The literature on organizational implementation of DFX is scarce, but it still shows clearly that Bralla's view is the most dominant, in most cases the DFX disciplines are implemented inside the product development organizations. The way of implementing them through the organization that actually pays for the costs of it, is much more reasonable, and it is a good way to implement the DFX within an organization.

This offers remarkable benefits over the traditional way, as our research has shown. That will answer the research question 2, "*What benefits does the new way provide?*" Similarly to traditional approach in the single program point of view, there are cross-functional teams with experts, program manager sets up business unit teams, each DFX discipline has guidelines etc., but the difference will be evident when there are requirements that will concern multiple programs. These "global" requirements will be more visible to all stakeholders, and they will be recognized more seriously. However, this requires a serious "twist of mind"; the traditional solution domain becomes the new problem domain, and DFX becomes the new solution domain.

One of the problems in product development as Lee and Billington [19] suggest, is that internal customers are not recognized or cared for as well as external customer. External customers bring in revenue and they are more visible [19]. However, the way of organizing DFX within operations stresses the importance of internal customers also, so that they are on equal level with external customers.

The transition of problem domain and solution domain means that from the DFX point of view, the solution domain is provided by the DFX management organization, and the DFX disciplines within that, and the problem domain is actually the product process.

A question "is DFX rather philosophical or rational approach" has been posed. We see that DFX is not only a philosophy, it also has practical implications. It is a way to organizing stakeholders inside the organization. DFX managers representing different stakeholders formulate general guidelines for the DFX based on the information in the corresponding platform. These guidelines are then implemented by the implementation manager in the product programs. As the requirements and solutions come from the organization funding the manufacturing, they are taken into serious consideration. The idea is to use DFX to make an effect to the product process, so that the DFX requirements, guidelines, principles, are implemented in the product process.

The platform managers are where the knowledge of the DFX disciplines is codified, for example in the form of documents, databases, lists of recommended suppliers etc., depending on the DFX. The main role of the discipline managers is to use that knowledge from the platform and form guidelines and principles to implement those requirements of that platform or general requirements. In addition, the responsibility of the discipline managers is also to train people who will take part of the DMPD process, which is part of the product process, and implement those guidelines and principles in a singular product.

Further benefits are, for example, the responsibility for DFX improvement will be distributed all over the organization. Thus, also other departments than R&D will be participating in the DFX improvement work. Table 1 summarizes our answers to the research questions.

Table 1. Summary table to answer the research questions

How does a large system provider successfully organize DFX contrary to the traditional way?	What benefits does the new way provide?
It can be organized systematically through the concept of DFX Management in Product Development (DMPD) and DFX capability management organization. In the case company, the emphasis is on Operations, but also taking into account Services, R&D and Marketing operations.	The responsibility for DFX improvement will be distributed all over the organization, thus helping long term planning and improvement. The way of organizing DFX within operations stresses the importance of internal customers also, so that they are on equal level with external customers.
Coordination of the activities of different DFX's through DFX management organization is required.	The DFX discipline managers train people who will take part at the product process, thus aiding process improvement and knowledge sharing.
The management, global responsibility for the processes, its existence, development and implementation for DFX concept resides with the internal stakeholder where it most matters, usually it will be the one who pays the costs.	DFX managers formulate general guidelines for the DFX based on the information in the corresponding platform. These guidelines are then implemented by the implementation managers in the product programs. As the requirements and solutions come from organization funding the manufacturing, they are taken into serious consideration, and they will be more likely implemented in the product process.
The DFX management organization formulates all the relevant DFX requirements into words and figures, and presents them to the product programs. They should also include the reasons for the requirements. The argumentation should be presented with similar criteria as external customer requirements.	Behind each DFX discipline, there is a platform of knowledge and technology to be adapted to the programs. These platforms are knowledge bases that include both product and the processes. The discipline managers use that knowledge from the platform and form guidelines and principles to implement those requirements of that platform or general requirements. Requirements that will concern multiple programs, product lines or families will be more visible to all stakeholders.

6 Conclusions

The general value adding principles of DFX management organization can be formulated in the following way based on the interviews and other research material:

-   Manage delivery capability and DFX implementation and maintenance in all case company products, solutions and platforms by efficient use of standard operations platforms as well as operations resources.
-   In order to ensure operations alignment with the product creation process, the DFX management organization will participate in programs to ensure seamless delivery of products.

- Starting from early planning phase, DFX management organization will make a strong contribution to business unit and R&D management structures throughout the product life cycle, driving DFX requirements analysis and decision-making in product proposals with end-to-end business case calculation support.
- During the maintenance phase, DFX management organization will manage delivery capability for all active products in the business units. DFX management organization will drive product change management from an operations point-of-view and, at the end of the product lifecycle, efficiently remove products with optimized assets and minimum scrap.
- When the same organization is also responsible for implementation and maintenance, the commitment is created more easily than in product programs, which are focusing on short term operations.

On the other hand, there are also advantages of managing and implementing DFX within one organization/function. For example, reporting; line of reporting would obviously be much shorter and straight forward, and another advantage would be having uniform practices. Thus, continuous discussions are held in the case organization concerning the most optimal way to manage DFX. This research is one concrete example of this continuous improvement work.

However, there are still challenges to be solved. Based on the interviews for example, converting requirements into costs or into a commensurable format to ease communicating and prioritizing requirements is challenging. The discipline managers of DFX's with a longer history have the benefit of being able to clearly describe the field in question, compared to newer disciplines. Only a minority of DFX requirements can be directly related to customers. This has been noticed annoying to many DFX discipline managers as the "voice-of-the-customers" is a powerful tool when negotiating with program managers about the importance of requirements. From the program's point of view, the company strategy and business target level requirements are not always seen very important – the requirements directly relevant to the program at hand go over the "abstract" requirements related to all programs. In general level the main processes seem to have descriptions that are well defined and documented. However, the utilization is a bit unclear because of the great amount of different sub processes, at least on all organizational units.

Comparison of different and sometimes conflicting requirements is difficult in practice, as they are lacking the common economic scale for comparison. For example, the desire to minimize the number of product titles, conflicts with customer requirements supporting increased number of these titles. End-to-end cost calculations provide the basis for requirements prioritization attempts. However, there is often skepticism concerning calculations made by other people. Currently requirements prioritization is often based on the individual's capability to sell their viewpoint. It is a fact that people are different and the processes still need standardization.

Identification of all important stakeholders is important, and it is a topic to be studied further; how to identify and manage the stakeholders and their needs. Another topic for further studies is providing implementation guidelines for actual implementation of this process.

References

1. Dodgson, M., Gann, D., Salter, A.: The Management of Technological Innovation. Completely Revised and Updated. Oxford University Press, New York (2008)
2. Bralla, J.G.: Design for Excellence. McGraw-Hill, New York (1996)
3. Sheu, D.D., Chen, D.R.: Backward design and cross-functional design management system. In: Proceedings of the 35th International Conference on Computers and Industrial Engineering, Istanbul, Turkey, pp. 19–22 (2005)
4. Eisenhardt, K.M.: Building theories from case study research. Academy of Management Review 14(4), 532–550 (1989)
5. Wiegers, K.: Software Requirements. Microsoft Press, Redmond (2003)
6. Leffingwell, D., Widrig, D.: Managing Software Requirements – A Use Case Approach. Addison-Wesley, Boston (2003)
7. Kotonya, K., Sommerville, I.: Requirements Engineering – Processes and Techniques. John-Wiley & Sons, Chichester (2003)
8. Maciaszek, L.: Requirements Analysis and System Design. Pearson Education, Harlow (2005)
9. Lauesen, S.: Software Requirements – Styles and Techniques. Addison-Wesley, London (2002)
10. Hall, J.G., Jackson, M., Laney, R.C., Nuseibeh, B., Rapanotti, L.: Relating Software Requirements and Architectures using Problem Frames. In: IEEE Proceedings of RE 2002 (2002)
11. Cybulsky, J., Reed, K.: Requirements Classification and Reuse: Crossing Domains Boundaries. In: Frakes, W.B. (ed.) ICSR 2000. LNCS, vol. 1844, pp. 190–210. Springer, Heidelberg (2000)
12. Jacobson, I., Booch, G., Rumbaugh, J.: The Unified Software Development Process. Addison-Wesley, Reading (1999)
13. Helo, P.: Managing agility and productivity in the electronics industry. Industrial Management & Data Systems 104(7), 567–577 (2004)
14. Kaski, T.: Product Structure Metrics as an Indicator of Demand-Supply Chain Efficiency: Case Study in the Cellular Network Industry, Doctoral Dissertation, Acta Polytechnica Scandinavica, Industrial Management and Business Administration Series, No. 13, Espoo (2002)
15. Holmström, J., Korhonen, H., Laiho, A., Hartiala, H.: Managing product introductions across the supply chain: findings from a development project. Supply Chain Management: An International Journal 11(2), 121–130 (2006)
16. Helms, M.M., Ettkin, L.P., Chapman, S.: Supply Chain Forecasting – Collaborative Forecasting Supports Supply Chain Management. Business Process Management Journal 6(5), 392–407 (2000)
17. Mentzer, J.T., Moon, M.A., Kent, J.L., Smith, C.D.: The need for a forecasting champion. Journal of Business Forecasting Methods & Systems 16(3), 3–8 (1997)
18. Meerkamm, H., Koch, M.: Design for X. In: Clarkson, J., Eckert, C. (eds.) Design Process Improvement – A review of current practice, pp. 306–323. Springer, London (2005)
19. Lee, H.L., Billington, C.: Managing supply chain inventory: Pitfalls and opportunities. Sloan Management Review 33(3), 65–73 (Spring 1992)

The Tool Coverage of Software Process Improvement Frameworks for Small and Medium Sized Enterprises

Filiz Çelik Yeşildoruk, Banu Bozlu, and Onur Demirörs

Middle East Technical University, Informatics Institute,
06531 Ankara, Turkey
filiz.celik@tcmb.gov.tr, {banu,demirors}@ii.metu.edu.tr

Abstract. Software Process Improvement (SPI) awareness is increasing among Small and Medium Sized Enterprises (SMEs). Conventional SPI frameworks are not appealing for SMEs since they are complex and costly. There are a number of frameworks, which address the problems of SMEs for SPI. This paper presents a comparative study of the most frequently referenced SPI frameworks established for SMEs from a SPI Tool coverage perspective.

Keywords: software process improvement, small and medium sized enterprises.

1 Introduction

Software industry has embraced the paradigm of achieving quality by improving processes starting from early 90s [1]. Since then, a number of tools for SPI have been evolved. Most of the current SPI studies focus on model-based improvement that aims to improve processes with respect to a reference model. To support the worldview, process improvement tools including process reference models, process assessment methodologies, process improvement methodologies and process modeling approaches are developed.

The software industry includes a considerable number of small and medium size companies. In all European countries, over 97 percent of Computer and Related Services enterprises have less than 50 employees and they account for over fifty percent of employment in the private sector [2]. Small software companies usually provide customer specific solutions targeted for businesses or specialized parts of larger systems. It is critical for these companies to produce quality software since it will determine the quality of the business or the quality of the whole system.

Although small companies are the majority and produce critical products, the software quality movement, in its early days, mainly targeted large organizations. Small enterprises were indifferent to the need in early days. However, pressures from acquirers, widening awareness on quality movement and the need to grow stimulated the need to establish quality infrastructures. During the last decade, specific needs of the SMEs derived the need for establishing frameworks targeted specifically at SMEs. Most of them can be considered as modified versions of process improvement frameworks such as CMMI [3] and ISO 15504 [4], each providing different tools and having different perspectives for process improvement requirements of SMEs.

F. Bomarius et al. (Eds.): PROFES 2009, LNBIP 32, pp. 290–302, 2009.
© Springer-Verlag Berlin Heidelberg 2009

In this paper we present the results of a comparative study on SPI frameworks established for SMEs. We defined the framework as a unifying approach that covers at least three significant SPI Tools. In this paper, we use the term Tool - starting with the capital letter - to cover notations, approach, techniques, methodologies and CASE tools. We identified significant SPI Tools as those, which are frequently utilized in model-based SPI initiatives. These Tools include process reference models, modeling methodologies and notations, assessment methodologies, improvement methodologies and automation environments, which are frequently utilized in model-based SPI frameworks. In addition to the utilization of the Tools, we also identified how and to what extent the Tool is utilized by each framework. In other words, we evaluate SME specific SPI frameworks by considering the Tools they have utilized.

The rest of the paper is organized as follows. Section 2 gives brief information about the previous research studies on SPI implementations in small settings. Section 3 includes the results of the comparative study. Finally, conclusions of the comparison are presented together with the future work planned.

2 Difficulties of SPI Implementation in Small Settings

Restrictions in applying conventional quality management tools in software domain, such as the lack of significant statistical data and improvement guidelines, have led practitioners to focus on development of model based improvement approaches. In model-based improvement approaches, organizations' processes are compared with the process attributes defined in a reference model. Based on the identified gaps between existing processes and the reference process attributes, improvement plans are established and executed [5]. As Sheard discusses, new standards or approaches for this purpose evolve regularly [6], yet most of these models are based on CMM or ISO 15504. However, there are a number of research studies which demonstrates that SMEs have difficulties in applying conventional model-based improvement frameworks [7][8][9].

In order to find solutions to overcome these difficulties, several researchers have focused on potential challenges facing small companies in process improvement activities [9][10][11][12][13][14][15]. The problems frequently occur due to the mismatch between utilized process improvement Tools and the organizational structure of SMEs. Current generic SPI Tools do not address structural characteristics of SMEs. Commonly used practices such as top down improvement approaches, lack of integrated frameworks and lack of detailed process libraries result in prolonged improvement cycles and complicate making timely process changes in response to the changes in the environment. Other significant problems that prevent SMEs from implementing SPI include high costs of improvement activities, and limited number of qualified personnel, which is one of the reasons why SMEs do not have expertise to choose and implement the improvement model [16].

Studies concentrating on specific requirements of SMEs resulted in development of a number of process improvement frameworks focusing on different aspects and aiming different goals. TOPS (Toward Organised Processes in SMEs) in Italy [17], SATASPIN (Software Process Improvement Network in the Satakunta region) [18] in Finland, INSPIRE in Estonia [19], SPIRE (Software Process Improvement in Regions of Europe) [20] in Europe, MoProSoft in Mexico [21], MPS in Brazil [22], PRISMS [23] in UK, MESOPYME [24] in Spain, TAPISTRY [16] in Europe, MARES [25] in Brazil, RAPID [26] are examples of SPI approaches specific to SMEs.

There are several studies in which SPI frameworks for SMEs are compared considering their specific properties in order to identify strengths and weaknesses of these frameworks. Such studies both help to reveal improvement opportunities for existing frameworks and assist SMEs to select relevant framework for themselves. Laporte's study introduces various centers and initiatives focusing on small enterprises in which the tools to be compared were selected based on a survey. Common requirements of SMEs are concluded as low cost solutions, staged approach and standardization of vocabulary [27]. Pino et al has conducted an extensive review on SPI efforts in SMEs by systematically reviewing published case studies on the topic. The focus is on usage of CMM, CMMI and ISO 15504, as they are found to be the mostly utilized approaches in published case studies [28]. Despite this situation, it is also concluded that these approaches are not suitable for SMEs since they have restrictive formal procedures for SMEs to follow. Mishra et al have compared a self-diagnosis methodology based on CMM, Software Process Matrix, ASPE-MSC, PRISMS and MESOPYME in their study [29]. Mishra underlines the fact that each SPI tool has its own benefits and limitations, which gives SMEs the burden of adapting and tailoring SPI tools according to their organizational needs. Several other comparative studies also emphasize that conventional standards are not appropriate and difficult to apply for SMEs [8][27][28][30].

In this study, we have chosen six SPI frameworks for comparison. These frameworks have different characteristics and offer guidance for SMEs in different SPI perspectives. SPIRE is one of the earliest projects to increase the awareness of best SPI practices and benefits among the top management, share experience with others and help SMEs maintain their improvement plans. It has been used widely with numerous documented case studies and it is important in the sense that it forms a basis for other improvement tools for SMEs. Although many countries or regions have software and systems process improvement networks[1], most of them are used to share ideas and experiences. SATASPIN, which involves SMEs working totally customer oriented, is a good example for the networked SPI efforts in the sense to demonstrate how these ideas were organized into a structured methodology for a group of SPI implementors. MoProSoft has been accepted as a national standard in Mexico, and also as an international standard by ISO/IEC JTC1/ SC7/WG24 for very small enterprises [31]. MPS offers a process centered software engineering environment to aid the SPI methodology it recommends. PRISMS and MESOPYME are included in the study as most frequently referenced CMM based SPI frameworks. PRISMS adapts CMM according to its business goals defined by top managers and MESOPYME focuses on reducing time and effort using action packages concept. It is observed that SME SPI frameworks are predominantly based on ISO 15504 rather than CMM. Main reason for this is that, ISO/IEC 15504 provides much flexibility than CMM because several processes can be managed at different capability levels [32]. Von Wangenheim underlines the fact that tailoring cost of CMM is more than the SMEs can bear [9]. Pino also states that usage

---

[1] http://www.sei.cmu.edu/collaborating/spins/spins.intl.active.html

of ISO/IEC 15504 is widening in SMEs due to the fact that it is a model which is easy to understand, flexible and fits the needs of SMEs [28].

3 Discussion of SME-Specific SPI Frameworks

The explained SME-specific SPI frameworks have different focuses and are divergent in characteristics. In model-based process improvement, reference models, process modeling notations and methodologies, assessment methodologies and automation of processes by means of CASE tools and workflow management systems are commonly used Tools.

- Most organizations use reference models as a source of best practices, as well as a means for improving education and communication. Furthermore, Holschke et al demonstrates that the use of reference models provide a systematic approach to planning, implementing and evaluating business process transformations [33].
- Assessment is a generic step in process improvement, it not only provides a baseline for organization's current status but also helps to check improvement progress as an audit tool [34][35].
- Software process improvement is a complicated activity which requires theory and models, skilled technical and managerial professionals [35]. The improvement methodologies enables organization's to plan SPI activities in alignment with strategic goals and customer expectations.
- Process modeling methodologies are useful in defining and studying existing processes for a better understanding and analysis to discover current problems as well as depicting the to be processes of the organizations. However, the dynamics between process modeling and improvement has not been examined in the literature thoroughly.
- The idea of combining process improvement with process automation is promoted, however, in its current state, many process improvement models are designed to be executed by humans, new approaches which would enable them to be interpreted by machines would be developed.

SMEs which operate on limited resources will preferably need SPI frameworks which would cover al these aspects as an integrated whole. However, current frameworks have structures, which concentrate on specific aspects rather than integrating different views. Rational [36] for example is a very effective modeling tool, however it does not offer a solution for process improvement. Similarly, Personal Software Process [37] or Team Software Process [38] concentrates on process improvement but they do not provide methodologies guiding organizations on implementation issues. Workflow management systems may be used to automate the processes, however continuity is not maintained (organizations do it once and leave as is since it is costly to keep the models and the reality in sync), therefore improvement is not supported. In this study, we have investigated the current SPI frameworks in terms of the extent of support for these different aspects. The frameworks are compared in a tabular view in Table 1, to highlight the improvement opportunities and significant similarities and differences among them. The comparison is done in six major categories with different characteristics to be investigated, which will be explained in this section.

3.1   General Properties

The characteristics in this category are generic to all frameworks. It includes historical information about the frameworks as most of them are based on best practices of previous SPI approaches and complement them with new properties to compensate the SME related challenges of the base approach. This category also gives information about the geographic scope of the methodology and for how long it has been in use.

The integrated Tools of the framework for process improvement are named in this category. Process improvement may be performed utilizing different Tools; some of which may be specifically intended for process improvement whereas others are utilized as supplementary aids. Complementary Tools such as process modeling and process automation may increase the efficiency of process improvement, especially when organizations have to react very quickly. Process modeling tools enable creating formal models by using visual representations, which can both be used in assessment and automation of processes. The generic properties reveal that none of the frameworks focus on modeling and automation tools, while they all have reference models, assessment and improvement tools.

3.2   Reference Model

Reference models include descriptions of process attributes so that each organization may use these descriptions to compare their processes with. Process attributes can be described at different abstraction levels. Some of the models include detailed descriptions such as best practices and implementation guidelines.

Tailoring guidelines may be used by organizations to adapt the reference model to specific organizational needs and situations. Glazer et.al. report that one of the reasons of failure in model-based improvement is the misuse of the model; most of the time models are applied rather than being implemented [39]. Applying a model imposes certain activities; however implementing a model utilizes models as learning and communication tools as well as media for organizing thoughts [39]. Implementation guidelines are also important for SMEs, as reference models are generic by definition; and SMEs can have difficulties in implementing those abstract definitions.

The process coverage is another issue that may differ among the reference models. As more processes are covered by the model, its application in different organizations is easier. Almost all of the existing models cover only the software life-cycle processes. SMEs on the other hand execute other processes such as service-desks and finances. Models with wider coverage will be beneficial for SMEs as the need to learn and execute multiple process models will decrease.

The dimension of a reference model describes the underlying structure and the relationships among process areas and with capability levels. A staged architecture includes process areas, which are associated with different organizational capability levels. A continuous architecture defines capability levels for process areas. Addressing strategic competencies in the market and focusing improvement actions in strategic process areas is especially important for SMEs; in which case a model with a continuous dimension structure can be applied by SMEs more efficiently. On account of this, all frameworks utilize a continuous architecture in which the selected processes that should be improved can be identified considering organizational goals and context.

Table 1. Comparison of SPI Frameworks

		SPIRE	SATASPIN	PRISMS	MESOPYME	MoProSoft	MPS
General Properties	Geographic Origin	Europe	Finland	UK	Spain	Mexico	Brazil
	Mostly used in	Europe	Finland	.	Spain	Mexico	Brazil
	Initiated in	1998	1998	2000	1997	2002	2003
	Designed especially for	Software	Software	Software	Software	Software	Software
	Intended Organization	SME	SME	SME	SME	SME	SME
	Popularity	Throughout Europe	In Finland	In UK	Spain	Chosen by ISO/IEC JTC1/SC7/WG24	In Brazil
	Based on	ISO/IEC 15504	ISO/IEC 15504 TR	CMM	CMM	ISO/IEC 12207 ISO/IEC 15504 ISO 9000:2000 CMMI	ISO/IEC 15504 ISO/IEC 12207
	Tools Utilized						
	• Reference Model	✓	✓	✓	✓	✓	✓
	• Modeling	X	X	X	X	X	X
	• Assessment	✓	✓	✓	✓	✓	✓
	• Improvement	✓	✓	✓	✓	✓	✓
	• Automation	X	X	X	X	X	X
Reference Model	**Level of abstraction**						
	• Detail of descriptions	Generic	ISO/IEC 15504 TR		Based on CMM	Detailed	Generic
	• Extend of coverage	Generic				Detailed	Generic
	Availability of tailoring guidelines	None				Available	None
	Availability of implementation guidelines	None				Available	Available
	Dimension	Continuous	Continuous		Continuous	Continuous	Continuous
Modelling Model	**Why to model**						
	• Prescriptive	N/A	N/A	N/A	N/A	N/A	N/A
	• Descriptive						
	Notation						
	How to model						

Table 1. (*Continued*)

	Tool Support						
	Measure	Process Capability Level	Process Capability Level	Process Capability Level	Process Capability Level	Process Capability Level	Process Capability Level
Assessment Methodology	Appraisal method	SPICE	ISO/IEC 15504-2	CMM assessment questionnaire	CMM based	EvalProSoft	ISO/IEC 15504-2
	Assessment team	Professionals	Internal and external professionals	Project Researchers	Domain experts		
	Assessment effort	High	High	High	Low	Low	
	Assessment cost	High	High	High	Low	Low	
	Tool support for self assessment	None	Tailored FISMA	Web-based tool recently developed			None
	Tool support for data collection	None	None	None	None	None	None
Improvement Methodology	Improvement Life-cycle	Waterfall-like	Incremental	Waterfall-like	Incremental	Agile	Incremental
	Application Paradigm	Top-down	Top-down	Top-down	Top-down	Top-down	Top-down
Automation Support	PCE Existence	N/A	N/A	N/A	N/A	N/A	N/A
	Notation • Functional • Behavioral • Structural						
	Tool support for • Process Definition • Process Execution • Process Follow-up						

3.3 Modeling Approach

Process modeling is one of the most significant means for transferring process experience into process knowledge. It is also a requirement of reference models at certain stages. It is frequently assumed that organizations may use any modeling approach. However, using 'any' does not guarantee improvement and modeling approaches to be in line with related tools. Why modeling is needed is important since different approaches focus on different goals. Descriptive modeling approaches are used for understanding the current processes. Prescriptive models on the other hand are generally used as guidelines or frameworks to organize and structure the desired process [40]. SMEs can benefit from descriptive modeling by transforming processes into tangible forms, which facilitate the understanding of current situations and provide a concrete view to identify improvement opportunities. SMEs can utilize prescriptive modeling by guiding and forcing the desired processes.

Tool support for modeling simplifies maintenance of the process descriptions, enables automated analysis of the processes and decreases ambiguity [41]. Modeling methodologies improve learning curve, increase reliability of the models and shorten the required effort [41][42]. Lack of guidelines for modeling activities result in ad hoc approaches, and most of the time a natural language based description of the process is formed. The resultant process descriptions are error prone and difficult for numerical analyses. Tools support is crucial for SMEs not only for reducing effort but also for reducing errors.

How to model processes is an important issue in the sense that it affects all the way down the improvement implementation. Process modeling as part of a process improvement initiative is usually performed in a top-down fashion, that is, the overall processes are identified primarily and then a process improvement team captures the processes one by one by interviewing stakeholders of each process and then detailing those processes by resolving inconsistencies. This approach requires a complete understanding of the context and therefore can create the problems that process modeling takes months and the contributions of actual performers remains minimal. The bottom-up process modeling requires a deep knowledge and understanding of detailed functions to combine into a single process. Modeling can also be performed using a combination of these two approaches in which each process owner in an organization models her activities and these partial models form the organization's process-base, which can be used to depict the process knowledge from different perspectives [43]. This style of process modeling may be of great value for SMEs since it does not require the effort of external modelers trying to understand the current processes, or trying to catch-up with the latest version of the processes.

Usage of notation in process modeling is important to integrate separately modeled processes easily and unambiguously. The notation is also important if models would be used as input for process execution tools.

None of the frameworks we have investigated integrates a modeling approach and its related Tools. Nevertheless, we have included the discussion to guide future studies on this specific Tool.

3.4 Assessment Methodology

In model-based improvement approaches, assessments are performed to identify the gap between the as-is processes of the organization and the attributes of the processes of the reference model and then improvement actions are planned to diminish the gap. The results of the assessment, measurement attribute, are defined in terms of process capability or organizational capability. As mentioned, SMEs tend to focus on strategic processes rather than the overall structure of the organization, therefore the focus is on process capability in SMEs rather than organizational capability. On account of this, for all the listed frameworks, the measure for process capability is capability level and in ordinal scale.

Appraisal is the systematic analysis conducted using a documented appraisal method and a reference model as a base. Appraisal method is closely related with the reference model and different appraisal methods are utilized by the frameworks. Assessment team is an important factor affecting the cost of the assessment. Although assessment team may include external professionals, internal participants, domain experts or researchers, generally external professionals conduct assessment, hence the cost is high. Moreover, some methods require the involvement of external professionals as well as trained participants in the assessed organization, which increases duration since not only the assessment team but also the participants within the organization spend time and effort. In SMEs, it is important for a successful SPI implementation to include the software development team members to reflect on the organizational concerns as well as establishing individual commitment to processes. Tool support for collecting data to be used in the assessment, as well as tool support for the assessment itself are helpful both to decrease costs and increase reliability of the assessment reports.

3.5 Improvement Methodology

The improvement methodology includes task definitions with sequence of tasks to be performed to plan and implement improvement activities in SMEs. The improvement methodologies in these model-based frameworks usually include similar activities, but the life cycles differ from one another. Improvement activities may be organized in waterfall-like, in incremental or agile styles. Traditional improvement methods use a waterfall-like approach, which carries all the disadvantages of the waterfall life cycle, most significant being the difficulty of managing change and establishing delayed outcomes. Contemporary SME specific SPI frameworks mostly prefer to use lightweight tools, which are iterative and incremental, since these approaches step forward as better responses to uncertainty and change, and enable short improvement cycles.

The application paradigm refers to the initiation and implementation patterns of SPI activities, which guides the organizations. Currently, top-down paradigm dominates the SPI activities in which the context is firstly examined to be able to detail into deeper levels later. The bottom-up paradigm requires a grass roots approach to SPI to initiatives. Distributed approach is also mentioned in which SPI implementations are supported by the top-management but initiated in all levels at the same time by process owners throughout the organization.

3.6 Automation Support

Automation helps to manage process complexity levels, improve quality by reducing errors and reduce time by delegating tasks [44]. Workflow management systems, business process management systems and CASE tools can be used for these purposes. Most of the time, process improvement frameworks suggest activities to explicitly define the processes, but do not offer how to do it. Process centered environments (PCE) provide solutions integrating the processes with the people, using the supporting technology, with specific focus on how work flows through the organization [45][46]. PCE can be supported by CASE tools in different levels of the automation such as defining, executing and controlling the processes. These environments require notations for functional, behavioral and structural views for defining the process in terms of executable languages.

As is the case for the modeling approach, none of the frameworks we have investigated integrates automation support approach and its related Tools. Nevertheless, we have included the discussion to guide future studies on this specific Tool.

4 Conclusion

In this paper, we performed a situational analysis based on existing studies. We have studied a selected set of SME-specific SPI frameworks and compared them to determine their coverage of software process improvement Tools. We have observed that in its current state, SPI frameworks for SMEs have accomplishments as well as some improvement opportunities.

All frameworks have well defined reference models, assessment and improvement methodologies. MoProSoft framework is distinct in this sense that it benefits from a wide class of process models and complements these models to be in line with SME needs. It is also noteworthy that the reference model in this framework includes detailed guidelines to facilitate process improvement in SMEs. Almost all frameworks utilize a continuous approach which enables SMEs to focus on process areas they want to improve.

MoProSoft is supported by EvalProSoft assessment methodology which is especially designed for assessment in small and medium enterprises however other frameworks utilize generic assessment tools. Except MoProSoft and MPS, frameworks require high effort and cost mostly because the required external know-how and experience. SATASPIN and PRISMS have considered the benefit of tool support for self-assessment and included supplementary tools in their framework.

It is notable that general trend in process improvement methodology is using incremental – rather than waterfall-like- approaches which is more suitable for SMEs. MoProSoft uses an agile SPI methodology which is formed after inspection of a wide variety of improvement methodologies. In agile methodologies, management may have the fear of loose of control [39], therefore to increase the management support in improvement activities, blending approaches may enhance the improvement by reassuring both the management and the employees that their concerns will be taken into consideration.

The major improvement opportunity is observed as integration of complementary Tools for process modeling and process automation to the frameworks. A framework utilizing all these Tools can act as an integrated solution, which would guide SMEs to address and tackle their problems and solve them in a faster and more cost effective way. Process models are assumed as the most significant means for transferring process knowledge into process improvement. Therefore integrating process modeling with process improvement activities can enhance the efficiency of SPI initiatives. Tool support is essential for modeling processes separately, and then integrating them identifying and resolving conflictions. Process automation is also not considered as an aspect in improvement frameworks. Especially for SMEs, which require minimum effort and expect maximum benefit, process automation support might help organizations to increase return on investment and ease process prescription. Process automation has a large potential of benefiting from process modeling. The quick change in processes makes it nearly impossible to execute the processes with modeling-only tools. However, modeling tools and notations which take subsequent steps of process models in improvement activities into consideration and interface with process execution systems; may enhance the maintenance of continuity in improvement activities.

A restriction in this study was the difficulty of finding the most recent versions of the documentation related to the frameworks, such as the reference models. This could imply that these frameworks are not necessarily maintained to reflect the recent developments in the field. It also means that we were not able to evaluate what advancements the models offer for different SPI Tools. In addition, there are not many documented case studies reporting the results of these SPI efforts except the SPIRE framework. Further work is required to implement these models and perform surveys on companies who implemented these models.

References

1. Paulk, M.C., Weber, C.V., Curtis, B., Chrissis, M.B.: The Capability Maturity Model: Guidelines For Improving The Software Process. Addison-Wesley, Reading (1995)
2. OECD, Organisation for Economic Co-Operation and Development, SME and Entrepreneurship Outlook (2005)
3. SEI. CMMI for Systems Engineering, Software Engineering, Integrated Product and Process Development, and Supplier Sourcing (CMMI-SE/SW/IPPD/SS, V1.1) Staged Representation. Technical Report CMU/SEI-2002-TR-012 ESC-TR-2002-012, Software Engineering Institute (2002)
4. ISO, Software Process Assessment - Part 2: A reference model for processes and process capability. Technical Report ISO/IEC 15504 TR2:1998, International Organization for Standardization (1998)
5. Thomas, M., McGarry, F.: Top-down vs. bottom-up process improvement. IEEE Software 11(4), 12–13 (1994)
6. Sheard, S.A.: Evolution of the frameworks quagmire. Software Productivity Consortium, Herndon, VA. Computer 34(7) (2001)
7. El Emam, K.: An Overview of Process Improvement in Small Settings. In: Web Engineering, pp. 261–275 (2006)
8. Miluk, G.: Results of a Field Study of CMMI for Small Settings Using Rapid Applied Ethnography. In: Proceedings of the First International Research Workshop for Process Improvement in Small Settings (2005)
9. von Wangenheim, C.G., Anacleto, A., Salviano, C.F.: Helping Small Companies Assess Software Processes. IEEE Software 23(1), 91–98 (2006)

10. Alexandre, S., Renault, A., Habra, N.: OWPL: A Gradual Approach for Software Process Improvement In SMEs. In: Proceedings of the 32nd EUROMICRO Conference on Software Engineering and Advanced Applications (2006)
11. Demirors, O., Demirors, E.: Software Process Improvement in a Small Organization. In: Gruhn, V. (ed.) EWSPT 1998. LNCS, vol. 1487, pp. 1–12. Springer, Heidelberg (1998)
12. Dyba, T.: Factors of Software Process Improvement Success in Small and Large Organizations: An Empirical Study in the Scandinavian Context. In: Proceedings of the 9th European Software Engineering Conference, Helsinki, Finland, pp. 148–157 (2003)
13. Garcia, S.: Thoughts on Applying CMMI in Small Settings. Carnegie Mellon University (2005),
    http://www.sei.cmu.edu/cmmi/adoption/pdf/garcia-thoughts.pdf
14. Garcia, S., Graettinger, C., Carmody, C., Penn, M.L.: Prototype for a Field Guide for Improving Processes in Small Settings. SEI (2008),
    http://www.sei.cmu.edu/iprc/ipss-field-guide.pdf
15. Paulk, M.C.: Using the Software CMM in small Organizations. In: Paulk, M.C. (ed.) Joint 1998 Proc. Pacific Northwest Software Quality Conf. and the Eighth Int'l Conf. On Software Quality, pp. 350–361 (1998)
16. Kuvaja, P., Palo, J., Bicego, A.: TAPISTRY- A Software Process Improvement Tailored for Small Enterprises. Software Quality Journal 8, 149–156 (1999)
17. Bucci, G., Campanai, M., Cignoni, G.A.: Rapid Assessment to Solicit Process Improvement in SMEs. In: Proc. 7th European Software Process Improvement Conf. (2000)
18. Mäkinen, T., Varkoi, T., Lepasaar, M.: A Detailed Process Assessment Method for Software SMEs. In: Proc. 7th European Software Process Improvement Conf. (2000)
19. Kalja, A., Oruaas, J.: An overview of SPI activities in Estonia. In: Proceedings of the EuroSPI 1999 conference: European Software Process Improvement (1999)
20. Sanders, M. (ed.): The SPIRE Handbook—Better, Faster, Cheaper: Software Development in Small Organisations, Dublin City. Univ. Center for Software Eng. (1998)
21. Oktaba, H.: MoProSoft: A Software Process Model for small enterprises. In: Proceedings of 1st International Research Workshop for Process Improvement in Small Settings (2005)
22. Weber, K.C., Araujo, E.R., Rocha, A.R., Machado, C., Scalet, D., Salviano, C.: Brazilian Software Process Reference Model and Assessment Method. In: Yolum, p., Güngör, T., Gürgen, F., Özturan, C. (eds.) ISCIS 2005. LNCS, vol. 3733, pp. 402–411. Springer, Heidelberg (2005) ISBN 3-540-29414-7
23. Allen, P., Ramachandran, M., Abushama, H.: PRISMS: an Approach to Software Process Improvement for Small to Medium Enterprises. In: Proceedings of the Third International Conference on Quality Software, Dallas (2003)
24. Calvo-Manzano, J.A., Agustin, G.C., Gilabert, T.S.F., Seco, A.D.A., Sanchez, L.Z., Cota, M.P.: Experiences in the Application of Software Process Improvement in SMES. Software Quality Journal 10, 261–273 (2002)
25. Anacleto, A., von Wangenheim, C.G., Salviano, C.F., Savi, R.: A Method for Process Assessment in Small Software Companies. In: Proc. 4th Int'l Software Process Improvement and Capability Determination Conf., pp. 69–76 (2004)
26. Rout, T.P., Tuffley, A., Cahill, B., Hodgen, B.: The Rapid Assessment of Software Process Capability in Software Process Improvement. In: Proc. of 1st Int'l SPICE Conf., Dublin City Univ. Center for Software Eng., pp. 47–56 (2000)
27. Laporte, C.Y., Renault, A., Alexandre, S.: The Application of International Software Engineering Standards in Very Small Enterprises. In: Oktaba, H., Piattini, M. (eds.) Software Process Improvement for Small and Medium Enterprises: Techniques and Case Studies, pp. 42–70 (2008)

28. Pino, F.J., Garcia, F., Piattini, M.: Software process improvement in small and medium software enterprises: a systematic review. Software Quality Control 16(2), 237–261 (2008)
29. Mishra, D., Mishra, A.: Software Process Improvement Methodologies for Small and Medium Enterprises. In: Jedlitschka, A., Salo, O. (eds.) PROFES 2008. LNCS, vol. 5089, pp. 273–288. Springer, Heidelberg (2008)
30. Habra, N., Alexandre, S., Desharnais, J.M., Laporte, C.Y., Renault, A.: Initiating software process improvement in very small enterprises: Experience with a light assessment tool. In: Information and Software Technology (2007)
31. ISO. ISO/IEC JTC1/SC7[1] Working Group 24, Life Cycle Processes for Very Small Enterprises,
    http://profs.logti.etsmtl.ca/claporte/English/VSE/index.html
32. Martins, P.V., da Silva, A.R.: A comparative study of SPI approaches with ProPAM. In: Proceedings of the Sixth International Conference on the Quality of Information and Communications Technology (2007)
33. Holschke, O., Gelpke, P., Offermann, P., Schröpfer, C.: Business Process Improvement by Applying Reference Process Models in SOA - a Scenario-based Analysis. Multikonferenz Wirtschaftsinformatik (2008)
34. Marciniak, J.J., Sadauskas, T.: Use of Questionnaire-Based Appraisals in Process Improvement Programs. In: Acquisition of Software-Intensive Systems Conference, Arlington, Virginia (2003)
35. Wang, Y., King, G.: Philosophies and Approaches to Software Process Improvement. In: Proceedings EUROSPI 1999 (1999)
36. IBM Rational Software, http://www-01.ibm.com/software/rational/
37. Humphrey, W.S.: PSP: A Self-Improvement Process for Software Engineers. Addison-Wesley Professional, Reading (2005)
38. Humphrey, W.S.: TSP: Leading a Development Team. Addison-Wesley Professional, Reading (2005)
39. Glazer, H., Dalton, J., Anderson, D., Konrad, M., Shrum, S.: CMMI or Agile: Why not embrace both! Technical Note. CMU/SEI-2008-TN-003 (2008)
40. Scacchi, W.: Process Models in Software Engineering. In: Marciniak, J. (ed.) Encyclopedia of Software Engineering, 2nd edn. Wiley, Chichester (2002)
41. Curtis, B., Kellner, M.I., Over, J.: Process Modeling. Communications of the ACM 35(9), 75–90 (1992)
42. Thörn, C., Gustafsson, T.: Uptake of Modeling Practices in SMEs. In: International Conference on Software Engineering. Proceedings of the 2008 international workshop on models in software engineering, pp. 21–26 (2008)
43. Turetken, O., Demiros, O.: Process Modeling By Process Owners: A Decentralized Approach. Software Process: Improvement and Practice 13(1), 75–87 (2008)
44. SEI. Software Process Automation: Experiences from the Trenches. Technical Report CMU/SEI-96-TR-013 (1996)
45. Christie, A.M.: Software Process Automation: A technology Whose Time Has Come? The Journal of Defense Software Engineering (1994),
    http://www.stsc.hill.af.mil/crosstalk/frames.asp?uri=1994/07/ xt94d07e.asp
46. SEI. Software Process Automation: Interviews, Survey, and Workshop Results. Technical Report CMU/SEI-97-TR-008 ESC-TR-97-008 Software Engineering Institute (1998)

Improving the Product Documentation Process of a Small Software Company

Anu Valtanen, Jarmo J. Ahonen, and Paula Savolainen

University of Kuopio, Department of Computer Science
P.O.B 1627, FI-70211 Kuopio, Finland
{anu.valtanen,jarmo.ahonen,paula.savolainen}@uku.fi
http://www.cs.uku.fi

Abstract. Documentation is an important part of the software process, even though it is often neglected in software companies. The eternal question is how much documentation is enough. In this article, we present a practical implementation of lightweight product documentation process resulting from SPI efforts in a small company. Small companies' financial and human resources are often limited. The documentation process described here, offers a template for creating adequate documentation consuming minimal amount of resources. The key element of the documentation process is an open source web-based bugtracking system that was customized to be used as a documentation tool. The use of the tool enables iterative and well structured documentation. The solution best serves the needs of a small company with off-the-shelf software products and striving for SPI.

Keywords: SPI, software product documentation.

1 Introduction

The importance of software process is well understood in the software industry, and in many companies serious work is done to improve the process used to develop software products. Software process is divided into many subprocesses and one of them is documentation process. The documentation process is often neglected [1] and the companies have problems keeping their documentation consistent and up-to-date [2]. Documentation is seen as "inevitable evil", extra work that does not bring concrete profit to the company, even though it should be seen as an essential subprocess and treated accordingly in the context of SPI. Studies show that important reasons for low software product quality and high development and maintenance costs are due to poor and missing documentation [3] [4].

The majority of software companies are small [5]. For example in Finland, the vast majority of companies operating in both data processing and software engineering fields, employ less than 50 people[1]. In a low hierarchy working environment, that small companies often have, every little thing does not necessarily have to be put on paper. However, the earlier mentioned studies [3] [4] apply

---

[1] http://www.stat.fi (2006)

F. Bomarius et al. (Eds.): PROFES 2009, LNBIP 32, pp. 303–316, 2009.
© Springer-Verlag Berlin Heidelberg 2009

also for smaller companies and some amount of documentation is necessary. It is shown that documentation is an important tool for communication and should always serve a purpose [6]. In small companies, the role of meaningful and relevant documentation is emphasized. They often have limited resources, both financial and human [5], and there is no time to create unnecessary documentation. Small companies do not have enough employees to perform complex tasks secondary to their products [5].

The eternal question is how much documentation is enough. It is not easy to determine what documents really are necessary to have a successful software process, what is needed to support the documentation process, and what level of precision documentation should have [7].

The companies should be able to decide what amount of documentation is really needed and with what accuracy it should be written to support their software processes in a way that documentation helps enhancing the software product quality cost-effectively. This is a problematic issue for what there is no simple answer. Different kinds of software process models, e.g. [8] [9] [10], try to help solving this problem but they do not provide specific rules what to document and how. A number of different kind of approaches for creating documentation are also planned out to help supporting the documentation process [1] [11]. Additionally, there is an extensive amount of ready-made documentation templates that can be applied. For example IEEE's documentation standards [12] [13], offer good template for creating consistent documentation. Nonetheless, fulfilling the requirements of the documentation standards usually requires a lot of resources. Even without aiming at comprehensively fulfill the requirements, ready-made templates have to be adapted to best serve the needs of the software process at hand. With small companies' limited resources, adopting the standards can be too challenging.

In the footsteps of CMM [14], there is a documentation process maturity model[15] in order to help enhancing the maturity of documentation process. However, the above mentioned problems that small software companies have adapting the process models, apply also in adapting the process improvement models in small companies. The limited resources make the usage of these models and methods quite difficult.

Despite the fact that documentation has been quite a popular research subject in recent years [16], there is not that much research done considering small companies' documentation needs. Previous research does not answer to the question: how small software companies should organize their documentation in practice, while following their own process model. In this article practical implementation of product documentation process suitable for small companies, and software process related to it, are presented. The processes are results of process improvement work done in the target company. The documentation process is custom-build in the target company's software process. The probleblematic resource issues can and must be diminished when planning the documentation process of a small software company.

This time the problem was dealt with:

1. Adopting a structured documentation process.
2. Introducing a new documentation tool, a modified open source bugtracking system.

The article is organized as follows. Section 2 describes the research problem and research methods. In Section 3, the company for whom the documentation process was planned is presented. Also the earlier modeled software process and problems that triggered the documentation process improvement are described. In Section 4, the improved documentation process is introduced. In Section 5, the Discussion, the results of the improvement work and the potential ways of applying the documentation process described here are analyzed. In conclusion the results are summarized.

2 Research Problem

The research presented in this article attempts to answer to the question:

– How a small software company, committed to process improvement work, should organize their documentation practices while following their own process model?

The main goals, of the research presented here, were to fix the documentation related problems detected earlier in SPI efforts [17] and to improve the documentation process the way it is possible to pursue towards more mature processes and better software quality.

Research method in this case was action research. Action research is "an iterative process involving researchers and practitioners acting together on a particular cycle of activities, including problem diagnosis, action intervention, and reflective learning" [18]. In this case the researchers and the target company worked in a very tight cooperation. One of the authors took part in the whole process of planning and implementing the improved documentation practices.

To introduce an efficient documentation process, following points had to be taken into consideration:

– What amount of documentation is really needed?
– How the documentation produced can be easily available for all the stakeholders?
– How to make sure that the documentation is kept up-to-date?

In a previous study contemplating the importance of documentation [19], four main reasons why documentation policy and updates of documents are necessary in software companies that aim at improving their software processes was proposed.

1. The documented project history serves as evidence of agreements made between customer and supplier throughout the project. It helps avoid misunderstandings over software requirements.

2. Tracked customer requirements support better project management and improve customer satisfaction. In fact, requirement traceability can save a software project. The prerequisite of establishing traceability is the existence of necessary documentation, where the sequential items are described and identified.
3. A small, successful software organization will grow and need to employ new people. It is easier to introduce the new employees to an order rather than to chaos. A well-defined process makes the growth smoother. A defined process is a process that has documented guidance and goals.
4. Documented software processes are needed in order to study how the processes work and how the process improvement action influences them. Without documented processes there is no possibility to monitor the performance of the process or to find out the gains of improvement.

The issues presented above were chosen as a basis for discussion while analysing the documentation needs and planning the documentation process presented here. These issues were deliberated throughout planning and implementing the documentation process. In Discussion, this subject is addressed further. The limitations of the study presented here are approached in Conclusion.

3   The Target Company

The company for whom the documentation process was created is a small software company in Finland. The company has less than twenty employees. It is a traditional software house that produces off-the-shelf products. Most of the company's workload consists of planning and releasing new versions of the existing software.

During process improvement efforts in the target company it became obvious that many of the problems in the company's software process were due to inadequate documentation [17]. Therefore, after modeling the company's software process and then streamlining it, the next step with the improvement efforts was to improve the documentation practices.

While modeling the company's processes there were major documentation related problems found, most notable issues being:

1. Problems with testing
2. Problems with decision making

Problems with testing were due to the fact that the software documentation while planning and implementing new versions of software was entirely inadequate. The requirements were not in written form, requirement based test cases were non-existent and performed tests were not documented. Basically, all the documentation related to new software version consisted of non-specific description of features to be implemented. As a result it was unclear what to test and when.

The issues leading to problems with decision making were in evidence e.g. when the company held a meeting of any kind, they usually did not make a memo out of it. As a result, the employees felt that they did not always stick to what was decided and, when there were no documented decisions, it was not always clear what the decision actually was. In addition, the planned releasing schedules of new software versions of did not exist in written form. Due to this the company could not always hold to their schedules because it was often unclear what had been scheduled.

The problems stated above could be ironed out by introducing new documentation practices. During the earlier process improvement phases the process documentation for SPI needs was already constructed. So the next step was to create a documentation process to support the actual software engineering and put the product documentation in shape.

4   The Documentation Process

In all SPI efforts the first step is to model and analyze the current situation [20]. The target company's processes were modeled and streamlined, using a lightweight technique described in [21], in earlier phases of the SPI project, see [17]. The current process model can be seen in Figure 1. As it can be seen, the planning (phases 1-3) and implementation/testing (phases 3-6) of the software happen in iterative circles. These iterations constitute the fondation of the software process and make sure that the implementation of new software features happen in a flexible and easily contorollable way[17]. To establish the documentation process the first task was to find out what documentation should be generated during the different phases of the company's software process.

Starting point with the company's documentation practices was that there were no official guidelines of how and what to document. However, the company had started to customize an open source web-based bugtracking system, Mantis², as a tool to support their software engineering. In addition to its intended use, bugtracking, Mantis already worked as an information storage of customer feedback, plans and ideas about possible new features of software. It was also loosely tied to testing phase. The advantages of customized Mantis were obvious, the system was already familiar to the employees of the company, they had the ability to adapt it to meet their future needs and the software was free of charge. Due to this the new documentation process was decided to realize the way it takes the most out of Mantis's advantages.

4.1   Creating the Documentation Process

Planning and implementing the documentation process described here was executed in a workshop like manner. The documentation problems detected worked as a starting point to documentation process improvement sessions in the target company. The steps taken in planning and implementing the documentation process are described in Table 1.

---

² http://www.mantisbt.org/

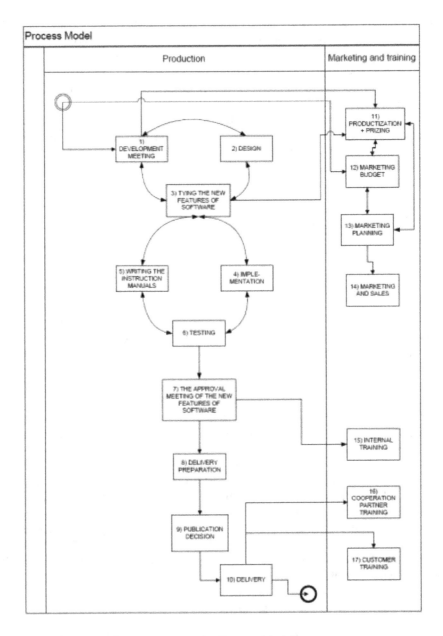

Fig. 1. The Process Model

While planning the improved documentation process the main goal was avoid unnecessary documentation. Because of this, the opinions of the employees using the documentation process were taken into account as much as possible. Most of the employees of the target company took part in planning the documentation

Table 1. Steps taken in planning and implementing the documentation process

No.	PHASE	DESCRIPTION
1	Session 1 –	Discussing and analyzing the documentation problems detected
2	–	Research on documentation templates, models and standards and possibilities of Mantis
3	Session 2 –	Finding solutions to problems
4	–	Adapting Mantis and creating documentation templates
5	Session 3 –	Assigning responsibilities and inspecting the documentation process
6	–	Implementation of the documentation process
7	Session 4 –	Analyzing and estimating the effect of the documentation process

process. In all of the sessions there were at least 6 participants from the target company and one SPI researcher, the main author of this paper.

Precise metrics to evaluate how well the documentation process served its purpose were hard to determine. However, when the documentation process improvement began there was a lightweight analysis done on testing and scheduling/decision making related issues already documented in Mantis, e.g. customer feedback on bugs that were due to inproper testing. The analysis supported the earlier made notions[17] and there were plenty of issues that could be categorized under testing and scheduling/decision making. Despite the very informal nature the analysis it was agreed that comparison of the amount of issues documented would be made after surveillance period beginning from the implementation of the new documentation process.

The fourth session was arranged to analyze and estimate the effect of the documentation process after the process had been in use for six months. In that session the team planning and implementing the documentation process had a look at Mantis's materials, made the comparison mentioned above and interviewed the users of the documentation process to form an opinion on how well did the documentation process actually serve the target company's needs (See Section 6).

4.2 The Documentation Process Template

The documentation process template produced during documentation process improvement described is presented in Table 2. The document types required in the documentation process and their storing places can be seen in Table 3.

4.3 The Improved Documentation Process

During the documentation process improvement Mantis was transformed to work as a project management, design and test documentation tool that also includes publication information while developing new versions of software. The customization was taken so far that it was possible to store almost all the

Table 2. The Documentation process template

No.	INPUT	PHASE	OUTPUT
1	Possible new features[3] Customer feedback[3]	**Development meeting**	Memo Inspected descriptions of possible new features[3]
2	Memo Descriptions of possible new features [3]	**Design**	Requirements specifications and design document[3]
3	Outputs of phases 1 and 2	**Tying the new features**	New features decision[3] Enhanced descriptions of the new features[3]
4	Outputs of earlier phases	**Implementation**	Technical descriptions [3] Test cases[3]
5	Existing Instruction manuals Technical descriptions	**Writing the instruction manuals**	Instruction manuals
6	Outputs of earlier phases	**Testing**	Test report[3]
7	Test report [3]	**Inspection**	Inspected test report[3]
8	Outputs of earlier phases	**The approval meeting of new features of software**	Memo of approval meeting Decision to start preparing delivery
9	Outputs of earlier phases Existing instruction manuals and user documentation	**Delivery preparation**	Instruction manuals User documentation Filled check-list
10	Outputs of earlier phases	**Publication decision**	Publication decision
11	Outputs of earlier phases	**Delivery**	

[3] = Document produced using Mantis.

information related to the company's software process in it. In addition to uses mentioned above, the same system works as an information storage and discussion forum.

The documentation process begins before the actual starting point of the software process. A lot of new development ideas and possible bugs emerge during the maintenance phase of the current version of software. These ideas and bugs come from customer feedback and inside the company. This valuable information is stored in Mantis.

The purpose of the development meeting, which initiates the actual software process, is to discuss the development ideas and possible bugs written down in Mantis. Because of the absence of proper meeting practices, the decisions made in the meetings tended to stay incoherent. To correct this, the meeting style was changed in to an inspection like fairly formal meeting where the possible new

Table 3. Document types

No. DOCUMENT	MANTIS[4]	LINKED[5]
1 Possible new features	x	-
2 Customer feedback	-	x
3 Memos	-	x
4 Descriptions of possible new features	x	-
5 Requirements specifications	x	-
6 Design documentation	x	-
7 New features decision	x	-
8 Technical descriptions	x	-
9 Test cases	x	-
10 Instruction manuals	-	x
11 Test report	x	-
12 Delivery preparation decision	-	x
13 User documentation	-	x
14 Check-lists	-	x
15 Publication decision	-	x

[4] = Document written in Mantis.
[5] = Document linked in Mantis (eg. Text documents, spreadsheets).

features are reviewed. The inspected possible new features and bugs to be fixed are marked in Mantis and preliminary prioritization of their implementation order is made.

The design phase's output was decided to be a compilation of requirements specifications and software design documentation. The design documentation adapts standards IEEE Std 830-1998 [12] and Std 1016-1998 [13] and is written in Mantis.

After the design phase the next step is to decide what new features will be implemented in the next version of software. The result of this phase was agreed to be a decision that declares the new features to be implemented. In this phase the implementation order of the new features is bound and this information is also written in Mantis.

Implementation phase results in specification documents that contain the technical descriptions of new features. The format of the technical descriptions also adapts IEEE Std 1016-1998 [13]. Also these specifications are written in Mantis. The test plans and the test cases will also be created at this point. Test documentation is written straight to Mantis and tied to existing design documentation. This way the documentation of a new feature is consistent. It is possible to see the details of the source that erupted the development of the particular feature, the different planning stages that it has gone through and it's technical implementation and the tests made to the feature from the same place by using search and grouping functions of Mantis. At the same time with the implementation phase software's instruction manuals are updated.

The documentation created during the testing phase is the test report that covers the new features. The report does not exist as a physical document but it is assembled from the information in Mantis. After this phase there will be a document inspection held to make sure that the testing is made properly and the test cases are extensive enough.

The approval of the new features follows the testing phase. From this phase the result is a memo of the approval meeting and decision whether the new version of software is ready for publication.

The delivery preparation phase includes writing the finalized version of the instruction manuals and other documents that are delivered to the customer. Also the pre-delivery check-list, created to make sure everything necessary is enclosed to the software version prepared for delivery, must be filled. When the new version is ready for delivery the publication decision has to be made. From the documentation viewpoint the decision is an official document with the signature of company's general manager.

Because the work done in the target company is mainly developing new versions of existing software majority of the documentation work is documenting the new features. It is important to remember that it is not enough to document just the features implemented, but that it is equally important to document the ones that were planned and discarded due to a reason or another. It was agreed that all the phases of planning a feature, not depending on whether it was realized or not, will be documented and stored in Mantis. This way it is possible to create an extensive knowledge database where it is possible to check in the future if some feature or solution has already been contemplated. The reason for rejection of some idea is also documented. This way the traceability of the documentation is improved. It is possible to avoid going through the same problems and poor solutions again. Also, by storing this information in Mantis, it is possible to collect an easily available knowledge database on features, solutions etc. for future reference.

5   Discussion

The new documentation process was designed the way creating documentation requires as small amount of resources as possible. Earlier SPI efforts had proven the importance of proper documentation. Because the company did not have any official documenting guidelines, the documentation was neglected and this had led to problems. Corresponding results have been reported in earlier studies. The documentation processes are immature and documentation practices nonsatisfactory [23]. Documentation is often done in a minimal way, producing only the user documentation. The reason for this is often that there is no established process that ties the documentation into product development. Furthermore, the organizations do not consider documentation as important as the "real" software product, the source code [1].

What distinguishes the case presented here from the others is partly the fact that the employees of the company were highly motivated to process improvement [24]. When it became obvious that some kind of formal documentation was needed to support their improved SE process, and make the improvement work possible in the future, the documentation work seemed to transform into a less unpleasant task. Furthermore, especially the employees testing the software products had identified the problems brought by the lack of documentation. Introduction of the new documentation process facilitated testing significantly. When the documentation of new features of software was made consistent, it became easy to assemble elaborate test plans and eventually test reports. This enhances the quality of testing and culminates in improved product quality.

The documentation process is presented in Table 2. The amount of documentation produced is quite minimal. The two iterations in the beginning of the SE process (Figure 1) are quick and the documentation practices must not make them longer. The same applies to the rest of the process, the new versions of software usually have short publication intervals. Even though quite a lot of design documentation is required, all of it is included in Mantis and is easy to keep up-to-date. Because of Mantis's structural form, writing the documentation required happens in short iterations and does not consume much time from the product development itself.

The documentation is easily available for all the stakeholders because using Mantis is compulsory for all the employees of the target company. The documents written using word processing software, e.g. memos and check-lists, are also linked to Mantis. Using Mantis's forms as a template for documentation reduces the amount of writing significantly and the documenting does not require special writing skills.

It is stated that process documentation alone does not make the process efficient. The process has to have some control and someone has to be responsible for it [20]. This applies for documentation process as well as any other process. In context of planning and implementing the documentation process, a lot of attention was paid to the roles and responsibilities in documenting. People responsible of keeping different documents up-to-date were assigned and it was emphasized that documentation is an essential part of the product development. There were also two inspections added to the documentation process to make sure that especially the planning and testing phases are properly documented.

Using the documentation process established, it is easy to present documented project history and track customer requirements using Mantis's search options. As a result of the company's former lack of documentation, there was no proper up-to-date descriptions of the software products of the company. This will also be corrected immediately to make the possible growth smoother. The company's software process was already documented, and people responsible of keeping the process descriptions up-to-date assigned, in earlier stages of SPI project. [19]

6 Conclusion

This article presents a solution how a small software company, committed to process improvement work, can organize their product documentation practices while following their own iterative and lightweight process model. In previous documentation research it is pointed out that the documentation processes are immature, but little is done to the problem [22]. In the research presented here actions are taken to remove the problems due to lack of documentation practices. In this case the need for a new documentation process came up during the company's process improvement efforts. Most of the problems detected while modeling and streamlining the target company's software process were documentation related. Starting point with the companys documentation practices was that there were no official guidelines how and what to document.

The documentation related problems were not least due to the fact that documenting was seen as an unpleasant task among the employees of the target company. Hence, while planning the new documentation process, the amount of documentation effort was kept nearest to minimal. This was accomplished by introducing a structured documentation process where documenting happens in small steps alongside the software product development. The documentation is made easy by customizing open source bugtracking system, Mantis, as a documentation tool. In Mantis, documentation is easily available for all the stakeholders. It is also kept up-to-date without extra effort, because of the documentation processes' structured nature and by assigning responsible people for individual documents produces along the process.

The traditional parts of software product documentation; requirements specification, design and technical documentation, user documentation, test plans and reports are all produced during the process described here, only in a different, structured and more lightweight way. There is no traditional documenting and planning phase before the actual software development begins. The documentation is written while the software development advances. Parts of, for example, requirement based test cases are already written into Mantis during the development meeting in the very beginning of the process (see Figure 1) and after that those parts are easily available to be constructed into a test report, used as the basis of the instruction manuals and so on. In addition to pieces of documentation mentioned above, decisions and schedules are also automatically documented while the memos of the meetings during the software process are linked to Mantis and part of the scheduling is done using Mantis itself. This way the software development cycles, that end up in publicizing new version of a software product, become coherent and traceable.

While analyzing and estimating the documentation process presented here (Table 1, Session 4) it was perceived that the documentation process helped to solve the target company's problems. While conducting informal interviews for the employees it appeared strongly that there was no reluctance for using Mantis. After establishing the documentation process, which supports their iterative planning and implementation/testing process phases, documentation happens in smaller and iterative steps. This way the documentation effort does not cause the stress and reluctance which seem to be quite common problems in producing the software product documentation.

The effort of producing the product documentation had diminished and the employees perceived that documenting happens almost automatically. When the software that they already were using for other purposes became the documentation tool, the step to start documenting was made easier. As a result of implementing the new documentation process, the earlier mentioned problems with decision making and testing do not exist anymore. This notion was also confirmed through analysing the issues reported in Mantis, e.g. the amount of testing related issues had diminished significantly. However, interesting notion considering the total amount of issues reported in Mantis was made. Despite the fact that the testing and decision making/scheduling related issues had diminished, the total ammount of documented issues was unchanged.

There are some limitations to the generalization of this study. Documentation process presented and the tool customized have only been tested in this one company. Despite the promising and quite reliable results presented here the approach needs further analysis to be more comprehensively validated. More precise metrics are needed in addition to more formal comparison on the documented issue amounts. Furthermore, more research on the reasons behind the notion on the unchanged amount of the documented issues would be interesting to conduct.

In addition, Mantis is not yet compatible with version control software (eg. CVS), which offers another limitation. Despite that using Mantis makes the version control of product and user documentation easy, the documentation process would be perfected by connecting the version control of the source code with it to make documentation more comprehensive. All these limitations are taken into consideration and planned to be confronted in the future research. The advantages of using customized Mantis seem to be quite notable and it would also be interesting to adapt the tool for other companies needs in the future. The presented documentation solution would best serve the needs of a company with off-the-shelf software products and the striving for SPI.

References

1. Bayer, J., Muthig, D.: A View-Based Approach for Improving Software Documentation Practices. In: Proceedings of the 13th Annual IEEE International Symposium and Workshop on Engineering of Computer Based Systems (ECBS 2006), pp. 269–278. IEEE Computer Society, Washington (2006)
2. Olsson, T., Runeson, P.: Document Use in Software Development: A Qualitative Survey. In: Software Engineering Research and Practice in Sweden, SERPS 2002 (2002)
3. Card, D.N., Mc Garry, F.E., Page, G.T.: Evaluating Software Engineering Technologies. IEEE Transactions on Software Engineering SE-13(7), 845–851 (1987)
4. Cook, C., Visconti, M.: Documentation is important. CrossTalk 7(11), 26–30 (1994)
5. Richardson, I., Gresse von Wangenheim, C.: Guest Editors' Introduction: Why are Small Software Organizations Different? IEEE Software 24(1), 18–22 (2007)
6. Forward, A., Lethbridge, T.C.: The relevance of software documentation, tools and technologies: a survey. In: Proceedings of the 2002 ACM symposium on Document engineering, pp. 26–33. ACM Press, New York (2002)
7. Briand, L.C.: Software documentation: how much is enough? In: Proceedings of Seventh European Conference on Software Maintenance and Reengineering (2003)

8. 12207.2-1997 Industry implementation of International Standard ISO/IEC 12207:1995. (ISO/IEC 12207 standard for information technology - software life-cycle processes - implementation considerations)

9. Kruchten, P.: The rational unified process: an introduction. Addison-Wesley, Boston (2000)

10. Beck, K., Andres, C.: Extreme Programming Explained: Embrace Change. Addison-Wesley Professional, Reading (2004)

11. Barker, T.T., Dragga, S.: Writing Software Documentation: A Task Oriented Approach. Allyn & Bacon, Inc., Needham Heights (1997)

12. Software Engineering Standards Committee of the IEEE Computer Society: IEEE Std 830-1998. IEEE Recommended Practice for Software Requirements Specifications. IEEE-SA Standards Board (1998)

13. Software Engineering Standards Committee of the IEEE Computer Society: IEEE Std 1016-1998. IEEE Recommended Practice for Software Design Descriptions. IEEE-SA Standards Board (1998)

14. Paulk, M.C., Curtis, B., Chrissis, M.B., Weber, C.V.: Capability maturity model, version 1.1. IEEE Software 10(4), 18–27 (1993)

15. Visconti, M., Cook, C.: Software system documentation process maturity model. In: CSC 1993: Proceedings of the 1993 ACM conference on Computer science, pp. 352–357. ACM Press, New York (1993)

16. Kajko-Mattsson, M.: The state of documentation practice within corrective maintenance. In: Proceedings of IEEE International Conference on Software Maintenance (2001)

17. Valtanen, A., Ahonen, J.J.: Big Improvements with Small Changes: Improving the Processes of a Small Software Company. In: Jedlitschka, A., Salo, O. (eds.) PROFES 2008. LNCS, vol. 5089, pp. 258–272. Springer, Heidelberg (2008)

18. Avison, D., Lau, F., Myers, M., Nielsen, P.A.: Action Research. Communications of the ACM 1, 94–97 (1999)

19. Lepasaar, M., Varkoi, T., Jaakkola, H.: Documentation as a software process capability indicator. In: PICMET 2001 International Conference on Management of Engineering and Technology, Portland, vol. 1, p. 436 (2001)

20. Zahran, S.: Software Process Improvement: Practical Guidelines for Business Success. Addison Wesley Professional, Reading (1998)

21. Ahonen, J.J., Forsell, M., Taskinen, S.K.: A modest but practical software process modeling technique for software process improvement. Software Process Improvement and Practice 7, 33–44 (2002)

22. Visconti, M., Cook, C.R.: An overview of industrial software documentation practices. Technical Report 00-60-06, Computer Science Department, Oregon State University (April 2002)

23. Visconti, M., Cook, C.R.: Assessing the State of Software Documentation Practices. Lecture notes in computer science. Springer, Heidelberg (2004)

24. Valtanen, A., Sihvonen, H.M.: Employees' Motivation for SPI: Case Study in a Small Finnish Software Company. In: O'Connor, R.V., et al. (eds.) EuroSPI 2008. CCIS, vol. 16, pp. 152–163. Springer, Heidelberg (2008)

Lessons Learnt from the Improvement of Customer Support Processes: A Case Study on Incident Management

Marko Jäntti

University of Kuopio,
Department of Computer Science,
P.O.B 1627, 70211, Kuopio, Finland
marko.jantti@uku.fi

Abstract. IT Infrastructure Library (ITIL) is the most widely used IT service management framework that provides guidelines how to create, manage and support IT services. Service support processes, such as incident management and problem management, are among the first ITIL processes that organizations start to implement. However, several challenges may exist in the process implementation. The research question of this study is: which issues are important in establishing an ITIL-based incident management process? The main contribution of this paper is to present lessons learnt from an ITIL-based process improvement project that focused on establishing an incident management process in an IS department of a university hospital. Our results show that key issues in implementing incident management are to 1) define the basic concepts of incident management with concrete examples and 2) define process interfaces between incident management and other support processes.

Keywords: customer support, incident, service desk.

1 Introduction

Many IT organizations start the implementation of IT service management processes from incident management. Incident management is a process that is responsible for operating the service desk function. The service desk extends the services that a traditional help desk provides. While a help desk focuses solely on dealing with software/hardware failures, a service desk acts as a single point of contact (SPOC) for all complaints, failure reports, service requests and change requests.

The goal of incident management is to resolve incidents reported by customers and users as soon as possible (however, within agreed service levels defined in service level agreement (SLA) [1]. An incident is "an unplanned interruption to an IT service or reduction in the quality of an IT service" [2]. The term *incident* can include software failures, hardware failures and service requests. Incident management is one of the service support processes within IT Infrastructure Library (ITIL) [3] and service operation processes in the latest ITIL version 3 [2]. ITIL is

F. Bomarius et al. (Eds.): PROFES 2009, LNBIP 32, pp. 317–331, 2009.
© Springer-Verlag Berlin Heidelberg 2009

the most widely used IT service management framework that consists of guidelines how to design, implement and manage IT services and IT service management processes.

In addition to the ITIL, several other IT service management frameworks can
be used to establish and improve the incident management process, such as IT
Service Capability Maturity Model [4], the Deliver and Support (DS) part of
the Control Objectives for IT and related Technology (COBIT) [5], the incident
management process of the Microsoft Operations Framework (MOF) [6] and
Kapella's Framework for Incident Management and Problem Management [7].

Background for the research problem: Although there are several IT service management frameworks and standards available, organizations face difficulties during IT service management development projects. They would need a
short summary which issues are especially important in establishing IT service
management processes, such as incident management and problem management.
Difficulties are mainly due to the following reasons. First, service management
frameworks and standards include too much information. There is a huge need
for persons who extract the essential information from heavy ITIL books. Second, IT service management concepts differ from those of traditional software
maintenance. There are concepts that are used in different ways than before (e.g.
problems and service requests) and a large number of new concepts that need
to be explained in training sessions (e.g. known errors, workarounds). Third, the
large number of process roles and responsibilities in the ITIL framework is a
big challenge for a small IT company. Finally, ITIL does not provide concrete
examples how an incident management tool should work.

Most of the research that has been conducted on this area has focused on
studying defect management, problem management, building help desks and
software maintenance. The research results reported in a Framework for Counting Problems and Defects [8], and in a Defect Management Process [9] indicate
that a jungle of defect management terminology and a lack of defined process
are the key challenges in managing software problems and defects. Some of the
traditional defect management methods, such as a fault tree analysis [10], and
causal analysis [11] can also be found in the ITIL processes.

Much has been written about establishing help desks [12,13] and introduction of knowledge base applications in help desks [14,15,16]. Additionally, there
are studies that have discussed the implementation of customer support systems [17,18]. In software maintenance studies, problem and defect management
activities are classified under corrective maintenance [19,20]. Problem management has been discussed, for example, in studies that deal with the maturity of
software maintenance [21,22].

However, there are few studies that have examined the implementation of
the incident management process. Niessink and van Vliet have examined the
maturity of IT service management processes, including incident management
[23]. The most interesting is their study that investigated software maintenance
from a service perspective and identified the problem in the interface between
incident management and problem management [24]. Additionally, Caldeira and

Brito e Abreu have studied the factors that affect the incident management lifecycle [25]. Because a large number of IT organizations are adopting IT service management processes, and will likely need help in implementing ITIL-based support processes, incident management is a very attractive research target.

1.1 Our Contribution

The main contribution of this paper is to

- describe how an incident management process was established in an IS department of a university hospital,
- discuss the ITIL-related questions that were raised in the process improvement meetings and
- present the lessons learned from establishing an incident management process.

A software process can be defined as "a set of activities, methods, and practices that are used in the production and evolution of software" [26]. Software maintenance is the last phase of the software evolution but perhaps the most expensive one. The main goal of this study is to improve customer support processes within corrective software maintenance by using IT service management framework ITIL. The main result of the study is the list of lessons learnt. Lessons learnt in our case are both recommendations how incident management should be implemented in order to meet the requirements of ITIL and observations of the most difficult issues in the process implementation.

The results of this study might be useful especially for people that are responsible for implementing customer support processes or are planning to improve existing processes based on IT service management frameworks. The target group of this study includes customer support managers, support process managers, IT service managers and quality managers.

The remainder of the paper is organized as follows. In Section 2, the research methods of this study are described. In Section 3, we describe how an incident management process was established and lessons learnt during the process improvement. Section 4 is the analysis of findings. The discussion and the conclusions are given in Section 5.

2   Research Methods

This case study is a part of the results of MaISSI (Managing IT Services and Service Implementation) research project at the University of Kuopio, Finland. The main research question of this study is: which issues are important in establishing an ITIL-based incident management process?

A combination of a case study research method and an action research method was used as a research method. A case study is "an empirical inquiry that investigates a contemporary phenomenon within its real-life context" [27]. The case study method was used to collect information of how Tekplus service desk works and information of service desk's stakeholders. Our study is partly action research because we participated in improving working practices of the organization. The MaISSI research team did not work only as an external observer but also created material for the incident management process description and process diagrams.

2.1   The Case Organization and Data Collection Methods

Our case organization is an IS department of the Kuopio University Hospital. They provide IT services for departments and clinics of the hospital. Currently, they have 4 full-time employees in the service desk but the number is likely going to increase in near future. When a case study started, the situation regarding IT service management processes was the following: the introduction of the ISO 20 000 standard had started but there were not yet complete process descriptions for any IT service management processes. The organization had received ITIL training from an ITIL consultancy company. Additionally, a tool development project for an incident management tool had started and was in the requirements specification phase. At the end of the case study, the incident management process description had received a version status 0.9. Support team members expected that the incident management process description will receive updates when the descriptions of other support processes become more mature.

Three important principles of data collection can be used to increase the quality of the case study: using multiple sources of evidence, creating a case study database and maintaining a chain of evidence. The sources of evidence in our study included documentation (ISOQ project plan, Plussa project plan, requirement specification for incident management system), archives (MaISSI project's research meeting memos, emails), and participant-observation in the following meetings that were held with the case organization:

- Goal definition meetings (26th March, 22nd April), participants: IS manager, MaISSI project manager, MaISSI project administrator)
- Process improvement meeting I - Concepts (8th May), participants: incident manager, 3 customer support team members, MaISSI project manager
- Process improvement meeting II - Roles (12th May), participants: incident manager, 3 customer support team members, MaISSI project manager
- Process improvement meeting III - Activities (19th May), participants: 3 customer support team members, MaISSI project manager
- Requirement specification meetings for incident management tool (26th May, 30th May), participants: 4 system designers incl. the coordinator, MaISSI project manager)
- Process improvement meetings IV, V and VI - Process diagram (9th and 18th June, 2nd July), participants: customer support team members, MaISSI project manager, MaISSI research assistants.

A standard Windows file folder with a restricted access was used as a case study database. The case study database included the documents received from the case organization, the work versions of process diagrams and memos from each case study meeting. The chain of evidence was maintained primarily through these memos. Each memo included the following information: date, location, participants, detailed description what was done or discussed in the meeting and the planned further work. Thus, the inputs for each lesson learnt can be easily traced.

2.2 Data Analysis Method

In a case study research method, there are two main approaches to analyze data: a case comparison analysis and a within-case analysis [28]. The basic idea of the within-case analysis is to examine cases carefully as stand-alone entities before making any generalizations. The cross-case analysis aims to search cross-case patterns and is suitable for multiple case studies. Because our study was a single case study, we used a within-case analysis to analyze the data.

The case study results were presented in chronological order. Only the most important questions and observations regarding the incident management process were taken into concideration and analyzed. We focused on the questions that were related to the goals, concepts, activities, and roles of the incident management process. The questions and observations were transformed into a list of lessons learnt. The most concrete result of the study was a process description document for incident management (version 0.9) with process diagrams for different incident types.

3 Lessons Learnt from Establishing an Incident Management Process

In this section, we describe how the incident management process description was created in cooperation between the case organization and MaISSI research team. Additionally, questions that were raised in process improvement meetings, and the lessons learned during the research process are presented. The IT service management framework IT Infrastructure Library (ITIL) version 2 was used as a basis of process improvement.

3.1 Goals for the Process Improvement

The research cooperation between the case organization and MaISSI research team started in the goal definition meeting on 26th March. The persons who participated in the meeting were a project manager and a project administrator of MaISSI, and an IS manager of the case organization. MaISSI team introduced the MaISSI research objectives and the IS manager presented the objectives of process improvement in the case organization. The IS manager reported that the organization had started the improvement of customer support processes according to ISO 20000 service management standard. Additionally, an external ITIL consultancy firm had consulted the case organization in improving processes. It was agreed that MaISSI helps the case organization in establishing a problem management process.

The second goal definition meeting was held on 22th April. Besides a project manager (MaISSI) and an IS manager, the person responsible for designing an incident management process (=Incident manager) participated in the meeting. As a result of meeting, it was decided that the process improvement work should start from incident management instead of problem management. After the meeting, MaISSI team received material from the case organization regarding process improvement, such as a project management plan for the process development project). For example, following goals for establishing a service desk were listed in the development project plan: customers shall receive single point of contact service, customers are able to monitor the status of their own support requests and send support requests through web, and customer support shall have effective problem resolution tools and communication tools.

3.2   Process Improvement Meeting I: Concepts and Terminology

The discussion of the first process improvement meeting (8th May) primarily focused on the current state of the help desk function, IT service management concepts and integrating those concepts into the case organization's incident management process description. An incident manager, three support team members and a project manager of MaISSI participated in this meeting.

Incident manager reported that one of the process goals was to combine different organizational units that provide support services under one service desk. In that model, each incident (a service request or a failure report), change request, or product development idea would go to a single point of contact (Tekplus service desk) that records them and assigns them to specialist teams if necessary. In the ITIL framework, a single point of contact is defined as "a single consistent way to communicate with an organization or business unit" [2].

In this meeting, the following process-related questions were raised:

- What is a service request?
- What is the difference between service requests and incidents?
- What is the difference between change request and service request?
- How can we convert an incident to a problem?
- Which activities belong to the 1st-level support and the 2nd-level support?

A standard ITIL definition for the incident is "any event which is not part of the standard operation of a service and which causes, or may cause, an interruption to, or a reduction in, the quality of that service" [3]. A service request in turn is an "incident not being a failure" [2]. Password queries and requests for information are typical service requests. Also events (automated alerts generated by the IT infrastructure) may cause incidents. There are two ways to put service requests into a category tree: 1) put service requests under the incident category (hardware failures, software failures and service requests), or 2) use incidents and service requests as parallel concepts and then define subcategories for both of them. Both ways seem to work well in practice.

The difference between a request for change (RFC) and a service request is small and unclear in many cases. An RFC is " a formal proposal for a change to be made" [29]. In fact, many routine and small-scale RFCs can be classified into service requests. Both 1st-line and 2nd-line incident management can generate RFCs to resolve incidents. An RFC could be, for example, a request for replacing a configuration item, installing hardware or software, making a code change etc.

Lesson 1. Define clearly what the following concepts of incident management mean in your organization: incident, service request, event, request for change. Reserve enough time for the introduction of IT service management concepts in the organization. ITIL concepts may sound familiar but can have different meaning than in traditional software engineering.

A frequently asked question regarding ITIL is, what is a 'problem'. The problem as as a concept belongs to the problem management process but must be understood by the incident management team. The definition of a problem is "an unknown underlying cause of one or more incidents" [2]. Note that customer's do not send problem reports but incident reports although an incident includes a description about the problem that a user has encountered. An incident may cause a problem but it should never become a problem. Incidents, problems and requests for change should be separate data records.

Lesson 2. The difference between incidents and problems is difficult to understand. The term 'problem' in the ITIL framework is reserved for the support provider organization's internal use.

Lesson 3. The interface between incident management and problem management is unclear and needs to be defined: who is responsible for suggesting and opening problem reports, and in which situations a problem record is opened.

3.3   Process Improvement Meeting II: Roles and Responsibilities

In this meeting (12th May), the roles and responsibilities within the incident management process were discussed. The following decisions were made in the meeting. The help desk concept was replaced with the service desk, four request categories were defined (incident, advice, order, feedback), and request for changes can also be related to the processes. Additionally, there was a long discussion whether the support requests can be generally called service requests because many customers like the term 'service request'. However, in the ITIL, the term 'service request' is reserved for information requests etc. and it is confusing to categorize service requests into service requests. The following questions were asked regarding the process improvement:

- Which roles does incident management process include?
- How can we close an incident?
- How should we handle resubmitted support requests?
- Which datafields regarding the customer should be included in the incident record?

The incident management process includes at least the following roles: an incident manager, a service desk worker and an incident specialist. In addition to these roles, a major incident handling team is needed. The incident manager is responsible for developing the incident management process and tools and coordinating the work of service desk workers and an incident specialists. Service desk workers record, classify, diagnose, resolve and close incidents. Their task is to provide initial support for customers and users.

Incident specialists perform 2nd-level support activities, such as detailed investigation and incident resolution. The same person who created the incident record is also responsible for closing the incident. If the incident resolution was produced by a specialist, the service desk must receive information about the resolution. The roles and responsibilities described by the ITIL were used in the process description of the case organization.

Resubmitted support requests can be processed using 'reopened' status. Datafields in the incident record regarding the customer information may include customer name, phone number, email, contact address and service level agreement.

Lesson 4. Incident management roles and responsibilities are easy to find in the ITIL framework. The 1st-level support should be responsible for closing the incident. Other support levels should avoid contacting customers because there is a risk that customers start contacting developers every time they have a problem.

3.4   Process Improvement Meeting III: Process Activities

The third process improvement meeting was held on 19th May. It started with a discussion whether a term 'service request' or an 'incident' should be used in the process diagram (see Fig. 1) and how many support levels are needed.

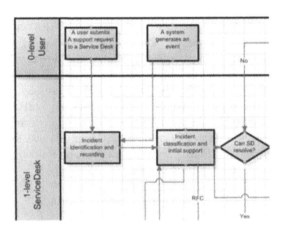

Fig. 1. A process diagram of the incident management process

Two support levels were defined for the incident management process (instead of original 3 levels). The service request handling was allocated to the first support level.

Lesson 5. There is no direct answer how many support levels are needed and how process activities are related to the support levels. From the very beginning, it is recommendable to divide incident management into 1st-level and 2nd-level support. A real problem is to find out which support level should contain problem management activities. One solution would be to put them under second-line support and reserve third-line support for product development, external service providers and subcontractors.

3.5 Requirement Specification Meetings for the Incident Management Tool

MaISSI participated in two requirement specification meetings for the incident management tool on 26th and 30th May. The case organization had decided to create its own tool for managing incidents. The role of MaISSI in these meetings was to answer the ITIL-related questions from designers.

In the first meeting, the coordinator of the tool development team presented the background, objectives and the current state of the tool development project. The second meeting focused on the incident classification and its effects on tool specification. We observed that the representatives of change management, problem management, release management and configuration management processes did not participate in the requirement specification meeting. The meetings resulted in the following questions:

- What is the relation between incident/problem/request for change records?
- How should we implement the charging for service requests?
- Can customer information be hierarchical?
- What is the incident lifecycle?
- Can we close several incidents at one time?
- Who is responsible for closing the incident?
- When is it possible to close an incident?
- Is it possible that an incident causes several change requests?
- When do we open a problem record?
- Which status information does an incident have?

Based on our observations in requirement specification meetings, we derived the following lessons. **Lesson 6.** Define interfaces between incident management and other support processes. Incident management has close interfaces to service request fulfillment, problem management, change management, configuration management and release management. **Lesson 7.** The process managers of the different ITSM processes should participate or give feedpack for the specification and design of the customer support tool. It is important that also other support processes are well-automated. **Lesson 8.** It is difficult to define incident status information. For example, the following statuses can be used: opened, in processing, waiting for delivery, closed.

3.6 Process Improvement Meetings IV, V and VI: A Process Diagram

The fourth, fifth and the last process improvement meeting were held on 9th June, 18th June and 2nd July. These meetings dealt with the draft of the incident management process diagram created by MaISSI. The diagram template and notation was provided by the case organization. As a result, incident management process actions were grouped under two main actions: 1) Receive incident (identify and record, classify and diagnose) and 2) Process incident (resolve, close and monitor). Additionally, the incident management process diagram was broken down into four different process diagrams by support request type: incident, order, feedback and information request. The final draft of the process diagram was sent to the case organization on 9th July which ended the case study. These meetings resulted in the following questions:

- When is a major incident created?
- How and when should we collect feedback from customers regarding incident resolutions?

A major incident is an incident that has a significant negative impact on the IT services. ITIL does not clearly define what is a major incident. However, an organization could decide that incidents with a highest priority level go into the major incident process. An easy way to collect feedback regading incident resolutions is to add a hyperlink of a customer satisfaction survey to the incident resolution message.

Lesson 9. Define what is a major incident and add a reference of a major incident process into a process diagram.

Lesson 10. If the incident management process diagram becomes too large, divide it into several subdiagrams that enable capturing details of handling different service request types.

4 Analysis

As a summary, the following list of lessons learnt was created during the case study:

1. Define clearly what the following concepts of incident management mean in your organization: incident, service request, event, request for change.
2. The difference between incidents and problems is difficult to understand.
3. The interface between incident management and problem management is unclear and needs definition.
4. Incident management roles and responsibilities are easy to find in the ITIL framework.
5. There is no direct answer how many support levels are needed and how process activities are related to the support levels.
6. Define interfaces between incident management and other support processes.

7. The process managers of the different ITSM processes should participate or give feedback for the specification and design of the customer support tool. It is important that also other support processes are well-automated.
8. It is difficult to define incident status information.
9. Define what is a major incident and add a reference to major incident process into a process diagram.
10. If the incident management process diagram becomes too large, divide it into several subdiagrams.

Difficult concepts and terminology is one of the major challenges in implementation of IT service management processes. The best way to avoid extra work is to read first the ITIL-based definitions of ITSM concepts, then take a look into the existing support requests stored by the help desk, and finally take at least five real examples for each concept. Practice has shown that achieving consensus regarding incident categories takes time and requires many process meetings.

One of the most difficult and important issues in the ITIL is to understand the incident lifecycle (Incident-> Problem -> Known error -> Request for Change), especially the difference between incidents and problems. In traditional software maintenance, a customer or a user sends a defect report or a problem report to a help desk. In the ITIL, a problem ticket is created by the second line support if they cannot find the solution to incident in the agreed time or if there are multiple incidents from the same issue.

There are several benefits of having separate records for incidents and problems. First, an incident reported by a customer can be rapidly closed with a good workaround (temporary solution) created by a problem management team. Thus, a customer does not have to wait a long time for a structural solution. Second, the investigation of the issue may continue as a problem although the original incident was closed. Finally, separate records also enable linking several similar incidents into one problem record. The most important thing is to remember that an incident never becomes a problem.

The third lesson learnt addressed that the interface between incident management and problem management is unclear and needs definition. The main objective of the incident management process is to restore the services used by customers as quickly as possible and minimize the adverse impact of incidents on business operations. The problem management process aims to find the root cause of an incident, create a work-around for the incident and thus convert the problem into known error. A problem record can be opened in the following cases: A service desk or an incident specialist expects that an incident will reoccur, multiple incidents have been received regarding the same issue, an incident specialist (2nd-level support) cannot find a solution to the incident, a tester/product developer/IT operator detects a fault, or a subcontractor or third-party service provider sends a fault report.

Regarding the fourth lesson, it is important to define roles for each IT service management process. The roles (an incident manager, a service desk worker and an incident specialist) and responsibilities within incident management are clearly written in the ITIL version 2 and easy to insert into a process description. Note that in the ITIL version 3 role definitions can be found in the attachment section.

Unfortunately, the organization must decide itself how many support levels it needs (usually three) for the incident management process and how process activities are located on the support levels. In large organizations, the second-level support consists of parallel teams that perform the same incident management activities but for different types of cases. If the problem management process must follow the ITIL version 2 (with problem control and error control), our recommendation is that problem control stays on the second level and error control on the third level as a part of the product development. In the ITIL version 3, there is no error control activity visible in the process guide.

The sixth and seventh lesson are both related to the interface between incident management and other support processes. These interfaces should be remenbered both in process improvement and in tool development. Each process description should include a section 'Interfaces with other processes'. In the tool development, the worst-case scenario is that the tool does not enable creating problem records for problem management or request for change records for change management. An incident management team also needs updated information about configuration items from the configuration management process and information about delivered release packages from release management.

According to the eighth lesson process people have difficulties in defining incident status information. Before the introduction of new statuses, one should create clear rules how to use statuses and test them with a pilot users.

Ninth lesson indicates that people who create incident management process descriptions often forget major incidents. Major incidents require a separate handling procedure. Additionally, a major incidents should not be transformed directly into a problem before a normal investigation and diagnosis because also a major incident could be resolved with an existing workaround. In such case, there would be no need to open a problem record and start a detailed investigation.

The last lesson is a simple advice for the process modeling work. After several months process modeling the incident management process diagram is full of boxes, arrows, lines, text and swimlanes. It is a challenge to get the detailed activities, support levels, and communication flows of incident mangement, problem management and service request handling to a single diagram. Instead of a single process diagram, it is useful to draw several subdiagrams.

Above mentioned lessons learnt were not presented in a priority order. Especially the lessons 1, 2 , 3, 5 and 8 are worth checking. It would be interesting to compare our results with other studies but by far we have not found a similar case study. In the traditional software maintenance and defect management a key challenge is that a research field includes many terms (defects, errors, bugs, faults, failures, and problems) that are difficult to distinguish from each other. The same challenge seems to appear also in the service-oriented software maintenance because people do not understand differences between incidents, service requests, problems and change requests. As as conclusion, defining these concepts clearly enough and with concrete examples is a key success factor in establishing an incident management process.

5   Discussion and Conclusions

Incident management is the process that manages all incidents, such as software and hardware failures, users' questions and queries. The main objective of the incident management is to restore normal service operation as quickly as possible. This study aimed to answer the following research question: which issues are important in establishing an ITIL-based incident management process?

The main contribution of this study was to present lessons learnt from an ITIL-based process improvement project that focused on establishing an incident management process. The study was carried out as a case study where the target was an IS department of a university hospital. The most important issues in establishing an ITIL-based incident management process are to

- define clearly the basic concepts of incident management in the organization: incident, service request, event, request for change,
- identify the difference between incidents and problems, and
- define interfaces between incident management, problem management and oter support processes.

The introduction of the IT service management concepts does not happen rapidly. The IT service management process improvement team will notice that people understand the ITIL concepts in different ways. Additionally, it is important to define the number of support levels and the communication between support levels and create rules for using incident statuses.

There are several limitations to this study. First, data were collected from one case organization during a relatively short research period. We have no real evidence that ITIL-based customer support would be more effective than the traditional customer support. Second, the case organization was a member of MaISSI research project and was selected for that reason. Third, we cannot generalize our research results to other organizations or derive any statistical generalizations based on case study results. However, our results can be used to expand the theory of incident management. Additionally, the preliminary results of our other case studies seem to show similar findings.

In conclusion, this study underlines the importance of concept definition in the beginning of the incident management process implementation. Further case studies are needed to replicate our results. Further research could also examine introduction of other IT service support processes, such as problem management, change management, configuration management and release management.

Acknowledgment

This paper is based on research in MaISSI (Managing IT Services and Service Implementation) and SOSE (Service Oriented Software Engineering) projects, funded by the National Technology Agency TEKES, European Regional Development Fund (ERDF), and industrial partners. Special thanks to Paula Mustonen, Anita Toivonen and Julia Järvinen for your contribution.

References

1. Office of Government Commerce: ITIL Service Design. The Stationary Office, UK (2007)
2. Office of Government Commerce: ITIL Service Operation. The Stationary Office, UK (2007)
3. Office of Government Commerce: ITIL Service Support. The Stationary Office, UK (2002)
4. Niessinka, F., Clerca, V., Tijdinka, T., van Vliet, H.: The it service capability maturity model version 1.0. CIBIT Consultants&Vrije Universiteit (2005)
5. COBIT 4.0: Control Objectives for Information and related Technology: COBIT 4.0. IT Governance Institute (2005)
6. Microsoft: Microsoft operations framework (January 2009),
   http://technet.microsoft.com/en-us/library/bb232042.aspx
7. Kapella, V.: A framework for incident and problem management. International Network Services whitepaper (2003)
8. Florac, W.: Software quality measurement a framework for counting problems and defects. Technical Report CMU/SEI-92-TR-22 (1992)
9. Quality Assurance Institute: A software defect management process. Research Report number 8 (1995)
10. Noda, A., Nakanishi, T., Kitasuka, T.: Introducing fault tree analysis into product-line software engineering for exception handling feature exploitation. In: Proceedings of the 25th IASTED International Multi-Conference Software Engineering, Innsbruck, Austria, pp. 229–234 (2007)
11. Card, D.N.: Learning from our mistakes with defect causal analysis. IEEE Software 15(1), 56–63 (1998)
12. Gonzalez, L.M., Giachetti, R.E., Ramirez, G.: Knowledge management-centric help desk: specification and performance evaluation. Decis. Support Syst. 40(2), 389–405 (2005)
13. Evans, K., Jones, W.T.: Building an it help desk: from zero to hero. In: SIGUCCS 2005: Proceedings of the 33rd annual ACM SIGUCCS conference on User services, pp. 68–74. ACM, New York (2005)
14. Graham, J., Hart, B.: Knowledge integration with a 24-hour help desk. In: SIGUCCS 2000: Proceedings of the 28th annual ACM SIGUCCS conference on User services, pp. 92–95. ACM Press, New York (2000)
15. Jackson, A., Lyon, G., Eaton, J.: Documentation meets a knowledge base: blurring the distinction between writing and consulting (a case study). In: SIGDOC 1998: Proceedings of the 16th annual international conference on Computer documentation, pp. 5–13. ACM Press, New York (1998)
16. Cheung, C., Lee, W., Wang, W., Chu, K., To, S.: A multi-perspective knowledge-based system for customer service management. Expert Systems with Applications 24(4), 457–470 (2003)
17. Wood, S., Howlett, R.J.: A web-based customer support knowledge base system. In: Lovrek, I., Howlett, R.J., Jain, L.C. (eds.) KES 2008, Part I. LNCS, vol. 5177, pp. 349–361. Springer, Heidelberg (2008)

18. Miller, A.: Integrating human factors in customer support systems development using a multi-level organisational approach. In: CHI 1996: Proceedings of the SIGCHI conference on Human factors in computing systems, pp. 368–375. ACM, New York (1996)

19. Lientz, B.P., Swanson, E.B.: Software Maintenance Management. Addison-Wesley Longman Publishing Co., Inc., Boston (1980)

20. Bennett, K.H., Rajlich, V.T.: Software maintenance and evolution: a roadmap. In: ICSE 2000: Proceedings of the Conference on The Future of Software Engineering, pp. 73–87. ACM Press, New York (2000)

21. April, A., Hayes, J.H., Abran, A., Dumke, R.: Software maintenance maturity model (smmm): the software maintenance process model: Research articles. J. Softw. Maint. Evol. 17(3), 197–223 (2005)

22. Kajko-Mattsson, M., Forssander, S., Olsson, U.: Corrective maintenance maturity model (cm3): maintainer's education and training. In: ICSE 2001: Proceedings of the 23rd International Conference on Software Engineering, Washington, DC, USA, pp. 610–619. IEEE Computer Society, Los Alamitos (2001)

23. Niessink, F., van Vliet, H.: Towards mature it services. Software Process - Improvement and Practice 4(2), 55–71 (1998)

24. Niessink, F., van Vliet, H.: Software maintenance from a service perspective. Journal of Software Maintenance 12(2), 103–120 (2000)

25. Caldeira, J., Abreu, F.B.: Influential factors on incident management: Lessons learned from a large sample of products in operation. In: Jedlitschka, A., Salo, O. (eds.) PROFES 2008. LNCS, vol. 5089, pp. 330–344. Springer, Heidelberg (2008)

26. Humphrey, W.S.: A personal commitment to software quality. In: ESEC, pp. 5–7 (1995)

27. Yin, R.: Case Study Research: Design and Methods. Sage Publishing, Beverly Hills (1994)

28. Eisenhardt, K.: Building theories from case study research. Academy of Management Review 14, 532–550 (1989)

29. Office of Government Commerce: ITIL Service Transition. The Stationary Office, UK (2007)

A Decision Model for Supporting Task Allocation Processes in Global Software Development

Ansgar Lamersdorf[1], Jürgen Münch[2], and Dieter Rombach[1,2]

[1] University of Kaiserslautern,
[2] Fraunhofer IESE
a_lamers@informatik.uni-kl.de,
{juergen.muench,dieter.rombach}@iese.fraunhofer.de

Abstract. Today, software-intensive systems are increasingly being developed in a globally distributed way. However, besides its benefit, global development also bears a set of risks and problems. One critical factor for successful project management of distributed software development is the allocation of tasks to sites, as this is assumed to have a major influence on the benefits and risks. We introduce a model that aims at improving management processes in globally distributed projects by giving decision support for task allocation that systematically regards multiple criteria. The criteria and causal relationships were identified in a literature study and refined in a qualitative interview study. The model uses existing approaches from distributed systems and statistical modeling. The article gives an overview of the problem and related work, introduces the empirical and theoretical foundations of the model, and shows the use of the model in an example scenario.

1 Motivation

More and more software products are being developed in a globally distributed way: Technological advances and the possible benefits of distributed development have made this not only a common practice but also a "business necessity" ([1], [2]). The expected benefits include cost savings, access to a worldwide resource pool, proximity to customers and markets, and a reduction in overall development time through a "follow-the-sun" approach [3].

However, global software development also imposes a set of problems and risks that are often overlooked [4]: For example, communication problems, caused by distance, language, and cultural differences, reduce productivity ([5], [6]) and quality suffers from inexperienced developers at remote sites or from a lack of trust between distributed teams [7]. These problems can even annihilate the cost reduction of sending work to low-cost regions [4].

In order to address the benefits and, at the same time, the risks and problems of global software development, effective project management is needed that actively considers the nature and characteristics of global software development. An important activity in global software development project management is task allocation: In addition to having to consider the characteristics and the availability of the workforce

F. Bomarius et al. (Eds.): PROFES 2009, LNBIP 32, pp. 332–346, 2009.
© Springer-Verlag Berlin Heidelberg 2009

(as in collocated development), task allocation in global software development must take into account the characteristics of the sites and their relationships (such as time zone differences or infrastructure).

Depending on the focus and the goals of a software development project, different allocations might be suited differently: In order to increase productivity, independent chunks of work should be assigned to every site [8]. On the other hand, assigning interdependent tasks to sites in different time zones might decrease the development time [3]. The lowest labor rates can be achieved by assigning as much work as possible to low-cost sites.

These goals and assignment strategies sometimes conflict with each other and have to be regarded systematically in order to identify the best task allocation for a particular project. In practice, however, allocation is not done systematically and often considers only single aspects such as labor costs [9]. Thus, there is a need for improving management processes in globally distributed software development processes.

This article presents a method for improving task allocation processes by developing a model for decision support. The model uses multiple criteria and weighted goals as input for suggesting a weighted list of possible task assignments. It is based on a systematic literature review and an interview study conducted in order to identify the factors that influence the success of distributed development projects.

The remainder of this article is structured as follows: Section 2 gives an overview of the related work in models for task allocation. The model is presented in detail in Section 3 together with its goals, a systematic literature review for determining its criteria and causal relationships, and a demonstration of its use within an example project. Section 4 names the limitations of the model and Section 5 concludes the article.

2 Related Work

In [8], a simple model for task allocation in global software development is presented. The underlying assumption is that software development can be described as a series of modification requests to a set of modules. Based on that, an algorithm is developed, which, for a given set of modules and modification requests, tries to find the optimal assignment of modules to sites. Optimal here means that the number of modification requests spanning multiple sites is minimized in order to reduce communication overhead.

The model represents a formal and well-defined approach for optimizing task allocation. However, its main drawback is the fact that it only considers one single criterion, namely, minimization of the communication needed between the available sites. It also uses the available resources per site as a constraint, but essential factors that influence project success (e.g., the available expertise or the cost rate per site) are not considered.

Another model for task allocation was developed by Setamanit, Wakeland, and Raffo [10]. Based on a combination of discrete-event and system-dynamic simulation, it allows for evaluating different allocation strategies. The model simulates software development at every site as well as the effects of the interaction between sites. Thus, it is able to make statements on the effects of different strategies on productivity.

However, the sites are only rudimentarily described in the model. Therefore, the model can only make general statements and cannot be used for concrete decision support. Besides, the factors influencing productivity are not identified empirically; thus, it remains unclear if they truly reflect the factors relevant in practice.

Other models for assigning tasks to a set of sites exist in other domains: In production, algorithms have been developed for allocating production work to a network of global sites with the goal of minimizing production and transportation costs. In the distributed systems domain, there are approaches for optimizing the allocation of computing tasks to a set of processors. An analysis and comparison of existing approaches was done in [11]. The approaches were evaluated against a set of requirements for a task allocation model in GSD. The result showed that none of the models fulfilled all requirements.

However, one algorithm for task allocation in distributed systems by Bokhari [12] satisfied most of the requirements compared to the other approaches. The algorithm tries to minimize the sum of the execution costs of the tasks at the processors and the costs of transmitting data between tasks at different processors. The main drawbacks for its application in GSD are: 1) The algorithm obviously does not contain empirical data on distributed development. Particularly, it does not contain a set of variables that represent the relevant characteristics of GSD. 2) The algorithm needs exact numbers as input. For example, the cost of processing a specific task at a specific processor has to be described with an exact number. Such a number can often not be specified when human behavior is modeled.

In the following, a model is proposed that reuses the algorithm while also addressing these drawbacks.

3   The Decision Model

The following section will introduce the decision model. First, the terminology and model goals are given. The model is based on a combined literature review and interview study on the criteria and causal relationships in task assignment that will be shown second. Afterwards, the theoretical foundations of the model will be presented, followed by the application of the model in an example project.

3.1   Terminology and Model Goals

The underlying assumption of the model is that every software development project consists of a weighted set of *goals* that define project success (e.g., project costs, software quality).

Project management in global software development aims at fulfilling these goals by assigning the tasks of a software development project to the appropriate sites during *task assignment*.

However, the effect of the task assignment on project goals depends on a set of *characteristics* of distributed software development. Time shift between sites, for example, is such a characteristic: If tasks are assigned to two sites with a large time shift between them, productivity may be reduced and thus project costs would increase. Task assignment should thus not only consider the project goals but also the characteristics of distributed development.

Project goals and characteristics of distributed development together represent the criteria that should be regarded in task assignment for global software development. This is the main goal of the decision support model presented here that considers these criteria.

More formally, the main goal can be described as follows: From the perspective of a project manager in a global software development project, it is the purpose of the model to support task allocation with respect to individual project goals and characteristics of distributed development.

From that goal, the following sub-goals are derived:

- Task allocation should be supported by suggesting several assignments of tasks to sites for a given project. Using these suggestions, the project manager can then make improved, systematic allocation decisions.
- The model should consider individual project goals. Therefore, the suggestions made by the model should be dependent on the priorities of the project.
- The characteristics of globally distributed development (e.g., the overhead of working and communicating in a distributed manner) should be taken into account systematically.

Further, more detailed, requirements for a decision support model are defined in [11]: A distribution model should support *multiple goals*, should be able to describe both *properties of tasks and sites* and *dependencies between tasks and sites*, and should be *adaptable* to different environments. An appropriate degree of *formality* should allow for making suggestions automatically and the criteria and causal relationships used in the model should be *empirically based*.

3.2 Empirical Identification of Criteria and Causal Relations

The empirical foundations of the model were laid using a combined literature review and interview study on distributed software development. These resulted in a set of criteria and causal relationships. The results were then used for the development of the task allocation model. The study is summarized in the following. (It is explained in more detail in [13])

The goal of the literature and interview study can be described as follows: From the perspective of a project manager in a global software development project, the criteria for task assignment and the underlying causal relationships should be identified. Three research questions were derived from that:

- Question 1: What are the goals of distributed development projects?
- Question 2: What characteristics of distributed development should be regarded during task assignment?
- Question 3: What are the relationships between the characteristics of distributed development and project goals?

The following steps were performed in the study:

1. Literature study: A literature study was conducted first. 26 publications from different journals, conferences, and workshops were analyzed. They can be classified into case studies, empirical studies (reporting the experiences of several distributed

Table 1. Analyzed literature

Case Studies	Empirical Studies	Other
[14], [15], [16], [17], [18], [19], [20], [21]	[22], [23], [24], [25], [26], [27], [7], [28], [29], [30], [31], [32], [33], [34], [35]	[36], [37] [38]

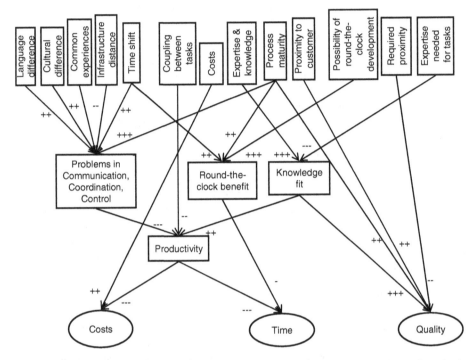

Fig. 1. Identified goals, influencing factors, and their relationship: strong (+++), medium (++), or soft (+) impact that is positive (+) or negative (-)

development projects), and other types of publications. Table 1 lists the analyzed literature. As a result, a first set of criteria and causal relationships was identified.

2. Questionnaire design: Based on the literature results, a questionnaire was designed for use in interviews with practitioners. In the questionnaire, the findings from the literature study were presented and the practitioners were asked to comment on these results.

3. Interview study: An interview study was conducted with managers of distributed software development. Interviews were conducted either in person or over the telephone. They usually lasted for approximately one hour. The interviews were part of a larger study on distributed development (see [13]), with ten of them being used for the work presented here. All interviews were recorded and transcribed literally.

4. Analysis: The transcribed interviews were analyzed question by question, comparing the answers with the literature study results. According to the practitioners' answers, the previous findings were weighted, new criteria and causal relationships were added, and irrelevant factors were removed.

The study resulted in a set of 13 influencing factors. These factors have an influence on four intermediate factors (problems in communication, coordination, and control; possible benefit of round-the-clock-development; productivity; fit between the knowledge needed for a task and that available at a site) and on three goals (cost, time, quality). Figure 1 shows the relationships identified between influencing factors and goals. It also gives a relative weight for the (positive or negative) influences.

3.3 Model Overview

Based on the results of the literature and interview studies, a model for supporting task allocation decisions was developed. The algorithms of the model reuse approaches from distributed systems and statistical modeling. In this section, the main elements and algorithms of the model are sketched.

3.3.1 Distributed Systems Algorithm for Identifying Optimal Assignments

In an earlier study [11], the distributed systems algorithm of Bokhari was identified as most promising for reuse in a GSD distribution model. A detailed explanation of the model can be found in [12].

The algorithm gets as input a set of modules (i.e., tasks) and a set of processors the modules can be assigned to. It considers two kinds of costs:

- Costs of executing module i on processor p. These are described as e_{ip}.
- Costs of transmitting data between module i and module j with i being assigned to processor p and j to q. These are described as $s_{pq}(d_{ij})$ with d_{ij} representing the amount of data transmitted between modules i and j and s_{pq} being the cost for transmitting one unit of data between p and q.

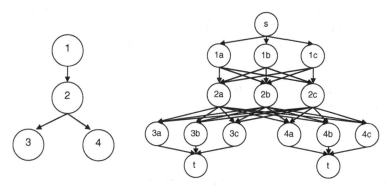

Fig. 2. An invocation tree and the corresponding assignment graph for three processors (a, b, c)

The tasks are assumed to be connected in a tree structure – every module is called by a single parent module and can call a set of other modules. This structure is called an *invocation tree*. The algorithm creates an *assignment graph* out of the invocation tree by creating a node for every combination of module and processor and connecting them in accordance with the invocation tree (see Figure 2).

The edges in the assignment graph are weighted with the combined execution and transmission costs. A graph algorithm developed by Bokhari then uses a dynamic programming approach for efficiently identifying the shortest paths through the graph. These paths represent the optimal assignment of modules to processors with a minimal sum of all execution and transmission costs.

On a high-level view, the algorithm solves a problem similar to the task assignment in GSD. Applying the model to GSD means:

- Modules and processors are represented by tasks and sites.
- The costs of executing module i on processor p are represented by the effort of doing task i of a software development project at site p (mainly depending on the characteristics of tasks and sites identified in Section 3.2).
- The costs of transmitting data between module i and module j with i being assigned to processor p and j to q are represented by the overhead being created between tasks i and j that are assigned to sites p and q (mainly depending on the dependencies between tasks and sites identified in Section 3.2).

The input variables describing the cost functions e_{ip} and $s_{pq}(d_{ij})$ in detail are given by the results of the empirical study. However, other problems remain:

- The algorithm can only handle tasks that are connected in a tree structure. However, tasks in a development project can have arbitrary connections.
- Costs are the only criteria for comparing different assignments. Therefore, the different conflicting goals that can exist in global software development have to be aggregated into one cost function.
- All costs are described by a single, distinct number, which does not represent the reality of human development that contains a large amount of uncertainty.

The first problem was solved by developing an extension of Bokhari's algorithm that contains an additional first step of transferring arbitrary graphs into a set of trees (however, with reduced efficiency). The other two problems were solved by describing the cost functions not by single numbers but using Bayesian networks.

3.3.2 Bayesian Networks for Evaluating Assignments

A Bayesian Network (BN) is able to formulate causal relationships under conditions of uncertainty. It consists of a directed acyclic graph representing discrete variables and their relationships and a set of probability tables. For every variable, one table describes the probabilities of its values as a function of the input variables [39].

The application of mathematical methods allows for inference within BNs: Using bottom-up and top-down reasoning, statements can be made on the probabilistic distribution of the values of any variable based on a set of observed values of other variables. In addition, it is possible to make reasoned statements even if not all independent variables have defined observed values. Thus, in software engineering research, BNs have been used to model and predict software development projects [40].

We used Bayesian networks in our model to represent the cost functions of the distributed systems algorithm of Bokhari: Both the cost of executing a task at a site and the cost of transmitting data between sites is represented by a BN. Figures 3 and 4 show the resulting networks.

Every BN models the impact of a set of input variables on three cost types (financial, time, quality). This is done for every combination of task and sites individually. For example, the BN for describing the cost at a site (Figure 3) can be instantiated for task t_1 and site s_1 with the according parameters of t_1 and s_1 (e.g., the size of t_1 and the process maturity at s_1).

BNs operate with discrete values for every input and output variable. We thus defined five steps from "very low" to "very high" for most variables (e.g., proximity to customer). For other variables (e.g., cost rate) that have numeric values, we defined intervals in order to get discrete values.

The probabilistic tables for the BNs were designed with help of the AgenaRisk tool [41]. It contains functions for calculating the table values by using the normal distribution and by representing the discrete values with numbers from 1 to 5. For example, the table for "development quality" is calculated by generating a normal distribution with the weighted average of "staff capability" and "process maturity" as mean value. The integration of this function between the intervals (0, 1)... (4, 5) then delivers the values for the probabilistic table.

Input variables, cost variables, causal relationships, and their weights (e.g., the weights of "staff capability" and "process maturity" on "development quality") were taken from the results of the literature and interview studies.

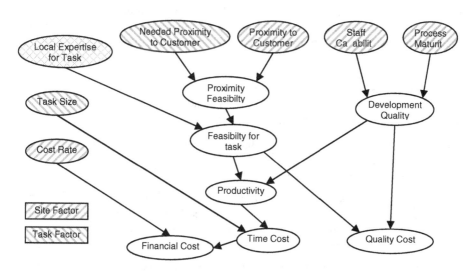

Fig. 3. Bayesian network for cost at site

In order to get one single cost function, all three costs (financial, time, quality) are normalized and added with different weights (which are dependent on project priorities) into one function.

The repeated application of the two networks for every combination of tasks and sites makes it possible to describe the needed cost functions of the distributed systems algorithm. However, the values of the functions are not distinct numbers but probabilistic distributions over a set of cost values. This makes the uncertainty in

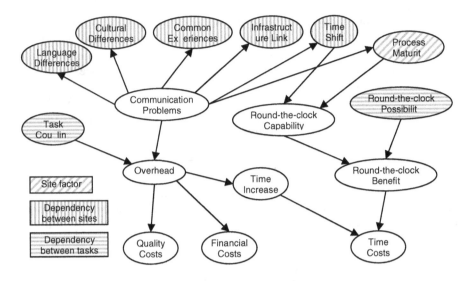

Fig. 4. Bayesian network for transmission cost

human behavior explicit. On the other hand, Bokhari's algorithm uses distinct values as input. Therefore, an algorithm was developed that is able to suggest assignments by using the distributed systems algorithm while taking the probabilistic cost distributions as input.

3.3.3 Algorithm for Suggesting Assignments
The link between the Bayesian networks results and the (adapted) algorithm of Bokhari is provided by a randomization algorithm. It basically consists of three steps:

- Collect the probabilistic distributions by executing the BNs for every combination of tasks and sites.
- Repeat for a large number of runs:
  - Randomly pick one number out of every probabilistic distribution. The probabilities for every random pick are provided by the probabilistic distributions. Store the numbers as cost functions for the distributed systems algorithm.
  - Execute the distributed system algorithm and store the returned assignment.
- Return the stored assignments in an ordered list with a decreasing number of occurrences.

In other words, the algorithm simulates a number of scenarios with randomly chosen numbers for the individual cost functions, based on the probabilistic distributions. This ensures, on the one hand, that across all scenarios, the costs reflect the predictions of the Bayesian networks. On the other hand, within each run, all costs are represented by distinct numbers, which makes the execution of Bokhari's algorithm possible.

As a result, the algorithm returns not one but several ordered assignments together with information on the number of scenarios in which each distribution was optimal. This makes the uncertainty in predicting human behavior explicit and gives the project manager the opportunity to choose from an ordered set of assignments.

3.4 Example

The model was implemented as a Java prototype with a Swing GUI and consisted of a generic and a model-specific part. The generic part contained implementations of the algorithm of Bokhari, the randomization algorithm, and the Bayesian networks. The BN implementation reused the JavaBayes framework [42] and extended it with functions for calculating the probabilistic tables similar to the functions used in the AgenaRisk [41] tool. The model-specific part implemented the BNs that were derived from the empirical study. As these were developed using AgenaRisk, they were transformed by hand into the implementation.

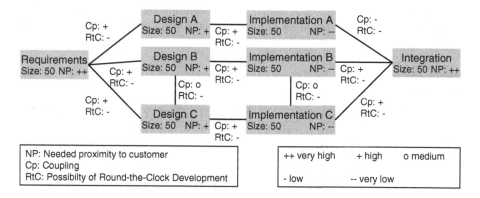

Fig. 5. Project example – Tasks to be distributed

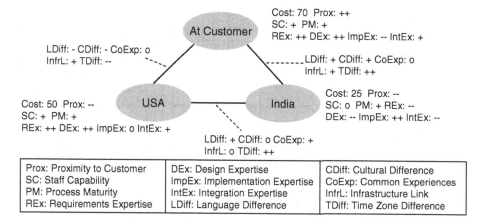

Fig. 6. Available sites

In the following, the use of the model will be shown in a hypothetical example. The tasks of the example project include requirements engineering, design and implementation of three different components, and integration. Three sites are available: One site at the customer, which is very expensive but has very good skills in requirements engineering and design. The second site is in the US. It is also expensive (but not as much as the customer's site) and also has good skills in requirements engineering and design. The Indian site has large differences (especially in language and culture) compared to the other two sites, but is very inexpensive. People there have very good skills in implementation but are inexperienced in requirements engineering and design. Figures 5 and 6 show the tasks and sites with their parameters in detail.

Table 2 shows the results of executing the model with three different weights on the goals. For every execution the three best results are presented together with the number of runs the assignment was optimal (e.g., in the first execution, the best assignment was optimal in 9% of the runs). In the first result, the focus was on all goals, with the highest weight on quality (Cost: 20%, Time: 30%, Quality: 50%). Here the model suggests doing the implementation in India and requirements and designing either at the customer's site or at the US site. Integration should be done at the customer's site (because it should be close to the customer) or in Asia (because it is closely coupled with implementation).

Table 2. Model results with focus on quality (left), development costs (middle), and development time (right)

1.: 9%

	Cust	US	Asia
Reqs	X		
Des A	X		
Impl A			X
Des B	X		
Impl B			X
Des C		X	
Imp C			X
Integr	X		

1.: 51%

	Cust	US	Asia
Reqs			X
Des A			X
Impl A			X
Des B			X
Impl B			X
Des C			X
Imp C			X
Integr			X

1.: 18%

	Cust	US	Asia
Reqs	X		
Des A	X		
Impl A	X		
Des B	X		
Impl B	X		
Des C	X		
Imp C	X		
Integr	X		

2.: 8%

	Cust	US	Asia
Reqs		X	
Des A		X	
Impl A			X
Des B		X	
Impl B			X
Des C		X	
Imp C			X
Integr	X		

2.: 7%

	Cust	US	Asia
Reqs		X	
Des A		X	
Impl A			X
Des B		X	
Impl B			X
Des C		X	
Imp C			X
Integr			X

2.: 11%

	Cust	US	Asia
Reqs	X		
Des A	X		
Impl A			X
Des B	X		
Impl B			X
Des C	X		
Imp C			X
Integr			X

3.: 7%

	Cust	US	Asia
Reqs	X		
Des A	X		
Impl A			X
Des B	X		
Impl B			X
Des C		X	
Imp C			X
Integr			X

3.: 6%

	Cust	US	Asia
Reqs			X
Des A		X	
Impl A			X
Des B			X
Impl B			X
Des C			X
Imp C			X
Integr			X

3.: 10%

	Cust	US	Asia
Reqs		X	
Des A		X	
Impl A		X	
Des B		X	
Impl B		X	
Des C		X	
Imp C		X	
Integr		X	

The next result shows the execution of the model with a very strong focus on the costs and very little regard for time and quality (Cost: 80%, Time: 10%, Quality: 10%). It can be seen that the model then suggests doing everything in India due to the low cost rate there. An alternative would be assigning requirements and design to the US site.

In the last run, the focus was set primarily on development time (Cost: 10%, Time: 80%, Quality: 10%). Now, the model favors assigning all tasks to one site, since this would reduce the overhead of distributed communication. Another alternative given by the model is to do every task at the site that has the best knowledge, which means assigning implementation to Asia and requirements and design to the customer site.

4 Limitations and Validity of the Model

There are several limitations regarding the applicability of the model:

The experiences gathered in the empirical study come from many different organizations and project environment. Therefore, the expressed relationships describe a general overview rather than a concrete environment. Within a specific organization, the relative weights of the criteria may differ, or additional criteria may be relevant. The model thus has to be adapted in order to be used in a specific environment. However, due to its modularization, this can be done by changing the Bayesian networks without having to modify the algorithms.

Underlying the model development was the assumption that project management can divide a project upfront into distinct tasks that can be independently assigned to the available sites. However, a project manager often has no clear information on the tasks of a project because, for example, an agile process is followed or there is not enough knowledge on the requirements or the technology. In these cases, it would be hard to use the model. This also implies that the model evaluation should start using historic project data as it is easier to identify distinct tasks in retrospective.

The model also assumes that there is enough knowledge in an organization for describing the characteristics of the sites (e.g., knowledge available, cultural differences). In Bayesian networks, it is possible to calculate probabilistic distributions without all input parameters having distinct values. Therefore, the model can be used even if not all variables are known. But the less information is known, the less useful are the suggestions made by the model.

The BNs operate with variable values from "very low" to "very high". As they are relatively fuzzy and subjective, an application of the model in a real-world environment needs to come with specific evaluation guidelines (e.g., which time zone distance is to be interpreted as "low" and which as "medium").

Although the criteria and causal relationships of the model presented here stem from an empirical study, the model needs further evaluation. It has so far only been used for simulating task assignment processes with hypothetical input data. Therefore, external validity needs to be carefully considered when applying the model and making conclusions in practice.

5 Conclusion and Future Work

The main goal of the work presented here was to find decision support for task allocation that considers multiple criteria for the decision. It is, however, not easy to clearly define the term "criteria" in a conceptual framework for a model. We distinguished between *goals* of software development projects (cost, time, quality) and *characteristics of distributed development* that have an impact on the goals. Based on that assumption and on an empirical study, we developed a model for decision support in task allocation that reuses an approach from distributed systems and Bayesian networks in order to suggest a prioritized list of assignments.

By conducting an empirical study on the goals and characteristics of distributed development, we assured that the model considered criteria relevant for task allocation. However, since the adapted distributed systems algorithm and the mechanism of selecting cost values according to probabilistic distributions work independently of the Bayesian networks, the model can be easily changed if other goals or influencing factors are relevant in a specific environment.

The model fulfills the goals stated in Section 3.1.: It results in a weighted list of *suggestions for task allocation* while systematically considering both *multiple project goals* and *characteristics of distributed development*. The requirements for a distribution model defined in [11] are also fulfilled:

- Multi-objectivity: The example shows how different weights put on the project goals can change the resulting assignments suggested by the model.
- Properties of tasks and sites, dependencies between tasks and sites: All of these types of influencing factors can be described in the Bayesian networks.
- Adaptability: The model can be adapted to different environments by changing the Bayesian networks.
- Formality: The model contains formal algorithms that can automatically suggest assignments.
- Empirically-based criteria: The influencing factors and goals were identified in an empirical study.

Future work will have to test the model in real-world environments. We therefore plan to evaluate and iteratively extend the model in case studies and experiments.

References

1. Herbsleb, J.D., Moitra, D.: Guest editors' introduction: Global software development. IEEE Software 18(2), 16–20 (2001)
2. Damian, D., Moitra, D.: Global Software Development: How Far Have We Come? IEEE Software 23(5), 17–19 (2006)
3. Carmel, E., Agarwal, R.: Tactical Approaches for Alleviating Distance in Global Software Development. IEEE Software 18(2), 22–29 (2001)
4. Seshagiri, G.: Point/Counterpoint: GSD: Not a Business Necessity, but a March of Folly. IEEE Software 23(5), 62–65 (2006)
5. Herbsleb, J.D., Grinter, R.E.: Splitting the organization and integrating the code: Conway's law revisited. In: 21st International Conference on Software Engineering, pp. 85–95 (1999)

6. Herbsleb, J.D., Mockus, A., Finholt, T.A., Grinter, R.E.: An empirical study of global software development: Distance and speed. In: 23rd International Conference on Software Engineering, pp. 81–90 (2001)
7. Smite, D., Moe, N.B.: Understanding a Lack of Trust in Global Software Teams: A Multiple-Case Study. Software Process: Improvement and Practice 13(3), 217–231 (2007)
8. Mockus, A., Weiss, D.M.: Globalization by Chunking: A Quantitative Approach. IEEE Software 18(2), 30–37 (2001)
9. Bass, M., Paulish, D.: Global Software Development Process Research at Siemens. In: Third International Workshop on Global Software Development, Edinburgh, Scotland (2004)
10. Setamanit, S., Wakeland, W.W., Raffo, D.: Using Simulation to Evaluate Global Software Development Task Allocation Strategies. Software Process: Improvement and Practice 12(5), 491–503 (2007)
11. Lamersdorf, A., Muench, J., Rombach, D.: Towards a Multi-Criteria Development Distribution Model: An Analysis of Existing Task Distribution Approaches. In: International Conference on Global Software Development, pp. 109–118 (2008)
12. Bokhari, S.H.: A Shortest Tree Algorithm for Optimal Assignments Across Space and Time in a Distributed Processor System. IEEE Transactions on Software Engineering 7(6), 583–589 (1981)
13. Lamersdorf, A.: Towards a global software development distribution model: Empirically-based model building for distributed software development. Master Thesis, University of Kaiserslautern (2008),
   http://wwwagse.informatik.uni-kl.de/staff/lamersdorf
14. Treinen, J.J., Miller-Frost, S.L.: Following the sun: Case studies in global software development. IBM Systems Journal 45(4), 773–782 (2006)
15. Battin, R.D., Crocker, R., Kreidler, J., Subramanian, K.: Leveraging Resources in Global Software Development. IEEE Software 18(2), 70–77 (2001)
16. Ebert, C., De Neve, P.: Surviving Global Software Development. IEEE Software 18(2), 62–69 (2001)
17. Mullick, N., Bass, M., Houda, Z., Paulish, D.J., Cataldo, M., Herbsleb, J.D., Bass, L.: Siemens Global Studio Project: Experiences Adopting an Integrated GSD Infrastructure. In: International Conference on Global Software Engineering, pp. 203–212 (2006)
18. Lindqvist, E., Lundell, B., Lings, B.: Distributed Development in an Intra-national, Intra-organizational Context: An Experience Report. In: International workshop on Global software development for the practitioner, pp. 80–86 (2006)
19. Casey, V., Richardson, I.: Uncovering the Reality within Virtual Software Teams. In: International Workshop on Global software development for the practitioner, pp. 66–72 (2006)
20. Heeks, R., Krishna, S., Nicholson, B., Sahay, S.: Synching or Sinking: Global Software Outsourcing Relationships. IEEE Software 18(2), 54–60 (2001)
21. Kobitzsch, W., Rombach, H.D., Feldmann, R.L.: Outsourcing in India. IEEE Software 18(2), 78–86 (2001)
22. Alami, A., Wong, B., McBride, T.: Relationship Issues in Global Software Development Enterprises. Journal of Global Information Technology Management 11(1), 49–86 (2008)
23. Oza, N.V., Hall, T.: Difficulties in Managing Offshore Software Outsourcing Relationships: An Empirical Analysis of 18 High Maturity Indian Software Companies. Journal of Information Technology Case and Application Research 7(3), 25–41 (2005)
24. Komi-Sirvio, S., Tihinen, M.: Lessons Learned by Participants of Distributed Software Development. Knowledge and Process Management 12(2), 108–122 (2005)

25. Espinosa, A., Slaughter, S.A., Kraut, R.E., Herbsleb, J.D.: Familiarity, Complexity, and Team Performance in Geographically Distributed Software Development. Organization Science 18(4), 613–630 (2007)
26. Herbsleb, J.D., Mockus, A.: An Empirical Study of Speed and Communication in Globally-Distributed Software Development. IEEE Transactions on Software Engineering 29(6), 481–494 (2003)
27. Herbsleb, J.D., Paulish, D.J., Bass, M.: Global software development at Siemens: Experience from nine projects. In: 27th International Conference on Software Engineering, pp. 524–533 (2005)
28. Pilatti, L., Audy, J., Prikladnicki, R.: Software Configuration Management over a Global Software Development Environment: Lessons Learned from a Case Study. In: International workshop on Global software development for the practitioner, pp. 45–50 (2006)
29. Ramasubbu, N., Balan, R.K.: Globally Distributed Software Development Project Performance: An Empirical Analysis. In: 6th Joint Meeting of the European Software Engineering Conference and the ACM SIGSOFT Symposium on the Foundations of Software Engineering, pp. 125–134 (2007)
30. Gareiss, R.: Analyzing the Outsourcers. Information Week (November 18, 2002)
31. Smite, D.: Global Software Development Project Management – Distance Overcoming. In: Dingsøyr, T. (ed.) EuroSPI 2004. LNCS, vol. 3281, pp. 23–33. Springer, Heidelberg (2004)
32. Kommeren, R., Parviainan, P.: Philips experiences in global distributed software development. Empirical Software Engineering 12(6), 1382–3256 (2007)
33. Espinosa, J.A., Nan, N., Carmel, E.: Do Gradations of Time Zone Separation Make a Difference in Performance? A First Laboratory Study. In: International Conference on Global Software Engineering, pp. 12–22 (2007)
34. DeLone, W., Espinosa, J.A., Lee, G., Carmel, E.: Bridging Global Boundaries for IS Project Success. In: 38th Hawaii International Conference on System Sciences, p. 48b (2005)
35. Coward, C.T.: Looking Beyond India: Factors that Shape the Global Outsourcing Decisions of Small and Medium Sized Companies in America. Electronic Journal on Information Systems in Developing Countries 13(11), 1–12 (2003)
36. Sakthivel, S.: Managing Risks in Offshore Systems Development. Communications of the ACM 50(4), 69–75 (2007)
37. Gurung, A., Prater, E.: A Research Framework for the Impact of Cultural Differences on IT Outsourcing. Journal of Global Information Technology Management 9(1), 24–43 (2006)
38. Carmel, E.: The Explosion of Global Software Teams. Computerworld 31(49) (1997)
39. Ben-Gal, I.: Bayesian Networks. In: Ruggeri, F., Kenett, R., Faltin, F. (eds.) Encyclopedia of Statistics in Quality and Reliability. John Wiley & Sons, Chichester (2007)
40. Fenton, N., Marsh, W., Neil, M., Cates, P., Forey, S., Tailor, M.: Making Resource Decisions for Software Projects. In: 26th International Conference on Software Engineering, pp. 397–406 (2004)
41. AgenaRisk Tool. Agena Limited, http://www.agenarisk.com/products/
42. Cozman, F.G.: JavaBayes - Bayesian Networks in Java, http://www.cs.cmu.edu/~javabayes/

Software Process Improvement: Supporting the Linking of the Software and the Business Strategies

Adriano Bessa Albuquerque[1], Ana Regina Rocha[2], and Andreia Cavalcanti Lima[1]

[1] University of Fortaleza, Washington Soares Avenue,
1321 - Bl J Sl 30 - 60.811-341 - Fortaleza, Brazil
[2] COPPE/UFRJ - Federal University of Rio de Janeiro,
P.O. BOX 68511 – ZIP21945-970 – Rio de Janeiro, Brazil
adriano.ba@terra.com.br, darocha@cos.ufrj.br,
andreia@bnb.gov.br

Abstract. The market is becoming more and more competitive, a lot of products and services depend of the software product and the software is one of the most important assets, which influence the organizations' businesses. Considering this context, we can observe that the companies must to deal with the software, developing or acquiring, carefully. One of the perspectives that can help to take advantage of the software, supporting effectively the business, is to invest on the organization's software processes. This paper presents an approach to evaluate and improve the processes assets of the software organizations, based on internationally well-known standards and process models. This approach is supported by automated tools from the TABA Workstation and is part of a wider improvement strategy constituted of three layers (organizational layer, process execution layer and external entity layer). Moreover, this paper presents the experience of use and their results.

Keywords: Software Quality, Software Process Improvement, Business Strategy.

1 Introduction

Nowadays, the world's software industry increases because the software became part of many products and activities. According to Nollen [1], the Indian software industry reached about $23.4 billion in sales revenue in the Indian fiscal year 2004-05. The Chinese software industry was $26.5 billion in 2004. And the worldwide software industry size was $1,045 billion in 2004.

Moreover, the software is becoming one of the most important assets to the organizations, because their products depend more and more of the software's services and their characteristics.

Prahalad et al. [2], emphasized that in all businesses, from the consolidated ones to the volatile, the information technology is a critical source of competitive opportunities and risks. They also said that the software products are determining the nature of the experiences that the clients, employees, partners and investors have with the company, their products, services and operations.

F. Bomarius et al. (Eds.): PROFES 2009, LNBIP 32, pp. 347–361, 2009.
© Springer-Verlag Berlin Heidelberg 2009

Reed [3] highlighted that 40% of the world population will suffer with the consequences, if some globally used systems fail.

In face of a context where the software product is a very important strategical component to the organizations, and knowing that the software process can influence positively the quality of this product, we defined an approach to evaluate and improve the organizations' process assets, integrated to TABA Workstation, where the business objectives and the product quality objectives are strongly considered to the planning and actions of the improvement cycle.

This paper presents this approach and the results of a real experience of use in a software organization of Rio de Janeiro.

Following this introduction, section 2 presents some relevant consideration related to organizational strategic planning. Section 3 presents some knowledge about software process improvement. Section 4 presents the proposed process. Section 5 presents the results of the experience of use and section 6 concludes the paper.

2 Business Strategy

On this competitive market, defining an adequate strategy is fundamental, because, the strategy can be seen as a headlight pointing out the direction of the investments. Without this, the initiatives can do not obtain the expected outcomes.

Moreover, as the software is an essential part of the products and services of the companies, the developer and the consumer should define specially strategies to acquire and develop their software products. Today, the matter "software" and their related actions must be introduced carefully on the strategic planning of any company.

Strategy is the choice of the market segment and clients that the business unities intends to serve, identifying the critical internal processes where the units should reach the excellence to accomplish their value proposition to the clients of the target-segments and selecting the individual and organizational capabilities to achieve the internal, of clients and financial objectives [4].

Wright, Kroll and Parnell [5] said that the strategy should be established with the participation of the high managers to obtain results in harmony with the organization's mission and objectives. At the same manner, Thompson Jr. and Strickland III [6] understand the strategy as the plan defined by the administration to reinforce the position of the organization on the market, promote the clients' satisfaction and achieve the performance objectives.

One of the most used approaches that deal with the strategic management is the Balanced ScoreCard (BSC), which is a methodology to facilitate the organizations to align their management processes and to focus all the organization on the strategy's implementation at long term.

This methodology has four operational perspectives, which are listed bellow. The objectives and measures of the scorecard of each perspective derive from the organization's vision and strategy.

- **Financial Perspective:** indicates if the implementation and execution of the strategy is contributing to improve the company's tangible outcomes. This perspective aims to evaluate the financial and economic outcomes of the business, considering the strategic objectives.

- **Customer Perspective:** indicates how to create values to the organization's clients, how to comply a demand satisfactorily and to identify the reasons which the clients want to obtain the products and services.
- **Internal Process Perspective:** analyzes the organization's internal processes, including the identification of the resources and capabilities that the company needs to raise their level of quality. The organizations should focus on the critical internal operations that permit to satisfy the clients and stockholders needs. According to Kaplan and Norton [17] the organizations should identify and measure their essential competences and the critical technologies necessaries to guarantee their permanence as the leader of the market, from the complete value chain of the internal processes which includes three main processes: Innovation, Operation and Pos-Sale Services.
- **Innovation and Learning Perspective:** ponders the organization's cultural attitudes related to development and retention of talents and the creation and systematization of the knowledge inside the organization [4]. This perspective permits the organization to guarantee its capability of renewing at long term.

However, nowadays, others models similar to BSC have emerged. Maisel [7] defined the Balanced Scorecard model, with the same name of the model created by Kaplan and Norton. This model consists of four perspectives (financial, client, commercial process and human resource) to measure the business. Mc Nair et al. [8] defined an approach called Performance Pyramid, which defined as its basic principle, the focus on the clients, linked with the organization's strategy. Adams and Roberts [9] defined the EP2M – Effective Progress and Performance Measurement, where they highlighted that the implementation of the strategy is not sufficient, but the organization should develop a culture to prepare the company to the changes, that are constants and to permit to make decisions in a rapid way. In 2005, Kim and Mauborgne [10] studying more than 150 strategic movements, created the Blue Ocean Strategy. This strategy tries to guide the organizations to the innovation and to markets not yet explored. The focus of this strategy is not the competition but rather the creation of new markets, aggregating values and reducing costs.

3 Software Process Improvement

The success of an Improvement Program depends of some factors that must be considered adequately. For example: (i) providing sufficient resources [11]; (ii) customizing the Improvement Program to the organization's characteristics [11]; (iii) adjust the improvement objectives to the business strategy objectives [12]; (iv) considering other type of factors besides only technical factors [11]; (v) investing in the human resources qualification [13]; (vi) obtain the engagement of all collaborators [11]; (vii) provide support of knowledge management approaches [11].

In the face of the complexity of some technical, cultural and environmental aspects related to software process improvement, standards and models were created or evolved aiming to guide the organizations to define and improve their processes [14] [15] [16] [17]. Besides, some effective approaches were already defined.

Komi-Sirviö [18] presented the approach Pr2imer, where the actual situation is analyzed, an ideal state and their indicators are defined, pilot projects are performed and according to the results, the improvements are institutionalized.

Birk et al. [19] defined an interesting improvement process approach, which the main characteristic is to be guided to the organization's specific software quality requirements. Birk and Pfhal [20] presented and approach based on system perspective, emphasizing the business objectives, the product objectives and the process objectives.

Caivano [21] defined a continuous process improvement approach using Statistical Process Control. Martins and Da Silva [22] defined the approach SPI – ProPAM, which is supported by the alignment between the processes and the projects management. This alignment is defined as the degree which the projects' plan and goals support and are supported by the processes' practices. Salo and Abrahamsson [23] presented an approach focused on knowledge management, which the objective is to provide, systematically, knowledge and experience mechanisms to help the project teams to define processes more adequate and to improve the engagement of the teams, including the software process group.

4 Process "Evaluation and Improvement of the Process Assets"

This reality, described above, motivated the following research assumption: how would be possible to define and implement on TABA Workstation an strategy able to guide the definition and execution of software process to improve the organizational standard processes using data from the projects.

This approach had to have the following requirements: (i) it must be part of a major strategy (Strategy in Layers to Define, Evaluate and Improve Software Processes); (ii) it must be integrated to the TABA Workstation; (iii) it must be guided by the business objectives; (iv) it must be guided by the product quality objectives; and (v) it must be executed on a real situation. The approach was defined and was called "Evaluation and Improvement of Process Assets". It encompasses four subprocesses: (1) Identifying improvement opportunities; (2) Planning and implementing improvements; (3) Identifying preventive actions; and (4) Concluding the improvement cycle.

Subprocess: Identifying Improvement Opportunities
The purpose of this subprocess is to identify the improvements to be implemented on the process assets aiming to satisfy the organization's vertical and/or horizontal improvement objectives. It encompasses the following activities which are made up of tasks:

1. **Characterize the improvement cycle:** the purpose of this activity is to characterize the actual improvement cycle of the organization. The process group, the high managers and the consultants (if exist) should to hold a meeting to identify important information to support this characterization.

   a. **Identify vertical improvements:** objectives related to reach some level on maturity models should be identified.
   b. **Identify horizontal improvements:** objectives related to the processes' performance or their suitability to the organization's needs should be identified.

c. **Identify business objectives:** the business objectives to support the selection of the organization's critical processes and the prioritization of the improvements should be identified. If the organization has already defined these objectives, it should review them.

d. **Identify product quality objectives:** product quality objectives to support the selection of the organization's critical processes, and the prioritization of the improvements should be identified. If the organization has already defined these objectives, it should review them. Before this definition, the process group should hold a meeting with the organization's collaborators to know their perception about the quality of the products. Besides, the organization could hold a meeting with the clients, a Forum of clients, to know the perceptions of them about its products and services.

e. **Identify and select the organization's critical processes:** the processes considered critical to the organization should be identified. As the problems of these processes are more relevant than others, these processes must be handled on this improvement cycle.

f. **Select projects:** the organization's projects, whose data should be analyzed on the actual improvement cycle to identify problems and improvement needs, are selected.

g. **Plan the process:** the execution of the process "Evaluation and Improvement of the Process Assets" is planned to the actual improvement cycle. On the planning, the activities and respective dates and resources should be defined. If some activity is not relevant to the actual cycle, it can be put out of the plan.

2. **Analyze processes to implement vertical improvements:** the purpose of this activity is to identify what are the improvements to be implemented on the organization's processes aiming to get a new level on maturity models, like: CMMI and MPS.BR.

   a. **Identify changes to the processes:** the processes should be analyzed, comparing them with the expected results of the models, to identify the changes to be implemented on the processes. The Gap Analysis technique [24] or the Compliance of Factors technique [25] can be utilized.

3. **Analyze data to implement horizontal improvements:** the purpose of this activity is to analyze data from the processes executed on selected projects, to identify problems that are making difficult achieve the business and product quality objectives. This activity is performed by the process group and consultants, if exist.

   a. **Analyze the results of the adequacy evaluations:** the results of the adequacy evaluations, which are always executed at the end of an activity, should be analyzed. The analysis should try to identify pattern of problems related to the training adequacy, support tool adequacy, template adequacy, activity's description adequacy and the activity's relevance.

b. **Analyze data from post mortem analysis:** data from the projects' post mortem analysis should be analyzed.

c. **Analyze results of the monitoring processes indicators:** results of the monitoring processes indicators should be analyzed.

d. **Select others data sources to be analyzed:** if necessary, others data sources can be selected, to improve the contextualization of the analysis. The following data source can be selected: (i) processes adherence evaluation; (ii) work products adherence evaluation; (iii) lessons learned; (iv) guidelines; (v) processes changes; (vi) processes changes demands and (vii) results of the official assessment MPS.BR or SCAMPI.

e. **Analyze others data sources:** if others data sources were selected on the anterior task, they should be analyzed.

f. **Evaluate problems:** all the found problems should be evaluated. Optionally, the Matrix to Analyze Problems can be filled out to each process, aiming to confirm or refute the evidences. This matrix is based on the method to support qualitative analysis, called Content Analysis [26]. This technique tries to identify, mainly, the frequency and intensity of some information on the documents.

g. **List the identified problems:** The problems identified during the analysis should be registered.

4. **Identify problems to be held:** the purpose of this activity is to identify the problems to be handled on the actual improvement cycle to achieve the vertical and/or horizontal improvement objectives. The tasks of this activity should be performed by all the process group's participants and if necessary, with the helping of the high managers.

a. **Present problems:** the collaborators which executed the activities "Analyze processes to implement vertical improvements" and "Analyze data to implement horizontal improvements" should present to the others members of the process group, the results obtained from their work, helping the process group to select the problems to be handled on this actual improvement cycle.

b. **Select problems to be handled:** the meeting's participants should select the problems to be handled, considering, mainly, the business objectives and product quality objectives.

5. **Identify the causes of the problems:** the purpose of this activity is to analyze the problems with the collaborators which performed any processes' activities, to find out the problems' root causes and to identify improvement opportunities to solve the identified problems.

a. **Analyze problems:** the identified problems are analyzed to identify the root causes. In a meeting, predefined cause and effect diagrams to each problem are presented, supporting the discussion between the participants and helping them to elaborate final versions of the diagrams. Other approach that can be executed to improve the understanding of the problems is to try to define the relationships between the causes using the Matrix to Discover Relationships or Influence Diagrams.

    b.   **Suggest improvements:** On the same meeting held to identify the root causes, the process group should capture improvement opportunities, which must come from the final version of the cause and effect diagrams.

6.   **Identify improvement opportunities to be implemented:** the purpose of this activity is to present the results of the anterior activity to all members of the process group, supporting them on the selection of the improvement opportunities that must be implemented on the actual improvement cycle. If convenient, the high managers can participate on the execution of this activity.

    a.   **Analyze and prioritize the improvement opportunities:** the analysis of the improvement opportunities should be performed using, firstly, the approach SWOT Analysis, to deepen the knowledge of the opportunities. Then, the level of prioritization must be defined using the most appropriate approach, considering, especially, the complexity of the improvements and the characteristics of the process group.

    b.   **Select the improvement opportunities to be implemented:** After the prioritization of the improvement opportunities, the meeting's participants should define the improvements which will be implemented on the actual improvement cycle.

    c.   **Work out the improvement report:** a member of the process group or the consultant, if exists, should work out a report containing the obtained results from this subprocess.

Subprocess: Planning and Implementing Improvements

The purpose of this subprocess is to plan the implementation of the selected improvement opportunities, and to implement and institutionalize them on the organization. It encompasses the following activities which are made up of tasks:

1.   **Change the process assets:** the purpose of this activity is to define and execute an action plan to implement the required modifications on the process assets. If exist high risky improvements to the organization, the action plan must consider the performance of pilot projects to evaluate them, before their institutionalization.

    a.   **Define the action plan:** the process group should define an action plan to guide the implementation of the improvement opportunities.

    b.   **Execute the action plan:** the collaborators of the organization should execute the actions defined on the action plan.

    c.   **Manage the action plan:** the process group should manage the execution of the actions defined on the action plan.

2. **Perform the pilot project:** the purpose of this activity is to perform one or more pilot Project to evaluate the high risky improvement opportunities, before their institutionalization. If they are not risky, the process group can do not execute this activity. All the tasks of this activity are performed by the process group.

   a. **Plan the pilot project:** the pilot projects should be planned, identifying the objectives, the assumptions and the data that must be collected.
   b. **Execute the pilot project:** the planned pilot project should be executed aiming to evaluate the effects derived from the modifications.
   c. **Analyze the results of the pilot projects:** the results obtained from the pilot project execution should be analyzed to decide if the improvement opportunities will be institutionalized. The analysis must verify if the effects are consistent with the assumptions defined on the planning.

3. **Implement the improvement opportunities:** the purpose of this activity is to implement the new process assets and institutionalize the improvements. All the tasks of this activity are performed by the process group.

   a. **Plan the implementation of the improvement opportunities:** the implementation of the improvement opportunities should be planned. When the improvement can not be implemented on the organization, like the creation of a new template, it will be required a new configuration of the TABA Workstation.
   b. **Perform the implementation of the improvement opportunities:** the new process assets are institutionalized on the organization in accordance to the planning and are incorporated on the Organizational Asset Library.
   c. **Training the team on the modified process:** the trainings required to guarantee the adequacy of the modified processes' execution are carried out and the implemented improvements are communicated to the stakeholders. These trainings can be carried out formally, inside the organization, by the members of the process group or by the consultants or can be performed more informally, with the support of a mentor. Besides, the implemented improvements should be published on the organization, informing, mainly, the objectives, the origin and the expected outcomes.

Subprocess: Identifying Preventive Actions

The purpose of this subprocess is to analyze historical data of the organization's processes and define preventive actions aiming to eliminate or reduce the probability of the occurrence of imminent problems. This subprocess can be executed whenever the organization considers convenient. It is not dependent of the execution of others subprocesses. It encompasses the following activities which are made up of tasks:

1. **Analyze data focusing in preventive actions:** the purpose of this activity is to analyze organizational historical data to identify possible preventive actions.

   a. **Select processes:** the processes, whose data will be analyzed, should be selected.

   b. **Identify imminent problems:** the relevant imminent problems of the selected processes should be identified. These problems should be identified from the risks which occurred on the organization's projects and from the audit reports. Besides, the results of the monitoring process indicators can be used too.

2. **Establish preventive actions:** the purpose of this activity is to establish preventive action to reduce the chances of the imminent problems to become a real problem.

   a. **Define preventive actions:** imminent problems should be analyzed by the process group to define preventive actions, which must be registered, along with the related problems, on the Matrix of Preventive Actions. The stakeholders can help on the identification of the preventive actions.

   b. **Define preventive actions plan:** a plan including the preventive actions, the respective responsible person, the beginning and final date should be defined by the process group.

   c. **Execute preventive action plan:** the preventive actions should be executed in accordance to the preventive actions plan.

   d. **Manage preventive action plan:** the preventive actions should be managed by the process group.

Subprocess: Concluding the Improvement Cycle

This subprocess has two purposes: the first is to identify, analyze and register the lessons learned during the execution of the processes to permit their reuse. The second aims to collaborate with the consultancy companies (external entities), to support the improvement of their process assets. It encompasses the following activities which are made up of tasks:

1. **Register lessons learned:** the purpose of this activity is to identify the lessons learned during the execution of this approach ("Evaluation and Improvement of the Process Assets"). All the tasks of this activity are performed by the process group.

   a. **Identify lessons learned:** relevant lessons learned during the execution of the approach should be identified.

   b. **Store lessons learned:** the identified lessons learned should be analyzed to choose those that must be stored on the organizational repository.

2. **Communicate results to the consultancy company:** the purpose of this activity is to send the results obtained on the actual improvement cycle and on the official assessments (CMMI, MPS.BR) to the consultancy company to collaborate with its process assets. The improvement report or only a part of it should be sent, including pertinent information.

a.   **Send the report:** if pertinent to the organization, the process
group should send, to the consultancy company, the improvement report or just a part of it. The results of the CMMI and
MPS.BR assessments are also important to be sent.

5   The Experience of Use

We executed The Process "Evaluation and Improvement of the Process Assets" on the
Software Engineering Laboratory (SEL) of COPPE, specifically on the Quality Sec-
tor, to evaluate its adequacy. This sector had implemented processes of MPS.BR level
E and soon would be assessed in this maturity model.

The Quality Sector team was composed of a doctor professor, a laboratory coordinator, three project manager, one technical coordinator, one quality assurance analyst,
one measurement analyst, two responsible for managing the configuration, one responsible to managing the reuse, analysts and programmers. The process group was
composed of the laboratory coordinator and three project managers.

The laboratory's activities included three families of projects: (i) projects related to
the development of the TABA Workstation; (ii) projects related to the development of
CORE-KM, a knowledge management environment and (iii) projects to develop tools
related to Master and Ph.D. thesis. All the projects used the software development
process and the others processes (Measurement, Configuration Management *etc.*).

Nowadays, the laboratory has implemented the following processes: Project Management, Requirement Management, Quality Assurance, Measurement, Configuration
Management, Organizational Process Definition, Reuse Management, Human Resource Management and Evaluation and Improvement of Organizational Process.

When this experience was carried out, there were three concluded projects and five
were still in process. The three concluded projects were related to the CORE-KM.
They were developed to an external client and one project manager and one analyst
participated of it. The quality assurance analyst has audited the products and the adherence of the processes, measures were collected and the activities of the Configuration Management were executed.

As the concluded projects had used the tool AvalPro, one of the tools of TABA
Workstation, we had data from the adequacy evaluations and post mortem analysis.
We had also the quality assurance reports and the measures collected during the exe-
cution of the processes.

The use of the process was restricted to the subprocess 1: Identifying improvement
opportunities and subprocess 4: Concluding the improvement cycle. The process
group decided do not execute neither the **subprocess 2: Planning and implementing
improvements** nor the **subprocess 3: Identifying preventive actions**. The subprocess 2 was not executed because none of the modifications were implemented before
the moment of the assessment. And the subprocess 3 was not executed because it was
not obligatory.

It is important to highlight that one of the authors of this paper participated on this
experience as consultant.

5.1   Execution of the Subprocess 1: Identifying Improvement Opportunities

Activity: Characterize the improvement cycle

Three members of the process group participated in the execution of this activity. A meeting with the process group was held, where the improvement cycle was characterized.

On the meeting, they defined the following horizontal improvement objective: "analyze the results obtained form the execution of the processes, aiming to convert the processes of level E (MPS.BR) more mature and adequate to the reality of the Quality Sector of the SEL, examining, mainly, the processes where the measures present greater deviation from the expected performance.".

On this moment, the group does not defined none vertical improvement objective, because all the processes of level E (MPS.BR) had already been implemented.

The process group defined the following business objectives: (i) increase the confidence of the clients on the quality of the products and on meeting the delivery deadline; (ii) create an experimentation environment to high maturity processes.

Moreover, they defined three product quality objectives: (i) Reliability: the products, when installed on the clients' environment, must have a high level of reliability, with a high time between failures, which must be quantitatively defined to each project in accordance to its characteristics. (ii) Maintainability: the products must be easy to maintain and evolve; (iii) Usability: the products must be easy to use, without any need to carry out training when the software is evolved.

The Project Management and Measurement were defined as critical processes, using as the main criterion the level of relationship between the processes and the business objectives. A third process (Quality Assurance), also related to business objectives, was not considered critical because they did not perceived problems on it. The process Measurement, although considered critical to achieve the second business objective, was excluded from the improvement cycle, because did not exist sufficient data to analyze its adequacy and performance. So, on this improvement cycle, only the Project Management was considered as critical.

Finally, the process group select three concluded projects related to CORE-KM. After the characterization, a member of the group worked out the Process Execution Plan. The next executed activity was "Analyze data to implement horizontal improvements".

Activity: Analyze data to implement horizontal improvements

A member of the process group and the consultant identified tendencies of problems, analyzing data of the selected projects and processes. The analysis included data from the adequacy evaluation, post mortem analysis and process monitoring indicators of the three selected projects. The data were obtained from TABA Workstation, using the tools AvalPro and Metrics. At the end of the activity, the report "Tendencies of problems" was worked out.

Activity: Identify problems to be held

The member of the process group and the consultant, who had analyzed the data, presented the report "Tendencies of problems" to all the participants of the process group. On this meeting, the problems were analyzed again. They also decided to perform a causal analysis on the problem "The timeline estimative precision is far from the expected", because it was considered important to the organization and it was extremely related to one of the business objective.

They observed that some problems were already being solved. Besides, they decided to handle some problems only on the next improvement cycle. Moreover, they established that two improvement opportunities should be handled on the actual cycle: (i) improve the template used on the activity Data and Communication Management and (ii) begin to use other support tool on the process Configuration Management, replacing the Bugzilla.

Activity: Identify the causes of the problems

This activity was performed in a meeting held with the participants of the three projects. During the meeting, the consultant presented a predefined cause and effect diagram to the problem described on the anterior activity. At the end, were produced: (i) the final version of the cause and effect diagram and (ii) a set of improvement opportunities.

Activity: Identify improvement opportunities to be implemented

This activity was executed in a meeting where the process group analyzing the results obtained on the anterior activities, prioritized and selected the improvement opportunities that should be implemented.

Firstly, a SWOT Analysis was performed in all the improvements, aiming to identify the barriers and the facilitators to the implementation. Then, the group decided that it was not necessary to define the level of prioritization of the improvement opportunities related to TABA Workstation and that they will be inserted automatically on the improvement report. On the same meeting, the group defined the level of prioritization of the others improvements: (i) develop the knowledge about the performance of the processes (quantitative models of process), (ii) improve the template used on the activity Data and Communication Management and (iii) begin to use other support tool on the process Configuration Management, replacing the Bugzilla.

To define the prioritization we used the Matrix to Prioritization (Table 1), where each participant of the meeting evaluated the improvements, considering the criteria of the matrix. When we defined the criteria of the matrix we tried to link the improvements to the business objectives and product quality objectives.

Table 1. Criteria used to prioritize the improvements

Criteria	Description
Seriousness	Seriousness of the problem.
Importance to the organization's business objectives	Importance of the improvement implementation to the organization's business objectives.
Impact on the quality of the software products	Impact of the improvement implementation on the quality of the organization's software products.
Impact on the productivity of the team	Impact of the improvement implementation on the productivity of the teams.
Impact on the satisfaction of the team	Impact of the improvement implementation on the satisfaction of the teams.
Impact on the satisfaction of the clients	Impact of the improvement implementation on the satisfaction of the clients.

After this, when the result of the prioritization was analyzed, we observed that they were very similar. So we used the Delphi technique [27] as a new approach to support the meeting of the consensus.

On this same meeting, the improvement opportunities were analyzed considering others criteria to choose the improvements that must be implemented, considering the short, medium and long term. The following criteria were used: (i) Effort: estimative in Men/Hour to implement the improvement; (ii) Resource Availability: availability of resources (financial, human and technological) to implement the improvement; (iii)Time: time to implement the improvement and (iv) Operational simplicity: simplicity to implement the improvement.

As the result of this activity's execution, was decided the following prioritization: (1) begin to use other support tool on the process Configuration Management, replacing the Bugzilla; (2) develop the knowledge about the performance of the processes (quantitative models of process) and (3) improve the template used on the activity Data and Communication Management. Finally, all the improvement opportunities were selected to be implemented on the actual improvement cycle.

5.2 Execution of the Subprocess 4: Concluding the Improvement Cycle

Some lessons learned were captured and registered during the execution of the approach: (i) The discussions between the members of the process group, occurred when the cycle is being characterized, is very important, because the objectives become more coherent with the organization; (ii) The definition of the critical process helps the data analysis to become more focused; (iii) The orientation of the decision must be always based on the business objectives and the product quality objectives, because the software is one of the most important asset of the companies; (iv) Structured data can speed the analysis up; (v) The predefined cause and effect diagrams helps the participants to remember others possible causes; (vi) The Delphi technique permits the decisions to be in accordance to the organization's needs and to the point of view of the majority of the members; (vii) All the points which were already defined, can be always improved in a new improvement cycle.

At the end, the members of the process group worked out the Improvement Report to be sent to the Consultancy (external entity).

5   Conclusion

Analyzing critically the experience of use in the Quality Sector of the SEL, we could observe, considering the execution of the subprocesses 1and 4, that the process was adequate. In spite of the subprocesses 2 and 3 were not executed, the process seemed feasible and useful, because the main subprocesses were performed.

The process group executed the approach easily. However, on the last activity of the subprocess 1, as the technique used was not adequate, we began to utilize the Delphi technique. Besides, the tools supported adequately the process, for example, the AvalPro. We could also observe that the definition of the business objectives and the product quality objectives were fundamental to the approach, because the it was executed on behalf of the company. As we could see on the Balanced Scorecard (BSC), the software process has to become a real perspective. So, all the organizations must define and execute their software process to support the achievement of the defined organizational strategy.

After the analysis of the experience we could identify the following limitations of the approach: (i) The qualitative analysis is not well structured; (ii) There is not a tool to support the activities related to the preventive actions and (iv) There are not tasks responsible to evaluate the effectiveness of the implemented improvement opportunities.

Other challenge is to define and implement an approach to software process improvement adequate to companies that invest on innovations and have their strategies focused on the creation of new markets. So, others experiences of use must be carried out. Probably, formal and planned use cases to verify in other context the adequacy of the approach.

References

1. Nollen, S.: Software Industry Performance in India and China. In: Amar, K., Nayak, J., Jomon, M.G. (eds.) INDIA in the Emerging Global Order, ch. 4. Tata McGraw-Hill Publishing, New York (2008)
2. Prahalad, C.K., et al.: The new meaning of quality in the information age, pp. 109–118. Harvard Business, Boston (1999)
3. Reed, K.: Software engineering – a new millenium? IEEE Software (July-August 2000)
4. Kaplan, R.S., Norton, D.: The Balanced Scorecard: indicators that drive the performance. Harvard Business Review (January/Febuary 2000)
5. Wright, P., Kroll, M.J., Parnell, J.: Strategic Administration. Atlas, São Paulo (2000)
6. Thompson Jr., A.A., Strickland III, A.J.: Dtrategic Planning. Pioneira, São Paulo (2000)
7. Maisel, L.S.: Performance Measurement Practices: A Long Way from Strategy Management. The Balanced Scorecard Report (May - June 2001)
8. Nair, C.J., Lynch, R.L., Cross, K.F.: Do Financial and Nonfinancial Performance Measures Have to Agree? Management Accounting 72(5), 28–35 (1990)
9. Adams, C., Roberts, P.: You Are What You Measure. Manufacturing Europe, 504–507 (1993)
10. Kim, W.C., Mauborgne, R.: Blue Ocean Strategy. Campus, São Paulo (1995)
11. Dyba, T.: Factors of Software Process Improvement Success in Small Organizations: An Empirical Study in the Scandinavian Context. In: Proceedings of the ESEC/FSE 2003, Helsinki, pp. 148–157 (2003)
12. Hefner, R., Tauser, J.: Things They Never Taught You in CMM School. In: Proceedings of the 26th Annual NASA Goddard Software Engineering Workshop, November 2001, pp. 27–29 (2001)
13. Cater-Steel, A.P.: Low-rigour, Rapid Software Process Assessments for Small Software Development Firms. In: Proceedings of the 15th Australian Software Engineering Conference (ASWEC 2004), Melbourne, April 2004, pp. 368–377 (2004)
14. SOFTEX: Brazilian Software Process Improvement – General Guide version 1.2
15. CMU/SEI: CMMI for Development version 1.2., CMU/SEI-2006-TR-008 (2006)
16. ISO/IEC: ISO/IEC PDAM 12207: Information Technology – Amendment 2 to ISO/IEC 12207 (2004)
17. ISO/IEC: ISO/IEC 15504-4: Information Technology – Process Assessment, Part 4: Guidance on use for Process Improvement and Process Capability Determination (2004)

18. Komi-Sirvio, S.: Development and Evaluation of Software Process Improvement Methods. In: Espoo 2004, p. 535. VTT Publications (2004)
19. Birk, A., et al.: PROFES: A Product Driven Process Improvement Methodology. In: Proceedings of European Conference on Software Process Improvement (SPI 1998), Monaco, December 1998, 9 p. (1998)
20. Birk, A., Pfahl, D.: A System Perspective on Software Process Improvement, IESE-Report No. 047.02/E Version 1.0 (2002)
21. Caivano, D.: Continuous Software Process Improvement through Statistical Process Control. In: Proceedings of the Ninth European Conference on Software Maintenance and Re-engineering (CSMR 2005), Manchester, March 2005, pp. 288–293 (2005)
22. Martins, V.M., Da Silva, A.R.: ProPAM: SPI based on Process and Project Alignment. In: Proceedings of the IRMA International Conference, Vancouver (May 2007)
23. Salo, O., Abrahamson, P.: Integrating Agile Software Development and Software Process Improvement: a Longitudinal Case Study. In: Proceedings of the 4th International Symposium on Empirical Software Engineering (ISESE 2005), Noosa Heads, November 2005, pp. 193–202 (2005)
24. Stalhane, T.: Root Cause Analysis and Gap Analysis - A Tale of Two Methods. In: Dingsøyr, T. (ed.) EuroSPI 2004. LNCS, vol. 3281, pp. 150–160. Springer, Heidelberg (2004)
25. Alloui, I., et al.: Advanced Services for Process Evolution: Monitoring and Decision Support. In: Conradi, R. (ed.) EWSPT 2000. LNCS, vol. 1780, pp. 21–37. Springer, Heidelberg (2000)
26. Bardin, L.: Content Analysis, Lisboa. Edições 70 (1977)
27. Boehm, B., et al.: Software cost estimation with COCOMO II. Prentice-Hall, Englewood Cliffs (2000)

Integrating Value and Utility Concepts into a Value Decomposition Model for Value-Based Software Engineering

Mikko Rönkkö[1], Christian Frühwirth[1], and Stefan Biffl[2]

[1] Helsinki University of Technology, Software Business Laboratory
Otaniementie 17, Espoo, Finland
[2] Vienna University of Technology, Institute of Software Technology,
Vienna, A-1040, Austria
{mikko.ronkko,christian.fruehwirth}@tkk.fi,
Stefan.Biffl@tuwien.ac.at

Abstract. Value-based software engineering (VBSE) is an emerging stream of research that addresses the value considerations of software and extends the traditional scope of software engineering from technical issues to business-relevant decision problems. While the concept of value in VBSE relies on the well-established economic value concept, the exact definition for this key concept within VBSE domain is still not well defined or agreed upon. We argue the discourse on value can significantly benefit from drawing from research in management, particularly software business. In this paper, we present three aspects of software: as a technology, as a design, and as an artifact. Furthermore, we divide the value concept into three components that are relevant for software product development companies and their customers: intrinsic value, externalities and option value. Finally, we propose a value decomposition matrix based on technology views and value components.

Keywords: Value-based software engineering, stakeholder value, software business.

1 Introduction

Researchers focusing on value-based software engineering (VBSE) have suggested that the economic and value perspectives should be integrated into the software engineering processes that until now have had a very technical focus. According to Biffl and his colleagues [1] and Huang and Boehm [2], software engineering is currently performed in a value-neutral setting, where the basis of methods and tools is on supporting development of technology, not on creating business value. This value-neutral approach makes it hard to create products that are valuable to people and make it difficult to make financially responsible decisions.

Based on the work of the Economics-Driven Software Engineering Research (EDSER) community, a VBSE research agenda has emerged aiming to integrate value considerations in all aspects of software engineering, and calling forth the development

F. Bomarius et al. (Eds.): PROFES 2009, LNBIP 32, pp. 362–374, 2009.
© Springer-Verlag Berlin Heidelberg 2009

of tools and methods to support the business side of software engineering [1]. Due to the novel nature of this idea, empirical evidence – currently being called for in software engineering [3] – supporting the feasibility of realizing value-based software engineering is limited.

Some of the most central work in the area of VBSE includes the initial theory of VBSE as presented by Jain and Boehm [4] and calculation methods estimating return on investment (ROI) of software development pioneered by for example Erdogmus, Favaro and Halling [5]. This work and the research in VBSE in general use several concepts and techniques from economics and accounting and apply them to the context of software engineering. While the inclusion of general business and management theories to the research of business aspects in software engineering can be considered a fundamental aspect of VBSE, we argue that the researchers in the area could significantly benefit from adapting more of the findings of the so-called software business research into their work.

Software business, as the authors of this paper define it, is a management research area, which focuses on software firms and develops knowledge to understand how and why these firms succeed. When defined this way, software business and VBSE share the phenomenon of interest but differ in the research paradigm. While researchers involved in VBSE use the engineering paradigm and develop tools and methods to help software firms succeed, researchers operating in software business area examine how and why firms succeed using the social sciences paradigm. Simply put, the models of VBSE are mostly prescriptive, while the software business research considers explanatory models as a central goal. We argue that these viewpoints are different sides of the same coin, and hence there is a great potential for cooperation and knowledge sharing.

The rest of the paper is structured as follows. First, we present some of the key theories used in the emerging software business research, particularly those related to value. Second, we review three different ways to conceptualize software based on the current paradigm employed by software business researchers. Throughout these two sections, we use software product development or market driven software development as the context. Finally, we will integrate the perspectives of value and the perspectives of software into a value decomposition matrix. The main contributions of this paper include linking VBSE and software business research as well as providing a conceptual tool to aid in different value considerations.

2   Concept of Value in Software Business Research

The concept of value is central to VBSE. Indeed, the main goal of this research movement is to assign a measure of value on decision making in the software process. This is seen as a complement to previous software engineering research that has mainly focused on technical aspects such as quality, cost, and development time. The concept of value is not strictly defined, but can be evaluated for example by a technique called Stakeholder Value Proposition Elicitation and Analysis [6]. From the perspective of economics, this resembles analyzing the utility function [see e.g. 7] of each stakeholder. After this, win-win technique, can be applied to negotiate the requirements.

Research by Briggs and Grünbacher [8] and Oza, Biffl, Fruehwirth, and Selioukova [9] have demonstrated the successful use of this approach in the elicitation of stakeholder values.

Another set of techniques focuses on valuating different features, requirements, or decisions on a single-dimensional measure (most commonly money) using mathematical formulas adapted mainly from accounting and finance[5]. However, the vagueness of the concept of value seems to be a central problem. If the researchers cannot agree on a common definition of value, we run the risk of producing incommensurable research, which seriously inhibits the progress of the field. We attempt to clarify the concept of value by anchoring it to the theory base used in software business.

The economic concept of value is most commonly defined as the amount of money that a unit of goods or services is traded for. Utility, on the other hand, is all the good and desirable that is created by consuming a product or a service. Hence the concept of value in VBSE is closer to economic utility than economic value. To avoid confusion with the terminology, we use the term "value" for value in VBSE context, and "economic value" when discussing the economic concept. The problem with utility, and value, is that good and desirable are highly subjective and idiosyncratic issues. Economics has solved the problem of diversity in utility between consumers by developing a multi-attribute utility theory [10] and using statistical distribution functions as utility functions. However, the abstract and generic nature of these theories limits their applicability to VBSE, as long as no relevant agreed on dimensions and measures exist for value components. In this paper we omit the philosophical of definition of value and assume that value exists, and we can use any definition that suits our needs. Hence, we rather ambiguously define "value is the degree of desirability". Agreeing that this definition sheds little normative light on the decision-making processes, we will now take a closer look what value means in different contexts. The discussion is structured around two central players in the software markets: utility-seeking customers and profit-seeking firms.

2.1 Values of Utility-Seeking Customers

From the customer perspective the value of software comes from its use, the utility it can create. While this is a seemingly trivial argument, it embeds much complexity: First, the utility is not only dependent on the intrinsic properties of the software, but also the skills of the user and several factors that are external to both the user and the software. Second, as discussed earlier, each customer values the software differently depending on for example her unique set of capabilities, and her own desires for different types of utility. Recent research by Oza and his colleagues [9] illustrates this value diversity in dynamic settings of software process improvement initiatives.

In a static setting where future is not considered, the value of the software comes from three different sources: intrinsic value, complementary value [11] and direct network externalities [12,13]. The intrinsic value is embedded in the software as functionality and attributes such as security and usability. This part of the value seems to have the closest match with the current concept of value in VBSE. A complement can be defined as a product or a service, which increases the value of another product or service [14] and here complementary value refers to value, which is created by combining a piece of software with another good or service. For example, a word processor is much more valuable when bundled in an office suite due to the possibility to embed objects created with other applications. Last, if the software can be used in communication, it is subject to network externalities – its value is dependent on the amount of other users of the software that are relevant to the focal user. For example, if two colleagues use compatible word processors, they can share files and collaborate benefiting both from the compatibility. A somewhat idealistic view of this phenomenon is known as Metcalfe's law "the value of a network is the number of users squared" [15]. Empirical evidence suggests that the value of network externalities can be in par with product features when a product's economic value is evaluated[11,16,12]. In other words, compatibility with other pieces of software can be as important as the features and quality of the software.

The problem with the above-presented decomposition of value is that it does not take into account the bounded rationality of people. Especially in the context of complex issues, people cannot base their decisions fully on facts. Hence, the purchase decisions are not based on real value, but perceived value [see e.g., 17]. We will first discuss the issue of where the estimate of real value comes from and then present some of the factors that may create bias between the real and the perceived value. In economics, a good whose value cannot be estimated without using the good is called "an experience good" [18]. While software is far from typical experience goods, like music, Messerschmitt and Szyperski [19] argue that software should be considered to be an experience good. This implies that the estimate for the value comes from using the good, referring to other users or reviews, or simply through advertisements. In the context of software, especially influential seems to be the experience with the prior generation or release of the product. However, even with perfect information gained through experience, the perceived value rarely equals the real value. One reason for this is that value contains also purely psychological parts. Often the market share correlates with the perceived value causing bandwagon effect [20], where the current user base drives adoption without any mechanism that would generate externalities. While the psychological part of the value has traditionally been considered as being solely in the domain of marketing, some recent work suggests that it should be taken into account also in the product development phase [21]. The significance of these psychological effects can be so strong as to enable firms with inferior products to capture the markets if they gain control of the bandwagon [13]. Product launch timing is an influential factor in creating these effects and hence at least release planning is affected by this market effect [22].

The last problem with estimating the value of a piece of software from the customer point of view is that software is an investment in a durable good and hence the expected future value matters. More concretely, the customer is interested on availability of complements in the future (including for example updates), and expected size of the user base. These both are issues, which can significantly affect which products are chosen and which firms' offerings prevail in the markets.

2.2 Values of Profit-Seeking Firms

Next we will discuss the concept of value from the perspective of a software firm. The objective of the firm is simple: to maximize the cumulative long term profits. However, this simple and uniform concept of value does not help much when trying to estimate the value of software development decisions. The reason is that the profits of the firm are realized in market transactions, and the evolution of the markets is an external facto that is largely outside the control of the firm. This is particularly true for the turbulent software markets, where standards, technologies, and even companies change rapidly. Due to this, attempts to generate systematic heuristics to optimize against the unknown future have not yet matched the use of managerial intuition in decision-making [23].

We will divide the further discussion of the value from the perspective of the software firm into two themes: market mechanisms and path dependency. In economics, market is a place where buyers and sellers exchange goods and services. If a buyer considered something as being more valuable than the seller, a transaction occurs. The purpose of the market is to create and divide surplus – the utility of the good for the buyer measured in money minus the cost of creating the good by the seller measured in money. Since the utility of different buyers varies, the seller usually prices the good in such a way that only a certain amount of users want to trade with the price. When a competitor with a similar product arrives, the optimal price that the seller should charge decreases. If the goods are sufficiently similar and there is sufficiently large number of sellers, the basic economic models predict that prices will fall to a level that equals the cost of production and sales by the sellers. If this so-called perfect competition situation occurs, no firm will create profit. To counter the effects of competition firms often deliberately create products that cause lock-in by means of creating extra costs when switching to other vendors or use advertising to make their product seem more advantageous than it actually is [24]. With these tactics, the firm is decreasing the surplus (value minus cost) that goes to the customer to create more profits. The importance of lock-in is that it enables software firms to extract more value from their products than would be possible if consumers could switch to competing products freely, thus explaining the voracious strive for market share in growing markets [25]. The phenomenon of lock-in and existence of network externalities create a challenge for evaluating the value of the software: Often several incompatible standards compete, and the outcome of this battle for dominance cannot be evaluated accurately ex ante [26]. The dilemma of a firm is that while it maximizes utility by being compatible with the dominant network, it can often capture more economic value by excluding competitors from the network by being incompatible with competing solutions [13]. The dilemma of compatibility and limiting the choice of the customer is something rather opposite to the win-win principle [27] used in VBSE. Another problem is that when technology is first developed and then sold at the markets, the value for the technology cannot be accurately defined at the time when the most value affecting development decisions are made since we cannot accurately predict how the market develops in the future [28].

Another issue with firms is that they have technological path dependency. That is, their future technological options are a function of the technology that they currently have in terms of not only technology assets but also knowledge. This means that sometimes firms need to optimize for longer term rather than following the most value-efficient approach for the current customers. If a firm fails to see this, it might end up in technological obsolescence or technological lockout [29].

To summarize the discussion in this section and the previous, we conclude that there probably cannot be a single unidimensional and measurable construct for value, but how value is seen depends on the context. However, we argue that just abstracting the value to a single figure can sometime be too simple solution since three different dimensions of value exits: intrinsic value of the software, externalities through compatibility and complements, and option value by enabling future development paths. Next we will look at the concept of value from a rather different perspective, that of software as a modular technology.

3 Three Perspectives on Software as Technology

After the initial discussion of value, we will now take an orthogonal view on the issue. If we are to understand what value means for software from the perspective of various management disciplines, we need to also understand how these disciplines conceptualize software. It is easy to define software as a technology without further considerations on the general nature of the term. To understand how software is presented in management research, we adopt a definition for the concept of technology by Schilling [30]

Technology refers to any manner of systematically applying knowledge or science to a practical
    application ... Technology in this context is generally understood to include information
    technology as well as technology embodied in products, production processes, and design
    processes.

Since the process of creating and the process of executing are systematic, and there is a practical application for software, we can indeed conclude that software fits well to this definition. The adopted definition links technology intimately but not exclusively to artifacts, that is, technology is both the artifacts that extend our capabilities and the skill to produce and efficiently use them. This definition is much more strict, than defining technology as knowledge that is intended for "use". If defined this broadly, technology would encompass virtually all useful routines and capabilities developed through organizational evolution.

In addition to artifacts and knowledge, technology can be considered from a third perspective: as a design. Design is a "blue print", a type of artifact that acts as a template for producing more artifacts. While not strictly correct, we distinguish between software design and software artifact by defining that software design is technology-in-development and the software artifact is technology-in-use, or technology which is embedded inside a medium and is ready to be executed or traded. We present each of these views in more detail and build link to VBSE.

3.1 Software Artifacts

Most notable property of software artifacts is that they are information. More precisely, software artifacts are a sequence of instructions that is codified in a form that can be interpreted and executed by computer hardware. Information artifacts have several distinct properties: First, information contains always two parts, message and the language, which it is codified with [31]. With software this naturally implies that the codification needs to be compatible with the hardware. However, in contrast to many other information goods, this codification is not readily comprehensible by people, and in the case of interpreted programming languages where the software is distributed in source code format and interpreted to machine language when executed, it still requires considerable effort to comprehend the code[24]. In this way, software does not suffer from the property shared by many other information goods, that is, software can be appropriated even if it has been once disclosed [32]. Hence, software should be considered as an experience good [19,18], but the implications of revelation are much less serious than with other more typical information goods.

Like any other information good, software does not wear out when used. However, it shares a characteristic with knowledge: Knowledge does not wear out, but competition can drive down the price even though the utility has not declined. The value can also diminish through obsoletion[33]. That is, the utility of the information does not decrease, but the market value is decreased through emergence of new and more advanced competing artifacts, or the environment where it is used changes so that the artifact is no longer useful for the purpose it was intended for. The speed of obsoletion can range from rapid to nearly inexistent. For example software that is run on the mainframes of financial institutions can be even several decades old, while anti-virus software needs to be updated several times a day to keep it on an adequate level of capability to block emerging and constantly developing threats. The value implication of this insight is that normal discounting methods that are used when evaluating economic value over time are not sufficient when considering value of software, which will be developed in the future, since the face value of the artifact does not stay constant over the time.

Software artifacts consist of two types of data: instructions for computer hardware and embedded information. The latter includes all text, images, sounds as well as information that is passed to external devices as forms of instructions [19]. The instruction part of the software artifact is what makes software behave like virtual machines that do things [34]. Software goods that consist mainly of instructions can be considered as tools that help people to get jobs done. Usually, when technology enables us to get things done, there emerges a dominant design [35], and hence there is in the longer run little variance in preferences – or the desire for utility - for software that is low in the information content. If there is no service component linked to the software, the offering of one firm scales easily and hence can result in capturing a monopolistic market share.

In contrast, when the embedded information content of the software is high, or the purpose of the software is to present information interactively, the preferences of the consumers behave very differently [see e.g., 36]. This is due to the fact that information and instruction content are valued differently: While the interactive part is valued for what it does, information is valued for what it teaches us or how it influences us [19]. Generally, there is a large variance in preferences for information, for both entertainment and education purposes. Moreover, these types of products suffer somewhat similar issues than information goods, once the users learn the information, the utility of the software artifact decreases. Prime examples of this kind of software artifacts are computer games. Indeed, computer games are no longer programmed, they are designed since the storyline, graphics, and environment of the game grow in importance related to technical aspects of the program [19]. Once a game is released, it might sell for only less than a year after its initial release. Moreover, once a person has completed the game once, his interest in the program is decreased since there is no element of novelty anymore in the information content.

3.2 Software Designs

As a system, technology is a collection of subsystems that are bound together with architecture, and each subsystem can be a system of other subsystems. The key insight from general systems theory is that a system cannot be comprehended as only through its parts, but needs to be considered as a whole.

According to Schilling [30]

Modularity is a general systems concept: is a continuum describing the degree to which a system's components can be separated and recombined, and it refers both to the tightness of coupling between components and the degree to which "rules" of the system architecture enable (or prohibit) the mixing and matching of components.

The level of modularity in software artifacts varies significantly, and it is not necessarily tied to modularity of the technology, which was used to generate the artifact. That is, a modular technology can result in highly integrated tightly coupled artifact systems. While this seems initially counterintuitive, it becomes clear after one considers the process of compiling software, where several source files are compiled and linked to become one binary executable. In this process the modularity of the technology is decreased and the modules loose their autonomy: it is no longer possible to easily exchange the compiled modules and in order for the system to work as designed, each module needs to work.

However, one software artifact can consist of several (executable and non-executable) files. In this case the system retains part of the modularity of the technology. For such modular product to be realized, several interfaces are required to define the architecture of the system [37,38]. In software, this modular design has several advantages: modular system can be upgraded or modified by exchanging modules to enhanced versions, and documented modular interfaces enable user driven innovation [39,40]. Modern computer games where users can create new scenarios or modifications are a prime example of the latter. Moreover, modularity enables the emergence of complements, which can be a significant source of value for a software product [41,42].

Modularity is a powerful concept, since modular designs include what Baldwin and Clark [38] call "option value". In their work combining the research streams of real options and complexity theory they identify six modular operations: splitting, substituting, augmenting, excluding, inverting, and porting. After developing theoretical measures of value for performing each of the operation, they present history of the computing industry as an example of how modularity works. The problem of modular design is, that while modularity enables more efficiently constructing a product family, it can lead to loosing the control of the design, that is, the parts of the design provided by the original vendor are no longer the value critical elements.

The power of modularity of design is that much of the complexity can be hidden under layers of abstraction. Modularity, measured often as coupling and cohesion in software engineering, has much benefits, including more comprehensible design and as a consequence result in better developer performance [43,44], can boost the innovation rate at each module, and enable better system reconfigurability [38]. However, this comes with a cost: First, even software with well defined architecture and internal interfaces tend to degrade over time. That is, incremental changes break the architecture and make the modules more tightly coupled if efforts are not spent to prevent this. This is a general property of technology and other complex systems and in software engineering it is known as Lehman's law [45]. When a complex system becomes more integrated, it looses its adaptability [46]. Moreover, the links become more numerous and less general, even to an extent that the abstracting effect of the modular system is lost. There is little use in modularity, if the software designer needs to be concerned with the internal structures of modules.

Clearly, not only the requirements, but also the architecture of the software needs to be value-based, if the long run value of the design is to be optimized. Unfortunately, this is not often the case when firms follow the client or market requirements to stay with the competition, especially when developing products on internet time [47].

3.3 Software Knowledge

The final aspect that we take on software as a technology is that of technological knowledge and competence. Currently, knowledge and technological capability are increasingly in the core of creating competitive advantage for companies [21,48,33] in high tech industries, like semiconductors, biotechnology, electronics, and software, where the development costs of new products can form a significant part of the cost structure of the entire company.

Defining the knowledge part of software is not straightforward unless one knows a bit of psychological aspects of programming. Hence, we start by briefly introducing a psychological view of how software is created. When a software engineer starts to write software that conforms to the previously designed requirements, he goes through a series of tasks. First, the problem is analyzed and formalized so that it can be solved with a computer, after which architecture and components of the solution are designed. This designing follows a cognitive problem solving process, where the software engineer combines external and codified knowledge to his own tacit knowledge creating a mental model of the solution [49-51]. After the model of the solution has been created, it is codified into a message using a programming language [31]. The result of the process of programming is a stream of textual information that resides on a computer or a similar platform. In this sense, the software code is only a projection of the solution developed by the programmer. Several finer aspects, especially why something is done like it is, remain tacit. In essence the codified form and the tacit form of software are intimately linked, and in this way software is tied to the people or organization that developed the software.

Clearly this knowledge is valuable and hence knowledge creation should be included in the value considerations, for example through integrating VBSE and experience factory [52], which is a general knowledge management framework for software engineering organizations. The value of knowledge comes from the fact that ability to learn is a function of what is already known and hence software firms who are on the edge of technology development often invest in projects for the main reason of learning. The downside for knowledge creation is, that it can lead to islands of specialization, where only one person or a small group holds a piece of tacit knowledge that is critical to the software development organization. If this happens it gives these employees an edge in the considerations of how the created value should be distributed among the stakeholders, thus enabling a potentially negative impact on the organizational knowledge distribution.

4 Synthesizing the Two Perspectives into a Value Decomposition Matrix

In the previous two sections we presented two views on value. First, we addressed the issue through three value components: intrinsic value, externalities, and option value. Second, we discussed three different views on software: as artifact, as design and as knowledge. Based on this discussion, we propose a value decomposition matrix to aid in considering the different aspects of value. The matrix is shown below in Table 1. Each cell in the cross-section of a view on software (rows) and value sources (columns) contains an illustrative question to aid in utilizing the nine different combinations in value considerations. The current limitation of the matrix is, that it mostly focuses on the view of the value to the customers and the organization, hence largely disregarding the value considerations that are relevant to employees. More work will be needed here in the future to integrate this third stakeholder group into the value decomposition matrix. Moreover, the framework is focused on market-driven development that takes place in software product firms.

Table 1. Value decomposition matrix

	Intrinsic value	Externalities	Option value
Software artifact	What is the direct value of this decision to the users of the software?	What is the indirect value of this decision to the users of the software through enabling connectivity to other users or software components?	What future software acquisition or enhancement options does this development decision provide for the users?
Software design	What is the direct value of this decision to our ability to create software artifacts?[1]	What is the value of this development decision on our ability to create connectivity and compatibility to our software artifacts?	What is the value of this development decision in terms of modular options?
Software knowledge	What do we learn directly by making this decision?	What do other parties that provide value for the users of our software learn if we take this decision?	What kinds of future learning options does this decision enable us to pursue?

---

[1] Consider that software design can be used to create several different artefacts (e.g. a product line).

Finally, we propose 5 potential avenues of future research in VBSE:

1. External value sources, like complements and network externalities need to be taken into account in value considerations.
2. Modularity, in terms of modular options and as an enabler for maintenance is a significant source for long-term value.
3. Market mechanisms have been the most successful institution in dividing utility in society and they provide a potential avenue for further research in VBSE.
4. Most firms do not create win-win, but win-loose less (firm-customer) situations, if they achieve lock-in. Hence, win-win does not necessarily create the most optimal solution for the stakeholder that has the most power in decision making.
5. Experience factory or some other knowledge management concept should be integrated in VBSE.

References

1. Biffl, S., Aurum, A., Boehm, B., Erdogmus, H., Grünbacher, P.: Value-Based Software Engineering. Springer, Heidelberg (2005)
2. Huang, L., Boehm, B.: How Much Software Quality Investment Is Enough: A Value-Based Approach. IEEE Software 23, 88–95 (2006)
3. Kitchenham, B., Pfleeger, S., Pickard, L., Jones, P., Hoaglin, D., El Emam, K., Rosenberg, J.: Preliminary guidelines for empirical research in software engineering. IEEE Transactions on Software Engineering 28, 721–734 (2002)
4. Jain, A., Boehm, B.: Developing a theory of value-based software engineering. In: Proceedings of the seventh international workshop on Economics-driven software engineering research, pp. 1–5. ACM Press, St. Louis (2005)
5. Erdogmus, H., Favaro, J., Halling, M.: Valuation of Software Initiatives Under Uncertainty: Concepts, Issues, and Techniques. In: Biffl, S., Aurum, A., Boehm, B.W., Erdogmus, H., Grünbacher, P. (eds.) Value-Based Software Engineering, Heidelberg, pp. 39–66 (2006)
6. Grünbacher, P., Köszegi, S., Biffl, S.: Stakeholder Value Proposition Elicitation and Reconciliation. In: Value-Based Software Engineering, pp. 133–154 (2006)
7. Parkin, M.: Economics. Pearson Education, Boston (2008)
8. Briggs, R., Gruenbacher, P.: EasyWinWin: Managing Complexity in Requirements Negotiation with GSS. In: Proceedings of the 35th Annual Hawaii International Conference on System Sciences. IEEE Computer Society, Big Island (2002)
9. Oza, N., Biffl, S., Frühwirth, C., Selioukova, Y., Sarapisto, R.: Reducing the Risk of Misalignment between Software Process Improvement Initiatives and Stakeholder Values. In: Industrial Proceedings of EuroSPI 2008, Publizon, Dublin, pp. 6.9-6.18 (2008)
10. Keeney, R.L., Raiffa, H., Rajala, D.W.: Decisions with Multiple Objectives: Preferences and Value Trade-Offs. IEEE Transactions on Systems, Man, and Cybernetics 9, 403 (1979)
11. Brynjolfsson, E., Kemerer, C.F.: Network Externalities in Microcomputer Software: An Econometric Analysis of the Spreadsheet Market. Management Science 42, 1627–1647 (1996)

12. Gandal, N.: Competing Compatibility Standards and Network Externalities in the PC Software Market. The Review of Economics and Statistics 77, 599–608 (1995)
13. Katz, M.L., Shapiro, C.: Network Externalities, Competition, and Compatibility. The American Economic Review 75, 424–440 (1985)
14. Brandenburger, A.M., Nalebuff, B.J.: Co-Opetition: A Revolution Mindset That Combines Competition and Cooperation: The Game Theory Strategy That's Changing the Game of Business. Doubleday, New York (1996)
15. Metcalfe, B.: Metcalfe's Law: A network becomes more valuable as it reaches more users. InfoWorld 17, 53 (1995)
16. Gallaugher, J.M., Wang, Y.: Understanding Network Effects in Software Markets: Evidence from Web Server Pricing. MIS Quarterly 26, 303–327 (2002)
17. Kotler, P., Keller, K.L.: Marketing Management. Prentice Hall, Upper Saddle River (2006)
18. Nelson, P.: Information and Consumer Behavior. Journal of Political Economy 78, 311 (1970)
19. Messerschmitt, D.G., Szyperski, C.: Software Ecosystem: Understanding an Indispensable Technology and Industry. The MIT Press, Cambridge (2003)
20. Rohlfs, J.H.: Bandwagon effects in high-technology industries. MIT Press, Cambridge (2001)
21. Boztepe, S.: Toward a framework of product development for global markets: a user-value-based approach. Design Studies 28, 513–533 (2007)
22. Lee, Y., O'Connor, G.: New product launch strategy for network effects products. Journal of the Academy of Marketing Science 31, 241–255 (2003)
23. Dane, E., Pratt, M.G.: Exploring Intuition and Its Role in Managerial Decision Making. Academy of Management Review 32, 33–54 (2007)
24. Shapiro, C., Varian, H.R.: Information rules a strategic guide to the network economy. Harvard Business School Press, Boston (1999)
25. Klemperer, P.: Markets with Consumer Switching Costs. The Quarterly Journal of Economics 102, 375–394 (1987)
26. Arthur, W.B.: Competing Technologies, Increasing Returns, and Lock-In by Historical Events. The Economic Journal 99, 116–131 (1989)
27. Boehm, B.W., Ross, R.: Theory-W Software Project-Management - Principles and Examples. IEEE Transactions on Software Engineering 15, 902–916 (1989)
28. Bowman, C., Ambrosini, V.: Value creation versus value capture: Towards a coherent definition of value in strategy. British Journal of Management 11, 1–15 (2000)
29. Schilling, M.A.: Technological Lockout: An Integrative Model of the Economic and Strategic Factors Driving Technology Success and Failure. Academy of Management Review 23, 267–284 (1998)
30. Schilling, M.A.: Toward a General Modular Systems Theory and Its Application to Interfirm Product Modularity. The Academy of Management Review 25, 312–334 (2000)
31. Cowan, R., Foray, D.: The Economics of Codification and the Diffusion of Knowledge. Industrial & Corporate Change 6, 595–622 (1997)
32. Varian, H.R., Farrell, J., Shapiro, C.: The Economics of Information Technology: An Introduction. Cambridge University Press, Cambridge (2004)
33. Teece, D.J.: Technology and Technology Transfer: Mansfieldian Inspirations and Subsequent Developments. Journal of Technology Transfer 30, 17 (2005)
34. Quintas, P.: Programmed Innovation? Trajectories of Change in Software Development. Information Technology & People 7, 25–47 (1994)

35. Anderson, P., Tushman, M.L.: Technological Discontinuities and Dominant Designs - a Cyclical Model of Technological-Change. Administrative Science Quarterly 35, 604–633 (1990)
36. Vogel, H.L.: Entertainment Industry Economics: A Guide for Financial Analysis. Cambridge University Press, Cambridge (2001)
37. Abernathy, W.J., Clark, K.B.: Innovation: Mapping the winds of creative destruction. Research Policy 14, 3–22 (1985)
38. Baldwin, C.Y., Clark, K.B.: Design Rules: The Power of Modularity. MIT Press, Cambridge (2000)
39. Franke, N., Hippel, E.V.: Satisfying heterogeneous user needs via innovation toolkits: the case of Apache security software. Research Policy 32, 1199–1215 (2003)
40. Schilling, M.A.: Intraorganizational Technology. In: Baum, J.A.C. (ed.) Companion to Organizations, pp. 158–180. Blackwell Publishers, Malden (2002)
41. Nambisan, S.: Complementary product integration by high-technology new ventures: The role of initial technology strategy. Management Science 48, 382–398 (2002)
42. Sengupta, S., Sengupta, S.: Some Approaches to Complementary Product Strategy. Journal of Product Innovation Management 15, 352 (1998)
43. Banker, R.D., Datar, S.M., Kemerer, C.F., Zweig, D.: Software Complexity and Maintenance Costs. Communications of the ACM 36, 81–94 (1993)
44. Kemerer, C.: Software complexity and software maintenance: A survey of empirical research. Annals of Software Engineering 1, 1–22 (1995)
45. Lehman, M., Ramil, J., Wernick, P., Perry, D., Turski, W.: Metrics and laws of software evolution-the nineties view. In: Proceedings of the Fourth International Software Metrics Symposium, pp. 20–32. IEEE Computer Society, Albuquerque (1997)
46. Orton, J.D., Weick, K.E.: Loosely Coupled Systems: A Reconceptualization. The Academy of Management Review 15, 203–223 (1990)
47. Cusumano, M.A., Yoffie, D.B.: Competing on Internet Time – Lessons from Netscape and Its Battle with Microsoft. Free Press, New York (1998)
48. Helfat, C.E., Peteraf, M.A.: The dynamic resource-based view: Capability lifecycles. Strategic Management Journal 24, 997–1010 (2003)
49. Vessey, I.: The role of cognitive fit in the relationship between software comprehension and modification. MIS Quarterly 30, 29–55 (2006)
50. Zhang, J.: The nature of external representations in problem solving. Cognitive Science 21, 179–217 (1997)
51. Zhang, J., Norman, D.A.: Representations in distributed cognitive tasks. Cognitive Science 18, 87–122 (1994)
52. Basili, V.: The Experience Factory and its relationship to other Improvement Paradigms. In: Sommerville, I., Paul, M. (eds.) ESEC 1993. LNCS, vol. 717, pp. 68–83. Springer, Heidelberg (1993)

On Business-Driven IT Security Management and Mismatches between Security Requirements in Firms, Industry Standards and Research Work

Christian Frühwirth

Helsinki University of Technology, Software Business Laboratory
Otaniementie 17, Espoo, Finland
christian.fruehwirth@tkk.fi

Abstract. Industry managers have long recognized the vital importance of information security for their businesses, but at the same time they perceived security as a technology-driven rather then a business-driven field. Today, this notion is changing and security management is shifting from technology- to business-oriented approaches. Whereas there is evidence of this shift in the literature, this paper argues that security standards and academic work have not yet taken it fully into account. We examine whether this disconnect has lead to a misalignment of IT security requirements in businesses versus industry standards and academic research. We conducted 13 interviews with practitioners from 9 different firms to investigate this question. The results present evidence for a significant gap between security requirements in industry standards and actually reported security vulnerabilities. We further find mismatches between the prioritization of security factors in businesses, standards and real-world threats. We conclude that security in companies serves the business need of protecting information availability to keep the business running at all times.

Keywords: Software Security, IT Security Management, security standards, software vulnerabilities.

1 Introduction

Managers in the software industry have long recognized the vital importance of information security for their businesses, but at the same time they perceived security as a technology-driven field rather then a business-driven one. Several developments in recent years have started to change this point of view: Rising costs of security measures [1] and an increasing risk of financial loss due to security incidents [2], [3], [4] are forcing companies to re-establish executive control over information security issues in their organization. Managers have taken action and today, the transition from a technical- to a business-oriented approach on information security is under full steam [5]. This transition however requires significant efforts and problems arise where business requirements for information security and standard practices are mismatched. This work investigates such mismatches by analyzing arguments from the literature and industry practitioners. We report on a series of 13 interviews that were conducted with a selected group of industry professionals of 9 different companies.

F. Bomarius et al. (Eds.): PROFES 2009, LNBIP 32, pp. 375–385, 2009.
© Springer-Verlag Berlin Heidelberg 2009

1.1 Terminology

Information security is defined by its objectives, as the assurance of confidentiality, integrity and availability of information. Literature refers to this concept as the "CIA triad" [6]. Confidentiality provides the secrecy of data to prevent unauthorized access or disclosure. Integrity refers to the reliability and trustworthiness of data. Availability ensures reliable and timely access to information for authorized individuals.

Security management strives to provide appropriate organizational and technological measures to fulfill these objectives. The failure to do so can result in a security vulnerability, threat or incident. A vulnerability is a point of weakness in a system. If this weakness is exposed and can be exploited it becomes a threat. The chance that such exploitation actually occurs is called risk. Security management thus acts as a distinct part of risk management and works on handling such risks in an economical way. A security incident is a violation a information security policy. It is any actual or anticipated act that threatens the confidentiality, integrity or availability of information in an unauthorized, unacceptable or illegal way. A vulnerability, which enables such a threat, can be considered an incident as well.

1.2 Objectives

Whereas there is strong evidence of a shift from technology to business driven security management in the practitioner literature [5], [7], [8], [9] our observation is that security standards and academic work have not fully taken it into account. We thus form the following proposition:

(P1) "The field of Information security management is transforming from a technology- to a business driven approach."

The key motivation of this research is to examine whether this disconnect has lead to misalignment of it security requirements in businesses versus in industry standards and research work. We formulate our research question as:

(Q1) "Is there a misalignment between the business requirements for information security by practitioners, current industry standards and academic research?"

We will conduct our investigation by examining the existing literature and conducting 13 interviews with practitioners from 9 different firms. The main contribution of investigating these issues lies in the possibility to identify the gaps between what businesses demand and what the actual work- and academic practices in information security provide. Knowing these gaps will allow researchers to better target their efforts towards industry's requirements in the future, hence increasing the applicability of their work.

The remainder of this text is structured as follows: In section 1 we present related literature from different research communities and analyze their findings in the light of our proposition and research question. Section 2 introduces the methodology and presents the main findings of the interview series. The last section compiles the output of section 1 and 2 and compares their findings to identify possible gaps between them.

2 Related Work

2.1 Transition towards Business Driven Security Management

The classic definition of security in software is to assure the confidentiality, integrity and availability of data [6]. We see that this particular concept of security is value neutral and contains no references to business requirements. More modern definitions of security, like the ISO 17799 standard address this shortcoming: ISO 17799:2005 adds a business perspective and refers to security as *"the process of protecting information from a wide range of threats in order to ensure business continuity, minimize business damage and maximize return on investment (ROI) by preserving confidentiality, integrity and availability of information"* [10]. We can take ISO's choice to recognize the business factor in security as the first argument to support *P1*. We will further refer to this argument as *(P1-A1)*.

Information security is further recognized as a significant cost factor in organizational budgets and international studies have shown, that company security investments have been steadily increasing for years [1]. One problem with increasing security investments in companies is the necessary budget authority. An organization's technical personnel, which is associated with such investments, has typically less budget authority then what would be required for bigger investments, hence managers or executives need to step in. Thus, as the size of investments increase, the responsibility for the investment decisions is gradually delegated towards higher levels of organizational hierarchy. This shift in security investment responsibilities towards the executive organizational levels, due to the increased investment size, is our second argument to support *P1 (P1-A2)*. How far up the hierarchy the investment decisions are being pushed will be laid out in the interview analysis of section 2.

While the investments in security grew, so has the number of published security vulnerabilities in software products. The "National Vulnerability Database (NVD)" of the U.S. department for Homeland Security collects newly published software security vulnerabilities since 2002. It showed a climbing number of new vulnerability reports from the very beginning [11]. By October 2008, 17 new vulnerabilities are published each day and the NVD now holds a record number of over 33.000 known software vulnerabilities. Disclosed security vulnerabilities are important to business executives and financial investors because of their impact on the market performance of the affected companies. Recent empirical research by Telang [4], Campbell [2], Cavusoglu [12] and Ishiguro [3] has demonstrated the negative effects of disclosed security vulnerabilities on a companies' performance on the stock market. Telang quantified this negative market impact with stock price drops between -0.63% and -2,1% [4]. Telang also identified cases where the timing of the software vulnerability's disclosure was used as a strategic weapon to influence the stock market price of a firm's competitor. [4] Alongside such punctual stock market losses, the average losses due to security incidents have risen as well since 2003 [13].

This is our third argument to support *P1*: Because the impact of security incidents now reaches beyond the operational level of a company, and literally into the pockets of shareholders and investors, business managers are highly incentivized to take control of security management issues *(P1-A3)*.

We can further extend the argument of manager incentives for public companies on the US market. In 2002 the U.S. government enacted the Sarbanes Oxley Act (SOX) as a reaction to the ENRON financial scandal. Section 404 of SOX requires companies to establish internal control systems that prevent financial fraud and specifies, that these controls include IT systems as well as business processes. Where companies fail to meet these legal requirements, their executives are held directly accountable. Hence, SOX provides additional incentives for executives to take on information security issues in their company.

2.2 Misalignment between Industry Requirements, Standards and Academic Research

There are numerous standards for information security in the industry. Well known examples are the early "trusted computer system evaluation criteria" (TCSEC)[1] from 1985 [14], the later ITSEC or today's "Common Criteria" (CC) [15] and ISO 17799 [10]. Empirical work by Myagmar [13] on the National Vulnerability Database has shown that there is a significant mismatch between these standards' requirements and the security vulnerabilities that are discovered in real life. Myagmar found that even the latest iteration of the CC standard put more emphasis on securing information *integrity* then the actual number of occurring integrity vulnerabilities would justify. At the same time the CC contains too little *availability* requirements, compared to the high number of availability related vulnerabilities recorded in the NVD. This quantitative gap between the requirements in industry standards and actually reported security vulnerabilities is our first argument to support *Q1* (*Q1-A1*).

The identified gap however seems to be slowly closing, as further work by Myagmar shows [13]. From 1996 to 2005 the extent of the mismatch between vulnerabilities and the standard's security requirements was continuously reduced. We argue that this is partly due to the increased involvement of the industry in the development process of security standards. While primarily governments developed the first major security standards for military purposes, newer versions, like the CC Version 3.1, are products of cooperation between industrial and governmental organizations and hence take business requirements into closer consideration. An additional argument to support *P1* is thus the shrinking gap between the real-world security vulnerabilities and industry standards, due to the increased involvement of industry stakeholders in standard development (*P1-A4*).

The academic community has also addressed the problem of mismatched requirements between industry and research work in its discussion. Recognized author Schneier [16] for example criticized investments in quantum cryptography by stating: *"[Quantum cryptography] as a product, it has no future"*. He explained his argument by noting that *"It's not that quantum cryptography might be insecure; it's that cryptography is already sufficiently secure"* [16]. Schneier implies that researches are sometimes looking to solve security problems in the wrong places. He raises the issue that security research tends to focus on improving security factors that are of less importance to businesses than others: The research in quantum cryptography for example emphasizes information confidentiality and integrity over availability. Scholars like

---

[1] TCSEC is also commonly known as "the orange book", referring to its origins in the "Rainbow" book series on computer security, published by the U.S. Department of Defense.

Neubauer [8] argue in a similar direction and suggest that security issues should be addressed from a value-based point of view, hence a business perspective. Neubauer's argument is supported by scholars from the software engineering literature, like Boehm [17] and Biffl [18], who have long called for stronger considerations of value concepts. We will take Schneier's example and the other author's call for increased value considerations as arguments to support both *P1* and *Q1* (*P1-A5, Q1-A2*).

3 Interviews with Industry Practitioners

3.1 Methodology

The presented interviews are part of a larger study on security management practices in the industry. To represent "the industry" we identified 6 different company types that took part in the study: Retail, Construction, IT, Trade, Consulting and Public services.

The study was conducted in 2007 through structured interviews, following a questionnaire with 69 questions. The duration of the interviews ranged from 50 to 90 minutes. Every interview-session was followed up by an open feedback conversation where the interviewees could explain their answers in more detail.

Each company type had to be represented by at least 1 interviewee, who either held a managerial-, operational-, or consulting position for at least 2 years that was related to IT security issues. The number of interviewees in each of these three job categories is shown in Table 1. A total number of 13 interviews were conducted. All questionnaires were complete and used for the analysis. All figures presented in this work are averages across the complete data set, unless stated otherwise. The size of the data set prohibits extensive regression analysis, thus the results are limited in their generalizability, but should be considered as indicators that invite future work with larger samples.

The 13 interviewees worked for 9 different companies. Out these 9 companies, 6 were large, multi-national corporations with computer networks of more then 1000 hosts. Although only 5 of 9 companies stated that information technology was among their core business areas, all (100%) described IT as vital for their business success. A dedicated IT Security department was employed by 6 out of 9. Those who had no security department where smaller companies, which instead employed dedicated individuals that took on security related tasks. None of the interviewees stated that they had no security caretaker whatsoever.

This work presents the first part of this study's results, hence only a subset of the total 69 questions in the questionnaire was used in this paper. The analysis of the remaining questions is subject to future work.

3.2 Managerial Versus Operational View of Security

In the beginning of the interview, the interviewees were asked to rate their approach towards IT security on a scale of 1 to 5, where 1 equals a completely technical approach and 5 equals an organizational one. The term "organizational" was used for reasons of readability in the questionnaire as substitute for "business- or value-driven approach" and explained verbally to the interviewees. Table 1 shows that interviewees in managerial roles generally rated their security approach as more business driven then people with operational roles. However, the average rating among all groups (mean average of each group dived by the number of groups) at 3,2 on a 1 to 5 scale shows that security issues are not perceived as a purely organizational issue. We interpret this result as a supporting argument for an ongoing transition from technology to business oriented approaches. Thus, this interpretation is considered as argument *(P1-A6)* to support *(P1)*.

Table 1. Interviewees and their view on security, categorized in three groups, according to the interviewee's role in the company

Interviewees role in the company	Operational	Managerial	Consulting	Total
Number of interviewees in group	3	9	1	13
Average answer to "What is your approach to security on a scale of 1-5?" 1 = technical, 5 = organizational	Mean: 2,3 (Median: 2)	3,2 (3)	4 (4)	3,2 (3)
"Do you know the concept of the CIA triad?"	1 Yes answer	4 Yes answers	1 Yes answer	6 Yes answers

As control question, the interviewees were asked whether they were familiar with the concept of the CIA triad (confidentiality, integrity, availability). Interviewee groups with a stronger organizational view on security were more likely to know the CIA concept then those with a more technical view.

It needs to be noted that the small number of interviewees and especially the single member in the group "Consulting" does not allow to identify global trends. The results should instead be considered as anecdotal evidence that encourage further empirical investigation.

3.3 Importance of Security Factors

In section 1 we have identified the arguments *(Q-1A1)* and *(Q1-A2)* that described the mismatch between the distributions of emphasis among the different security factors in real-life software vulnerabilities versus industry standards and academic research. So far though, we lacked the comparison with the practitioners' point of view. Hence, we asked the interviewees on which security factors they focus on in their companies. The interviewees answered by distributing 100 points among 5 security factors. Factors, which were more important to the company should receive more points then those, which were less important. The result is pictured in Figure 1.

Figure 1 shows that the interviewees clearly regarded data availability as the most important security factor. Because we analysed 5 different security factors, a direct comparison with Myagmar's [14] findings (see section 1, *Q1-A1*), who analyzed only 4 factors is not possible. Nevertheless, we can compare the relative ranking of the

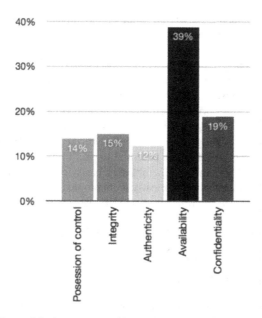

Fig. 1. Comparison of the importance of individual security factors to the interviewees

Table 2. Comparing the importance ranking of security factors between interviewees, industry standard and actual software vulnerabilities

Ranking of by interviewees	Ranking in industry standard (Myagmar 2006, Figure 6.)	Ranking in actual vulnerabilities (Myagmar 2006, Figure 6.)
1. Availability	1. Authentication	1. Authentication
2. Confidentiality	2. Integrity	2. Availability
3. Integrity	3. Availability	3. Integrity
4. Authenticity	4. Confidentiality	4. Confidentiality

4 factors both works have in common. Table 2 shows that the interviewees had very different priorities for their companies then Myagmar indentified in the Common Criteria (CC) industry standard and the National Vulnerability Database.

While the interviewees' companies had the strongest focus on data availability, followed by confidentiality, the CC industry standard ranked availability 3rd and confidentiality 4th. A similar mismatch is visible in the ranking of the actually recorded vulnerabilities in the NVD.

During the interview feedback session, one of the interviewees, an IT manager of a retail company, explained his decision to emphasize data availability over other security factors: *"Our stores have a combined sale volume of more then 1 million EUR per business day. A breach of data confidentiality would be horrible, but we would still be able to continue sales operations. We would loose sales though if data availability was suddenly interrupted."* Hence, from the companies' point of view, investing in availability is a simple business decision. The high availability rating was further not specific to the retail industry. Nearly all other interviewees chose similar priorities: 10 out of 13 interviewees had allocated 40% or more of their points to secure information availability.

The businesses' strong emphasis on availability clearly collides with the priorities set by the industry standards, however it is not unheard of that standards are not always applied as they are supposed to be. What is more surprising though, is the mismatch between the businesses' security priorities and real-world security vulnerabilities that were recorded by the NVD as shown in Table 2. We argue that this is due to the lack of a business-value based ranking of vulnerabilities in the NVD. While companies can prioritize security aspects based on the potential impact of a security breach on business value (e.g. sales), the NVD rates vulnerabilities based on the Common Vulnerability Scoring System (CVSS), which uses mostly technological metrics [19]. These different approaches in assessing the importance of security aspects might be responsible for the observed mismatch.

Hence, we can support Q1 *(Q1-A3)* by concluding that there is a clear mismatch between security requirements in businesses, standards and real-world vulnerabilities.

3.4 Who Drives Security Investments?

The problem of funding decisions in growing security investment was identified in section 1. We argued in *(P1-A2)* that due to the increased investment volume, the funding decisions are taken at higher levels of company hierarchy then before, thus by managers rather then technicians. The interviewees were asked to provide their experience on this issue by noting who drove past IT security investments in their company and who drives them now.

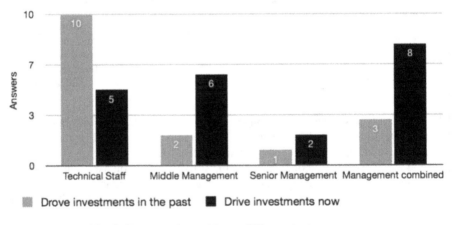

Fig. 2. Current and past drivers of IT security investments

The interviewees' answers are pictured in Figure 2. In the interviewees' experience, technical personnel used to be the strongest security investment driver and clearly outnumbered the combined senior and middle management 10 to 3. This finding is consistent with the notion that information security originated as a technology driven field. Today however, the emphasis has changed and security investments lie now in the hands of managers. Figure 2 further shows that this change is more visible in middle management then in senior management, where the increase of investment drivers is significantly smaller. The overall movement however presents a clear direction, towards more involvement of business executives in IT security. Hence, the interviewees' response confirms our initial claim in *(P1-A2)*.

4 Conclusion

In the course of this work we presented 5 arguments that support our proposition

(P1) "The field of Information security management is transforming from a technology- to a business driven approach."

P1-A1: Modern security standards adopt the concept of business value in their definition of security.

P1-A2: Increasing security investment costs move the investment responsibilities towards higher levels of management.

P1-A3: The financial impact of security incidents incentivizes managers to take control of security management

P1-A4: Businesses are increasingly involved in the development of security standards.

P1-A5: Authors in the academic literature are calling for increased value considerations in security research.

The purpose of this work was to analyze whether this transformation has led to misalignments between the requirements for information security by businesses, industry standards and academic research. We have presented three arguments, which addressed that question:

Q1-A1: Literature identified a quantitative gap between security requirements in industry standards and actually reported security vulnerabilities.

Q1-A2: Authors in the literature criticized a gap between academic security research and the security needs of companies

Q1-A3: The conducted interviews with industry practitioners showed a clear mismatch between businesses' security requirements, standards and actual security vulnerabilities.

Based on the presented arguments, we conclude that security management has indeed become a business issue and what used to be a technical domain is now handled by managers. Today's security standards showed misalignments with security vulnerabilities that are discovered in the real world. However, literature indicated that the gap between standards and real-world could shrink over time.

A strong mismatch was identified between standards, real-world vulnerabilities and the need of practitioners. We found that security in companies clearly serves a business need, the need to keep the business running at all times. One can argue that this strong focus on information availability will increase as more business-minded people replace technicians in the roles of security investment drivers. However, newer empirical research [3] suggests that confidentiality issues become more important as well, as confidentiality breaches get more costly for firms. Hence, it remains unclear whether the identified mismatches between businesses and standards and businesses and real-world vulnerabilities are going to grow over time. Future work in this area will thus help us to focus the development of security management and further increase its application value for businesses.

References

1. Larsen, A.: Global security survey: Virus attack, http://Informationweek.com/743/security.htm (visited, October 2008)
2. Campbell, K., Gordon, L., Loeb, M., Zhou, L.: The Economic Cost of Publicly Announced Information Security Breaches: Empirical Evidence from the Stock Market. Journal of Computer Security 11(3), 431–448 (2003)
3. Ishiguro, M., Tanaka, H., Matsuura, K., Murase, I.: The Effect of Information Security Incidents on Corporate Values in the Japanese Stock Market. In: The Workshop on the Economics of Securing the Information Infrastructure, WESII (2006)
4. Telang, R., Wattal, S.: An Empirical Analysis of the Impact of Software Vulnerability Announcements on Firm Stock Price. IEEE Transactions on Software Engineering (2007)
5. Egan, M., Mather, T.: The Executive Guide to Information Security: Threats, Challenges, and Solutions. Addison-Wesley Professional, Reading (2004) ISBN: 0321304519
6. Bishop, M.: Introduction to Computer Security. Addison-Wesley Longman, Amsterdam (2004) ISBN-10: 0321247442
7. ISACA, Information Systems Audit and Control Association (2000), COBIT, http://www.isaca.org/COBIT (visited, May 2007)
8. Neubauer, Klemen, Biffl: Business Process-based Valuation of IT-Security. In: Proceedings of the seventh international workshop on Economics-driven software engineering research EDSER 2005 (2005)
9. Roeckle, H., Schimpf, G., Weidinger, R.: Process-oriented approach for role-finding to implement role-based security administration in a large industrial organization. In: Proceedings of the fifth ACM workshop on Role-based access control table of contents, pp. 103–110 (2000) ISBN:1-58113-259-X
10. ISO/IEC Std. ISO 17799:2005, Information Technology – Security Techniques - Code of Practice for Information Security Management, ISO (2005)
11. NVD, U.S. National Institute of Standards and Technology: National Vulnerability Database (NVD), http://nvd.nist.gov/ (visited October 21, 2008)
12. Cavusoglu, H., Mishra, B., Raghunathan, S.: The Effect of Internet Security Breach Announcements on Market Value: Capital Market Reactions for Breached Firms and Internet Security Developers. International Journal of Electronic Commerce 9(1), 69 (2004)
13. Myagmar, S., Yurcik, W.: Why Johnny Can Hack: The Mismatch between Vulnerabilities and Security Standards. In: IEEE International Symposium on Secure Software Engineering, ISSSE 2006 (2006)
14. DoD, Department of Defense (1983), Trusted Computer System Evaluation Criteria, 1983. DoD 5200.28-STD, Library No. S225, 7ll, http://csrc.ncsl.nist.gov/publications/secpubs/rainbow/std001.txt
15. CC, Common Criteria, and Common Criteria Recognition Agreement, (CCRA) (2006), http://www.commoncriteriaportal.org/ (visited, January 2009)

16. Schneier, B.: Crypto-Gram Newsletter, Issue (November 15, 2008,
    `http://www.schneier.com/crypto-gram-0811.html#4`
17. Boehm, B.: Value-Based Software Engineering: Overview and Agenda. Value-Based
    Software Engineering: Overview and Agenda 15(3), USC-CSE-2005-504 (2005)
18. Biffl, S.: Message from the Track Chairs SPPI. In: 32nd EUROMICRO Conference on
    Software Engineering and Advanced Applications, EUROMICRO 2006 (2006)
19. Mell, P., Scarfone, P.: A Complete Guide to the Common Vulnerability Scoring System
    Version 2.0. National Institute of Standards and Technology 2007 (2007),
    `http://www.first.org/cvss/cvss-guide.pdf`

The Waterfall Model in Large-Scale Development

Kai Petersen[1,2], Claes Wohlin[1], and Dejan Baca[1,2]

[1] Blekinge Institute of Technology, Box 520,
SE-37225 Ronneby, Sweden
kai.petersen@bth.se, claes.wohlin@bth.se, dejan.baca@bth.se
[2] Ericsson AB, Box 518,
SE-37123 Karlskrona, Sweden
kai.petersen@ericsson.com, dejan.baca@ericsson.com

Abstract. Waterfall development is still a widely used way of working in software development companies. Many problems have been reported related to the model. Commonly accepted problems are for example to cope with change and that defects all too often are detected too late in the software development process. However, many of the problems mentioned in literature are based on beliefs and experiences, and not on empirical evidence. To address this research gap, we compare the problems in literature with the results of a case study at Ericsson AB in Sweden, investigating issues in the waterfall model. The case study aims at validating or contradicting the beliefs of what the problems are in waterfall development through empirical research.

1 Introduction

The first publication on the waterfall model is credited to Walter Royce's article in 1970 (cf. [1]). In literature there seems to be an agreement on problems connected to the use of the waterfall model. Problems are (among others) that the model does not cope well with change, generates a lot of rework, and leads to unpredictable software quality due to late testing [2]. Despite the problems identified, the model is still widely used in software industry, some researchers are even convinced that it will be around for a much longer period of time (see [3]). The following trends can be seen in research. First, the model seems to be of very little interest for researchers to focus on as it seems to be old-fashioned. Instead, recent studies have much more focus on agile and incremental development. Secondly, there is very little empirical research backing up what we believe to know about the waterfall model. In order to identify the evidence provided by empirical research on the waterfall model we conducted the following search on Inspec & Compendex:

- ("waterfall model" OR "waterfall development") AND ("empirical" OR "case study" OR "industrial")

F. Bomarius et al. (Eds.): PROFES 2009, LNBIP 32, pp. 386–400, 2009.
© Springer-Verlag Berlin Heidelberg 2009

Inspec & Compendex was selected as it integrates many full-text databases in computing and thus is considered a good starting point. The search resulted in 33 publications where none of the publications had an explicit focus on studying the waterfall model in an industrial setting. Thus, most of the problems reported on the waterfall model are mainly based on researchers' beliefs and experience reports. Consequently, in order to provide substantial evidence on the usefulness of the waterfall model in industry empirical studies are needed. Evaluating the usefulness empirically aids decision making of whether to use the model in specific context (here large-scale-development).

To address this research gap we conducted a case study focusing on identifying issues in waterfall development and compare them to what has been said in literature. Furthermore, the issues identified are ranked based on their criticality. The case being studied is a development site of Ericsson AB, Sweden. The waterfall model was used at the company for several years. The case study has been conducted according to the guidelines provided by Yin (see [4]). The case study makes the following contributions to research on waterfall development: 1) Illustration of the waterfall implementation in practice within large-scale industrial software development, 2) Identification of issues related to the waterfall model and their prioritization showing the most critical issues, and 3) Comparison of case study results with state of the art (SotA).

The remainder of this paper is structured as follows: Section 2 provides an overview of related work. Thereafter, Section 3 illustrates the waterfall model used at the company. Section 4 presents the case study design. The analysis of the collected data is provided in Section 5 (qualitative analysis) and Section 6 (quantitative analysis). Section 7 presents a comparison of the case study findings and state of the art. Section 8 concludes the paper.

2   Related Work

Literature identifies a number of problems related to the waterfall model. An overview of the problems identified in literature is shown in Table 1. In addition to the identified articles we considered books discussing advantages and disadvantages of the waterfall model.

The waterfall model is connected to high costs and efforts [2][5]. That is, it requires approval of many documents, changes are costly to implement, iterations take a lot of effort and rework, and problems are usually pushed to later phases [2]. Few studies are explicitly focused on the waterfall model and some reasons for the failures of the waterfall approach have been identified. One reason mentioned by several studies is the management of a large scope, i.e. requirements cannot be managed well and has been identified as the main reason for failure (cf. [7] [9] [8]). Consequences have been that the customers' current needs are not addressed by the end of the project [7], resulting in that many of the features implemented are not used [9].

Additionally, there is a problem in integrating the overall system in the end and testing it [10]. A survey of 400 waterfall projects has shown that the software being developed is either not deployed or if deployed, it is not used. The

Table 1. Issues in Waterfall Development (State of the Art)

ID	Issue	Reference
L01	High effort and costs for writing and approving documents for each development phase.	[2][5]
L02	Extremely hard to respond to changes.	[2][5][6]
L03	When iterating a phase the iteration takes considerable effort for rework.	[2]
L04	When the system is put to use the customer discovers problems of early phases very late and system does not reflect current requirements.	[1] [2] [7]
L05	Problems of finished phases are left for later phases to solve.	[2]
L06	Management of a large scope of requirements that have to be baselined to continue with development.	[8] [7] [9]
L07	Big-bang integration and test of the whole system in the end of the project can lead to unexpected quality problems, high costs, and schedule overrun.	[10][1][11]
L08	Lack of opportunity for customer to provide feedback on the system.	[10]
L09	The waterfall model increases lead-time due to that large chunks of software artifacts have to be approved at each gate.	[12]

reasons for this are the change of needs and the lack of opportunity to clarify misunderstandings. This is caused by the lack of opportunity for the customer to provide feedback on the system [13]. Specifically, the waterfall model fails in the context of large-complex projects or exploratory projects [3].

On the other hand, waterfall development comes with advantages as well. The waterfall model is predictable and pays attention to planning the architecture and structure of the software system in detail which is especially important when dealing with large systems. Without having focus on architecture planning there is a risk that design decisions are based on tacit knowledge and not explicitly documented and reviewed [14]. Thus, the probability of overlooking architectural problems is high.

3   The Waterfall Model at the Company

The waterfall model used at the company runs through the phases requirements engineering, design & implementation, testing, release, and maintenance. Between all phases the documents have to pass a quality check, this approach is referred to as a stage-gate model (see for example [15]). An overview of the process is shown in Figure 1.

We explain the different phases and provide a selection of checklist-items to show what type of quality checks are made in order to decide whether the software artifact developed in a specific development phase can be passed on to the adjacent phase.

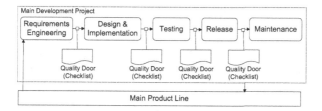

Fig. 1. Waterfall Development at the Company

Requirements Engineering: In this phase, the needs of the customers are identified and documented on a high abstraction level. Thereafter, the requirements are refined so that they can be used as input to the design and implementation phase. The requirements (on high as well as low abstraction level) are stored in a requirements repository. From this repository, the requirements to be implemented are selected from the repository. The number of requirements selected depends on the available resources for the project. As new products are not built from the scratch, parts from the old product (see main product line in Figure 1) are used as input to the requirements phase as well. At the quality gate (among others) it is checked whether all requirements are understood, agreed upon, and documented. Furthermore, it is checked whether the relevant stakeholders are identified and whether the solution would support the business strategy.

Design and Implementation: In the design phase the architecture of the system is created and documented. Thereafter, the actual development of the system takes place. The developers also conduct basic unit testing before handing the developed code over to the test phase. The quality gate checklist (among others) verifies whether the architecture has been evaluated, whether there are deviations from the requirements compared to the previous quality gate decision, and whether there is a deviation from planned time-line, effort, or product scope.

Testing: In this phase the system integration is tested regarding quality and functional aspects. In order to make a decision whether the the system can be deployed, measures of performance (e.g, throughput) are collected in the test laboratory. As the company provides complete solutions (including hardware and software) the tests have to be conducted on a variety of hardware and software configurations as those differ between customers. The outcome of the phase is reviewed according to a checklist to see whether the system has been verified and whether there are deviations from previous quality gate decisions in terms of quality and time, whether plans for hand-over of the product to the customer are defined according to company guidelines, and whether the outcome of the project meets the customers' requirements.

Release: In the release phase the product is brought into a shippable state. That is, release documentation is finalized (e.g. installation instructions of the system for customers and user-guides). Furthermore, build-instructions for the system have to be programmed. Build-instructions can be used to enable and disable features of the main product line to tailor the system to specific customer needs. At the quality gate (among others) it is checked whether the outcome meets the customers' requirements, whether the customer has accepted the outcome, and whether the final outcome was presented in time and fulfilled its quality requirements. A post-mortem analysis has to be performed as well.

Maintenance: After the product has been released to the customer it has to be maintained. That is, if customers discover problems in the product they report them to the company and get support in solving them. If the problems are due to faults in the product, packages for updating the system are delivered to the customers.

4   Case Study Design

The context in which the study is executed is Ericsson AB, a leading and global company offering solutions in the area of telecommunication and multimedia. Such solutions include charging systems for mobile phones, multimedia solutions and network solutions. The company is ISO 2001:2000 certified. The market in which the company operates can be characterized as highly dynamic with high innovation in products and solutions. The development model is market-driven, meaning that the requirements are collected from a large base of potential end-customers without knowing exactly who the customers will be.

4.1   Research Questions

The following main research questions should be answered in the case study:

- *RQ1: What are the most critical problems in waterfall development in large-scale industrial development?*
- *RQ2: What are the differences and similarities between state of the art and the case study results?*

The relevance of the research questions can be underlined as follows: The related work has shown a number of problems related to waterfall development. However, there is too little empirical evidence on the topic and thus more data points are needed. Furthermore, the criticality of problems is not addressed in any way so far, making it hard to decide in which way it is most beneficial to improve the model, or whether the introduction of a new way of working will help in improving the key challenges experienced in the waterfall model.

4.2   Case Selection and Units of Analysis

The case being studied is one development site of Ericsson AB. In order to understand the problems that occurred when the waterfall model was used at the company, three subsystems (S1, S2, and S3) are analyzed that have been built according to the model. The systems under investigation in this case study

Table 2. Units of Analysis

	Language	Size (LOC)	No. Persons
Overall System		>5,000,000	-
S1	C++	300,000	43
S2	C++	850,000	53
S3	Java	24,000	17
Apache	C++	220,000	90

have an overall size of approx. 2,000,000 LOC (as shown in Table 2). The LOC measure only includes code produced at the company (excluding third-party libraries). Furthermore, the number of persons involved in building the system are stated. A comparison of the system considered for this study and the size of the Apache web server shows that the system being studied is considerably larger and thus can be considered as large-scale.

4.3   Data Collection Procedures

The data is collected through interviews and from process documentation.

Selection of Interviewees. The interviewees were selected so that the overall development life cycle is covered, from requirements to testing and release. Furthermore, each role in the development process should be represented by at least two persons if possible. The selection of interviewees was done as follows:

1. A complete list of people available for the system being studied. Overall 153 people are on this list as shown in Table 2.
2. For the selection of persons we used cluster sampling. At least two persons from each role (the roles being the clusters) have been randomly selected from the list. The more persons are available for one role the more persons have been selected.
3. The selected interviewees received an e-mail explaining why they have been selected for the study. Furthermore, the mail contained information of the purpose of the study and an invitation for the interview. Overall, 44 persons have been contacted of which 33 accepted the invitation.

The distribution of people between different roles is shown in Table 3. The roles are divided into "What", "When", "How", "Quality Assurance", and "Life Cycle Management".

- *What:* This group of people is concerned with the decision of what to develop and includes people from strategic product management, technical managers and system managers.
- *When:* People in this group plan the time-line of software development from a technical and project management perspective.
- *How:* Here, the architecture is defined and the actual implementation of the system takes place. In addition, developers test their own code (unit tests).

Table 3. Distribution of Interviewees Between Roles and Units of Analysis

	S1	S2	S3	Total
What (Requirements)	2	1	1	4
When (Project Planning)	3	2	1	6
How (Implementation)	3	2	1	6
Quality Assurance	4	3	-	7
Life Cycle Management	6	4	-	10
Total	18	12	3	33

- *Quality Assurance:* Quality assurance is responsible for testing the software and reviewing documentation.
- *Life Cycle Management:* This includes all activities supporting the overall development process, like configuration management, maintenance and support, and packaging and shipment of the product.

Interview Design. The interview consists of five parts, the duration of the interviews was set to approximately one hour each. In the first part of the interviews the interviewees were provided with an introduction to the purpose of the study and explanation why they have been selected. The second part comprised questions regarding the interviewees background, experience, and current activities. Thereafter, the issues were collected through a semi-structured interview. To collect as many issues as possible the questions have been asked from three perspectives: bottlenecks, rework, and unnecessary work. The interviewees should always state what kind of bottleneck, rework, or unnecessary work they experienced, what caused it, and where it was located in the process.

Process Documentation. Process documentation has been studied to gain an in-depth understanding of the processes. Documentation for example includes process specifications, training material for processes, and presentations given to employees during unit meetings.

4.4   Data Analysis Approach

The problems related to the waterfall model at the company have been identified conducting the four steps outlined below. The steps are based on more than 30 hours of interview transcriptions and have been executed by the first author over a three month period.

1. *Clustering:* The raw data from the transcriptions is clustered, grouping statements belonging together. For example, all statements related to requirements engineering are grouped together. Thereafter, statements addressing similar areas within one group (e.g,. all areas that would relate to requirements engineering lead-times) are grouped.
2. *Derivation of Issue Statements:* The raw data contains detailed explanations and therefore is abstracted by deriving problem statements from the raw

data, explaining them shortly in one or two sentences. The result was a number of problem statements where statements varied in their abstraction level and could be further clustered.

3. *Mind-Mapping of Issue Statements:* The issue statements were grouped based on their relation to each other and their abstraction level. For example, problems related to requirements lead-times are grouped within one branch called "long requirements lead-times". This was documented in form of a mind-map. Issues with higher abstraction level are closer to the center of the mind map than issues with lower abstraction level.

4. *Validation of Issues:* In studies of qualitative nature there is always a risk that the data is biased by the interpretation of the researcher. Therefore, the issues have been validated in two workshops with three representatives from the company. The representatives have an in-depth knowledge of the processes. Together, the steps of analysis described here have been reproduced together with the authors and company representatives. For this a subset of randomly selected issue statements have been selected. No major disagreement has been discovered between the workshop participants on the outcome of the analysis. Thus, the validity of the issue statements can be considered as high.

After having identified the problems they are prioritized into A-problems (critical), B-problems (very important), C-problems (important), D-problems (less important), and E-problems (local). The actual limits on the classes is based on the results. The main objective of the classification is to systematize and structure the data and not to claim that these classes are optimal or suitable for another study.

A. The problem is mentioned by more than one role and more than one subsystem. Moreover, the problem has been referred to by more than $1/3$ of the respondents.

B. The problem is mentioned by more than one role and more than one subsystem. Moreover, the problem has been referred to by more than $1/5$ of the respondents.

C. The problem is mentioned by more than one role and more than one subsystem. Moreover, the problem has been referred to by more than $1/10$ of the respondents.

D. The problem is mentioned by more than one role and more than one subsystem. Moreover, it has been referred to by $1/10$ of the respondents or less.

E. The problem is only referred to by one role or one subsystem and thus considered a local or individual problem.

4.5   Threats to Validity

Threats to the validity of the outcome of the study are important to consider during the design of the study allowing to take actions mitigating them. Threats to validity in case study research are reported in [4]. The threats relevant to the study are: construct validity, external validity and reliability.

Construct Validity: Construct validity is concerned with obtaining the right measures for the concept being studies. One threat is the selection of people to obtain the appropriate sample for answering the research questions. Therefore, experienced people from the company selected a pool of interviewees as they know the persons and organization best. From this pool the random sample was taken. The selection by the representatives of the company was done having the following aspects in mind: process knowledge, roles, distribution across subsystems, and having a sufficient number of people involved (although balancing against costs). Furthermore, it is a threat that the presence of the researcher influences the outcome of the study. The threat is reduced as there has been a long cooperation between the company and university and the author collecting the data is also employed by the company and not viewed as being external. Construct validity is also threatened if interview questions are misunderstood or misinterpreted. To mitigate the threat pre-tests of the interview have been conducted.

External Validity: External validity is the ability to generalize the findings to a specific context as well as to general process models. One threat to validity is that only one case has been studied. Thus, the context and case have been described in detail which supports the generalization of the problems identified. Furthermore, the process model studied follows the main principles of waterfall development (see Section 3) and thus can be well generalized to that model. In addition, the outcome is compared to state of the art.

Reliability: This threat is concerned with repetition or replication, and in particular that the same result would be found if re-doing the study in the same setting. There is always a risk that the outcome of the study is affected by the interpretation of the researcher. To mitigate this threat, the study has been designed so that data is collected from different sources, i.e. to conduct triangulation to ensure the correctness of the findings. The interviews have been recorded and the correct interpretation of the data has been validated through workshops with representatives of the company.

5   Qualitative Data Analysis

In total 38 issues have been identified in the case study. The majority of issues is categorized in class E, i.e, they are only referred to by individuals or are not mentioned across subsystems (see Table 4). Furthermore, the distribution of issues between the phases requirements engineering (RE), design and development (DI), verification and validation (VV), release (R), maintenance (M), and project management (PM) is shown. The distribution of issues is further discussed in Section 7.

In the analysis of the issues we focus on classes A to D as those are the most relevant ones as they are recognized across roles and systems. Thus, they have a visible impact on the overall development process. However, this does not imply that local issues are completely irrelevant, they just have little impact on the

Table 4. Number of Issues in Classification

Classification	RE	DI	VV	R	M	PM	No. of Issues
A	1	-	1	-	-	-	2
B	-	-	2	-	-	-	2
C	1	2	-	-	1	1	5
D	1	1	2	-	-	-	4
E	1	1	2	3	8	10	25
Sum	4	4	7	3	9	11	38

Table 5. Issues in Waterfall Development

ID	Class	Process Area	Description	SotA
P01	A	Requirements	Requirements work is wasted as documented and validated requirements have to be discarded or reworked.	L02, L03, L08
P02	A	Verification	Reduction of test coverage due to limited testing time in the end.	L07
P03	B	Verification	Amount of faults found increases with late testing.	L05
P04	B	Verification	Faults found later in the process are hard and expensive to fix.	L07
P05	C	Requirements	Too much documentation is produced in requirements engineering that is not used in later stages of the process.	L01
P06	C	Design	Design has free capacity due to long requirements engineering lead-times.	L09
P07	C	Design	Confusion on who implements which version of the requirements.	-
P08	C	Maintenance	High effort for maintenance (corrections released to the customer).	L04
P09	C	Project Mgt.	Specialized competence focus of team members and lack of confidence.	-
P10	D	Requirements	The impact of requirements on other parts of the system are not foreseen.	L06
P11	D	Design	Design is overloaded with requirements.	-
P12	D	Verification	High amount of testing documentation has to be produced.	L01
P13	D	Verification	Problems in fault localization due to barriers in communication.	-

overall development process and thus are not recognized by other roles. Table 5 shows an overview of the identified issues in classes A to D and their mapping to literature summarized in Table 1.

5.1   A Issues

P01: The long lead-times of the requirements engineering phase led to the need to change requirements or discard already implemented and reviewed requirements as the domain investigated (telecommunication) is very dynamic. Furthermore, the distance to the customer caused misunderstandings which resulted in changed requirements or discarded requirements. Due to the complexity of the scope to be defined the number of requirements was too high for the given resources which resulted in discarding requirements (and sometimes this was done late in the development process). Furthermore, the interviewees emphasized that the decision what is in the scope and what is not takes a lot of time as a high amount of people that have to be involved.

P02: Test coverage in waterfall development was reduced due to multiple reasons. Testing is done late in the project and thus if there have been delays in development, testing has to be compromised as it is one of the last steps in development. Furthermore, too much has to be tested at once after the overall system has been implemented. Additional factors are that testing related to quality is often given low priority in comparison to functional testing, trivial things are tested too intensively, and test resources are used to test the same things twice due to coordination problems.

5.2   B Issues

P03: The later the testing, the higher the amount of faults found. The number of faults and quality issues is influenced negatively when using waterfall development. The main cause for this is late testing after everything has been implemented. This provides far too late feedback from test on the software product. Furthermore, basic testing is neglected as there has been low interaction between design and testing, resulting in lack of understanding of each other in terms of consequences of neglecting basic testing. Also due to communication issues, testing started verifying unfinished code which led to a high number of false positives (not real faults).

P04: Having late testing results in faults that are hard to fix, which is especially true for issues related to quality attributes of the system (e.g. performance). These kinds of issues are often rooted in the architecture of the system which is hard to change late in the project.

5.3   C Issues

P05: The interviewees emphasized that quite a lot of documentation is produced in the requirements phase. One of the reasons mentioned is limited reuse of documentation (i.e., the same information is reported several times). Furthermore, the concept of quality gates requires producing a lot of documentation and checklists which have to be fulfilled before passing on the requirements to the next phase. Though, in waterfall development the quality gates are required as they assure that the hand-over item is of good enough quality to be used as input for all further development activities.

P06: Design and implementation have free capacity, the reasons being that requirements have to be specified in too much detail, decision making takes a long time, or requirements resources are tied up due to the too large requirements scope. This has a negative impact on design, as the designers have to wait for input from requirements engineering before they can start working. As one interviewee pointed out *"For such large projects with so many people involved half the workforce ends up working for the rest"*. In consequence, the lead-time of the overall project is prolonged.

P07: From a design perspective, it is not always clear which version of the requirements should be implemented and by whom. The cause of this problem is that work often starts on unfinished or unapproved requirements which have not been properly baselined.

P08: Support is required to release a high number of corrections on already released software. This is due to the overall length of the waterfall projects resulting in very long release cycles. In consequence, the customers cannot wait for the corrections to be fixed for the next release, making corrections a time-pressing issue. Furthermore, the development model requires to handle parallel product branches for customer adaptations of the main product line. In this domain, products have a high degree of variability and thus several product branches have to be supported (see Figure 1).

P09: The competence focus of people in waterfall development is narrowed, but specialized. This is due to that people are clearly separated in their phases and disciplines, and that knowledge is not well spread among them. As one interviewee pointed out, there are communication barriers between phases. Furthermore, a lack of confidence has been reported. That is, people are capable but do not recognize their particular strength to a degree they should.

5.4 D Issues

P10: New requirements do not have an isolated impact, instead they might affect multiple subsystems. However, due to the large requirements scope, requirements dependencies are often overlooked.

P11: The scope of the requirements was too big for the implementation resources. In consequence, designers and architects were overloaded with requirements which could not be realized with the given resources. Furthermore, after the project has been started more requirements were forced into the project by the customer. In consequence, emergent requirements cannot be implemented by architects and designers as they already face an overload situation.

P12: Test documentation has been done too extensively as the documents became obsolete. The reason for the high amount of documentation was mainly that the process has been very documentation centric.

P13: When dealing with different subsystems, the fault localization is problematic as a problem might only show in one subsystems, but due to communication barriers not all subsystem developers are aware of the problem. In consequence, due to the lack of communication (see P09) the localization of faults reported by the customer is time consuming.

6   Quantitative Data Analysis

Table 6 shows the distribution of time (duration) in the development process. The requirements engineering phase takes very long time in comparison to the other phases. The actual implementation of the system seems to be the least time-intensive activity.

Table 6. Distribution of Time (Duration) over Phases (in %)

Req.	Impl.&Design	Verification	Release	Total
41	17	19	23	100

Furthermore, we measured the number of change requests per implemented requirement, the discarded requirement, and the percentage of faults found in system test that should have been found in earlier tests (function test and component test). The figures quantify the issues identified earlier. In particular, the high number of discarded requirements and the cause of change requests are related to issue P01. The long lead-times of requirements engineering increase the time-window for change requests and approximately 26 % of all requirements become obsolete. From a quality perspective the fault slip of 31 % is a symptom of P03 (increase of number of faults with late testing) and P04 (the types of faults found in system tests could have been found earlier and thus would have been easier to fix).

Table 7. Performance Measures

Measure	Value
CRs per implemented requirement	0.076
Discarded requirements	26 %
Fault slip to system test	31 %

7   Comparative Analysis of Case Study and SotA

Table 5 relates the issues identified in the case study to the issues mentioned in literature. If an issue from the case study is identified in literature the column SotA provides the ID of the issue identified in literature (listed in Table 1). Through this comparison it becomes apparent that four issues not mentioned in the identified literature have been discovered in the case study, namely P07, P09, P11, and P13. Vice versa all issues acknowledged in literature have been identified in the case study. Table 5 also shows that the highest prioritized issues (A and B) have all been mentioned in literature describing the waterfall model. In conclusion researchers and practitioners are aware of the most pressing issues related to waterfall development, while lower prioritized (but still important) issues have not been linked to the waterfall model to the same degree.

The issues in the case study are formulated differently from those identified in literature as the formulation is an outcome of the qualitative data analysis. Therefore, we explain how and why the issues of high priority from the case study and SotA are related to each other. The most critical issues are related to the phases of requirements engineering, and verification and validation (both identified in literature). We found that requirements often have to be reworked and or discarded (P01). The qualitative analysis based on the interviews explained the issue with long lead-times for requirements and large scope making responding to changes hard (related to L02), distance to the customer (related to L08), and change in large scope leads to high effort due to that many people are involved (related to L03). The quantitative analysis shows that 41 % of the lead-time is consumed for requirements engineering. Having to define a large requirements scope extends lead-time and thus reduces requirements stability. In consequence the waterfall model is not suitable in large-scale development in the context of a dynamic market. Regarding verification issue L07 identified in literature states that testing the whole system in the end of the project leads to unexpected quality problems and project overruns. This issue relates to the case study in the following ways: First, testing has to be compromised and thus test coverage is reduced when having fixed deadlines which do not allow for project overruns (P02). Secondly, the faults found late in the process are hard to fix, especially if they are rooted in the architecture of the system (P07).

The issues categorized as C are quite mixed, i.e. they include issues related to requirements, design, maintenance and project management. The issues categorized as D show a similar pattern as the most critical ones (A and B), i.e. they are related to requirements, and verification and validation. Furthermore, one issue is related to design. As mentioned earlier, less than half of the issues classified as C and D have been identified in literature before. An explanation of the issues not yet identified has been provided in the qualitative analysis (see Section 5).

It is also interesting to observe that a majority of local issues is related to project management and maintenance (see Table 4). Thus, it seems that there is a high number of issues which do not have such an impact on the process that knowledge about them spreads in the organization.

8 Conclusion

This case study investigates issues related to the waterfall model applied in the context of large-scale software development and compares the findings with literature. The results are that the most critical issues in waterfall development are related to requirements and verification. In consequence, the waterfall model is not suitable to be used in large-scale development. Therefore, the company moved to an incremental and agile development model in 2005. The comparison of the case study findings with literature shows that all issues found in literature are found in the case study. Though, the case study findings provide more detailed explanations of the issues and identified four new issues, namely 1) confusion of who implements which version of the requirements, 2) high effort for maintenance, 3) specialized competence focus and lack of confidence of people, and 4) problems in fault localization due to communication barriers.

References

1. Royce, W.: Managing the development of large software systems: Concepts and techniques. In: Proc. IEEE WESCOM. IEEE Computer Society Press, Los Alamitos (1970)
2. Sommerville, I.: Software Engineering, 7th edn. Pearson Eductation Ltd., London (2004)
3. Raccoon, L.B.S.: Fifty years of progress in software engineering. SIGSOFT Softw. Eng. Notes 22(1), 88–104 (1997)
4. Yin, R.K.: Case Study Research: Design and Methods, 3rd edn. Applied Social Research Methods Series, vol. 5. Prentice Hall, Englewood Cliffs (2002)
5. McBreen, P.: Software craftsmanship: the new imperative. Addison-Wesley, Boston (2002)
6. Pfleeger, S.L., Atlee, J.M.: Software engineering: theory and practice, 3rd edn. Prentice Hall, Upper Saddle River (2006)
7. Jarzombek, J.: The 5th annual jaws s3 proceedings (1999)
8. Thomas, M.: It projects sink or swim. British Computer Society Review 2001 (2001)
9. Johnson, J.: Keynote speech: Build only the features you need. In: Proceedings of the 4th International Conference on Extreme Programming and Agile Processes in Software Engineering (XP 2002) (2002)
10. Jones, C.: Patterns of Software Systems: Failure and Success. International Thomson Computer Press (1995)
11. Sametinger, J.: Software engineering with reusable components: with 26 tables. Springer, Berlin (1997)
12. Anderson, D.J.: Agile Management for Software Engineering: Applying the Theory of Constraints for Business Results (The Coad Series). Prentice Hall PTR, Englewood Cliffs (2003)
13. Cohen, D., Larson, G., Ware, B.: Improving software investments through requirements validation. In: Proceedings of the 26th Annual NASA Goddard Software Engineering Workshop (SEW 2001), Washington, DC, USA, p. 106. IEEE Computer Society, Los Alamitos (2001)
14. Boehm, B.: Get ready for agile methods, with care. Computer 35(1), 64–69 (2002)
15. Karlström, D., Runeson, P.: Combining agile methods with stage-gate project management. IEEE Software 22(3), 43–49 (2005)

Towards a Better Understanding of CMMI and Agile Integration - Multiple Case Study of Four Companies

Minna Pikkarainen

VTT Technical Research Centre of Finland
P.O. Box 1100, FIN-90571 Oulu, Finland
minna.pikkarainen@vtt.fi

Abstract. The amount of software is increasing in the different domains in Europe. This provides the industries in smaller countries good opportunities to work in the international markets. Success in the global markets however demands the rapid production of high quality, error free software. Both CMMI and agile methods seem to provide a ready solution for quality and lead time improvements. There is not, however, much empirical evidence available either about 1) how the integration of these two aspects can be done in practice or 2) what it actually demands from assessors and software process improvement groups. The goal of this paper is to increase the understanding of CMMI and agile integration, in particular, focusing on the research question: how to use 'lightweight' style of CMMI assessments in agile contexts. This is done via four case studies in which assessments were conducted using the goals of CMMI integrated project management and collaboration and coordination with relevant stakeholder process areas and practices from XP and Scrum. The study shows that the use of agile practices may support the fulfilment of the goals of CMMI process areas but there are still many challenges for the agile teams to be solved within the continuous improvement programs. It also identifies practical advices to the assessors and improvement groups to take into consideration when conducting assessment in the context of agile software development.

1 Introduction

There is an increasing need for software in all industrial domains in Europe [1]. There is even an increase in its part of everyday life as software is more used in ambulances, hospitals, mobile applications and home electronics. This need for software offers companies in smaller countries opportunities to work as software suppliers in international markets [2].

Even if there is a need for an increasing amount of software in the market, there is also high competition among software intensive companies. The profits are simply going to the company that can most rapidly produce customer value. This demands an organizational ability to respond to the changing customer requirements.

At the same time, there should not be any errors in the delivered software products. This is because, at the delivery stage, defect correction is extremely expensive

F. Bomarius et al. (Eds.): PROFES 2009, LNBIP 32, pp. 401–415, 2009.
© Springer-Verlag Berlin Heidelberg 2009

and time consuming. In fact, in traditional software development it takes more than 40 times longer to find and fix a defect if it is found in system testing as opposed to module testing [3]. Furthermore, in the safety critical product, even one error in the ready delivered system can lead to the loss of human life [2]. Thus, at the same time when the companies have demands for high quality software they also need to be agile.

Standards and models such as CMMI (Capability Maturity Model Integration) [4] provide ready, evaluated solutions for the software process improvement. [5-7]. It is shown that the CMM based software process improvement programs have brought companies even 28–53% of improvements in lead time and 70 to 74% of improvement in quality measured by the amount of defects [5]. One problem in the CMM model based software process improvement programs have been the high assessment costs [8] . It seems also that the actual developers are often forgotten in the software process improvement programs [9]. On the other hand, CMM based software development arguably leads to a situation in which the developers implement more documents than the actual software code [10] .

Agile methods have been increasingly used in software development companies. For example F-Secure[1] reported that the use of agile methods such as short cycles, continuous planning and daily meetings have brought them even 50% improvements in software quality [11][2].One problem in the agile methods is their time-consuming deployment which can lead to the situation in which one half of the company does not know what the other is doing [12]]. This is because the deployment of agile methods signifies a large change to companies [13]. Traditionally, a company should change both 1) their ways of action 2) and overall culture. In these situations most of the companies, however, may not have a possibility to invest in the large process assessments or programs [14]. Furthermore, the impact of the use of agile methods on the interaction between the teams, management, and customer have not yet been covered as a part of the real research [15]. There are, however, risks and challenges also in the projects using agile methods which can lead also to project failure. [16]

In general, people, especially in industries seem to believe that "CMMI and agile methods are like oil and water" [17] like opposite elements that should not be mixed together as a part of the software process improvement. SEI [18] has published a report arguing that there is compliance between the CMMI model and agile methods. The validity of this argument has not, however, yet been proved as a part of the empirical research. The goal of this research is to increase the empirical understanding in this research field. This is done by focusing on the research question: how to use a 'lightweight' style of CMMI assessment in an agile software development context. The research was done step by step based on the case study method that was applied in four case companies.

The structure of this paper is the following. Section 2 describes the research background including aspects of CMMI and agile software development. Section 3 presents the research design i.e. method used in the study. Section 4 presents an analysis of the cases, while section 5 concludes the paper with the key findings, research limitations and future work related to the CMMI and agile integration.

---

[1] http://www.f-secure.fi/
[2] This was reported directly by the F-Secure manager.

2 Background

This section describes the background to this study including the key concepts of CMMI and Agile and the empirical findings related to CMMI based SPI problems and agile software development.

2.1 CMMI

The main SPI model, investigated in this research, is the capability maturity model, CMMI [4]. CMMI was chosen as the focus of this research because CMMI based assessments are widely-used for evaluating the software processes within a company [19] and indicating key weaknesses needing immediate attention and improvement [20].The Capability Maturity Model® CMM is a model which is often used as a reference model in assessments to facilitate the organization to achieve a level where continuous, optimized improvement of the software development is possible [21]. CMM, as well as the numerous other IEEE standards and guidelines, integrates some of the wisdom in the software development industry [22]. The key differences between CMM and CMMI are 1) in CMMI the measurement and analysis process is added in the maturity level 2) there is more focus on software and product development, its risk management, verification and validation instead of the organizational level processes 3) in CMMI the organizational innovation and deployment process area is included in maturity level 5 instead of the change management process area.

CMMI includes both capability and maturity models, which means that it can be used in a staged and continuous way. The staged representation focuses on a set of key process areas, which are exclusively identified within the maturity levels (1–5) [4]. The assumption of the staged representation of the CMMI is that an organization cannot achieve the next maturity levels before achieving the previous level first. In the continuous representation, processes are measured using the same scale of capability levels [4]. CMMI includes 25 key process areas and each of them contains specific and generic goals that are again dealt with by specific and generic practices. [4].

Empirical studies have proven that assessments, integrated with the successful implementation of a change, can enable organizations to improve the speed and reduce the costs of the software development [5, 6]. CMM and more recently CMMI is regarded as the most popular reference model used in assessments as the first step of SPI [23] and it has been used, for example, to enhance the reduced costs of software development [5]. The assessments are also claimed to be wasteful, because the current assessment methods often tend to be too 'heavy' and expensive [8]. It has been reported that even 77% of process improvements take longer than expected [24]. There are many reasons why the assessment costs have risen too high. For example, organizations do not often know the process areas of higher levels before they have achieved the goals of the lower level [24].

The CMMI based improvement programs seem to demand a great deal of resources [25]. For example, the case study of 56 software organizations, that have conducted a CMM-based process improvement initiative, illustrates that the exploitation of the improvements is difficult [26]. It has been argued that in many cases it takes a long time and significant effort for organizations to show the benefits of the CMMI programs [6]. For example, a survey of 138 individuals in 56 software organizations shows that 72% of the SPI programs that successfully applied the CMM based identification of weaknesses, are not actually improved [27]. The reason for why the CMMI initiatives take so much time to be implemented might lie in the fact that the processes often produce an environmental change which means a shift in the whole process hierarchy to achieve the identified improvements [9]. This demands not only SPI team involvement but also efficient coordination and involvement of the developers. In most of the cases people in industries do not have much time for software process [9]. Often, processes get in the way of the developers and slow the pace of software development to a frustrating level [21]. The reason for this might lay in the wrong focus of improvement programs [9]. Although the assessments can involve the relevant people, the applied improvement programs have often focused too much on the process aspects at the expense of the people behind the actual development work [9]

2.2 AGILE Software Development

Although the initial ideas of agile software development have been created and used already in the 1970s and 1980s, the agile methods emerged in the late 1990s and the early 2000s. Since then, they have been introduced in companies as significant mechanisms to increase the organization's capability to respond to changes [34]. This study focuses on investigating eXtreme Programming (XP) [28] and Scrum [29]. These methods were chosen because they are considered to be the most popularly used of all the agile methods [30] and because studying these two methods in use gives a researcher possibility to examine both project management and engineering aspects of software development.

XP is an agile method originally presented by Kent Beck [28]. It is a 'lightweight' methodology with four key values: communication, simplicity, feedback and courage [28]. Scrum has been pioneered by Schwaber and Beedle [29]. It is a simple process mainly focused on project management of software development [30]. Scrum was originally influenced by Boehm's 'spiral' model, but it was developed based on industrial experiences to simplify the complexity of the project and requirements management in software organizations [31]. Scrum describes practices on an iterative, incremental time boxed process skeleton. At the beginning of the iteration, the team has a sprint planning meeting in which they decide what the team will do during the following iteration. At the end of the iteration, the team presents the results to all the stakeholders in the sprint review meetings to gain feedback on their work. The heart of Scrum is an iteration in which the self-organizing team builds software based on the goals and plans defined in the sprint planning meeting [31].

Both XP and Scrum define practices for the software development process. Beck [32] identifies 12 key practices for the software development process, which mostly focus on software engineering. Beck [28] argues that the XP practices are situation dependent, which means that the application of the practices is a choice which can be made based on the current development context.

During the 2000s, interest in agile methods has increased dramatically [13]. These methods have been adopted in different types of software projects and in wide-ranging application domains [33]. It has been shown that the use of agile methods can be beneficial for product manageability, visibility and team communication [34] as well as ensuring frequent feedback from the customer [35]. In Motorola, on the other hand a selected set of XP practices was used also in the field of safety critical systems [36]. In that case, the use of XP practices was reported to have 53% improved average quality compared to the plan-driven software development project.

3 Research Design

Case study research is appropriate in the situations when 1) actors of the case are important and the context of the case organization is critical [37] and 2) where control over behaviour is not possible as research data can be collected through observation in an unmodified setting [38]. Because the case context is considered critical in case studies [37] , it is important to select cases and researched entities carefully to make it easier and limit the analysis process [37]. This can be done, for example, by selecting companies for the case study research using some specific context factors (i.e. size, domain) [39]. The case study research has often been implemented and reported iteratively, for example, based on Yin [38] steps of case study research method. The case study has been said to be most suitable in the situations in which the researchers purpose to find answers to the explanation to some phenomena through how and why questions [37]. Answers to those questions can be created through the data analysis in which consistency is assured by collecting the research data from multiple settings [37]. Therefore, the collected data can be a combination of interviews, questionnaires and observations [39].

Table 1. Data collection

	Case1	Case2	Case 3	Case 4
Individual interviews	10	5	6	3
Group Interviews	5	1	3	7
Research Period	2005, 2006	2005	2005, 2006, 2008	2007, 2008
Number of Interviewed persons	6	5	6	18

During the period 2005–2008, the initial approach was to interview managers and employees in four firms that were in the process of implementing the XP and Scrum methods. Since this period was still early for software process improvement via agile practices, the firms were chosen opportunistically based on their business goals to adopt agile practices. During this research, a total of 40 interviews were conducted. All the individual interviews were semi structured and lasted for about 60–90 minutes each. All together 33 people from different industries participated in the assessments. This included developers, architects, project managers, customers and line managers from the case companies.

In case studies the data are typically collected from a few entities that can be a person, group or an organization [37]. In this study one project team was selected under analysis from each of the case companies. The case study research can be done using within-case and cross case comparison between these entities [39]. For example, analysing the selected entities first as a stand-alone entity 'within-case analysis' as described by Yin [38]. In this study, each of the cases were first analysed case by case and then compared to find the similarities and differences affecting CMMI and agile integration.

4   Empirical Analysis

This section describes the background of the analysed cases. It also presents an example of a brief analysis of each of the assessed organizations from the perspectives of integrated project management and collaboration.

4.1   Background of the Cases

This research was done in four companies producing software for telecom, information security and financial sectors (Table 2). All of the case organizations were working in the global markets in both Europe and USA. Additionally the case company 4 was working in distributed environments, having developers in Europe, India and USA. The sizes of the companies varied from 100 to 60,000 employees.

Table 2. Background of the cases

Company	Domain	Size of the company
Case 1	Telecom	100
Case 2	Telecom	60000
Case 3	Information security	300
Case 4	Financial	40000

All of the companies used a combined set of XP and Scrum practices as described by Fitzgerald et al [30]. Overall, the agile practices used varied quite considerably even between the teams between the companies but also inside of a company between the development teams. All the analyzed teams excluding case 1[3] used a Scrum framework (i.e. product backlogs, sprints, sprint planning and review meetings) and XP practices (i.e. continuous integration and collaborative code ownership). Some XP practices such as TDD, pair programming, were not used in any of the case companies for several reasons. For example, TDD seemed not to be useful for most of the cases. It was only used sometimes in cases 2 and 3 to support testing work but not as a regular part of development. Pair programming was analyzed as totally against the culture in case company 4 but useful in case company 2. In that case the project members also changed pairs on a daily basis. In case company 3, pair programming was used sometimes when doing complex tasks.

4.2   Implementation of the Assessments

Assessment planning started with the discussion of organization management of the assessed case company. In all cases, the common opinion of the management was that 'even if the assessments itself are useful, they need to be implemented in the lightest way possible' (i.e. not taking too much of the teams' and organizations' time). Therefore, the assessments were decided to be conducted as follows:

---

[3] The Scrum was used in case company 1 while conducting the second assessment.

- Assessments followed 7 of the 9 criteria outlined by Anacleto et al. [40] for the development of lightweight assessment methods: low cost, detailed description of the assessment process, guidance for process selection, detailed definition of the assessment model, support for identification of risks and improvement suggestions, no specific software engineering knowledge required from companies' representatives, and tool support is provided.
- Assessments were done purposing to lower costs [41] focused processes [42] simple assessment process [43] and modified use of assessment models [44].
- The assessment shared some of the requirements of the ADEPT and AHAA methods [2, 14] meaning that the assessment is implemented without the purpose of certification, both preparation and assessment time was minimized.
- Continuous representation of CMMI was used. This was because the goal of all evaluated companies was to achieve business goals through the improvement of software development process. Not, actually, to have official CMMI certification or to achieve certain maturity levels.
- Data used in the assessments were mainly based on the conducted group and individual interviews. In some of the cases (2 and 3) data from iteration retrospectives was also used in the analysis. Project plans and feature sheets were only documents that were checked during the assessments.

4.3   Assessment Results

In integrated project management aspects of CMMI specific goals were best achieved in company 2. Collaboration with stakeholders were efficient in cases 1, 2 and 4 but problematic also in agile case company 3.

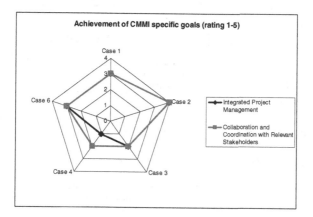

Fig 1. Integrated project management and coordination, (ratings 1-5 = 1 the CMMI goal not achieved, 3 partially achieved, 4 largely achieved, 5 fully achieved

4.3.1   Case 1

Integrated Project Management. In case 1 the company had two different process models one for customer tailoring work and another for the baseline product development. The company had separated software and hardware teams which were located close to each other. Interface dependencies were managed using an MS Word document. This document was created in several workshops with participation of both hardware and software development teams. *"We have workshops during the design phase, and (every) couple of days we get together and go through the decisions and modifications", developer.* At the beginning of the project, planning was done using detailed project plan which was not updated later on during the development. In agile mode, the plans were based on Excel sheets that were continuously updated in iteration planning meetings.

Coordinate and collaborate with relevant stakeholders. The fact that customers wanted just ready products instead of concurrent participation in development made it difficult to get customers involved in actual iteration planning meetings. *"and with our customers there is no commitment to be a part of the co-development", developer* . Therefore, the practice was rather that management was involved in weekly project meetings. Other stakeholders were involved when needed. Coordination such as feature management, task processing were based on iterative meetings and weekly discussions

A summary of the status of integrated project management and coordination process areas is provided in Table 3.

Table 3. Integrated project management and coordination in case 1

SG 1	Integrated Project Management	Status in case company 1
SP 1.1	Establish the Project's Defined Process	The company had two different process models one for customer tailoring work and another for baseline product projects
SP 1.2	Use Organizational Process Assets for Planning Project Activities	The use of the organizational level processes varied between the teams in the case company. In the evaluated team the company level process model was not used
SP 1.3	Establish the Project's Work Environment	The company had separated software and hardware teams which were located close to each others
SP 1.4	Integrate Plans	Plans were continuously discussed in iteration planning meetings
SP 1.5	Manage the Project Using the Integrated Plans	In the first phase, project was planned using detailed project plan which was not updated later on during the development. In agile mode, the plans were based on excel sheets that were continuously updated in Iteration planning meetings
SP 2.1	Contribute to the Organizational Process Assets	Organizational process assets were updated once a year based on the changed situation but feedback from projects were not systematically collected for this purpose
SG 2	Coordinate and Collaborate with Relevant Stakeholders	Status in the case company 1
SP 2.2	Manage Stakeholder Involvement	Customers were located in other countries and wanted just ready products instead of concurrent participation in development which made it difficult to get customers involved in actual iteration planning meetings. Management was involved in weekly project meetings. Other stakeholders were involved time to time
SP 2.3	Manage Dependencies	Dependencies were managed using word documentation that describes all the features and their interfaces. This document was created in several workshops with participations of both hardware and software development sites
SP 2.1	Resolve Coordination Issues	Coordination such as feature management, task processing were based on iterative meetings and weekly discussions

4.3.2 Case 2

Integrated Project Management. In case 2 the project manager defined agile based product development process for the specific project before the project started. The work process and practices were communicated to the developers in workshop and on the wall of the open office space. The information radiators (project status information on the wall) were used efficiently to communicate about project task status and overall progress. Plans were continuously updated and integrated into the project work status. Organization level processes did not, however, support the agile software development approach. *"In practice I made an exception to our standard process...I took customers in the steering group to watch milestones which was not actually a requirement of the milestone process"* Project manager. The project was monitored through the traditional state gate model.

Coordinate and collaborate with relevant stakeholders. In practice, project manager had separated milestone meetings with other stakeholders of the project in able to fulfil organizational level requirements. The architecture of the overall system was on developer's responsibility. At the beginning, developers had difficulties with the interface definition. This led to the situation in which the whole architecture was refactored and totally changed during the second iteration. A summary of the status of integrated project management and coordination process areas is given in Table 4.

Table 4. Integrated project management and coordination in case 2

SG 1	Integrated Project Management	Status in case company 2
SP 1.1	Establish the Project's Defined Process	Process for the project were defined before the project started and communicated to the developers in workshop
SP 1.2	Use Organizational Process Assets for Planning Project Activities	The evaluated team tailored the process model that they used based on the process model provided on company level
SP 1.3	Establish the Project's Work Environment	Project work environment was open office space, all information of project tasks and task estimations were located on the wall of open office space
SP 1.4	Integrate Plans	Plans were continuously updated
SP 1.5	Manage the Project Using the Integrated Plans	Plans were continuously integrated to the project work status
SP 2.1	Contribute to the Organizational Process Assets	Organization process did not supported the case team
SG 2	Coordinate and Collaborate with Relevant Stakeholders	Status in the case company 2
SP 2.2	Manage Stakeholder Involvement	Customer visited in project room daily to look at the task status with developers. Project manager had separated milestone meetings with other stakeholders of the project
SP 2.3	Manage Dependencies	Architecture was developers' responsibility. They had first difficulties with the dependency definition. The whole architecture was refactored and totally changed during the second iteration
SP 2.1	Resolve Coordination Issues	Feature and task processing issues were continuously discussed in iteration planning meetings

4.3.3 Case 3

Integrated Project Management. In case 3 the evaluated project was using a company-wide agile process model. The working environment was an open office space.

The project work tasks and task status was managed using an Excel sheet that was updated daily with the development team and Scrum master. According to the project manager the project status was continuously discussed in iteration retrospective meetings and then used to improve the organizational level process model.

Coordinate and collaborate with relevant stakeholders. One problem for the project members was the stakeholder involvement in the iteration planning and review meetings. In fact, both parties got frustrated because the management expected that their feedback would be taken into the project work on a daily basis but team members were expecting planning meetings before the decisions of the updates in the product backlog can be made. *"that made people confused, because they thought they had a voice, because they were in the daily meeting talking about something and then because that something didn't get done" project manager.* Dependencies between the features in the overall system were not well managed. In the end there were many unfinished features in the system which affected the output quality. One reason for the situation was that the requirements were not analysed in sufficient detail at the end of the project due to the short iteration planning meetings and lack of resources. A summary of the status of integrated project management and coordination process areas are described in Table 5.

Table 5. Integrated project management and coordination in case 3

SG 1		
	Integrated Project Management	Status in case company 3
SP 1.1	Establish the Project's Defined Process	Company had so called agile process model
SP 1.2	Use Organizational Process Assets for Planning Project Activities	The evaluated team tailored the company level process model based on their needs
SP 1.3	Establish the Project's Work Environment	Project working environment was open office space
SP 1.4	Integrate Plans	Project was managed using excel sheets
SP 1.5	Manage the Project Using the Integrated Plans	The project plans were updated daily by Scrum master and development team
SP 2.1	Contribute to the Organizational Process Assets	Project results were used to improve the organizational level process model
SG 2	Coordinate and Collaborate with Relevant Stakeholders	Status in case company 3
SP 2.2	Manage Stakeholder Involvement	Stakeholders could not always being able to participate in iteration planning meetings. They got frustrated because they were not used to a situation in which their change requests were taken part of the project work only in monthly iteration planning meetings
SP 2.3	Manage Dependencies	Dependencies were not well managed, there was unfinished features in the project outputs that affected to the quality of the project results
SP 2.1	Resolve Coordination Issues	Feature and task processing issues were not well solved due to the lack of time

4.3.4 Case 4

Integrated Project Management. In case 4 the project was using a so-called company wide hybrid process model which included aspects from both agile and plan-driven software development. Project members were working in the large open office space. The project was managed using Excel sheets and phone conference meetings with the people from US, India and Europe. Plans were continuously discussed and updated together with the team members and managers. Task allocation was made in Scrum meetings and the developers were responsible for the project tasks.

Coordinate and collaborate with relevant stakeholders. Project management was however, taking care of customer communication and in some projects the customers were not involved in the Scrum meetings. *"customer... they don't know too much. They're not very helpful." developer.* Therefore, the developers informed that there is a gap in the communication between the customer and product development team. Projects were short and established only for a short period at a time. The project manager stated that the requirements were defined in a large requirements definition document and then allocated to developers in Scrum meetings based on the manager's suggestions about their priorities. The allocation was done only by the development team without the customer support. A summary of the status of integrated project management and coordination process areas is given in Table 6.

Table 6. Integrated project management and coordination in case 4

SG 1	Integrated Project Management	Status of case company 4
SP 1.1	Establish the Project's Defined Process	Organization had a so-called hybrid process model
SP 1.2	Use Organizational Process Assets for Planning Project Activities	The evaluated team tailored the process model that they used based on the process model provided on company level
SP 1.3	Establish the Project's Work Environment	Project members were working in a large open office space
SP 1.4	Integrate Plans	Project was managed using excel sheets and phone conference meetings with the people from the US, India and Europe, Plans were continuously updated
SP 1.5	Manage the Project Using the Integrated Plans	Project feedback was not systematically used in the process model continuous development
SP 2.1	Contribute to the Organizational Process Assets	Project management took care of the customer communication, the customer was not involved in the Scrum meetings
SG 2	Coordinate and Collaborate with Relevant Stakeholders	Status of case company 4
SP 2.2	Manage Stakeholder Involvement	Design decisions were efficiently shared using Viki through the US and Europe. The business analyst and product management were not always involved in the Scrum meetings
SP 2.3	Manage Dependencies	Task allocation was done in Scrum meetings, developers were responsible for the project tasks
SP 2.1	Resolve Coordination Issues	Project managements 'took care' of the customer communication, the customer was not involved in the Scrum meetings

4.4 Deployment of the Improvements

In companies 2-4, both the software process improvement and agile practice deployment was first based on the management decision, but later tailored to the needs of the self-organizing development teams. In the longer term it was revealed from interviews that this caused a lot of process variations between the teams even in the same organization. Compared to the previous plan-driven situation both management and developers indicated that the use of agile methods really affected the developers' role in the assessment and software process improvement projects emphasizing the role of tailoring as a part of the deployment process.

6-12 months later the assessor went back to companies 1 and 3 to see the results of the assessment work. It seemed that integrated project management was becoming more systematic due to Scrum deployment especially in company 1. In company 3 the product management was now based on the group of people who were responsible for continuous feature analysis for the sprint planning meetings. All of the evaluated companies, however, reported that Scrum practices were adopted throughout the company during the two years after the assessment. In practice, however, the used agile activities varied significantly between the different development teams, even inside the same company.

6 Conclusions

Both CMMI and agile methods provide practical solutions on how to improve the speed of software development and quality of software products. There is not, however, much empirical evidence available on how to integrate these two aspects in practical assessments and SPI situations in the agile software development context. The purpose of this paper is to increase the understanding of CMMI and agile integration. As a result of this paper it was revealed:

The results of Iteration retrospectives can be utilized as a part of the assessment data. Iteration retrospectives were used in case companies 2-4. In case companies 2 and 3, the data of iteration retrospectives were collected and used also when in the analysis of the improvement needs of development teams during the assessments. This gave a much larger view of the project work in the longer period than the typical face-to-face interviews. Compared to the normal iteration retrospectives, assessments helped teams to come together and share information about the challenges and solutions inside and between the companies.

Agile software development needs to be improved using well established reference models. The analysis in section 4 was done using CMMI specific goals and agile practices. It is possible to integrate CMMI and agile in a framework that helps assessors to evaluate the status of the software development teams. All of the evaluated teams had major challenges that need immediate improvement to assure the rapid development of high quality software. There were some challenges that were common to most of the case companies:

- Component interface management is difficult in agile teams. There is a need for additional documentation of the components and their interfaces (companies 1-4)
- Organizational level processes do not support agile-type software development (companies 1, 2, 4, 5)
- Customer and part of the management are not committed to agile development, they are not involved enough in the project planning and monitoring work (companies 1- 5)

Self organizing is key when improving the development processes. It seems that there are some fundamental differences between the SPI programs that are conducted in the traditional software development teams and the SPI programs that are conducted in an agile context [45]. It has been argued, for instance that CMMI based improvement programs are often based on strong management control, whereas SPI in an agile context emphasizes the use of self organizing teams as the key for SPI implementation [45]. Thus, the process of conducting SPI in agile software development is based on team level improvements to daily working practices [45]. The same happened also in all of the evaluated cases in which the self organizing teams made the final decision about tailoring the process. In the longer term this may cause many process variations between the teams even in the same organization.

This research was carried out as a series of case studies to create a better understanding of agile practice adoption and improvement in software intensive organizations. Owing to the confidential nature of the data and the extended periods of data collection, the research team could not rely on more objective constructs to observe processes or process changes. The research team was also constrained by access to a few key informants in each organization who were managers or developers. Thus, it was only possible to triangulate across different observations of the same data point (interviews at different time points) and across other published material, and the researchers and research team's own observations In addition, due to the lack of a reference model for agile practices (e.g. a standard), the ratings presented in this study were achieved through the author's current knowledge gained from the literature and personal experience. Thus, the ratings presented are also subjective and context-specific. Furthermore, the author's role as a lead assessor in case companies 1, 2, 3 and 4 can be considered as a factor of bias in this research. However, the case study research method was considered a suitable and practical method in rapidly changing software development organizations.

Future research can go down two different routes. Firstly, the research can continue on other process areas of CMMI. For example, requirements development, technical solutions, product integration, validation and verification are process areas that could be mapped to XP and Scrum practices. Secondly, another possible avenue for further research is to examine agile method practices beyond those covered in this study i.e. XP and Scrum. Methods such as LSD, FDD, APM, Crystal and ASD are all such methods that could be assessed.

Acknowledgements. This work was partially supported by Science Foundation Ireland grant 03/CE2/I303_1 to Lero - the Irish Software Engineering Research Centre (www.lero.ie) and TEKES to VTT, Technical Research Centre of Finland. Special thanks also to Mikko Korkala about his valuable comments to this paper.

References

1. ITEA (2005),
   http://www.itea2.org/attachments/150/
   ITEA_SIS_in__the_future__Final_Report.pdf
2. McCaffery, F., Pikkarainen, M., Richarsson, I.: AHAA -Agile, Hybrid Assessment Method for Automotive, Safety Critical SMEs. In: ICSE 2008, Leipzig, Germany (2008)

3. Humphrey, W.S.: The Payoff from Software Quality. Computerworld (2002),
    http://www.computerworld.com/developmenttopics/
    development/story/0,10801,71222,00.html
4. CMMI, ed. Capability Maturity Model® Integration for Development, Version 1.2, Techni-
    cal Report CMU/SEI-2006-TR-008 CMU/SEI-2002-TR-002 ed, Software Engineering In-
    stitute (2006),
    http://www.sei.cmu.edu/publications/documents/
    06.reports/06tr008.html
5. Galin, D., Avrahami, M.: Are CMM Program Investment Beneficial? Analysing Past Stud-
    ies. IEEE Software 23(6), 81–87 (2006)
6. Niazi, M., Wilson, D., Zowghi, D.: A maturity model for the implementation of software
    process improvement: an empirical study. The Journal of Systems and Software, 1–18
    (2003)
7. Stelzer, D., Mellis, W.: Success Factors of Organizational Change in Software Process Im-
    provement. Software Process Improvement and Practice 4(4), 227–250 (1998)
8. Fayad, M., Laitinen, M.: Process Assessment Considered Wasteful. Communications of
    the ACM 40(11), 125–128 (1997)
9. Laitinen, M., Fayad, M.: Surviving a process performance crash. Communications of the
    ACM 41(2), 83–86 (1998)
10. Boehm, B., Turner, R.: Balancing Agility and Discipline. In: Balancing Agility and Disci-
    pline -A Guide for the Perplexed, p. 304. Addison Wesley, Reading (2003)
11. Agile Newsletter (2005), http://www.agile-itea.org
12. Cohn, M., Ford, D.: Introducing an Agile Process to an Organization. IEEE Computer 36(6),
    74–78 (2003)
13. Lindvall, M., et al.: Agile Software Development in Large Organizations. Computing Prac-
    tices 37(12), 38–46 (2004)
14. McCaffery, F., Taylor, P., Coleman, G.: Adept: A Unified Assessment Method for Small
    Software Companies. IEEE Software 24(1), 24–31 (2007)
15. Pikkarainen, M., et al.: The Impacts of agile practices on communication in software de-
    velopment. Empirical Software Engineering 13(3), 303–337 (2008)
16. Boehm, B., Turner, R.: Using Risk to Balance Agile and Plan-Driven Methods. In: Com-
    puter 2003, pp. 57–66. IEEE Computer Society, Los Alamitos (2003)
17. Turner, R., Jain, A.: Agile Meets CMMI: Culture Clash or Common Cause. In: 1st Agile
    Universe Conference, Chigago (2002)
18. SEI (2008),
    http://www.sei.cmu.edu/pub/documents/08.reports/08tn003.pdf
19. Trudel, S., et al.: The small company-dedicated software process quality evaluation
    method combining CMMI and ISO/IEC 14598. Software Quality Journal 14(3) (2006)
20. Daskalantona, M.K.: Achieving Higher SEI Levels. IEEE Software 11(4), 17–24 (1994)
21. Andersson, D.J.: Stretching Agile to Fit CMMI Level 3. In: Agile Development, Denver
    (2005)
22. Bamberger, J.: Essence of the Capability Maturity Model. Computer 30(6), 112–114
    (1997)
23. Agarwal, R., Chari, K.: Software Effort, Quality and Cycle Time: A Study of CMM Level
    5 Projects. IEEE Transactions on Software Engineering 33(3), 145–155 (2007)
24. Dangle, K.C., Larssen, P., Zelkowitz, M.V.: Software Process Improvement in Small Or-
    ganizations: A Case Study. IEEE Software 22(6), 68–75 (2005)
25. Hareton, K., Leung, N., Terence, C.F.: A process framework for small projects. Software
    Process Improvement and Practice 6(2), 67–83 (2001)

26. Niazi, M., Wilson, D., Zowghi, D.: Critical Success Factors For Software Process Improvement Implementation: An Empirical Study. Software Process Improvement and Practice 11, 193–211 (2006)
27. Herbsleb, J., et al.: Benefits of CMM-based software process improvement: Initial results, CMS/SEI-94-TR-013. Carnegie Mellon University, Pittsburgh (1994)
28. Beck, K.: Extreme Programming Explained: Embrace Change, p. 190. Addison Wesley Longman, Inc., Amsterdam (2000)
29. Schwaber, K., Beedle, M.: Agile Software Development With Scrum. Prentice-Hall, Upper Saddle River (2002)
30. Fitzgerald, B., Hartnett, G., Conboy, K.: Customising Agile Methods to Software Practices at Intel Shannon. European Journal of Information Systems 15(2), 200–213 (2006)
31. Schwaber, K.: Agile Project Management with Scrum. Microsoft Press, Washington (2003)
32. Beck, K.: Embracing Change with Extreme Programming. IEEE Computer 32(10), 70–77 (1999)
33. Karlström, D.: Introducing Extreme Programming - An Experience Report. In: XP 2002. Springer, Alghero (2002)
34. Larman, C.: Agile & Iterative Software Development, p. 340. Addison Wesley, Reading (2003)
35. Rising, L., Janoff, N.S.: The Scrum software development process for small teams. IEEE Software 17(4), 26–32 (2000)
36. Grenning, J.: Using XP in a Big Process Company: A Report From the Field. In: XP Universe, Raleigh, NC (2001)
37. Benbasat, I., Goldstein, D.K., Mead, M.: The Case Research Strategy in Studies of Information Systems. MIS Quartely 11 (1987)
38. Yin, R.K.: Case Study Research: Design and Methods. Thousand Oaks, California (2003)
39. Eisenhardt, K.: Building Theories from Case Study Research. Academy of Management Review 14(4), 532–550 (1989)
40. Anacleto, A., et al.: A Method for Process Assessment in small software Companies. In: Proceedings of the International SPICE conference of Process Assessment and Improvement, Portugal, Lisbon (2004)
41. Richardson, I.: Software Process Matrix: A Small Company SPI Model. Software Process Improvement and Practice 6(3), 157–165 (2001)
42. Wilkie, F.G., McCaffery, F.: Evaluation of CMMI Process Areas for Small to Medium-sized Software Development Organizations. Software Process Improvement and Practice 10(2), 189–202 (2005)
43. Horvat, R.V., Rozman, I., Györkös, J.: Managing the Complexity of SPI in Small Companies. Software Process Improvement and Practice 5(1), 45–54 (2000)
44. Kautz, K.: Software Process Improvement in Very Small Enterprises: Does it Pay Off. Software Process Improvement and Practice 4(4), 209–226 (1998)
45. Salo, O., Abrahamsson, P.: An Iterative Improvement Approach for Agile Development: Implications from multiple case study. Software Process: Improvement and Practice 12(1), 81–100 (2007)

ERP System Implementation: An Oil and Gas Exploration Sector Perspective

Alok Mishra and Deepti Mishra

Department of Computer Engineering, Atilim University,
Incek, 06836, Ankara, Turkey
alok@atilim.edu.tr, deepti@atilim.edu.tr

Abstract. Enterprise Resource Planning (ERP) systems provide integration and optimization of various business processes which leads to improved planning and decision quality, smoother coordination between business units resulting in higher efficiency, and quicker response time to customer demands and inquiries. This paper reports challenges, opportunities and outcome of ERP implementation in Oil & Gas exploration sector. This study will facilitate in understanding transition, constraints and implementation of ERP in this sector and also provide guidelines from lessons learned in this regard.

Keywords: ERP, Implementation, Oil and Gas Exploration, SAP.

1 Introduction

Business environment is becoming increasingly complex with functional units requiring more and more inter-functional data flow for decision making, timely and efficient procurement of product parts, management of inventory, accounting, human resources and distribution of goods and services [1]. To deal with these challenges Enterprise Resource Planning (ERP) came into existence. ERP is an integrated set of subsystems that integrates all facets of the business, including planning, manufacturing and logistics, sales and marketing. ERP systems are originated to serve the information needs of manufacturing companies. Over time though, they have grown to serve other industries, including financial services, customer good sector, supplier chain management and human resource sector. These systems provided integration and optimization of various business processes and this was what the companies looked for [2] along with tangible and intangible business benefits to organizations [3]. It is not wrong to say that ERP systems gained importance as they arrived at a time when process improvement and accuracy of information became critical strategic issues [4]. With this growth, ERP systems, which first ran on mainframes before migrating to client-server systems, are now migrating to the Web and include numerous applications. ERP is a product that helps automate a company's business process by employing an integrated user interface, an integrated data set, and an integrated code set. ERP systems are complex and implementing one can be challenging, time-consuming and expensive project for any company [5]. Motwani et al. [6] emphasized that ERP adoption involves initiating appropriate business process changes as well as information technology changes to significantly enhance performance, quality, costs,

F. Bomarius et al. (Eds.): PROFES 2009, LNBIP 32, pp. 416–428, 2009.
© Springer-Verlag Berlin Heidelberg 2009

flexibility, and responsiveness. ERP systems are widely adopted in a diverse range of organizations and define the business model on which they operate [7]. An ERP implementation can take many years to complete and cost tens of millions of dollars for a moderate size firm and upwards of $100 million for large organizations [8]. Implementing an ERP system is a major undertaking. About 90% of ERP system implementations are late or over budget [9] and the success rate of ERP systems implementation is only about 33% [10] [11]. The relative invisibility of the ERP implementation process is also identified as a major cause of ERP implementation failures [12]. Such invisibility is attributed to the unpredictably complex social interaction of IT and organization [13]. Volkoff [14] suggested that the critical challenge of ERP implementation is believed to be the mutual adaptation between IT and user environment. It is also interesting to note that ERP systems are large and complex, taking years to implement, the inclusion of today's strategic choices into the enterprise systems may significantly constrain future action. By the time the implementation of an ERP system is completed, the strategic context of the firm may have changed [7]. Mabert et al. [2] suggested that case studies and interviews facilitate to obtain reliable and detailed information on the current status of ERP practice and ERP implementations. They further argued that most implementation projects are unique in many ways in spite of many common underlying issues, activities and strategies. To meet on time and budget targets, ERP projects have to be planned very carefully and managed very efficiently [2].

Limited research has been conducted about ERP implementation issues and mainly in the form of individual organizations case studies only. Implementation failures, challenges and problems are still not documented in the literature [15]. In the context of ERP project implementation, challenges represent major pitfalls which if not addressed then a project stands little success. Therefore, it is important to understand the real life implementations, problems and related scenarios in detail.

Further to the best of our knowledge very few real life ERP implementations in oil and gas sector are documented in the literature. Therefore this paper will facilitate in understanding constraints, problems, success and pitfalls of implementation in this sector.

This paper is organized as follows: First ERP implementation related literature is reviewed. The next section follows real life ERP (SAP) implementation as case study, followed by lessons learned. Section 5 summarizes conclusions.

2 Literature Review

ERP systems, similar to other management information systems, are often perceived as very complex and difficult to be implemented [16][17]. System implementation success depends on many factors. ERP system evaluation, vendor selection, the ERP consultant, implementation plan and execution are all critical to the success of implementing an ERP system [18]. The inability of some firms to successfully implement and utilize enterprise systems to increase organizational outcomes has been a source of concern for both practitioners and academia [19]. The evidence of enterprise implementation failures go back to the late 1990s [20][21][5]. For many organizations, ERP systems are the largest systems they have worked with in terms of financial resources invested, the number of people involved and the scale of implementation [18]. Several recent cases of

ERP system implementation have experienced considerable difficulties [22][23][24][17]. The failure rate of ERP implementation is very high [25]. Among other obstacles, technical problems and people obstacles have been cited as the major barriers [26][23]. The types of problems and issues that arise from the implementation of ERP systems range from specific issues and problems that can come up during the installation of an ERP to behavioural, procedural, political and organisational changes etc. That manifests themselves once the system is installed. In case of ERP successful implementation is urgent, since the costs and risks of these technology investments rival their potential pay-offs [27]. Failure of ERP system implementation projects may lead to bankruptcy [5][28][29][30]. A study of 100 projects by Sirkin and Dikel [31] found that their sponsors considered them successful in only one-third of the cases and that tangible financial impact was achieved in only 37% of cases. Markus et al. [32] suggests that ERP systems are inherently flexible which means that stakeholders have many opportunities to influence the form of technology during the initial decision-making, development, the implementation and also the use of the system. They further argued that many problems related to ERP-implementation are related to a misfit of the system with the characteristics of the organization. This is supported by Davenport [5] that "ERP tends to impose its own logic on a company's strategy, culture, and organization' which may or may not fit with existing organizational arrangements". Although ERP systems are functionally wealth, standardizing organizational processes with these systems is often difficult [33]. It is found out that many firms that have experienced success with ERP, have comprehensively reengineered their organizational processes and structures as a method for enterprise–wide transformation [34]. In case of implementing ERP system we should put more effort in customizing ERP modules to compile with the existing workflow, report formats and data needs [18]. Involving users as early as possible in system implementation is generally a good strategy [35]. As an enterprise system, the success of ERP implementation requires a close cross-functional cooperation [6]. Further evidence from literature shows that, although many organizations are using some modules of an ERP system, they do not see themselves to be equipped with ERP [36][37][38].

In particular, IT integrators that specialize in energy are seeing more opportunities in what's termed as the "upstream" segment of the oil and gas sector. Upstream includes oil and gas exploration and the drilling and operation of wells. Drilling companies deal with large assets and work crews that move about the country or different ocean sites. Such companies use ERP to make sure their resources are deployed effectively. ERP solutions also help companies track equipment maintenance and keep tabs on employee certification and training. Drilling personnel may need certification to operate certain types of equipment [39]. Mergers and acquisitions are common in the upstream space, and integrators find opportunity in consolidation. The trend got underway a few years ago and continues apace. Consolidation begets complexity and generates interest in ERP. Moore [39] further suggests as oil and gas sector companies absorb others, operations may span several countries, each with its own statutory reporting requirements. Companies crossing international boundaries also need to deal with multiple currencies. Overall, combined organizations face rationalizing financial and accounting systems which requires ERP implementation.

The ERP system is an increasingly popular management tool to reshape a business or organization. Generally, the case study method is a preferred strategy when "how" and "why" questions are being posed, and the researcher has little control over events [40]. The case study method, a qualitative and descriptive research method, looks intensely at an individual or small participants, drawing conclusions only about the participants or group and only in the specific context [40]. The case study method is an ideal methodology when a holistic, in-depth investigation is required [41]. The Case study method has been proven a useful tool in investigating the problems of ERP implementation [42][43][44][6].

3 Case Study

3.1 Background of the Company

The Company was established in early 1970's to handle drilling operations required for exploration and field development as well as undertaking work-over and maintenance operations in both onshore and offshore areas. It has successfully carried out all drilling operations requirements and played an important role in the discovery of oil and gas. The main functions of the company are:

- **Operations:** This function includes two main divisions: Offshore and Onshore – each handles drilling operations. A Logistics division is also under this function and is responsible for providing logistics support in terms of transportation and civil equipment.
- **Technical:** Mainly responsible for providing technical support to the Operations function. The key divisions under this function are Commercial (procurement, inventory, tendering, warehouse, etc), Engineering & Projects, Maintenance, Business Support and a newly established division under the name of New Services. The field support services like two warehouses and two workshops are under Commercial and Maintenance divisions respectively.
- **Administration:** The role of this function is to provide administrative support including HR, Finance, IT and General Services. All of these divisions are located in head office.

3.2 IT Setup

The Information Systems & Technology (IS&T) department was formally established in the early 1990s with the mandate of providing computer and networking services to employees at Head Office. At that time, the company was running on Novel Netware and XT computers primarily used by Finance and Payroll services. The structure of the IS&T consisted of a networking unit and applications unit. The total number of IT staff, including network engineers, FoxPro programmers and customer support staff was under 20. The following in-house Foxpro based applications were being used:

- **Financial Applications:** General Ledger, Accounts Payable, Accounts Receivable, Payroll
- **Material Management:** Inventory Management, Fixed Assets
- **Miscellaneous:** Employee Database, Maintenance Work order Historical Database

Most of the above applications were developed by third parties and later on supported, maintained and enhanced by the internal development team of IS&T. Each application was dedicated to a particular group (department or process) and the exchange of data among these applications was very limited. The standard management reports were incorporated in the applications and those were printed and distributed to the management or concerned staff on a periodic or on-request basis. Management had to rely on the availability of the existing data and most of the decision making required a lot of manual information from various resources.

Initially the computers were only available to financial analysts, data entry operators and managers. During mid-90s, PC-based computing became popular and gradually all employees were provided PC workstations with Windows operating systems using word processing tools and other office applications. After all of the PCs were networked, the company decided to centralize the electronic files and hence the storage system (merely a dedicated file server) was added to the data centre.

3.3 Weaknesses of IT Applications

Following problems were faced in the old IT setup:

- Only a few functions / processes were automated using FoxPro-based applications.
- All the applications were working in silos without any exchange or integration among them.
- The maintenance of these applications was very difficult due to lack of documentation of source code, process information among development team, etc
- Most of the business areas were not automated – hardly any decision-making was fully supported by the existing applications.
- Most of the company's processes were cross-functional e.g. Material Requirement Planning, Procurement, Inventory, Maintenance, Invoices and Payments, Operations Planning, etc. However the existing applications were only supporting a small portion of the cross-functional process so the value generated by these applications used to be offset by the subsequent manual flow of the information.
- The architecture of the applications itself was weak. The system controls were inappropriate, allowing human error during data entry. As a result, the management had little confidence in the reports generated from the system resulting in a forced parallel-run of the manual registers and files for reconciliation and validation purposes.
- The core business areas were handled by manual processes. For example, more than 80% of staff was working in Operations (offshore and onshore), 10% were based in Head office and the remaining 10% were deployed in field support services (workshops, warehouses, base camps, etc) – all of these areas did not have any IT systems to support their processes.
- Long-employed staff with built-up tacit knowledge of the company became the only source of information. Lack of process documentation aggravated the problem and a few key positions held most of the process knowledge, creating critical organizational risk.

3.4 ERP Implementation

3.4.1 Objectives setting
In order to define clear goals and set expectations, the taskforce arranged a workshop with the management team to obtain their viewpoint. Participants were agreed on the following points:

- Timeframe – the implementation should not take a long time to complete.
- Cost – learning from industry experience, it was a general concern that any such implementation typically takes 3 times the initially estimated cost; the taskforce was asked to focus on the cost variance of the project.

3.4.2 ERP Selection
The first task was to finalize the selection of a particular ERP system. The task force had the following options to evaluate:

i)   Single ERP (SAP or Oracle) or
ii)   Best of breed (selecting the best module for each of its functional area)

Option (ii) was discarded quickly as it required more cost, time and skills to implement. In addition, it required building a comprehensive skill set for a variety of applications that was extremely difficult at the time. Therefore the option to go for a single ERP was selected. The next question was to choose between SAP and Oracle as these two ERP packages were amongst the most popular choices in that region and industry sector (i.e. Oil & Gas). Again the taskforce had the following options to consider:

i)   Conduct a self-study and choose between SAP and Oracle or
ii)   Hire a consultant to study company's requirements and propose a particular ERP system

After evaluating both options, the taskforce dismissed the second option as it required extra time (the tendering process itself could take many weeks) and cost. Therefore it was decided to:

- Arrange meetings with other sister companies who had already implemented an ERP to obtain their view point and lessons learnt.
- Arrange volunteers from each functional area to study the high-level features of a particular module of both ERPs.

After conducting the self-study and meetings with other operating companies, the task force agreed to proceed with SAP. The recommendation was presented to the management and they accepted it.

The task force then conducted a market research to find out the range of costs and timeframe. The initial data collected was not much encouraging as the minimum cost identified as USD 8 million (software license, hardware and implementation cost). The average implementation time was ranging from 18 months to 3 years which was also beyond the initial estimations as the company was aiming to complete the transition in 12 months.

3.4.3 Scoping and Approach Definition

The taskforce then moved to the Scoping and Planning phase in which a team of focal points (from each of the functional areas) was created to jointly develop a business requirements document for the ERP implementation. The focal points were selected based on their experience and knowledge of functional areas of the company. These focal points were required to allocate 80% of their business hours to work on this task as the deadline was in four weeks. Since most of the focal points were new to this type of work, they started working on their individual areas in their own style – the consolidated set of requirements produced by the team were clearly lacking the quality and consistency as the requirements were either too high-level/generic or too detailed. The team took another two weeks to refine those requirements further.

It was planned to implement the following SAP modules in the first round of implementation:

- Financial Accounting
    - General Ledger
    - Accounts Receivable
    - Accounts Payable
    - Book Close
    - Consolidation

- Controlling
    - Cost Elements
    - Cost Centres
    - Activity Based Costing (ABS)
    - Profit Centres

- Asset Management
    - Purchase
    - Sale
    - Depreciation
    - Tracking

- Human Resource
    - Employment History
    - Payroll
    - Succession Planning
    - Career Management

- Plant Maintenance
    - Labour
    - Material
    - Downtime and Outages

- Material Management
    - Requisitions
    - Purchase Orders
    - Goods Receipt
    - Inventory Management
    - Bill of Material

The taskforce had to address some of the strategic options:

- Big-Bang vs. Phased Approach: One of the questions was to finalize the implementation approach – whether to implement all modules in parallel or use a phased approach where each module would be implemented in a sequential manner. The later approach seemed to take longer time than big-bang therefore the team proposed to adopt a big-bang approach.
- Third Party vs. In-house Implementation: Where the first question was mainly addressing the timeframe, this question was concerning the cost as well. The taskforce evaluated various options and the most suitable appeared to hire SAP Consultants on a contract bases (as short-term employee) along with an experienced SAP Project Manager whose core responsibility would be to manage the SAP contract staff to deliver in the agreed time frame. Most of the SAP consultants were recruited from a body-shop (Indian resource costing maximum 20% of any SAP implementation consultancy firm).

During this phase, the new SAP project manager was recruited and a team of 10 SAP consultants were hired as contract employees. These included six functional resources specialized in different SAP modules, two SAP ABAP developers as technical resources, one SAP GUI and security administrator and one database administrator. At that time, SAP 4.6C version was bought. The license agreement included all SAP modules along with 200 initial user licenses.

3.4.4 Business Blueprints

The newly recruited project manager formed a functional team including the focal points from each of the business areas and the SAP Functional Consultants. The team was given the task to prepare the detailed business blueprints which were mainly the detailed definition of the company's processes and their mapping with the existing best practice-based processes defined in SAP. In most of the areas, company agreed to adopt the built-in processes of SAP as it gave the company an opportunity to implement the best practices simultaneously. The HR and payroll modules however required some customization as the certain local personnel policies were governed by government regulations and changing them was out of the question.

The task took eight weeks – with some known and unknown weaknesses in the blueprint document, the team decided to move to the next phase.

3.4.5 Design and Development

During the design phase, the complete definition of SAP GUI screens, transaction details, input/output layout and reporting formats were prepared. As most of the existing processes were manual, the major part of the design phase was actually aiming to a vanilla implementation of SAP. The design phase started in the 13th week of the project (measured from Scoping and Approach Definition Phase), and it took nearly eight weeks to complete. As time elapsed, the team was feeling a sense of urgency to complete the tasks-in-hand. As a result, some of the areas like detailed reporting requirements, test criteria, test cases and others did not get the attention they required. Nonetheless, the team produced a detailed design document at the end of the design phase. The role of the focal points was merely to review and sign-off the design document.

During the design phase, the technical team had completed the hardware sizing and specification. The platform choices were left open for the company and based on the long-term relations with the existing hardware vendors, a combination of Compaq and Dell servers were acquired. The backend database server was also kept open for the company to choose and the existing relationships with Microsoft business partner were leveraged to cut the deal for Microsoft SQL Server as the backend database server. Clearly the company's platform choice was Windows as all the PCs were equipped with Windows O/S, Microsoft Office, and Windows NT/2000 as network operating system. The company-wide email was supported by Microsoft Exchange server.

Towards the end of the design phase, the project team moved to the development phase. During this phase, the following activities were carried out:

- Hardware set up
- MS SQL Server installation and configuration on database server
- Installation and configuration of development and testing environment on separate servers
- Preparation for the test user machines
- Configuration of the SAP applications
- Data migration and conversion for the existing applications

At the end of this phase, the project had completed 32 weeks and the overall management was satisfied with the progress.

3.4.6 Implementation

Once the configuration of the SAP interfaces was completed, the initial user acceptance testing was conducted. The same team of focal points was used with a few added divisional users. Not much time was given for this testing as it was assumed that unchanged processes in SAP were already tested and confirmed. A list of target users was prepared for the system training in their respective areas. The project team struggled during this phase as the availability of the users was only 50% in all the training sessions despite the management instructions of giving full time to these training sessions. The project adopted a 'train the trainers' concept where it was assumed that the selected users would train the rest of the staff in their divisions.

The system finally rolled-out in the 40th week. The whole SAP team's contract was extended for another year to provide continuous technical and functional support until the system matured. The company had great expectations for SAP and was aiming to collect immediate benefits after the implementation.

4   Lessons Learned and Discussions

The overall project achieved both of the primary goals - timeline and cost. However, post-implementation progress did not occur as the company expected. Many areas remained 'out of SAP', data residing in SAP was questionable for its accuracy, certain controls were still missing in SAP, and transactions were taking more time to complete in SAP compared to the previous applications or manual processes.

When these issues were realized at the top-management level, a SAP Review Committee was formed to conduct an assessment of the current situation and to develop an action plan. The team started working on the task and after assessing the situation and meeting with key staff; the following was presented to management:

- The overall project lacked appropriate change management during its implementation. The SAP was definitely a transformational project for the company where its scope involved the company-wide processes and almost all the head office based employees were expected to use the system. Since ERP is a major investment of an organization and the implementation may involve substantial organizational changes, top management support has been found to be a key success factor of success, but more importantly top management need to develop a shared vision and to communicate it to the employees so that expectation is clear [18][45][35]. Thus the expectation of both peers and top management may influence the behaviour of the ERP users [18]. However in this case very little effort was spent in planning the transition from its legacy/manual processes to a sophisticated ERP arena. The project's core focus remained on the timely completion within the budget rather than achieving the results. Mabert et al. [2] also found in their case study that because of the investment required for an ERP project, both in terms of the resources and the resulting organizational changes, companies are very sensitive about implementation times and budgets.

- Another factor which was not considered was the employees' perception about the SAP. The rumour had already been spread in the company that after SAP, the warehouse staff will be truncated to just 20% of the original staff. Similarly, the support staff in other areas like Finance, HR, and Material Management had a similar impression. Focal points that were part of the project team were aware of the uncertain climate and may not have proactively quelled fears and rumours. As a result, the design phase remained weak and certain controls in SAP remained open. This allowed the system to accept inaccurate data in some of the transactions, which created doubts about the integrity of the system later on. Compatibility between the new system and the existing business procedures and data format are the major issues reported by the companies [46][47]. Reimers [48] also observed that implementing an ERP system implies that master data are maintained in one department but are actually used by other departments; smooth master data maintenance involves a high degree of cross-functional collaboration and also understanding which might be lacking in state-owned enterprises. Since ERP contains various modules that are intricately linked with each other, data should be managed properly to ensure their accuracy [49]. Here it is important to note that implementing an ERP will bring in changes to the way people work within the organization, processes will change and there may be job cuts and rationalization of responsibilities within departments [15].

- The third very important factor was the reduced training time for the end users. The project team wanted to complete the implementation phase and make an unfairly optimistic assumption about the 'train the trainers' approach. In order to provide a smooth access to ERP systems, a large number of elements must work closely together. These elements include supports in hardware, software, training and information provision [18]. Reimers [48] also identified training as one of the critical success factor in ERP implementation. The company had a mix of many nationalities and cultures and not all employees had influence over others to train or convince them in their respective areas. Moreover, some of the trained employees viewed their new status as one of increased power within the company, and were reluctant to pass their new-found knowledge to their colleagues.

5 Conclusions

This study provides valuable insights towards understanding ERP implementations and significant factors influencing success. Various case studies provide different findings which are unique to ERP implementations because of the integrative characteristics of ERP systems. Alignment of the standard ERP processes with the company's business process has been considered as an important step in the ERP implementation process [26]. After almost 7 years of implementation, company has mixed results in this case. Certain areas have seen great improvements after the implementation of SAP (e.g. Procurement, Maintenance, Financial) where certain areas remain weak (e.g. Employee Records, Contract Administration, Integrated Planning). From this implementation experience, it can be seen that it is not a particular technology platform or software application that can transform a company. Instead it is the way the company implements the technology that makes it successful.

References

1. Karsak, E.E., Özogul, C.O.: An integrated decision making approach for ERP system selection. Expert Systems with Applications: An International Journal 36(1), 660–667 (2009)
2. Mabert, V.A., Soni, A., Venkataramanan: Enterprise resource planning: Managing the implementation process. European Journal of Operational Research 146, 302–314 (2003)
3. Mishra, A.: Achieving Business Benefits from Enterprise Systems in Enterprise Resource Planning for Global Economies: Managerial Issues and Challenges, Carlos Ferran and Ricardo Salim, IGI Global, USA, ch. V, pp. 76–91 (2008b)
4. Yen, H.R., Sheu, C.: Aligning ERP implementation with competitive priorities of manufacturing firms: an exploratory study. International Journal of Production Economics 92, 207–220 (2004)
5. Davenport, T.H.: Putting the Enterprise into the Enterprise System. Harvard Business Review 76(4), 121–132 (1998)
6. Motwani, J., Mirchandani, D., Madan, M., Gunasekaran, A.: Successful implementation of ERP projects: evidence from two case studies. International Journal of Production Economics 75(1-2), 83–96 (2002)
7. Mishra, A.: Enterprise Resource Planning Systems: Effects and Strategic Perspectives in Organizations. In: Gupta, J.N.D., Sharma, S.K., Rashid, M.A. (eds.) Handbook of Research on Enterprise Systems, IGI Global, USA, ch. V, pp. 57–66 (2008a) ISBN:978-1-59904-859-8
8. Mabert, V.A., Soni, A., Venkataramanan: Enterprise resource panning survey of US manufacturing firms. Production and Inventory Management Journal 41(20), 52–58 (2000)
9. Martin: An ERP strategy. Fortune 2, 95–97 (1998)
10. Zhang, M.K.O., Lee, L.: Critical Success Factors of Enterprise Resource Planning Systems Implementation Success in China. In: Proceedings of the 36th Annual Hawaii International Conference on System Sciences (2003)

11. Arif, M., Kulonda, D., Jones, J., Proctor, M.: Enterprise Information Systems: Technology First or Process First? Business Process Management Journal 11(1), 5–21 (2005)
12. Griffith, T.L., Zammuto, R.F., Aiman-Smith, L.: Why New Technologies Fail? Industrial Management, 29–34 (1999)
13. Markus, M.L., Robey, D.: Information Technology and Organizational Change: casual Structure in Theory and research. Management Science 34, 583–598 (1988)
14. Volkoff, O.: Enterprise System Implementation: A process of individual metamorphosis. In: American Conference on Information Systems (1999)
15. Otieno, J.O.: Enterprise resource planning (ERP) systems challenges: A Kenyan case study. In: Schlender, B., Frielinghaus, W. (eds.) BIS 2008. LNBIP, vol. 7, pp. 399–409. Springer, Heidelberg (2000)
16. Liang, H., Saraf, N., Hu, Q., Xue, Y.: Assimilation of Enterprise Systems: The effect of Institutional Pressures and the Mediating Role of Top Management. MIS Quarterly 31(1), 59–87 (2007)
17. Xue, Y., Liang, H., Boulton, W.R., Snyder, C.A.: ERP implementation failures in China: Case studies with implications for ERP vendors. International Journal of Production Economics 97(3), 279–295 (2005)
18. Chang, M.K., Cheung, W., Cheung, C.-H., Yeung, J.H.Y.: Understanding ERP System Adoption from the User's Perspective. International Journal of Production Economics 113(2008), 928–942 (2008)
19. Kumar, V., Movahedi, B., Kumar, U., Lavassani, M.: A Comparative Study of Enterprise System Implementations in Large North American Corporations. In: Abramowicz, W., Fansel, D. (eds.) BIS 2008. LNBIP, vol. 7, pp. 390–398. Springer, Heidelberg (2008)
20. Hayes, S.: Providing Enterprise Systems. Practical Accountant 40(2), SR11 (2007)
21. Hendricks, K.B., Singhal, V.R., Stratman, J.K.: The Impact of Enterprise Systems on Corporate Performance: A Study of ERP, SCM, and CRM System Implementations. Journal of Operations Management 25(1), 65–82 (2007)
22. Goldberg, A.: The ERP trap. Upside 12(11), 32 (2000)
23. Krasner, H.: ERP Experiences and Evolution. Communications of the ACM 43(4), 22–26 (2000)
24. Wah, L.: Give ERP a change. Management Review 89(3), 20–24 (2000)
25. Yeh, T.M., Yang, C.C., Lin, W.T.: Service Quality and ERP Implementation: A conceptual and empirical study of semiconductor-related industries in Taiwan. Computers in Industry 58(8-9), 844–854 (2007)
26. Botta-Genoulaz, V., Millet, P.: A Survey on the Recent Research Literature on ERP Systems. Computers in Industry 95(2), 510–522 (2006)
27. Boonstra, A.: Interpreting an Erp-implementation project from a stakeholder perspective. International Journal of Project Management 24(2006), 38–52 (2006)
28. Fowler, A., Gilfillan, M.: A framework for stakeholder integration in higher education information system projects. Technol. Anal. Strategic Manage. 15(4), 467–489 (2003)
29. Markus, M.L., Tanis, C.: Multisite ERP implementations. Communications of ACM 43(4), 26–42 (2000)
30. McAfee, A.: When too much IT knowledge is a dangerous thing. Sloan Management Review 44(2), 83–89 (2003)
31. Sirkin, H., Diekel, K.: Getting value from enterprise initiatives. Boston Consulting Group, Boston (2001)
32. Markus, M.L., Axline, S., Petrie, D., Tanis, C.: Learning from Adopters' experiences with ERP: problems encountered and success achieved. Journal of Information Technology 15(4), 245–265 (2000)

33. Genoulaz, V.B., Millet, P.A.: An Investigation into the use of ERP systems in the service sector. International Journal of Production Economics 99, 202–221 (2006)
34. Mische, R., Bennis, W.: Reinventing through reengineering. Information Systems Management 13, 58–65 (1996)
35. Tchokogue, A., Bareil, C., Duguay, C.R.: Key lessons from the Implementation of an ERP at Pratt & Whitney Canada. International Journal of Production Economics 95(2), 151–163 (2005)
36. Keil, M., Tiwana, A.: Relative Importance of Evaluation Criteria for Enterprise Systems: A Conjoint Study. Information Systems Journal 16(3), 237–262 (2006)
37. Rikhardsson, P., Kraemmergaard, P.: Identifying the Impacts of Enterprise System Implementation and Use: Examples from Denmark. International Journal of Accounting Information Systems 7(1), 36–49 (2006)
38. Choi, J., Ashokkumar, S., Sircar, S.: An Approach to Estimating Work Effort for Enterprise Systems Software Projects. Enterprise Information Systems 1(1), 69–87 (2007)
39. Moore, J.: Oil and gas sector generates big business for systems integrators, SearchITChannel. com (2008),
    http://searchitchannel.techtarget.com/news/article/
    0,289142,sid96_gci1334850,00.html
40. Yin, R.K.: Case Study Research: Design and Methods, 3rd edn. Sage Publications, Thousands Oaks (2003)
41. Feagin, J., Orum, A., Sjoberg, G. (eds.): A Case for Case Study. University of North Carolina Press, Chapel Hill (1991)
42. Sheu, C., Chae, B., Yang, C.L.: National differences and ERP implementation: issues and challenges. Omega 32(5), 361–371 (2004)
43. Sarker, S., Lee, A.S.: Using a case study to test the role of three key social enablers in ERP implementation. Information & Management 40(8), 813–829 (2003)
44. Voordijk, H., Leuven, A.V., Laan, A.: Enterprise resource planning in large construction firm: implementation analysis. Construction Management & Economics 21(5), 511–521 (2003)
45. Motwani, J., Subramanian, R., Gopalakrishna, P.: Critical Factors for successful ERP implementation: Exploratory findings from four case studies. Computers in Industry 56(6), 524–544 (2005)
46. Soh, C., Kien, S.S., Tay-Yap, J.: Cultural fits and misfits: Is ERP a universal solution? Communications of the ACM 43(4), 47–51 (2000)
47. Van Everdingen, Y.: ERP adoption by European midsize companies. Communications of the ACM 43(4), 27–31 (2000)
48. Reimers, K.: Implementing ERP Systems in China. In: Proceedings of the 35th Hawaii International Conference on System Sciences. IEEE Computer Society, Los Alamitos (2002)
49. Ngai, E.W.T., Law, C.C.H., Wat, F.K.T.: Examining the Critical Success Factors in the adoption of enterprise resource planning. Computers in Industry 59(2008), 548–564 (2008)

11th International Workshop on Learning Software Organizations (LSO 2009) New Media in Transfer and Innovation

Andreas Jedlitschka[1] and Sira Vegas[2]

[1] Fraunhofer IESE, Germany
[2] Universidad Politécnica de Madrid, Spain
andreas.jedlitschka@iese.fraunhofer.de, svegas@fi.upm.es

1 Introduction

Software is one of the most important drivers of innovation. As organizations are becoming more dependent on software, the improvement of software quality and productivity becomes of essential importance for the competitiveness of an organization. Continuing the success of the LSO Workshop series since 1999, this workshop will provide a communication forum bringing together academia and industry for discussing the advancements made and addressing the challenges faced by continuous learning in software-intensive organizations.

Building upon existing work on knowledge management and organizational learning, the workshop will promote interdisciplinary approaches from computer science and information systems, business, management and organization science as well as cognitive science.

The LSO concept is not easy to implement because of the different nature of each organization, i.e., the fact that each organization is unique. In order to successfully implement LSO concepts, each organization has to find its own way, which requires the underlying concepts to be flexible. Some of these issues have been discussed in recent literature on organizational and individual learning. Recent developments in new media, such as everyone using new media for various business and private purposes, might pose the question to which extent these can support LSO. Do new media provide a means for solving at least parts of the issues?

Hence, the focus of this workshop will be on new media facilitating transfer of knowledge and supporting innovation. In economically difficult times such as today, it is important that knowledge management initiatives in software organizations are lightweight (i.e., do not place considerable additional burden on developers and end users), allow for an incremental adoption (i.e., do not require large up-front investment before any return of investment is at least visible), and are flexible regarding frequent changes in experts and topics.

This workshop invites researchers and practitioners to report on the current state of learning software organizations, share successes and failures, and discuss promising new ideas and approaches for using new media that enable organizations to systematically transfer experience and/or general knowledge in order to support innovation.

F. Bomarius et al. (Eds.): PROFES 2009, LNBIP 32, pp. 429–432, 2009.
© Springer-Verlag Berlin Heidelberg 2009

2 Topics of Interest

The following list gives the topics of interest to be discussed in the workshop:

- Social Software and Web 2.0 for LSO
- Practical applications of LSO approaches
- Success stories and failures in LSO
- Knowledge acquisition, generation, and transfer in software organizations
- Knowledge/skills representation and management in software organizations
- Knowledge distribution and feedback mechanisms
- Tacit knowledge capture and dissemination
- Process-oriented knowledge management approaches for LSO
- Learning software organization maturity
- Light-weight knowledge management approaches for agile software development processes
- Knowledge-generating software communities
- New media-based collaborative learning in software organizations
- New media facilitated technical infrastructures and technologies to support LSO
- Learning organizations related to innovation
- Lessons learned: becoming a LSO (positive and negative experience)
- How learning is shared in an organization across all networks: customers, internal staff, managers, key stakeholders
- The influence these networks have in an organization
- The relationship between networks and performance in an organization
- Evaluation techniques for knowledge management and LSO activities

3 Workshop Chairs

Andreas Jedlitschka
andreas.jedlitschka@iese.fraunhofer.de
Fraunhofer-Institute for Experimental Software Engineering (IESE), Kaiserslautern, Germany

Sira Vegas
svegas@fi.upm.es
Facultad de Informática, Universidad Politécnica de Madrid, Campus de Montegancedo, 28660 Boadilla del Monte, Madrid, Spain

4 LSO2009 Program Committee

- Althoff, Klaus-Dieter, University of Hildesheim, Germany
- Birk, Andreas, Consultant, Germany
- Bomarius, Frank, Fraunhofer IESE, Germany
- Conradi, Reidar, NTNU, Norway
- de Almeida Falbo, Ricardo, Universidade Federal do Espírito Santo, Brazil

- Dingsoyr, Torgeir, SINTEF, Norway
- Dieste, Oscar, University Politechnica Madrid, Spain
- Emrich, Andreas, DFKI, Germany
- Feldmann, Raimund, Fraunhofer Center Maryland, USA
- Gresse von Wangenheim, Christiane, UNIVALI Universidade do Vale do Itajaí, Brazil
- Grundy, John C., University of Waikato, New Zealand
- Lehner, Franz, University Passau, Germany
- Marçal de Oliveira, Káthia, Universidade Católica de Brasília, Brazil
- Menzies, Tim, West Virginia University, Canada
- Nick, Markus, Empolis , Germany
- Park, Shelly, University of Calgary, Canada
- Pfahl, Dietmar, SIMULA, Norway
- Rocha, Ana Regina Cavalcanti, Universidade Federal do Rio de Janeiro, Brazil
- Rodriguez, Daniel, University of Alcalá, Spain
- Sarcia, Alessandro, University Roma "Tor Vergata", Italy
- Schneider, Kurt, Leibniz Universität Hannover, Germany
- Steinbach-Nordmann, Silke, Fraunhofer IESE, Germany
- Varkoi, Timo, Tampere University of Technology, Finland
- Weber, Rosina, Drexel University, USA
- Weber, Sebastian, Fraunhofer IESE, Germany
- Wessner, Martin, Fraunhofer IESE, Germany

5 LSO Workshop History

1998: LSO" - first presentation by Althoff & Bomarius at the Workshop on Organizational Memories, ECAI'98, Brighton, England

1999: LSO'99 - 1rst Workshop held in Kaiserslautern, Germany at the 11th SEKE Conference (SEKE09)

2000: LSO2000 - 2nd Workshop held in Oulu, Finland at the 2nd PROFES Conference (Profes2000)

2001: LSO2001 - 3rd Workshop held in Kaiserslautern, Germany at the 3rd PROFES Conference (Profes2001)

2002: LSO2002 - 4th Workshop held in Chicago, IL, USA at the Conference XP/Agile Universe 2002

2003: LSO2003- 5th Workshop held in Luzern, Switzerland, at the 2nd KM Conference (KM2003)

2004: LSO2004 - 6th Workshop held in Banff, Canada at the 16th SEKE Conference (SEKE04)

2005: LSO2005 - 7th Workshop held in Kaiserslautern, Germany at the 3rd Conference Wissensmanagement (WM05)

2006: LSO2006 - 8th Workshop held in Rio de Janeiro, Brazil at the Int'l Symposium on Empirical SWE (ISESE06) and another LSO2006 Workshop in Hannover, Germany

2007: LSO2007 - 9th Workshop held in Potsdam, Germany at the 5th Conference Wissensmanagement (WM07) collocated with 4th German Workshop on Experience Management (GWEM2007)

2008: LSO2008 - 10th Workshop held in Rome, Italy at the 9th PROFES Conference (Profes2008)

A Half-Day Workshop on "Smarter Investment by Aligning SPI Initiatives, Capabilities and Stakeholder Values"

Yana Selioukova and Christian Frühwirth

Helsinki University of Technology
BIT Research Centre, Software Business Lab
P.O. Box 5500, FI-02015, TKK, Finland
{Yana.Selioukova,Christian.Fruehwirth}@tkk.fi

Abstract. Software companies who want to improve software process capabilities (SPCs)a systematic method to make informed investment decisions on software process improvement (SPI) initiatives. Such decisions should aim at creating maximum stakeholder values. To address this problem, we present a method with tool support that may help companies align stakeholder values with SPCs and SPI initiatives. The proposed method has been developed based on the well-established "Quality Function Deployment" (QFD) approach. The experience with the proposed method suggests that it particularly helps to reduce the risk of misalignment by identifying those SPI initiatives that are most beneficial to stakeholders. The tool support provided with the proposed method also generated positive experiences in increasing the usability of the method and helped companies in the elicitation and prioritization of stakeholder values. Therefore, we propose a workshop for the method work out named "Smarter Investment by Aligning SPI Initiatives, Capabilities and Stakeholder Values" in hypothetical case company.

Keywords: software process improvement, value-based software engineering, capabilities.

Introduction

Company executives need to invest in change initiatives that are most likely to improve those core capabilities of the company that have considerable impact on benefits provided to customers and other success-critical stakeholders. Change initiatives include, but are not limited to, SPI initiatives and aim at improving a company's performance in delivering stakeholder values. Software quality teams often struggle to convince senior management to grant funding for SPI programs for lack of getting a clear picture of tangible benefits [1]. Even if there is common understanding on needed investment in SPI programs, senior management and the SPI team still may fail to invest in "right" capabilities, i.e., capabilities that best improve the value to stakeholders. By investing in right capabilities companies may diminish risk of spending financial assets on change initiatives that do not provide evident advantages to stakeholders.

F. Bomarius et al. (Eds.): PROFES 2009, LNBIP 32, pp. 433–434, 2009.
© Springer-Verlag Berlin Heidelberg 2009

While there are many potential benefits of SPI initiatives, one of the major risks is to focus on initiatives that have only marginal effects on capabilities of the company and bottom-line benefits. We refer to such misleaded focus as "misalignment of SPI initiatives and stakeholder value". Software process assessment models, such as CMMI or Spice, are useful to give an overview on relevant target candidates in software process areas (SPAs) and provide feedback on process maturity to motivate SPI initiatives [2].

We present a method for eliciting and aligning stakeholder values with a company's software process capabilities to identify the most promising SPI initiatives. Stakeholder value is the part of value-based requirement engineering activities which includes: *"identification of success-critical stakeholders; eliciting their value propositions with respect to the system; and reconciling their value propositions into a mutually satisfactory set of objectives for the system"* [3]. The proposed method is largely based on "Quality Function Deployment" (QFD) principles and is supported with a prototype tool for more efficient data collection and analysis. The method comprises two iterations:

I) The first iteration helps to understand the alignment/impact between stakeholder values and SPCs,
II) The second iteration helps to understand the alignment between SPCs and SPI initiatives.

Based on the analysis of alignment data from both iterations, the decision makers are more likely to make an informed decision on investing in "right" capabilities, which shows a strong connection between SPI initiatives, SPCs, and stakeholder values. Furthermore, the accompanying tool support intrinsically fosters an improved common understanding between senior management and SPI teams on the value of SPI initiatives.

References

1. López-Cortijo, R., Guzmán, J.G., Amescua Seco, A.: ICharts: Charts for Software Process Improvement Value Management. In: Abrahamsson, P., Baddoo, N., Margaria, T., Messnarz, R. (eds.) EuroSPI 2007. LNCS, vol. 4764, pp. 124–135. Springer, Heidelberg (2007)
2. Dyba, T.: An Empirical Investigation of the Key Factors of Success in Software Process Improvement. Empirical Software Engineering 31, 410–413 (2005)
3. Boehm, B.: Value-Based Software Engineering: Reinventing "Earned-Value" Monitoring and Control. SIGSOFT Softw. Eng. Notes 28, 3 (2003)

Business Alignment: Measurement-Based Alignment of Software Strategies and Business Goals

Jürgen Münch[1], Jens Heidrich[1], and Vladimir Mandić[2]

[1] Fraunhofer IESE, Fraunhofer Platz 1, 67663 Kaiserslautern, Germany
jens.heidrich@iese.fraunhofer.de
[2] University of Oulu, Department of Information Processing Science, Rakentajantie 3, 90014 University of Oulu, Finland
vladimir.mandic@tol.oulu.fi

Summary

Most of today's products and services are software-based. Organizations that develop software want to maintain and improve their competitiveness by controlling software-related risks. To do this, they need to align their business goals with software development strategies and translate them into quantitative project management. There is also an increasing need to justify cost and resources for software and system development and other IT services by demonstrating their impact on an organization's higher-level goals. For both, linking business goals and software-related efforts in an organization is necessary. However, this is a challenging task, and there is a lack of methods addressing this gap.

The popular Goal Question Metric (GQM) approach has served the software industry well for several decades in defining measurement programs. However, it does not provide explicit support for motivating and integrating measurement at various levels of the organization. On the other hand, approaches such as Balanced Scorecard address mainly business-level goal-setting activities, and do not support the alignment of objectives at different levels of the organization with an integrated methodology. To fill this gap, we propose *GQM+Strategies®*: an integrated approach that is based on GQM and adds the capability to create measurement programs that ensure alignment between goals and strategies at different levels, from the highest strategic levels of the business to the level of individual development projects. The approach is based on rationales for deciding about options when operationalizing goals and for evaluating the success of strategies with respect to goals [1,2,3].

The tutorial will illustrate the *GQM+Strategies®* approach using practical examples from industry, present related approaches (like BSC, PSM, and CoBIT), and provide practical exercises on how to actually apply the method. The tutorial will focus on the following topics in detail:

Session 1: Principles and basics of goal-oriented measurement for quantitative management of an organization exemplified by the GQM approach.

F. Bomarius et al. (Eds.): PROFES 2009, LNBIP 32, pp. 435–436, 2009.
© Springer-Verlag Berlin Heidelberg 2009

Session 2: Effective linkage of goals and strategies on different organizational levels using the *GQM+Strategies®* approach.

Session 3: Utilizing the *GQM+Strategies®* approach in modeling organizational context to achieve an effective decision-making process on different organizational levels.

Session 4: Cost-efficient integration of measurement programs into organizational processes and their usage for transparent decision-making.

Furthermore, the tutorial will present related approaches for quantitative management of an organization, such as BSC (Balanced Score Card), PSM (Practical Software Measurement), and CoBIT (Control Objectives for Information and Related Technology). All topics will be illustrated with practical examples and experiences from industry.

Participants will learn how to apply the basic approach as part of practical exercises. This includes the following activities:

- Modeling and structuring of goals and corresponding strategies across different levels of an organization.
- Mapping goals and strategies to concrete metrics and indicators.
- Integrating measurement programs into the organization.
- Assessing the efficiency of strategies with respect to achieving goals.

Organization. The tutorial is planned for one day. The ideal number of participants is between 10 and 20; to ensure good discussions, we see 30 as a maximum practical figure. The tutorial will have three theoretical sessions and one practical exercise session, where the participants will apply the presented approach to their own business strategies and goals and exchange experiences with all participants.

Target Group. This tutorial addresses managers in the area of software development and IT, project managers, quality assurance managers, and controllers.

References

1. Basili, V., Heidrich, J., Lindvall, M., Münch, J., Regardie, M., Rombach, D., et al.: GQM+Strategies: A comprehensive methodology for aligning business strategies with software measurement. In: MetriKon 2007, Kaiserslautern, Germany, pp. 1–14 (2007)
2. Basili, V., Heidrich, J., Lindvall, M., Münch, J., Regardie, M., Rombach, D., et al.: Bridging the gap between business strategy and software development. In: Twenty Eighth International Conference on Information Systems, Montreal, Canada, pp. 1–16 (2007)
3. Basili, V., Heidrich, J., Lindvall, M., Münch, J., Regardie, M., Trendowicz, A.: GQM+Strategies–aligning business strategies with software measurement. In: First International Symposium on Empirical Software Engineering and Measurement, ESEM 2007, Madrid, Spain, pp. 488–490 (2007)

Customer Communication Challenges and Solutions in Globally Distributed Agile Software Development

Minna Pikkarainen and Mikko Korkala

VTT Technical Research Centre of Finland
P.O.Box 1100, FI-90571, Oulu, Finland
{Minna.Pikkarainen,Mikko.Korkala}@vtt.fi

1 Summary of the Tutorial

Working in the globally distributed market is one of the key trends among the software organizations all over the world. [1-5]. Several factors have contributed to the growth of distributed software development; time-zone independent "follow the sun" development, access to well-educated labour, maturation of the technical infrastructure and reduced costs are some of the most commonly cited benefits of distributed development [3, 6-8]. Furthermore, customers are often located in different countries because of the companies' internationalization purposes or good market opportunities.

Inefficient communication between customers and project teams can have a negative impact on the project outcome [9]. If the customer communication fails, it is likely that software products will be delivered late and over budget without meeting the needs of stakeholders and in particular end users. Customer communication is a significant challenge also in distributed agile software development, and it has been identified as one of the key issues that have to be taken into account [4, 10, 11]. Agile software development relies heavily on informal face-to-face communication over detailed documentation [12]. However, face-to-face communication and active customer involvement proposed by agile approaches do not often work as such in distributed environment. In such an environment, the customer can not necessarily participate in the face-to-face meetings with different stakeholders. Therefore, customer communication problems have tried to be solved by using different communication media, for example videoconferencing [11] and whiteboard software [4]. In addition, also more general level solutions have been proposed e.g. by Layman et al. [4] and Ramesh et al. [13]. These recommendations aim to create a communication rich environment and promote finding a balance between formal and informal communication in distributed agile context.

In spite of the communication challenges, there is not yet much research available focusing on the customer communication aspects of globally distributed agile software development. The purpose of this tutorial is to present some of the highlights related to this topic based on the in-depth, longitudinal research made in large software intensive company of 60000 employees during the years 2008 and 2009. After this introduction, the challenges and solutions of the customer communication will be discussed with the attendants. The discussion will be led based on the presenters' experiences on customer communication from 7 different companies during the years 2005-2009. This tutorial

F. Bomarius et al. (Eds.): PROFES 2009, LNBIP 32, pp. 437–440, 2009.
© Springer-Verlag Berlin Heidelberg 2009

will increase the knowledge of the attendees on this field and provide them solutions in order to tackle the problems related to customer communication.

2 Audience of the Tutorial

Since the agile methods are been increasingly used in the large globally distributed software development environments, this topic is relevant for all the companies working in this context. On the other hand, many small companies are pursuing for internationalization. One of the first steps in this process is often to find a customer group from international markets. This immediately creates the need for globally distributed customer communication.

Agile methods are also utilized by several consulting companies working in the field of software development. From their point of view, it would be significant to hear what kind of customer communication challenges companies are experiencing and how these challenges could be solved. Since customer communication in the context of agile software development seems to lack empirical knowledge, the topic would be also relevant for research organizations.

Attendees: industries: large and small; consulting companies; researchers.

3 How the Tutorial will be Structured and Run?

The tutorial will be composed of two different sections. During the initial 45 minute introduction, some of the key findings on the communication challenges in distributed agile environment are described. The discussed challenges are based on the empirical findings made by the presenters.

After the presentation, one hour workshop will be held. The goal is first to collect the challenges that the attendants have found of this topic and then discuss of the results together with the whole group. The purpose of the approach is to reveal both challenges and solutions that attendants have related to the customer communication in agile software development. After taking this tutorial, the attendees should have a more comprehensive view to the challenges on customer communication and solutions mitigating the risks related to this field.

During the discussions presenters will give examples based on the experiences of the companies that they have been working with related to this topic.

4 Biographies

Minna Pikkarainen has graduated from the Department of Information Processing Science, University of Oulu and finished her PhD about the topic of improving software development mediated with CMMI and agile practices at 2008. Minna has been working as researcher and project manager in VTT Technical Research Centre of Finland more than 11 years now. During that time she has worked in 18 industrial driven research projects doing close industrial collaboration with 8 organizations in Finland and in Ireland. Minna has participated as a key person for several large international ITEA project preparation work doing full project proposals and project outlines as collaboration together with large European level company networks (e.g. Flexi and Evolve projects). During 2007 and 2008 Minna has been leading VTT research group of the Large European projects called Agile ITEA (embedded agile software development) and Finnish consortium of ITEI (project about open innovations). So far Minna has provided several agile trainings, workshops with 10 different industries related to agile methods. Minna has been member of Lero, The Irish Software Engineering Research Centre since 2006. For the past 4 years, her work and publications have been focused on research in the area of agile software development.

Mikko Korkala is currently working on his doctoral dissertation on customer communication and collaboration in agile software development. Mikko has been involved with agile development since he started working on his Master's thesis in early summer of 2002. Mikko has worked at VTT Technical Research Centre of Finland as a research scientist since early 2007 and has previously worked at the Department of Information Processing Science and as a software engineer in software industry. In addition to research, Mikko has provided several agile trainings and has held invited agile talks both in Finland and abroad. Mikko has also worked as an onsite agile consultant for management in a large software company and helped to outline agile reference processes for software intensive companies.

5 History of the Tutorial

The tutorial will be based on the research of a large globally distributed software intensive company. Customer communication aspects in agile software development were studied in a longitudinal in-depth case study during the years 2008-2009. Furthermore, the presenters have experiences on customer communication challenges and solutions from 7 different organizations applying agile methodologies during the years 2005-2009. This experience will be utilized when discussing about the topic with the participants.

References

1. Herbsleb, J., Moitra, D.: Global software development. IEEE Software 18, 16–20 (2001)
2. Damian, D., Zowghi, D.: Requirements Engineering Challenges in Multi-site Software Development Organizations. Requirements Engineering Journal 8, 149–160 (2003)
3. Komi-Sirviö, S., Tihinen, M.: Lessons Learned by Participants of Distributed Software Development. Knowledge and Process Management 12, 108–122 (2005)
4. Layman, L., Williams, L., Damian, D., Bures, H.: Essential communication practices for Extreme Programming in a global software development team. Information and Software Technology 48, 781–794 (2006)
5. Taxén, L.: An integration centric approach for the coordination of distributed software development projects. Information and Software Technology 48, 767–780 (2006)
6. Ebert, C., De Neve, P.: Surviving Global Software Development. IEEE Software 18, 62–69 (2001)
7. Gorton, I., Motwani, S.: Issues in co-operative software engineering using globally distributed teams. Information and Software Technology 38, 647–655 (1996)

8. Battin, R., Crocker, R., Kreidler, J., Subramanian, K.: Leveraging Resources in Global Software Development. IEEE Software 18, 70–77 (2001)
9. Lee, G., DeLone, W., Espinosa, J.A.: Ambidextrous coping strategies in globally distributed software development projects. Commun. ACM 49(10), 35–40 (2006)
10. Schümmer, T., Schümmer, J.: Support for distributed teams in eXtreme programming. In: Succi, G., Marchesi, M. (eds.) Extreme Programming Examined, 1st edn., pp. 355–377. Addison Wesley, Boston (2001)
11. Kircher, M., Jain, P., Corsaro, A., Levine, D.: Distributed eXtreme programming. In: XP 2001, pp. 66–71 (2001)
12. Agile Manifesto (2001), http://agilemanifesto.org/
13. Ramesh, B., Cao, L., Mohan, K., Xu, P.: Can distributed software development be agile? Commun. ACM 49(10), 41–46 (2006)

Tutorial: Case Studies in Software Engineering

Per Runeson and Martin Höst

Lund University, Sweden
{per.runeson,martin.host}@cs.lth.se

Abstract. This document presents a tutorial on case study research methodology in software engineering, held at the 10th International Conference on Product Focused Software Development and Process Improvement (Profes).

Keywords: Case study, research methodology, tutorial.

1 Introduction

Software engineering and software process improvement are complex activities, which success or failure depends on many interrelated factors. This complex interaction cannot be fully studied in isolation, but needs empirical studies in real world settings. Case studies offer the opportunity to conduct this kind of studies. A case study is an empirical inquiry that investigates a contemporary phenomenon within its real-life context, especially when the boundaries between the phenomenon and context are not clearly evident. [1]

The area of software engineering involves development, operation, and maintenance of software and related artifacts. Research on software engineering is to a large extent aimed at investigating how this development, operation, and maintenance are conducted by software engineers and other stakeholders under different conditions. This means that the activities are carried out by individuals and groups of individuals, and social and political questions are of importance for this development. This means that many research questions in software engineering are suitable for case study research.

Case studies focus on phenomena in their context, especially when the boundary between the phenomenon and its context is unclear. This is particularly true in software engineering. This is to a large extent what is needed when conducting research in software engineering.

The term "case study" appears every now and then in the title of software engineering research papers. However, the presented studies range from very ambitious and well organized studies in the field, to small toy examples that claim to be case studies. However, case studies which are conducted and reported as stories of what a positive participant has experienced do not fulfill the criteria of solid independent research. This tutorial aims at presenting and applying guidelines for case study research that fulfill scientific criteria of good research.

Case study research focuses on the investigated case as such and does not have the same objectives of generalization as less flexile research approaches. This makes case study research an attractable research approach not only from a researcher's point of

F. Bomarius et al. (Eds.): PROFES 2009, LNBIP 32, pp. 441–442, 2009.
© Springer-Verlag Berlin Heidelberg 2009

view, but also for industry representatives. Industry representatives can conduct case studies as part of their ongoing improvement work in order to understand the benefits and costs of investigated new methods and ways of working. University researchers can take part in this process in order to investigate the suitability of investigated approaches in different environments.

2 Content

The tutorial is based on lectures, intertwined with practical tasks for the participants. The tasks involve analyzing published case studies and defining procedures for new ones.

The attendant is provided with a set of practical guidelines, which helps setting up new case studies as well as assessing the information in published case study reports, summarized in [2]. The following topics are covered in the tutorial

1. Definitions: What is a case study? What is action research? Quantitative and qualitative aspects of a case study. Fixed and flexible designs in empirical studies.
2. Setting up a case study: Defining scope and goal of a case study. Setting up contracts between the researcher and the studied organization. How to conduct a case study as part of an ongoing improvement process.
3. Data collection: Defining procedures for data collection. Questionnaire design. Interviews. Metrics collection. Archival data collection.
4. Data analysis and interpretation: Data filtering. Qualitative and quantitative analysis. Data interpretation in conjunction with the organization.
5. Reporting: What should be reported in a case study. Issues of secrecy and publicity.
6. Validity issues: Analysis of validity and actions to improve the validity of a case study.

References

1. Yin, R.K.: Case Study Research, 3rd edn. Sage Publications, Thousand Oaks (2003)
2. Runeson, P., Höst, M.: Guidelines for Conducting and Reporting Case Study Research in Software Engineering. Empirical Software Engineering 14(2), 131–164 (2009)

Author Index